THE COMPLETE BOOK OF
FOOTBALL

THE NEW YORK TIMES SCRAPBOOK
ENCYCLOPEDIA OF SPORTS HISTORY

FOOTBALL
BASEBALL
BASKETBALL
TRACK AND FIELD
GOLF
TENNIS
BOXING
SOCCER/PROFESSIONAL HOCKEY
WINTER SPORTS
OUTDOOR SPORTS
INDOOR SPORTS
WATER SPORTS
HORSE RACING/AUTO RACING

THE COMPLETE BOOK OF
FOOTBALL

EDITED BY
GENE BROWN

INTRODUCTION BY
FRANK LITSKY

ARNO PRESS
A NEW YORK TIMES COMPANY
NEW YORK/1980

THE BOBBS-MERRILL COMPANY, INC.
INDIANAPOLIS · NEW YORK

Library of Congress Cataloging in Publication Data

Main entry under title:

The Complete book of football.

(The New York times scrapbook encyclopedia of sports history.)

Issued also under the title: Football.
Collection of articles reprinted from the New York times.

Bibliography: p.

Includes index.

SUMMARY: Traces the history of football as presented in articles in the "New York Times."
1. Football. [1. Football] I. Brown, Gene. II. New York Times. III. Series.

GV950.F66   1979   796.332   79-92321
ISBN 0-405-12685-9 (Arno)
ISBN 0-672-52637-9 (Bobbs Merrill)

Manufactured in the United States of America

Appendix © 1979, *The Encyclopedia Americana.*

The editors express special thanks to The Associated Press, United Press International, and Reuters for permission to include a number of dispatches originally distributed by those news services.

Project Editors: Arleen Keylin and Christine Bent
Editorial Assistant: Jonathan Cohen

CONTENTS

Introduction   vii

1. College Football   1
   Origins of the Modern Game   2
   The Game Becomes Complex   33

2. Pro Football   85
   Growth of the NFL   86
   The Super League   128

3. Football and Society   173

Appendix   187

Index   194

American football had its origins in soccer and in rugby, a stepson of soccer. So did such sports as Canadian football (almost the same as the American game), Australian football and Gaelic football.

The game that developed in the United States required use of the hands to advance the ball, and the foot became almost incidental.

From its origins at Eastern colleges not sure what kind of game they wanted to play, American football developed into a sport that captivated millions of people. At the start of the 1970's, a Gallup Poll showed that football had replaced baseball as America's No. 1 spectator sport. Television audiences for the Super Bowl, the annual championship game of professional football, exceeded 100 million. Major colleges provided annual multi-million dollar budgets for football.

At the start of the 1970's, the 28-team National Football League (NFL), the only major professional league in the United States, had contracts with CBS, NBC and ABC, the three major television networks, to show its games. The four-year contracts brought the NFL teams $656 million, the largest entertainment package in television history. Each team was guaranteed $5.8 million a year from television, more than it derived from selling seats. To recoup their investment the networks sold 30-second commercial spots during games for prices ranging from $85,000 to $185,000.

Colleges also received large sums for television rights. The National Collegiate Athletic Association (NCAA), the major regulatory body for college sports, sold its television package to ABC for $118 million over four years. Millions more were paid by the three networks to televise post-season bowl games.

Football dominates autumn weekends. There are high-school games on Friday nights and Saturdays, college games on Saturdays and professional games on Sunday. The collegians and professionals play from September to December, with post-season competition in December and January.

Attendance has climbed steadily. In 1978, the 643 four-year colleges that played varsity football attracted more than 31 million spectators. The University of Michigan averaged almost 105,000 for home games. NFL attendance exceeded 11 million for the regular season and additional millions for preseason and playoff games. Average attendance at regular-season games was 56,000.

The early years of the antecedents of football are cloudy. Soccer was played in England about the 11th century but was banned for many years because it took warriors away from archery. The Irish played a form of Gaelic football in the 16th century.

Soccer was popular in England in the 19th century when William Webb Ellis, a frustrated college player, committed heresey. In a soccer game at Rugby College, Webb tried to kick the ball and missed. In anger, he picked up the ball and ran with it. His embarrassed team captain apologized for Webb's misconduct, but the concept caught on.

In 1841, the first game of "Rugby's football" was played. For more than 30 years, that variation remained in England. It developed slowly into the game now known as rugby, a direct descendent of soccer and the immediate forebearer of American football.

The first football game in the United States supposedly was the 1869 contest in New Brunswick, New Jersey, between Rutgers and Princeton Universities. Rutgers won, 6–4. In truth, the sport they played was soccer, with 25 men to a side. The ball could be kicked or advanced with the body, but not with the hands.

In 1871, this sport was modified by the "Boston game," in which running with the ball, as in rugby, was allowed. In 1873, Yale invited Harvard, Princeton, Columbia and Rutgers to organize a football league based on soccer rules. Harvard declined, preferring its "Boston game."

In 1874, Harvard found itself with a sport but no opponents, so it accepted an offer from McGill University of Montreal for a series of two games played under both the Boston rules preferred by Harvard and the McGill rules which were rugby.

Other American colleges were won over to the idea

of running with the ball. In 1876, the Intercollegiate Football Association was formed. Its rules were essentially rugby, and through the years they changed into the game now known as American football.

Though the sport was played mostly at prestigious Eastern universities, it became a game more for ruffians than for gentlemen. Muscles were more important than finesse. Protective equipment was primitive or nonexistent. Mass formations such as the flying wedge led to frequent injuries. In 1905 alone, when the game was played at relatively few colleges and sandlots, 18 players were killed and 159 seriously injured.

When President Theodore Roosevelt warned that he would ban football unless the roughness stopped, the rules committee made drastic changes. They not only saved the game but also laid the groundwork for its expansion and growth.

The new rules called for disqualifications of players guilty of slugging or kneeing. They created a neutral zone at the line of scrimmage, where every play began, making it more difficult for rival players to brutalize one another.

The old rules required a team to gain five yards in three plays (called "downs") or surrender the ball. Most teams used to run straight ahead, trying to gain two or three yards a down. The new rules required 10 yards, rather than five, for a first down, thus opening the game. (In 1912, the present rule allowing four downs was introduced.)

The most significant of the 1905–06 rules revisions legalized the forward pass. Here was a new skill and a new style. Defenses had to spread to cover potential pass receivers, opening the game further.

The forward pass was first used in 1906. Its potential was not realized until 1913, when Notre Dame, an obscure university from South Bend, Indiana, upset mighty Army, 35–13. Notre Dame's success came from the passes of quarterback Gus Dorais to end Knute Rockne, skills they perfected on the beach the previous summer.

That game changed the face of college football in several ways. The forward pass became an integral part of the game. Notre Dame became the most famous of all college football teams. And Knute Rockne, a Norwegian immigrant, became the most celebrated of all college football coaches.

College football's famous players include Jim Thorpe of Carlisle Indian School, Harold (Red) Grange of Illinois, Felix (Doc) Blanchard and Glenn Davis of Army and the Four Hoursemen backfield (Harry Stuhldreher, Jim Crowley, Elmer Layden and Don Miller) of Notre Dame.

The greatest innovator was Amos Alonzo Stagg, who played end for five years at Yale and then was head coach at Springfield College, University of Chicago and College of the Pacific for a total of 57 years. He pioneered the forward pass and the T formation. His inventions included the man in motion, shifts, quick kick, onside kickoff, field goal from placement, fake field goal, tackling dummy and the numbering of players. He was such an upright man that his son, Amos Alonzo

Stagg Jr., also a football coach, said, "To disagree with my father was like breaking with God."

One of Stagg's teammates at Yale was William W. (Pudge) Heffelfinger, an All-America guard for three years. In 1892, a few months after graduation, Heffelfinger received $500 to play one game for the Allegheny Athletic Association against the Pittsburgh Athletic Club. Allegheny won, 4–0, when Heffelfinger picked up an opponent's fumble and ran for a touchdown (a touchdown was worth four points then).

Heffelfinger was probably the first professional football player. In 1895, the Latrobe, Pennsylvania team paid $10 plus expenses to John Brallier to play quarterback against Jeanette, Pennsylvania. A decade later, the Canton, Ohio team paid $600 plus expenses to Willie Heston, an All-America halfback from Michigan, to play one game. Heston broke a leg on the first play and never played football again.

From these beginnings came professional football, but not without a struggle. College coaches denigrated the pro game, warning their players that it was not for gentlemen. Pro teams were loosely organized, and salaries were minimal.

In 1920, the American Professional Football Association, the first major league, was organized. Jim Thorpe was named president, a public-relations move the 12 teams hoped would help sell its product. But the public was uninterested. So were the club owners. The franchise fee was $100, but no one paid it. The league folded after one year. It was resurrected in 1921 with 13 teams. The champions were the Chicago Staleys, quarterbacked by Charlie Dressen, later a major-league baseball third baseman and manager. Franchises that sold for $50 eventually were worth up to $20 million.

In 1922, the league tooks its present name of National Football League. The Staleys changed their name to the Chicago Bears. Most teams were in or near Ohio, and the sport was still small time.

That changed in 1925 when Red Grange, the famous halfback from the University of Illinois, signed with the Bears. His manager, Charles C. (Cash and Carry) Pyle, arranged a barnstorming tour of seven games in 11 days. The New York game on that tour attracted 70,000 spectators and earned Grange $30,000. Grange made almost $100,000 that season and $100,000 in 1926.

After their 1925 success, Pyle, representing Grange, demanded a five-figure salary in 1926 and one-third ownership of the team from the Bears. When the Bears refused, Pyle leased Yankee Stadium in New York and attempted to get an NFL franchise. When the NFL refused, Pyle started the American Football League with nine teams, including Grange's New York Yankees. The league lasted one season, and Grange eventually returned to the Bears. Another American Football League started play in 1936 and lasted two years.

In 1936, the NFL conducted its first draft of college players. This annual draft, in which the weaker teams chose first, was designed to strengthen the weaker teams and eliminate bidding for college talent.

The NFL grew stronger under the leadership of de Benneville (Bert) Bell, its commissioner from 1946 until his death in 1959. Its greatest growth and refinement has come since 1960, when Alvin (Pete) Rozelle, the young general manager of the Los Angeles Rams, became commissioner.

Three other major leagues—the All-America Football Conference (AAFC) (1946–49), American Football League (AFL) (1960–69) and World Football League (WFL) (1974–75)—challenged the NFL with varied success.

The AAFC bid against the NFL for new and established players. The Cleveland Browns won the title in each of the league's four years, and eventually Cleveland, Baltimore and San Francisco were absorbed into the NFL.

The newest American Football League was founded in 1959 by Lamar Hunt when he was unable to buy an NFL franchise. It started play in 1960 with eight teams. It attained credibility because of two men—David A. (Sonny) Werblin and Joe Namath.

Werblin, a millionaire show-business agent and packager, headed a syndicate that bought the New York Titans' sinking franchise in 1963. In 1964, Werblin negotiated a television contract with NBC that gave AFL teams $36 million over five years. In 1965, Werblin signed Namath for his team, now called the Jets, for a then-record package of $427,000 over four years.

Namath was a charismatic quarterback whose success was a victory for the AFL in a costly bidding war for talent. The rival leagues agreed in 1966 to merge in 1970 into a 26-team NFL (it grew to 28 teams in 1976).

The Super Bowl game began in 1967. For the first three years, it matched the champions of the NFL and AFL; after that, it served as the NFL's championship game. The Green Bay Packers, coached by the legendary Vince Lombardi, won the first two Super Bowls. The Jets won the third by beating the NFL's Baltimore Colts, who were 17-point favorites, 16–7. The week before the game, Namath publicly "guaranteed" the Jets would win.

The World Football League began play in 1974, reinforced by such NFL players as Larry Csonka, Jim Kiick and Paul Warfield of the Miami Dolphins. Midway in the 1975 season, when losses totaled $20 million, the WFL folded.

Network radio first broadcast an NFL championship game in 1940, when 120 stations carried the Chicago Bears' 73–0 rout of the Washington Redskins. Television of NFL games, which started in 1939, was spurred by a Federal law that allowed professional sports leagues to negotiate contracts with one network. By 1979, the networks televised games regularly on Sunday afternoons and Monday nights and occasionally on Saturday afternoon, Sunday nights and weekday nights. Pro football had become big sport and big business.

Among the most celebrated professional players have been Bronko Nagurski, Jim Brown and O.J. Simpson, running backs, and Johnny Unitas, Sammy Baugh, Sid Luckman, Otto Graham, Fran Tarkenton and Joe Namath, quarterbacks. When Tarkenton retired in early 1979 after 18 seasons, he was the all-time leader in passes attempted (6,467), passes completed (3,686), yards passing (47,003), touchdown passes (342) and yards rushing by a quarterback (3,669).

—Frank Litsky

COLLEGE FOOTBALL

Knute Rockne at a Notre Dame practice, 1929.

ORIGINS OF THE MODERN GAME

ROOSEVELT CAMPAIGN FOR FOOTBALL REFORM

He Summons University Advisers and Asks Them to Agitate.

MAKERS OF RULES PRESENT

They Are Told That Brutality Should Be Eliminated and Fair Play Be Assured.

Special to The New York Times
WASHINGTON, Oct. 9.—Having ended the war in the Far East, grappled with the railroad rate question and made his position clear, prepared for his tour of the South, and settled the attitude of the administration toward Senator Foraker. President Roosevelt today took up another question of vital interest to the American people. He started a campaign for reform in football.

Around his table at luncheon were gathered the men who rule the game, Dr. D.H. Nicholas and W.T. Reid of Harvard, Arthur T. Hillebrand and John B. Fine of Princeton, and Walter Camp and John Owsley of Yale. They are athletic advisers of their universities, and John B. Fine and Walter Camp are members of the Rules Committee of the Intercollegiate Football Association.

The President has some personal interest in the game aside from his general interest in athletics, for his son has entered the freshman squad at Harvard and has already had cause to know how rough the sport may be, having received a black eye and other bruises in scrimmages.

Mr. Roosevelt, in beginning his talk to his guests, told them that he liked the game, but he felt that something should be done to reform the rules, especially in the interest of fair play and the discouragement of rough play, and asked them to undertake to start a movement to that end.

Public sentiment is yearly growing stronger against the brutality of the game, he declared, and the death of a man in order to win a game will result sooner or later in universal condemnation of it as a part of college athletics.

The President's sentiments and counsel were old friend Camp, who graduated from Yale in 1880—which was the President's year at Harvard. The two became acquainted in the athletic contests between the universities then, and have kept up the friendship ever since.

This is not the first time that Mr. Roosevelt has taken a hand in intercollegiate athletics. When he was Police Commissioner of New York, in 1896, he patched up a truce between Yale and Harvard, and brought about an agreement that has held good ever since.

Not a little significance is given to the incident today at the White House because of the persistent rumors that after leaving the White House Mr. Roosevelt will become President of Harvard.

October 10, 1905

The New Game of FOOTBALL

WITH the period for theorizing passed, college football teams must now face an entirely new condition of affairs on the gridiron. The universal outcry against brutality on the football field and the demand for a more open sytle of play have been met by a sweeping revision of the rules, the result of many conferences extending over nearly a year and participated in by representatives from colleges and universities all over the country. For months following the long Winter session of the rulemakers coaches have everywhere gone through the rules with the greatest care, racking their brains to analyze them and figure out their possibilities. Many predict the ruination of the game through the drastic reformation, while other profess to see a big improvemtnt. All agree on one point, however, that it will be harder for the un-sportsmanlike player to interfere with clean sport, while many of those who see in the coming game greater opportunities for open play believe that the elements of roughness and corresponding injury to players will be increased.

No one is in a position to foretell exactly what the outcome of the changes will be. This cannot be determined by a mere discussion of the rules or by the preliminary practice such as all of the college elevens have indulged in for the past two weeks. Nor are the early games likely to show up the points of advantage and disadvantage in the new rules. This year not only will the teams develop, but the game must needs develop as well, and it all should go to make the season one of the most interesting in the history of the sport. Notwithstanding the uncertainty of the outcome there are fundamental facts that have been developed on which the foremost strategists and tacticians of the game have practically agreed. But while the leading exponents of the game may entertain certain opinions, the great public, which makes the game possible, must be constituted the final court of judgment.

The changes are numerous and far-reaching. Many of them are of little real importantance, and others rather make platin the old rules that constitute new ones. The most important changes severely punish all rough play and provide for clean sport. Slugging and kneeing in future will bring disqualification; the neutral zone will greatly transform the scrimmage line; compact formations for mass tactics are discouraged; the forward pass will result in a more open style of game; the art of kicking will be an im-

portant feature; the tendency will be toward a new style of free running; the ten-yard gain will do much in preventing rough play, and the additional penalties will materially help the sport. There, in brief, are the principal elements which are expected to restore the great college game to public favor.

The main effort of the football reformers has been to "open up the game"—that is, to provide for the natural elimination of the so-called mass plays and bring about a game in which speed and real skill shall supersede so far as possible mere brute strength and force of weight. For years the game has been becoming less open, and the reason for this has been that coaches everywhere have shown themselves more proficient in planning methods for holding the other fellow back than for carrying the ball ahead. In recent years while end plays have often been attempted, what every college team has mainly relied on has been attack aimed somewhere inside the tackles, for success in advancing the ball has depended almost entirely on the sudden massing of half the team at one narrow spot on its opponent's line. And even if such plays could consistently gain only two or three yards they were considered successful.

The effort of the Rules Committee to prevent the further development of such a game was not taken to provide a more interesting contest, but to discourage a system of play which not only was responsible for many injuries, but placed a premium on the concentration, both offensively and defensively, of weight and beef rather than on quickness and real personal skill.

There has been no real alteration in the fundamental plan of the game. The underlying scheme has undergone no change. The first effort has been to provide for the detection of foul play and its stringent punishment. To this end there has been provided an extra umpire. This will be the first change noticed by the spectator. With the efforts made to enforce penalties there need be no great concern. They will not change the character of the spectacle much, though they will influence the method of coaching. This, however, is a consideration for the technical expert and not for the general public.

Cut at top of column illustrates: Illegal use of hands and arms by players of the side in possession of the ball. Player No. 1, in an attempt to obstruct an opponent, has his hand upon an opponent to push him away from that play.

The old style of starting the game has been retained, but there the old conditions cease, and the new features will at once be apparent. The first one of the most important changes will be when the opposing teams line up for a scrimmage. Instead of facing each other at close quarters, as in the past, the length of the ball will separate them, and this will affect the entire character of the defensive play. It will put an end to charging, and from a spectator's standpoint will materially improve the game, as it will reduce to a minimum mass plays, which made it next to impossible for the spectators to watch the progress of the ball with any degree of satisfaction. It will prevent one team securing a big advantage on their opponents before the ball is actually in play and favor a defensive rather than an aggressive game.

To eliminate brutality the mode of attack has undergone

Legal use of body in blocking; the player on the right has thrown his shoulder against his opponent's thigh, to block him away from the play, but is not using his hands or arms.

Legal use of arms by player of the side in possession of the ball; Player No. 2 is attempting to obstruct an opponent in keeping his arms close to his body.

Legal use of hands and arms by player of the side in possession of the ball; the player in the middle of the group, in attempting to obstruct an opponent, is keeping his hands together and his arms close to his body.

a sweeping change. Guards and tackles back and tandem plays are things of the past. Recognizing the principal element of danger, the committee limited the number of men to be drawn back to carry the ball to five, but to minimize the danger of accidents the men so drawn back must retire at least five yards. To students of the game this means that old mass and tandem plays will in future be impossible, and straight line plunging will be the favorite method of attack and ground gaining. Although many of the big teams in the past did not look with favor on this style of play, the fact that the defense had been weakened by the new rules and other changes effected will enable the teams to adopt this play with reasonable prospects of a fair measure of success, although the amount of ground actually gained

will be much less than formerly.

The forward pass and outside kick will help to make the new attack successful, as they will help to make the secondary line of defense, constituted by the backs supporting the linesmen, to withdraw behind the line distance of at least five yards, so as to be prepared for any quick change of position in the event of either of these plays being attempted. This will result, on the defending side, in the line-up being spread out somewhat on the order of the English Rugby game. With the defense thus weakened, it will be necessary for field leaders to resort to tricks and strategy to gain the necessary distance, which is now ten yards instead of five, as formerly.

CRUCIAL CHANGES IN FOOTBALL RULES.

1906.	1905.
Two lines of scrimmage, one for each team, and each through its own end of the ball.	One line of scrimmage through forward point of ball.
No centre, guard, nor tackle may drop back from line of scrimmage on offense, unless he is at least five yards back of line of scrimmage and another player of those ordinarily behind line of scrimmage takes his place in line of scrimmage.	Any of five centre men could be placed anywhere behind line of scrimmage.
When the ball has been kicked by a player other than the snapper back any player on the kicking side shall be on side as soon as the ball touches the ground.	Ball could not be put on side.
If in three consecutive downs (unless the ball shall have crossed the goal line) a team having constantly held the ball in its position, shall not have advanced the ball ten yards, it shall go to the opponents on the spot of the fourth down.	It was necessary to advance the ball but five yards to constitute the first down.
Before being snapped back the ball must be placed flat on the ground, with long axis at right angles to line of scrimmage.	Could be placed in any position.
One forward pass shall be allowed in each scrimmage, provided such pass be made by a player who was behind the line of scrimmage when the ball was put in play, and provided the ball after being passed forward, does not touch the ground before being touched by a player of either side.	Forward pass was not allowed.
The ball may not be touched by player who was on line of scrimmage when the ball was put in play, except by either of the two men playing on the ends of the line.	
A forward pass over the line of scrimmage within space of five yards on either side of the centre shall be unlawful.	
A forward pass by side which does not put ball in play in scrimmage shall be unlawful.	
A forward pass which crosses goal line without touching a player of either side shall be declared a touch-back for defenders of that goal.	

To retain possession of the ball the offense must find new plays, which must be open to conform with the new disposition of players on the field. It is in this particular that the quarter back kick, used with varying success for the past three years, or, as it in future will be known, the on-side kick, will be universally adopted.

The rule governing the on-side kick provides that the ball when kicked may be secured by any player of the side kicking it after it has touched the ground, whereas formerly the players of the kicking side were restrained by rule from touching the ball until it had been touched by one of the opposing side. If it be simply kicked down the field as formerly there is only the chance of getting the ball, provided it is not cleanly handled by the catching back, while if it is kicked short and to one side there is an excellent chance of one of the kicking side securing it before the defending side is able to reach it. This will result in a frequent use of the kick, which will be varied in execution according to the playing conditions.

While the two kicks are somewhat similar, there is really a big difference, which will have an important bearing on the game. The quarter back kick had to be secured by one of the kicking side who was behind the kicker when the ball was punted in order to be retained by the same side. Any man no matter how far he may be in his opponents' territory when ball is actually kicked, can now get it the instant it touches the ground. This will enable the man kicking the ball to place his kicks with judgment, and to one who is accurate in kicking this will be a big benefit and frequently enable him to aid his side in retaining the ball.

The forward pass is a radical departure. The old rule made it compulsory that the ball should not be passed toward the opponent's line. It had to be passed back before a player could run with it. Under the new order of things it can be passed forward at will, except that it may not be passed directly over the line of scrimmage within five yards of the centre either side. Then, too, it may be passed only to one of the back field players or to an end rush, six men in all, and may be passed to any part of the field.

The effect of this on the runner is incalculable, as he can at any time, when on the point of being tackled, pass the ball to one of his own side who may be some distance ahead and by these means it would be possible to carry the ball the entire length of the field. This is the one play that makes the English Rugby game so open and attractive. The carrying of the ball continuously is restricted, however, and the play can be used only once in each scrimmage, and the ball must be touched by a player of either side before touching the ground. The penalty for failing to touch a player is the loss of the ball. This requires the utmost accuracy in passing and handling the ball, prohibits long passes, and makes the dangers of the play very great. The forward pass is expected to result in long spectacular runs, especially as the defense must be weakened to be prepared to meet them.

The effect of these changes has resulted in the utmost conjecture and widest difference of opinion. The former spectacle of witnessing a team carry the ball the entire length of the field by short line plunges of two or three yards is no longer possible. It is now necessary to gain between three and four yards on every play to retain the ball, which under the changes will be a difficult matter. Line plunges are legislated out of existence, and the question whether open play will make it possible to gain consistently with forward passing and on-side kicking can only be determined when the big teams meet in competition and are somewhat evenly matched.

It is probable that the kicking will be developed with the hope of securing advantage from the fumbles of the opposing backs, but no matter what effect it may have on the scoring, it will bring into requisition speed, agility, and varying resources and from a spectator's point of view effect a wonderful and much desired improvement.

September 30, 1906

11 KILLED AT FOOTBALL.

104 Players Also Injured During the Season of 1906.

CHICAGO, Nov. 25.—Eleven players were killed and 104 were injured in the United States during the football season of 1906, according to The Chicago Tribune to-day. These figures are compared with the casualties of 1905, when 18 players were killed and 159 severely injured, and, according to The Tribune, show that "debrutalized" football has accomplished in a large degree the object aimed at, in rendering the game less dangerous to life and limb.

The decrease in casualties is especially marked among high school players. In the season of 1905 11 high school players were killed and 47 injured, while in the season just closed seven were killed and 25 hurt. All college and high school games this year were played under the new rules drawn up after the close of last season to satisfy the agitation for less dangerous football. This year not one fatality has occurred in the game played by the larger American colleges.

November 26, 1906

REVISED FOOTBALL RULES ARE READY

Committee Meet to Strengthen Weak Spots in Code.

Important Interpretation of Some Rules That Were Confusing Last Season.

The Intercollegiate Football Rules Committee completed its work of revising the football rules for next Fall at a meeting at the Murray Hill Hotel yesterday. Eleven representatives of the various colleges constituting the committee were in session from 10 o'clock in the morning until 4 in the afternoon reviewing the whole scope of the rules, and when they finished their work the rules were ready for publication. What the gathering really did was to review the work of its sub-committee, Walter Camp, Prof. L. M. Dennis, and E. K. Hall, which had been instructed to make such alterations in the code as were necessary to effect the changes decided upon at its February meeting. These alterations were modified in various inessential details and two additions made to the rules before they were approved in their final shape. The additions both referred to the forward pass.

It was decided that in case a forward pass were made near the goal line either on the bound or rolling, whether or not it had been legally touched before it crossed the line, it should go to the defending side as a touchback. It was also decided that in order to prevent any evasion of the rule defining which men were eligible to receive a forward pass, that all men should be considered on the line of scrimmage unless they were at least a yard behind the point at which the ball was put in play. The Carlisle Indians last year, by having three or four men withdraw a foot behind the line, qualified a number to receive a forward pass in controversion of the intention of the rule. The new measure seeks to obviate this. It was also decided that the extra official provided for in February should be called a field judge.

The meeting, after adpting the new code as prepared by its sub-committee appointed another Central Board of Officials to carry on the work which it so satisfactorily did last year. This committee consists of the same men: Prof. James A. Babbitt of Haverford, Chairman; Walter Camp of Yale, Prof. L. M. Dennis of Cornell, Prof. C. W. Savage of Oberlin, and Prof. J. B. Fine of Princeton. It was decided that this committee should call a conference of football managers and representatives of the various colleges to be held in New York about June 7, at which the whole question of enforcing the control of the Central Board over officials should be discussed. In a circular letter sent out last night those colleges which wish to organize the control of officials in the Central Board are requested to send representatives to the conference, where the appointment of officials, jurisdiction over them, uniformity of fees, and other similar matters will be arranged for. This conference is expected to avoid the misunderstanding that arose with reference to officials last year.

May 19, 1907

Walter Camp was Mr. Football at the turn of the century. He successfully pushed for changes in the rules that opened up the game and his All-American selections were eagerly awaited each year.

John Heisman, head coach at the University of Pennsylvania for many years, for whom the Heisman Trophy was named.

Many believe that Jim Thorpe was the greatest athlete of the first half of this century. He was outstanding in college football at Carlisle, later played pro ball with the Canton Bulldogs and was the track and field star of the 1912 Olympics.

RADICAL CHANGES IN FOOTBALL RULES

Four Periods of Fifteen Minutes Each, Flying Tackle Eliminated—Other Features.

After an extended period lasting nearly six months, the Intercollegiate Football Rules Committee yesterday announced in Spalding's Official Football Guide the rules which will govern the conduct of the game during the Fall season. Many of the changes are revolutionary in character and calculated to minimize greatly the danger of fatal accidents existing under the old rules.

The time of play is divided into four periods of fifteen minutes' duration instead of the traditional two halves of thirty-five minutes each. The usual intermission of fifteen minutes is maintained between the second and third period, but an intermission of three minutes only is allowed between the first and second and third and fourth periods. During this short intermission no player will be allowed to leave the field, nor will any one be permitted to come on the field save only the individual who looks after the physical condition of the players.

At the beginning of the second and fourth periods the teams change goals, but the down, the relative spot of the down, the possession of the ball and the distance to be gained remain as they were at the conclusion of the preceding period of play.

Another radical change is that governing the flying tackle. This has been entirely eliminated by a new ruling, which provides that a player must have one foot at least on the ground when tackling an opponent. The new legislation governing the forward pass, which a number of the experts were inclined to abolish altogether, will materially alter the play and aspect of the game.

This year's rules provide that a player is only qualified to receive a forward pass who is at least one yard back of his own line of scrimmage or occupies the position on the end of said line. No man may make a forward pass or kick the ball unless he is five yards back of the line of scrimmage.

The territory forward of the line of scrimmage, and consequently in the enemy's camp, is adjudged neutral for a distance of 20 yards pending the completion of a forward pass or kick. A forward pass is not legal if the ball crosses a line 20 yards in advance of the spot where it was put in play before touching the ground or a player.

In the case of a kick the players on the defense within the 20-yard zone must not interfere with the ends or other players in any way until these opponents have advanced 20 yards beyond the line of scrimmage.

Interlocked interference—that is, players of the side having the ball taking hold of each other, or using their hands or arms to grasp their teammates in any way—is forbidden, and it is also forbidden for any man on the side having possession of the ball to push or pull in any way the man running with the ball.

Another innovation is to be noted in regard to substitution of players during a game. A rule has been passed which provides that a player who has been removed for any cause except disqualification or suspension may be returned to the game once at the beginning of any subsequent period.

The longitudinal lines formerly marking the field are done away with, as the quarter back may now cross the line of scrimmage at any point.

The new rules have already been adopted by all the large colleges, nearly all of them being represented on the Rules Committee, which consists of L. M. Dennis, Cornell; E. K. Hall, Dartmouth; James A. Babbitt, Haverford; John C. Bell, University of Pennsylvania; Crawford Blagden, Harvard; Walter Camp, Yale; Paul J. Dashiell, Annapolis; W. L. Dudley, Vanderbilt; Parke H. Davis, Princeton; Lieut. H. H. Hackett, West Point; Dr. W. A. Lambeth, University of Virginia; C. W. Savage, Oberlin; A. A. Stagg, University of Chicago, and H. L. Williams, University of Minnesota.

August 18, 1910

SWEEPING CHANGES IN FOOTBALL RULES

After two long days of deliberation, the Football Rules Committee juggled and argued with many different suggestions to improve the gridiron game, and finally got down to business yesterday afternoon and changed the game radically, the main idea in the sweeping innovations being to give the offensive team a better chance to cross their opponent's goal line. Football men at the meeting, while they have had only a hasty glimpse of the decisive changes, predict that the game has been opened up, and that next year, under this new code, the football loving public will see a faster, better, and more open game.

Briefly, the changes include allowing the forward pass to cross the goal line for a distance of 10 yards; the length of the gridiron is shortened from 110 yards to 100 yards; a team is allowed four trials to gain 10 yards, instead of three trials; the onside kick is eliminated; the 20-yard zone which now restricts the forward pass is eliminated, and the ball may be thrown for any distance; the kick off at the beginning of the halves will be from the offensive side's 40-yard line, instead of the middle of the field; the loser of the toss of the coin is entitled to the same privileges at the beginning of the second half as the winner is entitled to at the beginning of the first half; after a touchback the ball will be put into play at the 20-yard line, instead of the 25-yard line; the position of field judge is eliminated, and there will be only three officials for each game, referee, umpire, and head linesman, who will also keep time; a touchdown to count 6 points instead of 5; only one representative allowed on the side lines during a game, instead of three; and, finally, a drop kick which first touches the ground and bounds over the goal posts does not count.

February 4, 1912

THORPE INDIANS' STAR.

Carlisle Captain Chief Point Getter in Victory Over Syracuse.

SYRACUSE, N. Y., Oct. 12.—The Carlisle Indian football team got sweet revenge on the Syracuse eleven for the victories which the local eleven got over the braves in 1910 and 1911, when Jim Thorpe and the redmen won today by a score of 33 to 0. Thorpe was the individual star of the hour's battle, and he was aided and abetted in the victory by Powell, Berglo, Arcasa and Welch. These five men played brilliant football and were in every play.

A heavy rain fell during the second period, making conditions unpleasant for the nine thousand spectators. At no time was the Syracuse team in danger of scoring. Thorpe scored three touchdowns, Powell and Welch one each. Thorpe kicked three goals.

October 13, 1912

Cornell to Number Football Men.

Special to The New York Times.

ITHACA, N. Y., March 8.—That he is in favor of numbering football players and is going to try the experiment next Fall with the Cornell football team was announced by Dr. Albert H. Sharpe, coach of the Cornell eleven, to-day.

Dr. Sharpe thinks that, sooner or later, the numbering of football players is bound to come. Meanwhile he says he is prepared to have the Cornell football team numbered in games if other big colleges will number their players. "In any event," he says, "the scheme will be tried out on the Cornell squad next Fall, and if it comes up to my expectations, it will become a permanent feature." Dr. Sharpe pointed out that the scheme had already been tried in intercollegiate basket ball and that it had been successful. "I think," he says, "that the scheme of numbering the men will aid the officials in the exercise of their duties and will help the spectators follow more closely the intricate plays of the game."

March 9, 1913

NOTRE DAME'S OPEN PLAY AMAZES ARMY

Cadets Unable to Break Up Accurate Forward Passing of Westerners.

Special to The New York Times.

WEST POINT, N. Y., Nov. 1.—The Notre Dame eleven swept the Army off its feet on the plains this afternoon, and buried the soldiers under a 35 to 13 score. The Westerners flashed the most sensational football that has been seen in the East this year, baffling the cadets with a style of open play and a perfectly developed forward pass, which carried the victors down the field thirty yards at a clip. The Eastern gridiron has not seen such a master of the forward pass as Charley Dorais, the Notre Dame quarter back. A frail youth of 145 pounds, as agile as a cat and as restless as a jumping-jack, Dorais shot forward passes with accuracy into the outstretched arms of his ends, Capt. Rockne and Gushurst, as they stood poised for the ball, often as far as 35 yards away.

The yellow leather egg was in the air half the time, with the Notre Dame team spread out in all directions over the field waiting for it. The Army players were hopelessly confused and chagrined before Notre Dame's great playing, and their style of old-fashioned close line-smashing play was no match for the spectacular and highly perfected attack of the Indiana collegians. All five of Notre Dame's touchdowns came as the result of forward passes. They sprang the play on the Army seventeen times, and only missed four. In all they gained 243 yards with the forward pass alone.

The topnotch forward pass performance of the game happened in the second period when Notre Dame carried the ball nearly the entire length of the field in four plays for a touchdown. Rockne caught McEwan's kick-off and was downed on the fifteen-yard line. Little Dorais then got five on a quarter back run. He then hurled a long pass to Pliska, which netted thirty yards. Dorais followed this with a beautiful placed heave of thirty-five yards to Rockne. Another forward pass to Rockne carried the ball to the five-yard line and then Pliska was jammed through the Army forwards for a touchdown.

Football men marveled at this startling display of open football. Bill Roper, former head coach at Princeton, who was one of the officials of the game, said that he had always believed that such playing was possible under the new rules, but that he had never seen the forward pass developed to such a state of perfection.

Except for a short time in the second period, when the Army team got going and hammered out two touchdowns by driving, back-straining work, the Cadets looked like novices compared with the big Indiana team. Just before West Point's second touchdown, Notre Dame made a great stand under the shadow of its own goal. The Cadets had the ball on the one-yard line and Hodgson, Hobbs and Capt. Hoge hurled themselves at the line, but it would not move. A penalty gave the Soldiers their first down and again the Army backs punched the rigid wall of last Westerners. Five times they hammered at the line and on the sixth crash, Prichard bulleted his way through for the touchdown.

This was the first time Notre Dame has ever been on the army schedule, and a crowd of 5,000 came to the reservation to-day to witness the game. Report had the Indiana team strong, but no one imagined that it knew so much football. Dorais ran the team at top speed all the time. The Westerners were on the jump from the start, and handled the ball with few muffs. The little quarter back displayed great judgment at all times, and was never at a loss to take the cadets by surprise. He got around as if on springs, and was as cool as a cucumber on ice when shooting the forward pass. Half a dozen Army tacklers bearing down on him in full charge didn't disconcert the quarter back one bit. He got his passes away accurately, every one before the cadets could reach him. He tossed the football on a straight line for 30 yards time and again.

The Army folks from Gen. Leonard Wood down to the youngest substitute on the scrubs were shocked at the way the Army team was put to rout. Head Coach Charley Daly paraded up and down the side lines nervously as he watched the depressing spectacle of the giant full back, Eichenlaub, tearing the Army line to shreds. The cadet corps in the stands yelled encouragement at the soldiers until they were hoarse, but it was a losing fight from the start.

There was little of encouragement in the Army's showing with the Navy game four weeks away. Their best playing was shown only in streaks. At times the Army backs punched through the Notre Dame line with genuine power behind their driving charge, but after they had hammered out two touchdowns, much of the snap was gone from their attack. In the last period the Notre Dame team also was pretty well played out. Going at top speed all the time slowed them up considerably at the end. But the wonder of it all was that covering all the ground they did didn't tire them earlier. They had the ball most of the time, and were always eating up the distance which separated them from the Army goal line.

McEwan kicked off for the Army and Dorais had taken only a few steps when he was buried under a pile of Army men. Eichenlaub tried the Army line, but it would not yield, and then the cadets let out a yell when the Army got the ball on a fumble. Both sides were penalized 15 yards for holding. Hodgson and Capt. Hoge jammed through the forward for big gains, but Hodgson was finally forced to kick. He booted the ball to Dorais on the five-yard line and the quarter back wiggled his way back to the 35-yard line before he was brought down. Pliska got around the end for five yards, and then Dorais tried his first forward pass, and it failed, so the quarter back punted to midfield.

Dorais was tackled so hard after catching Hodgson's return punt that he fumbled the ball, and the alert Meacham fell on the ball for the Army. Eichenlaub and Finnigan tore big holes in the Army's front and Dorais's second attempt at a forward pass failed. McEwan, the Army centre, was hurt in the mêlée which followed and had to retire for a while, but Trainer Harry Tuthill patched him up and he got back in the game in a few minutes.

Then Notre Dame cut loose. Some vicious line smashing by Eichenlaub and Pliska carried the ball down to the 25-yard line and Dorais hurled a beautiful forward pass to Capt Rockne, who caught it a few yards from the goal line and rushed it over for the first touchdown. Dorais kicked the goal. Before the first period ended, Dorais got off several spectacular forward passes to Pliska and Rockne. A successful forward pass by the Army, Prichard to Jouett, carried the ball to Notre Dame's 15-yard line, and from there Hodgson and Hobbs plowed their way to the goal line, Hodgson hurling himself over for the score. Woodruff was rushed in as a pinch kicker and booted the ball over the crossbar, tieing the score.

Soon after play was resumed Merillat was tackled so hard by Rockne that he was laid out, but came back into the game smiling just as soon as he got his wind again. Prichard then drove the Army team at top speed, and a fine forward pass, which he threw to Jouett, landed the leather on the five-yard line. Three times Hodgson and Hobbs tried to batter their way over the goal line, but got only as far as the one-yard mark. Here Notre Dame was penalized for holding and the Army fortunately got a first down. The Notre Dame team was making a desperate stand with the ball only six inches from the goal. Hodgson slammed himself into the scrimmage twice only to be turned back. On the sixth try, Prichard hurled his way over for a touchdown. Hoge missed the goal. The Cadets went wild with joy, but their happiness was short-lived, because Dorais then executed a string of forward passes which put the Army team completely up in the air.

After the Army's touchdown, Notre Dame, starting from the fifteen-yard mark, sailed serenely down the field for a touchdown, from which Dorais kicked the goal and put the Westerners in the lead, 14 to 13. Dorais fell back and the Notre Dame team spread out across the field. Dorais hurled the ball high and straight for twenty-five yards, and Rockne, on the dead run, grabbed the ball out of the air and was downed in midfield. Dorais lost no time in shooting another pass at Pliska, which netted thirty-five yards. The ball went high and straight, and Pliska was far out of the Army's reach when he caught it. The partisan Army crowd for the moment forgot that the Army was being defeated, and burst forth in a sincere cheer for the marvelous little quarter back Dorais and his record toss of thirty-five yards. The ball again shot up into the air and was grabbed by Finnigan a few yards from the Army goal line. Pliska, behind compact interference, skirted the Army tackle for a touchdown, and Dorais again kicked the goal.

Notre Dame had West Point on the run, and there was no stopping their wild, reckless advance. Dorais kept at his great work and had his ends and half backs dashing madly around the field chasing his long throws. Just before the end of the period Notre Dame had the ball on the Army's 45-yard line close to the east side of the gridiron. Dorais barked out a signal, and the whole western back field and ends rushed across to the west side of the field. Dorais received the ball from his centre and ran back several yards before he tossed the ball. He set himself and waited just a second too long. His throw was a wonder. It sailed far and straight through the air for nearly 40 yards, soaring toward the outstretched hands of Rockne. If this pass had been executed it would have been a dazzling trick, but just as Rockne was about to grab the ball Prichard hurled himself high over the Notre Dame Captain's head and caught the ball. Then the first half ended.

The teams fought stubbornly in the third period, the ball see-sawing up and down the field from one team to the other. The Army was fighting hard and stubbornly and threw back the Notre Dame charge. It was in this period that Dorais attempted a daring stunt. He dropped back to the midway mark, when Eichenlaub's tearing rushes had been stopped, and tried to kick a goal from the field. There wasn't a chance of his making it because the ball rose over the Army line only a few yards, and rolled down to the goal line.

Hodgson, Hobbs and Millburn then began to tear up the Notre Dame line for generous gains, and marched down to the Notre Dame 15-yard line. Millburn was fresh in the game, and on two plunges he carried the ball 12 yards.

Notre Dame was penalized for holding and it was the Army's ball on Notre Dame's two-yard line. Then the Westerners made the best stand of the game. As Hodgson threw himself into the scrimmage, he was lifted bodily by Rockne, who hurled him back for a loss. Millburn, too, was forced back for a loss by the fighting Notre Dame forwards. Prichard as a last resort tossed a forward pass over the goal line, where Merrilatt was waiting for it. The ever-awake Dorais was again on the job and caught the ball, saving Notre Dame from a touchdown.

In the last period Finnigan made a fine twenty-five-yard dash around Merrilatt's end, and after several bull-like rushes by Eichenlaub, the full back who would not be denied, the ball was finally carried over for a touchdown, after which Dorais kicked the goal. Notre Dame continued to run wild all over the field. The forward passes began to sail around in the air again, and hardly before the Cadets realized what was happening, Pliska, with the ball tucked under his arm, had galloped down the field to the five-yard line before the Army tacklers jumped on him and rubbed his leather-covered head onto the green turf. From here Dorais heaved a forward pass to Pliska, who caught it back of the goal line and scored another touchdown, and Dorais booted the ball over the cross-bar with graceful ease.

There was no stopping Notre Dame now. They had a score thirst which would not be quenched. A forward pass, which was received by Finnigan, brought the ball to the 30-yard line, and the Army was penalized 15 yards for off side play. From here the Notre Dame scoring machine got together and began to hammer and hammer relentlessly at the tiring line of stubborn soldiers. Yard by yard they fell back before the rushing Westerners. Notre Dame, through the fierce plunges of Finnigan and Eichenlaub, slowly but surely decreased the distance which separated them from another score. The Notre Dame full back pounded his way along without check until he was thrown over the line exhausted and as limp as a sack of meal. The line-up:

Army.	Position.	Notre Dame.
Jouett............	Left end	..........Rockne
Wynne..........	Left tackle	..........Jones
Meacham........	Left guard	..........Keefe
McEwan..........	Centre	...........Feeney
Jones..........	Right guard	.....Fitzgerald
Weyand........	Right tackle	......Lathrope
Merrilatt.........	Right end	........Gushurst
Prichard.......	Quarter back	.........Dorais
Hoge.........	Left half back	........Pliska
Hobbs........	Right half back	.....Finnigan
Hodgson........	Full back	......Eichenlaub

Referee—Mr. Morice of University of Pennsylvania. Umpire—Mr. Roper of Princeton. Head linesman—Mr. Leuhring of Northwestern. Time of quarters—Twelve and fifteen minutes. Army scoring: Touchdowns—Hodgson, Prichard. Goals from touchdown—Hoge. Notre Dame scoring: Touchdowns—Rockne, Eichenlaub (2,) Pliska (2.) Goals from touchdowns—Dorais (5.)

Substitutions—Army, Packard for Wynne, Waddell for McEwan, McEwan for Waddell, Goodman for Meacham, Huston for Goodman, Britton for Merrilatt, Ford for Hoge, Hess for Hobbs, Woodruff for Hess, Hobbs for Woodruff, Lanphier for Hodgson, Millburn for Lanphier; Notre Dame, Larkin for Finnigan.

November 2, 1913

Notre Dame Traveled 7,074 Miles.

Notre Dame's 1915 'Varsity football team created a record for traveling this year that has seldom if ever been equaled in the history of the sport. The team covered just 7,074 miles in traveling to complete the schedule of this season, and the eleven has passed through no less than twelve different States. The Notre Dame team has played as far east as West Point, on the Hudson River; as far west as Lincoln, Neb.; as far north as either Omaha, Neb., or South Bend., Ind., and as far south as Houston, Texas.

The team made a splendid showing during the season just closed, and their playing was all the more remarkable because the eleven was a traveling team, only three games of the season's schedule being listed for decision on Notre Dame's home grounds.

Notre Dame traveled to West Point, a distance of 1,688 miles for the round trip, and scored a victory over the Army by the score of 7 to 0. Later the team visited Nebraska and opposed the Creighton eleven in a game at Omaha, which resulted in a victory for Notre Dame by the score of 42 to 0. This contest entailed a journey on the part of Notre Dame of 1,108 miles. These journeys pale into insignificance, however, when compared with the traveling of the eleven last week to Austin, Texas, where they played the Texas State representatives.

December 4, 1915

FOOTBALL COACHES BARRED FROM LINES

Committee Does Little Tinkering with Code—Game Left Intact.

Two of the most spectacular features of football under the present rules—the forward pass and the goal from the field—were left unmolested by the Joint Rules Committee at its annual meeting, which ended at the Hotel Martinique yesterday. The game stands practically as it did during the last season, which was one of the most successful of recent years in point of exciting and thrilling competition. The only restriction placed on the forward pass was a minor detail, and prohibits a prospective thrower of the pass from rounding the ball when the defense breaks through and blocks the play.

Hereafter when the ball is thrown intentionally on the ground a penalty of ten yards will be inflicted from where the ball was put into play. The suggestion of Alonzo Stagg of Chicago that the field goal be reduced in value from three to two points was quickly squelched by the committee. It agreed with Coach Percy Haughton of Harvard that it was so difficult to devlop capable drop kickers that a team should receive full benefit of their kicking talent.

Football men who like the game in its present form rejoiced that the gridiron lawmakers left the game alone, and saved those features which were so much enjoyed by the thousands of spectators last season.

The most radical change which was made by the committee was barring the coaches from the side lines during the game. This will hit some of the teams pretty hard, for under the system of coaching followed at many of the colleges the head coach, walking up and down the line during the game, was a Czar of the situation, and, in many cases, absolutely controlled the campaign which was being carried on in the field. Some of the members objected strenuously to this change, and there was a warm discussion over the matter. Those who favored the new rule and finally carried it thought that it would reflect much greater credit on a team if each team was left to the judgment of the Captain.

In the past the head coach has sent in substitutes at will, and even now when barred from the side lines it will be impossible to entirely eliminate him from a part in the running of the game. Signals and messages may still be sent out to the Captain by means of substitutes. An effort was made to curb the frequent use of substitutes in the final period, but this measure was defeated.

February 8, 1914

BROWN'S ELEVEN LOSES AT PASADENA

PASADENA, Cal., Jan. 1.—It was an unkind greeting that California extended to Brown University this afternoon. Coming 3,000 miles across the continent to play one football game with the eleven of Washington State College, the Providence collegians were not only beaten by a score of 14 to 0 but they received an impression of California weather which will not be pleasant to relate when they return East.

The game, which was to be historic in that it came as the result of the longest trip ever attempted for a single contest, was played in dizzling rain on a field that was slippery and not at all one on which there could be a true test of football skill. Still for the most part the element of luck, which is conspicuous in many a battle of the gridiron, was not obtrusively present, but the game was slow and leaden alike to spectator and player.

There was no opportunity for either team to break loose with open play. The game had of necessity to resolve itself into a battering contest, much the same as those which were played when football was still undergenerated by the adaptation of new rules. Each team was deprived of circling attack around the wings. There was no footing to permit it. The runner could not get away from the lurching tackle or end who was able to hurl himself through before the man with the ball could gain the speed necessary in such plays. As a result, each realized that it must depend on line plunging, and that was uncertain.

The forward pass was relegated to the scrap heap of football temporarily. In fact, this was true of any of the trick plays which either team held in reserve for ground gaining when gains were necessary for touchdowns. All that had been expected failed of realization, and it was just an ordinary rain-soaked kind of football game that wouldn't have aroused a cheer from even the most loyal collegians.

When the teams came on the field for the first half they attempted to open up their play even under the adverse conditions. But it was useless, and then Washington started an attack against the Rhode Islanders that swept them back toward their own goal line. It was straight line plunging that was carrying Washington toward the Seattle goal, and while the gains were not big, still the Brown defense was not sufficient to enable it to hold off the three and four yard advantages for Washington.

It looked bad for the Easterners. They did not appear to find themselves in that first few minutes, and then suddenly there was the forging of a perfect defense. Back under the shadow of her own goal posts Brown halted the aggression of Washington, beat back the attack and took the ball. Washington began another attack that carried Brown steadily back. But it was a repetition of the first time the ball came dangerously near and then was forced the other way.

Near the end of the first half there was the first realization of the power in the Brown team. The men gathered themselves for a tremendous effort, and twice the spirit of the Eastern collegians almost carried them to touchdowns. But the Washington men were alert, powerful players, and Brown struck against a strengthening defense that eventually hurled the eleven back. At the end of the first half there was no touchdown for either side. There had been nothing but the hardest kind of playing on a sodden field.

With end running out of the question on the slippery field the Western eleven directed its attack against the left side of the Brown line and made repeated gains that brought the goal line of the Providence men many times in danger. Brown was really playing a defensive game for the greater part, though there were flashes of offensive work that were revelation of power.

The wet field changed the entire scheme of the Brown attack. It was expected that the negro half back, Pollard, a fast player, would gain many yards by skirting the ends and thus relive the deadly hammering through the line. But Pollard was of little avail. He could not get away for a fair start and his first failure was the indicator of the trend of the game. It was believed that the wet field would handicap Washington more than Brown, but it did not prove that way.

The closest that Brown came to a touchdown was in the second quarter, and then the brilliant work of Captain Andrews led the Providence men on their closest approach to the Washington goal, which was nineteen yards. It was Andrews's line plunging, a pretty forward pass, one of the few of the game, and several penalties against Washington that accomplished this result. It was at this point that Washington braced and took the ball on downs.

In reality Washington almost gained a bigger score against the Eastern colegians. Once it was a fumble when the ball was almost over the Brown goal line that robbed the Western eleven of a touchdown, and the ball was within twenty-five yards of the goal and a drop kick failed.

Each side made some costly fumbles, but they did not assume large proportions in estimating the merit of the two teams. If anything the breaks in this particular were even.

During the first period Brown had exhaused her strength, and while the Eastern eleven battled nobly, it could not hold back the fierce attack of the Western collegians. Strength and climate and other things were adding their mite to the defeat of Brown. In the third quarter Washington had the advantage of good substitutes, and it was one of these who, entering on the field fresh against the tired men from Providence, scored the first touchdown. Boone, who had replaced Henley, made the score after Brown had been forced steadily back to her own goal line.

Coach Robinson of Brown had seen the inevitable coming. He realized that his backs were tired and that it might avail something to run in substitutes. Seeing the determined attack of the Western eleven at the start of the third quarter, he resorted to heroic measures. The veteran back field was called from the game to give place to substitutes. And through this supposedly strengthened team Washington marched down the field to the first touchdown. Boone had discovered the weakness in Brown and he was sent crashing against the Eastern team time and again and always for a gain. Finally he scored and Durham kicked the goal.

Dietz scored the second touchdown and this again was the result of a march down the field. It started in the centre of the field, and with Boone, Dietz, and Bangs taking turns in carrying the ball the Brown line was forced back and the second touchdown secured by Washington.

After the game Walter Eckersall, the referee and former Chicago University quarterback, said that Washington State's team was the equal of Cornell's champion eleven. The line-up:

Washington State.	Position.	Brown.
Zimmerman	Left end	Butner
Clark	Left tackle	Ward
Applequest	Left guard	Stoff
Langdon	Centre	Sprague
Fishback	Right guard	Wade
Brooks	Right tackle	Farnum
Loomis	Right end	Weeks
Durham	Quarter back	Purdy
Bangs	Left half back	Pollard
Dietz	Full back	Saxon
Hanley	Right half back	Andrews

Touchdowns — Boone, Deitz. Goals from touchdowns—Durham (2.) Substitutes: Washington—Boone for Hanley, Finney for Applequest, Stiles for Fishback. Brown—Hillhouse for Andrews, Murphy for Purdy, Frazier for Pollard, Gemail or Saxton, Maxwell or Wade, Ormsby for Butner. Ward for Ormsby, Andrews for Hillhouse, Purdy for Murphy, Frazier for Pollard, Saxton for Gemail, Ormsby for Andrews. Referee—Walter Eckersall, Chicago; Dr. A. W. Smith, Michigan. Umpire—J. B. Ersfeld, Minnesota. Field judge—Clyde Holley, Pomona.

January 2, 1916

Football Michigan's Profitable Sport.

Profits from football receipts of the University of Michigan last Autumn were sufficient to cover deficits which each of the remaining athletic reports showed, it was announced at Ann Arbor yesterday. Football receipts totaled $55,852 and football disbursements were $40,548. Baseball fell $3,400 short of being self-supporting. The track athletic deficit was about $5,000. The report shows total athletic receipts of $90,935. and disbursements of $90,346. More than $12,000 was used to pay off the indebtedness on the new stadium and to improve the athletic fields.

March 4, 1916

TIBBOTT'S KICK MAY STAND.

Tiger Player's Field Goal Likely to be Season's Record.

Dave Tibbott's forty-six-yard drop kick in the Princeton-Tufts game last Saturday, which was just enough for the Tigers to triumph over the conquerors of Harvard, promises to stand as one of the longest field goals in the 1916 gridiron season, if not the longest that will be recorded this Fall. Tibbott's boot was the only score in the long battle, and it came after several of his teammates had endeavored in vain to hang up a tally of some sort over the Medfordites. His kick was perfect in direction from such a distance, and although as it sailed through the air it seemed to be destined to fall short of the crosspiece between the goal posts, it did not begin to drop until it had cleared the bar by about two yards.

The tabulation and analysis of field goal records have been annual hobbies of the followers of the greater American college game. Last year the experts saw the drop kicking mark, which had stood since 1898, shattered by Mark Payne o the Dakota Wesleyan eleven, who established the new world's record with a boot of 63 yards.

No one last season came within striking distance of the wonderful performance of J. T. Haxall in goals from placement. It was back in 1882 in the Princeton-Yale contest that Haxall scored for the Tigers when 65 yards away from the Elis' goal. In 1905 J. P. Davis of Dickinson scored a goal from placement against the University of Pittsburgh from the 58-yard mark, but last year the best records established for the season were of 48 yards, set up by J. G. Wilson of the Missouri School of Mines and Joseph Catlin and James Millikin. That the interscholastic placement kicking last season was of a higher calibre than in the collegiate games was shown in the work of Orson W. Wilcox of the Mansfield (Penn.) Normal School, who made one of 55 yards length.

Previous to Payne's drop-kicking record, a mark of one yard shorter—62 yards—had stood the test of time since 1898, when P. J. O'Dea of Wisconsin booted that distance in a game against Northwestern. The next mark is of 55 yards, and is held jointly by J. V. Cowling of the 1883 Harvard eleven and J. E. Duffy, a Michigan player, in 1891.

Drop kicking last year was not only longer, but more frequent. Charles H. McGuckin of Villanova holds two of the 1915 records. He had nine goals from the field by drop kicks for the season, and also tied with Howard Miller of Columbia and W. T. Vandegraaf of Alabama with four goals each for the most made in any one intercollegiate game.

October 18, 1916

FOOTBALL BACK IN 1869.

Rutgers Beat Princeton in First Intercollegiate Match.

Intercollegiate football is forty-seven years old this season, the first gridiron game having been played between Rutgers and Princeton on Nov. 6, 1869, at New Brunswick. Rutgers won by a score of 6 to 4. The game at that time was a very unwieldy affair and there were twenty-five players on a side. William J. Leggett, Captain of the Rutgers team, and William S. Gummere, afterward Chief Justice of New Jersey, devised the rules under which the match was played. This was the first football code formulated on this side of the Atlantic.

An account of the contest in The New Brunswick Daily Fredonia had the following to say about the game: "Our neighbor Princeton sent her chosen twenty-four stalwart men and one Goliath to combat our twenty-five striplings. Rutgers led off by winning the first inning amid the vociferous cheering of the bystanders. Princeton seemed to play a little wild at the beginning, but in the second inning they recovered themselves and came out the victors. So it continued, off and on, one gaining, then the other, until the ninth and tenth innings, when, notwithstanding the desperate efforts of the Princeton giants, Rutgers quickly and boldly followed in successive victory, giving them 6 runs to 4 of Princeton.

"The game thus ended in good feeling, although during the playing we observed some rather unnecessary sparring on the part of a few of the Princeton Phillistines. Princeton did well, but Rutgers did better, and let it continue to be, not alone in athletic sports, but also in the more energetic struggle of the mind."

Some of the rules under which the game was played were as follows: Goals must be eight paces. Each side shall number twenty-five players. No throwing or running with the ball; if either, it is a foul and the ball shall be thrown perpendicularly in the air by the side causing the foul. No holding the ball or free kicks allowed. No tripping or holding of players. The winner of the first toss has the choice of position. The winner of the second toss has the first kick-off. There shall be four judges and two referees.

November 26, 1916

STRICTER FOOTBALL RULES.

Big Nine Conference Aims at Professionalism in Any Form.

Apparently in an effort to stamp out anything that borders on professionalism in college football in the Middle West stringent new gridiron rules have been passed by the Big Nine Conference, and last week were ratified by the University of Wisconsin. One provision makes a false statement on a student's eligibility blank cause for his dismissal from the university. Another rule aims at the colleges in Ohio, Indiana, and Illinois, States where professional football is being played, and gives the colleges a warning against encroaches of the sport on a professional basis.

The new rules follow:

1. That a man making a false statement in his eligibility blank shall be dismissed from the university.
2. That the date for the opening football practice shall be moved from Sept. 20 to Sept. 15, and no facilities shall be provided for practice previous to that date.
3. (a) That all employes of the athletic department who take part in professional football games shall thereby be suspended from employment, and
   (b) That members of teams participating in professional football contests before graduation shall forfeit their letter and be recommended to the Faculty for further discipline.

March 4, 1917

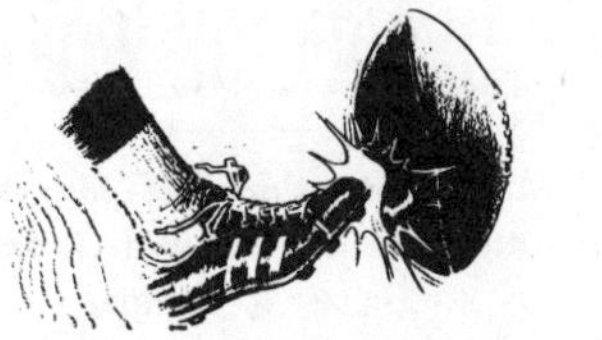

REVISED RULES BAR SIDE-LINE COACHING

The latest revision of the football rules, edited by Walter Camp, the Yale football mentor, has one new feature which will do away with one of the most objectionable features the game has developed during the past few seasons. This is the new rule which prohibits an incoming substitute from communicating with his team on the field until after the first play. In many of the big gridiron games the substitute subterfuge was carried on to unreasonable extremes. It was no uncommon sight to see a substitute sent from the side lines with information at a critical point of a game.

Side-line coaching has been a subject with which the rule makers have been grappling for the last few seasons. First, the side lines were cleared of the many assistant coaches and scouts, who used to crowd both sides of the field at the important games. The freedom of head coach was also restricted, and when the new rules permitted frequent substitutions, these players were used as a means of conveying information from the coaches to the players on the field. Gradually the initiative was taken from the players until the game was rapidly becoming a contest of automatons, which moved only at the beck and call of the coach on the side lines.

Prohibiting this objectionable feature will tend to throw the football players on their own resources and will develop strategy which heretofore has been dependent on side-line observation. There is but one exception to this rule and that is in the case of the quarter back. If the substitute replaces the quarter back, he is permitted to give the signal, but in no other way is he permitted to communicate with the players until after the first play.

The new restriction which has been placed on the forward pass will increase the value of this important play. One of the dangerous features of the forward pass has been the liability of the receiver of the ball being roughed. A new rule this season provides that when a player interferes with a player attempting to catch the forward pass, the penalty will be the loss of the ball to the offended side, at the spot where the foul was committed.

The place kick has been more clearly defined in the new code, and the play must be made by kicking the ball from its position when resting on the ground. This does away with the use of artificial tees, such as were used in some of the games last season. In one or two contests place kicks were made by placing a head gear on the ground and kicking the ball while it rested on the head gear. Gradually the rules makers are eliminating the objectionable features of the gridiron game. In the present edition of the rules the committee points out that the rules as they stand today should be allowed to crystallize as nearly as possible in their present from.

Each year new provisions have been made in the code to do away with side-line coaching, beating the ball, roughing the kicker and the receiver of the forward pass, talking to opponents, and disputing decisions of the officials. One by one these phases of the game are disappearing, and the standard of sportsmanship is unquestionably higher than it was in former days of the gridiron sport.

While no new rule was inserted in the code this year concerning holding, there was so much discussion about this feature of violation of the rules last season that officials this season will undoubtedly be instructed to enforce the rules against it more closely than ever before Holding is one violation of the rules which has never been rigidly enforced. There is no feature of the game which calls for more penalties during a game than holding. In pointing out the importance of eliminating this feature from the game the committee has incorporated in the rule book, under the interpretation of the code, the following:

"Holding is prohibited by the rules because it does not belong in the game of football. It is an unfair play. It eliminates skill. The slowest man in the world can make a forty-yard run in every play if the rest of his teammates would hold their opponents long enough. The game is to advance the ball by strategy, skill, and speed, without holding your opponent. Perhaps a good game could be invented the object of which would be to advance the ball as far as possible with assistance of holding your opponents, but it would not be football.

"It would probably become a team wrestling match and, unless drastic rules, rigidly enforced, prevented it, a free fight. If your coach cannot show you show to gain distance without holding your opponents get another coach."

September 2, 1917

LOCALIZE FOOTBALL IN COLLEGE WORLD

Many Institutions Planning Numerous Contests with Teams Close to Home.

Although 'Varsity football has been cancelled at Cornell and Dartmouth, it does not mean that the pigskin will be placed on the shelf at these colleges. There will probably be more football than ever before played at these places among the student soldiers. The schedules which were formulated with other colleges have been canceled, but plenty of impromptu games will be arranged for teams which can visit these places and return in a day's journey.

It is not and has never been the policy of the military officials to stamp out such a rugged, vigorous pastime as football among the students. There has been great delay, however, on the part of the officials in making it plain to the college authorities just what plan they mean to pursue. With the guarantees and other expenses involved in the arranging of the schedules at the end of last season, it was necessary for the student managers to cancel schedules to protect themselves from financial loss.

The manner in which the football situation at Pennsylvania has been rearranged to suit the military conditions will probably be followed at other institutions. The military officers realize the value of an hour or an hour and a half's football practice each day, and as the men will be in fine physical condition because of military training, this time can be given over to the development of play and gridiron tactics. Intramural and inter-regimental football will be played at the few colleges which have decided not to play any intercollegiate opponents.

September 27, 1918

Ohio State-Michigan Game Attracted a $100,000 Gate

ANN ARBOR, Mich., Oct. 27.—Approximately $100,000 in gate receipts was realized by the University of Michigan and Ohio State from the football game here last Saturday, according to Athletic Director Fielding H. Yost. Of this amount, about $80,000 resulted from the sale of reserved seat tickets, the remainder coming from student coupons. The sum, according to Yost, is the largest ever paid to witness a college athletic contest in the West. Paid admissions totaled more than 41,000, Yost announced, this figure also setting a record for Western universities. The money will be equally divided between Michigan and Ohio State.

October 28, 1921

EAST-WEST BATTLE ENDS IN 0-0 SCORE

W. and J. Eleven Outplays California Team at Pasadena, but Fails to Win.

OFFSIDE PLAY IS COSTLY

Deprives Easterners of Victory When Brenkert Crosses Goal Line —Crowd of 40,000 in Stands.

Special to The New York Times.

PASADENA, Cal., Jan. 2.—California's much-touted "wonder" football team was outplayed by Washington and Jefferson here this afternoon in the biggest intersectional clash of the year. While the game ended a scoreless tie, the Presidents from Pennsylvania outrushed, outgeneraled and generally outplayed the California Bears.

An offside play early in the first period robbed Washington and Jefferson of a victory. Halfback Brenkert broke through the right side of the California line, running from punt formation, and dodged through the entire California team thirty-five yards, going over the goal line. Umpire Thorp, however, detected a Washington and Jefferson lineman offside and the ball was brought back. That play would have registered a victory for the Presidents, as neither goal line was seriously threatened thereafter. Twice in the late stages of the game the Presidents rushed the ball well within California territory, and Captain Stein on both occasions tried for placement goals. Both attempts were failures.

A comparison of the relative strength of the two teams may be gained by the number of first downs registered, W. and J. getting 7 and California but 2. In the first half California showed a marked superiority in punting, Nisbet outkicking Brenkert on every exchange. Partly for this reason, and also because its running attack was stopped dead by the stalwart defense of the Presidents, California in the second half kicked usually on the first down.

Aerial Attack Misses Fire.

The much-vaunted aerial attack of the California Bears was conspicuous chiefly by its absence. Brick Muller, the famed hurler of passes, did not start the game, but he was injected early in the first half. California completed but two forward passes after he entered, one resulting in a loss and the catcher fumbling the other, W. and J. recovering. On the other hand, W. and J. made its longest single gain of the contest on a forward pass from Brenkert to Kopf.

Outstanding in the attack of the Presidents was the work of Halfback Erickson. Running from regular formation and also on a criss-cross play, the Minnesota Flash repeatedly reeled off substantial gains. The California tacklers seemed unable to stop him until three or four men had hurled themselves at him. He all but got away on several occasions, and as a threat kept the California defense puzzled througout. In running back punts, Erickson gave one of the greatest displays ever seen here, and in spite of the superior quality of Nisbet's kicking the net gain on the exchanges was not appreciable.

Toomey stood out as the best ground gainer of the Bears, but he could not consistently pierce the Red and Black defense, the Presidential front wall smothering him as well as the other backs most of the time.

The weather was ideal, cool and crisp, and with an absence of sunshine. But the field was in miserable condition. A twelve-hour rain had churned the grounds into a quagmire in many places, and frequently a runner slipped and fell for no gain without being tackled. The slippery condition of the ball also contributed to the fumbles, of which there were many by both teams. Usually the opposing side recovered the ball on the fumbles, but both suffered about equally.

Huge Crowd Attends.

The great stands were thronged, and it was estimated that about 40,000 persons saw what was termed one of the finest football games ever played in California. California was a long-odds favorite at the start, and even money was offered that the Bears would win by anywhere from 14 to 21 points. Large amounts were accepted on these terms by the Easterners, who carried away many thousands of dollars.

Washington and Jefferson flashed a superior brand of football at the start. The Presidents received the kick-off at their 25-yard line and marched straight down the field to the California 35-yard line without relinquishing the ball. Then came Brenkert's dart over the goal line when one of his men was offside. The Presidents again started their march, however, getting eight yards on the next play. Then a forward pass was true, Toomey, intercepting for California and running the ball back to the W. and J. 35-yard line. In four attempts the Bears could gain but two yards, the Presidents forcing back the onslaughts and taking the leather on downs on their 33-yard line.

Both teams then resorted to punting for the remainder of the period, W. and J. usually trying twice before kicking and California punting frequently on the first down. Washington and Jefferson kept edging continually towards the California goal, but seemed to lack the punch to make the necessary yardage for a first down. Just at the end of the first half Toomey on two plays made a first down for his team, the only one California made in the first two periods.

California's Strongest Threat.

W. and J. began a vicious assault at the start of the second half, but a fumble gave the ball to California, which rushed to the W. and J. 28-yard line, the nearest the Californians came to scoring. Here a fumble was recovered by the Presidents, who again opened up a relentless attack. The ball was carried to the 35-yard line and the Pennsylvanians seemed to be on their way to a score, when Brenkert fumbled, and again California saved itself by recovering inside its 40-yard mark.

Then, after receiving a kick and starting on its 40-yard line, W. and J. began another assault. A forward pass, Brenkert to Erickson, for thirty yards carried the ball to the California 30-yard mark shortly before the end of the third period. Here Captain Stein tried his first placement goal and missed. Nesbett immediately punted and Wash-Jeff cut loose with an off-tackle and end-play assault, frequently using a criss-cross with Erickson carrying the ball or Basista crashing into the line. A forward pass was uncompleted and again Stein tried for a placement goal. The slippery condition of the ball made it all but impossible to kick and the trial was a failure.

California was wholly on the defensive, except for a period near the close of the quarter, when the Bears' forwards rushed Brenkert so fast on his punt that the ball went almost straight up in the air and out of bounds on the W. & J. 22-yard line. It looked as if a break that might win for California had come and the California rooters with a mighty roar called for a touchdown. California then essayed a forward pass in a desperate effort to snatch the victory. Toomey caught the ball back of his scrimmage line, but as he seized it he was tackled so hard by two Wash-Jeff men, who hurled him back five yards, that the ball fell from his arms. Erickson picked it up and ran to his 22-yard line and California's only chance was lost.

Washington and Jefferson showed itself to be the same smart football team that went through its regular season undefeated. California plays were frequently diagnosed before they were well started and often the runner was smeared back of his goal line. Captain Stein of the Presidents, who directed his team personally in calling signals, mixed up his plays in bewildering fashion, while his line outcharged the Bear forwards all through the contest. With the exception of punting, California did not excel in a single department. At times Smith's team showed good interference to the line of scrimmage, but the Wash-Jeff forwards usually smashed the interfering wall and the backs got the runner.

Western football men were amazed at the ability of the W. and J. players and conceded that the Bears were downright lucky to stave off defeat.

Washingtond and Jefferson played through the entire game without making a substitution. California made a few substitutions, but both teams seemed to be in splendid physical condition. This was indicated in the first half when time was taken out but once for injuries, Fullback Basista of Washington and Jefferson getting a bump on the head. The Presidents covered Muller, the sensational All-America end of the Bears, so closely that he could not get going. It was the first time this year that the red-thatched end had met his match. He was never given an opportunity to hurl the long bullet-like passes which has featured the play of the Bears in earlier games. On one occasion he dropped back for a pass to an end speeding down the field, but the Red and Black forwards were upon him so quickly that he could not get the ball away and was forced to run with it, being hurled for a six-yard loss.

Game Cleanly Played.

The game, in spite of the intensity with which it was played and the stakes battled for, was characterized as one of the cleanest ever seen on the coast. The officials remarked on this phase of the contest, stating that no rough work of any kind was discovered. Numerous penalties were inflicted on account of the vigilance of the arbitrators, most of these coming for offside play. The only penalty for holding was drawn by Washington and Jefferson.

The line-up:

W. AND J. (0).		CALIFORNIA (0).
Kopf	L. E.	Stephens
Konvolinka	L. T.	Barnes
Neal	L. G.	Clark
Crook	C.	Latham
Vince	R. G.	Cranmer
Weldequist	R. T.	McMillan
Stein	R. E.	Berkey
West	Q. B.	Eri:
Erickson	L. H. B.	Toomey
Brenkert	R. H. B.	Nichols
Basista	F. B.	Nesbitt

Substitutions—California: Muller for Berkey, Schurr for Cranmer, Morrison for Nesbitt, Dunne for Nichols, Dean for Barnes.

Referee—George Varnell, Chicago. Umpire—Tom Thorp, Columbia. Linesman—H. H. Huebel, Michigan. Field Judge—Walter Eckersall, Chicago. Time of periods—Fifteen minutes.

January 3, 1922

CAMP FAVORS SLOW MOVIES ANALYSIS

Noted Football Authority Says Defects May Be Revealed by This Method.

Special to The New York Times.

NEW HAVEN, Conn., Feb. 17.—Yale coaches warmly favor the plan of analyzing the playing of football men by means of the eight-times-slow moving picture process. Defects have been revealed by this method which have been undetected in other ways.

Walter Camp, the former Yale head coach, said today of the plan: "This proposition resolves itself into an analysis of motion. Experiments along the same line have been tried before, but not in any definite form. It has been done for amusement rather than for instruction. Batters in baseball, for instance, show extraordinary divergences of form, while probably there are only at the most two vital characteristics which are common to all good hitters.

"In golf also, one point which is a factor common to all the best distance drivers is the straight left arm, and yet there are dozens of men whose peculiarities differ widely, all of whom, likewise, accomplish results. On the whole the proposal constitutes a most interesting study, and its development should, properly carried out, enhance greatly our detailed knowledge of methods in all sports."

February 18, 1922

THIRTY-ONE YEARS A COACH

Heisman, Now With Penn, Most Experienced of Grid Mentors.

Head Coach John W. Heisman of the University of Pennsylvania football squad undoubtedly holds the world's record for professional longevity. This season at Penn will mark his thirty-first year as a football mentor. The nearest approaches to this record have been made by Pop Warner, who is now coaching at Pittsburgh; Alonzo Stagg at Chicago and Dr. Williams, formerly at Minnesota, who have all coached over twenty-three years or more.

Heisman received his first experience as a college player at Brown University. He later transferred to the University of Pennsylvania, where he played left tackle on the Red and Blue varsity of 1890, and left end on the 1891 eleven, one of the greatest gridiron machines ever turned out at Penn.

It was at Oberlin College in Ohio that the veteran received his first experience as a coach in 1892. The eleven under his charge won eight straight games, including a victory over the University of Michigan, which boasted a great team that year. Heisman's greatest successes were achieved in the South, however. He coached four years at Clemson College, and it was his coaching ability that put that institution on the football map. In 1902 he won the Southern championship for Clemson. During his four years there his teams lost only four games.

It was Heisman's showing at Clemson that caused him to be the most-sought-after mentor in the South. He went to Georgia Tech in 1904, and remained there sixteen years as head football coach. In 1907 the Georgia Tech eleven defeated Pennsylvania, 41 to 0. It was this game that caused the Penn athletic officials to take notice of Georgia Tech's coaching work.

October 10, 1922

PRINCETON RALLIES AND BEATS CHICAGO

Avenges Defeat of Last Year With Brilliant 21-18 Victory at Stagg Field.

TRIUMPH IN LAST PERIOD

Special to The New York Times.

CHICAGO, Oct. 28.—The Princeton football team avenged its defeat at the hands of Chicago last season by beating the Maroon eleven at Stagg Field this afternoon in the most sensational intersectional battle of football history. Apparently beaten beyond all hope of even their most enthusiastic admirers at the end of the third period when they were trailing by 18 to 7, the fighting Tigers staged a desperate rally and rose to a glorious triumph by the score of 21 to 18. The immense throng of 32,000 which filled every available space within the confines of the limited enclosure, was stunned by the sudden change in the fortunes of battle.

With the Princeton line ripped and literally torn to pieces by the powerful line plunging of the Thomas boys and Sorn, the turning point came shortly after the start of the final period. Princeton was in possession of the ball on her own 1-yard line. Cleaves, standing fully 10 yards beyond the goal, pulled the unexpected by shooting a forward pass to Gorman, who sprinted to his own 40-yard mark before he was brought to earth. The Tigers failed to gain and Cleaves punted to Chicago's 42-yard line. Pyott, the Maroon left halfback, was stopped and then came the "break" of the game that eventually was to lead to Princeton's victory.

Zorn, a Chicago back, fumbled the ball on the next play and then Gray picked up the rolling sheroid and made a brilliant run for a touchdown. Smith kicked the goal and the Tigers were now within striking distance of their opponents. The score at this point was 18 to 14 in favor of the Maroon eleven. Before the stunned Chicago players could recover from this sudden change in the aspect of the battle, the Tigers uncorked another desperate assault which again carried the ball across the Maroon goal line. This touchdown gave the Tigers their victory, but the most thrilling and dramatic moment of this battle of battles was still to come.

Despite the fact that within several minutes more the game would pass into history, the Chicago players refused to concede defeat. In the closing minutes of the terrific struggle they fought brilliantly and with equal desperation to maintain their slim lead until the final whistle would assure them of their hard-earned victory.

Tigers Hold at Goal Line.

Shortly after the final kick-off, Chicago, with the help of two well-executed forward passes, advanced the ball to Princeton's twenty-five yard line. Another forward pass brought the pigskin to the six-yard mark and Chicago's followers still held out hope for a victory. Twice the Maroon assault was halted with a net gain of only three and a half yards. The brilliant John Thomas made another yard and with the ball scarcely more than a yard from the goal line Princeton stopped another charge by the same Thomas and it was the Tigers ball just feet from the goal. Princeton then kicked out of danger and before the teams could line up again the whistle blew and the great battle between the East and the West had ended.

Chicago outplayed Princeton both on the attack and on the defense in the first half of the contest. Although the Thomas boys made some spectacular runs these were due in no small measure to the magnificent line opening of Ponderlik and Rorke. Yet Princeton was playing what the East for years had called Western football-passing and running in open and risky style. It was this method of play which eventually gave the Tigers their triumph.

The Chicago players uncorked a whirlwind attack shortly after the start of the game and got off to an early lead. Several minutes after the opening whistle the Maroons were in possession of the ball on their own forty-yard line. Then they began a steady advance toward the Princeton goal. Brilliant line plunging and end running by John Thomas and Pyott brought the pigskin to the four-yard line. Two more plunges by Thomas put it across the line for the first score of the game. Pyott's try for the goal was partly blocked and Chicago was leading by 6 to 0.

Shortly before the close of the first period a brilliant forward pass from Snively to Gray for 45 yards put the ball on Chicago's 7-yard line. A penalty move it up to the 5-yard mark just as the quarter ended. When the second period opened Cleaves went across for the Tigers' first touchdown on the fourth down, but not until after the Chicago players had fought desperately to halt the Tigers' advance. Ken Smith booted the ball between the uprights, and Princeton was leading by 7 to 6.

Chicago Resumes Lead.

The Tigers' advantage was short-lived, however, as several minutes later the Maroons crashed through for another touchdown. Chicago marched steadily down the field to gain this score and advanced the ball to the Princeton 10-yard line on brilliant line plunging by Harry and John Thomas. The Princeton line was wavering badly at this point, and on two more plays John Thomas crashed across the goal line. Smith tried to kick a field goal for Princeton from the 25-yard mark later in the period, but the kick was blocked. Princeton advanced the ball as far as Chicago's 20-yard line toward the close of the period, but lost the spheroid on a fumble. The first half ended with the ball in midfield.

In the third period Princeton was held for downs on Chicago's 13-yard line. Later in the quarter, with the help of a Princeton penalty of half the distance to the goal line, Chicago advanced well into the Tigers' territory. With the ball on the Princeton 20-yard line John Thomas crashed through for fifteen yards, and in two more plays went across for Chicago's third touchdown. Pyott failed to kick the goal and the period ended with one score at 18 to 7 in favor of the Maroons. What occured in the final quarter has been told above.

The crowd was slow in assembling, although at 12:30 when the gates of Stagg Field were thrown open thousands of optimists who hoped to buy tickets were lined around the gates, to disperse slowly when the megaphone trumpeters announced no tickets were for sale.

The police regulations held the curious back for blocks from the stadium, and the gathering army of fans marched in comfort to the scene of combat, massing in colorful sections.

There was not much life until just an hour before game time, when a stocky gray-haired man walked slowly along the side lines and all of a sudden the Maroon side of the field arose with wild cheer. Hats came off and Chicago paid its tribute to Stagg, the beloved "old man," who did not hear, but walked quickly to the station from which he was to direct practice.

Maroon Welcomes Its Heroes.

Ten minutes later the Maroon first squad bounded out from the southwest of the stadium and the Chicago sections rose again, seething with noise and enthusiasm as the Maroon welcomed its heroes.

Half an hour later the Princeton squad, thirty-five strong, rushed onto the scene, and the same instant the blue and maroon clad band, escorting the biggest drum in the college world, marched around the field, and, while the teams practiced kicking, the band stood before the west stands and played "Wave the Flag of Old Chicago." The stands by that time were packed, masses of humanity banked the field in the boxes and, with the sun shining through a slight haze, a hint of a chill commenced to creep through the air. With the Black and Orange of the Tigers massed in the east stand, the Maroon of Chicago lending its color to the west stand, and with the great temporary stands at the ends of the field occupied by neutrals, the scene was set for the struggle between the East and the West.

The field was cleared while the teams retired for the final sessions with the coaches, and the cheer leaders took charge. Chicago sang "Go, Chicago-Go-Go!" and gave the Maroon "Fight" and the massed crowd in the west stand formed great "C" of maroon and white. Then suddenly from the east stand came the scream of the Tiger, the famous "Tiger, Tiger, Tiger!" of Princeton. The hosts of the East and West were battling in war of sound, sending their cheers, wave upon wave, across the field.

Between halves the Maroon band paraded, and marching to midfield, formed a huge "P" in honor of Princeton and played the Princeton hymn and then formed the "C" of Chicago. During the interim President Judson of Chicago crossed the field to call upon President Hibben, who accompanied him back to call at the Chicago official box.

October 29, 1922

Princeton Undergrads Celebrate Chicago Victory With Bells, Bonfires and Parade

Special to The New York Times.

PRINCETON, N.J., Oct. 28.—With bells tolling and bonfires burning on several parts of the campus, the Princeton undergraduates celebrated their team's victory over Chicago in enthusiastic manner here tonight. Never in the history of football at Princeton has an early season game created so much interest among students and townspeople as the intersectional classic in the Windy City today. When a Tiger team beats Harvard or Yale in football, the huge bell in the belfry of old Nassau Hall is pressed into service and the undergraduates take turns ringing it. But never has it been known to ring for an early season victory before.

When the news came through by radio and telegraph that Princeton had held the Maroons on their 1-foot line and the game was over, the hundreds of students formed an enthusiastic parade down Nassau Street singing the old Princeton songs, and the famous bell began to ring out the "Glory of Old Nassau."

A play-by-play account of the game came through at University Field during the game between Princeton freshmen and Fordham freshmen; the Western Union main office gave out the same thing: radio sets in the "Tiger Shop" and Palmer Laboratory also reported the game in detail. Each place was crowded with eager students, cheering madly one minute, groaning hoarsely the next. All agreed that never in football history has a game, outside of the big three, created so much fierce interest as this.

When the team and its followers return to jungle land tomorrow, a glorious homecoming is being planned by the undergraduate body. A parade will be formed and the victorious warriors will be escorted from the station to their rooms in state.

October 29, 1922

ROME'S COLOSSEUM OUTDONE BY OUR FOOTBALL BOWLS

SOME WILL SEAT 70,000

That Is 25,000 More Than Once Cheered the Gladiators

MANY STADIUMS TO RISE

It Is a Poor College Nowadays Without Amphitheatre Excelling Those of Old.

AMERICA'S college record is passing that of the Roman Empire in the number and size of amphitheatres built for games and athletic contests, and more great stadiums are planned or under construction in this country now than Rome ever had. Many of the American structures are far larger than anything in the ancient world, marking a new golden age of sport and outdoor amusement.

Added to the stadiums built in the last twenty years, the new group of structures will give to this country more than twice the number of the big amphitheatres of the old Roman days, and their seating capacity is far greater than the aggregate of the colosseums. The Roman Empire had between ten and fifteen larger stadiums and about 100 small structures, but every one of the larger amphitheatres can be matched now in this country. And there are countless smaller bowls.

He who thrills at reading of a gladiatorial contest can get the same thrill, experience the same "mob psychology," by attending a football game in the Yale Bowl, in the new stadium at Ohio State University, Columbus, or one of the numerous smaller American structures. Greater crowds attend. The spectacle is almost regal pomp, and interest in the great American game of football probably is even wider and more compelling than the Romans' interest in the water carnival and 100-day games with which Titus opened the Roman Colosseum in 80 A.D.

In two of these stadiums which have just been opened the crowds attending football games were larger than the combined seating capacity of the Roman Colosseum and the next largest structure of its kind in the Roman world, the amphitheatre at Capua.

One of the new structures was at Ohio State University, and the other was the Dudley Stadium built for Vanderbilt University at Nashville, Tenn. The next year will see at least ten more great stadiums rise on the grounds of American's universities and in the public parks of large cities, to say nothing of the professional baseball stadiums.

The largest crowd in football history witnessed the game between Ohio and Michigan at the dedication of the great stadium at Ohio State University. This was significant, because it showed as much interest in football in the Middle West as in the games of the Big Three, and added some weight to the arguments that football to a great extent has overshadowed col/scholastic activities. The crowd numbered more than 75,000, and additional thousands clamored for admission.

The seating capacity of this new horseshoe-shaped stadium is about equal to that of the Yale Bowl, which has 64,025 permanent seats, with temporary seats carrying the capacity to 70,657. Those are the approximate figures of the Ohio stadium, although it is of different shape, and the capacity may be increased by the erection of temporary stands at the open end of the horseshoe. Historians differ on the capacity of the Roman Colosseum, but the best opinion seems to be that it was capable of seating 45,000 persons, with additional standing room for 5,000. Both the Yale Bowl and the new Ohio Stadium are greater in dimensions. The Colosseum was 615 feet long and 510 feet wide. The playing field in the Yale is 933 feet long and 744 feet wide, and the arena of the Colosseum was 281 feet long and 177 feet wide.

25,000 Seats at Vanderbilt

The new Dudley Stadium at Vanderbilt University, also horseshoe shaped, seats 25,000 spectators and in general dimensions is about the size of the famous colosseum at Pompeii, where the gladiatorial contests were held before the city was buried under the ashes of Vesuvius. It is similar in appearance to the Ohio Stadium because it is the same shape, but smaller. Pennsylvania's new stadium, just dedicated, seats about 50,000 and cost $750,000.

All these stadiums have been built so they may be used extensively for field sports, baseball and other games. It is intended that the field shall not be reserved for the football contests, but also devoted to the general physical development of students.

Columbia University in its new stadium intends to centre interest on extensive facilities for all kinds of sports. President Nicholas Murray Butler has repeatedly declared that the athletic field rivalled the classroom in university life. Columbia was without football for years, so that other sports, particularly baseball and rowing, have gained an interest among alumni and students which football cannot soon overshadow.

This idea that the great athletic fields should be devoted to a variety of sports is gaining steadily. Spectacular football creates much interest and perhaps has some paralyzing effect on academic efforts just before the big contests, but diversified sport encourages participation by many students and does not affect studies.

Ohio, Pennsylvania and Vanderbilt have gone a step further than other colleges in working for this diversity, and Columbia intends to go another step in her plans for the new $3,000,000 Baker field and stadiums on the twenty-six acrea Dyckman tract at 218th Street and the Harlem Ship Canal. A football stadium will provide seats for 56,000 persons, but there will be separate stadiums for track athletics and baseball, so that the seating capacity of the three will be 73,000. The football stadium may be used for other sports.

This interest in sports, and particularly in college sports, as part of the "cooling off" process after the war, has found its expression in a well-defined movement among all colleges and universities, for the expansion of sports fields and stadiums, and virtually every college and universities, for the expansion of sports fields and stadiums, and virtually every college in the country has finished or is planning extensions of equipment.

The University of California plans a sports field and stadium. Wisconsion and Pennsylvania are working on the same lines. Iowa is starting a stadium campaign, and several large universities in the East have their plans under way.

Whether it has been wise to throw up these great structures so that thousands may view athletic contests, and particularly football contests, is a question frequently debated, especially among those who got their college training at the small institution where the work was heavy and closely supervised and every man took part for the fun of the game, and among those who were graduated from the harder school of experience. Some of these men think that stimulation of interest to too high a point diverts the minds of students from their collegiate work, and frequently affects those who most need the academic training. Others who look at the game and the colleges with more tolerant eye view this interest only as part of a desirable college life which may produce memories to be treasured, not too many regrets to be pondered over, and not too many flat failures in life.

Games for Thousands

Most of the educators who have spoken their thoughts on these subjects recently have expressed the opinion that great playing fields were as necessary as the laboratories of chemistry and physics. They have not meant stadiums where eleven men perform for the thousands who are not athletes, but the playing fields where thousands participate.

One of the first educators after the war to speak of the need of adequate sports fields for students, particularly in colleges situated in cities, was Dean William McClellan, Chairman of the Athletic Council at the University of Pennsylvania. He asserted that universities, particularly those in cities, were under obligation to supply recreation grounds.

"The war has taught the college world many lessons," he said. "It has also given us many hard problems to solve. In the early days of our war preparations too many find fellows were rejected because of physical defects which could have been prevented. The draft merely accentuted this condition.

"It was evident that the American college had developed the brains of the students, but had neglected their bodies. Then came the great cantonments, and with them the opportunity to show what men of vision could do to utilize athletics in the development of America's fighting machine. Mass athletics came overnight. It was shown that a whole camp could be organized so that every man could have his fun and make his athletics a direct contribution to his soldierly development. No man was neglected. There were no bleacherites, because every man was a participant.

"These former students will not tolerate the lack of vision with which so many of our colleges endeavor to crowd all their students into one little field for recreation. They will still want intercollegiate competition, but they will also demand that the student spectators shall likewise be athletes."

There are movements in several cities for the erection of stadiums with seating capacities far surpassing any of the college amphitheatres. Los Angeles has the most tangible as well as the most interesting plan of all, and is already at work on it. The seating capacity of this great Pacific Coast bowl is to be not less than 75,000, and the city has an eye open for the Olympic games. Infact, the International Olympic Committee has authorized Los Angeles to hold international games under the patronage of the committee in September, 1923, as part of the dedication exercises of the new stadium, but Los Angeles is out for the Olympic games of 1932. Those of 1924 are to be held in Paris and in 1928 the contest also will take place in Europe.

The Los Angeles Coliseum, which will be finished next Spring, is elliptical in shape and situated in a depression, just as the Yale bowl was built. The main entrance will be adorned with a concrete and stone peristyle, with colonades, and will be about 400 feet wide and 75 feet high at the loftiest point. The playing field will be 680 feet long and about 345 feet wide encompassed by a running track almost a third of a mile in circumference.

Interior playing fields are to be provided for football, baseball, soccer and other games, so that every foot of the players' space will be visible from all seats in the amphitheatre. Eighty-six entrances and exits will provide for speedy handling of the crowds, and there will be a driveway through the pile of stone and concrete for the entrance of pageants and parades, which may encircle the track and then file out again. Special lighting apparatus is to make night performances possible.

The stadium, to cost $2,5000,000, will be built under a unique arrangement. A Community Development Association is to build the structure, under agreement with the city, the county and several associations and city commissions. For an annual rental the city and county have equal rights with the development association for a period of years, then the property is to pass to the ownership of the city and county. Los Angeles banks are financing the plan, and the development association is a corporation with no profits, no capital stock, and all expenses met by subscription.

Big Plans for Chicago

Less tangible but just as vast in conception is Chicago's plan for a stadium seating 125,000 as a unit in a general scheme of beautifying Chicago by reclaiming a large part of the lake front. Chicago wants to do everything Los Angeles wants to do, even to having the Olympic games brought over from Europe. But completion of her plan is several years off. Los Angeles will be ready with her stadium next year.

It is not to be forgotten that New York City has several coliseums rivaling those of the ancient world in size and beauty. The Greek stadium at City College, built with the Lewisohn gift, is the best known, and the least known is the Rice Memorial Stadium in Pelham Bay Park.

Another large stadium now being constructed in the Bronx is the amphitheatre intended for the Yankees, which is to give the American League the finest baseball park in the country. It will have a seating capacity of 85,000 persons, or approximately 10,000 more than the Yale Bowl, the Ohio State University Stadium or the uncompleted Los Angeles Coliseum, so that it probably will be the largest arena in the world until Chicago finishes her stadium although the British Empire Exposition in London also plans a stadium with a seating capacity of at least 125,000.

The seating capacity of the grand stand in the Yankee stadium is to be 45,000 with 30,000 seats in the bleachers. At least 10,000 additional box seats can be provided at great football contests, such as the Army and Navy classic. A running track also will be provided so that the stadium may be used for games. The cost is to be more than $2,000,000.

The development of the idea for large stadiums began at Harvard about twenty years ago. The Harvard Stadium was completed in 1903. It was considered one of the wonders of the athletic world in its time, although its seating capacity is hardly more than half that of the Ohio stadium and the Yale Bowl. It is built in the form of a horseshoe, with an official seating capacity of 34,475, and additional room for about 3,500 extra seats. It cost $200,000, contributed by alumni.

Five years passed before another large stadium was constructed at any American university. Dr. James R. Day, then Chancellor of Syracuse University, induced the late John D. Archbold to build an amphitheatre for the university. It covers more than six acres and has a seating capacity of about 40,000. After this stadium was completed in 1908 a few smaller ones were constructed at other colleges, but it remained for Yale's graduates to set a mark in its big bowl.

Virtually all the great universities are falling in line, with principal activity in the Middle West, where interest in football has reached its highest pitch, and on the Pacific Coast, where football enthusiasts aspire to a great series of intersectional football games to determine the championship of the country, despite the fact that many of the larger universities already have foresworn intersectional contests and will confine their playing to teams in their own territory.

Alumni of the University of Iowa plan a big stadium; Wisconsin is building a stadium piece by piece with the income from football games; Leland Stanford Junior University has a bowl for its athletics, and the University of California plans a bowl to cost more than $1,000,000, with seats for at least 75,000. Many other colleges and universities have more or less ambitious plans.

Even the Marine Corps has its new stadium at Quantico, Va., with a seating capacity of 33,000. It is one of the most unique and cheapest of all the great arenas. General Butler of the Marine Corps conceived the idea for the stadium, and he carried it through without an appropriation by using reclaimed Government materials in its construction. The work was done by the marines. Only 10,000 seats are to be provided at first, but the eventual capacity will be 100,000.

November 5, 1922

67,000 SEE ILLINOIS BEAT MICHIGAN, 39-14

Red Grange Makes Five of Six Touchdowns Registered by Victors at Urbana.

SCORES ON FIRST KICKOFF

URBANA, Ill., Oct. 18 (Associated Press).—A flashing, red-haired youngster, running and dodging with the speed of a deer, gave 67,000 spectators jammed into the new $1,700,000 Illinois Memorial Stadium the thrill of their lives today, when Illinois vanquished Michigan, 39 to 14, in what probably will be the outstanding game of the 1924 gridiron season in the West.

Harold (Red), Grange, Illinois phenomenon, all-American halfback, who attained gridiron honors of the nation last season, was the dynamo that furnished the thrills. Grange double and redoubled his football glory in the most remarkable exhibition of running, dodging and passing seen on any gridiron in years—an exhibition that set the dumbfounded spectators screaming with excitement.

Individually, Grange scored five of Illinois' six touchdowns in a manner that left no doubt as to his ability to break through the most perfect defense. He furnished one thrill after another. On the very first kick-off Grange scooped up the ball bounding toward him on the Illinois five-yard line and raced ninety yards through the Michigan eleven for a touchdown in less than ten seconds after the starting whistle blew.

Grange Plays Sensationally

Before the Michigan team could recover from its shock, Grange had scored three more touchdowns in rapid succession, running sixty-five, fifty-five and forty-five yards, respectively, for his next three scores. Coach Zuppke took quarter ended. He returned later to heave several successful passes and score a fifth touchdown in the last half.

Michigan, bewildered by the catastrophe, unleashed a rain of forward passes, in an attempt to recoup, but most of them grounded when the receiver was covered by the Illinois defense.

Michigan was unable to stage a sustained rally and Illinois' lead was never in danger. This was largely due to the failure of the Wolverines to complete their passes, nine of their thirteen heaves being grounded and one intercepted. Michigan's three successful passes of the thirteen attempted were good for a total of 37 yards Illinois complete five passes for a total of 70 yards, two others grounding.

Grange surpassed all of his former exploits in every department. He handled the ball twenty-one times, gained 402 yards and scored five touchdowns. Unbiased experts agree that his performance was among the greatest ever seen on an American gridiron.

Grange Again Surprises

Running through a labyrinth of interference and tacklers, he crossed the field twice to gain the open on his first play. Britton made the point after touchdown. One the second kick-off. Grange received the ball and raced 10 yards before he was downed. Illinois lost the ball on downs but recovered by the same method on the 33-yard line. While the crowd was still breathless from cheering his first touchdown. Grange tore off 65 yards for a second, around right end.

A moment later, on the same play, he ran fifty-five yards for a touchdown and shortly after scored his fourth of the quarter from Michigan's ££-yard line. In each instance he started behind perfect interferences and sidestepped Michigan's safety men in the final spring. He has a way of dodging almost coming to a dead stop before whirling in another direction, that leaves his tacklers flat-footed and amazed.

The game was won and lost in this first thrill pocket moment when Grange, extricting himself repeatedly from seemingly hopeless tangles of tackers, crossed the goal line and permanently shook the Wolverine morale. The shock which his four touchdowns produced on the highly keyed Michigan team, dazed the Michigan crowd and team, and when the game was over many were still attempting to explain the defeat.

Steger scored Michigan's first touchdown in the second quarter after Briton's short punt had given Michigan the ball on Illinois's 25-yard line. Three drives at the line and a penalty for Illinois put the ball on the 15-yard line. Leonard made six Steger crashed off left tackle for the touchdown. Rockwell kicked goal.

Grange re-entered the game in the third period, and after an exchange of punts had given Illinois the ball, he passed 23 yards to Britton, who was downed on Michigan's 24-yard line. Leonard made six and Grange eight. On the next play Grange circled end for 10 yards and his final touchdown. Illinois obtained the ball on Michigan's territory shortly after the final quarter opened and Grange tossed the ball 23 yards to Leonard, who scored Illinois's final touchdown.

Michigan's opportunity for a rally came on the next kick-off, when an Illinois man clipped, the kicker and the ball was given to Michigan on Illinois's 20-yard line. Steger gained 5 and Heath made it first down with 3 yards to go. Rockwell and Steger were held to 1-yard gains, but on the next play Rockwell smashed across for Michigan's final touchdown.

Encouraged by this Michigan threw passes to all sections of the field without avail, and the game ended with Michigan holding the ball on her own 20-yard line.

The line-up:

ILLINOIS (39).		MICHIGAN (14).
Rokusek	L. E.	Marion
C.A. Brown	L. T.	Babcock
Slimmer	L. G.	Slaughter
Roberts	C.	Brown
Roy Miller	R. G.	Steele
R.L. Hall	R. T.	Hawkins
Xassell	R. T.	Grube
H.A. Hall	Q. B.	Rockwell
Grange	L. H.B.	Steger
McIlwain	R. H.B.	Parker
Britton	F. B.	Miller

SCORE BY PERIOD

Illinois	27	0	6	6—39
Michigan	0	7	0	7—14

Touchdowns—Granger (5), Leonard (substitute for Michigan), Steger, Rockwell. Points after touchdown—Britton (3) Rockwell (2)

Referee—C.J. Masker, Northwestern. Umpire—J.J. Schommer, Chicago, Linesman—N.E. Kearns, Depau. Field judge—J.M. Nichola. Oberlin. Time of periods—15 minutes.

October 19, 1924

NOTRE DAME TRIMS NEBRASKA, 34 TO 6

Wipes Out Defeats of Last Two Years With Largest Score in History of Series.

MILLER GOES OVER TWICE

NOTRE DAME, Ind., Nov. 15 (Associated Press),—Notre Dame defeated Nebraska, 34 to 6, today, wiping out the victories the Cornhuskers scored over Rockne's warriors in 1923 and 1922. It was the worst drubbing a Nebraska team ever received from Notre Dame in the ten years of football relations between the two universities. A colorful crowd of 26,000 saw the conquerors of Army and Princeton march to an easy victory.

The famous Notre Dame back field, consisting of Crowley, Layden, Don Miller and Stuhldreher, swung into action late in the first period, just before Nebraska crashed over with a touchdown, and, carrying the fight to Nebraska territory, slashed through the line for big gains and ran around the ends as they pleased, in addition to revealing a sensational forward passing attack.

Coach Rockne followed his practice of starting a team of shock troops composed of second string players, but as quickly as Nebraska pounded the ball dangerously close to Notre Dame's goal. Rockne gave the signal for new players to take the field. Layden, Crowley, Miller and Stuhldreher yanked off their sweaters and raced into the game behind a complete new line. From then on the contest was one-sided, and Nebraska, although fighting doggedly, was unable to match speed with the perfect Notre Dame machine.

The superiority of the Notre Dame team is revealed in the statistics, which showed Rockne's warriors making nineteen first downs as against one first down for Nebraska. Notre Dame made twelve attempts.

Nebraska won the toss and received the kick-off on its 15-yard line. Two small gains were followed by a punt to Scherer on Notre Dame's 46-yard line. Nebraska recovering Scherer's fumble. Myers fumbled on the first play, Hancusek recovering for Notre Dame. Connell and Cerney failed to make down and Cerney punted. Nebraska lost two yards on line plays and punted to Notre Dame's 25-yard line, but Nebraska lost two yards on line plays and punted to Notre Dame's 25-yard line, but Nebraska was offside and the ball was returned with a five-yard line, loss for Nebraska. The next punt went fifty yards to Ceney on Notre Dame's 18-yard line.

Robertson of Nebraska grabbed Layden's fumble of a pass from centre and ran to the Notre Dame 4-yard line. Rockne replaced his second team with the regulars, but Myers went over for a touchdown on the third play. Mandery missed goal. The first string backfield reeled off first downs to mindfield but missed a forward pass there and Layden punted to Nebraska's 33-yard line. Two plays lost five yards and offside set Nebraska Lack another five yards. Bloodgood gained back three yards as the period ended. It was Nebraska's ball on its 28-yard line and the score was 6 to 0.

Crowley Whips Around End.

At the start of the second period Nebraska punted to Walsh at midfield, and Crowley made eighteen yards around end. Layden added five and a Nebraska penalty five more. Stuhldreher passed to Crowley on Nebraska's 2-yard line and Stuhldreher went over for a touchdown. Crowley kicked goal.

Notre Dame kicked off and held for downs, receiving Nebraska's punt on the Notre Dame 49-yard line. Crowley passed to Stuhldreher, who ran to Nebraska's 32-yard line. Don Miller ran around end seventeen yards. Layden added seven, Crowley five more, and Miller made the touchdown. Crowley kicked goal.

Layden kicked off to Nebraska. Two end runs were blocked and an incomplete pass forced Nebraska to punt to Stuhldreher, who ran the ball back seventeen yards to midfield. Crowley passed eight yards to Miller, but Nebraska forced Notre Dame to punt, Nebraska punted back and the Notre Dame shock troops took up the goalward march. Layden tossed twenty-five yards to Stuhldreher. Bloodgood stopped Miller on Nebraska's 3-yard line as the half ended with the score 14 to 6 in Notre Dame's favor.

At the opening of the last half Layden kicked off—over the goal line as usual. Nebraska's punt was blocked and Layden took it on Nebraska's 48-yard line. Don Miller made twenty yards around end. Hutchison, Nebraska guard, was badly hurt on the play. On the next play Miller dodged through for a touchdown and Crowley kicked goal. Notre Dame received the kick-off and the procession started again with a 23-yard run by Miller, followed by short gains by Layden and Stuhldreher and a fake pass play by Layden which gained twelve yards. Don Miller got away for fifteen yards again after a Stuhldreher pass had crossed midfield.

Layden Misses Field Goal

Notre Dame's gains grew shorter and Nebraska took the ball on downs on its 8-yard line. Nebraska's punt was short and Layden tried to field goal from the 27-yard line, but missed. Bloodgood punted to Notre Dame's 20-yard line. On a pass from Stuhldreher, Crowley ran sixty-five yards for a touchdown, and the third period came to a close shortly after Crowley kicked goal, with Notre Dame leading by 28 to 6.

Bloodgood punted 60 yards to Stuhldreher, who ran the ball back to Notre Dame's 46-yard line at the start of the final period. Two Notre Dame passes were knocked down and Layden punted to Nebraska's ten-yard line. Myers made two short gains and Bloodgood ran to Nebraska's 23-yard line on a fake pass. Nebraska's rally was short lived and Bloodgood kicked another of his long punts. Rockne put in some substitutes, but left his first string backfield in. Layden ploughed through center for 15-yards to Nebraska's 48-yard line. The Notre Dame line smashing continued to Nebraska's five-yard line where Layden was stopped without gain, but he went over for a touchdown on the next attempt. Crowley's goal kick was blocked and the game ended with Notre Dame the victor, 34 to 6.

The line-up.

NOTRE DAME (34).		NEBRASKA (6.)
Collins	L. E.	Collins
Bach	L. T.	McLeson
Weibel	L. G.	J. Weir
Walsh	C.	Hutchinson
Kizer	R. G.	Ogden
E. Miller	R. T.	E. Weir
Hunsinger	R. E.	Robertson
Stuhldreher	Q. B.	Bloodgood
Crowley	L. H.B.	Looke
D. Miller	R. H.B.	Rhodes
Layden	F. B.	Myers

Touchdowns—Notre Dame: Miller (2), Stuhldreher, Crowley, Layden, Nebraska, Myers, Points after touchdown—Crowley, 4.

Referee—Ghee, Dartmouth, Uimpire—McCrary;, Kansas City, Field judge—Wyatt, Missouri, Linesman—Kirke, Iowa. Time of periods — minutes. November 16, 1924

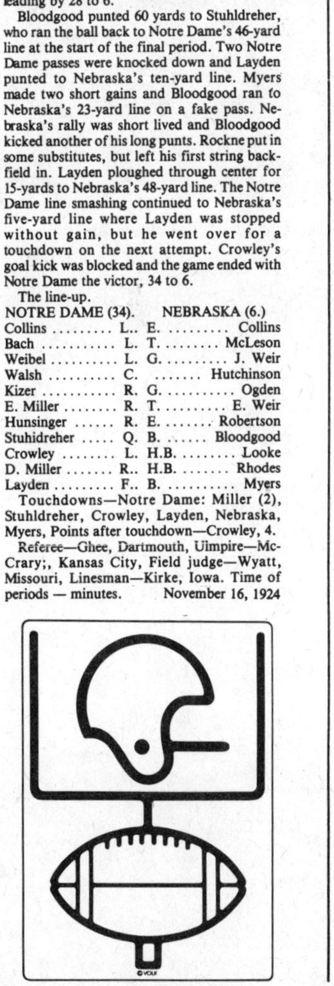

Red Grange, legendary halfback at the University of Illinois, shown here in 1924.

The sportswriter Grantland Rice immortalized several Notre Dame players of the early 1920's by calling them "The Four Horsemen." Elmer Layden was one of them.

100,000 SEE BATTLE AS CALIFORNIA TIES

Record Football Crowd for U. S. Watches Stanford Rally to Earn 20-20 Draw.

FORWARD PASSES SAVE DAY

Air Attack by Warner's Men Scores 2 Touchdowns in Last Few Minutes.

BEARS' LEAD IS WIPED OUT

Have 20-6 Advantage When Berkeley Warriors Make Stand in the Fourth Period of Contest.

PACIFIC COAST STANDING.

	W.	L.	Tied.		W.	L.	Tied
Stanford	3	0	1	Oregon	2	2	1
California	2	0	2	Oreg. Aggies	1	4	0
Washington U.	3	1	1	Wash. State	0	4	1
U. S. C.	2	1	0	Montana	0	3	0
Idaho	4	2	0				

Special to The New York Times

BERKELEY, Cal., Nov. 22.—Stanford's fighting football team electrified 100,000 spectators in the last few minutes of play in the big games this afternoon by scoring two touchdowns and tying up the score at 20 all.

After leading in the first half, 6 to 0, the Stanford team was literally torn to pieces by the California eleven in the third and part of the fourth quarters, the Bears gaining a 20-to-6 lead.

Then Stanford came through with an aerial attack that fairly swept California off its feet, and a beaten team went on even terms with its rival.

The crowd surpassed any that ever before saw a football game in the United States, it was stated here. The seating capacity of the Memorial Stadium, with the additional seats, is 76,000, and the remaining 24,000 persons, according to unofficial figures, saw the game from vantage points on "Tight Wad Hill," a section of the natural amphitheatre in which the stadium was erected. Two weeks ago arrangements were made to care for 12,000 persons on the hill, which overlooks the stadium, but twice this number can be accommodated.

The largest previous figures were the 80,000 attendance for a number of games in the Yale Bowl, and last year's 82,000 which saw the California-Stanford game from the stadium enclosure and hilltops.

Stanford scored its touchdown in the middle of the fourth period. After smashing down the field, the Cardinals scored when Shipkey caught Walker's 18-yard forward pass over the goal line, Cuddeback kicked the goal.

There was no score in the first quarter. California won the toss and Horrell kicked off. The wind was in favor of Stanford, and in the punting duel between Cuddeback and Dixon, Cuddeback had the advantage. Dixon tried a number of forward passes in the quarter and got away with one to Imlay for 24 yards, the best gain of the quarter.

Stamford played rings around California in the second quarter and scored 6 points on two place kicks by Cuddeback, his last one being from the 45-yard line.

In the third period Coach Andy Smith's Californians scored a touchdown. A forward pass from Dixon to Imlay paved the way. It was good for 18 yards and Imlay ran 30 yards more. Griffin carried the ball over, making 7 yards on one drive. Carlson kicked the goal.

California played all around Stanford in this quarter, just as Coach Warner's men had outplayed California in the second period.

The weather for the game was perfect, warm sunshine flooding a field which was a riot of colors. There was little wind to favor either team.

California's record this season is seven victories and two ties, counting the battle today.

Stanford has played fewer games but before today had not been tied. Stanford beat Occidental 20-6, Oregon 28-13.

The line-up:

STANFORD (20).		CALIFORNIA (20).
T. Shipkey	L. E.	L. Mell
H. Shipkey	L. T.	White
Swan	L. G.	Lau
Baker	C.	Horrell
Neill	R. G.	Carey
Johnson	R. E.	Cook
Lawson	R. E.	Huber
Mitchell	Q. B.	Carlson
Cuddeback	L. H.B.	Dixon
Kelly	R. H.B.	Imlay
Hey	F. B.	Young

SCORE BY PERIODS.

Stanford	0	6	0	14—20
California	0	0	7	13—20

November 23, 1924

ROCKNE'S RECORD IMPRESSIVE ONE

In Seven Years His Notre Dame Teams Have Won 57 Games, Lost 4, Tied 3

WON TWENTY-TWO STRAIGHT

Iowa Broke String in 1921, Then Hoosiers Won Next 17 in Row—To Make Debut on Coast.

Knute Rockne, seeking new worlds to conquer, will invade the Pacific Coast with his Nomads from Notre Dame on New Year's Day, there to meet the undefeated Stamford football team in what promises to be one of the greatest contests of the season. Should Notre Dame conquer Glenn Warner's eleven, the record of the Hoosiers, under the direction of Rockne, will be one of the greatest of all time, for since Rockne took charge of the Notre Dame's team as head coach seven years ago it has been defeated only four times and it has triumphed over some of the leading teams in every section of the country except the Pacific Coast, which it invades on Jan. 1 for the first time.

The Notre Dame record under Rockne is one of the most impressive ever made by a coach. During the 1918 season there was little high-class football because of the war and Notre Dame suffered one of its four defeats since Rockne has taken charge that season, bowing to the Michigan Aggies, 13 to 7. In 1921 it suffered its second setback, Iowa winning by a score of 10 to 7. In 1922 and 1923 the only games lost were to Nebraska. For the rest of the time that Rockne has been in charge the Normads have been unconquered, and only three teams have earned a tie. The Great Lakes Training Station eleven and Nebraska in 1918, and the Army in 1922.

Rockne has led his charges against Eastern teams twelve times and they have won eleven of the contests and the other was a 0—0 tie against the old rivals from West Point. Against Southern teams Notre Dame has won four games, all that they have played against representatives from that section. The Hoosiers have played fourteen contests with members of the Western Conference and have won thirteen of them, losing the other, 10—7, to Iowa. Altogether the Notre Dame team, playing in the East, South and Middle West since Rockne took charge as head coach, has played sixty-four games. Of these the Hoosiers have won fifty-seven, lost four and tied three.

Nebraska has been the particular Nemesis of the Normads ever since the great coach started his campaigning. Notre Dame has met the Cornhuskers seven times and Nebraska has been able to gain two victories and a tie in the series.

Has Trouble at Start

In 1918 Rockne sent his team into six games and it was then that he had his most trouble, despite the fact that the great George Gipp was a member of the backfield. Great Lakes and Nebraska earned ties and the Nomands were beaten by the Michigan Aggies. Notre Dame winning only three games. However, Rockne started his longest run with the last two contestants of that year and for twenty-two games in a row his team did not suffer a defeat. In 1919 Kalamazoo, Mount Union, Nebraska, Kalamazoo Normal, Indiana, Army, Michigan Aggies, Purdue and Morningside were met in turn and each was conquered. The string kept up through the 1920 campaign when Kalamazoo, Kalamazoo Normat, Nebraska, Valparaiso, Army, Purdue, Indiana, Northwestern and Michigan Aggies were defeated, and it continued for two games in the 1921 season, victories over Kalamazoo and De Pauw being added to the list.

Then came Notre Dame's second defeat since Rockne had taken charge, with Iowa ending the long string of victories. However, after that narrow setback by a margin of three points, Notre Dame started another long reign of terror and for seventeen games it was undefeated, finishing the 1921 season with victories over Purdue, Nebraska, Indiana, Army. Rutgers, Haskell, Marquette and Michigan Aggies. The following year the Army earned its tie, but Kalamazoo, St. Louis University, Purdue, De Pauw, Georgia Tech, Indiana, Butler and Carnegie Tech were defeated before Nebraska, with a 14—6 victory, broke the second long string in the last contest of the year. Except for Iowa's field goal in 1921 Notre Dame would have completed forty successive games without defeat.

Army Beaten Five Times

Notre Dame bowed again to Nebraska in 1923, but Notre Dame finished the season with three successive victories, and these, added to nine contests which were won this year, start another string of triumphs with twelve. The big test will come on Jan. 1 when Rockne leads his famous Four Horsemen against Stanford.

The Eastern teams that have been defeated by Notre Dame include the Army, which has been turned back five times; Rutgers, Princeton and Carnegie Tech. Notre Dame has conquered Georgia Tech three times and Valparaiso once in the South. The Big Ten teams that have fallen before Rockne's machines are Purdue, six times; Indiana, four times; North Eastern, twice; and Wisconsin, once. Now he travels farther West with the hope of adding Stanford to his string of victimes.

Following is Notre Dame's record since Rockne became head coach:

1918.
26—Case 6
66—Wabash.......... 6
7—Great Lakes 7
7—Michigan Aggies. 13
26—Purdue 6
0—Nebraska 0

1919.
14—Kalamazoo 0
60—Mount Union ... 7
14—Nebraska 9
55—Kalamazoo Nor.. 0
16—Indiana 3
12—Army 9
13—Michigan Aggies.. 0
33—Purdue 13
14—Morningside 6

1920.
39—Kalamazoo 0
42—Kalamazoo, N. .. 0
16—Nebraska 7
28—Valparaiso ..... 3.
27—Army .... 17.
28—Purdue 0
13—Indiana ....
33—Northwestern ... 7
13—Michigan Aggies.. 0

1921.
56—Kalamazoo 0
57—De Pauw 10
7—Iowa 10
33—Purdue 10
7—Nebraska 6
28—Indiana 7
28—Army 0
48—Rutgers 0
42—Haskell 7
21—Marquette 7
48—Michigan Aggies.. 0

1922.
46—Kalamazoo...... 0
26-St. Louis 0
20—Purdue 0
34—De Pauw 7
13—Georgia Tech ... 3
27—Indiana 0
0—Army 0
32—Butler..........3
19—Carnegie Tech .. 0
6—Nebraska 14

1923.
74—Kalamazoo 0
14—Lomnard 0
13—Army 0
25—Princeton 2
35—Georgia Tech ... 7
34—Purdue 7
7—Nebraska 14
34—Butler 7
26—Carnegie Tech .. 0
26—St. Louis 0

19240
14—Lombard 0
34—Wabash 0
13—Army 7
12—Princeton 0
334—Georgia Tech .. 3
38—Wisconsin 3
34—Nebraska 6
13—Northwestern ... 6
40—Carnegie Tech .. 19

December 26, 1924

PRESENT FOOTBALL SATISFIES N. C. A. A.

General satisfaction with the present football rules, with the conduct of the 1924 Olympics, with the advances made in all branches of athletics during the past year, condemnation of the use of still or motion pictures in coaching or scouting, decision to investigate Slummer baseball, a feeling of optimism for the future of sports, confidence that fears of over-commercialism are not founded in fact and a desire for harmonious cooperation with all other bodies engaged in the promotion of athletics were keynotes of the nineteenth annual convention of the National Collegiate Athletic Association at the Hotel Astor yesterday. The session-wound up with the annual dinner last night at which officers were elected for the ensuing year.

The branding of the practice of using movies in scouting as being unethical came in the form of a resolution passed unanimously by the delegates after a report on the subject had been read by J.P. Richardson of Dartmouth. The resolutions recommended that the practice be abolished. Formal notification of the action will be sent to the Presidents and other constituted authorities at the several institutions belonging to the association. Chairman Richardson declared that his committee had reached the conclusion that such usage is contrary to the spirit of fair play and, unless nipped in the bud, would tend to make football a business institution instead of a sport.

December 31, 1924

NOTRE DAME ROUTS STANFORD BY 27-10

52,000 See Rockne's Eleven End Season Unbeaten in Sensational Game at Pasadena.

PASADENA, Ca., Jan. '1 (Associated Press.)—Notre Dame's football eleven today swamped Stanford University's team under a 27 to 10 score. Notre Dame had the speed.

The famous Four Horsemen were pitted against Ernie Nevers of Stanford, and the Stanford star, although he covered himself with glory, could not offset their repeated charges. At that the red-shirted Stanford forwards outcharged the blue Jerseyed linesmen of Notre Dame, and it was owing to their work that the California institution was able to register ten points in the face of the fierce charging of the Hoosiers.

Notre Dame added to its list of honors that of having scored the first victory for the East in four intersectional games played on the Pacific Coast this season. For the first time in a number of years the Rose Bowl here was packed to capacity, and it was estimated that upward of 52,000 watched the contest. At almost every moment throughout the four periods the Notre Dame players lived up to their reputation for speed in foot and head.

The start was inauspicious for the Easterners. Coach Rockne sent in his second-string men to open the game, but Stanford shoved them steadily down the field. Then Rockne called on his stars and the real battle was on. Stanford's errors, which might not have been very costly against other opponents, were fatal when pulled against Notre Dame.

Stanford Scores Field Goal.

Stanford started the scoring by a placement kick off Cuddeback's toe in the first period.

In the second period, for the only time during the game, Notre Dame was able to gain consistently through the Stanford line. A prolonged drive ended when Layden bored through left guard three yards to a touchdown.

A few minutes later Layden came to the front again, pulled Never's pass out of the air and sprinted seventy yards for the second Notre Dame touchdown. Crowley kicked the goal. In the third period occured one of Stanford's costly errors. Solomon fumbled a punt on his own 20-yard line. He stooped to recover it when he might have played safely and fell on the ball. Huntsinger swooped down on him. shoved Solomon aside, grabbed the pigskin and ran unopposed to a touchdown. Crowley again kicked the goal.

Later in the period Notre Dame boldly attempted a forward pass within its twenty-yard line, and Never pulled down. Then followed a series of line bucks, nearly all of them featuring Never's, who worked his way to Notre Dame's eight-yard line. The Notre Dame players were set for another buck, but it did not come. Walker passed over the line to Ted Shipkey, and Stanford scored a touchdown. Cuddeback kicked the goal for the extra point. That ended Stanford's scoring.

Layden Stars Once More.

In the fourth period Stanford had another opportunity. An intercepted forward pass on Notre Dame's thirty-five-yard line put the ball in Baker's hands. Nevers was called on and in a succession of plunges carried the ball to Notre Dame's eight-inch line. The crowd thought it was a touchdown for Stanford, but when Referee Ed Thorp unscrambled the heap of players he found the goal line had not been crossed.

The last scoring play of the contest gave Layden another chance to show his speed. He intercepted a pass from Never's hands and led a chase all the way for thirty-five yards across the Stanford goal. Crowley's toe did the rest.

The Four Horsemen cantered, trotted and galloped with all the abandon expected of them. Harry Stuhldreher's play was handicapped when he twisted his left ankle early in the opening period and it slowed up his play during the remainder of the game. Layden and Crowley were the most effective ball carriers for Notre Dame. Don Miller performed well, but he did not quite reach the standard set by his teammates.

No one on the field today performed more brilliantly than Nevers. Except on the one occasion when he was halted on the eight-inch line, the Notre Dame line was unable to stop his terrific smashes that carried the force of every ounce of his 200 pounds.

Adam Walsh at centre and Boland at tackle were among the leading players on the Notre Dame line. Captain Jim Lawson, Stanford right end, was one of the day's individual stars, although the entire Stanford line performed with much credit.

Statistics Favor Coast Team.

Rockne made frequent substitutions at guard and tackle, the points at which the Stanford attacks were centred. The statistics of the game nearly all favor the losers. Stanford gained 164 yards from scrimmage as compared with Notre Dame's 134. The home players registered seventeen first downs, ten more than the South Bend team. Stanford completed twelve out of seventeen attempted forward passes and Notre Dame three out of seven. The Easterners' aerial attack resulted in a gain of 48 yards, while the Pacific Coast team gained 140 yards. Rockne's men were penalized four times for a total of 30 yards, while a single 15-yard penalty was inflicted against Stanford. Notre Dame made one fumble, by Harry Stuhldreher on the first play, and it was the only error made by Notre Dame players, while three misplays were registered by Pop

While the teams were changing goals between the first and second periods Referee Ed Thorp forced Captain Lawson of Stanford to remove the steel brace from his knee.

The game was fast and replete with many sensational plays. The pace was so speedy that it showed plainly on both teams shortly after the fourth period opened. The game was an open one and marked by daring play on both sides. It was a case of two fighting teams with plenty of class in a finish battle.

Notre Dame did not seem to suffer any more from the warm weather than the native team. The South Bend team spent a few days in Tucson, Ariz., and the training there seemed to have helped them get in shape for weather conditions here. At least, as far as observers here could see, the Notre Dame eleven suffered no form reversal.

Coach Rockne is scheduled to lead his team on the return journey tomorrow.

January 2, 1925

PENN ELBOW PADS RECEIVE APPROVAL

Special to The New York Times.

PHILADELPHIA, Pa., Oct. 25.—Although Illinois has objected to the elbow pads worn by Pennsylvania players, claiming they look like a football, Back Field Coach Bert Bell said today that the Eastern Football Rules Committee has given its O. K. to them. Bell and the other Penn coaches insist they are absolutely legal.

Coach Bob Zuppke asked for a

sample of the pads and one was forwarded to Champaign, Ill. The three Illinois scouts who attended the Penn-Williams game at Franklin Field last Saturday inspected the elbow pads in the dressing room and will make a report to Zuppke. The pads are made of a lightweight brown leather and used as an elbow protection.

Penn's preparations today for the trip to Illinois consisted of a mock defense against the Orange and Blue plays. The scouts who saw Michigan beat Illinois warned the Red and Blue of overconfidence. They claim Zuppke's team will be hard to beat on its home field.

All the Penn players are in good physical condition with the exception of Joe Laird, substitute quarterback, who is still nursing a bad knee. Dick Odiorne, who was out for a while with a sore ankle, is romping around again and ready for hard work.

It was planned to stage a scrimmage today, but the soggy condition of Franklin Field caused the coaches to change their mind. They did not wish to risk any injuries.

October 26, 1926

Big Stop-Clock and Announcing Device To Guide Fans at Wisconsin-Iowa Game

Special to The New York Times.

MADISON, Wis., Nov. 10.—Spectators at the homecoming game between Iowa and Wisconsin on Saturday will not be in the dark as to the number of minutes left to play. There will be a big clock on the scoreboard to show them.

The clock, which is electrically operated, is constructed like a stop-watch such as is used by the officials. It is controlled from the sidelines and can be stopped whenever time is taken out by the field judge and started when the ball is again put in play. George Levis, the business manager of the University of Wisconsin Department of Athletics, announced today

that a contract had been signed for the installation of the clock and that it would be ready for Saturday's game with the Hawkeyes, and will also be used for basketball games.

Another feature that has been provided to keep the 42,000 seat holders informed as to what is going on is an electric announcing system. Amplifiers have been installed at various parts of the stadium, and the play-by-play description will be broadcast by an experienced man, assisted by representatives of the two teams. The ball carrier, tackler, kicker, passer, &c., will be called and the more intricate plays explained.

November 11, 1926

Michigan Leads the Big Ten In 13-Year Football Rating

CHICAGO, Dec. 18 (*P*).—The thirteen years' campaign toward the enemy goal posts, since the Big Ten reached its present status in 1913, gives the University of Michigan the best record in the Winter review of football glory. The Wolverines dropped out of the Conference the same year Ohio State was admitted as the tenth member in 1913, but came back again four years later, and have now won twenty-seven of their thirty-eight Big Ten contests.

The thirteen-year Conference standing, Big Ten games only considered, and excluding 1918, the war season, follows:

Team.	G.	W.	L.	T.	P.C.
Michigan	38	27	10	1	.730
Chicago	75	44	24	7	.647
Illinois	68	40	22	6	.645
Ohio State	58	32	22	4	.593
Iowa	53	28	24	1	.538
Wisconsin	63	28	25	10	.528
Minnesota	57	27	25	5	.519
Northwestern	65	19	45	1	.297
Indiana	50	12	35	3	.255
Purdue	55	12	37	6	.244

December 19, 1926

FOOTBALL GOAL POSTS SET BACK TEN YARDS

Rules Committee Leaves Field 100 Yards, but Makes Kicking for Goal Harder.

LATERAL PASS IS CHANGED

Offensive Side Retains Ball at Point It Is Grounded, Except on Fourth Down.

INCREASE SHIFT PENALTY

Team Allowed to Remain in Huddle Only 15 Seconds—Ball Now Dead on Fumbled Punt.

By ROBERT F. KELLEY.

Intercollegiate football will enter the season of 1927 under rules which should result 'n the most radical changes in the game that have occurred since the installation of the forward pass.

The annual meeting of the National Rules Committee drew to a close at the Hotel Roosevelt yesterday afternoon with the announcement of unexpected and drastic changes made in the playing code.

Major Fred Moore's lateral pass rule was written into the book and the goal posts were moved back ten yards, though this affects only field goal kicks, the touchdowns still to be made at the same point and the playing field remaining 100 yards in length.

These were probably the most important of the changes, though actual usage through a season will have to be awaited as the means of proof. They were of sufficient importance to thrust into the background the shift play legislation, important as this was.

Increase Penalty on Shift.

The officials took care of the shift by increasing the penalty for violation from five yards to fifteen yards and by making every official on the field equally responsible in the handling of this play. Heretofore the referee and the linesman have been the sole arbiters on the play. Violation shall come where any teams or member of a team fails to come to a full stop for one second before the ball is snapped back. There is the exception of one player who may be in motion, but toward his own goal.

There will be no more snatching up of fumbled punts and long runs to touchdowns therefrom, such as featured the past year's Army-Navy game, for a fumbled punt, with exceptions, is declared dead when recovered by the kicking side. The exceptions are on kickoffs, kicks from safety and kicks from fair catches.

Stalling was hit at by the reduction of the number of legal times out in either half from four to three. Also it was decreed that any delay of thirty seconds between the time the ball is ready for play and the time it is snapped or the remaining of a team in the huddle for more than fifteen seconds shall constitute intentional delay.

The committee, many of them former football stars and present coaches, ran through signals behind the doors of the conference room to test out the huddle and found, says Edward K. Hall, Chairman, that five to ten seconds were enough for this system, but gave it fifteen to be on the safe side. The huddle, by the way, is named in the shift legislation, the first formal recognition that it is a variation of this play.

These were the important changes. There were several minor ones, including a note to be inserted in the rules saying that the committee has no objection to any teams that may so desire arranging a game on the forty-play system. This is the plan for eliminating the time element, making forty plays constitute a game instead of dividing it into quarters and halves.

This scheme, which has been tried by Brown and Boston University, came in for discussion during the talk on stalling, but the committee ruled that it would not do anything which might be called formuating a set of rules for a new game.

The committee gave the referee sole jurisdiction over his ruling on any act where a player or person not legally permitted on the field interferes with play. This is to cover cases possible at smaller games where an overexcited partisan might rush out on the field and does not affect present ruling on substitutions.

The referee now will have complete jurisdiction on the size and shape of cleats. Rubber cleats were legalized. Junior high schools and elementary schools were advised to limit their games to eight-minute periods. Last year the committee advised senior high schools to play only twelve-minute periods.

The moving back of the goal posts was the original suggestion, according to one committee member, of no member of the committee, but came from a former Yale star. It was done, basically, so that the try for point after touchdown would not continue to be the mere formaility of kicking. The added distance of the kick, Chairman Hall said, might now tend to increase the number of times teams would try for this point through the medium of the rush and the pass.

It also will remove plays from the sector of the goal posts, such as the kicking out from behind. Also, without changing the point totals allowed, it gives the touchdown a bit more value than two field goals. It means that teams without exceptional kickers very seldom will try for field goals with any real hope of success from points further back than the 30-yard line.

The lateral pass rule reads as follows: "Any player may at any time hand or throw the ball in any direction except toward his own goal. If any such pass made on the first, second or third down strikes the ground within the field of play or goes out of bounds either before or after having been touched by a player of either side it shall belong to the side which made the pass at the point where it first strikes the ground within the field of play, or if it goes out of bounds before striking the ground, at the point where it crossed the sidelines; on the fourth down the ball shall go to the opponents at the same point. The pass from the snapper back to put the ball in play is excepted from this ruling."

The possibilities of this ruling are vividly apparent. It is probably the most important rule made at the meeting and is, in a great many respects, a step toward the game of Rugby. It may take several seasons before the possibilities are exhausted and new plays ought to abound during next season.

The rule on fumbled kicks tends further to lessen the importance of punting in the present-day game and the ruling on the shift, say the committee members, will keep this in bounds. Critics of this plan—who included Hall himself before the meeting—feel that it places too much of a burden on the official.

In the ruling on the shift the officials are not asked to hold a watch on the play, but the wording suggests the rapid counting of 1-2-3-4 as about the time required for an approximate second.

March 6, 1927

NIGHT SCHOOL GAME A SUCCESS IN SOUTH

Draws Record Crowd for Junior Contest at Montgomery, Ala.—Thirty Lights Used.

Special to The New York Times.

MONTGOMERY, Ala., Sept. 24.—The first night football game in the South, which was staged here last night at Cramton Bowl before a record crowd for high school contests, was pronounced a success by officials of the bowl, who predicted that many of the high school contests this season would be played at night.

Thirty lights, each of 1,000 watts and 1,500 candlepower, were strung lengthwise across the field at a height of fifty feet, five yards apart. Two giant floodlights, one focused on the scoreboard and the other above the two strands that held the field lights, completed the illumination scheme. The spectators were in darkness and barely discernible by the players.

The floodlight spread across the field at a height of fifty-five feet was to care for high punts. On one occasion the ball shattered a field light, but aside from this incident the game moved as smoothly as a daylight contest.

The novelty of the spectacle was said by the officials to be a strong factor in bringing the crowd, but aside from this, they pointed out, there is also the consideration that more persons are free during the night hours and can attend games without any loss of time for business. The crowd was estimated from 5,000 to 6,000. Montgomery's usual high school football crowds do not exceed 4,000.

The game proved to be a one-sided affair, the Cloverdale High School winning over the Pike Roads School by a score of 71 to 0. From the first the Cloverdale youngsters took the ball and romped across the field for touchdown after touchdown.

September 25, 1927

PITTSBURGH LOSES COAST GAME, 7 TO 6

Stanford Wins When Wilton, Whose Fumble Put East Ahead, Tallies on Another.

BOTH SCORE IN 3D PERIOD

Hagan Picks Up Loose Ball and Goes 19 Yards to Place Panthers in Lead.

By The Associated Press.

PASADENA, Cal., Jan. 2.—In a glorious finale to an up-and-down season Stanford's Cardinals defeated the great Pittsburgh team in the annual East-West Tournament of Roses football game here today, 7 to 6.

A colorful throng of 55,000 spectators saw the Cards make a thrilling comeback in the third period after a heartrending touchdown had set them on the short end of a 6—0 count. A fumble by Wilton of Stanford was picked up by Hagan and the stocky Panther halfback rushed 19 yards to plant his cleats in Stanford scoring turf.

Lashed into fury by the sudden reverse, and after they had outplayed their rivals for two periods, the Cards threw everything into one great offensive. A 31-yard pass by Hoffman, which fell into Worden's waiting arms, paved the way. On the 29-yard line, line play after line play, with Hoffman carrying the oval almost continuously, brought Stanford two yards from the goal.

Wilton Gets the Touchdown.

A fumbled ball brought groans, then cheers from the Cardinal rooting section. Hoffman's short pass was caught by Sims, who fumbled when tackled after he had gone a short distance; but little Frank Wilton, whose bobble earlier in the period had resulted in the Pittsburgh touchdown, snatched the ball and dashed three yards across the goal line. Hoffman's successful try for the extra point was the margin of victory.

With the minutes slipping away, Pittsburgh made one smashing effort and the sky was filled with passes that either fell too far ahead of receivers or were knocked down by Cardinal hands.

The central figure in today's gridiron drama was Coach Pop Warner of Stanford. The strategy of the master was pitted against that of the former pupil. Eleven years ago Jock Sutherland, Panther coach, was a star player under Pop when the latter directed the destinies of the Eastern university.

Big Biff Hoffman, Stanford fullback, was the outstanding player in the smashing wind-up that turned back an eleven that had been undefeated during the season until today.

Hoffman Hits Line Hard.

Hoffman cracked the vaunted Panther line almost every time he carried the ball, and he was called on frequently. Eighty-eight yards from scrimmage followed his efforts, while nearly all passing and punting duties fell to him.

Gibby Welch, Pitt's star halfback, was a tower of strength for his alma mater, but Stanford had been coached to watch him. Welch broke away several times for runs that totaled firty yards, but eighteen yards was his best individual effort, while Booth, fullback, and another famed Eastern warrior, was held to a total of thirty-nine yards.

Stanford led its rival in yards gained from scrimmage. The Cardinals reeled off a total of 154 yards against 139 for Pittsburgh. Stanford crashed through for fourteen first downs. Pittsburgh turned in half that many. Warner's men also had an edge in passing, completing three out of ten forwards for a total of thirty-two yards, while the Panthers tried the air eleven times, completing two for twenty-two yards.

Punting honors went to Pittsburgh. Hagan booted the oval for an average of fifty-one yards, while Hoffman's average was forty-seven yards.

The panthers were penalized seven times for a total setback of sixty-five yards, Stanford four times for thirty-five yards.

Pitts Wins the Toss.

The teams went out on a dry field to start the game. Pittsburgh won the toss and chose to receive.

Stanford made a first down on the old Statute of Liberty play after Hagan had kicked the ball out of danger. The Palo Alto team made another first down on line plunges. Hoffman got another first down when he pierced Pittsburgh's centre. Montgomery of Pittsburgh replaced Fox at guard who was injured.

Stanford lost the ball to Pittsburgh on the latter's 5-yard line and Hagan kicked from behind the goal. Stanford lost the ball when Welch caught Hyland's long pass on his 31-yard line and ran out of bounds. Pittsburgh went back 15 yards for holding as the period ended with the score 0 to 0.

At the start of the second period Pittsburgh, by line plunges, made a first down and pushed the ball to Stanford's 49-yard line. Murphy of Stanford then grabbed a Pittsburgh pass. A plunge by Wilton and a run by Hoffman gave Stanford a first down. The same combination again made another first down.

Wilton hit guard and Hoffman cleared another hole through centre and placed the ball on the 7-yard line. Wilton, on a faked pass, put the ball on Pittsburgh's 2-yard line. The hidden ball trick failed to work and Stanford lost the ball on downs.

Hagan kicked out of danger for Pitt and the teams struggled about midfield for several minutes, penalties, intercepted passes and short drives marking the play, with fortune favoring neither side. When the half ended Pitt had the ball near the centre of the field. There still had been no scoring.

Murphy took Pitt's kick to Stanford's 34-yard line at the start of the third period. The teams exchanged kicks as line attacks netted scant yardage. Pitt started a rush from the East's 19-yard zone. The attack swept down the field with heavy gains by running plays, interrupted only when Wilton knocked down Welch's pass over the goal line.

Pitt scored on the next play when Wilton fumbled and Hagan scooped up the ball, racing 19 yards to the goal. Booth's kick failed and Pitt led, 6 to 0.

Stanford Goes on Attack.

Stanford came back with a rush. The West's deceptive passing, running and driving attack drove quickly across the goal on consistent gains. Stanford took the lead and the game, 7 to 6, when Hoffman kicked goal.

The Stanford touchdown was registered by Wilton, who scooped up the ball after Sims caught and then fumbled Hoffman's pass.

Hoffman kicked off for Stanford and for half the final period the two teams swayed over midfield. Post, Stanford guard, carried the ball 30 yards to Pitt's 31-yard point on a guard-around play.

Both teams used numerous substitutes as the Stanford men plunged ahead toward the goal. Twice they threatened to score, but the Pitt defense held near the goal.

Taking the ball near their goal, the Panthers drove to midfield on a passing attack, but their desperate aerial attempt failed, as passes fell incomplete, and Stanford received the ball on downs just before the gun ended the game.

The line-up:

STANFORD (7).		PITTSBURGH (6).
Preston	L. E.	Donchess
Sellman	L. T.	Kern
Post	L. G.	Fox
McCreery	C.	Cutler
Robesky	R. G.	Roberts
Freeman	R. T.	Wasmuth
Harder	R. E.	Guarino
Murphy	Q. B.	Edwards
Hyland	L. H.	Welch
Hill	R. H.	Hagan
Hoffman	F. B.	Booth

SCORE BY PERIODS.

Stanford	0	0	7	0—7
Pittsburgh	0	0	6	0—6

Pittsburgh scoring—Touchdown, Hagan.

Stanford scoring—Touchdown, Wilton (sub for Hyland). Point after touchdown—Hoffman.

Referee—Evans, Millikan. Umpire—Sharpe, New York. Linesman—Egan, Pittsburgh. Field judge—Dolan, Notre Dame. Time of periods—15 minutes.

January 2, 1928

MILLIONS LISTEN IN ON ROSE FESTIVAL

Audience in New York Shivers as Announcer Describes Game in Pacific Sunshine.

S O S INSURANCE PLANNED

Lloyd's May Underwrite $67,000 Broadcast Tomorrow Night by Dodge Brothers.

While 69,000 persons sat in the "Bowl of Roses," at Pasadena, Cal., yesterday, and watched the football game between the University of Pittsburgh and Stanford University that crowned Pasadena's Tournament of Roses, Graham McNamee stood before a microphone linked-up with forty-six transmitters, embracing the entire country, and gave a play-by-play description of the game.

In Pasadena a warm sun smiled down on the gay crowd. In New York, 4,000 miles away, a cold sun dropped below the horizon as the city shivered on one of the coldest days of the Winter.

An official of the National Broadcasting Company which arranged for the hook-up estimated that more than 25,000,000 persons listened in.

The broadcast was wired direct from the Bowl of Roses to the National Broadcasting Company's headquarters at 711 Fifth Avenue, whence it was sent back over leased wires to the stations taking the program. This arrangement called for the use of two distinct lines from the West Coast, one to bring in the program and the other to send it back to the company's Pacific Coast network.

"Here we are," Mr. McNamee began. "Just above the edges of the Bowl are the banks of the valley, which are absolutely green, verdant and beautiful. A warm sun is shining, with here and there the shadow of a cloud. Over the 50-yard line Old Baldy rears his massive head. Right from here I can see roses blooming and orange trees, lemon trees and all kinds of trees. Can some of you people back in New York imagine this 'extreme heat,' if you know what I mean."

Then Mr. McNamee apologized as he removed his coat and vest.

January 3, 1928

CALIFORNIA BEATEN BY GEORGIA TECH, 8-7

60-Yard Run Toward Wrong Goal by Riegels of California Helps Tech Win Before 70,000.

OWN MAN STOPS HIS DASH

But Georgians Tackle Him on 3-Yard Line and Maree Blocks Kick for Safety.

TOUCHDOWN FOR THOMASON

Goes Over in Third Quarter on 15-Yard Gallop—Losers March 98 Yards to Tally in 4th.

Special to The New York Times.

PASADENA, Cal., Jan. 1.—In a thrilling football game before a capacity crowd of 70,000 in the Rose Bowl here today, the Golden Tornado of Georgia Tech defeated the University of California football team by a score of 8 to 7, the victors scoring on a safety and a touchdown. The Western eleven tallied in the fourth quarter after a straight march from its own 2-yard line.

The game was marked by an unusual play, which, it ultimately developed, was of great importance in the final score. It led to Georgia Tech's safety. Captain-elect Riegels of the Golden Bears, playing centre, snatched up a Tech fumble in the second quarter and started toward the Georgia Tech goal. There had been no scoring thus far in the contest and Riegels broke into a dead run.

Tech men sprang up in front of him and in eluding them he cut back across the field. He turned again to escape the opposition and in so doing apparently became confused and started down the field to his own goal, 60 yards away. As he pounded down the side line both California and Tech players stood amazed in their tracks.

Lom Pursues Him.

Benny Lom, halfback for the Golden Bears, sensed the situation almost immediately and sprang into action. Down the field he went after the flying Riegels, who only put on more speed as he heard feet pounding the turf behind him. Finally Lom grabbed hold of his mate at the California 3-yard line and turned him around. Making interference for Riegels, Lom started back down the field, but Tech was alert and a wave of tacklers hit Riegels before he could more than turn around, hurtling him back to the 1-yard line.

California immediately took up the punt formation, but Riegels, at centre, was nervous, and Lom, receiving the ball to kick, was little steadier. As the ball was snapped, Maree, Georgia Tech tackle, stormed through the line and blocked the punt. The ball rolled out of the end zone, but the officials ruled that Breckenridge, California quarterback, had touched it and that a safety would be scored against California.

The annual New Year's Day classic was played under an azure blue sky, with the thermometer standing at 80

degrees and the great crowd in holiday spirit, cheering both teams and the brilliant plays.

Tech's touchdown came in the third period. Shortly after the start of the second half, Lom got off a 50-yard punt that went to Tech's 23-yard line. Mizell punted back and Breckenridge fumbled. Waddey, Tech end, recovered on the Bear 27-yard line.

Jones Blocks Bears' Kick.

Mizell fumbled on the first play and Fitz, California tackle, recovered on the Bear 29-yard line. Lom made half a yard on the first play and on the next Jones broke through to block his kick and recovered the ball on the California 9-yard line. Four times Tech smashed the line and wound up just a foot shy of a touchdown. Lom retreated behind his goal line and punted to Thomason, who was downed in his tracks on the California 45-yard line. Mizell blazed around right end for thirty yards to the 15-yard line. On the next play Thomason went through tackle, reversed his field and went over the goal line standing up for a touchdown. As the try for point was missed the score became 8 to 0.

The Bears did not get their passing attack organized until the closing minutes of the final quarter and with just one and a half minutes to play, Captain Irving Phillips took a pass from Lom for a touchdown.

The Bears had advanced the ball from their 2-yard mark, Lom hurling long and accurate passes to Phillips and Eisan in the 98-yard march for the touchdown. Barr kicked goal, making the score 8 to 7.

The contest was marked by an unusual number of breaks in addition to Riegel's dash for his own goal. There also were several fumbles of consequence as in the first quarter when Lom threw a forty-yard pass to Barr, who dropped the ball while standing, all alone on the Tech goal line.

Lom Is Called Back.

Then in the second quarter Lom scooped up a fumble and raced sixty yards to the Tech goal, only to have the ball called back, Referee Dana ruling he had blown his whistle before the fumble.

In the third quarter, Breckenridge fumbled a punt, Waddey recovering for Tech on the California 27-yard line. Mizell fumbled the ball right back into California's possession, only to have Jones block Lom's kick on the 9-yard line, which ultimately led to Tech's touchdown.

In the same quarter Captain Phillips hurled a 40-yard pass to Eisan on a reverse play, only to have the Bear quarterback stumble and fall just as he was about to catch the ball deep in Tech territory.

The fourth quarter saw Rice, racing after another perfect pass from Lom, with a clear field ahead of him, stumble and fall. Eisan took another

pass from Lom, took two steps and fumbled, Lumpkin recovering for Tech on the Engineers' 45-yard line.

However, there were shining lights aplenty in the contest. The two rival captains were in brilliant form. Captain Peter Pund was a tower of strength in Tech's hard battling forward wall and Phillips was a hero in defeat at end for the Bears. Warner Mizell and Stumpy Thomason of Tech turned in several sensational dashes. Thomason's runbacks of punts, when he managed to escape Phillips and Avery, were spectacular.

Lom was the outstanding hero for the losers. He played smart football, was in every play and carried the ball on sweeping end runs with dash and vigor. He shot through tackle and over guard, hurled long passes to the ends, or short, snappy passes behind the line of scrimmage to the other backs. His kicking was excellent.

Jones, at end, and Maree, at tackle, were equally good with Pund in the Tech line. Likewise, Steve Bancroft, the bulky Bear tackle, played a rousing game.

How Georgia Tech-California Lined Up for Football Game

Georgia T. (8).		California (7).
Waddey	L.E.	Avery
Maree	L.T.	Fitz
Drennon	L.G.	H. Gill
Pund	C.	Riegels
Westbrook	R.G.	Schwarz
Thrash	R.T.	Bancroft
Jones	R.E.	Phillips
Schulman	Q.B.	Breckenridge
Thomason	L.H.	Lom
Mizell	R.H.	Barr
Lumpkin	F.B.	Schmidt

Score by Periods.

Georgia Tech......0 2 6 0—8
California ....0 0 0 7—7

Scoring.

Touchdowns—Thomason, Phillips. Point after touchdown—Barr. Safety—By Georgia Tech on California.

Substitutions.

California—Miller for Riegels, Schlicting for Barr C. Handy for Schwarz, Cockburn for Schmidt, Rice for Schlicting, Norton for Avery, Riegels for Miller, Breckenridge for Eisan, Beckett for Gill.

Georgia Tech—Durant for Schulman, Dunlap for Mizell, Watkins for Maree, Holland for Jones.

Officials.

Referee—Herbert Dana. Umpire—Arthur Badenoch. Linesman—T. M. Fitzpatrick. Field judge—William Streit.

January 2, 1929

BOOTH HERO AS YALE DEFEATS ARMY, 21-13, BEFORE 80,000 FANS

By ALLISON DANZIG.

Special to The New York Times.

NEW HAVEN, Conn., Oct. 26.—A mere mite of a youth, dwarfed with his 144 pounds and his 5 feet 6 inches in height by the towering giants around him, turned in one of the most amazing performances ever seen in the Yale Bowl today to lead a faltering Yale team out of the wilderness of defeat over the prostrate

form of a Goliath Army eleven.

Hurled into a maelstrom that found his six-foot team-mates fighting on the short end of a 13 to-0 score, Albie Booth, Yale's sophomore quarterback, wrote his name in imperishable letters among the moleskin heroes of the Blue as he ran rings around and through Army's demoralized tackles, ends and secondaries, to score three touchdowns and gain for Yale a totally unlooked-for 21-to-13 victory.

Eighty thousand spectators jammed in the huge saucer to its farthest structures beneath a benign welkin, witnessed the downfall of an Army eleven that entered the game a 2-to-1 favorite.

Among those 80,000 was Mrs. Albert J. Booth, the mother of the hero of the day, sitting in at a football contest for the first time.

Not even a Belasco could have staged the scene more dramatically.

This action sequence recalls one of the strangest events in the history of college football. Roy Riegels of California ran 60 yards the wrong way in the 1929 Rose Bowl against Georgia Tech. From top to bottom, left: Riegels (number 11) gets the ball and takes off for what he thinks will be a touchdown. Top to bottom, right: one of his teammates gives chase and stops him just short of disaster.

nor could an Alger or a Henty have charted a more heroic course for young Booth than he blazed this afternoon.

Picture the scene. It was early in the second period. Army had scored twice—once through a 45-yard run by Cagle on an interception of a pass in the opening quarter and again in the second per period on a 35-yard run by Murrel. The Yale cheering section was in the doldrums, while the 1,200 cadets across the field were roaring forth their victorious chant. There didn't seem to be the ghost of a chance for the Bulldog. Apparently he was as hopelessly licked as every one had expected him to be.

Right after that second Army touchdown Head Coach Mal Stevens gave Booth the signal to warm up. Instantly the Yale stands came to life and the atmosphere became almost electric as the diminutive sophomore unlimbered his legs along the sidelines. A moment more and he was rushing on the field and one name was on every one's lips.

It was remarkable that so many thousands could find their ebbing hopes upon so comparatively frail a pair of shoulders. It was an impressive testimonial to the magic of Booth's name, but it seemed that they were expecting too much of him. Army's giant line would crush him.

How Yale and Army Elevens Lined Up for Their Contest

YALE (24).		ARMY (13).
Hickof	L. E.	Carimark
Ferris	L. T.	Price
Stewart	L. G.	Humber
Palmer	C.	Lazar
Greene	R. G.	Hillsinger
Vincent	R. T.	Perry
Barres	R. E.	Messinger
Bob Hall	Q. R.	Gibner
Snead	L. H.	O'Keefe
Miller	R. H.	Cagle
Duna	F. B.	Murrel

SCORE BY PERIODS

Yale	0	7	14	021
Army	7	6	0	0—13

Touchdowns—Booth 3. Murrel. Cagle. Points after touchdowns—Booth 3. (dropkicks), O'Keefe (place kick).

Substitutions—Yale: Loeser for Stewart. McLennan for Suead, Austen for Hall Booth for McLennan, Hare for Loeser, Philips for Palmer, Godman for Hickof, Hickok for Godman, Taylor for Duna, Elis for Miller, Palmer for Philips, Reane for Eilis, Hawley for Vincent, Loeser for Hare, Marting for Ferris, McLenna for Boot, Hall for Austin, Godman for Hickof, Linehan Miller for Laxar, Parkam for Price, Trice for Hillsinger, Suarez for Humber, Miloy for Messinger, Spengler for Perry, Glattly for O'Keefe, Park for Miller, Humber for Suarez, MacLean for Sprenger, Kenny for Carimark. Carlpark for Kepay, Hillberg for Carlmark, Laxar for Miller, Miller for Messinger, O'Keefe for Glattly, Glattly for O'Keefe. Caryer for Gibner, Suarez for Humber, Gletcher for Malley.

Referee—W.G. Crowell, Swarthmore, umpire—Tom Thorp, Columbia, Linesman—H. A. Fisher, Pennsylvania, Field Judge—Hill Hollenback, Pennsylvania, time of periods—15 minutes.

Eli Team Is Inspired.

But as remarkable as was the effect of Booth's appearance upon the stands, it was nothing compared to the transformation that took place in the Yale team. From the moment that their new pilot rushed into their midst the wearers of the blue became eleven entirely different men.

Inspired by his presence, the line lost its sluggishness, the attack developed a coordination that had been lacking. The machine had gained a spark-plug, and away it went high. Army, confident of victory and glorying in a manpower that was expected to smother Booth before he could get started, found itself, almost in the twinkling of an eye, forced on the defensive.

Before the end of the second period, in which Booth scored his first touchdown almost single-handed on a march of 32 yards, the cadets were reeling, and with the third quarter they collapsed completely.

Army Put to Rout.

The entire left side of their line became demoralized, and the spidery little Yale quarterback, taking the ball on almost every rush, had the Yale cheering section delirious with joy as he broke loose time after time, sidestepped tackle after tackle and carried the ball 35 yards for his second touchdown.

When Booth followed this score with a second drop-kick for the extra point to put Yale in the lead for the first time, the scene in the Bowl was as close to bedlam as any that has been staged there since Yale won its last-minute victory over Princeton in 1927. But the biggest ovation for the amazing little quarterback was yet to come.

Army, badly disorganized and helpless to advance the ball, was forced to punt right after the next kick-off by yale. The ball nestled in the arm of Booth on his 35-yard line near the right side of the field and his progress seemed to be blocked by the whole Army team. Apparently headed for the side line. Booth almost miraculously evaded one tackler after another without stepping outside and breaking out of a knot of Army men, dodged and sidestepped until he found open territory.

How he got out of such a swarm of gold jerseyed Giants is almost inexplicable, but gt out he did, and with his team-mates clearing out the last few cadets, he raced 65 yards for his third touchdown.

Not only the cheering section but the whole Yale team now did tribute to Booth. Captain Greene, towering over him like a Great Dane over a terrier, almost picked him off the ground to pound him on the back and the rest of the team rushed to him joyously to do a little more pounding.

It was Booth's day all the way. Not in years has a Yale back scored so tremendous a personal triumph as the New Haven youth did this afternoon. Cagle, the pride of Army and hero of her victory in the Bowl last year, was totally eclipsed.

From the time that Booth entered the day, the ace of the Army team was bottled up by a rampant Yale line that was throwing him for losses behind the line and that was swarming in on him so fast on his end runs that he was continually having to throw passes from fifteen to twenty yards behind the line as he did in the Stanford game last year.

Not even Stanford could smother Cagle's passes and runs in such an annihilating fashion as the Blue forwards did today. From that, it may be gathered how utterly the whole Army machine disintegrated for when Cagle is given any kind of a chance at all he is likely to score one way or another. Army was so badly outclassed in the third period as to look almost like a high school team.

Yale piled up six first downs in that period, to none for Army, and registered thirteen in all, to seven for Army. Five of those seven were made in the final quarter after Booth had been withdrawn.

Out of the eleven passes that Cagle threw, only three were completed, two of them in the closing minutes, while Yale had even less success with the pass, completing only one out of eight and losing three by interception. One of the three interceptions led to Army's first touchdown, while Yale profited by Gibner's fumble on his thirty-two yard line that paved the way for the Elis' first score.

It was a sorely disappointed regiment of cadets that assembled quitely on the field after the final whistle and marched out of the bowl on the way back to West Point.

In the morning, they had arrived with supreme confidence in their team to pass in review before the start of the game they had put on another of their impressive parades in the bowl marching with martial step like conquerers. The stage, it seemed, was all set for a big day for Army and Red Cagle and for the third victory for a Biff Jones eleven over Yale in the four years he has been at the helm on the Plains.

One man spoiled the day for the cadets, made a mockery of the strength of their giants and frustrated the hopes of Jones for an unbeaten eleven in the last year at West Point and that man was the smallest one on the field.

But it would be unfair not to give due credit also to the men on the Yale line whose inspiring play opened the way for Booth's brilliant runs and also to the lads whose interference mopped up ahead of him.

Taylor at fullback was a big ground gainer when he went in to relieve Dunn; McLennan stood out in the first line and Miller and Bob Hall also earned their share of glory.

And last but not least give credit to Mal Stevens, Yale's stout-hearted coach, who has brought the Blue back to the heights in the face of the storm of criticisms that was heaped upon him following the Georgia defeat.

October 27, 1929

NOTRE DAME DEFEATS ARMY, 7-0, AS ELDER MAKES 96-YARD RUN

85,000 See Fleet Back Intercept Pass for Touchdown on Frozen Stadium Field..

CARIDEO ADDS EXTRA POINT

Score Comes in 2d Period of Stirring, Hard-Fought Game in Which Cadets Star.

LOSERS USE ONLY 11 MEN

Victors Pressed to Finish Season Undefeated — Cannon, Carideo, Cagle and Murrel Shine.

By ROBERT F. KELLEY.

Jack Elder, standing on his own 4-yard line in the middle of the second quarter, grabbed a forward pass that had left the hands of the attacking Chris Cagle of Army and raced ninety-six yards over turf frozen as hard as concrete to bring Notre Dame to the end of the trail unbeaten and holding the slim margin of 7 to 0 in its final game. That one stabbing run that brought a crowd of 85,000 to its feet was all there was to the scoring in the last game of the Eastern football season, and it brought defeat to a great and gallant Army football team that contributed its share to one of the best football games of history.

Never again during the course of the hard, bitter struggle played in icy, arctic winds did the famous team from South Bend threaten the Army goal. Notre Dame's first and second string back fields were set back on their heels by the surging Army defense, but the team found the courage and the skill to make those few points count.

Army Twice Near Score.

On two occasions Army stood at the threshold of scores, but both times Notre Dame managed to turn the Cadets back—once with that amazing, brilliant interception and run and once when another Cagle pass, in the closing period, fell through the frost-stiffened fingers of Hutchinson as he sprawled face downward on the semi-ice that formed yesterday's playing field.

The huge mob that piled into the Yankee Stadium for this last game, scheduled before Winter took complete charge of things, remained to the bitter end, held there by the thrilling, fighting efforts of Army to offset that one knife blow and by the stubborn, game resistance of the team from South Bend that has gone undefeated and untied through one of the hardest schedules of modern history.

A great string of beaten teams is on this Notre Dame victory list, but certainly one of the highest points along that list must be reserved for the golden-clad players of Army who fought so well and so gamely without a single substitution.

Ground Frozen Hard.

No football game has ever been played under harder conditions for the men in action. The ground underneath was as hard and unyielding as the surface of the finest automobile road in the country. The cleats of the backs and the linemen slid over its frigid surface, and fingers were turned into numb stumps by the frost-laden wind that whipped down from the top of the towering stands and frequently blew the ball out of position between plays as it lay innocently on the ground.

There would have been no possible blame attached to any one for fumbling or playing only fair football, but in the face of this, the men of Notre Dame and Army turned in one of the best games the current season has seen, a game in which fumbling was scarce, in which the centres of both sides passed well, and in which the lines and the ends of both sides played superb, fighting football.

It was a frozen, solid sort of game. Passes were tried but they were useless. Three of Army's were intercepted and none completed. Notre Dame tried only four and these went astray. A receiver couldn't get to the ball and the defense backs had all the better of it, coming up on the run and watching the ball throughout.

Army Line Has Edge.

In the face of this, the game dropped into a stubborn fight with the lines of both sides doing herculean service, but with the Army line, if credit must be given to one side or the other, coming out on top. Time and again a golden swarm of players surged through to blot out Notre Dame's famous back field which had been compared to the "Four Horsemen" of a previous year. Not more than two or three times did any of these Notre Dame backs get away for a gain of any appreciable size.

At the start of the second quarter, Tom Lieb, acting in place of the crippled Rockne, sent in Notre

Dame's first string backs. But Moon Mullins, Frank Carideo, Jack Elder and Martin Brill made just a single yard on attack all through that period and not the slightest vestige of a first down. Army slammed into them, Murrel and Cagle storming up often to make tackles in the enemy back field. But there was that one heart-breaking play of Elder's, the fastest man on the Notre Dame team.

Army had worked out this situation for itself. After a first period in which the two teams battled around the middle of the field, Murrel sent one of his great punts deep into Notre Dame territory. Schwartz punted back and his kick was short, Army taking the ball just beyond mid-field. Here Lieb sent in his first string backs. He had started his first string line.

Murrel began the berserk, thrusting dives into the line which were to feature the game, and with Cagle helping him, the Army jammed through to the 20-yard line. Here Notre Dame, led by the bare-headed Jack Cannon, who yesterday was one of the greatest linemen of the season, stood up at last and stopped the Army attack. Notre Dame took the ball on downs.

But Army was tasting great things and three plays later, Price, Army's left tackle, went slamming through to shove a Notre Dame defense man into a punt, blocking it. Notre Dame recovered, but the ball belonged to Army on downs on the 14-yard line.

Murrel plunged through centre for a few precious feet, but this was too long a process, and Cagle dropped back for one of his passes. He shot the ball away from his cold fingers dead for the Army receiver, waiting almost on the Notre Dame goal line in the northwest corner of the field.

Elder Intercepts Pass.

But Elder was there, too. He chose a gamble and the gamble worked. Instead of playing in the orthodox fashion for a goal line defense and knocking the ball down while covering receivers, Elder drove through boldly, grabbed the ball on his own 4-yard line and started like mad up the sidelines.

For a few brief, breath-catching strides he struggled and fought to maintain his balance and keep inside the field. Referee Ed Thorp ran over behind him to watch, and the great Notre Dame back succeeded in setting himself and sailed away.

Two Army players cut across the field and dove at him, but they were a scant few inches short and he stepped into the open with one interferer looking out for trouble. There was no dodging, just straight and very fast running, and the ball carrier was never threatened again until the 8-yard line was reached and one more Army player dove at him and missed, to lie there, his face buried in his arms, as Elder ran across the goal line with the touchdown and the football game.

Carideo Adds Extra Point.

Carideo, who was a superb figure in the Notre Dame back field all afternoon, then sent over his placement for the extra point and the scoring for the day was finished.

But that came nowhere near telling the story of the game. Certainly there is enough glory for Notre Dame in the magnificent undefeated season it has been through to concede the unscored honors of the day to Army. Army might well have won this game. Save for that one valuable run, Army outplayed Notre Dame for the most part, and always there was the superb sight of eleven Army players starting this fight and finishing it without a single substitution. It was an Army team that started action with no thought of shock troops or anything else but the single thought of coming back from the ruck of a real hard-luck season.

No football crowd anywhere in the United States can claim any edge on the huge throng which watched the struggle, for those present sat half-frozen and spellbound by one of the greatest exhibitions of courage that any athletic field in this country has seen, and it was courage on both sides.

Cannon's Play Stands Out.

It seems unkind to single out any players above the rest for praise in this icy epic of football, but certainly Cannon was a magnificent guard and certainly Joe Nash filled capably the shoes of the injured Moynihan, and Carideo was everything he had been called—a brainy, hard-running quarterback, full of gameness and football instinct—and his punting throughout the last three quarters was one of the prime reasons for the success of Notre Dame.

The rest of the Notre Dame team, running into stubborn, amazing resistance from Army, deserves all the credit in the world for playing fine football. But to the Army team, starting and finishing on the attack—the game ended deep in Notre Dame territory, with Notre Dame, after taking the ball away on downs, hugging it like a precious jewel on short quarterback runs until the final whistle blew—go the tributes of the season.

They started Carlmark, Price, Humber, Miller, Hillsinger, Perry, Messinger, Carver, Hutchinson, Cagle and Murrel, and they finished that way. In a few days they start for the West and a post-season game with Stanford as a real representative of the best of Eastern football, for yesterday they were a team which ranked high with any who hav better records throughout the season.

Cagle and Murrel Star.

If it is necessary to pick out names in that Army team, the names of Cagle and Murrel must go to the top. Cagle, playing his last game in the East, paid a fitting and perfect farewell to the game he has featured. He was a great football player, and if he had been able to get his passes to successwul endings, the game might have had another ending.

For a running mate he had John Hertz Murrel, who had the greatest football afternoon he has ever had. when there were holes he made he bulled through, anyway, and when there were holes, he made yard after yard. Only a great, fighting and real football team could have turned back the Army yesterday, and Notre Dame can throw all of its other games of the season away and point to this one alone as sufficient claim to greatness. Knute Rockne, held to his bed by illness, had sent another brilliant and fully first-rate football team into action.

Army gave an indication of what was to be expected in the first period when, after a punt or two, Murrel, who matched Carideo in his great kicking all afternoon, sent away a beauty that rolled to Notre Dame's 27-yard line, which was recovered by Army after it hit a rival back. Right there Notre Dame began the defense that saved the day, but it needed a break or so at that.

On the first play into the line, Murrel fell on the frozen turf. On the next play Cagle fumbled the ball and recovered. On the next Notre Dame came through to nail Cagle and then Cagle sent away a pretty pass that was just a shade too far for the two frantic Army men, loose in front, to get to as their cleats slid over the frozen ground.

That was the last time either team had a scoring chance in the first period. Then came the second with Army pushing through to open what promised to be a scoring spot, only to have the Cagle pass turn into a boomerang. Neither team was inside the other's 40-yard line for the rest of that second period.

It was brilliant defensive football on both sides, fine football that kept the crowd keyed up, but for the most part it was with gasps of astonishment as the Army forwards surged through with no respect at all for the famous first-string back field of Notre Dame and threw them for losses. There was only a 1-yard gain for Notre Dame during this period, aside from the long run to touchdown.

Ball Remains in Midfield.

In the third period the play remained in the centre of the field except when punts temporarily sent the ball into the territory of one team or the other.

Notre Dame never threatened in the fourth either, and the only time either side was near to a score was when Cagle, shaking off tackler after tackler came back about 40 yards with a punt toward the close and gave the Army the ball on Notre Dame's 38-yard line. Notre Dame, fighting madly to protest that 7-point advantage, stopped the Army short and forced a pass from Cagle.

Cagle sent it away perfectly, but Hutchinson could not stand up. He was clear on the 19-yard line, but when he tried to move up to the ball he fell flat on his face and the last chance of Army to make its gallant fight pay dividends went glimmering.

Only twice during the game was Notre Dame in possession of the ball inside Army's 35-yard line. Army drove deep into Notre Dame territory three times, that was all. It had to be a combination of luck and skill to end this game with one side on top, and the luck and the skill to take advantage of it were with Notre Dame.

Two great and gallant football teams struggled for two hours over a frozen, brutal playing surface and one of them won, but there was certainly honor enough to go around for each side.

Wintry Setting for Game.

New York has never had a more wintry setting for a football game. It is doubtful if any place in the East has had one more so. Only the 21-to-21 tie which Army and Navy played in Chicago had anything like this to offer to its spectators, though the snowstorm that featured the Chicago battle was missing from this one.

New York awoke yesterday morning morning to clear skies, the color of the blue steel that goes into the blades of fine duelling swords and just as cold looking. The sun was a pale yellow and went across the sky as though it were just fulfilling a formality and not bothering much with turning on heat.

Where, in other big-game towns, the crowds of the day head into town in special railroad trains and thousands of automobiles, New York goes to its big games via the subway. This game started earlier than any other of the district and a half hour before the start, at 1 o'clock, there was to be the important business of the entry of the cadets. No one who had managed to get his hands on tickets wanted to miss this, so before the morning was half way through, the subway began to take on the aspect of a mad rush.

It was the typical evening and morning rush that the millions of office workers in the city know each day, but it was a different one. Here was a crowd which was not heading for steam-heated offices or for well-kept homes. It was a crowd going out to brave the rigors of an afternoon under conditions that would bother some polar explorers.

Little Bunting Is Seen.

New York, blasé and used to great spectacles, had not dressed up much for this affair. Only a few store windows bore colors and ribbons and here and there a hotel had a banner or two stretched across its lobby.

But the color and excitement of the game were on hand as soon as the voyagers reached the subway entrances. A few ordinary mortals, trying innocently to reach their homes after work in the morning, found themselves enveloped in a rushing, good-natured but very bulky crowd.

On the steps of most of the express stations the ubiquitous vendor of winning colors and souvenirs stood, very much in the way, but standing his ground and screaming his wares.

Men and women pushed into the underground platforms looming huge in fur coats, galoshes, blankets, woolen, skating caps and great driving-mittens. A vast army of people was starting out through a peaceful city for an afternoon's battle with the weather. Winter had shut down hard with everything at his command, but the crowds were not going to have this day they had been waiting for so long spoiled for them.

Ushers Arrive Early.

At the stadium, long before noon, hundreds of ushers and hot dog and coffee vendors, looking forward to a great afternoon of business, reported for work, the vendors looking very cold indeed in their white coats. But they had work to do before they had been on hand very long.

The wide, extra-sized sidewalks placed all around this gigantic stand of the Yankee Baseball Club, looked bare and roomy early in the morning, but by the middle of the day they were jammed deep. The streets filled up with taxicabs and autos, extra police wrestling with them, and the confused, noisy sound of a great crowd filled the air, set to the steady monotonous undertone of more subway trains grinding into the station overhead to deposit more thousands.

In the meantime, up at Rye and at Travers Island the players of Notre Dame and Army had risen, breakfasted and run out into the biting, icy winds for a bit of exercise. Then, just before noon, they were loaded into special buses and, with motorcycle police weaving and lurching before them, headed for the stadium.

Kept From Excitement.

The players had been closely guarded from all this excitement and it wasn't until they drew in sight of the stadium that the noise and crowds came on them. Their escorts cut a clean line through the traffic and pulled up before the doors in the rear of the stadium marked "New York American League Baseball Club, Office."

The players jumped out of their cars, bundled up to the eyes in great coats, and ran up the few steps to the doorway to disappear until they ran out on the field inside.

The tall, almost dangerous looking steep sides of the big grand stand began to fill slowly. Extra wooden seats had been placed behind the last rows in the lower and mezzanine and behind these the standing room filled first with people looking for the best places. The holders of the reserved seats lingered around the coffee stands and munched sandwiches, taking their time about filling up the bare spaces of the stands with their multicolored clothing and white appearing faces.

How Army-Notre Dame Lined Up In the Yankee Stadium Game

NOTRE DAME (7).		ARMY (0).
Colrick	L.E.	Carlmark
Twomey	L.T.	Price
Cannon	L.G.	Humber
Nash	C.	Miller
Law	R.G.	Hillsinger
Leahy	R.T.	Perry
Conley	R.E.	Messinger
Gebert	Q.B.	Carver
Savoldi	L.H.	Hutchinson
Schwartz	R.H.	Cagle
O'Connor	F.B.	Murrel

SCORE BY PERIODS.

Notre Dame	0	7	0	0	7
Army	0	0	0	0	0

Touchdown—Elder. Point after touchdown—Carideo (placement kick).

Substitutions—Notre Dame: Carideo for Gebert, Brill for Savoldi, Elder for Schwartz, Mullins for O'Connor, Donaghue for Leahy, O'Brien for Colrick, Collins for O'Brien, Savoldi for Mullins, Colrick for Collins, Mullins for Savoldi, O'Connor for Brill. Army: none.

Referee—Ed Thorp, De La Salle. Umpire—John Schommer, Chicago. Linesman—N. E. Kearns, De Paul. Field judge—A. W. Palmer, Colby. Time of periods—15 minutes.

The stands were still only about three-quarters filled when a sudden exciting blare of music burst into the field and a roar came to welcome the blue-coated bandmen at the head of the cadets of the United States Military Academy.

Marching at Steady Pace.

Marching steadily into the cold wind, their deep blue capes set back to show the white facing, the band strode in and stood in a corner of what is ordinarily the baseball outfield, but which yesterday was the end of the gridiron. Then, behind them, in a steady, precisely even flow came the blue-gray corps of cadets.

They were the only people in the place that did not appear half frozen. They marched with their faces straight ahead into the cold air and

their shoulders thrown back as though they were defying the weather as well as the players of Notre Dame They kept coming, swung around and marched in company front across the field until they blotted out its discouraged looking grass with the color of their uniforms. Then suddenly they stopped and became a frozen, absolutely motionless picture as a great throaty roar of admiration came from the stands.

They stood there silently while four white-shirted cheer leaders ran through them toward the Notre Dame side, which they were facing. The cheer leaders formed a pyramid, one of them climbing on top, and there came a terrific bark of noise from the cadets as they cheered the enemy. Then they were silent and suddenly, as one man, about-faced to their own stands. The formality was ended. On one knee,

they cheered their own team, leaping into the air, hats in hand, with the final note. Then to a cheerful, pumping quick march, they ran to their places in the stand and started the unceasing roar of noise which they kept up all afternoon.

They had hardly been seated when the players came running out to the field. They punted and ran through signals, blowing on their fingers, with their coaches and substitutes following them about covered with blankets and great sheepskin-collared coats like some tribe of Eskimos.

Finally they withdrew to the sidelines, the captains met in the centre of the field, a coin flashed in the air and the teams ran out for the kick-off, dancing and slapping themselves against the cold.

December 1, 1929

Players of the Game

Knute Rockne—Notre Dame's Great Coach

By ALLISON DANZIG.
All Rights Reserved.

FROM Norway, the land of sagas, there came to America shortly after the turn of the century an immigrant boy who was, in the course of time, to write a saga of success as vivid in its appeal to the youth of today as the Icelandic exploits of Leif, the son of Eric the Red.

Knute Kenneth Rockne is the name of this carrier forward of Scandinavian traditions, and wherever football is played or discussed in the United States no figure is held in greater esteem.

The boy of tender age who was thrown upon his own resources before he went to high school, who worked as a brakeman on a railroad in Illinois to pay his college tuition, has contributed a chapter to football history which marks him as one of the game's real geniuses and assures him of a fixed place as part and parcel of its tradition. He is, of course, one of its transcendantly successful coaches.

Planning for Next Year.

Today, in South Bend, Ind., Knute Rockne sits in his wheel-chair with his crippled leg, planning for the year that is ahead, while telegrams and letters of congratulation still pour in upon him following Notre Dame's successful completion of probably the most exacting schedule ever undertaken by an eleven. Every one loves a winner and Notre Dame was one for nine successive Saturdays against teams that represent a cross-section of the country's best football talent.

In turn the Rockne men met and defeated Indiana, Navy, Wisconsin, Carnegie Tech, Georgia Tech, Drake, Southern California, Northwestern and Army. Not one of those nine opponents, all of whom were met away from home, constituted a "soft spot." Not one of those games offered the opportunity for a letdown or a breathing spell.

The final returns, following the stirring battle with Army at the Yankee Stadium, show 145 points for Notre Dame to 38 for its opponents. It is not to be wondered at that Dr. Frank Dickinson of the faculty of the University of Illinois has com-

Times Wide World Photo.

KNUTE ROCKNE.

puted Notre Dame to be the winner of the Jack F. Rissman trophy, "emblematic of the national intercollegiate championship," and that there is a general disposition to award the mythical crown to the South Benders, in spite of the fact that there are other strong claimants in Pittsburgh, Purdue, Tulane, Tennessee and St. Mary's.

Had Four Unbeaten Teams.

This is not the first time that Rockne has brought a team through an arduous schedule undefeated. In the twelve seasons that he has been at the helm at Notre Dame since he succeeded his chief, Jess Harper, as head coach in 1918, he has had four unbeaten teams, in 1919, 1920, 1924 and 1929.

In only two of those twelve years has his team lost more than one game. The total reckoning for the period is 95 games won, 12 lost and 5 tied, while Notre Dame has piled up 2,582 points to 593 for its 112 opponents.

Until this year, the greatest of all the Rockne teams, certainly the most celebrated, was his Four Horsemen combination of 1924. It was on this great outfit that Stuhldreher, Miller, Layden and Crowley rode to a national championship behind a line that pivoted around probably the greatest Notre Dame centre, if not one of the greatest of all centres, Adam Walsh, now line coach at Yale.

But Rockne's fame does not rest solely upon the victories turned in by his teams. In the fifty-odd years' history of football there has been no coach whose concepts of strategy have been more highly respected than those of the South Bend wizard.

His Plays Widely Copied.

His formations and plays have been copied as much as those of almost any coach that can be named. His pupils have been more in demand as coaches than those from any other college. His coaching schools have been the mecca of college and high school coaches, his books on the game have circulated widely and there has been no other coach who has been so much in demand both as a lecturer on the technique and strategy of football and as a raconteur with an inexhaustible mine of amusing stories about the game.

Wherever football men assemble, whether at formal coaches' meetings or informal gatherings, if the thick-set, bald-headed, flat-nosed Rockne is present he is certain to be the centre of the group. To see him stand in front of a blackboard before a gathering of his colleagues and diagram his plays, often for the edification, he announces dryly, of a rival in the group, is an entertaining and profitable experience that is not soon forgotten.

Although he has been heard to remark often that "they call me a rough-neck," Rockne has an erudition and culture that make him equally at home whether he is speaking in the vernacular of the football field, addressing a Back Bay gathering in Boston or engaging in a learned discourse on eurythmics with Bob Zuppke, the poet-painter of Champaign, Ill. As an undergradu-

ate he took honors in chemistry, of which he is an instructor at Notre Dame.

There is never anything half-hearted or faint-hearted about what Rockne says. He is a man with intense convictions and the courage of those convictions, who speaks forcibly and fearlessly. Football is of his very fiber and being. Both as a player (he was one of the best ends turned out at Notre Dame) and as a coach he has acquired a deep and abiding affection for the game and he has emphatic ideas of its worth as a school of training for shaping the character of the boys under him.

Praises the Game Highly.

"Football," he said on one occasion, "teaches a boy a sense of responsibility—responsibility as a representative of his college, responsibility to his team-mates, responsibility in controlling his passions, fear, hatred, jealousy and rashness. Football brings out the best there is in every one."

As intense as is his devotion to the game, just as fierce is his hostility to those who seek to disparage its benefits, while withering is his scorn for a certain type of collegian whom he terms "powder puff youths," "rumble seat cowboys" and "mezzanine floor hurdlers."

Fraternities and co-eds also have drawn his ire. He has no objection to them academically, but both of them he regards as nuisances around a football camp. The latter, he says, take too much of the players' time and the former bring about athletic politics, which are a distinct handicap to a coach.

It is to the fact that Notre Dame neither is co-educational nor allows fraternities that Rockne attributes in part the success of his teams. Another factor, he states, is the isolation and cohesiveness of the university; still another is the system of mass athletics that he, as athletic director, has built up at South Bend, where a dozen dormitory teams play regular schedules with each other.

Wants All Students to Play.

"If football is a good sport for the varsity player," he argues, "why isn't it a good sport for the entire undergraduate body? Granted that it is, I want every boy at Notre Dame who cares to kick a football to have some place in which to kick it."

Rockne teams have always been noted for their speed, alertness and intelligence, the chief reason being that he is so careful in choosing the right type of youth to fit his system. There are six cardinal points he keeps before him in selecting his material and in molding it. They are:

1. Brains, "resiliency of mind, resourcefulness, power of analysis."
2. Spark, "the emotional urge that lifts a man out of the commonplace."
3. Hard work. "No one has ever succeeded without it."
4. Sense of responsibility. "Chores pay dividends and clearing the path for a team-mate comes under the heading of chores."
5. Proper point of view. "To play fairly, to respect the rights of opponents and the rules of the game."
6. Mental and moral courage.

December 10, 1929

FIELD GOAL BEATS NOTRE DAME, 16-14, AS 52,000 LOOK ON

Baker's 33-Yard Placement in Final Minute Gives Southern California Triumph.

THREE-YEAR STREAK ENDS

Shaver's Two Touchdowns in Last-Period Rally Precede the Deciding Kick.

BANAS AND SCHWARTZ TALLY

Count After Long Marches in the Second and Third Quarters— Walker Watches Struggle.

	So. Cal.	Notre Dame.
First downs	18	10
Yards gained rushing	117	169
Forward passes	11	10
Forward completed	2	1
Yards gained, forwards	73	25
Forwards intercepted by	1	2
Laterals	4	3
Laterals completed	4	3
Yards gained, Laterals	25	43
Number of punts	5	11
*Distance of punts, yards	229	496
Run-back of punts, yards	75	14
Fumbles	6	0
Own fumbles recovered	4	0
Penalties	0	10
Yards lost, penalties	0	89

*From point where ball was kicked.

By ALLISON DANZIG.

Special to The New York Times.

SOUTH END, Ind., Nov. 21.—One of the greatest winning streaks compiled in football since the time of Michigan's point-a-minute teams of a generation age came to an end with one minute left to play today as Notre Dame's all-conquering horde, unbeaten in three years, went down in stunning defeat before one of the hardest-running, fiercest-tackling elevens that ever stepped upon a gridiron.

With 52,000 spectators looking on thunderstruck in the beautiful new red brick stadium that stands as a monument to Knute Rockne, Southern California, the team that had last defeated the Ramblers in the final game of 1928, performed the almost incredible feat of spotting its opponent a 14-0 lead going into the final period and then proceeding to pile up sixteen points in the space of fifteen minutes to win the game, 16-14.

A 33-yard field goal from placement from the 23-yard line by Johnny Baker in the last sixty seconds of play won this savagely-fought battle just when it seemed that Notre Dame, for the fourth time in six years, was to carry the day by the margin of a point after touchdown.

Stage Two Long Marches

Two long marches by the rugged, tremendously aggressive Trojans, one for 47 yards and the other for 57 yards with the brilliant Gaius Shaver carrying the ball over each time, had preceeded Baker's electrifying kick but, in spite of the fact that Southern California was stampeding Notre Dame's defenses with long forward passes and laterals and ripping its heretofore impregnable line to shreds, it looked as though the Trojans were doomed to suffer defeat again through the blocking of Baker's first kick for the extra point by Joe Kurth, the Ramblers' magnificent tackle.

With four minutes left to play after their second touchdown, the Trojans, a desperately inspired team if ever there was one, started another march down the field from deep in their own territory, and in two tremendous passes, one thrown 50 yards by Shaver in Sparling and the other hurled by Shaver to Hall for a 23-yard gain, the first two actually completed by the Californians all day, carried the ball to the 17-yard line.

A -yard penalty, one of the many costly setbacks that Notre Dame suffered all afternoon, advanced the ball to the 12-yard mark, but then Notre Dame's powerful line rose up in its might and hurled Sparling back on a reverse to the 15-yard mark, and Clark fumbled Mohler's succeeding pass. Time was fleeting and it seemed that Southern California's dangerous uprising had been squelched and its last chance had gone aglimmering.

Mohler Holds the Ball.

But on third down Orville Mohler, the Trojan quarterback, cunningly called for a field goal, knowing the Ramblers would be on guard against a pass instead of concentrating entirely on rushing through to block the kick, and big Johnny Baker dropped back to the 23-yard mark with Mohler holding the ball, and sent the pigskin high and squarely between the uprights.

That pigskin parabola through the air, which gave Southern California its first victory over Notre Dame in three years and a thoroughly deserved one if Leonine courage, berserk tackling on the defence and reckless abandon in running on the offense are football virtues, left the great throng stunned and over-whelmed with despair, save for the handful of Trojan rooters, who were fairly delirious with joy.

It was almost unbelievable. Here was the great Notre Dame team, the most dreaded in the land, a team that had won twenty-five consecutive games, with the single interruption of a tie score against Northwestern in the rain and mud, and which had given the impression of having an inexhaustible mine of power as yet untested, humbled on its own playing field.

Only once before in twenty-seven years had the Ramblers tasted defeat on their own turf, in the 1928 game with Carnegie Tech, and never before had they gone down in their new stadium, dedicated in the Navy game a year ago.

Notables in the Throng.

Mayor Walker of New York, who was in the stands with Mayor Cermak of Chicago, Edsel Ford, Mr. and Mrs. John Hertz of Chicago and a host of notables of the stage and screen, was probably as downcast as any one present in the great throng, the largest crowd ever to see a sporting event in this city, for there is no more loyal Notre Dame rooter than New York's Mayor.

It was a stunning disillusionment to see victory that appeared to be within grasp suddenly turned into defeat on a single play, with the final whistle only a minute away. The defeat was all the more galling after the apparently unsurmountable lead that Notre Dame had gained in the second and third quarters. If any one had been so bold as to predict before the game that there was any team that ever wore cleats that could spot the South Benders fourteen points and defeat them in a fourth period he would have been laughed to scorn.

Notre Dame had scored its first seven points in the second period, after being outplayed in the first, on Banas's touchdown, climaxing a 55-yard march, and Jaskwich's place kick. Its next score came with startling abruptness and in the characteristic Notre Dame fashion before the second half was two minutes old.

In just four plays after Schwartz had taken Shaver's kick and run it back to the Notre Dame 37-yard line, the Ramblers had marched sixty-three yards to their second touchdown.

Laterals Figure Prominently

Brancheau gained nine yards on a reverse. Schwartz, the finest back Notre Dame had on the field, who fully measured up to his All-America laurels of 1930, went around left end for fourteen yards, and then came a lateral pass, one of many of these plays that figured prominently in the game, from Schwartz to Banas.

Going around his left end after taking the lateral, Banas streaked down the field, cut in, evaded tackler after tackler, picked himself up twice after being hurled to the ground, and fought his way to the 3-yard line for a gain of thirty-seven yards. On the next play Schwartz went off his own right tackle, cut back slightly, and went over for the score on the fourth scrimmage of the advance, after which the unfailing Jaskwich again kicked the goal for the extra point.

At the end of this spectacular march, which found the Notre Dame attack functioning in its customary manner in the power of its blocking and the synchronization between the line and backs in working toward the perfect play, the game seemed to have been won and lost.

Probably no one among the 52,000 in the stands thought Southern California had a ghost of a chance and the prospect was that now that the Ramblers had found themselves and their true stride they would run away with the game.

Here was the Notre Dame team that every one had seen or read about for three years, a team so dangerous and powerful that it could strike a fatal blow at any given moment with its flawless technique and precision in the execution of its shift plays. It called for courage of the nth degree to stand up against such a team and to prevent it from turning the game into a rout, but this Southern California team of Howard Jones's had that courage and it showed it by coming back with a surging rush to take command of the game from this point and maintain it all through the rest of the play.

It wasn't any later than the next kick-off that the Trojans, who had shown their mettle by the manner in which they went down under the very first kick-off of the game behind Rosenberg to hurl themselves savagely upon Schwartz, started their amazing comeback.

Before the crowd could get over the startling turn in the situation they had rushed the ball from their own 30-yard mark to Notre Dame's 10-yard line, with Mohler and Shaver ripping through for long gains and Sparling, the end, coming around on reverse plays. Notre Dame stopped this advance of 60 yards and took the ball away on downs.

The Ramblers had stopped the Trojans' advance of 50 yards to their 3-yard line in the first period and had taken the ball away on downs again on the Ramblers' 11-yard mark a minute later. Apparently the Californians lacked a goal-line punch.

Start Another March.

But right after that 60-yard march had come to grief, the Trojans started another that was to lead to their first score on the third play of the final period. A lateral from Mohler to Shaver accounted for 16 yards, a reverse with Sparling picked up 11 more and the rest of the ground was made by the irrepressible, hard-running Shaver, who barely got over the goal line in the very corner of the field.

A damaging penalty played a big part in the Californians' next touchdown. Mohler hurled one of his long passes down the field and the ball was grounded. But the officials ruled t[illegible] Shaver was interfered with in [illegible]eceiving the pass and the ball was given to Southern California on Notre Dame's 24-yard line for a first down and a gain of 32 yards on the penalty.

There was a storm of protest from the stands, but the decision stood, and in three plays Mohler and Shaver carried the ball to the 10-yard line for another first down. On the next play the lateral pass made its appearance again. Mohler, going into a spin that threw Notre Dame off, suddenly started back and tossed the ball out to the side to Shaver, who thundered around his own left end and fought his way across the goal line, carrying a Notre Dame back with him.

That long penalty was one of ten that were called on Notre Dame during the afternoon, for a total of 89 yards. Many of the penalties were inflicted for interference with the pass receiver and the two passes that the Trojans made for 50 and 28 yards in the closing minutes were the only ones they completed all day out of eleven thrown.

Passer Is Hurried.

Notre Dame completed only one pass out of ten attempted, which seemed almost incomprehensible, the one gaining twenty-five yards in the Ramblers' march to their first score. The reason for this poor showing with the pass was partly because the thrower was hurling the ball too far or his receiver was a step or two short in getting down under it. But the chief reason was the fact that the Southern California ends and tackles were rushing in to hurry the passer.

The Trojan line showed itself to be the equal of Notre Dame's today. It was a line that had tremendous power and all sorts of fight and that went for the Notre Dame line, too. In fact, no game in years has witnessed so ferocious and bruising a battle between lines as took place in the South Bend stadium today.

So great was the wear and tear in this struggle that Hunk Anderson, in the final quarter, was constantly sending in reserves to bolster his line, but fresh troops, even though they were regarded as good as the first line, could do little more than the men they replaced.

The Southern California attack, one of the most mystifying ever exploited by a football team, was much more difficult to solve than Notre Dame probably expected. In practice against their scrubs, the Ramblers had their defense worked out perfectly, but it did not work that way in the game.

The Trojans, going into a huddle, circled around and intermingled, then lined up in three waves, 4—4—3, and then shifted into their starting formation. The starting formation some times found the line balanced, but most of the time unbalanced.

Sometimes there were two men on the short side, sometimes there was only one. The ends were split most of the time, but were spaced in tight from the double wing-back formation, which was used along with the single wing-back alignment.

There were no less than five different bases of the Southern California attack, and with the men shifting around, backs and linemen jumping up and back, the formation changing with almost every play, and the lateral pass thrown in to add to the uncertainty of the defense, it is not to be wondered that the Ramblers failed to diagnose the plays as well as they had expected to.

Weather Clears Unexpectedly.

The ground was firm and dry, for the weather cleared unexpectedly, and the day was perfect for football, so that neither team found any difficulty in executing its plays except the difficulty presented by two fighting lines.

Notre Dame used its conventional 7-2-2 defense, the linemen standing up and some of them a yard back of the line until Southern California had shifted into line, when they would hop up into their places. The Trojans, on the defense, played a six-man line, with the secondary in 3-1-2 or 3-2-1 alignment. Both defenses were stronger against the pass than they were against the running attack, except that in the final quarter the Notre Dame backs allowed Sparling and Hall to get behind them.

It would hardly be fair to single out men for meritorious service in a game so desperately fought all along the line, but Kurth was certainly a great tackle today in every respect,

as was also Krause, and Schwartz was a magnificent back, save that his kicking suffered by comparison with Shaver's at times.

Shaver stood out vividly for the Trojans all the time he was in the game, and Mohler and Sparling did yeoman work, too, while the whole Southern California line covered itself with glory in the manner in which it stood up to Notre Dame's forwards and often outplayed them.

The line-up:

Southern Cal. (16).		Notre Dame (14).
Sparling	L. E.	Kosky
Brown	L. T.	Culver
Rosenberg	L. G.	Harriss
Williamson	C.	Yarr
Stevens	R. G.	Hoffman
Smith	R. T.	Kurth
Arbelbide	R. E.	Devore
Shaver	Q. B.	Jaskwich
Mallory	L. H.	Schwartz
Pinckert	R. H.	Sheeketski
Musick	F. B.	Banas

SCORE BY PERIODS.

| Southern California | 0 | 0 | 0 | 16—16 |
| Notre Dame | 0 | 7 | 7 | 0—14 |

Touchdowns—Shaver 2, Schwartz, Banas. goal from field—Baker (place kick). Points after touchdown—Jaskwich 2, Baker (all place kicks).

Substitutions—Southern California: Mohler for Shaver, G. Clark for Mallory, Erskine for Smith, Baker for Rosenberg, Rosenberg for Baker, Baker for Rosenberg, Shaver for Mohler, Mohler for Musick, Mallory for Clark, Clark for Mallory, Smith for Erskine, Erskine for Smith, Hall for Brown, Palmer for Arbelbide. Notre Dame—Krause for Culver, Brancheau for Sheeketski, Host for Kosky, Kozak for Kurth, Mahoney for Devore, Wunch for Hoffman, Culver for Krause, Kurth for Kozak, Devore for Mahoney, Hoffman for Wunch, Kosky for Host, Wunch for Hoffman, Leahy for Banas, Krause for Culver, Kozak for Kurth, Leonard for Leahy, Mahoney for Devore, Sheeketski for Brancheau, Culver for Krause, Millsoam for Sheeketski, Murphy for Jaskwich.

Referee—Frank Birch, Earlham. Umpire—H. E. Gillett, Oregon. Linesman—Jay Wyatt, Missouri. Field Judge—Norman Barker, Chicago. Time of periods—15 minutes.

November 22, 1931

Players of the Game

Howard Jones—Southern California's Coach

By ALLISON DANZIG.
All Rights Reserved.

TEN years ago a Hawkeye team from Iowa went up against a Notre Dame eleven that had won twenty-two consecutive games. On that Notre Dame team, coached by Knute Rockne, were Eddie Anderson, Paul Castner, Roger Kiley, Harry Mehre, Tom Lieb, Chet Wynne, Glenn Carberry and Johnny Mohardt, all players listed on Notre Dame's scroll of honor.

Also playing on the South Bend eleven, as one of the best guards of the season, was Heartly Anderson. The coach of the Hawkeyes was Howard Jones and in that game Notre Dame's long winning streak was brought to an end by the score of 10—7, the only defeat suffered by the Ramblers in forty successive games beginning with the last two of 1918 and extending up to the final one of 1922.

Last Saturday a Notre Dame team coached by Heartly Anderson that had gone undefeated in twenty-six consecutive games had its winning streak broken, and again it was an eleven directed by the same Howard Jones that snapped the string, a string that had started after Southern California had vanquished the Ramblers in the last game of 1928.

It is not to be wondered at then if Notre Dame men look upon Howard Harding Jones as something of a supercoach, a master mind who alone has been able consistently to shatter their ambitions for national dominion, a nemesis whose predilection is for ending their all-conquering rampages.

Warner Dominating Figure.

A year ago, the two most celebrated football coaches in the country were Rockne and Glenn Warner of Stanford. When the wizard of South Bend passed on, Warner was left as the dominating figure in the game, with his wing-back formations in vogue at almost every major college save those where the many disciples of Rockne were teaching the Notre Dame shift.

But out on the Pacific Coast, the

Times Wide World Photo.

HOWARD JONES.

nursery of great football teams, this categorical reduction of winning football to the systems of two men was not accepted as it has been in the other sections of the country. How could it have been when down in Los Angeles there was another coach, with ideas of his own, whose teams were defeating both Stanford and California and annually giving Notre Dame a terrific battle with the exception of 1930?

Howard Jones has probably been the most under-recognized coach, from a national standpoint, the game has had in many years. When one looks back upon his record, takes into consideration the fact that he has been coaching for twenty-four years and the added fact that he played and coached with distinction at Yale, it seems incomprehensible that he should have received so little attention as has been accorded him.

Geographical propinquity has a large bearing on the publicity given to a football coach, but Stanford is 3,000 miles from New York and yet Warner has been publicized more in the Eastern press than has any coach on the Atlantic seaboard.

Seven Years With Trojans.

In the seven years that Jones has been at Southern California, his teams have won or tied for the Pacific Coast conference championship four times, finished second twice and third once—this in his first year at Los Angeles. They have won 61 games to date, tied 2 and lost 10, four of the ten being lost to Notre Dame, and in four instances the defeat was inflicted by a margin of a point after touchdown.

In the last four years Stanford has scored only 12 points against the Trojans, being shut out three times, and in six games California has scored only 15 points, winning from Southern California by 15—7 in 1929 after a scoreless tie in 1928. What other team, with the exception of Notre Dame, can point to as good a record as this, taking the character of the opposition into consideration?

Long before he went to the Pacific Coast, Jones had shown his ability as a coach. After graduating from Yale, where he played end on the same teams with his illustrious brother, Tad, who was all-America quarterback in 1907, Howard Jones coached at Syracuse in 1908 and then came back to Yale. His 1909 eleven was one of the greatest defensive combinations ever to step upon a gridiron, worthy of comparison with the famous Michigan point-a-minute teams of a few years before.

Held Opponents Scoreless.

This Yale team won all ten of its games without being scored upon, playing Harvard, Princeton, Army and Colgate among others, and not one of its opponents ever had the ball inside the Elis' 28-yard line. There were six all-America players on this Blue outfit—Ted Coy, fullback; Steve Philbin, halfback; Johnny Kilpatrick, end; Heinie Hobbs, tackle; Andrus, guard, and Carroll Cooney, centre.

Jones coached four years at Yale, not all of them consecutively, and also served at Ohio State, Duke and Iowa before going to Southern California. His 1921 team at Iowa won the Big Ten championship, the first time the Hawkeyes had taken the title since 1900, and his 1922 team defeated his brother, Tad's, Yale eleven, 6—0. Aubrey Devine, who is Jones's chief scout; Fred (Duke) Slater, Gordon Locke and Leland Parkins were among the famous players developed by Jones at Iowa.

Much is printed and heard of the personal rivalry between Jones and Warner on the Coast. That rivalry goes back to 1908, when the former was at Syracuse and the Stanford Sachem was coaching the Carlisle Indians.

Syracuse and Carlisle met that year and the story is that Jones understood, when the game was arranged, that twenty-minute halves were to be played. Warner, however, said that he knew of no such understanding when the teams came to the field, and so Syracuse had to play thirty-five-minute halves. The rivalry has been going on ever since, though it is not as personal as some of the accounts make out. At least the coaches always shake hands after the meetings between their teams.

Complex Attack Employed.

For all of his success, Howard Jones has never had a system named after him, as has Warner and as did Rockne. And yet, his is one of the most ingenious and progressive minds in the game. The attack employed by his team against Notre Dame is one of the most complex in the history of the game, entirely individual to Southern California and fabricated by Jones since the close of the 1930 season.

While it embraces features of both the Notre Dame and Stanford systems, utilizing the shift, the single and double wing-back formations, both the balanced and unbalanced line and spinners, reverses and other plays indigenous to South Bend and Palo Alto, the Trojans' offense has no parallel in the multiple alignments into which Jones deploys his men.

It is the kaleidoscopic change in the pattern of his offense, screening the direction and nature of the thrust, to the confusion of the defense, that makes his attack so difficult to stop, plus the sound principles of line play inculcated and the tremendous power generated by heavy, mercury-footed backs who run with a stark fury that is almost appalling.

It was after his team had suffered its humiliating 27-0 defeat at the hands of Notre Dame last year that Jones decided to experiment anew with his offense, and it was only one of several times during his career that he had shown the same progressiveness in scrapping the old and seeking something better.

Jones Changed the Defense.

After his first two years on the coast, during which he lost both times to Stanford, Jones changed his defense to smash the wing-back attack, playing his ends in close in a six-man line and sending them in fast to mess up the slow-forming plays behind the line of scrimmage, and also adding to his own offense until it put Warner's "57 varieties" in the shade. The result has been that Stanford has never beaten Southern California since.

Back in 1913, too, Jones showed his ingenuity in devising an offense suited to the needs of the occasion. After serving at Ohio State he went back to Yale in 1913 to find that the situation had changed radically from what it had been in 1909. Under Percy Haughton and with such stars as Brickley, Hardwick and Mahan, Harvard had succeeded to Yale's place at the top of the pack and the Elis were even finding it difficult to defeat small college teams.

When Maine held Yale to a score-less tie at the start of the 1913 season, Jones decided that his material was not powerful enough to use the attack it was employing and boldly gambled on changing to a different type of offense.

In this new attack, from a balanced line, he spaced his tackles out from the guards, put his ends opposite the defensive ends, his half backs four yards back of the offensive tackles, the quarterback behind centre and the fullback eight yards back of centre. With this new attack, Yale held Princeton to a 3-3 tie and lost to Harvard only through the uncanny kicking skill of Brick-

ley, who made five drop kicks in the game.

Jones is the quiet type of coach who says little and lets his team do his talking for him. Reticent by nature, he finds coaching football teams too taxing a work to permit him to be distracted by anything else and it is only when stung by unjust or unfair criticism that he allows himself the indulgence of a reply. There is one subject, however, on which he has no hesitation in expressing himself and that is "overemphasis" in football.

"Those who say players spend too much time on football when they

should be studying," he remarked recently, "should remember that a student who lets the game come between himself and an education wouldn't study anyway.

"As far as overemphasis goes, when most teams of today get through practice in the afternoon they are through. On the other hand, when Tad and I played at Yale, we often were called to the gymnasium at night to run signals."

November 24, 1931

SWEEPING CHANGES MADE IN FOOTBALL

Rules Committee Acts to Lessen Hazards—Orders Six Drastic Modifications.

By ALLISON DANZIG.

The outcry raised during the season of 1931 against the mounting toll of gridiron casualties, the most violent excoriation football has been subjected to since 1905, brought forth yesterday the most far-reaching mod-

ifications adopted in the playing rules of the game in a quarter of a century.

From Hanover, N. H., where the National Football Rules Committee has been in session, came the eagerly awaited report, through Chairman E. K. Hall, to set up additional safeguards against the hazards of the game and establish new rules affecting the technique of the play without exacting any serious sacrifice from the fascination and virile character of football.

The changes are six in number and are designed to reduce or eliminate the danger from the use of hard protective equipment, the illegal use of the hands on the head of an opponent and the employment of the so-called "flying wedge" on the kick-off and the flying tackle and block. In addition, they liberalize the substitution rule to make more frequent

replacements possible, and bring the scrimmage to an end more quickly by declaring the ball dead the instant any portion of the carrier's body other than his hands or feet touches the ground.

Summary of the Changes.

Briefly summarized, the changes are as follows:

1. Equipment—Hard and unyielding substances used in the construction of protective devices must be covered on the outside with padding at least three-eighths of an inch thick.

2. Kick-Off—At least five players on the receiving team must remain within fifteen yards of the restraining line of the kicking side until the ball has been kicked, and the kick-off may be made by either a punt or a drop kick as well as by a place kick.

3. Blocking and Tackling—The flying block and tackle are made ille-

gal. The player may leave his feet only at the instant of contact with his opponent. Penalty of five yards provided for infraction.

4. Substitutions—A player withdrawn from the game may return in any subsequent period, "time out" being charged against the team for the substitution.

5. Dead Ball—The ball now becomes dead the instant any portion of the carrier, excepting hands or feet, touches the ground, regardless of whether he is within the grasp of an opponent or not.

6. Use of Hands—Players on the defense are forbidden to strike an opponent on head, neck or face, but may use palm of hands to ward off or push such opponent in effort to get to the ball or the carrier. Penalty for infraction is disqualification of the player and loss by his team of half the distance to the goal line.

February 16, 1932

Columbia Football Team Upsets Stanford

Special to THE NEW YORK TIMES.
PASADENA, Calif., Jan. 1.—Those roaring Columbia Lions were sea Lions today and they splashed their way to a surprising and clear-cut victory over the Stanford football team, 7—0, in the annual Tournament of Roses classic.

Thus a season marked by many reverses was climaxed by probably the greatest upset of them all.

Surging through a drizzling, disheartening rain to a one-touchdown lead in the second period, the Lions four times thrust back the furious onslaught of Grayson, Hamilton, Van Dellen and the rest of Stanford's super-backs in a last-half struggle.

Sixteen first downs for Stanford; six for Columbia. Two hundred and seventy-two yards gained for Stanford; 114 yards for Columbia. Six scoring chances for the Cardinals; three for the Lions. But that scoreboard read: Columbia 7, Stanford 0, at the finish.

The bad weather of the last few days cut the attendance considerably. About 40,000 hardy fans showed up for the game. Most of them sat huddled under umbrellas throughout the first half. Former President Herbert Hoover, an alumnus of Stanford, was an interested spectator.

Lions Display Gameness.

No gamer, more determined bunch of football players ever appeared in the Rose Bowl than this furious crew Coach Lou Little loosed on the unsuspecting Indians. Twice turned back from the Cardinal goal line in the first period, they kept on plugging until Al Barabas, left halfback, raced across the line for a touchdown.

Then the visitors clung to this precious margin in the face of the same powerful attack that a scant two months ago had tripped the mighty Trojans of the University of Southern California. The Lions succeeded where the Trojans failed. They stopped Stanford.

Six different times during the contest—twice in the first half and four times in the second — the mighty Red team crashed and drove its way to the shadow of the Columbia goal, and six times Columbia staved off those threats.

Fumbles and penalties contributed to stopping the Indian drives, but the Easterners always were on hand to take advantage of every break offered them.

So magnificent were these defensive stands of the Lions that they overshadowed the lone touchdown of the day, which Barabas scored on a 17-yard dash that still has the California fans baffled—not to mention Stanford.

Starts From Blocked Kick.

It all started from a blocked kick. Alustiza got a bad pass from centre, was hurried, and a trio of Colum-

bians sifted through to block the kick. It was only third down, so when young Bob Reynolds, Stanford tackle, fell on the ball, it was still in Indian possession.

Alustiza, of course, kicked again, and Montgomery returned five yards to the Indian's 45-yard line. Stanford was penalized five yards on the next play, and then Montgomery hurled a pass to Tony Matal.

The end made a leaping catch, came down sliding, and skidded along three more yards before he was stopped, eventually coming to rest on the 17-yard stripe.

On his first try Barabas fumbled, but he recovered for a half-yard loss. On the next effort Montgomery took the ball from centre, wheeled in a deceptive reverse and handed to Barabas.

Thereupon hostilities seemed to halt for an instant. Every one stood around and looked at every one else. A Columbia back sifted through between right tackle and right end, drawing the secondary away. So Barabas, using the hidden-ball ruse, took off around Stanford's right end. There were no Stanford men in the way and Barabas loped the 17 yards to the goal line.

Amid tremendous jubilation on the part of the Columbia players, Wilder took aim at the uprights and calmly booted the ball from placement for the extra point.

That touchdown was the reward of tremendous valor and determination. Twice in the first period the "Sea Lions" had splashed down to within hailing distance of the Indian goal line, only to be halted by fumbles. Once Barabas was at fault, and later the slippery pigskin eluded Montgomery after he was tackled.

Stanford opened the game with a drive to the Columbia 29-yard line that bogged down when Matal made two consecutive tackles to hold Indian runners for no gain. In the second quarter the Cardinals smashed their way to the 25-yard line before being halted.

In the second half the Indians reached the 15-yard line, where a penalty stopped them: the 14, where they lost the ball on a fumble; the 1-yard stripe, where another fumble halted the attack, and the 8-yard stripe, where Columbia's stalwart line refused to yield.

The game reminded many old-time Rose Bowl veterans of the 1925 contest, in which Knute Rockne's Four Horsemen triumphed over Stanford, 27 to 10. The Indians made all the ground on that day, and Notre Dame made most of the points.

Grayson Likened to Nevers.

Curiously alike, too, were Ernie Nevers, the great fullback of 1925, and Bobby Grayson, Stanford's latest line cracker. Grayson, using that same churning foot motion that Nevers made famous, banged his way over centre, raced through tackle and rushed around end for a total of 160 yards—more than all of Columbia's backs made.

Columbia had two great stars in action today. One was Captain Montgomery, whose shifty swivel hips carried him through the Stanford defense time and time again.

The other was Barabas, who lunged and smashed his way along for frequent gains. And it was a tackle by this sensational sophomore back that halted one Stanford touchdown drive.

Aside from these two, the work of the Columbia ends—McDowell, Matal and Chase— was outstanding. Matal was injured just before the close of the first half and saw no additional action, Chase substituting with more than usual efficiency.

During the third and fourth periods the rain fell only intermittently. The soggy ball made passing almost impossible and the fact that each team completed a long toss at critical times was astonishing.

Stanford tried twelve and completed two for a net gain of 23 yards. The Lions tried only two and made one good—the Montgomery-to-Matal affair.

Punting was exceptionally good, considering the circumstances. Alustiza averaged 30 yards with his boots, while Montgomery turned in a 37-yard average in fourteen attempts. He had the hard luck of twice seeing well-placed efforts roll over the goal line just a foot inside the sidelines.

Game Cleanly Played.

The game was fought savagely, but was cleanly played on the whole. Stanford lost 66 yards on penalties, much of the losses coming from incomplete passes, while the Lions lost 5 yards on four separate occasions.

Columbia's victory today evened up the score somewhat for the Rose Bowl competition. It was the East's seventh victory in the nineteen games played between college teams since Washington State defeated Brown in 1916. The West has won nine contests, while three have ended in ties.

Today's appearance was the first made by Columbia and it was the fourth for Stanford. The Indians have won one, lost two and tied one in their defense of the West's prestige. Columbia also had the distinction of being the first team from New York to play in the Bowl.

After a short exchange of punts, Stanford launched the first real offensive when Maentz, on a reverse, skidded his way deep into Columbia territory, being dragged down on the 26-yard line.

But here Red Matal swung into action, smashed two plays in a row, and Stanford bogged down on the 30-yard stripe, Alustiza punting out of bounds on the 20-yard line.

Montgomery swept loose for a ten-yard gain, but the Lions were held. The Lion captain then punted and the slippery pigskin eluded Maentz's grasp. Al Barabas pursued the ball and recovered it on the Stanford 38.

Barabas Runs 26 Yards.

Buoyed by this exhibition of his own skill on a soggy gridiron, Barabas promptly took a reverse from Montgomery and dashed 26 yards before Grayson finally tackled him on the 12-yard line.

However, Barabas fumbled on the next play and Reynolds recovered for Stanford on the 18-yard line. The Cardinals were penalized for holding, but Alustiza got off a terrific kick of 58 yards to Columbia's 39-yard marker.

A short time later Montgomery decided it was time to show the fans that Columbia had other carriers besides Barabas and he sprinted twenty-six yards. Cliff and Barabas then alternated at tak-

Times Wide World Photo.

Al Barabas, Who Made Touchdown.

ing the pigskin, but the drive ended when Montgomery fumbled on the 10-yard line, where Maentz recovered just as the quarter ended.

Alustiza's kick was blocked shortly after play was resumed, but it was only third down and Stanford retained possession of the ball when Reynolds recovered.

New Offensive Starts.

Montgomery returned Alustiza's next effort to the Stanford 45 and another Lion offensive hurriedly got under way. A pass, Montgomery to Matal, put the ball on the 17-yard line.

Barabas almost fumbled on the next play, but recovered and was thrown for a half-yard loss.

This so embarrassed Al that he scored a touchdown on the next play, all of which left Stanford, and the natives, considerably baffled.

Montgomery took the ball, handed it to Barabas, and every one on the Cardinal team stood around looking at one another for a second or two.

Then Al started chugging out around his own left end. Topping, Stanford right end, was flat on his back, and "Bones" Hamilton, right halfback, was nowhere in sight, so Al just galloped along, crossing the goal line without difficulty. Wilder converted the extra point.

Somewhat nettled, Stanford open

Columbia-Stanford Line-Up.

COLUMBIA (7).		STANFORD (0).
McDowell	L.E.	Smith
Jackel	L.T.	Callaway
Pinckney	L.G.	Corbus
Wilder	C.	Muller
Dzamba	R.G.	O'Connor
Richavich	R.T.	Reynolds
Matal	R.E.	Moscrip
Montgomery	Q.B.	Alustiza
Barabas	L.H.	Hamilton
Brominski	R.H.	Maentz
Nevel	F.B.	Grayson

SCORE BY PERIODS.

Columbia .... 0 7 0 0—7
Stanford .... 0 0 0 0—0

Touchdown—Barabas. Point after touchdown—Wilder (placement).

Substitutions — Stanford: Topping for Smith, Van Dellen for Maentz, Drown for Callaway, Adams for O'Connor, Trompas for Moscrip, Moscrip for Trompas, Bates for Muller, Sim for Hamilton, Callaway for Drown, Hillman for Alustiza. Columbia: Linehan for Barabas, Chippendale for Nevel, Chase for McDowell, Tomb for Montgomery. McDowell for Chase, Nevel for Chippendale, Montgomery for Tomb, Barabas for Linehan, Ciampa for Wilder, Chippendale for Nevel, Demshar for Jackel, Linehan for Barabas, Barabas for Linehan, Jackel for Demshar, Wilder for Ciampa, Nevel for Chippendale, Chase for Matal.

Referee—Tom Louttit, Oregon State. Umpire—Ed Thorp, De La Salle. Linesman—W. R. Crowley, Bowdoin. Field judge—Tom Fitzpatrick, Utah.

ed up with a terrific drive a few minutes later, smashing 36 yards in seven plays to the Columbia 34, but there the Lions rallied and they had possession of the ball as the half ended.

Stanford opened the second half with a bludgeoning attack that saw Grayson and Hamilton advancing the ball 60 yards in five plays to the Lion 20-yard marker. A 15-yard penalty for holding upset the attack, however, and Alustiza was forced to punt.

After receiving Montgomery's return kick, the Indians cracked right back again, with Grayson passing to Topping for 20 yards. Plunges by Hamilton and Grayson netted a first down on the 13-yard line, but Grayson fumbled and Columbia recovered to stave off the attack on its own 14-yard stripe.

Crashes Over Centre.

Nothing daunted, the Indians drove back a third time when Grayson, on a fake reverse, crashed over centre, bowled right into Referee Tom Louttit and continued on 22 yards to Columbia's 12-yard mark.

In two plays Grayson made it a first down on the 3-yard mark, in three more plays the Cardinals lost

a yard and then Grayson fumbled, Brominski recovering on his own 1-yard stripe.

Early in the fourth quarter the Indians launched a fourth drive, with Grayson and Hamilton doing most of the gaining, until they arrived at the 14-yard stripe.

Here Coach Little sent in five substitutes, which time out cost Columbia a 5-yard penalty to its own 8-yard line. But the Columbia line tightened, with McDowell and Chase smashing in to break up plays, and the Stanford march wound up on the 10-yard line.

January 2, 1934

ALABAMA DEFEATS STANFORD, 29 TO 13

Displays Great Aerial Attack to Win as Record Crowd of 85,000 Fans Looks On.

HOWELL IS PACE-SETTER

Scores Twice, Once on Run of 67 Yards—Indians Strike First in Rose Bowl Game.

STATISTICS OF THE GAME.

	Alabama.	Stanford.
First downs	13	14
Yards gained rushing	167	204
Forward passes	13	5
Forwards completed	10	2
Yards gained, forwards	216	86
Forwards intercepted by	4	1
Number of punts	6	6
*Distance of punts, yards	261	227
Run-back of punts, yards	54	34
Opponent's fumbles recovered	0	4
Penalties	4	4
Yards lost, penalties	40	40

Individual Yardage.

Stanford—Grayson 96, Hamilton 59, Van Dellen 49, Alustiza 7.
Alabama—Howell 111, Angelich 23, Demyanovich 11, Boozer 22.
*From line of scrimmage.

By The Associated Press.

PASADENA, Calif., Jan. 1.— Aerial sleight of hand met football power on the ground today and 85,000 excited spectators saw legerdemain win as Alabama defeated Stanford, 29 to 13.

The visitors from the South put on the greatest exhibition of forward passing seen in the twenty-year history of the annual competition in the Rose Bowl. The winners had nothing to match the tremendous drive of the losers, but they tossed the ball with an accuracy that left the record-breaking crowd—and Stanford players — gasping for breath. The Crimson compiled the amazing record of completing ten out of thirteen attempted passes for a total of 216 yards.

With the exception of one sixty-seven-yard sprint for a touchdown by Millard (Dixie) Howell, all the counters were scored or made possible by the astonishingly effective overhead attack.

The capacity crowd, a new record for the Rose Bowl, and the largest attendance of the current football season, first marveled and then cheered as Howell threw pass after

Times Wide World Photo.

Three of the Backs: Brominski, Nevel and Montgomery.

pass right into the hands of his receivers, principally Don Hutson, Paul Bryant and Jim Angelich.

An Ace Sharpshooter.

Howell scored two touchdowns, half of his team's total, but it is not merely as a runner that he will be remembered in the Rose Bowl. Every Stanford supporter will think of him as an ace shapshooter when he recalls his standing with a ball poised for flight.

There was nothing Stanford could do about Howell's deadly pitching as he threw strikes most of the afternoon. Not until late in the fourth period was one intercepted, and then the passer was rushed. His receivers caught many of the passes on the run, but the ball was there for them most of the time.

To complete a busy day, Howell did some sensational punting.

Alabama won the game in a second period packed with enough action for a dozen football games. Stanford was ahead, by virtue of a first-period touchdown, when without warning the game exploded in the Indians' faces. In fifteen minutes the lads from Tuscaloosa piled up 22 points—three touchdowns and a field goal.

Fail to Stop Grayson.

Bobby Grayson's driving power was the big cog in Stanford's offensive and the visitors never were able to stop the big boy with the pistonlike legs. They slowed the Portland (Ore.) youth up from time to time, but they did not stop him. Stanford showed that the old football adage that touchdowns cannot be made on running plays the length of the field was all wrong. The Redskins did it once and almost repeated.

The big rose-decorated stand was spotted with volunteer alumni from every Southern State. They helped the 2,500 Alabama supporters who came all the way from home to cheer the Crimson victory and whooped it up after the game as the bands played "Dixie."

The first period was far more Cardinal than Crimson. At the start Alabama had the ball only twice and lost on its two running plays.

Howell's booming kicks from deep in the shadow of his own goal posts saved his team temporarily and then a fumble gave the Westerners the ball in scoring territory. Stanford at once turned on the heat and, as the power was generated, fast and furiously rode to a touchdown.

Alabama Starts Rolling.

Alabama didn't get started in the first period but the second found it under way. Howell started passing and the Alabama receivers were there to catch his throws. The Stanford cheers over the first touchdown were still echoing from the canyons outside the Bowl when Alabama scored. The goal was missed and Stanford held its lead but not for long.

The Crimson took the next kick-off, marched down to the five-yard line and, when Stamford stopped three plays, kicked a field goal to take the lead, which never was given up.

On the next kick-off Howell made his sixty-seven-yard run on the third play and Stanford had lost the ball game and the amazing Southerners had scored two touchdowns and a field goal without giving up the ball.

Although Stanford led in first downs, 14 to 12, Alabama gained more ground from combined passes and rushes, 383 to 290. Stanford's power gave it the rushing advantage, 204 to 167. Alabama had an edge in the kicking, each team punting six times, Stanford totaling 227 and Alabama 261. Stanford got all the fumbling breaks, recovering the ball every time it was fumbled by either side.

Alabama kept its Rose Bowl escutcheon unblotted with three victories and one tie. Stanford, playing for the fifth time in the Rose Bowl, has won only one game and tied one. The tie was with Alabama eight years ago. Alabama's Tournament of Roses victories have been scored at the expense of Washington, Washington State and Stanford.

Howell, doing everything a football player is called on to do, was the outstanding player on the field. He passed, ran, kicked, intercepted passes, backed up the ends and tackled in the open. Howell gained 111 yards rushing.

Grayson confined his activities to running in the main, but he did a great job of that, getting 98 yards during the game.

The game showed the packed stands some great end play. Hutson and Bryant were better offensively than defensively but they played well enough on defense and any gains made around them were more than offset by their sensational pass-catching.

Monk Moscrip was a Stanford defensive star throughout, his only misplay coming when Howell ran by him as the Stanford player slipped trying to get close enough to make the tackle. Larry Rouble, at guard, played a great game for the losers.

Blocking Backs Applauded.

The unsung heroes, the blocking backs, Riley Smith for 'Bama and Bones Hamilton for Stanford, contributed some great work and the crowd, usually reserving its cheers for the ball carriers, gave them both big hands.

An Alabama fumble gave Stanford a chance to score late in the first period. Joe Demyanovich dropped the ball when tackled and Keith Topping fell on it on the Alabama 27-yard line.

Grayson ran to the 20-yard line and Buck Van Dellen picked up eight yards on the next play. A reverse, Grayson to Hamilton, moved the ball to the 5-yard line and Grayson then plunged to the 1-yard line. Grayson went over for the first touchdown of the game and Moscrip added the extra point with a placement.

Alabama came right back to score without giving up the ball. Howell ran the kick-off 24 yards to the 45-yard line and on the next play passed to Hutson on Stanford's 27. On the next play, a pass, Howell to Angelich, placed the ball on the 16. An end-around play lost five yards and Howell passed to Bryant on the 5-yard line.

Howell dashed over the goal line for the touchdown on the next play, but Smith's try for the extra point by a placement kick failed.

Howell Runs 19 Yards.

On the next kick-off, Stanford kicked over the goal line. On the first play from scrimmage, Howell ran 19 yards and then passed to Hutson on Stanford's 32-yard line. Howell made two yards and then passed to Hutson on Stanford's 5-yard line. Hutson fumbled when tackled but Bryant recovered. Howell lost two and Smith then dropped back to the 20 and kicked a field goal from placement.

Stanford again kicked off and Howell ran to the 26-yard line. Angelich ran to the 33 and Howell then broke away and ran 67 yards for a touchdown, finishing the sprint with no Stanford man near him. Riley Smith kicked the goal.

With a minute to play in the second period, Riley Smith intercepted a Stanford pass on Stanford's 46-yard line. On the next

Alabama-Stanford Line-Up.

ALABAMA (29).		STANFORD (13).
Hutson	L.E.	Moscrip
Whatley	L.T.	Reynolds
Marr	L.G.	Adams
Francis	C.	Muller
Morrow	R.G.	Rouble
Lee	R.T.	Callaway
Bryant	R.E.	Topping
Smith	Q.B.	Alustiza
Howell	L.H.	Van Dellen
Angelich	R.H.	Hamilton
Demyanovich	F.B.	Grayson

SCORE BY PERIODS.

Alabama	0	22	0	7—29
Stanford	7	0	6	0—13

Touchdowns—Howell 2, Hutson 2, Grayson, Van Dellen. Field goal—Smith (placement). Points after touchdowns—Smith 2, Moscrip (placements).

Substitutes—Alabama: Ends, H. Walker, Gandy, J. Walker; tackles, McGahey, Boswell; guards, Danuletti, Peters, Dahlkamp, A. White; centre, Dildy, Moye; quarterback, Campbell, Goldberg; halves, R. White, Stapp, Boozer. Stanford: Ends, Monsalve, Smith, Schott, Trompas; tackle, Lettunich; guards, Callahan, Walton, Black; centre, Brandin; quarterback, Anderson, Maentz; halves, Reisner, White; fullback, Anderson.

Referee—Bob Evans, Milliken. Umpire—Cort Majors, California. Linesman—G. M. Phillips, Georgia Tech. Field judge—R. J. Ducote, Alabama Poly. Time of periods—15 minutes each.

play Joe Riley passed to Hutson, who caught the ball on the Stanford 30-yard line and ran for a touchdown. Hutson missed the goal.

Stanford took the kick-off to open the third period and marched straight to a touchdown. Grayson ran to the Stanford 33-yard line. Hamilton ran to the Alabama 48 and Van Dellen went to the 41. Grayson on a sprint around right end was chased out of bounds on the 22.

Reverse Brings Results.

Van Dellen smashed through the line to the 16 and Grayson made a first down 12 yards from the goal. A tricky reverse play, Van Dellen carrying the ball, brought Stanford another touchdown. Moscrip missed the goal.

The last 'Bama touchdown came in the final quarter, Francis intercepting a pass to take the ball from Stanford on Alabama's 26 late in the third period. Howell made nine yards in two plays and then a penalty for roughing Howell gave Alabama 15 yards for which it didn't have to work.

Angelich ran to Stanford's 44 as the period ended.

Howell failed for the second time in the game to complete a pass. Alabama was caught holding and penalized to its own 41. Howell passed to Hutson on Stanford's 30 and he went on over the goal line. Smith kicked the goal and the scoring was over for the day.

January 2, 1935

TULANE CONQUERS TEMPLE BY 20-14

Takes Inaugural Sugar Bowl Football Game Before 30,000 at New Orleans.

SIMONS IN STELLAR ROLE

Runs 75 Yards for First Green Wave Marker—Hardy Scores Twice for Victors.

STATISTICS OF THE GAME.

	Tulane.	Temple.
First downs	10	13
Yards gained rushing	160	215
Forward passes	16	13
Forwards completed	7	3
Yards gained, forwards	88	19
Forwards intercepted by	1	1
*Average distance of punts, yards	35	30
Run-back of kicks, yards	65	39
Opponent's fumbles recovered	1	4
Yards, lost, penalties	20	7

*From line of scrimmage.

By The Associated Press.

NEW ORLEANS, Jan. 1.—Pop Warner's powerful and deceptive Temple Owls bowed before the fire and dash of Tulane's Green Wave, 20 to 14, in the inaugural Sugar Bowl football game today before 30,000 spectators.

The game produced sixty minutes of downright excitement that turned the stands into howling frenzies as the tide of battle did as many reverses as the back fields. Temple opened an attack of power and back-field deception that threatened to sweep the Wave off the field and ran up a score of 14 to 0 that left the Greenies groggy.

Most of the spectators would not have given 2 cents for Tulane's chances early in the second quarter, but in a flash the situation was upset when McDaniel, Tulane back, caught the Temple kick-off and started off to the right with the whole Owl squad swinging over for the attack.

Simons Shows His Speed.

Little Monk Simons came racing over to the left and on the 25-yard line caught a lateral pass from McDaniel. A team-mate took Temple's end, Wise, out of the play.

Running with the speed of a deer, Little Monk flanked the Owls and went over the goal line for Tulane's first touchdown after a 75-yard run. Barney Mintz, the brilliant team-mate of Simons, kicked the extra point and the Wave began to roll.

The half ended, 14 to 7, in favor of Temple but the Wave was at full tide. The Owls opened a charging running attack in the third quarter behind their powerful back, Dave Smukler.

The drive opened on Temple's 25-yard line and the Owls carried the ball on reverses, spinners and line bucks alternately among Smukler, Testa and Mowrey to the 11-yard line, where the Green Wave took it on downs. The ball see-sawed until the fleet Bucky Bryan took the ball in mid-field and rushed it to Temple's 27-yard line.

Pass Brings a Score.

McDaniel and Lodrigues hit the line to the eleven-yard point where Bryan shot a neat pass over the goal line to Hardy, Tulane's star end. Mintz again kicked the extra point.

But the fourth quarter brought the greatest football of the game. Frey, Temple's quarterback, punted to Tulane's 30-yard line, Tulane moved it to the 40-yard line on two line plays and 13 yards were picked up on a pass, Simons to Hardy. Another line play placed it on Temple's 43-yard line.

Mintz threw a 27-yard pass to Hardy but Mowrey, Temple back, ped it with his fingers and the ball shot in the air. Hardy grabbed it on the 15-yard line and whirled for the goal line. He rolled over the goal line by scant inches with Frey hanging onto his legs, but Frey and Bongsdoff blocked Mintz's attempted place-kick for the extra point.

The game opened with a punting duel between Smuker and Simons but in the last two minutes of the first quarter Frey punted from Tulane's 45-yard line over the goal line. The ball was put in play on the 20-yard line. On a backward pass, Mintz fumbled and Gurzynski recovered on Tulane's 10-yard line. Smukler hit the line for three yards and then pressed over the goal line to Testa. Smukler kicked the extra point.

Hurtles Both Lines.

The second Temple touchdown also was made off a Tulane fumble, this time by Lodrigues, who dropped it on his own twenty-yard line where Frey recovered it for Temple. In a powerful push Smukler carried the ball over, hurtling both lines on the last play. He then kicked the extra point.

This ended Temple's scoring but the Owls never ceased to threaten Tulane's goal. In their drives across the field with gains of five or more yards almost each time they hit the line, they seemed certain to score again.

The Owls threatened in the fourth quarter when they took the ball on Temple's thirty-seven yard line and drove it straight as an arrow on running plays to Tulane's five-yard line. Tulane rose to great heights of defensive football and aided by a five-yard offside penalty against Temple, it managed to hold the vicious Owls and took the ball on downs on the thirteen-yard line.

Here Tulane launched another drive and had the ball on Temple's 19-yard line and moving fast when the game ended.

A Great Football Game.

The fans saw a great football game, and Little Monk Simons brought his brilliant football career to a glorious end. It was his spectacular run that turned the tide of battle to Tulane, when defeat was staring it in the face, and Dave Smukler can go back home with the plaudits of New Orleans football fans, whom he nearly scared to death.

Before the game and at the half a pageant was held on the field. A huge sugar bowl, with two little girls dressed in the colors of the two colleges standing inside, was brought to midfield. There they were greeted by Father New Orleans, dressed in the costume of the Cavalier, while the Temple and Tulane bands played.

Coaches Warner of Temple and Cox of Tulane expressed satisfaction with the performances of their teams. Cox was grinning happily when he said immediately after the game, "It was a great game. I'm just tickled to death we won."

Warner, somewhat reticent, hurried off the field to ascertain the condition of his players.

"It was a nice ball game, a good game," Pop said, "but we got some igh breaks."

The line-up:

TULANE (20).		TEMPLE (14).
Hardy	......L.E.	Wise
Moss	......L.T.	Dougherty
Evans	......L.G.	Boyd
Robinson	......C.	Stevens
Smither	......R.G.	Gurzynski
Ary	......R.T.	Russel
Kyle	......R.E.	Anderson
Brownson	......Q.B.	Frey
Mints	......L.H.	Stoalk
Simons	......R.H.	Testa
Loftin	......F.B.	Smukler

SCORE BY PERIODS.

Tulane .... 0 7 7 6—20
Temple .... 7 7 0 0—14

Touchdowns—Smukler, Testa, Simons, Hardy 2. Points after touchdown—Smukler 2 (placements), Mintz 2 (placements).

Substitutions—Temple: Mowry for Stonik, Miller for Boyd, Boyd for Miller, Miller for Boyd, Bongsdoff for Testa, Zanin for Anderson. Tulane: Lodrigues for J. Loftin, McDaniel for Brownson, Preissler for Kyle, Mentass for Hardy, Thomas for Simons, Bryan for Mints, Brownson for McDaniel, Strobell for Moss, Hardy for Mentass, Kyle for Preissler, Moss for Strobell, G. Tessier for Smither, Monk for G. Tessier, N. Loftin for Robinson, Simons for Thomas, Mints for Bryan, McDaniel for Brownson, J. Loftin for Lodrigues.

Referee—Everett Strupper, Georgia Tech. Umpire—Tom Thorp, Columbia. Linesman—W. M. Hollenback, Penn. Field judge—Walter Powell, Wisconsin.

January 2, 1935

BERWANGER GAINS TROPHY.

Downtown A. C.'s Football Award Voted to Chicago's Star Back.

The Downtown Athletic Club's trophy for "the most valuable football player in the East" will go to Jay Berwanger, captain and right halfback of the University of Chicago football team, it was announced yesterday.

All football players east of the Mississippi River were eligible under the "Eastern" classification in the poll taken among Eastern sports writers to determine the trophy winner. Berwanger received 84 votes. Monk Meyer of Army was second with 29 and Bill Shakespeare of Notre Dame placed third with 28.

A luncheon in honor of Berwanger will be held at the Downtown A. C. on Tuesday and he will fly here to attend it. Mayor La Guardia has been invited to present the trophy to the Chicago star.

December 5, 1935

Colleges Searching for Check On Trend to Goal Post Riots

Eastern 'Ivy' Group Disturbed by Outbreaks During and After Games—Steel and Electric Shock Uprights Fail to Curb Attacks—Police Presence Harmful at Times.

By The Associated Press.

Colleges throughout the country have welcomed increased interest in football this year, especially as reflected in mounting box-office receipts, but the problem of confining spectators' enthusiasm to the stands has become an acute and critical issue.

The Associated Press learned yesterday that athletic authorities of the so-called Eastern "Ivy League" are considering drastic measures to curb the increasing tendency toward riotous attacks on goal posts or other encroachments by spectators on playing fields. Echoes of this year's disturbances also have reached officers of the National Football Rules Committee.

Bowl Posts Dismantled.

The growing feeling that "something should be done" before the situation gets completely out of control was emphasized by the turbulent scenes in the Yale Bowl at the end of the Yale-Princeton game. Spectators razed the goal posts at one end of the gridiron before the game was over, and were stopped from doing the same thing to the other set of uprights only after officials fought them off.

This was the second occurrence of the kind in the Bowl during the season. The goal posts were ripped down in the last few minutes of the Yale-Dartmouth game.

A free-for-all was narrowly averted during the Fordham-New York University game at the Yankee Stadium, touched off by a fist fight between rival players. At New Orleans, Tulane and Louisiana State cohorts waged a general mêlée after the game and the goal posts were taken apart despite the precaution of the home forces in having them wired and charged with electricity.

Serious Consequences Feared.

It is with such episodes as these that college authorities are mainly concerned rather than such instances as that of the Dartmouth rooter who leaped out of the stands and took a place in the line-up facing Princeton at the goal line. They fear the possibility of dangerous consequences if measures are not adopted to keep spectators under control.

Suggestions have gone so far as to include elimination of the goal posts and, along with it, the point after touchdown, but it is not likely the rules committee will give this serious consideration.

"This would mean the elimination of the field goal as well as the try for extra point with a kick and hardly seems justified," said William S. Langford, secretary of the rules committee. "We still want to keep the foot in football."

Additional police protection on the field may appear an obvious solution, but college leaders have discovered by experience that there is also danger in this arrangement. In some localities, in the first place, the entire constabulary would not be sufficient in numbers to cope with a mass demonstration.

Second, it has been demonstrated on several occasions that the presence of police, assigned to guard goal posts, merely aroused the competitive spirit of spectators.

Steel goal posts, set in concrete, also have failed to furnish the answer to this particular phase of the problem. In addition, they are costlier to replace.

December 6, 1935

Northwestern Victor, 6-0; Ends Gopher Streak at 21

By The Associated Press.

EVANSTON, Ill., Oct. 31.—The supposedly impregnable citadel of Minnesota's football power fell today before the furious charge of Northwestern's Wildcats, carrying with it the demolition of the game's most celebrated winning streak and the 1936 championship dreams of the galloping Gophers.

Taking advantage of a sequence of extraordinary breaks, Northwestern pushed over a last-minute touchdown to beat Minnesota, 6 to 0, in a battle that was savagely fought in the mud and rain before a shrieking crowd of 47,000 spectators in Dyche Stadium.

A penalty for slugging by big Ed Widseth, star tackle and co-captain of Minnesota, followed the recovery of a Gopher fumble on the visitors' 13 and paved the way for Steve Toth, Northwestern fullback from Toledo, Ohio, to plow across for the winning score on the second play of the final quarter.

"Widseth, in the pile-up of a line play, hit an opposing player twice in the face after the whistle blew," said Referee John Getchell of St. Thomas after the game.

The offense called for a 15-yard penalty, but since the Wildcats had the ball only 13 from the goal line the actual penalty amounted to 12 and left the home team with four chances to put the ball across from the 1-yard stripe.

Minnesota twice thrust back-line plunges, with Don Geyer and Toth carrying the ball, before and after the teams changed sides of the field for the final quarter. Toth, on the third play of the series and second play of the last quarter, plunged across his own right tackle for the touchdown.

Toth's attempt to place-kick the extra point was blocked by Antil, Gopher end, but the mudcaked Wildcats took the 6 points that the break had aided them in collecting and then proceeded to fight off Minnesota's most furious counter-charges throughout the last period.

The Gophers went down with colors flying, throwing all their manpower into the game in their furious efforts to turn the tide, but they were stopped by a combination of the mud, the rain, their own loose handling of the slippery ball and the sensational defense of the Wildcats.

The defeat brought a dramatic finish to the Minnesota winning streak, which had extended through twenty - one successive games, perched the Gophers on top of the football world and made the system taught by Bernie Bierman the standard by which gridiron production was measured.

28 Games Without Defeat

The mighty men of Minnesota, under Bierman's shrewd tutoring, had gone through twenty-eight consecutive matches without defeat. Just a week ago, in taking their fourth straight game of the current campaign from Purdue by a 33-0 margin, they were hailed as another invincible machine headed for national championship heights.

Minnesota's first setback since the Gophers lost to Michigan in the final game of the 1932 season not only rocked the entire American football world but gave Northwestern command of the Big Ten championship race. The Wildcats also entered the game unbeaten and untied, and their triumph stirred a rain-soaked crowd of partisan rooters to wild heights of celebration.

Led by the brilliant Andy Uram, bright star of their back-field array, the Gophers outrushed Northwestern nearly 2 to 1, gaining 225 yards from scrimmage to their opponents' 120, but the Wildcats had the stuff they needed on the defense. The home team not only refused to crack under the stiffest kind of pressure but rarely missed opportunities to capitalize Minnesota's mistakes.

Three times, in the last period alone, wild lateral passes by Minnesota resulted in recoveries by bruised and tired but nevertheless alert Wildcat players. Three times, throughout the game, Minnesota was within apparently easy striking distance of the opposing goal, only to have the furious Northwestern defense, led by Quarterback Fred Vanzo and John Kovatch, end, turn back these threats.

Thrills in Third Period

The thrills of the game were packed into the late stages of a turbulent third period. The first of the series of bad "breaks" that led to Minnesota's downfall was a hurried punt by Ray King, lanky Gopher end, which carried only about 30 and rebounded a dozen yards to Minnesota's 46, just as though there was backspin on the ball.

Seeing their opportunity, the Wildcats shook Don Heap loose for a 26-yard run to the 20, while the crowd leaped to its feet in a frenzy

Statistics of the Game

	N.W.	Minn.
First downs	7	9
Yards gained rushing	120	225
Forward passes	2	7
Forwards completed	0	1
Yards gained, forwards	0	16
Forwards intercepted by	3	0
Lateral passes	1	9
Laterals completed	0	3
Yards gained, laterals	0	26
*Av. dist. of punts, yds.	40.9	30
†Run-back of kicks, yds.	41	102
Opponent's fumb. recov.	4	0
Yards lost, penalties	5	30

*From line of scrimmage.
†Includes kick-offs and punts.

of anticipation. The Gophers yielded stubbornly to three line plunges by Don Geyer and Bernie Jefferson, Negro halfback, putting the ball on Minnesota's 12.

Here Geyer attempted a place-ment field goal, with Heap holding the ball. He got the kick away beautifully, but the pigskin sailed a few feet to the right of the uprights.

This looked like a life-saver for the Gophers, but things continued to go wrong. They were penalized five yards for delaying the game after putting the ball in play on their 20. Then Julius Alfonse, half-back and co-captain, fumbled a behind-the-line pass from Andy Uram and DeWitt Gibson, big left-tackle of the Wildcats, fell on the ball during a terrific scramble, on the 13.

Then came the incident that finally set the Gophers right back up against their own goal. Geyer plunged into the line, where he was tackled by Widseth.

There was a terrific pile-up in the mud, the whistle blew and then, as the players were untangling, Referee Getchell said he detected Widseth striking Geyer. It didn't look like a serious mix-up from the stands, but the official unhesitatingly rushed over, issued a sharp warning and picked up the ball to administer the penalty that led to Toth's touchdown three plays later.

The game throughout was hard fought, with the inspired Wildcats rising to superb defensive heights against a team that carried a heavier offensive punch and which simply could not put together enough successful plays to get results.

Two Northwestern stars, Heap and Kovatch, were knocked groggy by the impact of Gopher tackles. Heap was forced from the game in the first half, but returned to star in the second half, Kovatch, in the third quarter, flatly refused to quit the field after nearly having his ribs caved in by the force of a running tackle. The substitute sent out for him was recalled and the star Wildcat end continued to help wreck opposing plays.

Long Runs by Uram

Uram, the ground-gaining star for Minnesota, twice pulled the crowd to its feet with long runs. Early in the first period Uram dashed 48 yards to Northwestern's 23, where he was forced out of bounds, but the Wildcats smeared four plays and took the ball on downs on their own 25. Again, in the final quarter, Uram broke loose and galloped 34 yards before being brought down on the 29.

The Gophers gambled with long forwards at this point but Northwestern broke them up and took the ball on downs after a fourth down pass was grounded in the end

zone. Misdirected laterals, at three other stages of Minnesota's final rally, proved costly. Ollie Adelman, Erwin Wegner and Hi Bender of the Wildcat defense, recovered fumbles of laterals in the last period.

Northwestern, aside from its touchdown, rarely produced any offensive fireworks, although Heap twice got away for good runs of 16 and 26 yards and Kovatch on an end around play galloped 22 yards to Minnesota's 37-yard line in the opening period.

Otherwise the ability of Jefferson and Toth to outpunt Minnesota's King proved a decisive factor, although the latter got away one tremendous boot covering 85 yards that pulled the Gophers out of a bad hole in the first period.

No Intentional Roughness

Coach Bierman said Widseth told him there was nothing intentional in the mix-up that resulted in Minnesota being penalized for unnecessary roughness just before Northwestern scored its touchdown.

"It looked like one of those things where there may have been a little hot-headed play, and, of course, it was unfortunate under any circumstances," said Bierman. "Widseth has had a fine record for three years for clean play and sportsmanship, and I'm sure he had no intention of hitting Geyer."

Bierman offered no alibi for Minnesota's defeat. He said the breaks simply caught up with the Gophers and that the team got a little panicky in the handling of the ball in the closing stages.

The line-up:

NO'WESTERN (6)		MINNESOTA (0)
Kovatch	L.E.	Antil
Gibson	L.T.	Widseth
Schreiber	L.G.	Weld
Fuller	C.	Svendsen
Reid	R.G.	Twedell
Burnett	R.T.	Midler
Zitro	R.E.	King
Vanzo	Q.B.	Wilkinson
Heap	L.H.	Uram
Hinton	R.H.	Alfonse
Toth	F.B.	Spadiccini

SCORE BY PERIODS
Northwestern .... 0 0 0 6—6
Minnesota 0 0 0 0
Touchdown--Toth.

SUBSTITUTES
Northwestern — Ends: Deibl, Bender. Tackles: Burnette, Voigts, Malloy. Guards: Calvano, Devry. Center: Wagner. Half-backs: Jefferson, Adelman. Fullback: Geyer.
Minnesota—End: Reed. Tackle: R. Johnson. Guards: Schulz, Bell. Halfbacks: Matheny, Gmitro, Thompson. Fullback: Butler.
Referee—John Getchell, St. Thomas. Umpire—H. G. Hedges, Dartmouth. Field judge—George Simpson, Wisconsin. Linesman—H. W. Huegel, Marquette. Time of periods—15 minutes.

THE MINNESOTA RECORD

Gophers Undefeated in 28 Games Prior to Yesterday.

Minnesota's last defeat prior to the setback by Northwestern yesterday was by Michigan, 3—0, in the final game of the 1932 season. The Gophers' undefeated string had extended through twenty - eight games, with the last twenty-one resulting in victories. Four tie games were played in 1933.

The twenty-eight-game no-defeat Minnesota record:

1933
19—South Dakota State........ 6
6—Indiana 6
7—Purdue 7
7—Pittsburgh 3
19—Iowa 7
0—Northwestern 0
0—Michigan 0
6—Wisconsin 3

1934
56—North Dakota State........12
20—Nebraska 0
13—Pittsburgh 7
48—Iowa 12
34—Michigan 0
30—Indiana 0
35—Chicago 7
34—Wisconsin 0

1935
26—North Dakota State........ 6
12—Nebraska 7
20—Tulane 0
21—Northwestern 13
29—Purdue 7
13—Iowa 6
40—Michigan 0
33—Wisconsin 7

1936
14—Washington 7
7—Nebraska 0
26—Michigan 0
33—Purdue 0

November 1, 1936

Texas Christian Halts Marquette By 16-6, With Meyer in Star Role

End Catches Two Touchdown Passes, Boots Field Goal and Extra Point, Scoring All Frogs' Points in Cotton Bowl—Art Guepe Runs Sixty Yards to Tally—Baugh Also Stars.

By The Associated Press.
DALLAS, Texas, Jan. 1.—Slingin' Sam Baugh, that passing man from Texas Christian University, paired with L. D. Meyer, unheralded end, to bury Marquette's Golden Avalanche, 16—6, in the Cotton Bowl football game today.

Seventeen thousand fans sat under overcast skies and witnessed a thriller that showed every play in the books.

Baugh ended three years of spectacular college play with a liberal dash of passing, kicking, running and tackling that had the stands shrieking for his re-entrance into the game as he sat on the bench in the last minutes.

But it was Meyer, 168-pound nephew of Coach Leo (Dutch) Meyer, who, in a wild afternoon of pass receiving and placement kick-ing, produced every point the Christians scored.

The game was not five minutes old when Baugh shot a 23-yard aerial to Scott McCall to place the ball on the Marquette 15. Then Meyer propelled a placement kick from the 23-yard stripe over the bar for a field goal.

Cuff Makes Long Boot

Three plays later Marquette scored. Cuff slammed a long kick to Baugh on the Christian 15 and Baugh retaliated with a long boot which Art Guepe, Avalanche quarterback, caught on his 40. Guepe started to the left, cut back into the center and brushed through diving Texans in a 60-yard sprint to a touchdown.

That was only the beginning. Roberts and Montgomery, line smackers for the Horned Frogs, alternated on spinners and reverses to work the ball to midfield and then Baugh and Meyer connected on a 30-yard pass. The little end sprinted down the sideline and Ray (Buzz) Buivid, Marquette's All-America halfback, trailed him to the 2. There Buivid gave him a shove that helped him across the line. Meyer personally added the extra point.

Ground plays, with Roberts, Montgomery and McCall crushing the Marquette line, took the Christians from the Marquette 40 to the 18 before Montgomery, on a fake reverse, suddenly reared up and hurled a touchdown pass to Meyer. He outjumped two Marquette backs for the ball.

The Frogs worked on the theory that a good offense was the best defense, clinging to the ball and hurling dangerous and tricky passes even when they boasted a 10-point lead.

Passers Stage Duel

Baugh and Buivid, rated as two of the nation's greatest passers, put on their aerial show. Baugh tried thirteen heaves, picked up a touchdown from one, worked the ball down field for the field goal, completed five and came off with 110 yards gained from hurling. Buivid three times was dropped for 10-yard losses while trying to find an open receiver. He passed nineteen times, saw three of his tosses intercepted and completed ten for 130 yards.

The line-up:

TEXAS CHR. (16)		MARQUETTE (6)
Meyer	L.E.	Anderson
Hale	L.T.	Siefert
Holt	L.G.	Czernecki
Aldrich	C.	Schoemann
Harrison	R.G.	Reif
Ellis	R.T.	Hansen
Roach	R.E.	Muth
Baugh	Q.B.	Art Guepe
McCall	L.H.	Sonnenberg
Montgomery	R.H.	Buivid
Roberts	F.B.	Cuff

SCORE BY PERIODS

| Texas Christian | 10 | 6 | 0 | 0—16 |
| Marquette | 6 | 0 | 0 | 0— 6 |

Touchdowns—Meyer 2, Art Guepe. Point after touchdown—Meyer (placement). Field goal—Meyer (placement).

SUBSTITUTES

Texas Christian—End: Needham. Tackles: Linne, Hensch, White. Guards: Kline, Rogers, Dunlap, Mayne. Center: Tittle. Backs: O'Brien, Wilkerson, Clifford, McClure, Hall, Farrell.

Marquette — Ends: Cooper, Higgins. Tackles: Lumb, Kun. Guards: Mosovsky, Jennings, Lauterbach. Back: Al Guepe.

Referee—Boynton, Williams. Umpire—Getchell, St. Thomas. Field judge—Minton, Indiana. Linesman—Morton, Michigan.

Statistics of the Game

	T.C.U.	Mar.
First downs	16	10
Yards gained rushing	178	95
Forward passes	20	21
Forwards completed	9	10
Yards gained, forwards	151	130
Forw'ds intercepted by	3	3
Lateral passes	1	3
Laterals completed	1	1
Yards gained, laterals	0	8
*Av. Dist. of punts, yds.	32½	39 1-3
†Runback of kicks, yds	50	70
Opponents' fumb. recov	0	0
Yards lost, penalties	35	25

*From line of scrimmage.
†Includes punts and kick-offs.

January 2, 1937

from Tipton to George McAfee, and set the stage for the appearance of Tony Ruffa, place-kicking star of the Blue Devils.

With the ball on the 23, Ruffa kicked it high and squarely between the uprights. The 3 points looked big.

U. S. C. suddenly caught fire; Duke seemed caught in the fire. Bob Spangler, safety man, fumbled a Trojan punt, Phil Gaspar recovered it and it was U. S. C.'s ball on Duke's 10. But the Dukes refused to yield and the Trojans tried a field goal from the 25. Gaspar's boot missed.

Lansdell Leads Advance

Tipton kicked out to the Californians' 39, and Grenville Lansdell, quarterback and running star, engineered a drive that took the ball into Duke territory. Lansdell made 5 yards, Bob Peoples 1, Lansdell 7 and a first down on the Duke 48. He made 5 more off right end and Krueger picked up 4 on an end-around play. Lansdell fired a short pass over the line to Peoples for 5 to reach the Duke 35.

Howard Jones, U. S. C. coach, suddenly sent in Nave to replace Lansdell. Jones was going by air for that touchdown, and Nave was to pilot the attack. A penalty for too many times out put the ball on the 40 and Nave started to work.

Fading far, keeping out of range of Duke's rushing ends, he passed for 14 yards to Krueger. Changing his direction, he whipped the ball for 10 to Krueger, and still another was completed to Antelope Al, but it lost 2 yards.

The clock was ticking off the seconds, and the huge crowd was roaring with excitement. Nave again called a pass, drifted far back and fired. The ball cut diagonally across the field and was clutched by Krueger.

Tipton's Punting Excellent

What followed was anti-climax. Gaspar kicked the extra point but few saw it. The gallant Dukes took the kick-off and tried desperately to win the game they thought

91,000 See So. California Topple Duke

LAST-MINUTE TOSS DEFEATS DUKE, 7-3

Nave's Fourth Straight Pass Caught by Krueger in End Zone for U. S. C. Triumph

MARCH SPANS 61 YARDS

Follows Field Goal by Ruffa, Aerials Covering 40—Blue Devils Yield First Score

STATISTICS OF THE GAME

	U.S.C.	Duke
First downs	13	8
Yards gained rushing	135	86
Forward passes	31	13
Forwards completed	13	6
Yards gained, forwards	84	53
Yards lost, forwards	8	1
Forwards intercepted by	2	2
Yards gained, int. passes	30	26
*Av. dist. of punts, yds.	32	40.5
†Run back of kicks, yds.	75	87
Opponents' fumbles rec.	1	0
Yards lost, penalties	40	30

*From line of scrimmage.
†Includes punts and kick-offs.

By The Associated Press.

PASADENA, Calif., Jan. 2.— Southern California's mighty Trojans, with a sixty-one-yard touchdown drive in the last minute of play, defeated Duke University's eleven, 7 to 3, before 91,000 spectators today.

Wrecking Duke's proud record of no defeats, ties or points scored against it in nine games of the 1938 schedule, U. S. C., celebrating its return to the Rose Bowl after an absence of six years, traveled through the air to victory about forty-five seconds before the final gun.

The overflow throng, gathered under bleak skies for this twenty-fourth consecutive Tournament of Roses football spectacle, saw an unheralded substitute back and a sophomore end spoil the clean standard of the Iron Dukes from North Carolina with four straight passes.

The story-book substitute back was Doyle Nave and the sophomore end Antelope Al Krueger from Antelope Valley. Krueger took Nave's last long pass, good for eighteen yards, as he waited in a corner of the end zone, and there went Duke's hope of victory in its anaugural appearance in the big bowl.

For three quarters it was a battle between the Trojans, fighting for the fifth U. S. C. triumph in the bowl, and Eric (the Red) Tipton, Duke's one-man offensive. For three quarters neither team could get inside the other's 35-yard line, but Duke finally drove to Southern California's 15 after a 23-yard pass

Wired Photo—Times Wide World

MacLeod of Dartmouth about to be stopped after running back punt twenty-five yards in East-West event. The tacklers, left to right, are Means, Boyd and Nielsen. Daddio is on the ground.

they had won a minute before. Tipton, whose tremendous kicking should have been the feature of this grueling clash, was tossed for a 12-yard loss. He passed the Dukes back toward midfield, but the gun sounded.

The game was over and the Dukes were driven into their first defeat, the first score tallied against them and a long, weary train ride back to Durham, N. C.

Duke was stubborn and as strong as its record foretold, but the Blue Devils went the way of other great undefeated teams—Notre Dame and California—before the slashing, spectacular, persevering Trojans.

It was a brilliant victory for Jones and a sad one for Wallace Wade of Duke. Wade had never been beaten in the Rose Bowl, although one of his three Alabama teams had been tied, but this Blue Devil aggregation, which yielded 13 first downs to 8 and was outrushed 135 yards to 86 and outpassed 84 yards to 53, was up against an unbeatable team today.

Duke in the first half failed to capitalize on a pair of blocked Trojan punts. Aside from Tipton, it hardly presented an offense worthy of the name, but its defensive strength and Tipton's towering punts kept the Trojans in their back yard.

The murky skies sprinkled rain intermittently until late in the game and then the sun peeked through.

Duke's scoring drive was started in midfield. Tipton made 1 yard and passed 13 down a sideline to McAfee. Robbie Robinson made 5 yards to reach the 20 and Tipton made 2. O'Mara, big Duke fullback, crashed over tackle for 3, and on fourth down Ruffa booted his field goal.

Duke won the toss at the start and took the north goal, with Harry Smith booting the ball. Bob Spangler ran back the kick-off from his 7-yard line to the 28. Tipton lost 6 and punted to Lansdell, who ran 13 yards to his 43.

U. S. C. made a first down in midfield on a pass and end run, but Tipton intercepted Lansdell's long toss on his 9. Tipton punted right back to the Trojan 40. Southern California punted out on Duke's 30.

Bob O'Mara and Tipton drove to the 37 before Tipton kicked to the Trojan 25. Two passes to Bob Winslow and Bill Sangster took the ball to the U. S. C. 48.

Lansdell and Sangster advanced to the Duke 46. Another throw to Bob Hoffman took the ball to the 37. Then Lansdell's kick went over the goal line.

Tipton promptly booted back to the Trojan 31. A quick kick and a clipping penalty gave Duke possession again on its 25. A 15-yard penalty gave Duke a first down on its 46. Tipton went to midfield around left end.

After Tipton booted out of bounds on the Trojan 10, Landsell raced 25 yards. He had to punt and Spangler made a 10-yard return to his 36. Tipton punted to the 18 and Lansdell ran around left end for 21.

Kicking Game Continues

George McAfee returned Mickey Anderson's punt 7 yards to his 36 as the second quarter opened. Tipton punted to the Trojan 37 and in two sweeps Anderson ran to midfield. He smashed to the Duke 42, but had to punt. Bailey blocked the kick and Duke took over on its 45.

Once more Tipton kicked after two plays failed and U. S. C. swung into action on its 25. Jack Banta sent the ball to the Trojan 40. Anderson's quick kick went out of bounds on the Duke 40.

Rose Bowl Line-Up

U. S. C. (7)		DUKE (3)
Fisk	L.E.	Darnell
Stoecker	L.T.	Maloney
Smith	L.G.	Johnson
McNeil	C.	Hill
Tonelli	R.G.	Yorke
George	R.T.	Haas
Stanley	R.E.	Perdue
Lansdell	Q.B.	Spangler
Morgan	L.H.	Eaves
Hoffman	R.H.	Tipton
Sangster	F.B.	O'Mara

SCORE BY PERIODS

U. S. C.	0	0	0	7—7
Duke	0	0	3	3—3

Touchdown—Krueger. Point after touchdown—Gaspar (placement). Field goal—Ruffa (placement).

SUBSTITUTES

U. S. C.—Ends: Krueger, Winslow, Stonebreaker. Tackles: Gaspar, Fisher. Guards: Phillips, Thomassin. Center: Dempsey. Quarterbacks: Anderson, Day, Nave. Halfbacks: Jesse, Shell. Fullbacks: Jones, Banta, Peoples.

Duke—Ends: J. Marion, Bailey. Tackles: F. Ribar, Winterson. Guards: R. Alabaster, R. Baskerville, Ruffa. Centers: S. Robb, G. Burns. Quarterback: G. McAfee. Halfbacks: W. McAfee, J. Davis, C. Deane. Fullback: R. Robinson.

Referee—Bob Morris, Seattle. Umpire—Paul Menton, Loyola of Baltimore. Linesman—Ralph Coleman, Oregon State. Field judge—Battle Bagley, Washington and Lee.

With a clear field in front, Spangler dropped Tipton's pass. Tipton and O'Mara drove to midfield and a first down. Then Tipton kicked over the goal line.

Perdue blocked Day's quick kick, but it was third down and Day recovered on his 10. He punted to Spangler, who raced 14 yards to the Trojan 38. Jones intercepted Tipton's pass and ran to his 29.

Southern California had to kick and Duke started on its 35. On two fake passes, Tipton ran to the Trojan 48-yard line. Duke lost the ball on the Trojan 35 with ten seconds to play in the half.

The Trojan kick-off went only to the 24 and Bailey ran to the 34. Tipton punted to the Trojan 28. Lansdell broke away for 10. They exchanged kicks, with Duke getting possession on the 20. Tipton slipped on the 10-yard line but punted to the Trojan 36 and Lansdell returned to the Duke 49.

Lansdell had to kick and Duke took over on its 31. Again Spangler dropped Tipton's long pass in the open. Tony Tonelli blocked Tipton's kick but Duke recovered on the 20.

After another boot, Lansdell broke loose to the 36. But Don Hill intercepted Lansdell's pass and ran to U. S. C.'s 45. McNeil intercepted Tipton's pass on his 35.

George McAfee returned a U. S. C. punt 15 to midfield. He caught Tipton's pass on the Trojans' 25. It was the first time the Californians' goal was in danger. Roger Robinson smashed the line for 5. The ball was on the 18-yard line as the third period ended.

O'Mara went to the 15, and it was at this stage that Ruffa kicked his field goal. Then came U. S. C.'s winning drive.

January 3, 1939

A KICK-OFF ON THE AIR

By ORRIN E. DUNLAP Jr.

SCIENCE has scored a touchdown at the kick-off of football by television. So sharp are the pictures and so discerning the telephoto lens as it peers into the line-up that the televiewer sits in his parlor wondering why he should leave the comforts of home to watch a gridiron battle in a sea of mud on a chilly autumnal afternoon.

With one all-seeing electric camera perched on the rim of the stadium for a birdseye view and the other for close-ups along the sideline, so amazing are the results that the majority of colleges in and around New York are shunning the idea of permitting a telecaravan to camp within the gates to toss the scenes over the fence to a non-paying audience. Managers of athletics contend that it is not fair to those who buy tickets, and, furthermore, if the games are telecast successfully, ticket buyers will diminish.

It must be remembered, they say, that football in many colleges supports all other branches of sport, so the collegians are aware that they must not "bite the hand that feeds" them by permitting radio cameras to gobble up the performance gratis. It is pointed out that numerous colleges now sanction commercial sponsors to underwrite their football broadcasts, and this goes a long way to offset deficits, in fact, to erase them.

Yale was among the first to welcome commercial radio sponsors. Princeton has frowned upon the idea, but recently flirted with it by circulating a questionnaire among the student body to learn the sentiment in regard to inviting radio sponsors to enter the Tiger's lair. And, now before all colleges have settled the radio broadcasting question, telecasting is upon them.

THE Fordham ram bucking the Waynesburg line was the first to be seen on the telescreens. Twelve miles from the gridiron a precocious 10-year-old lad as he watched the warriors plunge, punt and tackle through the air, was heard to remark, "Well now won't this keep people away from paying to see the game?" And on Monday morning the manager of a New York department store reported that he thought he had seen the

Wheeled up to the sidelines, the television camera's telephoto eye peers into the football line-up and tosses close-ups of the plays into the air for home reception.

ball and the plays in the Fordham-Waynesburg game clearer by television than if he had been at the stadium.

With the camera on a dolly at the 40-yard line, the coach himself has nothing on the televiewer at home. Both are on the sidelines. When the players gallop directly in front of the camera the televiewer feels that he is plunging right through the line or sliding out of bounds with the ball runner.

Football by television invites audience participation. The spectator at the gridiron does not have that intimacy with the players; he knows the game is separate from him because he is sandwiched in the crowd; the gladiators are out on the field. But by television the contest is in the living room; the spectator is edged up close. His eye is right in the game. The quarterback is heard calling the signals.

At the kick-off the camera is focused on the ball in the center of the field. Then the "eye" swings to the team about to kick and follows the players as they rush down the field to attack. Or if the teams are in formation for a line play, the "eye" watches them, sees the ball snapped back, and the play or the punt is followed. After the touchdown the lens is trained on the player standing back for the kick, and from his toe to the goal posts the camera traces the pigskin's arc.

IN football as in baseball and other sports telecasts the announcer is a vital link with the audience. It is noticed, however, that the announcer at the gridiron is following a new technique. He is calm and factual. There is nothing emotional about his tongue. The generation of excitement is left to the audience. Nevertheless, without the voice the game would be stripped of much of its life.

The trained observer at the microphone alongside the camera is needed to name the substitutions, to explain delays in the game, to point out trick plays and to announce the yardline placement of the ball. He tells the number of downs, the yards gained and the yards to go. He names the player kicking off, the runner, the tackler and the hero who makes the play. Without the announcer football by television would be a flat, silent picture, except for cheers, the band and clamor of the crowd.

Typical of the announcer's comment, which justifies his presence at the televised game, are such expressions as follow: "The ball is on the eight-yard line, second down, two yards to go. Blumenstock carries the ball on a straight buck and picks up a yard on the play."

Or he may say something like this: "Stefanic carrying around his own right end is thrown for a three-yard loss. The ball is on the eight-yard line . . . Brooks is back to kick. He kicks high in the air. It's out of bounds on the 34-yard line."

It is such information that makes the telecast as interesting as a broadcast, plus the picture. The listener sees more of the plays. He need no longer sit at the radio de-

pending upon his imagination to visualize the scene on a mental make-believe gridiron. Television takes him to the sidelines, right up to the white lines that run over the grass.

* * *

IF football becomes a television feature, as it holds every promise of being, providing that the economic riddle can be solved satisfactorily, the collegians may find it necessary to dress for the benefit of the radio audience. For example, if both teams are garbed so that they look alike on the screen it is confusing to the remote spectator. Harvard in crimson and Cornell in red look alike in a telecast. Colors do not solve this problem, although the different colored shirts are, of course, easily identified by spectators at the game.

Green, black and blue look alike by television, so some of the old college colors may have to be cast aside in favor of white and black shirts or else resort to stripes, polka-dots or checks, while the opposing team wears a solid color. Incidentally, the white summery outfits of the referees are ideal for television. The rotund officials are prominent figures scampering across the screen against the dark background of the grass, and it is easy to follow their wigwagging as they signal to the scoreboard attendants.

For a person or event, be it a parade, sports contest or banquet, to qualify for broadcasting there must be entertaining or informative sounds. Telecasting calls for action. That is why a prizefight has 100 per cent television value. There is plenty of action on the gridiron and that is why football is classed as a "natural" for the cameras.

The cavorting cheer leaders, the band and panoramic views of the grandstand add realism to the scene. The high-stepping drum major and the twirling baton thrown high in the air belong to television; he brings life into the picture as the band swings down the field playing "The Beer Barrel Polka."

THE screen is dull during huddles or when a player is injured. The trainers are seen to rush out on the field with the bucket of water to administer with sponge and towel. Then when the player gets up, limps around and then runs back in the line-up the televiewer, too, feels like joining in the handclaps; so intimately does the camera make him a part of the scene. The band is important in television for it re-

stores life and keeps action flowing on to the screen when time is out. Music gives the eye a chance to wander from the screen and rest a bit. When the band stops and the whistle blows the televiewer has the signal that the play is about to be resumed.

The collegiate curtain-raiser between Fordham-Waynesburg was played under what might be called television weather. It was hot; the same blazing conditions under which the studio actors perform. On such a sunny Autumn afternoon the televiewer may wish he were at the game, but when he sits comfortably at home and sees snow flurries, rain and the players covered with mud while the spectators in the stands are shivering and huddled in robes and raincoats, he has the edge on things. When the final whistle blows the weather matters not to him, he has no long trek home, no crowd with which to jostle. And he has seen the game so clearly that it is no wonder that the telecasters report that they are encountering resistance all along the line in trying to arrange with college athletic associations to pass football forward to the home.

October 15, 1939

Chicago Abandons Intercollegiate Football in Surprise Move by Trustees

BIG TEN HIT BY LOSS OF MAROON ELEVEN

Special to THE NEW YORK TIMES.

CHICAGO, Dec. 21—The University of Chicago, in the past one of the powers of the Western Conference, tonight decided to abandon intercollegiate football.

The decision to drop the sport, in which Chicago ranked high for nearly half a century, was made upon a unanimous vote of the university board of trustees in a meeting tonight. The action was announced by Harold Swift, chairman of the board, and Robert Maynard Hutchins, president of the university.

The board's statement included the suggestion that all of the university's football opponents for the 1940 season release the Maroon eleven from the scheduled engagements.

Only Tuesday night T. Nelson Metcalf, athletic director at Chicago, announced next season's program, listing eight games and including three with other members of the Big Ten.

This schedule follows:
Sept. 28, Wabash; Oct. 5, De Pauw; Oct. 12, Miami at Miami, Ohio; Oct. 19, Purdue at Lafayette, Ind.; Nov. 2, Michigan; Nov. 9, Ohio State at Columbus; Nov. 16, Virginia; Nov. 23, Brown at Providence.

The Big Ten opponents on this card are Purdue, Michigan and Ohio State.

Stagg Retired in 1933

Mr. Metcalf expressed himself as surprised by the announcement, although admitting he was aware of the proposed abandonment yesterday. Clark D. Shaughnessy, who has coached football on the Midway since Amos Alonzo Stagg was retired in 1933, was the most astounded figure involved in the sudden move, stating he was unaware of it until today.

Shaughnessy said he had made no plans for the future and could not comment on the move. When asked if he would remain as a member of the faculty, he said:

"I can't be sure of anything; as far as I know, I will remain with the university."

He appeared to be under great strain.

Mr. Metcalf said he had expected some action, because of the controversies created by Chicago's poor showing in football in recent years, but that he had not known until yesterday that the trustees were planning to abolish intercollegiate competition.

"I had hoped to get the opinions of all the other Western Conference athletic directors before any publicity was given the trustees' action," Mr. Metcalf said. "In so far as I know, the university will continue to engage in Conference competition in all other sports, but I cannot be sure of that until I learn whether or not the other schools will consent to meet the Maroons in those sports and not in football."

A statement by Mr. Swift and Dr. Hutchins read:

The university believes in ath-

letics and in a comprehensive program of physical education for all students. It believes its particular interests and conditions are such that its students can derive no special benefit from intercollegiate football.

The university looks upon all sports as games which are conducted under its auspices for the recreation of the students.

The university will continue to promote intramural sports and will encourage all students to participate in them.

This emphasis on athletics for all students at the university has been steadily increasing during the last fifteen years, and there are more students taking part in the twelve intramural sports now sponsored by the university than ever before.

Effect on Other Sports

The university trusts that its withdrawal from intercollegiate football will not require termination of its long and satisfactory relationship with the other members of the intercollegiate conference known as the Big Ten.

The University of Chicago at present is the only institution in the Big Ten that competes in all thirteen sports sponsored by the conference.

Except for football, the university will continue to maintain intercollegiate teams in all sports which the conference sponsors. The decision is effective at once and institutions with which football games have been scheduled for 1940 and 1941 will be asked to release the university.

December 22, 1939

Stanford Overcomes Nebraska Before 90,000 in Rose Bowl

COAST TEAM STOPS CORNHUSKERS, 21-13

STATISTICS OF THE GAME

	Stan.	Neb.
First downs	14	9
Yards gained rushing	254	56
Forward passes	14	14
Forwards completed	7	3
Yards gained, forwards	98	72
Forwards intercepted by	4	1
*Av. dist. of punts, yds.	35	37
‡Run-back of kicks, yds.	166	104
Rival fumbles recovered	0	2
Yards lost, penalties	58	20

*From line-of scrimmage.
‡Includes punts and kick-offs.

By The Associated Press.

PASADENA, Calif., Jan. 1—Stanford University's magicians of the gridiron swept to victory for the tenth consecutive time today as the Palo Alto eleven reached the peak of a spectacular comeback campaign with a stunning triumph over Nebraska in another stirring chapter in Rose Bowl football history.

The down but ever stout-hearted Cornhuskers, striving for victory in their first appearance in the big bowl, made a gallant stand, but they failed to solve the wizardry or stave off the lightning thrusts of this Stanford T-Model machine, and trudged wearily off the emerald green floor of the stadium, the roar of 90,000 persons echoing over the Arroyo Seco, with the score board reading: Stanford 21, Nebraska 13.

It was a glorious triumph for Stanford, a team that couldn't win for losing in 1939 and then came back to astonish the football world in 1940 with an uninterrupted streak of victories and a parade into this Bowl game today.

It was also a triumph for the Indians' popular coach, Clark Shaughnessy, a fugitive from football-frowning Chicago University, who took over downtrodden Stanford last Fall and piloted it to this promised land.

Batter the Huskers

Twice Nebraska's valiant Cornhuskers forged ahead, and each time Stanford, with Frankie Albert, Hugh Gallarneau, Pete Kmetovic and Norm Standlee battering and befuddling the Huskers, came from behind and then roared on to a decisive triumph.

Nebraska sent a shudder down the Stanford backs in the first two minutes of the game. Taking the kick-off, it blasted like dynamite down field to a quick touchdown. Halfback Butch Luther ran the kick-off back 27 yards to the Stanford 48, Harry Hopp lost two, but the Husker Hurricanes went to work. Vike Francis, 200-pound fullback, barged 14 yards on one play, 13 on the next, and Luther smashed the Stanford right side for 14. Quarterback Roy Petsch made two, and from the Indians' 7 Luther hit for five. Big Francis went through his right guard for the touchdown, and then added the extra point.

Stanford played around and then drove across into Husker territory. Standlee was hit hard on the Nebraska 28, however, and fumbled, Center Bob Burrus recovering. Nebraska kicked, and the T-Model machine began to click from midfield.

Little Kmetovic skipped 29 yards off his right end on a play that few saw, including the Nebraskans. Gallarneau lost two but Kmetovic knifed through for 10 yards to the 10. Gallarneau, on the next play, shot through the Husker left tackle for 10 yards and a touchdown, scoring standing up. Albert then kicked the first of his three conversions for the afternoon.

Hauled Down by Taylor

Midway in the second quarter Nebraska punted and Kmetovic, trying to catch it over his shoulder in the sun, fumbled and Allen Zikmund, a reserve, pounced on it on the Stanford 33. Petsch called for a pass and Herman Rohrig let it fly—a long one that found Zikmund on the 10 and literally sent him flying over the goal line. Rohrig tried for the place kick, Taylor blocked it, Rohrig tried to run it across and Taylor hauled him down. The point was missed, but Nebraska held a 13-7 lead.

It wasn't held long. Stanford took the out-of-bounds kick-off from its 35, pounded on up to the Husker 40 and then All-America Albert fired a hard, high pass to Gallarneau. He made the prettiest catch of the day, stretching far into the air over the clutching hands of the Husker secondary, brought the ball down and raced on over the goal, 10 yards away.

That tied the score, but Albert broke the tie with a place-kick conversion.

Nebraska sent in reserve after reserve, but this Stanford line wouldn't give and the Stanford pass defense was air tight. Early in the third period the Indians traveled from their own 24 into the Husker side of the field. Albert's flat pass to the fleet Kmetovic went for 36 yards, another was good for 14. Down the Indians went, and finally the ball rested only 8 inches away from a touchdown. That stout Husker line held, however, for four downs inside the 2-yard line, and then took the ball.

Brings Crowd to Its Feet

Hopp booted the ball out of danger; Kmetovic caught it on the Husker 40 and brought the shouting crowd to its feet with that sensational touchdown run of the game. He ran first to the left, wheeled and headed to the right, and the downfield blocking that followed was a sight to behold. Huskers were strewn like cornstalks over the turf. Francis was somersaulted by one block and was injured, and meanwhile Kmetovic was squatting on the ball across the goal stripe.

The methodical Albert again kicked the extra point. It ended the scoring. Nebraska never threatened again, but managed to hold off another scoring threat by Stanford.

Thus passed into Rose Bowl history another post-season game. Stanford now has won three, lost three and tied one in its Bowl appearances.

January 2, 1941

THE GAME BECOMES COMPLEX

Football Rules Committee Adopts Three Important Changes to Speed Offense

FREE SUBSTITUTING WRITTEN INTO CODE

By The Associated Press.

CLEMENTON, N. J., Jan. 3—The National Collegiate Football Rules Committee gave the game's offense a break today with three major rule changes affecting substitutions, behind-the-line ball-passing and forward passes.

After a three-day committee session at the near-by Pine Valley Country Club, Chairman Walter R. Okeson of Bethlehem, Pa., announced these major changes:

1. Players may be substituted as many times as desired during a game; elimination of the rule prohibiting an incoming substitute from communicating with his team until after the ball has been put into play; when substitutions are made in the last two minutes of play in the first or second half, the watch will be stopped as usual when the substitute comes on the field, but will be started again as soon as the substitution is completed.

2. The ball may be handed forward at any point behind the line of scrimmage to any player and will be treated as though it were a backward pass.

3. Fourth-down forward passes which become incomplete in the opponent's end zone will be treated as though they became incomplete on the field of play instead of being ruled touchbacks. On such plays, the ball will go to the defending team at the point where the ball was put into play instead of the 20-yard line as in the past.

Uniform Numbering Urged

The committee also recommended standard numbering of players in the various positions as an aid to spectators, but said it recognized that "several years will be necessary to effect this change."

Okeson said groups of colleges throughout the country would test the standard numbering during the 1941 season and "on the basis of this research the committee expects next year to be in a position to define what such numbering must be."

"The general aim of the committee," Okeson said, "was to give the offense greater power without injuring the defense too much.

"We feel the free substitution rule will not only be a great help to the smaller colleges but will still further reduce injuries. The rule covering substitutions in the last two minutes of play will prevent the present practice of coaches sending in players in an attempt to delay the game."

Okeson said the second change, covering handing the ball forward, would eliminate a difficult foul which officials have had to call. Any lineman, provided he comes out of the line, will be eligible to handle the ball, Okeson explained.

The chairman added that in such plays the ball must be handed, rather than passed, and that both players must have a hand on the ball during the transfer.

The new fourth-down forward pass rule, Okeson pointed out, goes even further than the professional football rule in that under the pro rules the ball is given to the defensive team on the 20-yard line unless the incomplete pass was thrown from outside that line.

Return of the goal posts to the goal line and widening of the posts to encourage field-goal kicking, the latter recommended by the American Football Coaches Association, were rejected by the committee, Okeson said. He said return of the goal posts would be dangerous to the players as well as handicap to the offensive tea

January 4, 1941

Spread of T Formation Vexes Shaughnessy; Rivals May Tax Stanford Defense With It

By The United Press.

Clark Shaughnessy is afraid he may have helped create a football monster that will menace him and his Stanford team next season.

The genial coach of the Rose Bowl victors was a visitor in New York yesterday, and told reporters about his menace, the widely publicized T formation, which was used in 1940 with such success by Stanford and the Chicago Bears, professional champions.

Shaughnessy, a tall, sturdy chap with sparse, iron-gray hair, said, "unquestionably many college teams throughout the country will shift to this brand of play for next season, and particularly on the Pacific Coast because of the simultaneous success of Stanford and the Bears.

"Accordingly, Stanford will be stacking up against teams using a system of play similar to that which helped the Indians so much in 1940. Already I'm trying to figure out defenses for my favorite type of offense. And it's a difficult job to work out a good defense for it."

The Indians' pilot pointed out that Stanford had played against ten types of defense last season and that none could quite fill the bill. Likewise, the Washington Redskins thought they had doped out the proper defense, but were walloped, 73-0 by the Bears.

Shaughnessy said the sturdiest defense Stanford had encountered was Southern California's five-man sliding line, in which the Trojan line-men did not attempt to break through but merely "slid" sideways in the direction of play, standing up and holding back the Stanford men.

"They used our men to block our own plays," he said, "but when the second half opened, this defense too proved futile because the Indians began passing and running around the ends."

What effect will increased use of the T formation have upon the college game?

Shaughnessy predicted it would result in greater scoring and more action for the fans.

The coach will be guest of honor tomorrow night at a dinner given by the Stanford Alumni of New York.

January 28, 1941

Football No Slower Despite Use Of Unlimited Subs, Survey Shows

By The United Press.

The professional pessimists who greeted the football rules changes with gloomy predictions of four and five-hour games can stop worrying right now. Although substitutes are being employed more often than a bottle opener at an alumni reunion, they haven't slowed up the action—at least not enough to matter.

A United Press survey of Saturday's fourteen major games disclosed yesterday that although in some instances the coaches substituted as many as 128 times no contest ran longer than 2 hours 55 minutes and the average playing time—2 hours 23 minutes—is no higher than that of contests of last year, 1939 or what have you.

The Lone Conclusion

This is the only conclusion to be drawn from the gathered facts. Although the rules changes lifted the lid on substitutes in an avowed effort to relieve the pressure on smaller schools with sparse reserves, the survey failed to disclose any trend in this direction.

For instance, North Carolina used seventy-nine substitutions while being beaten, 52–6, by Tulane, yet Pitt used only twenty-eight while being drubbed, 39—0, by Minnesota.

Here are the average figures: In the fourteen games, coaches substituted eighty-eight times, for a grand total of 1,239 changes. The winners averaged forty-eight shifts apiece, for a total of 678,

while the losers were lower with forty, or a total of 561. This indicates, if anything, that beaten teams are just as badly off this year as ever.

128 Substitutions Made

The Tulane-North Carolina game produced the most changes of the day—128—as Tulane substituted 49 times against Carolina's 79, but the game took only 2:38 to play, the same length of time used up in the contest between Minnesota and Pitt, in which only 91 substitutions were employed.

The shortest game of the day was Harvard-Dartmouth at 2:06, but these teams used 48 substitutes, or five more than Ohio State and Purdue, who played thirteen minutes longer.

The largest number of substitutes used by a winning team was the 77 by the Texas Aggies in defeating T. C. U. The smallest was the 21 employed by Ohio State in shading Purdue. The largest number for a loser was North Carolina's aforementioned 79, and the smallest was the 22 used by Columbia and Purdue, both of whom, incidentally, were beaten.

Specialists Are Used

The rate of substituting is much higher than in previous years as coaches are making more frequent use of "one-play" specialists and also are shifting men on offense and defense.

Against Villanova, Frank Kimbrough of Baylor switched his half-

backs every time the ball changed hands—using two specific men on defense and two others on the attack. However, since virtually all of these changes are being made when time is normally out the length of the games is not being affected greatly.

The figures' (which do not include the eleven men who started the game, but do include every substitution made after the whistle blew):

Winner.	No.of Subs.	Loser.	No.of Play. Subs. Time.
Texas Aggies..	77	T. C. U......	36	2:55
U. S. C......	55	W. S. C.....	36	2:22
Notre Dame..	45	Carnegie	38	2:21
Minnesota ...	63	Pitt	28	2:38
Wisconsin ...	42	Iowa	23	2:27
Ohio State...	21	Purdue	22	2:19
Texas	56	Arkansas	61	2:30
Tulane	49	N. Carolina....	79	2:38
Alabama	51	Tennessee ...	38	2:25
Fordham	48	W. Virginia..	53	2:25
Michigan	27	Northwestern..	50	2:09
Georgia	56	Columbia	22	2:30
Navy	63	Cornell	52	2:21
Harvard	25	Dartmouth ...	23	2:06
Total 678			561

October 22, 1941

Irish to Use T Formation

SOUTH BEND, Ind., Feb. 26 (AP) —The famed backfield shift which Knute Rockne developed while an undergraduate at Notre Dame and improved later as coach will be scrapped by the Irish football team. Coach Frank Leahy disclosed today he would use the T formation when his protégés begin Spring practice because he believes his speedy backs can operate more effectively when running from that line-up.

February 27, 1942

FOOTBALL DROPPED BY 189 COLLEGES

61 in East, 49 in South Listed in Associated Press Survey

With the East and South topping the list, close to 200 colleges, large and small, have abandoned football for the duration.

A nation-wide survey by The Associated Press yesterday showed that 189 institutions of higher learning have felt the drain of manpower and transportation problems to such an extent that they will not attempt to play the game until after the war.

A few of them dropped by the wayside a year ago, but the majority have canceled the sport this year, many of them since the Army said its trainees would not have time to participate in intercollegiate athletics.

The list is expected to be increased considerably by the time September rolls along, for many schools indicated they planned to play but actually didn't know what the situation would be until the fall term starts.

The survey showed sixty-one schools had dropped the sport in the East, forty-nine in the South, thirty-four in the Southwest, twenty-six in the Midwest, ten in the Rocky Mountain area and nine on the West Coast. The latter does not include California's many junior colleges, practically all of which will not field teams this fall.

While, naturally, the list is composed largely of small schools, it also includes such bulwarks of the gridiron sport as Harvard, Georgetown, Duquesne, Lafayette and the Little Three, Williams, Wesleyan and Amherst, in the East.

Also Kentucky, Mississippi, Mississippi State, Florida, Auburn and Tennessee of the bowl-minded Southeastern Conference; Creighton, St. Louis and Washington University of the Missouri Valley and Baylor in the Southwest Conference.

July 14, 1943

ARMY AND NOTRE DAME BATTLE TO 0-0 TIE BEFORE 74,000

IRISH STAGE MARCH

Move 85 Yards but Are Halted on the Army 3 in Second Period

CADETS HAVE SIX CHANCES

Unable to Capitalize on Them, Failing to Triumph After 25 Victories in a Row

By ALLISON DANZIG

Army, the scourge of the gridiron for three years, remained undefeated and unbowed but was still looking for its first point in four meetings with a Notre Dame team coached by Frank Leahy as the intersectional rivals fought to a scoreless tie at the Yankee Stadium yesterday.

The football game of the year between the nation's two top-ranking elevens resolved itself into a crunching battle of powerful lines. In vain 74,000 onlookers waited for an eruption of the explosive punch that each was expected to turn loose upon the other in a high-scoring duel dominated by the offense.

For the first time in three seasons of uninterrupted and overpowering success against twenty-five opponents, Doc Blanchard and Glenn Davis, the celebrated Mr. Inside and Mr. Outside, found themselves shackled and crushed to earth like ordinary mortals through their full sixty minutes of devotion to duty.

Stopped Time and Again

The Army attack that had rolled up 107 points in the two previous meetings of the teams—the most humiliating disasters suffered by Notre Dame in modern times—was stopped time and again deep in the opponent's territory by the powerful Fighting Irish line.

Johnny Lujack who, an equally tireless worker who, without any sign of lameness in his ankle, directed the Notre Dame attack, passed, picked, ran and did defensive duty throughout the entire bruising game, except for two plays, was accorded the same lack of respect and rough treatment.

The horde of hard-running backs that were expected to pour through the Army line, as the cadets

weakened and crumbled before the far greater replacement strength of their rival, never brought the ball into scoring territory except on two occasions.

Army Fails to Sag

All of the pre-conceived notions and theories went out the window. Notre Dame did not flood the field with substitutes, using the same number of linemen as Army and only four more backs. The West Pointers did not sag in the fourth quarter, holding the Fighting Irish to one first down in that period while getting one themselves, and the greater individual brilliancy and threat of Blanchard and Davis did not materialize.

So furiously did the Kelly Green line swarm upon the renowned B. & D. and also upon Quarterback Arnold Tucker and Davis when they passed that never once was Army able to break a man loose from scrimmage for any great distance. The Notre Dame carriers and receivers likewise were stopped abruptly.

Blanchard made a run of twenty-one yards, and Davis never went that far from scrimmage. Tucker got away for thirty yards and that was the longest gain of the day. Terry Brennan's run of twenty-two yards was the only one of any length made by Notre Dame. Only two passes carried for any distance, one tossed by Lujack to Bob Skoglund netting twenty-five yards, and Davis throwing to Blanchard for twenty-three.

Ends on Same Note

It was not the thrilling offensive spectacle that had been looked for. Nevertheless, the battle was so fiercely waged and the lines and the backers-up rose up so nobly when their goal lines were endangered that the crowd never found the play lacking in excitement, particularly when Army stopped a Notre Dame advance of eighty-five yards three yards short of a touchdown—the only sustained march put on by either side all afternoon.

So the resumption of the rivalry between Earl Blaik and Frank Leahy, back from two years' service in the Navy, ended on the same low note that it began in 1941. That year, too, when Leahy went to South Bend from Boston College and Blaik was called to West Point from Dartmouth by General Robert Eichelberger to revive Army's sunken fortunes on the gridiron, their teams played to a scoreless deadlock.

In 1942, Notre Dame won by 13—0. In 1943, one of the great teams of all time, Leahy's last before he went into the service

smashed Army by 26—0 and was established the national champion. So four times Blaik has sent an Army team out against a Leahy eleven without a single point accuring to the West Pointers.

It was a bitter disappointment to the Army coach, in view of the many chances his team had to score yesterday. Six times the cadets had the ball inside Notre Dame's 33-yard mark, once on the 15, again on the 20 and also on the 23. But never could Blanchard or David carry it over or Tucker or Davis pass it across to capitalize the numerous breaks gained through interception and the recovery of fumbles.

Notre Dame, aside from its eighty-five-yard mark, once on the 15, again on the 20 and also on the 23. But never could Blanchard or David carry it over or Tucker or Davis pass it across to capitalize the numerous breaks gained through interception and the recovery of fumbles.

Notre Dame, aside from its eighty-five-yard march to Army's 3-yard mark in the second quarter, on which Gerry Cowhig was the big gun and Lujack passed twenty-five yards to Skoglund, never approached the West Point goal line again except on one occasion.

The recovery of the ball on an Army fumble gave the fighting Irish possession on the 34 in the third period, but they could get only two yards. Then Tucker, a worthy rival for Lujack for All-America honors and one of the most brilliant figures on the field, ended the threat with one of his three interceptions of the afternoon.

Teams Expertly Scouted

The defense was simply too strong for the offense on each side and both teams had been scouted so expertly and thoroughly that neither was able to surpass the other with its operations from the T formation.

Leahy did not appear to take the tie quite as much to heart as did Blaik. Considering the many times that Army threatened, probably he had no cause to feel sad over the outcome, though it must have been a keen disappointment to him when his team put on its long march, only to fail of a first down at the 3 by a yard. Also considering what Army had done to the Fighting Irish the past two years, as well as to all others, the scoreless tie might be regarded as a moral victory for Notre Dame.

On the basis of the statistics, which are remarkably even and show a difference of not thirty yards—in Notre Dame's favor—in total gains from scrimmage between the contesting forces, a draw was the logical verdict.

The big crowd that filled the Stadium to the last seat included an impressive assemblage of distinguished guests. Seated in the Superintendent's section with Maj. Gen. Maxwell D. Taylor of the United States Military Academy were Secretary of War Robert P. Patterson, Secretary of the Navy James Forrestal and Attorney General Tom Clark, who received an urgent summons and made his departure during the game.

Statistics of the Game

	Army.	N.D.
First downs	9	11
Yards gained, rushing	138	173
Forward passes	16	17
Forwards completed	5	6
Yards gained, forwards	57	52
Forwards intercepted by	3	2
Number of punts	7	8
*Av. dist. of punts, yds.	40	40
Run-back of punts, yds.	86	46
Fumbles	3	5
Own fumbles recovered	1	2
Penalties	2	1
Yards lost, penalties	30	5
*From line of scrimmage.		

Also seated in the Superintendent's boxes were General of the Army, Dwight D. Eisenhower, Army Chief of Staff; Generals Jacob L. Devers, Carl Spaatz, Omar Bradley and Courtney Hodges, Maj. Gen. Anthony McAullife, Admiral Thomas C. Kinkaid and a host of officers of lesser rank, from both branches of the services.

O'Donnell at Contest

Brig. Gen. Rosy O'Donnell, Col. Red Reeder and Edgar Garbisch, Army football heroes of other days were present.

A hundred wearers of the Purple Heart from the New York area attended the game as guests of the United States Military Academy. Col. Lawrence M. (Biff) Jones, graduate manager of athletics at West Point, sent the tickets to Col. B.B. Millenthal, officer of the First Army Special Services Division at Governors Island.

The weather was just about made to order for the game to which the whole football world had looked forward all season. The threat of rain which caused a good part of the crowd to delay its arrival at the Stadium was dissipated as the sun broke through the clouds just as Captain Blanchard and Co-Captains Lujack and Cowhig met in the center of the field for the toss of the coin.

Before the play got under way and during the intermission between the halves, the gathering was entertained by the United States Military Academy band and the Notre Dame band and by the circus acts put on by the latter organization with clowns and simulated wild animals going through stunts.

The West Point corps of 2,1000 cadets entered the Stadium exactly on the dot as scheduled at 12:40. Their faultless files on parade and maneuvers on the field, with all 2,100 moving as one in absolute precision, won the usual pounds of applause. The Army mules, Mr. Jackson and Skippy, the diminutive gift of the Ecuadorean Ambassador some years ago, went galloping around the sidelines under the expert bareback riding of cadets.

Contrary to Practice

Captain Blanchard won the toss and, contrary to Army's usual practice, elected to receive the kick-off. Heretofore, Army has kicked off when it had the honor. Yesterday, it had too much fear of Notre Dame's offensive power to give it the first crack at the ball.

Not only in this departure from its usual custom did Army show its respect for its rival's attack but also in its willingness to gamble by rushing the ball on fourth down even in its own territory, rather than to kick. Notre Dame did likewise but only on one or two occasions.

Army had its first chance to score early in the opening quarter. Steve Sitko fumbled and Tackle Goble Bryant recovered for West Point on Notre Dame's 24. A pass from Tucker to Davis, who had gone in motion, netted eight yards, but Blanchard was stopped just short of a first down on the 15 and the ball changed hands.

Notre Dame then put together two first downs with Sitko and Brennan hitting the left side of the Army line. Army braced and got two first downs with Blanchard and Davis carrying for short gains and Davis passing for five to Barney Poole, who, with Hank Foldberg, were tremendous in guarding Army's flanks. Joe Steffy and Art Gerometta did yeoman work in stopping plays to the inside. Notre Dame's defense stiffened at midfield and there was no further threat of a score in the first period.

The action picked up violently in the second quarter and the Stadium roared with cheers from both sides as first Army drew near a score, then Notre Dame and then Army again.

A reverse pass from Davis to Blanchard, who went tearing down the field alone to the left, netted twenty-three yards and a first down on the Notre Dame 23. The cadet corps was standing to a man and roaring for a touchdown, but the Fighting Irish rose up and treated Davis scandalously.

Davis Is Smothered

On an attempt to turn Notre Dame's left flank, the Army halfback was smothered for a 5-yard

Notre Dame-Army Record

1913—N. D. 35, A. 13	1930—N. D. 7, A. 6
1914—A. 20, N. D. 7	1931—A. 12, N. D. 0
1915—N. D. 7, A. 0	1932—N. D. 21, A. 0
1916—A. 30, N. D. 10	1933—N. D. 13, A. 12
1917—N. D. 7, A. 2	1934—N. D. 12, A. 6
1918—No game	1935—N. D. 6, A. 6
1919—N. D. 12, A. 9	1936—N. D. 20, A. 6
1920—N. D. 27, A. 17	1937—N. D. 7, A. 0
1921—N. D. 28, A. 0	1938—N. D. 19, A. 7
1922—A. 0, N. D. 0	1939—N. D. 14, A. 0
1923—N. D. 13, A. 0	1940—N. D. 7, A. 0
1924—N. D. 13, A. 7	1941—A. 0, N. D. 0
1925—A. 27, N. D. 0	1942—N. D. 13, A. 0
1926—N. D. 7, A. 0	1943—N. D. 26, A. 0
1927—A. 18, N. D. 0	1944—A. 59, N. D. 0
1928—N. D. 12, A. 6	1945—A. 48, N. D. 0
1929—N. D. 7, A. 0	1946—N. D. 7, A. 0

RECAPITULATION

	W.	L.
Notre Dame	21	4
Army	7	4

loss. His pass to Blanchard failed and then he sought to get off a lateral to Blanchard as he was hemmed in.. A half dozen opponents buried him on the 37-yard line, a further loss of 9 yards. Davis then kicked and Cowhig returned the punt 7 yards to his 12. It was there that Notre Dame started on its 85-yard march.

With Cowhig making most of the gains, Lujack passing to Skoglund for 25, and Bill Gompers contributing, Notre Dame looked unstoppable on the attack. Army's defense was being ripped asunder.

After Cowhig had smashed twenty yards through tackle, with a cordon of blockers clearing the way, Blaik rushed in Harvey Livesay in place of Rip Rowan to give Army a second center in backing up the line. Rowan was playing in the injured Ug Fuson's place at fullback, while Blanchard played the entire game at right half.

Lujack passed to Cowhig for two yards. Gompers got five. Then Lujack, on a quarterback sneak, got one. The place was in an uproar. The ball was on Army's 4, and it was fourth down and two to go for a first down.

On a fake at the middle, Gompers sped around Army's right end and for a moment it seemed he would make it, but he was hauled down after his long lateral run on the 3, a yard short of a first down. Army was saved and the finest offensive effort of the day had gone for nought.

Bill West, the only backfield substitute Army used except for a two-minute period of relief of Tucker by Bob Gustafson, and whose kicking was so valuable to his team, booted the ball out to midfield. After that, Army was in no danger again in the half and had the chance again to score when Tom Hayes recovered a fumble on Notre Dame's 35.

Blanchard got two yards and then Tucker's three passes were knocked down. Just before the end of the half, Tucker intercepted a pass, and on the last play before the intermission, ran thirty yards to Notre Dame's 30.

Blanchard turned in some magnificent defensive work in the third period, tackling with terrific impact. The play was mostly in Notre Dame territory, although the Fighting Irish were making most of the gains.

Then came Notre Dame's first and only break of the game. John Mastrangelo recovered an Army fumble on the Cadets' 34. Two plays netted only two yards and then Lujack fired a pass. The ever-vigilant Tucker snared the ball and went snaking up the field thirty-two yards to his own 42. On the next play Blanchard made his longest run of the day for twenty-one yards, and a first down on the 37. The Cadet corps was in an uproar. Davis and Blanchard got four yards and then Tucker passed over the middle to Foldberg for thirteen and a first down on the Irish 20. Surely the deadlock was to be broken now. Army seemed definitely on its way, on its longest march of the day. Then came frustration once more. Terry Brennan gathered in Davis' pass on his 8, to end the threat, and on the next play sped twenty-two yards around end as the third quarter ended.

Early in the fourth quarter Army failed of a first down by inches on Notre Dame's 33. Shortly after Sitko intercepted a pass on his 10, fumbled and Lujack recovered on his 5. From behind his own goal line the Notre Dame quarterback got off a superb kick of fifty-five yards.

Davis brought the ball back to Notre Dame's 39 and there Martin grabbed the ball out of the air as Tucker's pass was partially blocked at midfield. A minute before the end of the game Tucker made his third interception of the day near midfield.

Ball Brought Back

With forty-eight seconds left, Davis fired a long pass to Blanchard, who made a spectacular catch at the 20, with two defenders on top of him. The place was in an uproar again, but Blanchard had stepped out of bounds in catching the ball and it was brought back. That was all.

Despite the overheated rivalry that was looked for, the game was one of the most cleanly played of the year. So far as is known, there were no injuries of consequence and only three penalties were inflicted.

Indicative of the strength of the defense, Davis gained a total of 30 yards in seventeen tries, Blanchard 50 yards in eighteen, Tucker 37 in nine. Brennan gained 69 yards in fourteen attempts, Cowhig 37 in seven, Sitko 24 in five and Lujack made 9 yards in carrying the ball eight times. Six of his seventeen passes were completed for 52 yards, all going to different receivers, and three were intercepted.

The line-up:

ARMY (0)	NOTRE DAME (0)
Poole	L.E.	Martin
Biles	L.T.	Connor
Steffy	L.G.	Fischer
Enos	C.	Strohmeyer
Gerometta	R.G.	Royal
Bryant	R.T.	Fallon
Foldberg	R.E.	Zilly
Tucker	Q.B.	Lujack
Davis	L.H.	Brennan
Blanchard	R.H.	Sitko
Rowan	F.B.	Mello

SUBSTITUTES

Army—Ends: Hayes, Rawers. Tackles: Anderson, Tavzel. Guards: Ray, Drury. Centers: Yeoman, Livesay. Backs: Gustafson, West. Notre Dame—Ends: Skoglund, Koskowski. Tackles: Sullivan, Urban. Guards: Signiago, Mastrangelo. Center: Wendell. Backs: Cowhig, Swistowicz, Ashbaugh, Panelli, Slovak, Gompers. Referee—Rollie Barnum, Wisconsin. Umpire—E. C. Krieger, Ohio University. Linesman—Paul Goebel, Michigan. Field judge—William Orwig, Michigan.

November 10, 1946

ARMY CHECKS LATE NAVY RALLY TO WIN THRILLER, 21-18

MIDDIES JUST MISS

Drive to 3-Yard Line in Dying Minutes of Game Before 100,000

By ALLISON DANZIG
Special to The New York Times.

PHILADELPHIA, Nov. 30—The clock ran out on Navy. By the margin of a few precious yards the greatest record in Army football history was saved in the Municipal Stadium today.

Three yards stood between Navy and the upset of the ages over the team that had stood invincible for three years. One hundred thousand spectators, President Harry S. Truman among them, were making a bedlam in the huge horseshoe enclosure as the fighting midshipmen ripped and passed their way 64 yards down the field.

The great Army eleven was the overwhelming favorite by 28 points over an opponent that had lost seven successive games. And Army was being swept off its feet in a desperate fight to stem the tide of defeat that had set in after the cadets had led by 21—6 at the half.

Close to Defeat

The team that had conquered twenty-six foes and tied Notre Dame over a three-year period was hanging on the ropes. Nothing it seemed, could save it against the surging power and clever resourcefulness of its rampant rival from the Severn.

From their 33-yard line the amazing midshipmen, who had swept 78 yards and then 35 in the third period to make the score 21—18 at the start of the final quarter, stormed 64 yards to Army's 3-yard line. It was first down and goal to go, with a minute and a half remaining to play.

Throughout the tremendous enclosure, to its farthest reaches, the multitude was standing in a turmoil of mad excitement, cheering,

pleading, urging its heroes on, or to stand and hold that line. It was drama as nerve-wracking and pulsating as anything within memory in the long history of this bitter rivalry between the service academies.

Hope Seemed Gone

All hope seemed gone for Army. The team that had scored on three of the first four times it had the ball and apparently was going to win in a rout was being hammered into helplessness.

The renowned Doc Blanchard and Glenn Davis, who had scored Army's three touchdowns and turned in one of their most dazzling twin performances in this last appearance of their college ca-

Glenn Davis (left) and Felix (Doc) Blanchard, Army's dynamic duo of the 1940's.

reers, were completely forgotten. There were new idols holding the stage and sending the crowd into convulsions of happiness or chilling its heart with fear—Reaves Baysinger, Pistol Pete Williams, Leon Bramlett, Lynn Chewning, Al McCully, Bill Hawkins and Bill Earl.

First down and 3 yards to go. Nine feet to go for the touchdown that would make history and send Army toppling from the lofty pedestal it has occupied for three years in the finale for Earl Blaik's invincible Black Knights of the Hudson.

The teams lined up and 193-pound Chewning, who had been held in reserve until the last quarter by Capt. Tom Hamilton, was called on by Quarterback Baysinger to carry the ball on first down. It was Chewning who had just brought the ball down to the 3 with a 20-yard end run on fourth down.

The powerful fullback from Richmond hurled himself at the sagging Army line as the crowd screamed with what voice it had left. Goble Bryant and Hank Foldbert tore through and nailed him at the line of scrimmage. Again Chewning carried, and this time big Barney Poole smashed him down in his tracks.

The suspense was almost unbearable. The clock showed less than a minute left to play. It still didn't seem possible that Navy could be stopped.

At this critical juncture Referee Bill Halloran stepped in, picked up the ball and carried it back five yards. The midshipmen had been penalized five yards for delaying the game. A groan went up from the Navy stands, but there was still time to do it, so it seemed.

Tosses to Williams

On third down, Navy went into single wing formation, into which it had been shifting from time to time from the T. Hawkins took the snap from Dick Scott, Navy's superb center, and took two steps toward the line, then flipped the ball out to Williams.

The Army line was not fooled this time, as it had been on other buck laterals. It surged in on the fast halfback and nailed him on the five-yard line. Before another play could be run, a pistol barked, sounding the end of the game.

Army's great goal-line defense, one of its noblest efforts of the year, had saved the day. West Point was the winner by 21—18, by the margin of Navy's failure to kick a single one of its three tries for the extra point following its touchdowns.

Such was the tremendously dramatic ending of the forty-seventh meeting between the midshipmen and the cadets. Thus did Army wind up the three most glorious years it has known on the gridiron, with a record of twenty-seven victories and one tie.

Finale for Great Stars

So did Blanchard and Davis and Arnold Tucker, probably the greatest backfield triumvirate in modern times, if not of all time, con-

President and Mrs. Truman, who were among the spectators

The New York Times

clude their glamorous record of triumph.

And so did Navy redeem itself for all the misfortune that had dogged it from the second day of the season in September. This was one of the poorest of all Annapolis teams, on the record, but the midshipmen of 1946 will long be remembered and honored for the spirit that scorned odds and came within an inch of bringing down the scourge of the gridiron—closer than even Notre Dame came in its scoreless tie with Army.

And a salute is in order to Captain Hamilton, a brilliant war leader whose fighting spirit matched his men's, whose faith in them never dimmed at any time during the campaign and who sent them into battle with expressions of confidence in their ability to win.

Army and Navy furnished the perfect ending to the football season with their enthralling rivalry. The weather was perfect for both the players and for the year's record gathering. The sun shone in a clear sky, the temperature was in the forties and the crowd, warmly clad, enjoyed the spectacle in complete comfort.

Spectacle for Crowd

The spectacle included not only the rousing fight but all of the side show that goes with an Army-Navy game. The gathering thrilled to the sight of the corps of 2,100 cadets and the brigade of 2,700 midshipmen swinging along on the field in faultless files.

It revelled in their unrivaled lung power in keeping up a constant roar of songs and cheers and was entertained by the parade of an Army tank and a Navy battleship. Bill X, the Navy goat, and Mr. Jackson and Poncho, the Army mules, emerged from the ship and

tank as the tank fired blank salutes and the battleship belched forth smoke.

The gathering was not only the year's largest but one of the most distinguished to attend an Army-Navy game. Surrounding President Truman were members of his Cabinet, the highest ranking flag officers of the Army and the Navy, Senators, Congressmen, Governors and members of the diplomatic corps.

The President, arriving shortly before the West Point corps paraded into the stadium, was escorted with Mrs. Truman and the members of his party to his box, roped off by a square cordon of Pinkertons and Secret Service men. Mr. Truman sat on the Navy side for the first half of the game.

During the intermission, he was escorted by Vice Admiral Aubrey V. Fitch, Superintendent of the Naval Academy, and Rear Admiral Stuart H. Ingersoll, commandant of midshipmen, to the center of the field. There he was met by Maj. Gen. Maxwell D. Taylor, Superintendent of the Military Academy, and Brig. Gen. Gerald J. Higgins, commandant of the corps of cadets.

The President then was convoyed to his box on Army's side for the second half. As it turned out, the President was sitting on the wrong side each half. While he was on the Navy side Army was squarely in command of the play, and once he joined the cadets, Navy took over control of the game.

The turn in the tide came shortly after the second half got under way. Army took the opening kick-off after the intermission and went down to Navy's 31-yard mark. It seemed that the cadets were going to increase their 21-6 lead by another touchdown. But on fourth

down, with 2 yards to go for a first down, Army elected to kick.

That decision, and another that came just before the end of the third period, had a vital bearing on the transformation that took place in the play.

Might Have Gone On

Had Army chosen to gamble for a first down, and it would not have been much of a gamble with the ball well in Navy territory, it might have continued on to score. It was after Davis had kicked out of bounds for only ten yards that Navy started on its 78-yard touchdown march.

The decision that came later was a real gamble, and it turned out badly. Probably influenced by the great offensive strength that Navy had shown on its touchdown march, Army elected to try for a first down deep in its own territory. Less than a yard was needed on the fourth down and Blanchard was sent into the line.

The midshipmen stopped him like a stone wall, and as a result the cadets gave up possession on their own 35. It was from there that the middies went on to their third touchdown, which came on the third play of the final quarter.

The touchdown play was one of the cleverest of the day and was typical of the resourcefulness and enterprise of Captain Hamilton's team. On fourth down, with the ball on the three, Earl took a lateral and fired the ball straight into the arms of Bramlett in the end zone for the score.

To start at the beginning, Navy took the opening kick-off, after Captain Bramlett had won the toss, and went down to Army's 45. Baysinger kicked into the end zone and Army started on its 20. Blanchard made a first down and then Davis fumbled, Newbold Smith recovering for Navy on Army's 32. The middies got to the 26 and then Baysinger fumbled as he was tackled by Poole, and Art Gerometta recovered for Army on his 37. Now Army was on its way.

In four plays the cadets went sixty-two yards for their first touchdown. After a buck had gained two yards, Tucker fired a pass to Davis, who had gone in motion from the T-formation. The rapid halfback streaked down the sideline 46 yards. Blanchard got a yard and then Davis took a pitchout pass from Tucker, shook off three tacklers and went the 13 yards to the goal line.

Navy's answer to this characteristic example of Army striking power was to take the next kickoff and go all the way, 81 yards. Baysinger, who was an unknown until the Notre Dame game and who covered himself with glory with his passing, running of the team and kicking today, engineered the touchdown drive with the skill and poise of a veteran.

Williams and Myron Gerber did most of the carrying. Baysinger fired a pass to Art Markel for 11 and another to Bramlett for 32, putting the ball on the 2. Baysinger then made the touchdown on a quarterback sneak from a foot out. Bob Van Summern's try for the extra point was blocked, and Army led by the conversion of Jack Ray.

Ray was to kick the extra point after all three of Army's touchdowns to furnish the margin of victory. So he stood as one of Army's heroes of the day.

Army now proceeded to answer Navy in kind. And it went exactly the same distance that the Middies had gone, 81 yards, and took fewer plays. After Blanchard and Davis had carried to the 40, Tucker pitched out to Davis for 11. The scoring play was a 52-yard gallop by Blanchard. The Army fullback burst through the line and sprinted almost with the speed of Davis in outdistancing his Navy pursuers.

A break set up Army's third touchdown, which followed in this second quarter. Bill Yeomans intercepted Baysinger's pass. Army started on Navy's 38-yard mark. In just three plays the ball was across.

Davis Fires to Blanchard

Davis passed to Poole for 8 and then ran for 4. On the next scrimmage, Davis, taking a direct pass from center, fired like a flash to Blanchard, who had gone in motion to the left. The big fullback went 26 - yards, and Army led, 21—6, after Ray had booted the extra point.

Before the half ended, the ball changed hands rapidly on an amazing one-hand interception by Davis, Jim Carrington's recovery of an Army fumble, and Rip Rowan's interception of another pass.

The second half started with Army going to the Navy 32 and then kicking. Navy, taking the ball on its 22, went 78 yards, with Williams, Gerber and Hawkins carrying. An interference penalty against Army kept the march alive.

Baysinger passed 18 yards to Markel over center, Williams got down to the 4 on a shovel pass, and Hawkins scored from the 2-yard mark. Hawkins failed on the try for the extra point and the score was 21—12.

Statistics of the Game

	Army.	Navy.
First downs	8	20
Yards gained, rushing.	185	163
Forward passes	10	19
Forwards completed	6	11
Yards gained, forwards.	106	136
Forwards intercepted by	3	1
Number of punts	3	3
*Av. dist. of punts, yds.	30	32
Run-back of punts, yds..	0	12
Fumbles	3	3
Own fumbles recovered.	1	2
Penalties	5	5
Yards lost, penalties....	29	25
*From line of scrimmage.

On the next kick-off, Blanchard ran the ball back to his 25 and then he and Davis carried to within inches of a first down. Army decided to gamble on a first down and Blanchard was stopped without gain. Navy took over on Army's 35 and went on to its third touchdown.

Earl passed to Bramlett for 14 and Hawkins, who was wearing a brace on his knee but was surprisingly fast, broke through the middle for 16, putting the ball on the 5. A play failed to gain as the quarter ended.

Hawkins made two yards to start the final period, and then Bramlett took the pass from Earl for the touchdown. Again Hawkins' try for the extra point failed and the score was 21—18.

Crowd Is Stirred

The crowd was in a state of high excitement now. Navy had completely taken the play away from Army, and it was a question whether the middies could be held in check.

Army now started as though it would put an end to the middies' uprising. After Rowan had brought the kick-off back to his 32, Davis broke loose around left end, streaking along sideline 29 yards to Navy's 39. Now it was the cadet corps' turn to do some whole-hearted cheering for the first time in a long spell.

Apparently Army was on the way again. But on the next play Davis fired a long pass and Pete Williams intercepted. That was the last time Army made any kind of offensive gesture. The first down that Davis had made on his long run was the Army's first and last of the quarter. It had made only one in the third period, while Navy was to roll up eleven in the second half.

Navy started its final thrilling march after Davis had kicked and Williams had returned the punt to Navy's 33. Captain Hamilton, who made clever use of his substitutes, sent in Chewning, who was fresh and eager for heavy duty. A pass from Williams to Phil Ryan, substitute end, netted 17. Williams and McCully, who also had been on the injured list, carried the ball to the 23. Army held here, but on fourth down Chewning broke away for 20 yards to the 3, as previously related.

Then came the maddest ninety seconds any ball game could possibly know, ending with the ball on Army's 5 and Earl Blaik's badly expended but dead game team the winner by 21—18.

With their handful of reserves, the cadets just barely made it, to save their great record. Blanchard and Davis played the entire sixty minutes in their farewell to college football, and Tucker was in for all but a minute or two. Bay-

singer, the find of the year at Navy, played almost the entire game and turned in a job to swell the heart of his father, Syracuse's famous Ribs Baysinger.

The whole Navy team did a tremendous job, and there was nothing wrong with an Army team that fought under fearful pressure all year with few replacements and still had enough to stand off the terrific challenge of the midshipmen. It was only by an eyelash that the cadets prevented repetition of the stunning upset the midshipmen sprang at Annapolis in 1942.

The line-up:

ARMY (21)		NAVY (18)
Poole	L.E.	Markel
Biles	L.T.	E. N. Smith
Steffy	L.G.	Emerson
Enos	C.	Scott
Gerometta	R.G.	Carrington
Bryant	R.T.	Shimshak
Foldberg	R.E.	Bramlett
Tucker	Q.B.	Baysinger
Davis	L.H.	Williams
Rowan	R.H.	Schwoeffermann
Blanchard	F.B.	Gerber

SCORE BY PERIODS

Army .... 7 14 0 0—21
Navy .... 0 6 6 6—18

Touchdowns—Blanchard 2, Davis, Baysinger, Hawkins, Bramlett. Points after touchdown—Ray 3 (placements).

SUBSTITUTES

Army—Ends: Hayes, Rawers. Tackles: Tavzel, Feir. Guards: Ray, Drury. Centers—Livesay, Yeomans. Backs—Fuson, Gustafson.

Navy—Ends: Tatom, Russell, Ryan. Tackle: Lawrence. Guards: Golding, Hunt. Center: Jesse. Backs: Van Summern, Welsh, McCully, Chewning, Schiweck, Earl, Ambrogi, Hawkins. Referee—William T. Halloran. Providence. Umpire—Frank S. Bergin, Princeton. Linesman—James J. Allinger, Buffalo. Field judge—Fred R. Wallace, Washington.

December 1, 1946

DAVIS, BLANCHARD SCORED 537 POINTS

Paced Army's 3-Year 1,179 on Totals of 306, 231, Aiding With 89 Touchdowns

WEST POINT, N. Y., Dec. 1 (AP) —Glenn Davis and Doc Blanchard, who ended their college football careers at Philadelphia yesterday, scored 537 of the 1,179 points rolled up during the past three seasons by unbeaten Army. Between them they scored eighty-nine touchdowns to pace the cadets to twenty-seven victories and one tie through the 1944, 1945 and 1946 seasons.

Davis crossed the goal line fifty-one times to score a total of 306 points, while Blanchard crashed into pay dirt thirty-eight times and booted three conversions to amass 231 points.

Davis' greatest season was in 1944 when he scored twenty touchdowns. Blanchard's best year was 1945 when he crossed the goal line nineteen times and added a point after touchdown.

Their scoring record by years:

	TD.	Pat.	T.		TD.	Pat.	T.	Year.
	20	0	120		9	0	54	1944
Davis..	18	0	108	Blanchard	19	1	115	1945
	13	0	78		10	2	62	1946
Total..	51	0	306	Total..	38	3	231	

December 2, 1946

COLUMBIA TOPS ARMY, 21-20

LIONS SCORE UPSET

Army Has 20-7 Lead at Half-Time, but Bows to Columbia Rally

By LOUIS EFFRAT

Columbia 21, Army 20!

A typographical error? No—a thousand times no—and the 35,000 fans at Baker Field yesterday will attest to the authenticity of Columbia's greatest gridiron achievement: a totally unexpected victory that overshadowed even the magnificent Rose Bowl conquest of Jan. 1, 1934, when the Lions beat Stanford.

After thirty-two straight games in which Army had not known defeat, Earl Blaik's cadets appeared to be en route to another triumph yesterday. They battered Columbia almost at will throughout a lopsided first half and enjoyed a 20-7 margin at the intermission. Up to that point the Lions had had no ground attack to speak of and most of their gains overhead were made possible because of spectacular catches rather than by the passing of Gene Rossides.

True, the West Point offense, overpowering though it was, lacked smoothness, but it still was potent enough to grind out the yardage. Army's speedy backs, operating behind so rugged a line, had, it seemed, a comfortable lead that was likely to be widened later. Apparently Columbia once again had been overmatched.

Dominates Third Period

However, a half is only 50 per cent of the whole, and Columbia proceeded to prove this truism after the rest period. Except for one drive that brought Army to the Lions' 15-yard line, where the defense tightened and took over, the Light Blue dominated the scoreless third period. Lou Little's men then took charge of the last quarter and won going away, after having fashioned two touchdowns and conversions.

When the game ended with Columbia deep in Army territory, but more concerned over clinging to its 1-point margin than increasing it, the victors hoisted one of their mates on their shoulders and carried him from the field. He was Bill Swiacki, a pass-catching end who, more than any individual, was responsible for one of the biggest upsets of this, or any, campaign.

Swiacki caught eight passes. Half of these were the result of his own individual brilliance, and the one he snared in the end zone, the one that brought the Lions into contention at 3:32 of the final period, will have to rank with the great catches of all time. Nothing like it has been seen here since Al Gionfriddo robbed Joe DiMaggio in the sixth game of the 1947 world series.

Set All-Time Mark

It was Swiacki, who hails from Southbridge, Mass., and is playing his last season at Morningside Heights, who helped make possible an all-time Columbia passing record. Rossides and Lou Kusserow, who were on the firing end, completed twenty aerials. Eighteen of them were by Rossides. The old mark of eighteen completions was set by Sid Luckman against Army in 1937 and tied by Paul Governali against Michigan in 1941 and Colgate next season.

Swiacki it was, too, who paved the way for the deciding tally when he made another great catch of a twenty-six-yard pass by Rossides, good for a first down on the Army 3-yard line, midway in the closing chapter. Two plays later Kusserow went over. Ventan Yablonski, who hadn't failed on his first two conversion attempts, booted the vital extra point and Columbia was on top, 21—20.

This was a sad moment in Army football history. It was the first time since Oct. 12, 1946 that the cadets had fallen behind. About six and a half minutes later, when

Bill Swiacki reaching out to make a diving catch of pass tossed by Gene Rossides for a 26-yard gain, putting the ball on the 3-yard line and setting the stage for the third Columbia touchdown, the scoring of which is shown at the right. *Associated Press*

the gun barked, they still were in the red and one of the most amazing "defeatless" strings had been snapped.

The poise that had been so characteristic of Blaik's teams through the four-season span of the streak was missing yesterday, even when the West Pointers were showing the way. Rip Rowan, Arnie Galiffa and Bill Gustafson showed sporadic speed and power, especially Rowan.

When it came to filling the shoes of the departed Doc Blanchard, Arnold Tucker and Glenn Davis, however, they were dwarfed. The yardage was amassed and at times a cadet got off a long run but virtually all of Army's destructive offense was crowded into the first thirty minutes.

Columbia, of course, must have had something to do with the eclipse of the visitors' attack—and the collapse of the heretofore perfect defense. Rossides, after a wobbly start, improved his pitching and, with Swiacki and Bruce Gehrke contributing handsomely on the receiving end, Columbia was the aggressor—determined, confident, irrepressible.

That the Lions were confident was evident in the closing minute of the first half. At that stage, though trailing by 14—7, they elected to try for a field goal by Yablonski from the 13-yard line. It failed, but this was the tip-off that the Light Blue felt certain it would score later. It did—more than once.

Rowan, Blanchard's understudy last year, did some excellent running for a futile cause. The second-half let-down by the Black Knights nullified all his good work. Rowan, who must rate alongside the fleetest fullbacks in the nation, scored two touchdowns. Galiffa accounted for the other, the first in the contest.

The game was less than five minutes old when Army tallied, going all the way the first time it had the ball. A 55-yard advance, sparked by Rowan, was climaxed on the ninth play when Galiffa went over from the 2-foot line on a quarterback sneak. Jack Mackmull added the point.

Army's Long Football Streak

1944		1946	
Army...46	North Carolina 0	Army...35	Villavona 0
Army...59	Brown 7	Army...21	Oklahoma 7
Army...69	Pittsburgh 7	Army...46	Cornell 21
Army...76	U. S. Coast G. Acad.. 0	Army...20	Michigan 13
Army...27	Duke 7	Army...48	Columbia 14
Army...83	Villanova 0	Army...19	Duke 0
Army...59	Notre Dame........ 0	Army...19	West Virginia 0
Army...62	Pennsylvania 7	Army... 0	Notre Dame.....(tie) 0
Army...23	Navy 7	Army...34	Pennsylvania 7
		Army...21	Navy 18

Totals—Army nine victories, no defeats. Army points 504, opponents 35.

Totals—Army nine victories, one tie. Army points 263, opponents 80.

1945		1947	
Army...32	Pers'nel Dist. Comd. 0	Army...13	Villanova 0
Army...54	Wake Forest........ 0	Army...40	Colorado 0
Army...28	Michigan 7	Army... 0	Illinois ....(tie) 0
Army...55	Melville (R. I.) Pt.	Army...40	Virginia Tech....... 0
	Boat School 13	Army...20	Columbia 21
Army...48	Duke 13		
Army...54	Villanova 0		
Army...48	Notre Dame......... 0		
Army...61	Pennsylvania 0		
Army...32	Navy 13		

Totals—Army nine victories, no defeats. Army points 412, opponents 46.

Totals—Army three victories, one tie, one defeat. Army points 113, opponents 21.

Grand totals—Army 30 victories, 2 ties, 1 defeat. Army points 1,292, opponents 182.

Gustafson Intercepts Pass

It continued to be all Army in the opening period. After Gustafson's interception of a Columbia aerial, Win Scott and Bobby Jack Stuart went to a first down on the Columbia 15. Two plunges by Rowan brought the cadets to the 9. There, Charley Gabriel's pass was thefted by Al Kachadurian on the goal line to frustrate the visitors.

Amos Gillette, Gustafson and Rowan sparkplugged an Army drive that was good for 61 yards and a touchdown in the second quarter. After Gustafson gained

28 yards to the 1, Rowan bulled his way over his own right guard and Mackmull place-kicked the point for a 14-0 margin.

Stymied by the hard-rushing Army line, the Lions had been accomplishing next to nothing until Rossides completed three successive aerials, the first to Gehrke and the next two to Swiacki. Every catch was sensational. In less than two minutes, the Lions gained 53 yards overhead before Kusserow, taking a hand-off from Rossides, crashed over the right side for 6 yards and a tally. Yablonski's kick was perfect.

The remaining minutes of the half produced a series of thrills as George Kisiday recovered a Galiffa fumble on the Army 4-yard line. Kusserow bucked to the 1, but the referee ruled that it was no go because he had not put the ball in play. Columbia did not get that close in three tries and Yablonski unsuccessfully attempted to get three points via a field goal.

Longest Run of Day

Army took over at the 20, Gabriel made a yard, but on the next efforts the Cadets were penalized to their 16 for illegal backfield motion. Then came the day's longest and best run, an 84-yard touchdown dash along the sideline by Rowan. It started as a routine off-tackle slant, but Rip switched to the outside and he was off. On the way Rowan shook off at least three would-be tacklers.

Statistics of the Game

	Colum.	Army.
First downs	18	12
Yards gained, rushing	100	302
Forward passes	30	10
Forwards completed	20	4
Yards gained, forwards	263	42
Forwards intercepted, by	2	1
Number of punts	6	5
*Av. dist. of punts, yds.	39.7	31.8
Run-back of punts, yds.	23	71
Fumbles	2	2
Own fumbles, recovered	1	1
Penalties	4	11
Yards lost, penalties	30	74

*From line of scrimmage.

Army's bad break, though it didn't strike home at the moment, was Mackmull's failure to add the point.

The third chapter was scoreless, but Rossides completed eight passes and Kusserow one, an omen of what was in the offing.

Early in the fourth period Rossides passed twice to Bill Olson for 16 and 11 yards. Rossides picked up 5 on a sneak and then Swiacki came through with his acrobatic catch in the end zone. It was a diving, sliding execution that won the admiration of all except Army followers. Yablonski's boot was good and now only six points separated the teams.

Stuart ran the kick-off from his end zone 32 yards to the Army 27.

Rowan added 18, Stuart 7 and a Galiffa-to-John Trent pass made it first down on Columbia's 34. When Stuart gained 6 it appeared as if Army was headed in the right direction. There, however, the Lions stopped the cadets cold and took over.

With eight and a half minutes left, the home team was confronted with the problem of negotiating sixty-six yards. It did, in six plays and in exactly 1 minute and 27 seconds. The quarterbacking of Rossides in this drive was flawless, clever.

Spotting Army spread out in a 5-man-line defense, Rossides sent Yablonski off tackle for a first down on the Lion 45. Then he sneaked twenty-two yards himself to the Army 33 and Kusserow went to the 29. Now the cadets were back in a 6-man line, so Rossides fired a pass to Swiacki and it was first down on the 3. The rest is history.

A Deafening Roar

Rossides gained a yard, and then handed the ball to Kusserow for the touchdown. The roar that greeted Yablonski's conversion—the winning point—was deafening.

Army desperately went aloft then, and Galiffa hit Rowan with a thirty-yard pass, but that one was recalled for offside. Galiffa then fired to Trent for eight yards, but when he tried to click with another aerial Kusserow intercepted and that was the end of the streak.

The line-up:

COLUMBIA (21)		ARMY (20)
Swiacki	L.E.	Rawas
Briggs	L.T.	Galloway
Karas	L.G.	Steffy
Hampton	C.	Yeoman
Klemovich	R.G.	Henry
O'Shaughnessy	R.T.	Bryant
Gehrke	R.E.	Trent
Rossides	Q.B.	Galiffa
Kusserow	L.H.	Stuart
Olson	R.H.	Shelley
Yablonski	F.B.	Mackmull

SCORE BY PERIODS

| Columbia | 0 | 7 | 0 | 14—21 |
| Army | 7 | 13 | 0 | 0—20 |

Touchdowns—Galiffa, Rowan 2, Kusserow 2, Swiacki. Points after touchdowns—Mackmull 2, Yablonski 3.

SUBSTITUTES

Columbia—Ends: Kisiday, Rakowski. Tackles: Hasselman. Guards: Bacauskas, Chaky. Center: Shekitka. Backs: Kachadurian, Lincoln, Nork, Russell, Van Bellingham.

Army—Ends: Aton, Kellum. Tackles: Davis, Feir. Guards: Barnes, Lunn. Center: Livesay. Backs: Dielens, Gabriel, Gillette, Gradoville, Gustafson, Rowan, Scott.

Referee—Joseph H. Williams (Bucknell). Umpire—Frank S. Bergin (Princeton). Linesman—William J. McConnell (Middlebury). Field judge—Raymond J. Barbuti (Syracuse).

October 26, 1947

ARMY UPSETS MICHIGAN, 21 TO 7

CADETS STUN 97,000

Break 25-Game Winning Streak Begun in 1946 by Michigan Eleven

ARMY LEADS AT HALF, 14-0

Fischl, Cain, Kuckhahn Score as Team Extends Unbeaten String to 14 Contests

By ALLISON DANZIG
Special to The New York Times.

ANN ARBOR, Mich., Oct. 8—The longest winning streak compiled by a major college football team in twenty-five years ended today as Michigan, the nation's top-ranking eleven, was toppled by Army, 21—7.

Before 97,000 stunned Wolverine fans, Earl Blaik's Black Knights from the Hudson, underdogs by from one to three touchdowns, showed the Middle West some of the most savage tackling, hardest running and finest pass offense and defense ever exhibited by a team from the East to gain a smashing victory.

With 250 West Point cadets from the senior class roaring their approval in an ecstasy of joy, Army went 88 yards in ten plays to score in the first quarter and capitalized a fumble to go 10 yards in one swoop for another touchdown early in the second period. After a scoreless third quarter Michigan, profiting by a fumbled pass from center on fourth down by Army, went 31 yards to score early in the final period. Then, with less than three minutes remaining, the cadets broke the hearts of the huge crowd by going across a third time on an advance of 29 yards in two plays.

Mackmull Adds 3 Points

Karl Kuckhahn, filling in for the injured Gil Stephenson and doing a tremendous job with his powerful running through the middle; Jim Cain and Frank Fischl scored the Army touchdowns, and Jack Mackmull, old reliable among extra-point specialists, booted the ball through the uprights each time. Don Dufek, hard-hitting fullback, tallied for Michigan.

The defeat, a bitter pill for Western Conference football, was the first for the Wolverines since the middle of the 1946 season and ended a winning sequence of twenty-five games. Had they triumphed, they would have tied the modern record set by Cornell from 1921 to 1924.

The setback was all the harder for Michigan to swallow since it had lost to Army on the occasion of their only two other meetings, in 1945 and 1946. No other football team on record has beaten the Wolverines three times in succession.

In downing the eleven ranked with Notre Dame as the top team of 1947 and again in 1948, Army extended its sequence of games in which it has gone undefeated to 14. Rated seventh in the current national ranking, the cadets, who had won from Davidson and Penn State in their first two games, now will take their place again near the head of the parade, where they were entrenched in the days of Doc Blanchard and Glenn Davis.

Galiffa at His Best

There was no Blanchard or Davis to lead the cadets to victory over Michigan as in the two previous clashes of the teams, but Army had a superb quarterback in Arnold Galiffa, who ran and passed as he never had before; a battering fullback in the 190-pound Kuckhahn, a brilliant running halfback in Cain and a sterling pass catcher in End Bill Kellum.

But the undoing of mighty Michigan, which had given so hard a thumping to Stanford last week, definitely was not the handiwork of any individual so much as a team job. From the first play, this Army outfit demonstrated that it could play the rough and tough football indigenous to the Middle West, and it shut down so hard on the Wolverines with the fierceness of its tackling that the crowd sensed forthwith that this was to be no picnic for its heroes.

On the second scrimmage, Charley Ortmann, brilliant halfback and one of Michigan's most valuable operatives, went down and had to be carried from the field on a stretcher. Up to then, the crowd probably had felt a bit sorry for Army and the licking it was expected to take.

It had reveled and taken pride in the tingling spectacle provided by its magnificent marching band of 125 pieces before the hostilities started, and it had every confidence that its stalwarts in maize and blue would give the same sort of superior performance. The little band of West Point seniors, a pinpoint of slate gray in the huge panorama of shirt-sleeved humanity on this Indian summer day, hardly was more engulfed than its team was expected to be.

The bitter disillusionment of the huge throng can be attributed simply to Army's solid grounding in the fundamentals of blocking and tackling and to the soundness of its coaching. It was beautifully trained physically and expertly equipped with attacking plays from the T formation and with a

Jim Cain of the cadets (running in white shirt) breaking away from a Michigan player as he swept end for 10 yards and a touchdown in the second quarter at Ann Arbor yesterday.

Associated Press Wirephoto

defense, mainly 6-2-2-1, that was particularly throttling against passes, but in the final analysis it was the toughness with which the cadets played the game that proved too much for Michigan wits its big line and dangerous backs.

Bruce Ackerson at tackle, Ralph Kaseman at guard and the ends who were throwing themselves so recklessly at the Michigan blockers won this game for Army as much as did the offensive heroes. Outstanding, too, were Hal Shultz, who intercepted two passes and knocked down more; the backers-up, Don Beck and Elmer Stout; and Tom Brown, with his punting, fine work as safety and an interception that turned the tide in Army's favor again when it was running heavily against the cadets.

Brown's interception occurred a few minutes after Michigan had scored early in the final quarter. Walter Teninga, work-horse of the Wolverine backfield, intercepted a pass on the cadets' 42 immediately following Army's return of the kick-off and Bennie Oosterbaan's team was on the way to what seemed the tying score. Leo Koceski, fast wingback in the single wing attack, made a first down on the 25 on one of his many reverses and Dufek went through a big hole to the 17.

The stadium was in an uproar. It seemed that Army finally was breaking under the strain and no longer had the physical strength to contain the speed and power which had been threatening over and over, only to fizzle out up to the end of the third period.

Then, suddenly, the bedlam ended with a gasp of stunning disappointment. Charley Lentz, substitute left halfback, fired a pass into the end zone, where Brown

snatched the ball and touched it down. Michigan had missed its big chance and every one sensed that this must be the end of its hopes. Why Michigan resorted to the pass on second down when its running attack was going so irresistibly was not easy to understand. Its passing had been dismally unsuccessful throughout the afternoon, as shown by the fact that it completed only three aerials of twenty-three attempted for 16 yards. In its drive of 31 yards to its touchdown it had gained 7 yards through the air, but it was its running attack that was shattering Army's defenses, and possibly had it continued to run it would have tied the game.

In the second period the Wolverines were so futile in their passing, both because of the inability of the receivers to hold the ball as well as Army's defense, that they abandoned the air arm to start the second half. The difference in their favor was immediately noticeable.

Penalty Checks Advance

Dufek and Koceski took the ball all the way down to Army's 18 after Koceski had run back the kick-off to his 30. That threat was halted by a penalty for illegal use of the hands, the only one inflicted on the Wolverines all afternoon.

Army's opening period touchdown march of 88 yards was the work largely of Galiffa and Kuckhahn, who played almost all of the game as offensive fullback, with Stephenson limited to a couple of plays because of his leg injury. Galiffa threw three passes for 52 yards to Kellum and Dan Foldberg and picked up ground on clever delayed runs.

Kuckhahn started the assault with a 10-yard smash and put the ball on the 5 with another dash.

through right tackle. On the next play Fischl raced around his left end for the score. Teninga and Tony Momsen had shots at him, but neither could hold him.

Michigan had a big chance late in this period after it had moved the ball 35 yards past midfield. Teninga punted and Shultz ran the ball back to his 12. Army was penalized to its 1-yard line and Brown kicked from his end zone.

The punt was partially blocked and Michigan took over on Army's 16, but Army's might on the defense and Michigan's weak passing attack ruined this opportunity. Three successive aerials by Teninga failed to reach their mark.

Army moved the ball from its 15 to Michigan's 28 early in the second quarter, but a penalty, one of many the cadets suffered, nullified Galiffa's 25-yard pass to Kellum, so Brown had to kick. On the first play afterward, John Ghindia, unknown quarterback who had been moved up to the first string in the Stanford game and had been expected to play so important a role for Michigan, fumbled.

Ackerson recovered the ball in the air on the 15 and ran to the 10. On the next scrimmage Cain went around his right end to score, with the help of a block thrown by Bruce Elmblad on Lentz at the line of scrimmage.

For the rest of the period Michigan was bottled in its territory, throwing passes that never succeeded. Two were intercepted, one by Stout and the other by Shultz. Army had the ball on the Wolverines' 20, but Lentz intercepted there to prevent a score.

A double dose of bad luck for Army late in the third period put Michigan in position for its score. Brown got off a superb kick of

Statistics of the Game

	Army.	Mich.
First downs	13	12
Yards gained, rushing	171	187
Forward passes	12	23
Forwards completed	5	3
Yards gained, forwards	76	16
Forwards intercepted by	4	3
Number of punts	7	8
*Av. dist. punts, yds.	33	38
Run-back of punts, yds.	81	85
Fumbles	4	2
Own fumbles recovered	4	1
Penalties	9	1
Yards lost, penalties	71	15

*From line of scrimmage.

sixty-two yards that went out of bounds on the 3, in spite of the fact that he had to reach high for the pass from center.

The ball was taken back because of Army's illegal use of the hands. Brown dropped back to kick again, and this time he was unable to hold the pass from center. Unable to kick, he tried to run and was downed on his 31. It was from there that the Wolverines went for their score, Dufek leaping across from the 1-foot mark.

The line-up:

ARMY (21)
Left Ends—Lehlein, Foldberg, Kuyk.
Left Tackles—Shira, Elmblad, Henn, McDaniel.
Left Guards—Kaseman, Lunn, Mackmull.
Centers—Maladowitz, Stout, Henrickson.
Right Guards—Galloway, Irons, Thieme, Cox, Kelly.
Right Tackles—Ackerson, Davis, Kimmel, Haas.
Right Ends—Trent, Kellum, Stone, Roberts.
Quarterbacks—Brown, Galiffa, Blaik.
Left Halfbacks—Shultz, Cain, Pollock.
Right Halfbacks—Abelman, Fischl, Martin.
Fullbacks—Beck, Kuckhahn, Johnson, Stephenson.

MICHIGAN (7)
Left Ends—Allis, Clark, Sutherland.
Left Tackles—Johnson, Wistert, Hess.
Left Guards—Jackson, Heneveld.
Centers—Erben, Momsen, Farrer, Sauls.
Right Guards—McClelland, Wolter.
Right Tackles—Atchison, Wahl.
Right Ends—Wisniewski, Hollway, Ray, Skala.
Quarterbacks—Ghindia, Pubick.
Left Halfbacks—Ortmann, Tennings, Lentz.
Right Halfbacks—Koceski, Van Summern.
Fullbacks—Kempthorn, Dufek, D. Peterson, T. Peterson.

October 9, 1949

Thorpe Hailed as Greatest Player On Gridiron in Past Fifty Years

Jim Thorpe, whom his Indian mother named Bright Path, was the greatest football player thus far this century in the United States, in the opinion of sports writers and broadcasters who participated in the Associated Press' poll.

Thorpe combined the Irishman's love of combat, which he inherited from his father, with the Indian's cunning and grace to gain his place in the sport's hall of fame in 1911 and 1912, playing left halfback for the now defunct Carlisle, Pa., Indian School.

None of the modern players, benefited by the game's amazing growth through the intervening four decades, could nudge the 6-foot-2-inch 190-pound Sac and Fox warrior from first place.

Of 391 experts who took part in the midcentury poll, 170 put Thorpe on top for his almost legendary feats. Harold (Red) Grange, Illinois' Galloping Ghost of the mid-Twenties, was second with 138. Bronko Nagurski, Minnesota's strong man of the Grange era, was third with 38, followed by Ernie Nevers of Stanford and Sammy Baugh of Texas Christian. Each had seven votes.

Three Votes for Trippi

Charles Trippi of Georgia, whom Thorpe rates as the greatest player he, ever saw, got only three votes and finished eighth in the ranking. The Dixie Dynamo also was surpassed by Don Hutson of Alabama and George Gipp, Notre Dame immortal. Hutson received six votes, Gipp four.

Strangely enough, Thorpe bowed out of football in 1928 after his team, the Chicago Cardinals, lost to Grange and the Chicago Bears, 34 to 0. An Associated Press account of the game says Thorpe "was unable to get anywhere. Now in his forties and muscle bound, he was a mere shadow of his former self."

Thorpe was born near Prague, Okla., in 1888, one of twin boys. The brother died of pneumonia shortly after his eighth birthday. By 1903 the budding athlete was at Carlisle, hoping to become an electrician. When it was discovered that Carlisle did not offer such a course, he switched to the tailoring school and thus got his first chance to play football as a guard on the tailor eleven.

But it was nearly two years later that he first attracted attention of the school's coach, Glenn (Pop) Warner, and then as a high jumper. Warner, at the time, rated himself more a track coach than a football mentor.

During virtually the entire 1907 season Thorpe sat on the bench, but in 1908, when the Indians' regular halfback was injured, he sped 65 and 85 yards for touchdowns that brought the tiny school an upset triumph over mighty Pennsylvania.

Played Pro Baseball

By season's end he was the most talked about athlete in Pennsylvania and Warner looked ahead with pleasure. But Thorpe failed to return to school in 1909 and again in 1910. Subsequent athletic history reveals that he was playing professional baseball—an action that later cost Thorpe his Olympic medals and trophies after having been called the world's greatest athlete by the King of Sweden.

He was lured back to Carlisle in 1911 by Warner, still track minded, who promised Thorpe that if he returned and practiced, the Indian could make the 1912 Olympic team.

Then followed two of the greatest football years ever enjoyed by any athlete, capped by being named to Walter Camp's All-America team for both years.

For many football followers Thorpe's exhibition in the 1911 game against Harvard, then the ruler of the football universe, was the greatest of his career. Thorpe himself rates the 1912 game with Army as the greatest thrill of his football career.

He finished that day by gaining 22 of the Indians' 27 points. Army, second only to Harvard in Eastern rankings, had 6.

Against Harvard, with his legs encased in bandages because of the pounding they had taken in victories over Lafayette and Penn, Thorpe kicked four field goals and plunged 70 yards in nine plays for a touchdown that brought the Indians an 18-to-15 victory. The decisive field goal was booted from the 48-yard line.

After his college career, he turned to professional football with the Canton, Ohio, Bulldogs.

The complete poll follows:

Jim Thorpe with Carlisle Indian School team forty years ago

Associated Press

	Votes
James Thorpe, Carlisle	170
Harold (Red) Grange, Illinois	138
Bronko Nagurski, Minnesota	38
Ernie Nevers, Stanford	7
Sammy Baugh, Texas Christian	7
Don Hutson, Alabama	6
George Gipp, Notre Dame	4
Charles Trippi, Georgia	3

Others receiving votes were Sid Luckman, Columbia, Steve Van Buren, Louisiana State, Willie Heston, Michigan, and Chick Harley, Ohio State, two each; Bill Henry, Washington and Jefferson; Bennie Oosterbaan, Michigan; Niles Kinnick, Iowa; Glenn Dobbs, Tulsa; Glenn Davis, Army; Clyde Turner, Hardin Simmons; Doak Walker, Southern Methodist; Frank Albert, Stanford; Felix (Doc) Blanchard, Army, and Charley Brickley, Harvard, one each.

January 25, 1950

NOTRE DAME UPSET BY PURDUE, 28-14

By The Associated Press.

SOUTH BEND, Ind., Oct. 7—Purdue today ended Notre Dame's reign of terror on the gridiron which had gone unchecked through thirty-nine games without defeat, the greatest record in modern college football.

The sophomore-dominated Boilermakers buried the Irish giant, 28—14, in a stunning upset that shocked the Notre Dame campus and left 56,748 fans shaking their heads in disbelief.

It was no fluke. Purdue, a 20-point underdog, outplayed the Irish in every category—including an overpowering fighting spirit and confidence.

The Boilermakers lashed to a 21-0 halftime lead. Notre Dame cut it to 21—14 by the outset of the fourth period.

This rally, unleashed as drizzle slicked the field, only pumped more fire into Purdue. The pent-up wrecking crew struck right back to score on a 56-yard pass play, Sophomore Dale Samuels to Mike Maccioli, and slam the door in Notre Dame's face.

The Notre Dame giant died without his seven-league boots on. Missing was his vaunted aerial attack and pulverizing running that had geared the gridiron Goliath through four seasons without a setback.

Last Loss to Service Team

The last time the Irish had been beaten was by 39-7 by the Great Lakes Naval Service team on Dec. 1, 1945. Since then thirty-seven teams folded before them. Army, with a 0-0 deadlock in 1946, and Southern California, with a 14-14 standstill in 1948, were close to victory but that was all.

It was Notre Dame's first loss at home since Michigan won, 32—20, in the eighth game of the 1942 season.

It was only the fourth defeat for a Frank Leahy-coached team in eight seasons. His Irish have won 62 and tied five.

Leahy's pre-season plaint that Notre Dame would drop several engagements had been taken with a bit of salt, but after the Irish had to go all out to shade North Carolina, 14—7, in the opener a week ago, observers could see that Leahy might be right. Purdue's victory over the nation's top-ranking team proved it.

Notre Dame's line was ripped unmercifully, its pass attack and offense failed miserably. The giant was thoroughly whipped.

All-America Bob Williams, the great clutch shooter, tried 20

Record of Notre Dame Streak

SOUTH BEND, Ind., Oct. 8 (AP) —Notre Dame was defeated in the final game of the 1945 football season and escaped defeat again until today. Here is the string:

1946
Nothe Dame 26, Illinois 6.
Notre Dame 33, Pittsburgh 0
Notre Dame 49, Purdue 6.
Notre Dame 41, Iowa 6.
Notre Dame 28, Navy 0.
Notre Dame 0, Army 0.
Notre Dame 27, Northwestern 6.
Notre Dame 41, Tulane 0.
Notre Dame 26, Southern California 6.
Won eight, tied one.

1947
Notre Dame 40, Pittsburgh 6.
Notre Dame 22, Purdue 7.
Notre Dame 31, Nebraska 0.
Notre Dame 21, Iowa 0.
Notre Dame 27, Navy 7.
Notre Dame 27, Army 7.
Notre Dame 26, Northwestern 19.
Notre Dame 59, Tulane 6.
Notre Dame 38, Southern California 7.
Won nine.

1948
Notre Dame 28, Purdue 27.
Notre Dame 40, Pittsburgh 0.
Notre Dame 26, Michigan State 7.
Notre Dame 44, Nebraska 13.
Notre Dame 27, Iowa 12.
Notre Dame 41, Navy 7.
Notre Dame 42, Indiana 6.
Notre Dame 12, Northwestern 7.
Notre Dame 46, Washington 0.
Notre Dame 14, Southern California 14.
Won nine, tied one.

1949
Notre Dame 49, Indiana 6.
Notre Dame 27, Washington 7.
Notre Dame 35, Purdue 12.
Notre Dame 46, Tulane 7.
Notre Dame 40, Navy 0.
Notre Dame 34, Michigan State 21.
Notre Dame 42, North Carolina 6.
Notre Dame 28, Iowa 7.
Notre Dame 32, Southern California 0.
Notre Dame 27, Southern Methodist 20.
Won ten.

1950
Notre Dame 14, North Carolina 7.
Purdue 28, Notre Dame 14.

passes and completed only seven

A recovered Purdue fumble set up the first Irish touchdown. After two minutes in the third period, Williams passing four yards to End Jim Mutscheller.

Bill Barrett's 33-yard run ignited the second, made in the first 10 seconds of the finale. John Petitbon jarred over from the 6. This capped Notre Dame's only sustained drive, 57 yards in five plays.

Purdue's one touchdown in the first period and two in the second left the outcome inevitable. While the Boilermakers rolled up the 21-0 margin, Notre Dame was pushed from pillar to post and pierced beyond midfield only once.

That was in the second quarter with the help of a 15-yard roughing infraction against Purdue's high-spirited brigade — one thoroughly drilled by Coach Stu Holcomb in crisp downfield blocking and tackling and supercharged in the line. The Irish outrushed Purdue, 237 yards to 201, but most of the efforts were in midfield and out of threatening territory.

Purdue, led by the sensational sophomore, 161-pound Samuels from Chicago, gained 158 yards in the air. The Irish mustered only 46.

Purdue's veteran John Kerestes and Neil Schmidt picked up 81 and 80 yards, respectively, through and around the once-famed Notre Dame forward wall. Maccioli added 37 on the ground and 80 more with three of Samuels' passes. Schmidt, 170-pound ball of fire, traveled 71 yards with three other catches.

The outcome rested largely with the fact that Purdue pulled 58 rushing plays in all. Notre Dame had the ball long enough for only 38.

The clincher of the whole affair was Samuels' 56-yard scoring pass to Maccioli in the fourth period. It came after Notre Dame had

STATISTICS OF THE GAME

	Purdue	N. D.
First downs	18	17
Yards gained, rushing	201	237
Forward passes	21	22
Forwards completed	9	7
Yards gained, forwards	158	46
Forwards intercepted by	3	1
Number of punts	4	3
*Av. dist. of punts, yds.	42	34
Rival fumbles recovered	2	1
Yards lost, penalties	47	106

*From line of scrimmage.

shown signs of staging a typical comeback from a Leahy half-time pep talk.

Dick Cotter of Notre Dame recovered sophomore Phil Klezek's fumble on the Purdue 10 to touch off Williams' scoring toss to Mutscheller at the start of the third.

After the Irish had held Purdue on the 1, Notre Dame surged 57 yards for its second marker, to cut the lead to 21-14 with 10 seconds gone in the finale.

Following the ensuing kick-off, Samuels tried two unsuccessful tosses. Then he faded back and catapulted to Maccioli. He caught the ball on a dead run and galloped the 40 remaining yards with Petitbon nearly tackling him just short of the pay-off line.

The end of the Notre Dame victory march was accomplished by the oldest rival on the current schedule.

Home Winning Streak Ends at 28

Purdue's victory, which snapped the Irish home winning streak of 28 games, was its first after five consecutive losses and only its fifth in a series that began in 1896.

Purdue opened its season a week ago by losing, 34—26, to Texas.

Purdue made its sting felt in the first four minutes. Schmidt went 86 yards for an apparent touchdown but it was nullified by a ruling he had stepped out of bounds on the Purdue 26.

After that blow, the Boilermakers stormed 85 yards in 11 plays to the Notre Dame 1 before being stopped.

With one minute left in the first quarter, Purdue's high-spirited team capped a 74 yard push by springing Kerestes off tackle from the 2 on the tenth play of the drive. Schmidt's 18-yard sprint and Samuels' 28-yard toss to Schmidt, ruled complete on interference by Captain Jerry Groom, set up the first touchdown.

Purdue boosted the lead to 21—0 at half time. Kerestes again jammed off tackle from the 2 to score at the outset of the second period. Samuels' 35-yard pitch to Schmidt touched it off.

Just prior to this pay-off, Dale Schnaible's 45-yard runback of Williams' pass began a Purdue surge which reached the 4 before ending. Schmidt bobbled Samuels' lateral and lost seven yards.

One minute before half time, Samuels hit Schmidt with a 30-yard scoring toss to complete a 54-yard assault in five plays.

The line-up:

PURDUE (28)
Left Ends—Flowers, Sugar, Bringer.
Left Tackles—Janosek, Considine.
Left Guards—Deem, Jackson.
Centers—Knitz, Reed.
Right Guards—Hager, Skibinski.
Right Tackles—Beletic, Bruner.
Right Ends—Brewster, Banas, Crncic.
Quarterbacks—Samuels, Curtis, Schnaible, Jones, Mateja.
Left Halfbacks—Maggioli, Klezek.
Right Halfbacks—Schmidt.
Fullbacks—Kerestes, Montgomery, Kasperan, Heninger, Young.

NOTRE DAME (14)
Left Ends—Ostrowski, Kapish.
Left Tackles—B. Flynn, Zambroski, Zancha, Weithman.
Left Guards—Burns, Boji.
Center—Groom.
Right Guards—Wallner, F. Johnston.
Right Tackles—Toneff, Dunlay.
Right Ends—Mutscheller, Jonardi, Helwig, Kelly.
Quarterbacks—Williams, Mazur.
Left Halfbacks—Petitbon, Gay.
Right Halfbacks—Barrett, Flood, Bush, Marchand.
Fullbacks—Landry, Cotter, Gander, Caprara, Paolone.

SCORE BY PERIODS
Purdue .... 7 14 0 7—28
Notre Dame .... 0 0 7 7—14
Touchdowns—Kerestes 2, Schmidt, Maggioli, Mutscheller, Petitbon. Points after touchdown—Samuels 4, Caprara 2 (placements).

October 8, 1950

NAVY UPSETS ARMY, 14-2, ENDING CADET 28-GAME STREAK

ZASTROW IS STAR

Crosses First, Then His Pass to Baldinger Clicks for Navy

ARMY'S BACKS SHACKLED

By ALLISON DANZIG
Special to THE NEW YORK TIMES.

PHILADELPHIA, Dec. 2—The lightning of an infuriated band of Navy demons struck an overwhelmingly favored Army eleven, not a second but a third time, in

the same place at the Municipal Stadium today. Thus the team that had bowed to no foe since 1947 finally met its master in possibly the most shocking verdict of a season of bewildering reversals.

Battered and outplayed in almost every category by an opponent it was expected to humble by three touchdowns, Army came to the end of its twenty-eight-game sequence without defeat in a stunning 14-2 setback that marked Navy's first victory over the cadets since 1943.

A gathering of 101,000 spectators, among whom were President Truman, members of his Cabinet and generals and admirals galore, watched in amazement as the oft-beaten sailors from Crabtown tore into the second-ranking team of the country to give it a thumping

physical beating from which it will not soon recover.

Like so many wildcats, the gang-tackling midshipmen hurled themselves upon the big-name Army backs, to smother their running operations, and knock down and intercept their passes while their own fiery ball carriers were tearing loose and scoring through the air with their cleverly executed flanker T-formation attack.

The Clock Runs Out

It was 1946 and 1948 all over again. Four years ago a despised Navy team went on the rampage against the great Blanchard-Davis outfit, only to lose by 21—18 as the clock ran out with the middies inside the cadets' 5-yard line. In 1948 a West Point eleven that had won eight games, while Navy was losing eight, could do no better

than hold the rampant tars to a tie.

This time the long-suffering eleven from the Severn, playing under the direction of a new head coach, Eddie Erdelatz, finally broke the back of Army's resistance and won a glorious victory that was earned on merit beyond any question of doubt.

President Truman was a winner with Navy today and Truman "luck" came through for the third successive time. The Commander in Chief initiated the practice of remaining seated on the side of the host team in 1948, instead of crossing to the other side of the field at halftime, and that year he rejoiced with the midshipmen around him as the sailors gained a moral victory with their 21-21 tie. Last year Mr. Truman sat with Army as Earl Blaik's Black Knights gave Navy the worst beating in the fifty-one game history of the rivalry, a 38-0 decision.

Today, heavily guarded by an extra-large detail of Secret Service men, as well as by F-51 Mustangs patroling the skyway because of the attempt made on his life a month ago in Washington, the President was the guest of Vice Admiral Harry W. Hill, Superintendent of the Naval Academy. He had a royal good time again, even though the Commander-in-Chief is theoretically supposed to be neutral when the cadets do battle with the midshipmen.

It was Navy's day this drab, overcast but dry afternoon, from the time the captains of the teams, Tom Bakke of Annapolis and Dan Foldberg of West Point, assembled at the Presidential box with the coaches and Referee Paul N. Swaffield, for the spin-of the coin. The toss was won by Captain Bakke, who received, as did Folberg, a silver dollar from Mr. Truman, and that was an omen of what was to come, though there was no way of knowing it at the time.

It was not until the second quarter began that anyone had a real inkling of the disaster that was in store for an Army team that was seeking to complete its third successive season and its sixth in seven years without defeat and that was bent on demonstrating, at Navy's expense, that it had as much right as Oklahoma to rank as the No. 1 eleven of the country.

There was indication enough in the first quarter that the cadets were mixing with a lot of furies as they were stopped dead four times, once at the Annapolis 15 after taking possession on Navy's 22 as Quarterback Bob Cameron, who kicked so superbly all afternoon, was unable to get off a fourth-down punt and fumbled the ball. But even though Army could not move the ball and failed to make a first down in the quarter, Navy was not making any offensive threats, with the ball deep in its territory.

Early in the second period, after Halfback Frank Hauff, one of Navy's numerous heroes, had intercepted the first of five passes by Bob Blaik that went into enemy hands, the midshipman attack began to get up a full head of steam, and now it was that the vast crowd came to a realization of the fate that was in store for the team that was supposed to win by a lopsided score.

Day of His Life

From then on it was Navy's game, the game of Hauff, Fullback Dave Bannerman, Quarterback Bob Zastrow, who had the day of his life with his running and passing and scored the first touchdown on a 7-yard buck; End Jim Baldinger, who made a great catch in the end zone of Zastrow's 30-yard pass for the second score twenty seconds before the end of the half; End John Gurski, who intercepted two passes in the fourth quarter and the game of those embattled sailors in the line and secondary who swarmed in and all but tore the cadet backs limb from limb with the ferocity of their tackling.

The 3,700 midshipmen in the stands were in a delirium of happiness over the seeming miracle they beheld until they stormed down from the stands on the final play

to raise Coach Erdelatz, Captain Bakke and their other heroes to their shoulders.

They had waited seven long years—almost two undergraduate generations—for this day of retribution, which wiped out the mortification of the adversity they had suffered season after season.

They saw their line, in which some of the men were playing on both offense and defense against the Army platoons, knock the Army backs loose from the ball with their savage tackling, harry Blaik in his attempts to pass as he has never been harried before, and stop such feared carriers as Al Pollard, Vic Pollock, Gil Stephenson, Jim Cain, Frank Fischl, Jack Martin and Gene Filipski stone dead in their tracks, limiting them to 77 yards, to Navy's 200.

They also saw their secondaries back up the line violently and cover Foldberg, a great pass catcher, and the other receivers with amazing thoroughness, and their interferers open the way for their carriers with berserk blocking that even as fine an end as Hal Loehlein could not resist.

Another Pass Interception

Army, able to make only one first down in 3 yards by running in the opening half, while Navy was going 32 yards and then 63 in five plays for its two scores and a 14-0 lead, was expected to do something drastic about the situation after the intermission. But right off the bat another Blaik pass was intercepted and Navy, reaching the cadet 21-yard line, threatened to score again, only to fail as Roger Drew's attempted field goal from the 30 fell short.

A Navy fumble, which Herb Johnson recovered near mid-field, contributed to Army breaking into the scoring column on a safety in this third period, Zastrow being hurled back 14 yards into his end zone for the two points after Blaik had punted out on the 12, one of his numerous good spot kicks.

At the very end of the quarter the cadet attack started to roll for the first time as Pollard went 24 yards for a first down, the second one Army had made up to this point. The attack carried to the Navy 21 as the final period opened and the 2,400 cadets in the stands were roaring in the hope that their team had finally set sail. There was still time to save the day, and the way the West Pointers were battling it seemed that they might possibly do it.

Then came one of the wildest final quarters any football game has produced. In those last fifteen minutes three Army passes were intercepted, each team lost the ball twice on fumbles, a Navy kick was blocked by Charley Shira and Elmer Stout, the middies were penalized time and again. On the very last play, with Army three yards from a touchdown, Gurski intercepted, ran the ball back nearly to midfield and fumbled for the fifth bobble of the period.

Army, in this last quarter, was on Navy's 21, 15, 6 and 3-yard marks and it could not get across once, marking the first time the cadets have failed to register a touchdown since 1947.

Gurski's first interception stopped them at the 21. After getting the ball on the 20 on a Navy bobble, they gave up the ball on downs on the 22. They got the ball again on the 29 on Gerald Hart's recovery of a fumble, after Pollard

and Pollock's march had been stopped by Martin's fumble, and went to the Navy 6, where Cain lost the ball on a bobble.

The blocked kick gave the cadets their last chance, with less than a minute remaining, Army taking possession on the 9. But, after Cain had carried to the 3 and two plays had failed, Gurski made his second interception of the quarter on the final scrimmage.

Navy's special defense was partly responsible for Army's utter frustration on the attack. The middies were looping and charging on a slant in the line and shooting in the backers-up in the 6-2, 2-1 alignment. The cadets attacked from their usual straight T formation and did not appear to have any new devices. At any rate, Navy seemed to be ready for anything sent at them—rough and ready, that is.

On the offense, the sailors confined themselves to the T formation, abjuring the single wing, of which there had been talk and which they have used briefly during the season. Most of the time they had one or two flankers, either a halfback alone or paired with an end.

From this alignment they had a wide variety of plays, hitting both through the middle and sweeping off the tackles or outside, and passing. Zastrow has never been more effective than he was on quarterback sneaks and all of the backs, particularly Bannerman and Hauff, ran with a drive and determination that carried them on after they appeared to have been stopped.

Zastrow scored from the 7 in the second period after he had apparently been stopped at the 5, digging and churning to get across. His touchdown was set up by two passes he threw to Art Sundry for 18 and to Hauff for 5.

Makes Spectacular Catch

On the second march of 63 yards Zastrow went 11 yards and Bill Powers, a yeoman worker on both offense and defense, reversed around right end for 22. Then Zastrow passed 30 yards into the end zone to Baldinger. The Navy end was covered by Gene Gribble, but he leaped high into the air and snatched the ball in a spectacular catch.

That score, making the count 14—0 after Drew's second extra-point kick, almost broke the heart of Army. It had been trying desperately to make a tying touchdown and seemed to be on the

Statistics of the Game

	Navy.	Army.
First downs	13	5
Yards gained, rushing.	200	77
Forward passes	10	24
Forwards completed	5	6
Yards gained, forwards.	68	60
Forwards intercepted by	5	1
Number of punts.	8	8
*Av. dist. of punts, yds.	40	40
Run-back of punts, yds.	23	65
Rival fumbles recovered	3	4
Penalties	9	3
Yards lost, penalties.	65	35

*From line of scrimmage

way when Blaik passed 26 yards to Foldberg, but that effort went for naught. Thereafter, until the mad last quarter, Navy had possession of the ball and gave the cadets few chances to go on the attack.

The 14 points that Navy scored were the most made against Army by any team all season. The victory, in all probability, marks the dawn of a new era for football at Annapolis.

After all their years of adversity, the midshipmen should now be on their way to regaining the stature they enjoyed prior to 1944. Nothing could be a greater tonic for them than a triumph over Army, which has stood for the best in Eastern football, if not in the country, for most of that period.

The line-up:

NAVY (14)

Left Ends—Treadwell, McDonald.
Left Tackles—Tetrault, Davis
Left Guards—Fischer, Denfeld, McCowan.
Centers—Bryson, Sieber, Kukowski.
Right Guards—Steele, Parker, Pertel, Lowell.
Right Tackles—Hunt, Gragg, Dumont.
Right Ends—Bakke, Gurski, Baldinger.
Quarterbacks—Zastrow, Cameron.
Left Halfbacks—Hauff.
Right Halfbacks—Powers, Brady, Sundry, Etchison.
Fullbacks—Bannerman, Botula, Drew, Franco, Owens.

ARMY (2)

Left Ends—Foldberg, Loehlein, McShulakis, Denman.
Left Tackles—Zeigler, Shira.
Left Guards—Elmblad, Bara, Brian, Hart, Volonnino.
Centers—Haas, Stout, Bretzke, Guess.
Right Guards—Roberts, Malavasi, Cox.
Right Tackles—Ackerson, Kimmel.
Right Ends—Weaver, Rowekamp, Krobock, Conway.
Quarterbacks—Blaik, Reich.
Left Halfbacks—Pollock, Schultz, Cain, Gribble.
Right Halfbacks—Fischl, Johnson, Martin, Filipski.
Fullbacks—Pollard, Beck, Stephenson.

SCORE BY PERIODS

Navy	0	14	0	0—14
Army	0	0	2	0— 2

Touchdowns—Zastrow, Baldinger. Points after touchdown—Drew 2 (placements). Safety—Army.

Referee—Paul N. Swaffield, Brown. Umpire—Leonard Dobbins, Fordham. Linesman—William J. McConnel, Middlebury. Field judge—Clifford Montgomery, Columbia. Electric clock operator—Charles G. Eckle.

December 3, 1950

Kentucky Upsets Oklahoma in Sugar Bowl

WILDCATS' PASSES STOP SOONERS, 13-7

Parilli's Superb Air Tactics Enable Kentucky to Cut Oklahoma String at 31

CONTEST THRILLS 32,000

Yowarsky Shines on Defense in New Orleans Struggle— Jamerson Scores Twice

STATISTICS OF THE GAME

	Kentucky.	Okla.
First downs	7	18
Yards gained, rushing	84	189
Forward passes	12	8
Forwards completed	9	3
Yds. gained, forwards	105	38
Forwards intercepted by	1	1
Punts	8	6
*Av. dist. of punts, yds.	41.7	33.4
Fumbles	0	5
Yards lost, penalties	40	30

*From line of scrimmage.

NEW ORLEANS, Jan. 1 (AP)—Oklahoma, the Goliath of college football and holder of the greatest victory streak in modern times, fell in the Sugar Bowl today before Kentucky, 13—7, on the passes of Babe Parilli and the superb line play of Walt Yowarsky. A capacity crowd of 82,000 watched.

The defeat was Oklahoma's first since the opening game of the 1948 season—32 games ago. Two of those victories were in thhe preceding two Sugar Bowl games.

The mightly Sooners ranked first in the nation in The Associated Press poll, started toward their downfall this chilly, windy day in the first quarter when Yowarsky recovered a fumble by Oklahoma quarterback Claude Arnold on the Oklahoma 25. On the next play, Parilli passed to Wilbur (Shorty) Jamerson for a touchdown.

Four other Oklahoma fumbles kept the national champions in trouble and not until late in the fourth quarter could the Sooners score.

Five times in nine games this year Oklahoma trailed opponents. Each time Oklahoma came back to victory and late in the game today it looked like the Sooners might do it again.

Rock-Ribbed Defense

Oklahoma's only touchdown came very late and they might have challenged again, but the Southeastern Conference champions from the Bluegrass stood like a rock wall in the final minutes.

An Oklahoma runner bobbled the ball after a Kentucky punt and Yowarsky was there to cover it for Kentucky. That cut the life out of Oklahoma and gave even

greater spirit and dash to the Wildcats from Lexington.

Yowarsky was by far the greatest lineman on the field where three All-America stars were in action. He made at least twenty decisive tackles in addition to being in the right place when Oklahoma fumbled.

As a result Right Tackle Yawarsky received the Warren V. Miller Memorial Trophy as the outstanding player of the game. Yowarsky, selected by sports writers at the contest, was the first lineman to win the trophy.

Parilli, a second-string All-American, passed far less than usual. Apparently Kentucky was satisfied to play it safe with a 13-point lead. However, when Parilli passed, he usually connected. His long toss to Al Bruno set up the Wildcats' second touchdown.

The first half was a clear story of Oklahoma's superior running versus Kentucky's outstanding passing and the passing was by far the more productive.

Fumbles on Sixth Play

On the sixth play of the game, Arnold fumbled on his 23 and Yowarsky recovered. Then Parilli, "The Kentucky Babe," was rushed badly when he jumped to throw and couldn't spot a receiver. But he squirmed around among Oklahoma tacklers until Jamerson was deep in Oklahoma's end zone. Then

he jumped again and fired. Jamerson was well guarded but he made a great leaping, finger-tip catch for the touchdown.

Kentucky's all-America Tackle Bob Gain, made the conversion and Kentucky had a 7-0 lead after 2 minutes and 50 seconds. For the next 15 minutes the game was fluid but fruitless in touchdowns.

Kentucky End Ben Zaranka dropped a pass from Parilli in the end zone to cut away another Kentucky touchdown. Just a few minutes later, however, Kentucky made up for Zaranka's flub. The Wildcats got the ball on their 19 and went 81 yards down the field in seven plays. Their second touchdown was set up principally on another brilliant Parilli pass. The Babe threw down the middle to Bruno who finally was knocked down by Jack Lockett on Oklahoma's 1-foot line. Jamerson banged across for his second scoring honor. Gain's kick was wide, but Kentucky had 13 points.

Losers in Trouble Again

Two other Oklahoma fumbles in the half—another by Arnold and one by Leon Heath—put the Sooners in trouble but Kentucky failed to cash in after the recoveries.

The Sooners, usually a five or six touchdown production outfit, finally managed to get going in the fourth quarter. Gain tried a field goal for Kentucky and missed.

Oklahoma took over and blasted 80 yards, mostly on the fine running of Billy Vessels and Heath. Twice Heath made first downs on fourth-down power smashes.

Arnold, with nothing like the passing and ball handling wizardry of Parilli, took the ball from center and flipped a short pitchout to Vessels who threw a looping pass to Merrill Green for the touchdown. The play covered 17 yards. All-America Tackle Jim Weatherall kicked the point.

Kentucky stood off an Oklahoma thrust in the third quarter which reached the 2-yard line. Here, again, Yowarsky was in the right place at the right time. He tackled Vessels for a vital 5-yard loss and on the next play Arnold threw poorly toward All-America Frank Anderson, end, who couldn't get to the ball.

The line-up:

KENTUCKY (13)
Left Ends—Zardaka, Fry
Left Tackles—Gain, Lukawski, Pope.
Left Guards—Donaldson, Wannamaker.
Centers—Rogers, Moseley, Fuller.
Right Guards—Ignarski, Conde, James.
Right Tackles—Yowarsky, McKenzie.
Right Ends—Bruno, Fucci, McClendon.
Quarterbacks—Parilli, Varley.
Left Halfbacks—Webb, H. Jones Clark.
Right Halfbacks—Jamerson, Martin.
Fullbacks—Leskovar, Wooddell.

OKLAHOMA (7)
Left Ends—Keller, Lockett.
Left Tackles—Weatherall, Janes.
Left Guards—McNabb, Clark, Harkey.
Centers—Moore, Catlin.
Right Guards—Mayes, F. Smith.
Right Tackles—D. Smith Cole.
Right Ends—Anderson, Cisak, Reddell.
Quarterback—Arnold.
Left Halfbacks—Vessels, Silva, Heatly.
Right Halfbacks—Gray, Crawford, Green.
Fullbacks—Heath, McPhail.

SCORE BY PERIODS
Kentucky .... 7 6 0 0—13
Oklahoma .... 0 0 0 7— 7
Touchdowns—Jamerson 2, Green. Points after touchdown—Gain, Weatherall.

January 2, 1951

AN OKLAHOMA PLAYER HIT HARD AFTER GAINING A YARD

Halfback Frank Silva is stopped by Bill Wannamaker of Kentucky in the last quarter of Sugar Bowl game in New Orleans.

Associated Press Wirephoto

OHIO STATE NAMES HAYES HEAD COACH

Trustees Confirm Appointment, Ending Mad 2-Month Quest for Fesler Successor

COLUMBUS, Ohio, Feb. 18 (UP) —Ohio State University named Wayne (Woody) Hayes of Miami (Ohio) University as its new head coach tonight, ending a melodramatic two-month search for a successor to Wes Fesler in this football-mad community.

The board of trustees approved the amiable, dark-haired coach from Oxford, Ohio, on the second try. Hayes had been recommended for the job by the athletic board, but the trustees refused to approve his name at a previous meeting last Monday because only four of its seven members were present.

The naming of Hayes was a hard blow to the forces who were lustily campaigning for the return of Paul Brown, coach of the professional Cleveland Browns. Brown coached at Ohio State from 1941 to 1943 and thousands of fans, alumni, students and a segment of the press waged a ceaseless fight to bring him back.

Six of the seven trustees were on hand at this afternoon's brief session and they lost no time in confirming the coach to what is generally considered the hottest football spot in the Big Ten Conference.

Fesler resigned his $15,000-a-year post Dec. 9 because he said the demands for winning teams nearly drove him to a nervous breakdown.

Hayes will receive a salary of $12,500 on a one year contract, but with a "gentlemen's agreement" that the agreement will be continuing, University President Howard L. Bevis said. Fesler was paid $15,000 at the time he resigned.

February 19, 1951

One Saturday Football Telecast For Each Area Set by N.C.A.A.

Committee Unanimously Approves Limit of Two Games on Video for Any Team— No Anti-Trust Violation Seen

WASHINGTON, April 18 (AP)— The television committee of the National Collegiate Athletic Association, in what it said was a move to save intercollegiate sports, today approved a plan for limited telecasts of next fall's college football games.

Under the plan adopted by the association group, this will be in store for the television fan:

1. Only one game will be televised in any area on any given Saturday.

3. On at least one Saturday a blackout may be imposed and no game will be brought into the area at all.

3. No team will be seen more than twice, once at home and once when it plays away from home.

These plans had been drawn previously by a four-man steering committee, and were approved unanimously today by the full, twelve-man committee.

Rear Admiral Tom Hamilton of the University of Pittsburgh, the committee chairman, explained that the program is experimental for one year only.

He believes that television has lowered football gate receipts.

"And remember," he said, "that some 72 per cent of our athletic programs, including our intramurals, depends on football receipts."

Hamilton said that if athletics are of any value they must be in all colleges and "not restricted to the eight or ten colleges" which could sell games to television sponsors.

Under the plan adopted by the committee today, the sponsors will choose the games they want to produce, within the limits laid down for them.

Hamilton said college representatives had discussed the plans with the Department of Justice and expect to see H. Graham Morison, Assistant Attorney General, tomorrow. He said he was sure the colleges were not violating anti-trust laws. The only lawyer on the committee, Bob Hall of Yale, said: "We are assured we are well within the bounds of the law."

Hugh Willett of Southern California, president of N. C. A. A., told the news conference:

"We approach this problem from the conviction that our athletic program is worth preserving. We believe there is a solution. We believe we can live with television."

April 19, 1951

Ivy League De-emphasizes Football; Bars Spring Drill, Post-Season Play

An eight-point program governing football, including the abolition of spring practice and post-season games, was announced simultaneously yesterday by the presidents of eight Ivy League colleges— Brown, Columbia, Cornell, Dartmouth, Harvard, Pennsylvania, Princeton and Yale.

The joint statement said that spring practice was being eliminated because of the peculiar pressures on football and a desire to avoid intensity of athletic specialization in a single sport.

The new program was patterned after the policies adopted recently by the American Council of Education.

Under the new program coaches and players in the Ivy League are barred from participating in football games that settle sectional or other championships.

This includes, according to an official of the circuit, such contests as the North-South in Miami, Fla., and the East-West at San Francisco. Players and coaches from the Ivy loop have been active in these annual post-season games down through the years.

Yale's Herman Hickman coached the North team at Miami last December and Tuss McLaughry of Dartmouth was one of the East's coaches at San Francisco. Dick Kazmaier, the All-America back from Princeton, played in the last East-West game. Ivy League teams have not participated in post-season games in a number of years.

While many of the coaches preferred limitation, rather than abolishment of spring training, Ivy League officials generally decided to go along with the stricter controls in the interests of keeping football "in the proper academic perspective."

The Ivy League presidents agreed:

1. To abolish so-called football clinics, that is, the practice of assembling high school coaches to explain and demonstrate coaching methods of the staff.

2. To abolish spring football practice because of the peculiar pressures on football and their desire to avoid intensity of athletic specialization in a single sport. In taking this action the committee recognizes that the same evils may exist in other major sports, and they are proceeding with a study of this matter.

3. To start fall football practice for all institutions on Thursday, September 4, 1952.

4. That beginning with the fall of 1953, each institution would play every other institution in the group at least once every five years.

5. To study ways and means of reducing the number of games scheduled.

6. To reaffirm the principle of the control of athletics by the academic authorities, this control to include scheduling policy, eligibility, the award of scholarships and student aid.

7. To amend the eligibility rule in the present agreement by including the following: "Beginning in 1954 no student shall be eligible whose secondary school education was subsidized or whose post-college education is promised by an individual or group of individuals not closely related to the family as a consideration for his attending the college which he now attends."

8. To amend the rule in regard to post-season football contests to read as follows: "The subscribing institutions shall not engage in post-season football contests or any contests designed to settle sectional or other championship, and no player representing these institutions shall participate in such contests, and no coach shall undertake to coach teams entered for such contests.

It was noted that the agreement for each institution to play every other institution in the group at least once every three years beginning in 1953 would automatically restore Penn to the schedules of those who have voiced reluctance at one time or another to meet the Philadelphians on the gridiron.

No Criticism Involved

Dr. Grayson Kirk, vice president and acting head of Columbia University, said the group viewed the decisions as "not involving any criticism or admission of guilt on the part of the schools in the league, but rather as a policy reaffirming their position on these matters, which will help the Ivy League to maintain its leadership in the area of football ethics." He said also: "I think it is a good thing for the Ivy League to set the standards."

At Princeton, Dr. Harold Dodds, president, said Princeton will go along with the Ivy group although many connected with football here, including Head Coach Charlie Caldwell, were in favor of the extra practice sessions.

He said: "Although Princeton believes that the four weeks of spring football practice under the limitations as to hours and other restrictions that have prevailed since the war have not distorted the real values of the sport, we shall abandon the practive in accordance with the prevailing opinion of the Ivy group.

"In eliminating this period of voluntary practice, which has had the unanimous support of the members of our varsity football squad for the past three years, we reaffirm Princeton's conviction that only through cooperative effort is it possible to establish and maintain football as part of a sound college eeducational program."

At Ithaca, N. Y., Cornell President Deane W. Malott said, according to The Associated Press:

"While from the point of view of Cornell athletic policies some of these steps are of comparatively little significance, it seemed important to support the 'Ivy League' in its effort to maintain football in proper academic perspective."

Harold E. Stassen, president of the University of Pennsylvania, said he was "pleased with the constructive step which the unanimous agreement represents."

Wants Enforcement Teeth

The new back-to-purity sports code for college athletics drawn up by the American Council on Education drew sharp criticism yesterday from several university officials but others promised full compliance and said it appeared to be a workable solution.

George L. Cross, president of the University of Oklahoma, thought the code was so restrictive that "we may have created another Volstead Act," The United Press reported.

The code's chief de-emphasizing features were a complete ban on all post-season bowl fooball games and elimination of spring practice.

Mr. Cross believes that bowl games and spring practice should be banned, despite the fact that Oklahoma has been a major football power and a participant in post-season contests on a number of occasions. But he does not think the A. C. E. program will work unless stronger enforcement provisions are provided.

"I'm not in favor of Oklahoma becoming an experimental school where all these things are tried out," Mr. Cross said. "This thing can work only if it is put into effect on a universal basis. If you just put it into effect at one school or conference it would only make those teams inferior."

Mr. Cross said if the A. C. E. proposal to accrediting agencies to withdraw recognition from schools which fail to follow the code were put into effect "the code will have real teeth in it."

"However, I'm not sure they can do that. The code looks a little rough to me. We may have created another Volstead Act."

[The Volstead Act was passed in 1919 in an effort to enforce the Eighteenth Amendment to the Constitution, which prohibited the sale of alcoholic liquors.]

Arthur S. Adams of Washington, president of the council said that it was true they had no power to enforce the code, but that he hoped regional accrediting agencies would without academic recognition from schools failing to observe it.

"It is a standard of performance which all schools should observe," Mr. Adams said.

Hugh Willett, president of the National Collegiate Athletic Association, said he thought the code would not bring about any changes in college athletics until after January of 1953, when the next N.C.A.A. convention will be held. On that basis there would be a full schedule of New Year's Day bowl games next season and spring football practice would be eliminated only in certain sectors this year.

Vote on Policy Needed

"Policies of our organization can be changed only by vote of our 343 member universities and colleges and the twelve allied conferences," Mr. Willett said.

Asa Bushnell, commissioner of the Eastern College Athletic Conference, said he opposed only the elimination of spring football practice. He thought it would be more practical merely to curtail it.

Bernie Moore, commissioner of the Southeastern Conference, said except for the bans on bowl foot-

ball and spring practice "everything else is in line with what we already are doing."

Reeves Peters, secretary of the Big Seven, said his conference would make a thorough study of the plan and discuss putting it into effect in the meeting of athletic directors at Kansas City on Feb. 28-29. Artie Eilers, commissioner of the Missouri Valley Conference, said his schools would cooperate 100 per cent with N. C. A. A. policy on the matter. Commissioner Dick Romney of the Rocky Mountain Skyline Conference said, "Sentiment has been expressed which confirms my feeling we will go

along with the new rulings."

In Peoria, Ill., Bradley University dropped plans for the 1952 National Campus Basketball tournament.

February 19, 1952

Sports of The Times

By ARTHUR DALEY
Grand Old Man

JUST before the second Battle of Bull Run was fought, Amos Alonzo Stagg was born in West Orange, N. J. That's a staggering long time ago. But that same Amos Alonzo Stagg, still spry and hearty, will celebrate his ninetieth birthday tomorrow. Truly can it be said that the Grand Old Man is one of the most remarkable persons the world of sports has produced.

He began his football coaching career at the University of Chicago in 1892 and developed the Maroon into one of the most formidable gridiron forces in the land. When the mandatory retirement age of 70 beckoned Stagg to the sidelines, he refused.

"I'm not too old," he insisted, "and I can't see any sound reason for my quitting football. I know too much."

So off he went to the little College of the Pacific to resume his life's work. And in 1943, when Stagg was 81 years old, he produced a team that upset mighty California, 6 to 0, and came perilously close to upsetting unbeaten and untied Southern California. He probably would have achieved that as well if it had not been for the fact that two Pacific touchdowns were called back by whistle-tooting officials. His fellow coaches then proudly voted him "Coach of the Year."

Still in Harness

Life has been a bit quieter of recent seasons. But he still is extremely active as assistant to his son, Paul, at Susquehanna. The mention of Paul Stagg brings to mind an incident that typifies the character of this noblest Roman of them all.

Back in 1922 Chicago and Princeton were locked in a titanic battle, with the Maroon driving to within two yards of the winning touchdown. The wily Lonnie Stagg knew precisely what play would click. All he had to do was send it in to his embattled heroes, as every other coach in the business positively would have done. What made it easier for him was that he merely had to whisper it to his substitute quarterback, his own son, Paul.

"That would violate the spirit of the rules," said the Grand Old Man—and he refused. Princeton won, 21 to 18.

Overly Scrupulous

Only a hair-splitter could have been so uncompromising. A substitute quarterback merely calls a play, which was perfectly legal in that era when coaching from the sidelines was forbidden. He wasn't bootlegging information from the bench to others. He was calling it himself. To Stagg that violated the spirit of the rules. He just couldn't permit it.

Profound have been the effects of this man of character on the game. In view of his unflinching integrity, his unyielding adherence to every tenet of pure amateurism and his emphasis on the character-building qualities that football can offer, it's extraordinary that he should have compiled so remarkable a record for success down through the years, winning the admiration, re-

Amos Alonzo Stagg

spect and love not only of his players but of his fellow coaches as well.

Once when Illinois and Chicago couldn't agree on a referee, the Illinois coach suggested that Stagg referee the game himself, knowing full well that the Illini would get a fairer shake from Lonnie than from anyone else.

The man never smoked, drank or used a stronger epithet than an explosive "Jackass!" The droll Bob Zuppke once listened to him for a full afternoon and wryly commented, "By the time practice is over, there isn't a human being left on the field. The whole squad is *grazing*."

Imaginative Strategist

Stagg had a great football mind and was a shrewd innovator. He was the first man to use the spiral pass from center, the first to use a flanker, the first to use fake and multiple ball-handling, the first to use the unbalanced line and the first to use the man-in-motion.

The Chicago Bears are generally credited with the man-in-motion maneuver but Stagg was experimenting with it at Chicago even before Red Grange first used it. It probably was borrowed unconsciously and unthinkingly after watching a Maroon practice, not that that's any crime.

Stagg placed the forward pass in his repertoire in 1906, the same year Eddie Cochems was developing it in St. Louis. The Grand Old Man worked out sixty-three pass plays and hoped to upset Minnesota with them. But they played in a driving rainstorm and passing was impossible, Chicago losing 4—2. Later, though, the pass was exploited in crushing strong Illinois, 63 to 0.

It wasn't only as a sideline genius that Lonnie gained fame. He was a superb athlete in his undergraduate days at Yale. Not only did he gain a place on Walter Camp's All-America team at end but he was a pitcher of such class that the Giants offered him the unheard of sum of $4,200 to turn professional. This occurred after he had fanned twenty Princeton batters.

And now Lonnie Stagg is about to reach 90, every candle in his birthday cake a shining beacon of what's noble and decent in the world of sports.

August 15, 1952

Southern California Downs Wisconsin on Coast

PASADENA, Calif., Jan. 1 (AP)—Traveling 73 yards on a victory parade led by second-string halfback Rudy Bukich, the Trojans of Southern California defeated Wisconsin, 7—0, today and finally, in the seventh year, ended the succession of Big Ten triumphs over the Coast Conference in the Rose Bowl.

The magnificent march came midway in the third period and sank the Badger hopes of making it seven in a row for the Big Ten in this, their first appearance in the classic.

Bukich, a rangy senior from St. Louis, sent the Trojans sailing by air 65 of those 73 yards in a near perfect demonstration of passing accuracy—five out of six throws.

The touchdown, plus the conversion, was hardly safe from then on, and not a soul of the estimated 100,000 fans left the place. Nor, it is safe to say, did many of the millions of television watchers around the nation leave their seats.

Twice in the fading moments the gallant Badgers drove deep into Trojan territory. Big Alan (The Horse) Ameche hammered through the Trojan line for a total of 133 yards and quarterback Jim Haluska kept the Trojans in a flurry with his throwing.

No Last-Quarter Jinx

But it was not to be. The fourth-quarter jinx in the series, which saw California twice lose in the closing moments, and Stanford collapse entirely, did not prevail today.

Both teams encountered hard luck in the early minutes. Southern California lost its star left halfback, Jim Sears, after three minutes and thirty-three seconds with a broken leg bone. Later Wisconsin lost its No. 1 left halfback, Bill Hutchinson, who did not return until the closing minutes.

The Trojan touchdown was launched after the most dramatic run of the day. It was the first play from scrimmage after the kick-off opening the second half.

Ameche, the leading ground gainer in the Big Ten this season, rolled off the left side and kept rolling for fifty-four yards before he was hauled down on the Trojan 33 by the two linebackers, Marvin Goux and George Timberlake.

The Badgers were on the go, but so was Southern California's Terrific defensive platoon. Badger Halfback Roy Burks fumbled when hit by Tackle Bob Van Doren and End Bob Hooks recovered the ball on the Trojan 27.

Bukich, understudying Sears, went into high gear. He fired Striken to Left End Ron Miller for fourteen and two for nine apiece. He found Tom Nickoloff, the right end, for 11, and in eight plays U.S.C. was on the Badger 22. The next strike was the pay-off—to Right Halfback Al Carmichael, who was standing wide open in the end zone.

Rose Bowl Line-Up

SOUTHERN CALIFORNIA (7)
Left Ends—Miller, Hattig, Stillwell.
Left Tackles—Thompson, Ane, Ashcraft, Fouch.
Left Guards—Willhoite, Pucci.
Centers—Welsh, Timberlake.
Right Guards—Cox, Pevlani, Pavich.
Right Tackles—Weeks, Van Doren, Da Re.
Right Ends—Nickoloff, Hooks, Petty.
Quarterbacks—Bozanic, Gour, Riddle.
Left Halfbacks—Sears, Bukich, Welch, Dandoy.
Right Halfbacks—Carmichael, Crow, Kirkland, Exley.
Fullbacks—Sellers, Han, Koch, Tsagalakis, Clayton.

WISCONSIN (0)
Left Ends—Peters, Wuhrman, Esser, Lundin.
Left Tackles—Prchlik, Hoegh, Ursin.
Left Guards—Steinmetz, Kennedy, Brandt.
Centers—Simkowski, Durkin, Messner.
Right Guards—Stensby, O'Brien, Amundsen.
Right Tackles—Suminski, Berndt, Martin, Gulseth.
Right Ends—Andrykowski, Voss, Locklin.
Quarterbacks—Haluska, Hable.
Left Halfbacks—Hutchinson, Canny, Carl, Shwaiko, Gingrass.
Right Halfbacks—Witt, Dornburg, Burks.
Fullbacks—Ameche, Lamphere, Dixon.

SCORE BY PERIODS
Southern California .... 0 0 7 0—7
Wisconsin .... 0 0 0 0—0

Touchdown—Carmichael. Point after touchdown—Tsagalakis.

Kicking specialist Sam Tsagalakis added the extra point and thus ended the scoring and the end of the Big Ten domination in this event.

Wisconsin's T-formation attack went well on the ground despite the vaunted U.S.C. defensive platoon—211 yards to a mere 48 rushing by So. California—but the Badgers couldn't stop Bukich and his record of twelve completions out of twenty throws for 137 of the 185 yards the Trojans collected in the air.

Ameche netted his 133 yards in 28 times lugging the ball and was the leading crown gainer.

But time and again the stout Trojans, possessing vastly more reserve strength, stopped the Badgers in scoring range—once on the 7, again on the 14, twice more inside the 30, and with the excitement mounting in the fading moments, on the 20.

Thus were the heroic but outmanned Badgers stopped on the deepest thrust, to the seven, they faked a field goal and Witt ran to the Trojan two—short of a first down by one short yard.

Late in the fourth period, Haluska, Ameche, Jerry Witt and Burks swept from their own 20 to the Trojan 17 and the Badger rooters roared for a score. But the Trojans drove them back to the 23 and took the ball.

Injured Player Helps

In the final threat Wisconsin went from its 18 to the Trojan 24. Even the injured Harland Carl came off the bench to help. But the Trojans held again.

One game record was broken. Desmond Koch of U.S.C. boomed off one kick for 72 yards that spelled gloom for the Badgers. It bettered a 68-yard punt made by Galus Shaver of U.S.C. against Pitt in 1930. The Trojans' punting average was a sensational 51.37 yards. The versatile Bukich got off one for 60 yards. The other seven were Koch's.

The Trojans, with their "horse-and-buggy" single-wing attack, as Coach Jess Hill describes it, were a happy lot as they left the field and fans swarmed in to congratulate them. And it was a tired but dead-game Badger squad that headed for the dressing room in this, the thirty-ninth, Rose Bowl game.

The pass play that won the game was a brand new one for the Trojans, Coach Hill disclosed.

"It was the first time we'd use that pattern," he said. "This undoubtedly was the best game of Bukich's career. We had plenty of potential receivers downfield on the toss. But Carmichael was all alone on the goal line and Bukich's toss was right in his hands."

STATISTICS OF THE GAME

	U.S.C.	Wisconsin
First downs	16	19
Rushing yardage	48	211
Passing yardage	185	142
Passes attempted	27	26
Passes completed	18	11
Passes intercepted by	2	2
Number of punts	8	5
Punting average, yds.	51.37	39.2
Fumbles lost	0	1
Yards penalized	62	20

January 2, 1953

College Football Ends Two-Platoon System

By The Associated Press.

ST. PETERSBURG, Fla., Jan. 14—College football's costly two-platoon era, which introduced the gridiron specialist and bankrupted the football programs of many small colleges, came to a sudden end today.

After three days of vigorous discussions behind closed doors, the Football Rules Committee of the National Collegiate Athletic Association killed the free substitution rule by a unanimous vote.

The new regulation, which brings back the era of the all-around "iron man" offensive and defensive performer, states that players removed from the game during the first and third periods may not return to action in those periods.

Players withdrawn before the final four minutes of the second and fourth periods may go back into the game in the last four minutes.

The rules make no provision for the extra-point kicker, which means he is under the same restrictions as other players.

In another change, the committee altered the defensive pass interference regulation to give the offensive team only enough yardage for a first down. Previously, the defensive team was penalized 15 yards from the point of infraction.

The fair-catch rule remains unchanged, but the committee indicated the player must have signaled far enough in advance to prevent opposing players tackling him. The decision will be left up to officials.

"This is the end of the two-platoon system," said Columbia's coach, Lou Little.

"It was a radical action, but when we thought it over thoroughly, we decided we could have as good a game as we had before, and this is going to help the colleges with financial problems."

Small Colleges Suffered

Fifty small colleges have been forced to abandon football because of the huge squads and the big coaching staffs demanded by the two-platoon system with its many offensive and defensive experts.

Little said the action was expected also to bring renewed interest in football to the colleges that have de-emphasized the sport in recent years.

"These schools won't have to keep up with their neighbors now by maintaining so many coaches and players," he said. "They can come back now, within their means and restore football without trying to overextend themselves."

The committee's surprise action ignores a recommendation by the nation's college coaches, who voted four to one in a recent survey for keeping the substitution rule the way it was or making it even more liberal.

On the other side of the dispute were college presidents and administrators, who believed it was necessary to eliminate the fabulous costs of the two-platoon system. Many fans also have spoken out against the system, declaring that the constant stream of players on and off the field was confusing and decreased the interest in the game.

The system was legalized in 1941, with the adoption of a rule permitting coaches to make unlimited substitutions any time the clock was stopped and to make single substitutions between players while the clock was running.

Before 1941, no player removed from a game could be sent back in the same quarter.

Subject Discussed 3 Days

The committee chairman, H. O. (Fritz) Crisler, the Michigan athletic director, said the subject was discussed for three days "without thinking of our teams and our schools, but with the best interests of football and its future in mind."

Crisler said the committee was "gravely concerned" about the schools that had been forced to abandon football because of the two-platoon system.

"This is going to mean a great and sudden change in the organization of football programs," said K. L. (Tug) Wilson, Big Ten commissioner, who attended the committee meetings in an advisory capacity. Others at the meetings agreed that thousands of college coaches would have to discard their present programs.

"They're going to have to start considering now who their best

49

eleven players are." Crisler said. "Obviously, the boys now will have to play the game both ways."

Little said that while the new rule would cut down on the size of varsity squads, just as many boys will be able to play football as before, because the rule will mean the rejuvenation of junior varsity teams.

The new rule, which ends a colorful and controversial era of college football, reads:

"A player withdrawn from a game during the first or third periods may not return during the period from which he was withdrawn.

"Players withdrawn from the game before the final four minutes of the second or fourth periods may return during the final four minutes of the period in which they were withdrawn, but if withdrawn during the final four minutes of either the second or fourth periods, they may not return during that four-minute period."

known a single topic to be discussed so thoroughly and to have so many angles involved as the two-platoon system. We had a free exchange of views from all sections of the country—from players, coaches, college administrators, spectators, officials and the press.

More Than Technical Change

"We recognized this as not just a technical change in a football rule but one that involves the administration of college athletics and the whole philosophy behind it. In the end, we tried to recognize all the arguments pro and con."

The committee said it felt the present rule on "false starts" covered the so-called "sucker shift," a maneuver intended to draw the opposition offside in scoring territory, but re-worded the rule in an effort to strengthen it.

"It's just a matter of the officials calling it," Crisler said.

The term "sucker shift" was introduced into football vocabulary during the past season after Notre Dame's victories over Oklahoma and Southern California. The Irish were accused of using unethical tactics by employing a shift to draw the opposition offside and get 5-yard penalties near the goal line.

The committee rejected a proposal to make T-quarterbacks eligible to receive forward passes after handling the ball from center. This action may have been in response to a plea from Amos Alonzo Stagg not to make any changes in the rules "which will add strength to the offense."

January 15, 1953

Rice Wins, 28-6, Despite Tackle By Player From Alabama Bench

DALLAS, Tex., Jan. 1 (UP)— Halfback Dicky Moegle scored on runs of 79 and 34 yards and had another 95-yard touchdown dash marred by an Alabama bench-warmer's tackle today as Rice crushed the Tide in the Cotton Bowl, 28 to 6.

Moegle ripped through Alabama's touted defenses for 265 yards in one of the most dazzling one-man shows in the Bowl's 18-year history, but he had to share top billing with his unexpected sideline foe, Fullback Tommy Lewis.

The slender Rice speedster was 57 yards downfield from the line of scrimmage and pulling away from all Alabama defenders. Then Lewis leaped from the bench and pulled Moegle to the ground on the Tide 38-yard line with a tackle that brought the capacity crowd of 75,504 to its feet.

Fourth Straight Bowl Victory

Referee Cliff Shaw immediately made one of bowldom's most momentous decisions by awarding a touchdown to Moegle.

That gave the Southwest Conference co-champions the working edge they needed to score their fourth straight bowl triumph. Moegle was unanimously chosen as the outstanding back in the game in a vote of fifty-nine sports writers present.

The football rules permit the referee to "make such ruling as in his judgment justice may require" when play is interfered with by some act "palpably unfair." In elaboration, the "approved rulings" section of the

Associated Press Wirephoto

TWELFTH-MAN TACKLE: Dicky Moegle, Rice halfback, crossing the 50-yard marker on what probably would have been a 95-yard touchdown run in the Cotton Bowl at Dallas yesterday, only to be downed at the 38-yard line by Alabama's Tommy Lewis (arrow), who is coming up off the sideline bench. Moegle was credited with the score. Rice Tackle Dick Chapman (78) is streaking up to block out Alabama Halfback Bill Oliver, in the left foreground.

rule book states that a touchdown is to be awarded when "anyone other than a player or official * * * tackles a runner who is in the clear and in his way to a reasonably assured touchdown."

Alabama had shocked the favored Owls with a 47-yard first-quarter scoring surge, capped by Lewis' one-foot scoring plunge. But the Southeastern Conference champions never were in the ball game after Lewis' "boner."

Rice, its high-velocity ground game stymied early by the loss of fullback Kosse Johnson with a first-period ankle injury, turned the chore over to Moegle and the 19-year-old junior from Taylor, Tex., delivered the goods.

On the first play of the second quarter, he slashed inside right tackle, cut away from three would-be tacklers and sped 79 yards unmolested for the tying points. Leroy Fenstemaker kicked the first of three straight conversions and Rice was ahead to stay.

Alabama whipped back on a 54-yard run by halfback Bill Oliver, but quarterback Bart Starr fumbled away a scoring chance and Rice got the ball on its 5.

On the first play, Moegle

Statistics of the Game

	Rice.	Ala.
First downs	14	11
Rushing yardage	379	188
Passing yardage	59	67
Passes attempted	10	16
Passes completed	4	7
Passes, intrcptd by.	0	2
Number of punts	8	7
Punting average, yds	25.1	32.7
Fumbles lost	0	4
Yards penalized	89	65

knifed through that same narrow gap on the right side of the line and weaved untouched up to midfield.

Suddenly, out popped Lewis from the bench and he threw a jarring tackle that left Moegle and the crowd stunned. After the officials awarded Rice the touchdown, Fenstemaker again converted to stretch Rice's lead to 14 to 6 and that's where it stood at half-time.

Alabama didn't offer the whirlwind passing attack expected of it, but when Starr did try to pass he found himself being crowded backward by a charging Rice

line, spearheaded by tackle Dick Chapman.

Lewis, Corky Tharp and Starr were the big guns in a sometimes effective Alabama running game that netted 188 yards, but four costly fumbles nullified much of this gain.

The line-up:

RICE (28)
Left Ends—Hart, Holland, Ward.
Left Tackles—Chapman, Goleman.
Left Guards—Hudson, Rayburn, Treadway.
Centers—Rucka, Lundstedt, Wilson.
Right Guards—Paul, Lee, Rayburn, Harphold.
Right Tackles—Schueble, Cox, Riviere.
Right Ends—Bridges, Crawford, Wortham, Costa.
Quarterbacks—Fenstemaker, Grantham, Nesbitt, Proctor.
Left Halfbacks—Moegle, Nesrsta, Rogers.
Right Halfbacks—Kellogg, Laviage, Burk, C. Johnson, Stone.
Full backs—K. Johnson, Taylor, Garbrecht, Whittaker.

ALABAMA (6)
Left Ends—Cummings, Tillman.
Left Tackles—Mason, Shipp.
Left Guards—Lee, Wilga.
Centers—Carriagah, Delaurentis.
Right Guards—Eckerly, Morrer.
Right Tackles—Youngelman, Culpepper, Smalley.
Right Ends—Willis, Lynch.
Quarterback—Starr.
Left Halfbacks—Luna, Ingram, McBridge.
Right Halfbacks—Tharp, Oliver, Hollis.
Fullbacks—Lewis, Stone.

SCORE BY PERIODS
Rice .... 0 14 7 7—28
Alabama .... 6 0 0 0— 6
Touchdowns—Lewis, Moegle 3, Grantham.
Points after touchdowns—Fenstemaker 3, Burk.

January 2, 1954

waits on the line or floats wide as the quarterback slides out, the quarterback will keep and run inside of him. If the end crashes to meet him, the quarterback will pitch out wide to a trailing halfback.

Whereas a tight T quarterback seldom carries and often will go through a game without getting his uniform soiled, the split T quarterback is one of the workhorses of the attack and is more likely to be selected for running than passing ability.

SINGLE WING. The single wing has been a bread-and-butter formation since football's Neanderthal era. It features power and passing.

Tailback Key Player

With the line unbalanced and the backs in a wedge array, it is set up to get two-on-one blocking at the point of impact. And, in the wingback, it provides an additional pass receiver who is in a position to break clear fast. Another passing advantage is the fact that the tailback, unlike the T quarterback, is in passing position at the snap.

The tailback is the key player of the single wing backfield. The formation's strongest power plays are built around him, he is the principal passer and should also be at least a good enough kicker to get off a quick kick when strategy dictates one.

The modern single wing blends a high degree of deception with the straightforward application of power that is inherent in the formation. Bewildering buck-lateral, fullback-spin and reverse sequences have been developed Flanker and spread variations are used widely.

Among the leading current exponents of single wing are U. C. L. A., Tennessee, Michigan, Michigan State, Princeton and Harvard.

WING T—The wing T, which can be run from either balanced or unbalanced line, represents an attempt to combine in one formation the best features of T and single wing. Lou Little was one of the first coaches to see its possibilities and has been using it off and on at Columbia for the last fifteen years. Buff Donelli at Boston University and Rip Engle at Penn State are other leading exponents.

Another recent football trend is the use of what is called the "multiple attack." This involves the alternate use of T in some variety and single wing. The usual procedure is to come out of the huddle in T formation and run from that or to shift to single wing and run from that.

Michigan, under Fritz Crisler, and Michigan State, under Biggie Munn, were among the first colleges to exploit the multiple attack. Other prominent users are Iowa, Southern California and Pennsylvania.

October 2, 1955

Football Hard Work for Fans, Too

4 Basic Formations Used on Offense Are Clarified

Many readers of articles on football and those who follow games on radio and television may not understand, or sometimes may be confused by, references to the various formations employed by attacking (the ball-carrying) teams.

The diagrams printed herewith, depicting the positions of the offensive players before the ball is snapped, may be of help. There are variations, of course, but studying these four basic formations should make it easier to follow an account of a game with better understanding.

TIGHT T—One of the oldest football formations, the T was all but abandoned for a number of years. It returned to popularity shortly before World War II as the result of the spectacular success the Chicago Bears and Stanford University had using it with the man-in-motion series of plays developed by George Halas and Clark Shaughnessy.

From its balanced set-up, the T features quick, deceptive thrusts in any direction and concealed-intent, delayed pass plays. A deft quarterback is a prime requisite of a successful T-formation attack. He handles the ball on almost every play and much depends on his ability to keep the defense off balance with his whirling fakes and feints.

The T is the basic formation of professional football and also is used by many college teams. The current trend is to station one or more ends or backs wide in flanking positions. This puts a potential pass-receiver out in the open and spreads the defense.

Interior Linemen Split

SPLIT T—The Split T, developed at Missouri by Don Faurot during the World War II years, is probably the most popular college formation today. Such leading teams as Maryland, Oklahoma and Notre Dame are among those that employ it as a basic formation.

It gets its name from the fact that the interior linemen are

split, rather than stationed shoulder-to-shoulder, as in the tight T. This is done to spread the defense, widen the lateral range of effective attack and provide better blocking angles.

However, the important difference is not in the initial physical alignment. It is in the sliding action of the quarterback. Whereas the tight T quarterback makes his spinning fakes virtually in place, the split T quarterback ranges laterally behind his line after taking the snap.

The key split T play is the quarterback "keep option." On this play, the quarterback retains the ball until the defensive end commits himself. If the end

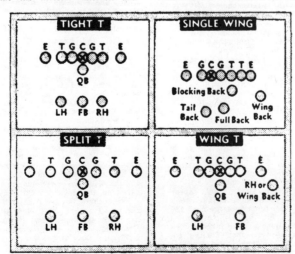

Here are four basic formations used in college and professional football as drawn by Lou Little, Columbia coach.

NOTRE DAME TOPS ARMY, 23-21

LATE KICK DECIDES

Stickles Gets 32-Yard Field Goal as Irish Rally to Nip Army

By ALLISON DANZIG
Special to The New York Times

PHILADELPHIA, Oct. 12—Trailing, 20 to 21, with seven minutes to play, Notre Dame kicked a field goal from the 28-yard line today to defeat favored Army, 23—21, as football's most famous intersectional rivalry was renewed after a ten-year interval. It was a thrilling climax to a thunderously played game.

It was a game that kept the 95,000 spectators in the Municipal Stadium seething and roaring throughout the boiling action. Never before had each team registered so many as three touchdowns in their thirty-five meetings. Each score brought forth riotous cheers.

The greatest outburst occurred as Monty Stickles, a third-string sophomore end, booted the ball from off to the left 38 yards through the uprights, 10 yards beyond the goal line. Since the play started on the 22-yard line, Stickles, under college rules, was credited with a 32-yard field goal.

Stickles' failure to kick the extra point following Notre Dame's third touchdown had appeared to spell the doom of the Fighting Irish two minutes before. But instead of being the goat of the game, the 6 foot 4-inch, 215-pound end from Poughkeepsie, N. Y., turned out to be a hero.

First Attempt Clicks

Stickles' superb effort, the first field goal he had ever attempted, was a heart-breaking checkmate to the West Point cadets. Never behind in the game and leading by 21—7 with a minute left in the third period, they appeared to have victory in their grasp until the ball from Stickles' toe sailed over their helpless outstretched hands.

Until the field goal, Bob Anderson, Army's blazing sophomore halfback, seemed destined to win the Grantland Rice Award, set up by the Four Horsemen of Notre Dame. Twice he had gone across the Fighting Irish goal line. The

first time he scored was on a stirring 81-yard run, the second time Army put the ball in play from scrimmage.

Anderson, who was off the field at the end of the game, possibly with an injury, also scored on a 1-yard plunge. However, Nick Pietrosante, a 210-pound Ansonia, Conn., received the Rice award as the game's outstanding player by the vote of the occupants of the press box.

The powerful fullback, who was on the bench with injuries most of the year, well deserved the honor. He, too, scored twice, the second time on a 65-yard dash in the last minute of the third period, when Army's second team was on the field.

Pietrosante was a bull all afternoon with his pile-driving rushes inside. He got off tremendous punts and his interception of a pass was a key play in Army's defeat.

The interception was made in the final quarter, after Stickles had failed on his try for the extra point. That left Notre Dame trailing by 21—20. Army, deep in its own territory, surprisingly elected to take to the air, instead of protecting its lead.

Quarterback Dave Bourland got off a jump pass over the center of the line. Frank Geremia knocked the ball down and it appeared to be an incompleted pass. But Pietrosante managed to grab the dropping ball just before it struck the ground. Bedlam broke loose in the Notre Dame stands as the Irish took possession on Army's 26-yard mark.

The cadets put up a furious defense to stop Notre Dame. It seemed they had saved their lead and the victory. But on fourth down, with the ball on the Army 22, Stickles dropped back to the 28.

With Quarterback Bob Williams, who was second only to Pietrosante among Notre Dame's heroes, holding the ball, Stickles booted the winning kick.

Pietrosante was one of the half dozen Fighting Irish who had been afflicted with the flu at South Bend before the team's departure for the game. He and all of the others, including the brilliant Dick Lynch, all played their alloted parts without any noticeable slackening of their efficiency.

Pietrosante gained 139 yards in twenty rushes. Lynch made 52 yards in fourteen carries. Anderson was the top ground-gainer of the game.

Fifteen times the superb Army sophomore halfback took the ball for a total gain of 186 yards. His 81-yard touchdown dash, on which he faked Lynch beautifully before cutting towards the middle and speeding ahead of Bob Scholtz, caught Notre Dame by surprise.

For the first time in the fif-

teen years that Coach Earl Blaik has used the T formation at West Point, Army attacked from an unbalanced line. Notre Dame could hardly have been prepared for it. A big opening developed at left tackle, through which Anderson shot to head for the sideline before reversing himself.

Army Scores Quickly

In scoring its three touchdowns, Army went 81 yards in three plays in the first quarter; 72 in seven, and 81 in eleven in the third period. The Fighting Irish went 80 yards in thirteen plays to make the score 7—7 at the end of the opening quarter.

Neither team scored in the second period, in which Army lost the ball on the 14 after going 56 yards. Notre Dame was stopped on the 20 after an advance of 66 yards.

Pietrosante's 65-yard dash was made forty-eight seconds after Army had scored its third touchdown in the third quarter. The teams changed sides with Army leading by 21—14.

Notre Dame got its third tally right after the start of the final quarter. It went 56 yards in twelve plays.

Army's failure to make a first down by about a yard just before this Notre Dame score was a turning point in the game. The cadets had to kick, and it was after receiving the punt that the Fighting Irish went for their score.

Again, after Stickles' field goal, Army was short of a first down by a yard at midfield. Desperate, it ran on fourth down. Fullback Harry Walters was overwhelmed as green-jersey men swarmed in to gang-tackle him.

This was a game in which the offense predominated. With both sides clobbering one another, Army gained 303 yards on the ground, to 254 for Notre Dame. The passing distance was about the same.

In addition to Pietrosante, Lynch and Williams, who was a strong runner, a good passer, a clever ball-handler in carrying out fakes and a decisive blocker; and Frank Reynolds also did good work on offense for Notre Dame. Reynolds filled in at left half for Aubrey Lewis, Notre Dame's fastest back, who had to be left at South Bend with an injured ankle. Co-Captain Ed Sullivan was also out of the game with a bad ankle.

For Army, Anderson, Pete Dawkins, Bourland, Walters and Vin Barta stood out. Dawkins, stationed as a flanker, got off on a run of 39 yards as he took a fast pitchout from Bourland, faked Reynolds and raced to the 7-yard mark. From there he swept around right end on the next play as he took another toss from Bourland and went across. Barta and Bourland threw hard blocks ahead of him. That was one of numerous times that Bourland helped open the way for the ball carrier.

Irish Vary Attack

Notre Dame ran the split T from a balanced line. At times the spacing was conventional, but on others the slot was used. This had the ends or a back and an end out wide and after a back or an end in the wingback position. At times the Irish had an end and a back both stationed wide on one side.

It called for quick, heady defensive play on the part of Army to meet this varying attack. And at times the cadets were spread well across the field. They defended well on the flanks and against passes, but they could not stop Pietrosante and Lynch inside.

It was a day of marvelous weather for football, with a warm sun offsetting the slight chill. The crowd did not quite fill the big horseshoe stadium, but it was the largest gathering to see these rivals play since their 1930 meeting at Chicago.

The West Point Cadet Corps, 2,320 strong, marched in an hour before the play started. The cadets thrilled the crowd with their faultless maneuvers on parade. Then the Army mules went racing around the track as the cheer leaders kept the incipient generals bursting into song and cheers.

On the other side of the field there was a big gathering of Notre Dame followers, some of them from as far away as Los Angeles. They were much in evidence with their cheers, particularly when their marching band was in action. After the game, hundreds of them poured out to swarm around and congratulate their team and tear down the goal posts in quick time.

Notre Dame won the toss and received Maurice Hilliard's kickoff. Reynolds, taking a pitchout, passed to Lynch for 22 yards on the second scrimmage and Notre Dame seemed on its way. But three plays later Dawkins intercepted Williams' pass and Army took possession on its 17.

Cadets Stopped on 14

In two plays the Cadets had a score. Dawkins got 2 yards and then Anderson was off on his 81-yard dash for a touchdown. Hilliard kicked the extra point and Army led by 7—0 in less than three minutes.

When Notre Dame was stopped without gain after receiving the next kick-off, it appeared that Army was too strong for the Fighting Irish. But right after the cadets had quick-kicked across the goal line, Notre Dame took over on its 20 and went all the way.

Williams threw three passes for 36 yards on the advance of 80 yards. He also broke loose for 17 yards on a clever fake. Pietrosante went over from the 1 and Don White kicked the extra point to make the score 7—7.

Army went 56 yards to the 14, with Anderson and Dawkins making the gains. Army was stopped short of a first down on the 14 on the first play of the second quarter.

Notre Dame took possession there and went 66 yards with Pietrosante and Reynolds the big gainers. The Irish were stopped after reaching the Army 20.

In the third period, Army took the kick-off and went 72 yards. Bourland and Anderson carried to the Notre Dame 46 and then Dawkins got loose on his 39-yard run with a pitchout. He scored from the 7 on the next play.

Hilliard kicked the point and Army led, 14—7. Reynolds took the next kick-off and sped 52 yards up the middle behind a wedge of blockers. Bourland nailed him on the Army 38 when it seemed he might go all the way. Notre Dame advanced the ball to the 18 and there lost it on downs.

After an exchange of kicks, Army was off to its third touchdown. It went 81 yards in eleven plays. Notre Dame was using a nine-man line. Bourland, noting this, called on the air arm, which he had employed sparing-

Statistics of the Game

	N. D.	Army
First downs	15	16
Rushing yardage	254	303
Passing yardage	81	83
Passes attempted	15	9
Passes completed	7	5
Passes intercepted by	1	1
Punts	4	4
Av. dist. of punts, yds.	37	32.5
Fumbles lost	0	0
Yards penalized	45	20

ly up to this time.

Three passes were completed on the march, two to Army's fine end, Bill Graf, before Notre Dame changed its defenses. Then Anderson went crashing through center with terrific drive and was stopped less than a yard from the goal line. On the next play, he took a pitch out and swept around left end, with Bourland blocking for him. Walters kicked the point and Army led, 21—7.

With one minute remaining in the quarter, Blaik sent in his second team. In forty-eight

seconds Notre Dame had a touchdown. It took just one play.

Pietrosante broke away when he seemed to be surrounded in the center of the field and raced toward his left, to go all the way, 65 yards. Stickles kicked the extra point and it was 21—14.

The teams changed sides for the final quarter, and Army, failing to make a first down after taking the kick-off, punted. Notre Dame swept 56 yards to score. It stayed on the ground entirely and Lynch, Williams, Reynolds and Pietrosante carried. Army's line was overpowered and Lynch went over from the 1.

Stickles missed on the conversion and it seemed Army's game, with the score 21—20. But then Pietrosante's interception enabled Notre Dame to gain a reprieve. Taking the ball on the Army 26, the Irish moved to the 22. Then followed the winning field goal by Stickles.

With less than seven minutes

left the Army took the kick-off and went to midfield. There it was stopped, falling just short of a first down. That was its last chance.

NOTRE DAME (23)
Left Ends—Royer, Stickles, Prendergast.
Left Tackles—Geremia, Puntillo.
Left Guards—Schaaf, Hurd, Sabal.
Centers—Sholtz, Corson.
Right Guards—Ecuyer, Gaydos, Adamson.
Right Tackles—Lawrence, Nagurski.
Right Ends—Myers, Wetoska.
Quarterbacks—Williams, Izo, White.
Left Halfbacks—Reynolds, Selcer, Ward.
Right Halfbacks—Lynch, Just, Ward.
Fullbacks—Pietrosante, Toth, Lima.

ARMY (21)
Left Ends—Usry, Warner.
Left Tackles—Melnik, Millick.
Left Guards—Novogratz, Rowe.
Centers—Kernan, Oswandel.
Right Guards—Slater, Lytle.
Right Tackles—Hilliard, Wilmoth, Millick.
Right Ends—Graf, Morrison.
Quarterbacks—Bourland, Douglas.
Left Halfbacks—Anderson, Roesler.
Right Halfbacks—Dawkins, Waldrop.
Fullbacks—Barta, Walters.

Army	7	0	14	0—21
Notre Dame	7	0	7	9—23

Notre Dame scoring—Touchdowns: Pietrosante 2 (1 plunge, 65, run), Lynch (1, plunge). Field goal—Stickles (32). Conversions: Stickles, White (placements). Army scoring—Touchdowns: Anderson 2 (41 run, 1 run), Dawkins (6, run). Conversions: Hilliard 2, Walters (placements).

October 13, 1957

College Football Notes

'Ride Series' Aims to Fool Defense

By JOSEPH M. SHEEHAN

Many new technical terms have crept into football's vocabulary while some fans weren't listening. Among them is "ride series." That's the designation for one of the most effective play sequences of the modern T formation.

In some centers of gridiron culture, the ride series is called the "ride-'em," "drive" or "belly" series. Under any name, it's an ingenious set of plays featuring split-second timing and a shell-game brand of ball-handling by the quarterback.

For a practical demonstration of how the ride series works, Saturday's Yale-Army game at New Haven is recommended. The Black Knights and Bulldogs both rely heavily on the sequence and have developed it to a high degree.

So spectators at the Bowl can get attuned in advance to its operations, Col. Earl Blaik sketched Army's ride series. The West Point coach isn't divulging any tactical secrets in the diagram that appears in the adjacent column. It could just as well have been copied from Jordan Olivar's Yale play-book.

Here's the step-by-step procedure in the ride series left halfback slant off tackle that is illustrated:

The quarterback takes a hand-to-hand snap from center. He whirls to his right and takes a long step to the rear. With arms extended, he plunks the ball into the middle of the fullback, who has started forward with the snap.

Then comes the "ride." Keeping his hands on the ball, the quarterback rides in toward the line with the hunched-over fullback. In this particular play of

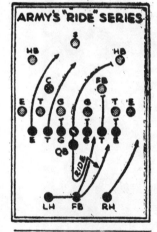

the series, the quarterback removes the ball from the fullback's covering grasp just short of the point of contact.

Meanwhile, the left halfback, also taking off at the snap, has cut across through the starting position vacated by the fullback and turned toward the line on a slightly wider slant. If the timing is right, he will be about a step behind and a step outside the fullback when the quarterback finishes his ride.

The quarterback then steps to the right and hands off to the left halfback, who hits between the left defensive tackle and end. To keep the defense wary of the other possibilities in the situation, the quarterback also will make an after-the-act feint of a pitch-out to the right halfback and finally retreat as though to pass.

The series embraces pitch-out sweeps to either halfback and the pass, too. And, of course, to set up the sequence, the quarterback must now and then give the ball to the fullback. When the series is well-executed the

fullback almost always is tackled when he hits the line and it would be a shame to disillusion the defense completely.

The key to the whole series is the ride because it involves a "deliberate fake" to which the defense has a chance to react. The threat of the fullback plunge pins the line-backer and defensive tackle at the point of impact and helps set them up for blocks.

It may be noted that, as diagrammed for use against a conventional six-man line, this play shows no block on the defensive left end. He'll be screened out, if necessary, by the right halfback. However, the chances are that the right halfback can maneuver the end out of the play without contact by flaring wide. In today's fluid football, where defensive alignments and tactics vary from play to play, blocking assignments have to be adjusted on the field.

November 2, 1955

College Football Notes

Variety of Defenses Keeps Attack Alert

By JOSEPH M. SHEEHAN

Time was when a football team's only worry about the rival defense was whether the backs would be deployed in box or diamond array behind the basic seven-man line.

Today an attacking team must be prepared to cope with anything from a four to a nine-man line. An added problem is that the initial defensive alignment is likely as not serves just as

camouflage for the real intent of the defense.

For instance, a seven-man line defense in which the ends retreat to take outside responsibility against passes is little different from a five-man line defense with the linebackers posted wide.

Similarly, a five-man line defense with the linebackers shooting the gap (charging across the scrimmage line at the snap) does not vary greatly from a seven-man line defense. And so on through all the numerous variations.

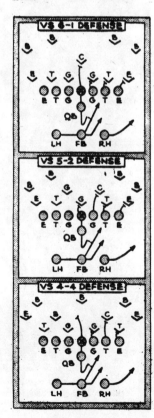

As an antidote to offensive line splits designed to isolate blocking targets at the pre-planned point of impact, modern defense emphasizes fluidity and pursuit rather than rigid territorial responsibility.

An increasing number of teams are using defense-in-depth arrays, such as the 4-4 and 5-2 set-ups diagrammed in the adjacent column. The 6-1 defense has many similar characteristics.

Along with the depth principle, these defenses feature loaded frontiers. Aggressive linebacking gives the 4-4 the effect of an eight-man line. With the corner backs of the secondary only a few steps behind the scrimmage line, the 5-2 and 6-1 almost

might be called nine-man line defenses.

How does the attack cope with the changing defensive picture?

It, too, must emphasize flexibility. Linemen are drilled to make on-the-spot adjustment of blocking assignments in accordance to the defense.

The general principle of line blocking, at least on inside-tackle plays, is to block the man directly opposite or, if unopposed, to block the closest man on the side away from the planned course of the ball carrier.

The accompanying diagrams give a rough idea of how this principle is applied. The play used for the purposes of illustration is a fullback slant inside tackle from the T-forma-

tion "ride series." To simplify matters, only the blocking assignments near the point of impact are charted.

Against even-number line defenses, where no rival plays him head-to-head, the offensive center picks off a linebacker. It's the single linebacker against the 6-1 defense, the "off" or "away" linebacker against the 4-4. The center's assignment against the 5-2 is to block the so-called middle guard.

The offensive right guard blocks straight ahead when directly opposed, as in the 6-1 and 4-4. He goes for the near linebacker when unopposed, as in the 5-2.

The offensive right tackle blocks the defensive tackle, sta-

tioned on his outside shoulder in the 6-1 and head-to-head with him in the 5-2. With no lineman opposite him in the 4-4, he goes for the linebacker straight ahead.

The plot thinckens when the defense supplements varied alignments with slanting charges (looping), cross charges (stunting) and gap-shooting linebackers (deals).

There are answers to those, too. A smart quarterback can make the defense look bad by calling a play that catches it zigging when it should be zagging. It's a great chess game that goes on down on the field.

November 10, 1955

Georgia Tech Tops Pitt

Pass Interference Against Grier Helps Engineers Triumph, 7 to 0

Associated Press Radiophotos

Officials ruled that Bobby Grier, on ground, Pitt's fullback, pushed Don Ellis of Georgia Tech as Ellis reached for pass from Wade Mitchell, quarterback. Tech took ball on one-yard line on penalty and then registered the only touchdown of the Sugar Bowl contest.

Georgia Tech Scores Following Controversial Play—Pitt Near Goal as Game Ends

NEW ORLEANS, Jan. 2 (UP) —Georgia Tech scored a touchdown on pass interference called against Bobby Grier, Negro fullback, and then stopped drive after drive for a 7-0 victory over Pittsburgh in the Sugar Bowl today. The Panthers were less than five yards from a touchdown when time ran out.

The touchdown came in the first five minutes after Tech had recovered a Pitt fumble on the Panthers' 33-yard line. On the next play, Quarterback Wade Mitchell threw toward End Don Ellis in the end zone and the official ruled Grier, the first Negro ever to play in a Sugar Bowl, had pushed Ellis and prevented the Tech player from catching the ball.

Tech got the ball on the 1-yard line, as a touchdown could not be awarded, and two plays later Mitchell plunged over for the touchdown. He also kicked the extra point.

After the game, Grier said, "I don't know how they called it. He was pushing me all the way down the field and finally pushed me across the goal line. And they called interference on me."

Tech Players 'Fine Sportsmen'

Grier, weeping openly in the dressing room, said the Tech players treated him wonderfully and added: "They are all fine sportsmen."

Johnny Michelosen, Pitt coach, said he didn't see the play and added: "The game is over. Sure I'd like to see the movies, but what can be done about it?"

A crowd of 80,175 watched Tech put up brilliant stands against the running power of the Panthers. In the fading minutes of the first half, Pitt drove to the Tech 1 but couldn't get it over on fourth down.

Pitt pulled a comeback in the last two minutes that almost succeeded on the southpaw passing of Darrell Lewis, a third string quarterback. Lewis, almost trapped by charging Tech defenders, shook off tackler after tackler and swept to the 4½-yard line from the Tech 30.

But the game ended before Pitt could stage another play.

Tech's kicking game kept Pittsburgh in the hole for most of the first half. Fullback Ken Owens kicked one 63 yards to the Pitt 2-yard line. Johnny Menger booted another out of bounds on the Pitt 5.

Quarterback Pete Neft of Pitt suffered a head injury early in the third period. Grier sustained an injury to his left leg and left the game in the fourth period.

Outside of the touchdown it was a defensive contest from start to finish.

Grier was cheered repeatedly for a gallant performance after his team was penalized on the interference play. He broke loose in the third period for 26 yards, longest run of the game, and made a spectacular catch of a pass by Quarterback Cornelius Salvaterra.

Engineers' Reach 7

With Quarterback Toppy Vann directing the attack, Tech staged only one sustained drive. That came in the fourth period when the Engineers drove to the Pitt 7. But Pitt's terror twins at the ends, Joe Walton and John Paluck, slowed the Engineers there.

Vann then threw a pass and Halfback Ray DiPasquale of Pitt intercepted it on the 5.

With Neft and then Salvaterra directing the offense, Pitt drove 79 yards but Tech's defensive unit, headed by Guards Franklin Brooks and Allen Ecker, took over on the 1.

Brooks later was voted the

Statistics of the Game

	Ga.Tech	Pitt
First downs	10	19
Rushing yardage	142	217
Passing yardage	0	94
Passes attempted	3	18
Passes completed	0	8
Passes intercepted by	1	1
Punts	6	4
Punting average, yds.	33.8	38.7
Fumbles lost	0	2
Yards penalized	15	72

most valuable player in the game.

Ironically, Pitt won the battle of statistics. The Panthers got 19 first downs to 10 for Tech, gained 217 yards rushing to 142 for Tech and also gained 94 yards passing to no passing gain for Tech.

The line-up (AP):

GEORGIA TECH (7)
Left Ends—Rose, Nabors, Huff.
Left Tackles—Vereen, Christy, Gossage.
Left Guards—Brooks, Fulcher, Baum.
Centers—Morris, Stephenson.
Right Guards—Ecker, Miller, Glazier.
Right Tackles—Thrash, Anderson, Askew.
Right Ends—Ellis, Bagwell.
Quarterbacks—Mitchell, Vann.
Left Halfbacks—Rotenberry, Flowers, Menger.
Right Halfbacks—Volkert, Thompson, Noe.
Fullbacks—Mattison, Owen, Gookin.

PITTSBURGH (0)
Left Ends—Walton, Glatz, Kiesel.
Left Tackles—Pollock, McCusker.
Left Guards—Scorsone, Hunter.
Centers—Cenci, Bose, Bruckman.
Right Guards—Schmitt, Bolkovac.
Right Tackles—Canil, Kissel, Linn.
Right Ends—Paluck, Rosborough.
Quarterbacks—Neft, Salvaterra, Lewis.
Left Halfbacks—Bowen, Cost.
Right Halfbacks—DiPasquale, Cimarolli, Jelic, Passodelis.
Fullbacks—Grier, Jenkins.

Georgia Tech	7	0	0	0—7
Pittsburgh	0	0	0	0—0

Touchdown—Mitchell (1, plunge). Conversion—Mitchell.

January 3, 1956

Michigan State Halts U.C.L.A. in Closing Seconds

KAISER'S KICK NIPS COAST TEAM, 17-14

Field Goal in Last 7 Seconds Wins for Michigan State Before 100,809 Fans

STATISTICS OF THE GAME

	Mich. St.	U.C.L.A.
First downs	18	13
Rushing yardage	251	136
Passing yardage	130	61
Passes attempted	18	10
Passes completed	6	2
Passes intercepted by	1	2
Punts	2	7
Punting average, yds.	40	39.5
Fumbles lost	1	0
Yards penalized	98	60

PASADENA, Calif., Jan. 2 (UP)—Michigan State's brilliant football team today scored one of the wildest Rose Bowl victories in history, defeating the University of California at Los Angeles, 17—14.

The finish was so frenzied that there was doubt as to the identity of the player who kicked the Spartans' winning field goal with 7 seconds to play. Dave Kaiser, an end, was credited with the deciding boot.

Fullback Gerry Planutis had attempted one field goal and missed from the 30-yard line in the hectic fourth period. Then Kaiser went in to the game to kick the game-winning goal, but all the announcers at the field gave Planutis the credit. The error was not corrected officially until the players reached the dressing room.

Planutis' Attempts Fail

Probably most of the 100,809 fans were unaware as they left the Stadium that the hero was Kaiser instead of Planutis. Kaiser was called on because Planutis' efforts on two previous attempts had failed.

Planutis teamed with Clarence Peaks and Walt Kowalczy to lead Michigan State to the victory after U. C. L. A. had rallied in the final period to tie the score at 14—14.

Except for the field goal, tailback Ronnie Knox of U.C.L.A., just recovered from a broken leg, might have emerged the hero for leading the Bruins to the tying touchdown.

In the final seconds of the game, the capacity crowd was on its feet while U. C. L. A. was penalized to its 1 and a short punt set up the winning kick.

Kowalczyk and Peaks were the Spartans' running stars of the game. Michigan State riddled the Bruin line, then scored on two passes.

Peaks was involved in both efforts. He caught one aerial for a touchdown and connected on a 67-yard play with End John Lewis for the other.

The victory was the ninth for the Big Ten in the ten years of the Big Ten-Pacific Coast Conference pact.

Bruins Get Break

U. C. L. A. capitalized on a break at the start of the game. Earl Morrall's pass was intercepted on the Spartan 19 by Halfback Jim Decker, who returned the ball to the 16. Sam Brown and Fullback Bob Davenport alternated in carrying to the 2. Davenport plunged over from there, Decker converted and U. C. L. A. led, 7—0, with three minutes of play gone.

The Bruins got another break in the first period when Morrall fumbled and U. C. L. A. recovered on the 36. The Coast team

worked the ball down to the Spartan 13, but was shoved back to the 21.

Decker tried a field goal from the 27 but missed. From that point, the Spartans started moving. Kowalczyk broke loose for 30 yards on the drive, during which Morrall completed his first pass of the game to Jim Hinesly. Morrall passed again on the 13 and tossed a scoring strike to Peaks on the goal line. Michigan State was on its own 9 when the half-time gun cracked with the scored tied at 7—7.

Neither team could score in the third period. Michigan State exercised ball control and drove to the U. C. L. A. 2 only to be shoved back to the 8. Planutis attempted a 15-yard field goal, but the kick was wide. U. C. L. A. then got into Michigan State territory, but was stopped on the 39.

Starting from the 20, the Spartans drove to the 33, where Peaks took a pitchout from Morrall and threw a pass to Lewis. The end caught the ball on the 20 and broke away from a defender to score after 49 seconds of the final period.

Shortly thereafter, Brown was hurt and Knox entered the game. After an exchange of punts, Knox completed U. C. L. A.'s first pass, a 14-yard toss to End Rommie Loudd. He followed that with his 47-yard pass to Decker to the 7. Knox worked the ball to the 1 on two running plays and a substitute fullback, Doug Peters, dived over.

Penalty Sets Back Bruins

Then the Spartans, with Planutis and Peaks carrying, reached the U. C. L. A. 24 and Planutis attempted the field goal that failed. An unsportsmanlike conduct penalty set U. C. L. A. back to the 1.

Knox' punt was to the U. C. L. A. 40, but the Bruins were penalized for interfering with

the receiver to the 19. Michigan State was penalized 15 yards.

Morrall passed for 10 yards, then a delaying-the-game penalty set Michigan State back another 5 yards before Kaiser kicked his field goal from the 31.

Kaiser, a 200-pound transfer student from Notre Dame, never before had kicked a field goal in college competition. The six-foot player from Alpena, Mich., had made two unsuccessful tries earlier this season. Kaiser's kick carried forty-one yards, since the goal posts are set ten yards behind the goal line. The ball was booted on a slight angle.

Kowalczyk was chosen the player of the game by the Helms Athletic Foundation. He carried thirteen times for 88 yards and an average of 6.7.

The line-up (UP):

MICHIGAN STATE (17)
Left Ends—Lewis, Kolodziej, Jones, Jewett.
Left Tackles—Masters, Rutledge.
Left Guards—Currie, Matsos.
Centers—Badaczewski, Matsko.
Right Guards—Nystrom, Hellern.
Right Tackles—Haidys, Burke.
Right Ends—Kaiser, Hinesly.
Quarterbacks—Morrall, Wilson.
Left Halfbacks—Peaks, Mendyk.
Right Halfbacks—Kowalczyk, Wulff, Zysk, Gaddini.
Fullbacks—Planutis, Lowe.

U. C. L. A. (14)
Left Ends—Hermann, J. Smith, O'Garro.
Left Tackles—White, Shinnick, Hampton.
Left Guards—Cureton, Birren.
Centers—Palmer, Matheny.
Right Guards—J. Brown, Harris.
Right Tackles—Moreno, Penner.
Right Ends—Loudd, Adams, H. Smith.
Quarterbacks—Ballard, Berdgahl.
Left Halfbacks—S. Brown, Bradley, Knox.
Right Halfbacks—Decker, Holloway.
Fullbacks—Davenport, Peters.

Michigan State	0	7	0	10—17
U. C. L. A.	0	7	0	7—14

Michigan State scoring—Touchdowns: Peaks (13, pass from Morrall), Lewis (67, pass from Peaks). Field goal: Kaiser (41). Conversions: Planutis 2.
U. C. L. A. scoring—Touchdowns: Davenport (2, plunge), Peters (1, plunge). Conversions: Decker 2.

January 3, 1956

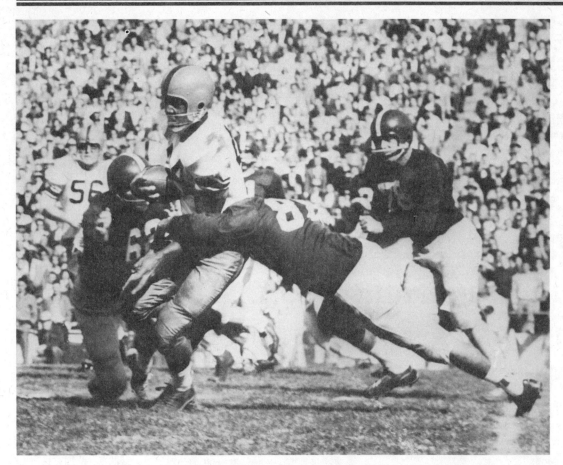

Syracuse's Jim Brown is shown here being tackled in the 1957 Cotton Bowl. It usually took several men to bring him down.

The 1958 Army team had a formation that featured a "lonesome end." Bill Carpenter (number 87) stayed out of the huddle and got his signals from the sideline.

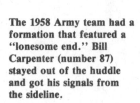

Brown Scores 43 Points In Last Game for Orange

By LINCOLN A. WERDEN
Special to The New York Times.

SYRACUSE, Nov. 17—As far as the Colgate football team was concerned, there was just too much Jimmy Brown in the game today. The crushing Syracuse left halfback from Manhasset, L. I., in an individual performance of All-America proportions, led his team to a 61-7 triumph before a sellout crowd of 39,701.

In his final game for the Orange, Brown accounted for 43 points, scoring six touchdowns and kicking 7 extra-point placements. No other team in this fifty-seven-year-old series had tallied as many points as the Syracuse aggregation did in Archbold Stadium this cold gray afternoon.

The highest total credited to any previous Syracuse squad came in 1944. That was 43 points, the total that Brown amassed by the time he made his final exit early in the fourth period.

In 1898, Colgate defeated Syracuse, 58 to 0, and that was the scoring mark shattered by Brown and this alert, fast-moving squad that rolled on to accumulate 511 yards by rushing.

Davis' Record Broken

Brown's share of this figure was 197 yards on twenty-two carriers. As a result, the senior left half sent his season's ground-gaining yardage to 986 yards. This erased the previous best by any Syracuse player, which was the 805 yards compiled by George Davis in 1949.

Syracuse was on the way to a touchdown after taking the opening kick-off. During the first half, Syracuse scored four of the five times it had the ball. On the other occasion, a fumble on the 2-yard line enabled Colgate to gain possession. But the Orange attack was soon rumbling goalward again.

In the second half, Syracuse scored five of the six times it had possession. An intercepted pass momentarily stalled Syracuse on the Red Raiders' 20. But then, as in the second quarter, the Orange recovered quickly from this error and pounded out a touchdown.

Jamison Scores on Pass

On the Colgate side, Guy Martin, the team's top quarterback and passing ace, tried mightily to overcome the Syracuse line and hit his receivers. He completed four out of four in the initial quarter and hit his left end, Al Jamison for the Raider touchdown in 14:00 of the opening period. Martin converted with a placement.

Martin fought doggedly on defense. Although pressed as the game wore on, he completed six-

teen of thirty-five for 195 yards.

With Governor Harriman among the spectators, the Syracuse fans enjoyed this concluding game of one of the Orange's successful football seasons. There are rumors on the campus that their team may be selected for a post-season bowl game.

Colgate, victor over Yale earlier in the season, had been beaten thrice before this contest. Syracuse was the pre-game favorite, having lost only once, by 14-7, to Pitt. But no one anticipated the stunning show that Brown was to put on.

Ridlon's Pass Surprises

This victory put Syracuse's string at six over the Raiders, a record. At half-time, the press box announcer jocularly said: "The score is now Brown 27, Colgate 7." Brown was responsible for scoring all of his team's points in the first half.

In the first period Brown scored at the end of Syracuse's initial 75-yard drive from the 1-yard line. A 43-yard running pass, Jim Ridlon to Dick Lasse, right end, surprised Colgate and was the highlight of this march. Brown converted to make it 7—0 in 4:54.

Syracuse kicked off but Colgate was soon forced to punt. Moving from its 29, Syracuse went 71 yards in ten plays. Brown went the concluding 15 yards around his left end for the touchdown. His conversion made it 14—0. The time was 11:14.

It was Colgate's turn to score as Martin began firing with extreme accuracy. Colgate moved 76 yards in six plays, the biggest chunk being a 33-yard gain on an aerial to Dick Randall.

The Syracuse alternate team was in on defense during this Colgate attack. The starting line-up returned to the game and Syracuse had the ball at midfield after two Colgate kick-offs went out of bounds. Taking a pitch-out from Quarterback Chuck Zimmerman, Brown raced down his right sideline 50 yards for the touchdown. It was 20—7

and Brown's try for the extra point was wide.

After the three touchdowns in the first quarter, Syracuse bagged one in the second. Colgate penetrated to its rival's 19, only to have Zimmerman intercept a Martin pass to give Syracuse the ball on the Orange 13.

Alan Cann, Syracuse fullback, carried twelve times in the first half for 91 yards and was a constant threat before he hobbled off with a knee injury in the third chapter. Brown gained a first down on the Colgate 3. Here Ridlon fumbled as he appeared to be going for the touchdown.

Martin of Colgate recovered and Syracuse was momentarily thwarted. Martin tried to connect with a receiver and after failing twice, punted to Brown on fourth down.

From the Colgate 29, Syracuse went on to score by 11:27. Brown went to his right for the last 8 yards. His conversion made it 27—7.

Pass by Martin Fails

John Call, Colgate right half, went 45 yards on a big bid by the Raiders before the half ended. Colgate was down to the Syracuse 4 as Martin tried to pass for a touchdown in the last fifteen seconds, but failed.

Brown had carried thirteen times for 127 yards in the first half.

In the third period Syracuse added 21 points.

Syracuse went 74 yards on fourteen plays, with Zimmerman keeping the ball on a quarterback sneak for the fifth touchdown. Brown converted again. The time was 8:21 and the score 34—7.

When Syracuse had the ball a little later Brown went 19 yards to his left and then 19 yards to his right for the touchdown on the last two of four plays that were required for this score.

Brown avoided all tacklers on this touchdown sprint. He then kicked the placement to make it 41—7 at 10:50.

Before the third period was over, Syracuse went 46 yards on six plays, with Fred Kuczala, a reserve quarterback, going over from the one-foot line.

Dean Danigelis attempted to convert and Colgate was charged with roughing the kicker. Brown came in to replace Danigelis and kicked the placement for a 48-7 margin at 14:56.

Syracuse recovered a Colgate fumble at the outset of the final quarter. From the Raiders' 20, Syracuse went for its eighth touchdown in 1:54 after Brown had charged through from the 1-yard line. Brown's placement was good and the score was 55—7.

The Orange began from their 24 in a drive midway through the fourth session, but Martin's interception gave the ball to Colgate on the Syracuse 20. With reserves in the line-up for most of this period, Syracuse headed goalward immediately after the Martin interception.

Ed Coffin, Syracuse fullback, grabbed a subsequent Martin toss and Syracuse had the ball on the Colgate 9. Three plays later and Dan Ciervo, one of Brown's replacements at left half, knifed through from the 2 yard line. Dan Fogarty's placement was wide and the score was 61—7. Colgate went all the way to the Orange 9 before the game closed, but Syracuse was moving again after Danigelis intercepted a pass on his goal line and raced back 45 yards.

The Line-Up

November 18, 1956

Statistics of the Game

	Syr.	Col.
First downs	31	14
Rushing yardage	511	95
Passing yardage	99	195
Passes attempted	7	35
Passes completed	4	16
Passes intercepted by	5	0
Fumbles lost	1	2
Number of punts	0	4
Av. dist. of punts, yds.	0	33.7
Yards penalized	44	16

NOTRE DAME TOPS OKLAHOMA, 7-0

By The Associated Press.

NORMAN, Okla., Nov. 16—Oklahoma's record streak of forty-seven football victories was ended today by a Notre Dame team that marched 80 yards in the closing minutes for a touchdown and a 7-0 triumph.

Oklahoma, ranked No. 2 in the nation and an 18-point fa-

vorite, couldn't move against the rock-wall Notre Dame line and the Sooners saw another of its streaks shattered—scoring in 123 consecutive games.

The defeat was only the ninth for the Oklahoma coach, Bud Wilkinson, since he became head coach at Oklahoma in 1947. It virtually ended any

chance for the Sooners of getting a third straight national championship.

Although the partisan, sellout crowd of 62,000 came out for a Roman holiday, they were stunned into silence as the Sooners were unable to pull their usual last-quarter winning touchdowns—a Wilkinson team trademark.

Rousing Cheer for Irish

As the game ended when Oklahoma's desperation passing drive was cut off by an intercepted aerial, the crowd rose as one and suddenly gave the Notre Dame team a rousing cheer.

It was a far cry from last year when the Sooners ran over Notre Dame, 40—0. The victory gave the Irish a 3-1 edge in the five-year-old series dating back to 1952.

The smashing, rocking Notre Dame line didn't permit the Sooners to get started either on the ground or in the air.

The Sooners were able to make only 98 yards on the ground and in the air just 47. Notre Dame, paced by its brilliant, 210-pound fullback Nick Pietrosante, rolled up 169. In the air, the Irish gained 79 yards by hitting nine of twenty passes. Bob Williams did most of the passing for Notre Dame.

Notre Dame's touchdown drive, biting off short but consistent yardage against the Sooners' alternate team, carried from the 20 after an Oklahoma punt went into the end zone.

Sooners Call First Team

Time after time, Pietrosante picked up the necessary yard he needed as the Irish smashed through the Oklahoma line. Notre Dame moved to the 8 and the Sooner first team came in to try to make the third Sooner goal-line stand of the day.

Pietrosante smashed four yards through center and Dick Lynch was stopped for no gain. On the third down, Williams went a yard through center.

Then Lynch crossed up the Sooners and rolled around his right end to score standing up. Monty Stickles converted to give Notre Dame the upset and end collegiate football's longest winning streak.

The closest Oklahoma could get to Notre Dame's goal was in the first quarter when the Sooners' alternate team moved to the 3 before being held on downs.

In the third period, brilliant punting by Clendon Thomas and David Baker kept Notre Dame back on its goal line but the Sooners couldn't capitalize.

Thomas sent punts down on the Notre Dame 15 and 4 and

Statistics of the Game

	N. D.	Okla.
First downs	17	9
Rushing yardage	169	98
Passing yardage	79	47
Passes attempted	20	11
Passes completed	9	4
Passes intercepted by	1	1
Punts	8	10
Av. dist. of punts, yds.	38.5	36.5
Fumbles lost	1	1
Yards penalized	45	35

Baker put them down on the 3 and 7.

This time there were no breaks as Notre Dame shook off last week's jitters that saw the Irish fumble away the ball five times in losing to Michigan State, 34—6.

Pietrosante gained almost a third of Notre Dame's rushing yardage as he made 56 yards on seventeen carries. Lynch was just two yards behind with 54 in seventeen carries. The best an Oklahoma player could muster was 36 yards in ten tries. This was made by Thomas.

Williams completed eight of nineteen passes for 70 yards. In Oklahoma's last-minute desperation drive, Quarterback Bennett Watts made two of three aerials for 31 yards.

Notre Dame was the last team to beat Oklahoma, at the start of the 1953 season on the same field that it smothered the Sooners today. Then Coach Frank Leahy's Irish beat Oklahoma, 28—21. The next game, Oklahoma and Pittsburgh tied at 7—7. Then the Sooners set sail through the forty-seven games until Terry Brennan's Irish stopped the string today.

Wilkinson, the nation's winningest, active coach, had amassed 101 victories in his ten years at Oklahoma. There were three ties.

Oklahoma started as if it would stretch its string. It marched the first time it got its hands on the ball from the Sooner 42 down to the Irish 13, but the big Notre Dame line stiffened at the 13.

Oklahoma continued to play in Notre Dame territory the rest of the first quarter. It had another chance when a fumble, with nine minutes gone, was recovered by Guard Dick Corbitt on the Notre Dame 34. However, the Sooners were stopped cold and finally Baker had to punt on fourth down.

In the second quarter another Sooner drive got down to the 23 but on the first play of the second quarter, Carl Dodd fumbled. The ball was punched around in the Sooner backfield and Pietrosante finally smothered it on the Notre Dame 48.

Then Williams started his passing attack to three different receivers and piloted the Irish down to the 3 with first and goal. Pietrosante picked up a yard in each of two plunges, Frank Reynolds went to the one-foot line and then Jim Just was held for no gain.

Later Notre Dame came back with its bruising ground game and moved to the 16. With fourth down Stickles came in for his fake place kick but instead Williams hit Just on the 6 for a first down. It was then on the second play that Reynolds' pass was intercepted by Baker in the end zone.

NOTRE DAME (7)
Left Ends—Royer, Prendergast.
Left Tackles—Puntillo, Geremia.
Left Guards—Schaaf, Adamson, Sabal.
Centers—Scholtz, Kuchta.
Right Guards—Ecuyer, Djubasak.
Right Tackles—Lawrence, Nagurski, Dolan.
Right Ends—Stickles, Wetoska, Colosimo.
Quarterbacks—Williams, Izo, White, Hebert.
Left Halfbacks—Reynolds, Doyle.
Right Halfbacks—Lynch, Just.
Fullbacks—Pietrosante, Toth, Lima.
OKLAHOMA (0)
Left Ends—Stiller, Coyle.
Left Tackles—Searcy, Thompson.
Left Guards—Northcutt, Owjesky, Gwinn.
Centers—Harrison, Davis.
Right Guards—Krisher, Corbitt.
Right Tackles—D. Jennings, Lawrence, Ladd.
Right Ends—Rector, S. Jennings.
Quarterbacks—Dodd, Baker, Watts, Sherrod.
Left Halfbacks—Sandefer, Boyd, Hobby.
Right Halfbacks—Thomas, Carpenter, Gautt, Pellow.
Fullbacks—Morris, Rolle.
Notre Dame .... 0 0 0 7—7
Oklahoma .... 0 0 0 0—0
Touchdown—Lynch (3, run). Conversion—Stickles.

November 17, 1957

College Football to Give 2 Points For Conversion on Pass or Run

By The Associated Press

FORT LAUDERDALE, Fla., Jan. 12 — College football rule-makers adopted a revolutionary change in the game's scoring system and relaxed substitution barriers another notch today. Both changes take effect immediately.

Recalling the scoring rule from a subcommittee, the football lawmakers voted to give 2 points for a conversion scored on a run or a pass and one point if scored on a kick.

This surprise move—designed to add drama to the dull conversion play—was the first change in football scoring rules since 1912.

Under the old rule only one point was awarded for a conversion, no matter how it was scored.

The football rules committee of the National Collegiate Athletic Association (N. C. A. A.) approved the scoring and substitution revisions by a unanimous vote.

The rules changes will affect all institutions playing football under N. C. A. A. rules, whether colleges or high schools. Many high schools use other rules, however, and some of those which use N. C. A. A. rules in general do not use all of them.

The substitution change permits every player to re-enter a game once during each quarter. For the past three seasons, only the eleven players of each team who started a quarter could re-enter. Substitutes were allowed only one appearance per quarter.

This change was adopted primarily to aid small colleges with limited squads, said the retiring committee chairman, Herbert Orrin (Fritz) Crisler, the athletic director of Michigan.

January 13, 1958

Army Eleven Launches Space Man

New 'Lonesome End' Quickly Invades Enemy Ground

By JOSEPH M. SHEEHAN

Army's "lonesome end" formation, introduced with such striking success against South Carolina last Saturday, has football fans buzzing.

Wherever gridiron aficionados gather, table cloths soon are chicken-tracked with the "X," "O" and other cabalistic symbols of diagrammaticians ready and willing but not always able to explain Col. Earl Blaik's latest stratagem.

To save grandstand quarterbacks laundry bills, Capt. Barney Gill of the Army coaching staff drew the "lonesome end" formation as it really is. It is presented here, in right and left aspects, for all to see.

For security reasons, Gill withheld one item of highly pertinent information. He did not divulge how the "lonesome end," who remains aloof from the huddle in which his ten team-mates cluster for play instructions, is apprised of the maneuver selected.

The suspicion, undenied at West Point, is that Army, perhaps with the help of Lieut. Col. Red Reeder, an old diamond buff, has adapted a set of baseball signs to pass the word to the quarantined flankman.

To do a little supposing: "Skin against skin" (i.e., rubbing of hand against face by a designated signaler) might mean a run to the right (if it were the right hand to the right cheek). "Skin against cloth" (i.e. plucking at jersey) might mean a certain type of pass, etc.

Army's football G-2 undoubtedly changes sender and code from game to game, if not quarter to quarter or even play to play.

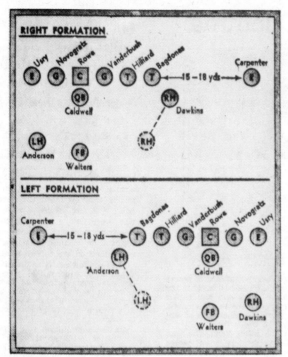

The New York Times   Oct. 1, 1958

Army's new "lonesome end" formation. Note how the cadet linemen reverse positions from right to left.

One clarifying point has been permitted to seep through the solid wall of communications security. How does the "lonesome end," who languishes in solitude on either side, know on which side to take station?

The position of the ball at the end of the preceding play determines that. If it is spotted to the right of the field's vertical center line, Army, with the "lonesome end" in the van, will line-up to the left, or wide side. And vice versa.

As the diagrams show, more clearly than words, the "lonesome end" formation is an unbalanced-line (four linemen to one side of center) wing-T or T formation (depending whether the lead (strong side) halfback moves up close to the line or fills out the bar of the T.

Cadet Lineman Rotate

To simplify blocking assignments, the linemen rotate with the shift to right or left. In other words, Bill Carpenter always is the "lonesome end;" the same tackle, Ed Bagdonas,

always is next to him, and so on all the way along the seven-man frontier.

The halfbacks interchange duties but not positions. On right formation, Pete Dawkins, the right half, is the wingback. On left formation, Bob Anderson, left half, moves up.

Spread formations such as Army's new set-up are not unusual in modern football. But Blaik seems to have made a strategical "breakthrough" by having his flanker posted in advance. With the "lonesome end" already in place when the rest of the team wheels out of the huddle, the Black Knights can strike much faster than if they had to wait for him to take his station.

South Carolina was caught completely by surprise. Now that the secret is out, it will be interesting to see whether Penn State and Notre Dame on the next two Saturdays will be able to keep closer company with the "lonesome end."

October 1, 1958

Villanova Excels in I Formation

By JOSEPH M. SHEEHAN

In this season of fresh approach to offensive football, Villanova has come up with one of the more interesting variations from the norm.

Coach Frank Reagan's Wildcats, currently sporting a four-

Notes on College Sports

game winning streak and a 5-1 won-lost record for the campaign, have turned to the I formation with spectacular results. This alignment, which gets its name from the perpendicular de-

ployment of the four backs behind center, is not new. Few things are in football.

Tom Nugent, Florida State's coach, devised it some years ago and still uses it, effectively enough for his team to have beaten Tennessee in one of last Saturday's major upsets.

Frank Leahy, while he still was at Notre Dame, also gave it a brief trial, but soon reverted to the split-T formation.

However, in this area, the I formation has not often been on display. For this reason, Coach Reagan was persuaded to sketch a couple of plays that indicate how it operates.

For obvious reasons, Frank describes the running play diagrammed at the top as the "middle wedge." It is a straight-ahead thrust by the right halfback, Dave Intrabartolo, the deep back in the I.

Double-team blocking by Villanova's center and left guard on the opposing right guard, and left halfback on the opposing left guard wedges open the hole.

Villanova's tackles shoot through to screen off the opposing linebackers, and Intrabartolo, led by his fullback, blasts through the middle after taking a hand-off from the quarterback.

The pass play diagrammed has been another "money play" for Villanova. Fakes by Jim Grazione, the quarterback, to the left halfback and the fullback hold the defensive linebackers in place.

The right halfback's flare to the right and the threat of a roll-out sweep by Grazione, who is an excellent runner, influences the defensive left halfback to edge in close.

Villanova's right end, Tom Heron, feints a block on him and then slips by to take a pass from Grazione in the deep right flat.

Unlike most modern offensive variations, which employ flanking ends and backs to spread and isolate the defending players, the I formation, by its concentration of backfield strength in the middle, compresses the defense.

Theoretically, this gives the offense, which holds the initiative by virtue of knowing in advance where it is going to strike, an opportunity to exploit the outside.

At the same time, I-formation teams space (split) their linemen to get running room and provide better blocking angles for plays up the middle, such as the wedge play diagrammed.

Aside from its inherent assets, the I formation gives Villanova the benefit of attacking from a set-up against which few defenses have had previous experience.

It should be remembered, however, that formations don't win football games. Good execution of the fundamentals does. Obviously, Villanova is dotting its I with solid blocking and tackling.

October 29, 1958

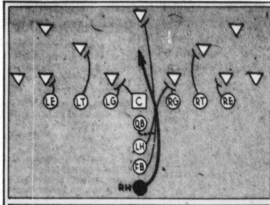

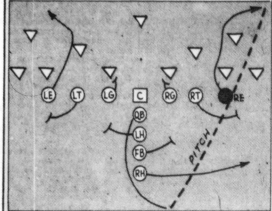

The New York Times   Oct. 29, 1958

I-formation run and pass used by Villanova

Rutgers' Option Is Rivals' Dilemma

By JOSEPH M. SHEEHAN

An ingenious short-side option play that capitalizes on the special talents of Bill Austin and Bob Simms has helped Rutgers maintain a pristine record in football this season.

The Scarlet Knights have scored three touchdowns by passing and three by running on this play, the details of which, as supplied by Coach John Stiegman, appear in the accompanying diagram. The play, which can be run to either side, is shown as Rutgers works it from its normal single-wing formation, with the line unbalanced to the right (four men on the right side of center).

From this set-up, Rutgers sends its fullback in motion to the left before the snap. After the fullback clears, a lead pass to the left is snapped to the left halfback, or tailback, who is Austin.

Behind the blocking of the fullback and the left guard, who pulls out of the line to lead the play, Austin sweeps toward the left sideline.

Meanwhile, the Rutgers left end, who is Simms, goes downfield and breaks out and the Rutgers right end, Dutch Wermuth, cuts downfield and across to the left, also penetrating the defensive right halfback zone.

Depending on the reaction of the defensive right halfback, Austin runs or throws. The decision is left to his snap judgment. If the halfbacks comes

Notes on College Sports

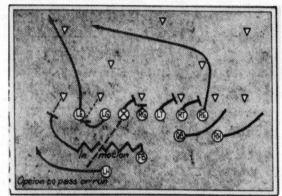

The New York Times   Nov. 5, 1958

Rutgers' single-wing short side pass-run option play

up to meet the threat of a run, Austin will pass. If the halfback retreats to guard against a pass, Bill will keep the ball and run.

This play represents a classic example of how the offense works at isolating a defender and confronting him with an insoluble dilemma.

That Rutgers is able to do so is a function of its use of the unbalanced-line single wing. The inherent strength of the lop-sided formation to the right obliges the defense to overshift to that side. This leaves the right halfback exposed to the counter-move toward the left.

Of course, drawing such a play and making it work are different things. With all its virtues) this is not a strong

play. There's not much power in front of the ball and, if the defensive right end and tackle charge aggressively enough, they have a good chance of nipping it in the bud.

On the other hand, the lead pass Austin gets from center gives him a half-step of breathing room. So clever a runner and deft a passer doesn't need much more. Also, Simms has the knack of getting loose quickly. That's why he's the East's leading pass receiver.

Lafayette will be well advised to be on guard against this play when it meets Rutgers for the Middle Atlantic Conference title and the Middle Three Brass Cannon Trophy at New Brunswick on Saturday.

November 5, 1958

COLLEGE ACTIONS WILL SPEED GAME

Wider Posts to Help Field Goal Kickers—Blocking Rule Is Clarified

LOS ANGELES, Jan. 14 (UPI)—The National Collegiate Athletic Association Rules Committee today widened the goal posts by 4 feet, 10 inches to invite more field goal attempts. The committee also relaxed the substitution restrictions to speed up football on the college level.

The committee unanimously approved a proposal to place the goal post uprights 24 feet apart, instead of the 19 feet, 2 inches as now is the case, to give field goal kickers a better target.

On the substitution rule, the committee voted to allow one man to enter the game anytime the clock is stopped without having his entry counted against his team.

This means that whenever the clock is stopped, except during an excess time out, one man and one man alone may be substituted. It will permit a coach to insert a field goal kicker or other specialist when the clock is stopped and then remove him without penalty.

January 29, 1959

NAVY BEATS ARMY BY 43-12, RECORD SCORE IN SERIES

100,000 SEE ROUT

Bellino Scores Three Times as Middies Trounce Cadets

By ALLISON DANZIG
Special to The New York Times.

PHILADELPHIA, Nov. 28—Navy perpetrated another of its shocking uprisings against a favored Army football team today. This time it was a massacre.

Rolling up the biggest score ever registered by either team in the service rivalry as Bullet

Joe Bellino went berserk and tallied three times, the midshipmen won all the way in this sixtieth meeting since 1890. The awful reckoning was 43—12.

The East's biggest football crowd of the year, numbering 100,000 and including most of the members of the Presidential Cabinet, saw the embattled town Tars take command at the outset. Before the game was eight minutes old they were leading by 13—0 as the streaking, shifty Bellino, the first Navy player ever to score three touchdowns against Army, sped 15 yards for his first touchdown and 46 yards for the second.

Army, which failed to make a first down in the opening period, scored twice in the second period, on a 29-yard pass from Joe Caldwell to Bill Carpenter,

and on Bob Anderson's 12-yard dash through his right tackle. But Navy added a third touchdown in this quarter. Tranchini went 11 yards on a clever bootleg play at the end of a drive of 66 yards, and Navy led, 21—12, at half-time.

Caldwell Has Bad Day

Thereafter, Army never was in the game. Navy, using four fast halfbacks on defense in concentrating on stopping the cadet passing attack, made the day a miserable one for Caldwell, Army's record-breaking passer. He was harried and overshooting his receivers and had three of his throws intercepted.

Navy shut down on the cadet running offense so solidly, with the line rising to its greatest

performance of the year, that Army had a net of minus 14 yards by rushing in the second half.

Anderson, Army's all-America halfback who has been handicapped by a bad knee most of the season, was limited to 11 yards in the second half. He was completely overshadowed by Bellino, who gained 110 yards in the first two periods and was voted the outstanding back in the game.

Gaining 151 yards by rushing and 66 by passing in the second half, Navy tallied its fourth touchdown in the third period to widen its lead to 29—12, and two more in the final quarter while holding the cadets scoreless.

Bellino set up the touchdown in the third period as he

snatched a tipped Caldwell pass and raced 37 yards before carrying the ball across from the 1-yard mark. A. Caldwell punt that went only 11 yards and gave the ball to Navy on the Army 29 started the Middies on the way to their fifth score.

Quarterback Goes Over

A pass by Joe Tranchini, who had one of his best days in completing nine of fifteen throws for 117 yards and who scored two touchdowns, accounted for 23 of the 29 yards just before the third period ended. The Navy quarterback carried the ball over from the 1 on a sneak. The final touchdown came a few minutes after the following kick-off.

Caldwell's pass was intercepted by Ron Brandquist, another fine performer for Navy. He was used as a fullback flanker on offense, with Dick Pariseau in the right halfback position. Brandquist grabbed the ball on the Army 30 and returned it to the 25.

Tranchini passed to George Bezek, who excelled with Tom Hyde on the Navy flanks, for 11 yards; and after Bellino had carried to the 1, Bandquist went across.

Tranchini passed to Bezek for 2 extra points, the fourth time he had completed a conversion pass, but this time Navy did not get the points. It was penalized for a personal foul, the third inflicted upon the Middies for being too rough in their plays, and the kick for the extra point from the 20-yard mark was blocked.

Just before the game ended, Army had its first scoring chance of the half. Caldwell now found his target consistently, for the first time in

the game, and four aerials to Carpenter, Anderson and Frank Gibson advanced the ball from the cadet 22 to Navy's 10. But the opportunity went for nought as Jim Honeywell intercepted another Caldwell pass in the end zone.

Scoring Drives Reviewed

A recapitulation of the scoring shows that Navy went 67 yards in six plays and 63 yards in three plays for its touchdowns in the first period; 66 yards in twelve plays in the second quarter; 18 yards in five plays after Bellino's interception in the third period; 29 yards in six plays in the third and fourth quarters; and 25 yards in six plays, following Pariseau's interception, for the last score.

Army advanced the ball 65 yards in nine plays for its first touchdown and 66 yards in twelve plays for its second.

Tranchini did not throw a touchdown pass, but he fired to Hyde, voted the outstanding lineman of the game, for 11 yards on the first touchdown advance; to Hyde for 12 yards on the second; to Tom Albershart for 11 and to Matalavage for 14 on a screen pass down the middle on the 66-yard march; to Brandquist for 23 on the 29-yard advance, and to Bezek for 11 on the final scoring drive.

In addition to his nine completions, the Navy quarterback passed for three 2-point conversions.

Caldwell threw one touchdown pass. Only six of his twenty-three serials reached the mark. Time and again he threw the ball beyond his receiver, in part because of the pressure put upon him by the Navy line and the thoroughness with which the middies in the secondary covered the receivers.

ACROBATICS: Roger Zailskas of Army lands on his back after intercepting pass aimed for Frank Dattilo of Navy during first period. Glen Adams of Army is other player.

CENTER OF ATTENTION: Joe Bellino of Navy gains 12 yards before Army catches him during the first period.

It was an unhappy day for the famed Army quarterback, who has broken Academy records this year and is rated by his coach, Dal Hall, as best passing quarterback Army ever had.

Nevertheless, Caldwell broke the Academy record of Glenn Davis for total gain. He brought his total to 1,258 yards today. The old mark, set by Davis in 1945, was 1,182 yards.

In scoring 43 points today, Navy exceeded the total of 42 it registered in 1951, the highest either team had made in the series. The combined total for the two teams, 55, also established a record. The old mark was 49, also made in 1951.

That was the second year of Eddie Erdelatz' tenure as Navy's head coach. The year before, Navy had administered a shock to a highly favored Army team with a 14-2 victory, the same kind of a shock Navy produced in 1946 when it came within an

Statistics of the Game

	Navy	Army
First downs	23	13
Rushing yardage	278	62
Passing yardage	117	138
Passes attempted	23	27
Passes completed	9	7
Passes intercepted by	3	3
Punts	3	9
Av. dist. of punts, yds.	35	29.1
Fumbles lost	2	0
Yards penalized	48	31

eyelash of beating the famous Doc Blanchard-Glenn Davis invincibles.

A Disappointing Finish

For Army, it was a disappointing finish to a season in which its high hopes were wrecked by a succession of injuries that almost decimated the backfield. The Cadets were in better shape today than they had been in weeks, with Carpenter, and Anderson who ruined Navy a year ago, ready

to show in close to peak form.

But Navy, which also had recovered from injuries, played as it had not all season, and Army's best was not good enough. More than anyone else, it was Bellino, one of the greatest ball-carriers ever to come out of Annapolis, who wrecked Army.

Injured for a good part of the season, Bellino had led Navy to victory in every game in which he was sound, and he did it again today with perhaps the most shining performance of his career, to the unalloyed joy of the 3,800 midshipmen and the dismay of the 2,500 cadets.

Wayne Hardin, who succeeded Erdelatz as head coach this year, has thus started out in the same way that Erdelatz did against Army.

The young Navy coach had said that his team was equal to Army in passing and in the running strength, and that it could win if the line played its best game of the year. The line did just that, with Hyde, John

Hewitt, the only sophomore on the first two teams, and Frank Visted in stellar roles.

NAVY (43)
Left Ends—Dattilo, Mather, Albershart.
Left Tackles—Boyer, Driscoll, Butsko, O'Donnell.
Left Guards—Thomas, Falconer, Lucci, Blumbo.
Centers—Visted, Stackhouse, Dunn.
Right Guards—Hewitt, Blockinger, Solak, Gansz.
Right Tackles—Erchul, Huffman, MacDonald.
Right Ends—Hyde, Bezek, Luper, Schriefer.
Quarterbacks—Tranchini, Maxfield, Spooner, Kisiel.
Left Halfbacks—Bellino, Correll, Pritchard, Mankowich.
Right Halfbacks — Brandquist, Pariseau, Hardison, Honeywell.
Fullbacks—Matalavage, Zenyuh.

ARMY (12)
Left Ends—Usry, Gibson, Everbach.
Left Guards—Jezior, Miller, Butzer.
Centers—Oswandel, Joulwan.
Right Guards—Vanderbush, Casp.
Left Tackles—Kuhns, Brown.
Right Tackles—McCarthy, Whitehead.
Right Ends—Carpenter, Waters, Fuellhart.
Quarterbacks—Caldwell, Blanda, Douglas.
Left Halfbacks—Anderson, Blumhardt, Minor, Adams.
Right Halfbacks—Kirschenbauer, Zailskas, Culver.
Fullbacks—Rushatz, Eielson.

Navy	13	8	8	14—43
Army	0	12	0	0—12

November 29, 1959

ALERT U.S.C. DEFEATS WISCONSIN IN ROSE BOWL, 42-37

100,000 THRILLED

Unbeaten, Top-Ranked Trojans Withstand Badgers' Rally

By BILL BECKER
Special to The New York Times.

PASADENA, Calif., Jan. 1—Southern California's national champion Trojans scored early and often and then hung on for dear life to edge the University of Wisconsin, 42, to 37, today in the all-time high-scoring parade in the Rose Bowl.

The Badgers, Big Ten champions and rated second only to the Trojans, almost ran U.S.C. out of the Pasadena pasture with 23 points in the final quarter. But they just couldn't catch up.

The wild finish, sparked by a superb quarterback, Ron Vanderkelen, had 98,698 spectators limp and hoarse. The total of 79 points far surpassed the previous Rose Bowl record set in 1930 when U.S.C. defeated Pittsburgh, 47-14.

Vanderkelen, magnificent in adversity, set another Rose Bowl record by completing 33 of 48 passes for 401 yards, including two touchdowns. He also scored on a 17-yard run himself.

But Pete Beathard, his opposing quarterback, was almost as flashy, if

not as prolific. Beathard threw four touchdown passes in completing eight of 12. That gave him a record, too.

The touchdowns and records were as plentiful as popcorn as the two top elevens put on a genuine professional show. Wisconsin ran up 32 first downs to 15 for the Trojans—and got only the consolation of chalking up another for the books.

Richter, Bedsole Score

Vanderkelen's payoff passes went 19 yards to his favorite target, Pat Richter, the All-America end, and four yards to Gary Kroner, a workhorse halfback.

Beathard's scoring shots went 57 and 23 to Hal Bedsole, Troy's All-America wingman; 13 yards to Fred Hill, another end; and 13 yards to Ron Butcher, a tackle who was eligible on a shift.

The last enumerated bought Troy's first touchdown in the first five minutes 37 seconds and set the tenor for the rest of the long, wild afternoon.

Vanderkelen and Beathard were named co-players of the game, quite deservedly, by a board of sportswriters.

The 11-touchdown extravaganza was an offensive coach's delight and a statistician's nightmare. It was topped by 11 successful conversions and even a safety. Only a field goal was lacking.

A poor pass from center Larry Sagouspe sailed over Ernie Jones' head as he tried to punt and he was downed in his end zone by Ernie Von

Heimburg, Wisconsin guard, for a two pointer.

Trojans Killed Clock.

That made it possible, mathematically, for the Badgers to pull the game out. There were still five minutes left to play.

But Vanderkelen and his fighting mates could only get one touchdown. The game ended with the thankful Trojans running backward deliberately to kill the clock and then punting on the final play.

Besides Beathard and Bedsole, Willie (the Wisp) Brown, a fleet halfback, stood out for the men of Troy. Brown made several fine receptions, kickoff runbacks of 41 and 31 yards and stopped one Badger drive with an interception for a touchback in the end zone.

Richter caught 11 passes for 163 yards total for one of his finest days. Little Lou Holland grabbed eight for 72 yards and scored on a 13-yard scamper around end.

Vanderkelen wound up with five net yards gained by rushing to give him a total of 406 yards gained, surpassing the previous high of 279 yards set by Bo Chappuis of Michigan in 1948. The young man's coolness under fire with a garland of Trojans around his neck was colossal.

Big Ben Wilson, fullback, led ground gainers with 57 yards in 17 carries. But Brown carried for 19 and caught three passes for 108 yards, the longest a 45-yard gainer from Bill Nelson, Beathard's alternate. Bedsole snagged four passes for 101 yards.

The marches were legion, and though the action occasionally was bogged down by 170 yards in penalties, the game never lacked for offensive thrills.

Doubtless the 5,5000 Badger rooters who came from Wisconsin for the game will discuss a second-quarter called-back touchdown the rest of the winter. Vanderkelen completed a 30-yard pass to Holland in the end zone, but a Badger was detected clipping and the score was nullified.

That left the halftime score 21-7 in favor of U.S.C. Anything closer could have meant ultimate victory for Wisconsin's persistent Badgers.

Southern California closed out its first all-winning season in 30 years with 11 victories in 11 games. Wisconsin wound up with an 8-2 record and still was looking for its first Rose Bowl triumph.

Wisconsin lost 7 to 0 to U.S.C. in 1953 and 44 to 8 to Washington in 1960 in two previous appearances.

Troy's most successful Rose record now reads 10 wins and three defeats.

SCORING SUMMARY:
Southern Cal: Touchdowns—Butcher (13-yard pass from Beathard), Wilson (1-yard plunge), Heller (25-yard run), Bedsole 2 (57 and 23 yard pass from Beathard), F. Hill (13-yard pass from Beathard). Conversions—Lupo 6 (all placekicks).
Wisconsin: touchdowns — Kurek (1-yard plunge), Vanderkelen (17-yard run), Holland (13-yard run), Kroner (4-yard pass, Vanderkelen), Richter (19-yard pass, Vanderkelen). Conversions — Kroner 5 (all placekicks). Safety — Ernie Jones, tackled by Von Heimburg in end zone.
By Quarters:

Wisconsin	7	0	7	23—37
U. S. C.	7	14	14	7—42

January 2, 1963

N.C.A.A. RESTORES 2-PLATOON SETUP

FORT LAUDERDALE, Fla. Jan. 12 (AP)—Virtual unlimited substitution was restored to college football today, making possible for the first time since 1952 the use of the two-platoon system.

The football rules committee of the National Collegiate Althletic Association moved a long way toward granting the desires of a majority of the nation's coaches for completely free and unlimited substitution.

Only a single restriction was left. A team must sacrifice a time-out when it sends in a platoon when the clock is running.

"This is the nearest you could possible come to what the coaches wanted," said Jack Curtice, the rules committee chairman of the American football Coaches Association.

"This fulfills their wishes. This is a reasonable rule on which the committee spent a great deal of time."

Platoons Can Come In

The new rule provides that platoons may be sent into a game at any time when the clock is stopped. Two players may enter when the clock is running.

Platooning is prohibited only when the clock is running and a team has used all its timeouts.

The clock is stopped when the ball goes out of bounds or over the goal, after a score, when a penalty is assessed, after an incompleted pass and during a measurement for a first down.

Unlimited substitution, which allows coaches to put together separate offensive and defensive platoons and increases the use of specialized players, has been used with great success by the pros.

College football abandoned unlimited substitution in 1953 to bolster the chances of the smaller schools that did not have the manpower to match the larger universities.

Coaches Favor New Rules

The coaches, however, whose please were virtually ignored by the N.C.A.A. rules committee, remained steadfastly in favor of two-platoon football. They insisted that unlimited substitution enabled them to field more effective teams, made for more exciting football and, most importantly, allowed many more boys to play.

The rule was changed from year to year to find a workable compromise, but with little success. Three years ago, the setup was such that Paul Dietzel, then at Louisiana State, was able to develop a three platoon system—one offensive team, one defensive team and one two-way team.

Dietzel's system gained wide favor and considerable success—notably by Wayne Hardin at Navy—but even that became unworkable when the rule was changed again last year to further restrict substitutions.

A Strong Indication

At a meeting of the N.C.A.A. in New York two weeks ago nearly 90 per cent of the coaches present indicated their desire for a return to unlimited substitution. They had done this in the past to no avail, but today was different.

Two-platoon football on a college level is now back, and few will be more delighted than the professionals. Now they can go back to selecting defensive and offensive specialists from the college ranks and forget about converting two-way stars to one-way experts.

One says that "No player can deliberately or maliciously use his helmet or head to butt or ram an opponent's neck, head or face." The penalty is immediate expulsion from the game.

The other safety rule stipulates that "no player of the team, any member of which has called for a fair catch, shall carry the ball more than two steps in any direction." The new rule does allow the ball to be carried if it touches the ground or an opponent.

January 13, 1964

RHOME SETS MARKS AS TULSA WINS, 19-7

TULSA, Okla., Nov. 7 (AP)—Jerry Rhome set two national football record and tied another and then got help from Tulsa's defense to down Memphis State, 19—7, here today.

Rhome completed 25 of 35 passes—11 of them to Howard Twilley, the nation's leading pass catcher — to set a new career pass completion record of 392 and a new mark for most points accounted for in a season, 190.

But it was Tulsa's defense—led by Willie Townes and linebackers Jeff Jordan and Charles Hardt—that preserved the victory. The defense never permitted the Tigers past the Tulsa 40 until the fourth quarter.

Rhome passed to Twilley for two touchdowns to tie the national season record for scoring passes. He scored himself on a two-yard keeper.

| Tulsa | 0 | 0 | 13 | 6—19 |
| Memphis State | 0 | 0 | 0 | 7— 7 |

Tul.—Twilley, 4, pass from Rhome (Twilley, kick).
Tul.—Rhome, 2, run (pass failed).
M.S.—Wright, 65, pass from Fletcher (Fletcher, kick).
Tul.—Twilley, 13, pass from Rhome (run failed).
Attendance—13,692.

November 8, 1964

U.C.L.A. BOWL VICTOR

MICH. STATE BOWS

Bruins Win, 14-12— Beban Tallies Twice —Stiles Excels

By BILL BECKER
Special to The New York Times

PASADENA, Calif., Jan. 11 —There is still room for Cinderella stories in the teeming lore of college football and the University of California, Los Angeles, Bruins wrote one of the greatest chapters in that vein today.

The Bruins, five times beaten in five previous Rose Bowl assignments, rose up to defeat the all-but-crowned national champions from Michigan State, 14 to 12, in one of the major upsets in the 52-year run of this production.

Showing great team speed, spirit and swarming ability, the much smaller Bruins hustled to a 14-point lead in the second quarter. Then Tommy Prothro's battlers staved off the Spartans' 12-point surge in the final period to prevail.

In clinching victory, the stanch Bruin defenders twice set back Michigan State power attempts for 2-point conversions—the last on the next-to-the-final play of the game.

Early Defeat Avenged

It was a thrilling season finale before 100,087 for the Bruins, who went into this game 14½-point underdogs. The victory also avenged their season-opening loss to Michigan State, 13-3, in East Lansing, Mich., last Sept. 18.

For Prothro, it marked the first victory in five Rose Bowl appearances as player, assistant coach and head mentor. Prothro was coach of the Oregon State Beavers, who lost, 34-7, to the University of Michigan here last New Year's Day.

But his players today were of a different stripe. Outweighed 17 pounds a man, they forced the Spartans into errors, fumbles and intercepted passes that turned the tide of battle.

Gary Beban, the Bruins' sophomore quarterback, was superb both passing and running against the Michigan State behemoths. He scored both Bruin touchdowns, on sneaks of 1 yard each, Kurt Zimmerman's two conversions sealed the decision.

However, in the final showdown, the victory was forced by the fine defenders headed by Bob Stiles, a halfback from Glen Ridge, N. J., and Dallas Grider, an alert linebacker. Stiles was voted player of the game by the Helms Athletic Foundation, a rare honor for a defensive player.

The sellout crowd thrilled to the Bruin heroics, which reached a positive crescendo in the fourth quarter as Duffy Daugherty, Michigan State coach, pulled out all stops and shuttled quarterbacks in an effort to win, or at least tie.

Held in their own half of the field for most of 3½ quarters, the Spartans struck quickly midway in the fourth period for their first touchdown.

Steve Juday, the Spartan quarterback, passed 42 yards to Gene Washington, the end, and then Bob Apisa, the Hawaiian fullback, ran 38 yards around right end with a pitchout from Jim Raye, an alternate quarterback, for the touchdown.

Juday, attempting to pass for a 2-pointer, was swarmed under by Jerry Klein, an aggressive Bruin end.

After an exchange of kicks, the Spartans started rolling from their own 49-yard line with less than four minutes to play. With Daugherty sending in each play with alternate quarterbacks, the Spartans moved 51 yards in 15 plays, with Juday sneaking over center from six inches out to make the score 14 to 12.

There remained only 31 seconds to play as the Spartans lined up for the conversion attempt.

With all spectators standing, and the stands in almost complete bedlam, Raye, at quarterback, pitched out to Apisa who dashed for the right side line and the coffin corner. Up came Stiles — down went Apisa, about 1 yard short of the goal line—and 2 points short of a face-saving tie.

It was the final play for Stiles, who was shaken up severely. But it was a fitting climax for the 22-year-old junior, who earlier had come up with two timely interceptions and a touchdown-saving interference. The game ended one play later with Michigan State essaying a vain onside kickoff attempt.

Fumble Is Recovered

The first quarter was scoreless, but at the end of the period a Bruin center, John Erquiaga, pounced on Don Japinaga's fumble of a punt on the Spartan 6-yard line. Beban circled left end for 5, and then, on the first play of the second quarter, hit right guard for 1 yard and the touchdown.

Immediately afterward, Zimmerman executed an onside kickoff and Grider fell on it on the Michigan State 42. In five plays, including a 27-yard pass to Kurt Altenberg, Beban moved the Bruins to their second touchdown. Beban went over left guard from the 1. Zimmerman's second conversion sent the Bruins to their dressing room with a 14-0 lead at half-time intermission.

Stiles, a former New Jersey all-state prep back, first spiked the Spartans by intercepting Juday's long pass and running it back 42 yards in the opening period.

Later, he barged into Washington when the big end had him beaten on a long pass in the second period. Stiles said after the game he deliberately hit the big end to break up "a sure touchdown." Interference was called on the play. But the Bruins then held and Dick Kenney, Michigan State's barefoot place-kicker, missed a field goal attempt from the 13-yard line. In the third quarter, the 5-foot 9-inch, 175-pound defender came up with another theft of a Juday pass into his left defensive sector.

No Alibi for Losers

Daugherty refused to alibi for the Spartans, who were No. 1 in The Associated Press and United Press International polls.

"It's an old gag," he said, "but this is a game of inches, just like baseball. We missed that field goal just by inches, and the final conversion try the same way."

"I want to give U.C.L.A. full credit for a great game. They kept us off balance and forced us into mistakes."

"But," he added, "I'm still proud of my boys. They were behind two touchdowns with seven minutes to play, and they gave it a big effort only to lose by inches."

Prothro, equally magnanimous said: "This is my most exciting victory. It was the highest we've been all season and definitely our greatest game."

He said Michigan State "has improved since we met them early this year—every team does. I think they earned their rating of No. 1.

"We were the better team today, but you have to judge a team on the whole season and so far as I'm concerned they're still No. 1."

The Bruins wound up their season with a record of eight victories, two defeats and a tie. But most important in Western eyes was the fact that the Pacific Athletic conference champions managed to bring the West its fifth victory in the 20-year-old series with the Big Ten. The Big Ten holds 15 victories. There have been no ties—but the Big Ten would have settled for that gladly today.

Statistics of the Game

	U.C.L.A.	Mich.St.
First downs	10	13
Rushing yardage	65	204
Passing yardage	147	110
Passes	8-20	8-22
Interceptions by	3	0
Punts	11-40	5-42
Fumbles lost	2	2
Yards penalized	86	14

U. C. L. A.	0	14	0	0—14
Michigan State	0	0	0	12—12

U. C. L. A.—Beban, 1, run (Zimmerman, kick).
U. C. L. A.—Beban, 1, run (Zimmerman, kick).
M. S.—Apisa, 38, run (pass failed).
M. S.—Juday, 1, run (run failed).
Attendance—100,087.

January 2, 1966

NOTRE DAME AND MICHIGAN STATE PLAY 10-10 TIE

SPECIAL DELIVERY—ONE TOUCHDOWN: Regis Cavender gets 6 points for Spartans in second quarter of game

Irish Gain Standoff On Late Field Goal

By JOSEPH M. SHEEHAN
Special to The New York Times

EAST LANSING, Mich., Nov. 19—Who's the nation's No. 1 college football team now?

There was no immediate, clear answer to that burning question today after Notre Dame, which had been rated No. 1, and Michigan State, which had been rated No. 2, played to a 10-10 standstill before an emotion-wracked overflow crowd of 80,011 at Spartan Stadium.

Michigan State got its scoring punches first. On a march initiated in the first quarter, the Spartans drove 73 yards to a touchdown in 10 plays. Regis Cavender smashed over for the score from 4 yards out at 1:40 of the second period.

About 7½ minutes later, after having penetrated to Notre Dame's 25 and having been set back to the 30, Michigan State tallied again, on a 47-yard field goal by Dick Kenney, the barefooted kicker from Hawaii who also had kicked the extra point after the touchdown.

Notre Dame Strikes Back

Notre Dame retaliated after the second Michigan State score by moving 54 yards to a touchdown on three successive pass completions by Coley O'Brien, a sophomore who took over at quarterback midway in the first period after his classmate, Terry Hanratty, had been knocked out of action by a shoulder separation.

The payoff toss was a 34-yard beauty into the end zone to Bob Gladieux, who filled in at left halfback for Nick Eddy, whose previously damaged shoulder would not permit him to play.

Joe Azzaro kicked the extra point after this touchdown and also made Notre Dame's equalizing field goal, from 28 yards out, on the first play of the fourth period after Notre Dame had moved the ball from its 20 to Michigan State's 12.

Azzaro, who had made all three of his previous field goal attempts this season, had a further chance to be a hero, but he muffed it.

With six minutes to play, Tom Schoen of Notre Dame made his second successive interception of a pass by Jimmy Raye, Michigan State's slick and nimble quarterback, and ran the ball from midfield to the Michigan State 18.

But the aroused Spartan defense threw the Irish back to the 24, forcing Azzaro to try a kick from 41 yards out. The kick was long enough, but it veered right and flew wide of the posts by a considerable margin.

This long-awaited clash of unbeaten and untied titans, which undoubtedly had one of the largest television audiences ever attracted by a sports event, was defense-dominated, as had been expected.

Michigan State had no other scoring opportunities other than those on which it capitalized and only once, other than on its scoring drives, did Notre Dame threaten. That was in the first period, when the Irish reached the home 37 on a 25-yard pass from Hanratty to Gladieux.

This march floundered on the 34 when rushes by Larry Conjar and Hanratty picked up only 4 yards and a pass by Hanratty missed connections.

Hanratty was injured on his running play. Charlie Thornhill, Michigan State's fine linebacker, slammed him down hard and 283-pound Bubba Smith, in hot pursuit, fell atop him.

For what it was worth, Michigan State had the better of the battle of the statistics. The Spartans had the edge in first downs, 13 to 10; in rushing, 142 yards net to 91; in passing, 142 yards to 128, and in total yards gained, 284 to 219.

But the Spartans gained most of their yardage in their own territory, in which they were kept pinned for much of the game by the superior punting of Kevin Hardy, Notre Dame's left-footed, 270-pound tackle.

While Raye could not keep his team moving consistently in attacking territory, he did a magnificent job of extricating the Spartans from sticky situations.

In the third quarter, for instance, Michigan State fumbled away the ball on its first play after the second-half kickoff. Notre Dame, in possession on the home 30, went to the air immediately, but the Spartans got the ball back right away when Jess Phillips picked off a pass by O'Brien intended for Rocky Bleier on the Michigan State 2.

This was a chance for the Irish to bottle up the Spartans —sit on them and play for a break.

But Raye, carrying three times himself, worked the ball out to a first down on the 13, passed to Gene Washington for another first down on the 28, and Notre Dame's territorial advantage was lost.

Michigan State's junior quarterback piloted his team out of danger again the next time the Spartans had the ball. Another booming punt by Hardy forced Michigan State back to its 5, and the Spartans once more were in trouble.

Raye met the challenge by tossing a 41-yard pass to Washington on first down and the Spartans were out of the pocket again.

Long Pass Starts Spartans

Another long first-down pass from Raye to Washington, this one for 42 yards, started Michigan State rolling to its first touchdown on the Spartans' third turn with the ball in the first period.

This play put Michigan State on Notre Dame's 30. Clint Jones and Raye punched out a first down on the 18 and, after the teams changed goals for the second quarter, Cavender roared 10 yards up the middle for another.

From the Notre Dame 8, Cavender bulled through to the 5. Jones hit over his left side for a yard and Cavender found a hole inside Notre Dame's left tackle and crashed through for the score.

Michigan State gave Notre Dame's vaunted tackles—Pete Duranko and Hardy—a working-over on this drive, but thereafter the Spartans were able to make only sporadic progress on the ground.

The next time it had the ball, on its 18, Michigan State began the drive to its field goal, which was a continuous drive only in a manner of speaking.

The slippery Raye got the Spartans moving with a 30-yard rollout sprint around end to his 48. Dwight Lee then broke around his left end for 16 yards to the Notre Dame 36.

After a short gain by Cavender, Jim Lynch, Notre Dame's stalwart linebacker, intercepted a pass by Raye. But before the play was over, Michigan State was back in possession. Jones tackling Lynch and knocking him loose from the ball.

A penalty set the Spartans back to the Notre Dame 43, but Raye passed to Washington for a first down on the 27. There the Irish braced and, after incurring a 5-yard motion penalty, Michigan State lined up on the Irish 30 for Kenny's field-goal attempt.

His boot split the uprights and gave him a total of 19 field goals for his three-year varsity career.

Tom Quinn's 38-yard return of the kickoff that followed Kenney's field goal put Notre Dame on the way to its touchdown. From his own 46, O'Brien opened up immediately.

Jim Seymour, Notre Dame's celebrated sophomore end (who didn't catch a pass today), dropped O'Brien's first throw. The next three connected.

Gladieux circled out of the backfield to take the first for a first down on Michigan State's

The Line-up

MICHIGAN STATE (10)
Left Ends—Brenner, C. Smith, Chatlos.
Left Tackles—Przybycki, Ruminski, Bailey.
Left Guards—Conti, Bradley, Gallinaugh.
Centers—L. Smith, Ranieri, Redd, Richardson, Brawley.
Right Guards—Techlin, Pruiett, Jordan.
Right Tackles—West, McLoud, Hoag.
Right Ends—Washington, Haynes, Thornhill.
Quarterbacks—Raye, Wedemeyer, Kinney, Webster, Super.
Left Halfbacks—Lee, Berlinski, Summers, Lawson.
Right Halfbacks—C. Jones, Waters, Armstrong, J. Jones, Ware.
Fullbacks—Cavender, Phillips, Garrett, Apisa.

NOTRE DAME (10)
Left Ends—Seymour, Rhoads.
Left Tackles—Seiler, Duranko.
Left Guards—Regner, Hardy.
Centers—Goeddeke, Monty, Kelly, Page.
Right Guards—Swatland, Pergine.
Right Tackles—Kuechenberg, Lynch.
Right Ends—Gmitter, Stenger, Horney.
Quarterbacks—Hanratty, O'Brien, Martin, Azzaro.
Left Halfbacks—Gladieux, O'Leary, Belgener, Criniti.
Right Halfbacks—Bleier, Smithberger, Quinn, Haley.
Fullbacks—Conjar, Schoen, Dushiney.

Michigan State	0	10	0	0—10
Notre Dame	0	7	0	3—10

M.S.—Cavander, 4, run (Kenney, kick).
M.S.—FG., Kenney, 47.
N.D.—Gladieux, 34, pass from O'Brien (Azzaro, kick).
N.D.—FG., Azzaro, 28.
Attendance—80,011.

STATISTICS OF THE GAME	M.S.	N.D.
First downs..........	13	10
Rushing yardage...	142	91
Passing yardage...	112	128
Passes	7-20	8-24
Interceptions by...	1	3
Punts	8-38	8-42
Fumbles lost......	1	1
Yards penalized....	32	5

42. Bleier, from wingback, took the second for an 8-yard gain.

Then came the bomb to Gladieux. Again circling out of the backfield, but running a deeper pattern, Eddy's stand-in got behind the Spartans' deep defenders and O'Brien laid the ball in his arms in the end zone over a desperate lunge by Phillips, the safetyman.

O'Brien's passing also figured prominently in Notre Dame's drive to its field goal. Completions to Bleier for 10 yards, Conjar for 16, and Dave Haley for 24 swiftly moved the Irish from their 20 to Michigan State's 30.

After a Michigan State off-side, Haley and Conjar punched out another first down on the home 17. But against Michigan State's stiffening resistance, Notre Dame could get no farther than the 10. It was from there, on the right-side hash-mark, that they set up Azzaro for his field goal.

For the rest of the way, neither team made any substantial penetration of rival territory under its own momentum.

Notre Dame had its shot at victory on the Schoen interception—but missed the field goal —and then decided to settle for the tie, running out the clock with four running plays after getting the ball for the last time on its 35 with a minute and a half to play.

This was the end of the 1966 trail for Michigan State, Big Ten champion for the second straight year. Notre Dame has one game to play, against Southern California next Saturday.

November 20, 1966

Purdue Tops U.S.C., 14-13, in Rose Bowl

By ALLISON DANZIG
Special to The New York Times

PASADENA, Calif., Jan. 2—From the humiliation of its 51-0 massacre by Notre Dame in its regular-season finale, Southern California regained the might of its October form to come within a point of tying heavily favored Purdue in the 53d Rose Bowl game today.

The Boilermakers, making their first appearance in the most ancient of all bowl games, gained the victory, 14-13, by virtue of the Trojans gambling to win, rather than settling for a tie, and failing on a 2-point conversion pass after scoring their second touchdown less than three minutes before the end of the game.

A crowd of 101,455, filling the bowl on a day of warm sunshine, thrilled to the tense, exciting action of a game that was expected to be pretty much of a procession for Purdue, piloted by the celebrated Bob Griese, one of the top passers of the year and the runner-up for the Heisman Trophy.

For the first 17 minutes, the play was as overwhelmingly one-sided as the Trojans' calumniators had predicted. During that time, Southern California had the ball only on four plays and failed to make a first down while the Boilermakers were scoring a touchdown and compiling nine first downs.

Dropped Pass Stalls Drive

From the opening kickoff Purdue utterly dominated the field as it went 68 yards to the 5 and failed on a pass dropped in the end zone, then came back to go 57 yards in 16 plays for a touchdown and a 7-0 lead at 2 minutes 17 seconds of the second quarter.

The Trojans, to this point, had been helpless to stop both Purdue's running attack and Griese's rollout and quickly released passes and had been futile on the attack the few times they had the ball. But following the Purdue touchdown the Trojans underwent a metamorphosis that had the vast crowd in an uproar as they so completely took charge as to make nine first downs before the Boilermakers could register another.

First, U. S. C. went 57 yards as Troy Winslow, who was to closely rival Griese for quarterback honors, fired passes of 7,

Rose Bowl Line-Up

PURDUE (14)
Ends—Beirne, Griffin, Olson, Homes.
Tackles—Barnes, Burke, Calcaterra, Rafa, Olssen.
Guards—Erlenbaugh, Sebeck, Kyle, Piper.
Center—Labus.
Linebackers—King Burke, Marvel.
Quarterbacks—Griese, Conners, Emch.
Halfbacks—Baltzell, Finley, Hurst, Charles, Catavolos, Frame, Keyes.
Fullbacks—P. Williams, Cirbes.

U. S. C. (13)
Ends—Rossovich, Almon, Cahill, Klein, Mays, Miller, B. Hayhoe.
Tackles—Yary, Magner, Moore, J. Hayhoe, Wells, Crane.
Guards—Oliver, Petrill, Homan, Blanche, Scarpace.
Center—Baccitich.
Linebackers—Young, Snow, King.
Quarterback—Winslow.
Halfbacks—McCall, Sherman, Lawrence, Cashman, Shaw, Jaronyck, Salness, Nyquist.
Fullbacks—H. Williams, Hull.

Purdue	0	7	7	0—14
Southern California	0	7	0	6—13

Pur.—Williams, 1, run (Griese, kick).
U.S.C.—McCall, 1, run (Roosovich, kick).
Pur.—Williams, 2, run (Griese, kick).
U.S.C.—Sherman, 19, pass from Winslow (pass failed).
Attendance—101,455.

and 39 yards to reach the 10-yard line, only to lose the ball on a fumble. Then the Trojans went 44 yards to score the tying touchdown less than two minutes before the end of the half.

As the second half got under way the Trojans continued to hold the upper hand until another fumble, which gave Purdue the ball on its 39, brought a turn in the play. From then on, the Boilermakers held the upper hand, but the Trojans had so much fight that the outcome remained in doubt until the goal posts went crashing down just before the last play of the game.

Purdue took the lead, 14-7, late in the third period as it went 37 yards in six plays. Perry Williams carried from the 2 for his second touchdown. Just prior to the advance, Griese had fired a 39-yard pass to Jim Beirne, who was knocked loose from the ball as he was tackled crossing the goal line, costing the Boilermakers a score.

Then came another startling reversion in the final quarter, as in the second period. Winslow threw the longest pass of the day, for 52 yards, to Rod Sherman, who was pulled down on the 4. With the crowd in an uproar, the Trojans failed on three running plays, and then their attempt for a field goal from the 18 on fourth down was blocked.

That seemed to be the end of the Trojans' hopes. But immediately they had the ball again as their defense stopped Purdue hard, and, with the stadium in boiling excitement, they went 64 yards in 14 plays and Winslow fired 19 yards to Sherman for what was taken to be the tying score.

An offside penalty against Purdue was heavily instrumental in the touchdown drive. Southern California was in kick formation on fourth down when the offside was called. The Trojans thus were able to maintain possession of the ball, with the first down it gave them at midfield, and they went all the way.

Instead, however, of falling into kick formation to try for the tying point, the Trojans elected to go for 2 points and victory.

Pandemonium broke loose in the big Purdue cheering section when George Catavolos, behind whom Sherman had caught the touchdown pass, redeemed himself by cutting in front of Jim Lawrence, the intended receiver, and intercepted Winslow's pass.

So Catavolos saved the victory for the Boilermakers and the Big Ten Conference, which had been left crushed when Michigan State's overwhelmingly favored Spartans were beaten here by the University of California, Los Angeles, 14-12, last New Year's Day.

January 3, 1967

United Press International Telephoto
At another point in the contest, Jaronyck rides **Jim Beirne** so jarringly that Beirne drops a pass in the end zone.

HARVARD TIES YALE, 29-29, ON LAST PLAY OF THE GAME

By STEVE CADY
Special to The New York Times

CAMBRIDGE, Mass., Nov. 23—Unbeaten Harvard turned The Game into The Miracle today by scoring 16 points in the last 42 seconds and gaining a hysterical 29-29 tie with unbeaten Yale.

If the capacity crowd of 40,280 still can't believe what it saw, it could hardly be blamed.

With the ball on the Yale 38, the score 29-13 and the Eli stands chanting "We're No. 1," most of the record corps of 400 reporters in the press box already had their accounts of the game well under way.

Then Frank Champi, a second-string Harvard quarterback who had already thrown one touchdown pass, decided that maybe he, not Brian Dowling of Yale, really was the reincarnation of Frank Merriwell.

Just Enough Just in Time

His 15-yard scoring pass to Bruce Freeman and a 2-point conversion run by Gus Crim put the Crimson within tying range. Then, on the last regular play of the game, after a fumbled onside kickoff had given the Crimson possession, Champi hit Vic Gatto with an 8-yard scoring pass.

After the field had been cleared of demonstrative Harvard fans, the substitute quarterback threw a perfect 2-point conversion strike to Peter Varney.

Out came the paper in the press-box typewriters, out came articles that had begun, "Brian Dowling completed a spectacular Yale football career today by passing for two touchdowns and running for two more..."

Dowling, the 21-year-old senior who would have been playing for Ohio State against Michigan today if he had not decided to go to Yale, was spectacular beyond the wildest expectations of his admirers. Calvin Hill, too, had a big day for Yale, for he scored one touchdown and passed the fabled Albie Booth for most points (144) in a Yale career.

Dowling, who closed his career with eight Yale records, completed 13 of his 21 passes for 116 yards. He sent the Elis ahead by running 3 yards on a bootleg play in the first period, and in the second he threw a 3-yard touchdown pass to Hill and a 5-yarder to Del Marting. And after Harvard had scored on a 1-yard plunge by Crim in the third, his 5-yard touchdown run in the fourth looked like the clincher.

Just the Move Just in Time

But it was Champi, completing six of 15 passes for 82 yards and three touchdowns, who sent ancient Harvard Stadium into bedlam and turned a plaintive plea of "10,000 men of Harvard want victory today" into a boisterously understanding, if slightly inaccurate, mass singing of "With

Crimson in triumph flashing."

Champi, a 5-foot-11 junior from Everett, Mass., replaced George Lalich late in the first half after Yale had taken a 22-0 lead.

With 44 seconds to go in the half, he managed to put the Crimson on the scoreboard with a 15-yard pass to Freeman, a second-string end. The conversion kick was muffed, and Yale went to the dressing room with a comfortable 22-6 lead.

This was the first time in 59 years the two schools had gone into their traditional showdown undefeated and untied. The unexpected result left each with a won-lost-tied mark of 8-0-1 and a share of the Ivy League title on league records of 6-0-1.

Harvard, salvaging its first unbeaten season since 1920, has never won the Ivy crown outright.

Today's eagerly awaited clash was the 85th in a series that began in 1875, and the deadlock was the first since 1951.

Ironically, it was Harvard's belatedly inspired offense, not its top-ranked defense, that saved the day and prevented Dowling from completing a perfect 23-0 record at Yale for games in which he played.

Dowling, a 195-pounder from Cleveland, missed 11 games in his four years at Yale because of injuries. Watched by pro scouts today, he has been described as a "born winner."

But he couldn't do anything to stop Harvard today in the last frantic 42 seconds. Like Hill, he was sitting on the bench.

A Boston Massacre Fails

Harvard's defense, stingiest in the nation among major colleges in the matter of points allowed, had been advertised in widely distributed handbills here as being "wanted for massacring Yale's offensive football team on Saturday, Nov. 23, 1968."

But the way Dowling and Hill operated, that billing would hardly have stood up in court. The evidence, particularly in the first half, was somewhat circumstantial.

In the final desperate moments, it was the neglected Harvard offense that turned Yale jubilation into frustration.

And it was a bad break for Yale, which had been getting most of the good ones, that set the stage for the wildest finish in the 63-year history of this concrete horseshoe.

Dowling, in charge as completely as Merriwell, Yale's fictional superstar, flipped a screen pass from the Harvard 32 to an open receiver, who started toward the goal line. But the receiver fumbled and Steve Ranere of Harvard pounced on the ball at the Crimson 14.

Champi then got the Crimson going on the nine-play, 86-yard drive that resulted in the first of the miracle touchdowns. The big gainer, again reflecting the sudden turn of fortune, came on a fumble by Champi.

Fritz Reed, a junior who had been switched from end to tackle this season, grabbed the ball and took off toward the Yale goal. He might have thought he was an end again and had just caught a pass. Anyway, he rambled from the Yale 32 to the 15.

Nobody paid much attention, because only 42 seconds remained. In the Yale stands across the field from the press box,

old Blues and young Blues waved white handkerchiefs and chanted, "We're No. 1" (in the Big Three, in the Ivy League and to some of the more dedicated football buffs, in the nation). Even Percy Haughton Harvard's legendary coach, might not have had the courage to ask a Crimson team to pull one out in that situation.

But Champi must have been listening to Mr. Merriwell. On the next play, he looked for an open receiver, failed to find one, tried to lateral, dodged some white-jerseyed Elis—and threw to his right. Freeman, the sophomore end, snagged the pass on the Yale 3 and went into the end zone.

The 2-point plunge by Crim, a junior fullback, reduced the volume of the "We're No. 1."

Now Harvard tried what it had to try—an onside kick. It worked. Yale fumbled the skittering kick and Bill Kelly, another Harvard sophomore, recovered on the Yale 49.

Champi, apparently trapped on a pass attempt, decided to do what Dowling had been doing with remarkable success most of the chilly, but clear, afternoon. He ran. He went for 14 yards to the Yale 35 and a face-mask penalty against the Elis advanced the ball to the 20.

Time remaining: 32 seconds. Harvard fans: in an uproar. Yale fans: apprehensive.

8 They Want, and 8 They Get

Champi threw two passes into the endzone. Both were broken up. Champi surprised everybody, including Yale, by sending Crim up the middle on a draw play. It went for 14 yards to the Eli 6.

"We want 8," the Harvards screamed.

Champi, trapped trying to pass, was nailed on the 8 for a 2-yard loss. Four seconds remained, enough for one play.

Trapped again, the amazing substitute played ring-around-a-rosy with Yale's defenders. He tried to lateral, as he had attempted to do on the previous drive. He ran around in circles for what seemed like 10 seconds before spotting Gatto alone in the end zone. Gatto, the senior captain and the first back in Harvard history to rush for 2,000 yards, clutched the ball surely in the most dramatic moment of a dramatic career. Touchdown!

Spectators swarmed onto the field to mob the Harvard captain.

"Quiet, please!" the public-address announcer implored the fans. The field was cleared. Champi fired a bullet pass into Varney's midsection.

Merriwell couldn't have done it any better.

Yale	7	15	0	7—29
Harvard	0	6	7	16—29

Yale—Dowling, 3, run (Bayless, kick).
Yale—Hill, 3, pass from Dowling (Bayless, kick).
Yale—Marting, 5, pass from Dowling (Marting, pass from Dowling).
Harv.—Freeman, 15, pass from Champi (kick failed).
Harv.—Crim, 1, run (Szaro, kick).
Yale—Dowling, 5, run (Bayless, kick).
Harv.—Freeman, 15, pass from Champi (Crim, run).
Harv.—Gatto, 8, pass from Champi (Varney, pass from Champi).
Attendance—40,280.

November 24, 1968

TEXAS BEATS ARKANSAS ON DARING GAMBLES, 15-14

LONGHORNS RALLY

Score Twice and Make 2-Point Conversion In Last Quarter

By NEIL AMDUR

Special to The New York Times

FAYETTEVILLE, Ark., Dec. 6 —Trailing by 14-0 in the fourth quarter, unbeaten Texas parlayed two daring gambles into a 15-14 victory over Arkansas today for the Southwest Conference title, a berth in the Cotton Bowl and a giant step toward the national championship.

A successful 2-point conversion run and a long fourth-down pass brought the Longhorns from behind for the second time in 10 games, much to the distress of Penn State fans, who had prayed for a tie or an upset, and Razorback rooters caught up in the tumult of Arkansas' biggest event since it rejoined the Union.

Before a capacity crowd of 44,000 that included President Nixon, and with millions watching on national television, the Longhorns registered their 19th consecutive triumph and dealt Arkansas, an underdog, its first setback after nine victories.

The Razorbacks, cheered by a raucous majority in Razorback Stadium, will settle for a New Year's Day berth in the Sugar Bowl against Mississippi.

Nixon Presents Plaque

Texas received a championship plaque from Mr. Nixon after the game. The Longhorns could solidify their claims to the No. 1 spot by beating Notre Dame in the Cotton Bowl on New Year's Day.

The game was in doubt until the final 73 seconds, after Texas had taken the lead for the first time on Happy Feller's 43d conversion in 45 attempts with 3 minutes 58 seconds left. A brilliant 44-yard pass on fourth down from James Street to Randy Peschel had moved the Longhorns into scoring position. Jim Bertelsen pounded through left guard from the 2-yard line for the touchdown.

But Bill Montgomery, a superb competitor throughout the game at quarterback, brought the Razorbacks from their 20 to the Texas 39 in the closing minutes. On second down at the 39, he passed to his favorite receiver, Chuck Dicus, who had caught one touchdown pass, had another nullified by a pass-interference penalty and in all made nine receptions for 146 yards.

But Tom Campbell, a defensive back, moved in front of Dicus and made his sixth interception of the season.

The margin of victory was a run for a 2-point conversion earlier in the period by the ubiquitous Street, a 175-pound senior, who completed a second season at quarterback without tasting defeat.

After an aggressive defense had contained the awesome Texas ground game for three quarters, Street broke away on a 42-yard scamper for the Longhorns' first score. It came on the opening play of the final period.

The 21-year-old senior retreated for a pass. Finding no open receivers, he slipped through the pocket, avoided tacklers and slanted past the last defender into the end zone.

It was the 56th touchdown of the season for the Texas scoring machine that had averaged 44 points a game. After all the 44 points a game. After all its other touchdowns Texas had converted the extra point by a place-kick. Coach Darrell Royal this time decided to try for 2 points, rather than try it later if Texas scored again.

On the play that has become the Texas trademark, the option, Street slid along the left side of the line and, seeing a shred of daylight at tackle, cut inside and struggled into the end zone.

"We felt that was the time for the 2-point conversion," Royal said afterward. "If we had missed it, we could have still gone for 2 again and gotten a tie. But if we had kicked after the first touchdown and gone for 2 after the second, then the pressure is really on us."

The pressure was on, anyway, after Arkansas had turned two Texas fumbles into a 14-0 lead. A recovery at the Longhorn 22 on the second play of the game was followed by Bill Burnett's 1-yard scoring smash with less than two minutes gone and the crowd still buzzing over the landing of helicopters on the practice field south of the stadium and the appearance of President Nixon.

Dicus Catches 29-Yarder

Another fumble early in the third quarter gave Arkansas field position, and it moved 53 yards in five plays for its second score.

The 180-pound Montgomery, who completed 14 of 22 passes for 205 yards on the synthetic playing surface, threw a 29-yarder to the slick-stepping Dicus for the tally, and the Arkansas cheering section waved placards and shouted the familiar "We're No. 1."

Despite the deficit, the strange surroundings and memories of 1965, when another unbeaten Longhorn team was upset in the same stadium, Texas refused to panic.

It was Royal who called the crucial fourth-down pass with 4:47 left. Needing 2½ yards at the 43-yard line, Street faked, dropped back and threw down the sideline.

Two Arkansas defenders were following Peschel.

"I looked back over my shoulder and thought the pass was gonna be over my head," the 200-pound senior tight end said. "I lowered my head and kept running and looked up, and there it was."

Said Royal:

"Every now and then you just have to suck it up and pick a number. You don't use logic and reason; you just play a hunch. I never considered punting."

He said his coaching staff sat around until 1 A.M. this morning talking about the 2-point conversion. With good reason. In 1964 the Longhorns scored in the closing minute to trim an Arkansas lead to 14-13. They went for 2, failed and lost. Texas was No. 1 then.

"I'm glad it's over," said Frank Broyles, the dejected Arkansas coach, in the dressing room. "We lost on the scoreboard, but we're proud. The turning point was on fourth down when they went for the bomb."

Texas 0   0   0   15—15
Arkansas 7   0   7   0—14

Ark.—Burnett, 1, run (McClard, kick).
Ark.—Dicus, 29, pass from Montgomery (McClard, kick).
Tex.—Street, 42, run (Street, run).
Tex.—Bertelsen, 2, run (Feller, kick).
Attendance—44,000.

STATISTICS OF THE GAME

	Tex.	Ark.
First downs	19	18
Rushing yardage	244	103
Passing yardage	124	205
Return yardage	47	—2
Passes	6-10	14-22
Interceptions by	2	2
Punts	2-36	7-31
Fumbles lost	4	0
Yards penalized	30	40

December 7, 1969

By Invitation Only

39 Colleges Have Monopolized Bids To 4 Major Football Bowls in 20 Years

By GORDON S. WHITE Jr.

NOTRE DAME made a sound financial decision to break its long-standing policy against football bowl appearances when it accepted a bid to the Cotton Bowl game set for Jan. 1. The university claims to be searching for funds to support scholarships for minority students and a bowl game now and then may be the answer.

There is money to be made in a bowl game—as much as $350,000 a team.

Notre Dame, which will be invited time and again in the future, has broken into an elite group of colleges and universities that have had the four major bowl games all to themselves for the 20 years ending this winter.

Only 39 colleges have been invited to the Orange, Sugar, Cotton or Gator Bowl games in the last two decades.

The Rose Bowl is not counted. That once premier bowl game is limited by contract to a team from the Big Ten against a team from the Pacific Eight Conference.

118 Major Teams

There are 440 football playing colleges in the National Collegiate Athletic Association, which votes approval of the bowl games. There are 118 major college teams, the ones most likely to get a bid to one of the four bowls mentioned. Thus, only one third of the major N.C.A.A. football teams have played in these games and shared in the wealth.

Each college, which is headed to the Gator, Orange, Sugar or Cotton Bowl this

Woody Hayes, former controversial coach of Ohio State, makes a point at a 1978 practice session.

Sweet victory: University of Alabama players carry coach Paul "Bear" Bryant off the field after their 1975 Sugar Bowl triumph against Penn State.

season, with the exception of Notre Dame, will have been to postseason money country at least five times in 20 years. Mississippi, a Sugar Bowl team this winter, is making its 11th appearance in one of these four bowls. Texas is headed there for the 10th time. Arkansas and Tennessee are going there for the ninth time and Florida for the eighth. Penn State and Missouri, opponents in the Jan. 1 Orange Bowl, are making their fifth bowl game.

The four major bowls have staged a total of 80 games in 20 years. This means there have been openings for 160 colleges but only 39 have reached the lucrative games.

From the winter of 1950-51 through the 1970 bowl games, nine colleges have been asked only once. Eight of the 30 repeaters have gone only twice in the last 20 years so that there are 22 colleges that might be called "regulars."

Of the "regular," four colleges have gone to one of these four bowls 10 or more times. Thus, of the 80 bowl games played in 20 years, four colleges have performed in 41 of the 160 team games of more than 25 percent.

The Cotton Bowl saves the host team spot for the Southwest Conference champion—Texas most of the time. But Texas has appeared in two other bowl games during the last 20 years and Arkansas, another Southwest team, has been to five other major bowls.

Obviously, the rich get richer and the majority of colleges around the nation approve. N.C.A.A. policy, established by its more than 600 members, permits the bowl colleges to take in hundreds of thousands of dollars each year.

This is the same N.C.A.A. membership policy that permits a handful of colleges to earn millions of dollars for their televised games while the majority goes begging.

Most conference teams must share their bowl receipts with the other members of the league. This might sound as if Penn State, an independent, can come away from the Orange Bowl with about $350,000 this winter while Mississippi gets only about a tenth of that after sharing its Sugar Bowl receipts with the other nine Southeastern Conference colleges.

But in the last 20 years, the S.E.C. has been represented in these four major bowls 62 times, including some games where both teams were S.E.C. colleges such as the Tennessee-Florida game set for the Gator Bowl Dec. 27.

The S.E.C. can't cry poverty as a result of its bowl games. The Southwest Conference does well, too, since it is assured of half of the Cotton Bowl receipts each season and usually half of another bowl or two as is the case this winter.

Bowl games were worth much less in 1951. But that may be all relative because of cost increases.

For a long time some observers have voiced displeasure with the manner in which a small number of colleges get the high profits from weekly television appearances. The same thing has been going on for a longer time in the bowl scene.

The colleges that have played in the Orange, Sugar, Cotton or Gator Bowls from 1951 through 1907 and the number of appearances:

College	Appearances	College	Appearances
Mississippi	11	Maryland	3
Alabama	10	Rice	2
Georgia Tech	10	Air Force	2
Texas	10	Colorado	2
Arkansas	9	Kentucky	2
Tennessee	9	Miami (Fla.)	2
Florida	8	Pittsburgh	2
Oklahoma	8	Texas A. & M.	2
L.S.U.	7	Texas Tech	2
Syracuse	6	Wyoming	2
Missouri	5	Kansas	1
Nebraska	5	Florida State	1
Penn State	5	North Carolina	1
Auburn	4	Notre Dame	1
Baylor	4	S.M.U.	1
Clemson	4	Tulsa	1
Navy	4	Vanderbilt	1
T.C.U.	4	W. & L.	1
Duke	3	West Virginia	1
Georgia	3		

December 7, 1969

Texas Hands Notre Dame 21-17 Cotton Bowl Loss

PASS ON 4TH DOWN IS KEY TO VICTORY

Street Hits Speyrer on the 2 and Dale Takes Ball Over With 68 Seconds to Play

By NEIL AMDUR

Special to The New York Times

DALLAS, Jan. 1—Texas began the new decade the way it left the old today, gambling for a late victory.

Displaying the competitive trademarks of a true national champion, the Longhorns responded from deficits of 10-0 and 17-14 to score a 21-17 victory over Notre Dame in the 34th Cotton Bowl classic. The winning touchdown came on a 1-yard run by Billy Dale with 68 seconds left in the game.

Two successful executions of fourth-down plays in the closing drive carried Texas to its 20th straight victory and frustrated Notre Dame's return to postseason bowl activity after 45 years.

After Joe Theismann, the Notre Dame quarterback, had improvised a 24-yard touchdown pass to Jim Yoder for a 17-14 Irish margin with 6 minutes 52 seconds left, Texas drove from its 24-yard line to the Notre Dame 28, with its winning streak and No. 1 ranking in jeopardy.

Time Running Out

Three running plays gained 8 yards, before Coach Darrell Royal, faced with another crucial fourth-down play, called time out with 4:26 remaining.

Last Dec. 6, in Fayetteville, Ark., the Longhorns turned a similar situation, fourth down and 3 yards to go at their 43, into a daring 44-yard pass play that produced a 15-14 victory over Arkansas and earned them the Cotton Bowl berth and the No. 1 spot.

Today, before an overflow crowd of 73,000 that included former President Lyndon B. Johnson, and with millions watching on national television, the Longhorns shunned a field-goal attempt and tried a pitchout to the left side, away from Notre Dame's 274-pound defensive standout, Mike McCoy.

The carry, by Ted Koy, gained the required 2 yards and set the stage for more fourth-down drama, this time from the 10-yard line, again 2 yards short of a first down.

Royal's decision was an option pass-run, and James Street, the 175-pound senior quarterback, responded with the same tenacity under pressure that he showed in guiding the Longhorns through 10 regular-season games.

Speyrer Grabs Low Pass

Street dropped back and threw along the life sidelines to Charles (Cotton) Speyrer, the stringy split end. The pass was low and to the outside, but Speyrer caught the ball on his knees, in front of Clarence Ellis, the Notre Dame defender, at the 2-yard line.

Notre Dame held for two plays. But on third down, again running away from McCoy, Dale moved through the left side of his line for the touchdown.

The script did not end here, however. Theismann, who completed 17 passes for 231 yards and two touchdowns in a magnificent performance, completed two passes for first downs to the Texas 38.

But in another replay of the Texas-Arkansas finish, Tom Campbell, the son of Mike Campbell, the Texas defensive coach, intercepted Theismann's 27th pass at the Longhorn 14 with 38 seconds left.

It was Campbell, a defensive back, who thwarted Arkansas' last drive in the closing minutes with an interception deep in Texas territory.

"I forced the pass," a dejected Theismann said afterward in the solemn Notre Dame dressing room. "I had plenty of time, but I threw it high."

The national importance of the game was portrayed in the intensity and desire with which both teams played. On several occasions, officials had to re-

Statistics of the Game

	Texas	N.D.
First downs	25	25
Rushing yardage	331	189
Passing yardage	107	231
Return yardage	33	0
Passes	6-11	17-27
Interceptions by	2	1
Punts	4-39	7-36
Yards penalized	50	50

strain players from exchanging more than words. After Campbell's interception, tempers became so strained that Royal ran onto the field and into the huddle to calm his orange-shirted players.

Koy, younger brother of Ernie Koy of the New York Giants, was knocked unconscious in the first half after a tackle and did not return until the fourth quarter.

During another confusing exchange in the first half, Notre Dame appeared to have recovered Street's fumble at the Texas 6-yard line. But officials ruled Randy Stout, an offensive tackle, had signaled the field judge for a time out before the snap of the ball.

The victory was Royal's fifth straight in bowl activity and the 500th for the school.

"It was a tremendous football game," said Ara Parseghian, who finished his sixth season at Notre Dame with an 8-2-1 won-lost-tied record. "They came up with two clutch plays on fourth down," the coach said. "I thought the pass to Speyrer was a poor pass, too low, and favorable for us. But it was a great catch."

Notre Dame was an underdog, by 7 points, for only the second time in Parseghian's tenure. When Scott Hempel kicked a 26-yard first-quarter field goal and Theismann fired a 54-yard scoring pass to Tom

Gatewood early in the second quarter, the Irish had Penn State rooters in ecstasy.

But Texas had rallied from 14-0 deficits twice this season, and Street, a senior with an eye toward a professional baseball career, preserved his record of never having quarterbacked a losing college game.

A 74-yard scoring drive in nine plays wiped out the sting of Gatewood's touchdown grab and dispelled Royal's pregame fears that Texas would have trouble moving on the soft stadium turf, which, incidentally, resembled a cow pasture.

Jim Bertelsen's 1-yard rush over left guard made it 10-7 in the second quarter. Texas was even more impressive with a 77-yard scoring march that consumed eight minutes of the second half without the Longhorns throwing a pass.

Thirteen of the 18 plays on that drive were run at Notre Dame's right side, away from McCoy. Koy scored from the 3, but it was Steve Worster, named the game's outstanding offensive player with 155 yards rushing in 20 carriers, who maintained momentum for the 14-10 margin.

But Theismann, the junior from South River, N. J., was Street's equal en route to a single-game Cotton Bowl passing record. On the next series, the Irish drove 80 yards for a score, with Theismann accounting for 60 running and passing.

"Yoder was the key receiver," Theismann said, of his scrambling 24-yard scoring toss. "I thought we had it then, but Texas never quit.

"If I had to do it all over again, I wouldn't do anything differently. But they got the big plays and that's the name of the game."

```
Texas ...............0  7  0 14—21
Notre Dame ..........3  7  0  7—17
 N.D.—FG, Hempel, 26.
 N.D.—Gatewood, 54, pass from Theismann
(Hempel, kick).
 Tex.—Bertelsen, 1, run (Feller, kick).
 Tex.—Koy, 3, run (Feller, kick).
 N.D.—Yoder, 24, pass from Theismann
(Hempel, kick).
 Tex.—Dale, 1, run (Feller, kick).
 Attendance—73,000.
```

January 2, 1970

O. J. Simpson, the piston-legged running back who became a Heisman Trophy winner and Consensus All-America while at the University of Southern California, has been adjudged college football's greatest player of the nineteen-sixties by National Collegiate Sports Services.

In a midsummer poll, Simpson, now a member of the Buffalo Bills of the National Football League, received 267 votes. His nearest competitor in the balloting was Gale Sayers, the former Kansas University ball-carrier who had 131 votes. Next was Archie Manning of Mississippi with 47.

The same poll of 518 college head coaches, athletic directors and sports information directors, selected Paul (Bear) Bryant of Alabama as the top college coach of the decade. Bryant received 127 votes to 121 for Darrell Royal of the University of Texas.

August 23, 1970

Notre Dame Snaps Texas Streak With 24-11 Victory

THEISMANN RUNS FOR TWO SCORES

Back Also Passes for Tally —Irish Recover 5 Texas Fumbles in Cotton Bowl

STATISTICS OF THE GAME

	Notre Dame	Texas
First downs	16	20
Rushing yardage	146	216
Passing yardage	213	210
Return yardage	0	26
Passes	9-19	10-27
Interceptions by	1	1
Punts	8-46	5-33
Fumbles lost	1	5
Yards penalized	52	33

By NEIL AMDUR
Special to The New York Times

DALLAS, Jan. 1—A wishbone defense stopped the wishbone offense today, as Notre Dame ended college football's third longest winning streak with a 24-11 victory over Texas in the 35th annual Cotton Bowl game.

Lining up on defense to mirror the offensive players in the Texas backfield, the inspired, underdog Irish reversed last year's 21-17 loss to the Longhorns and snapped a 30-game Texas victory string that had spanned three seasons.

Also ended was the modest record of five consecutive post-season bowl triumphs for Coach Darrell Royal.

The victory marked the second time in the last 25 years that Notre Dame played the role of spoiler against teams with long victory streaks. On Nov. 16, 1957, the Irish ended Oklahoma's national collegiate record 47-game string by winning 7-0, in Norman Okla.

Today's game, viewed by a somewhat stunned capacity crowd of 73,000, was a strange turnabout from the thrilling 1970 finish that highlighted the Longhorns' comeback in the final 68 seconds. After its first series of plays last year Texas trailed, 10-0; today the Longhorns led, 3-0, after their first series—on a 23-yard field goal by Happy Feller.

Texans Need a Shamrock

But Notre Dame countered with three touchdowns in the next 13 minutes on a 26-yard pass from Joe Theismann to Tom Gatewood, and two Theismann runs of 3 and 15 yards.

The Texas Wishbone-T, which had averaged 41 points and 374 yards rushing through 10 regular-season victories, needed a shamrock in the backfield today. The Longhorns were limited to 216 yards on the ground, fumbled nine times and lost five, had one pass intercepted and failed to convert the big possession plays that had characterized their dramatic victories in the last two seasons. On 19 occasions, the Notre Dame defense stopped Texas with no more than a 1-yard gain.

Steve Worster, the all-America fullback, showed the effects of a knee injury that had limited his practice time in recent weeks. Worster fumbled four of his 16 carries and gained only 42 yards against an aroused Irish squad, which had yielded 331 yards on the ground last year.

The 11 points were the lowest scoring total for Texas in three years. The Longhorns' last loss was to Texas Tech, 31-22, in the second game of the 1968 season.

Opportunities Abound

"We had our opportunities," said Royal, who was bidding for a second successive national championship. "They were there. We were not beaten so bad that we did not have opportunities."

Notre Dame produced a group of surprising heroes, besides the defense and Theismann, who completed nine of 16 passes for 176 yards.

The Irish played without Gatewood for most of the game, after the all-America junior strained a hamstring muscle running out the fourth-down touchdown toss from Theismann with 7 minutes 58 seconds left in the first quarter.

A 74-yard quick-kick by Jim Yoder midway through the second quarter stunned Texas and forced the Longhorns to spend the next seven minutes driving 86 yards for a touchdown. A 2-yard pitchout from Eddie Phillips, the courageous quarterback, to Jim Bertelsen accounted for the Texas score.

But rather than settle for a 21-11 half-time lead, Notre Dame came out throwing in the last 105 seconds. The big gainer that helped produce a 36-yard field goal was not a Theismann-to-Gatewood pass, but a Jim Bulger-to-Clarence Ellis hookup.

Ellis in Offensive Debut

Bulger, a 6-foot, 5-inch, 200-pound sophomore quarterback from Pittsburgh, made his first appearance of the season with 54 seconds left. He came into the line-up after Theismann injured some fingers on his throwing hand.

Ellis, named the game's outstanding defensive player at cornerback, also ran into the line-up with Bulger and then raced behind a Texas defender to catch a 37-yard pass. It was the first appearance on offense for the fleet Ellis this year.

Coach Ara Parseghian then sent in Pat Steenberge, Theismann's understudy. Steenberge, another sophomore from Erie, Pa., passed 6 more yards to Ed Gulyas. Scott Hempel kicked the placement with 24 seconds left that gave Notre Dame more points in the first half than anyone had scored in an entire game against the top-rated Longhorns this year.

"We tried to mirror their wishbone with the same type of defense," Parseghian said. "We wanted Texas to pass."

The victory was Notre Dame's 10th, the most for any Parseghian-coached team, against one loss.

The Texas misfortunes began

in the opening series, after Phillips broke away from a 63-yard run on the first play. On second down from the 8, Phillips pitched out to Bertelsen, but the ball was fumbled out of bounds, and the Longhorns had to settle for 3 points.

Texas fumbled three kickoff returns, including a line-drive after the first Notre Dame touchdown that the Irish recovered on the Longhorn 13-yard line. Theismann scored six plays later on a rollout from the 3.

The strength of the Notre Dame defense was particularly evident early in the second half. When Texas reached the Irish 35-yard line needing 1 yard for a first down, the Longhorns gambled and Bertelsen cracked at left guard.

But Jim Musuraca, another Irish sophomore, closed up the hole and pushed Bertelsen back.

"They changed their defensive pattern and threw a lot of beef at us on that play," Royal said. "It worked."

Phillips was magificent in defeat. He rushed for 164 yards and lobbed nine of 17 passes like a shot-putter for 199 yards. He left the game with an injury

with 8:54 left and Texas at the Irish 22.

Notre Dame	14	10	0	0—24
Texas	3	8	0	0—11

Tex.—FG, Feller, 23.
N.D.—Gatewood, 26, pass from Theismann (Hempel, kick).
N.D.—Theismann, 3, run (Hempel, kick).
N.D.—Theismann, 15, run (Hempel, kick).
Tex.—Bertelsen, 2, run (Lester, pass from Phillips).
N.D.—FG, Hempel, 36.
Attendance—73,000.

January 2, 1971

Nebraska, on Late Rally, Stops Oklahoma for 21st in Row, 35-31

4th Touchdown by Kinney Is Difference

STATISTICS OF THE GAME

	Neb.	Okla.
First downs	19	22
Rushing yardage	59-297	64-279
Passing yardage	65	188
Return yardage	80	7
Passes	6-13	6-11
Interceptions by	0	0
Punts	5-36	3-36
Fumbles lost	1	3
Yards penalized	5	0

By NEIL AMDUR
Special to The New York Times

NORMAN, Okla., Nov. 25—Unbeaten, top-ranked Nebraska scored a touchdown in the final 98 seconds today to outlast Oklahoma, its national challenger, 35-31, in a college football classic that surpassed expectations for Thanksgiving Day excitement.

The Orange Bowl-bound Cornhuskers, who had never trailed through 10 previous victories, had to come from behind twice to register their 21st consecutive victory and 30 game without a loss.

It took a pressure-filled 74-yard drive that consumed more than five minutes of the final period for Nebraska to regain the lead from the aroused Sooners, who also had trailed, by as many as 11 points, earlier in the game.

Jeff Kinney, a 6-foot-2-inch, 210-pound running back who seems destined for greater achievements as a professional, carried the last four times and 15 yards in the drive, including the final 2 for the decisive touchdown through a hole carved by Larry Rupert, the all-America guard.

Glover Finishes It

It was Kinney's fourth touchdown of the afternoon, and he finished with a shredded white jersey, 174 yards rushing in 30 bruising carries and totally "exhausted."

Oklahoma, with a 9-1 won-lost record and headed for the Sugar Bowl on New Year's Day against Auburn, had one final chance at its 19-yard line after the fifth Nebraska score.

But Nebraska made a strategic change in its defensive secondary and applied a hard rush on Jack Mildren, the Sooner quarterback. On fourth down, Rich Glover, a junior middle guard from Jersey City, and a standout all day, rushed Mildren and deflected his attempt to throw long to Jon Harrison, his fleet wide receiver.

A record and raucous Owen Field crowd of 63,385 and an international television audience (the game was beamed by satellite to Europe and the Far East) had little time to let their midday holiday meals settle.

Johnny Rodgers, the Cornhuskers' explosive back, weaved 72 yards for a touchdown on a thrilling punt return after the Sooners' first offensive series. The furious pace continued for the entire game.

Almost No Foul Play

The two teams accounted for nine touchdowns and 829 yards total offense, including 311 in the first half by Oklahoma, which scored with five seconds left to take a 17-14 halftime lead on a 24-yard pass from Mildren to Harrison, his high school teammate from Abilene, Tex.

In a tribute to the consistency and quality of play throughout, only five yards in penalties were assessed against both schools.

Nebraska, the nation's No. 1 defensive team, spent 10 days trying to defense the various options and subtleties of the Oklahoma Wishbone offense. Yet Mildren, the 6-foot, 190-pound senior, was magnificent in defeat, running for touch-downs of 2 and 3 yards, throwing to Harrison behind a frustrated cornerback, Bill Kosch, for two more and amassing 267 yards total offense.

The Cornhuskers limited Greg Pruitt, Oklahoma's speedy all-America back, to his lowest output of the season, 53 yards in 10 carries. But Mildren's efficiency on the option and his ability to sustain long drives with crucial third-down calls reaffirmed the efficacy of the Sooners' attack.

Oklahoma scoring drives covered 70, 80, 78, 73 and 69 yards, and the Sooners averaged over 6 yards a play, incredible statistics against a team that had not yielded more than 17 points in a single game and had been called by Chuck Fairbanks, the Oklahoma coach, "one of the most complete college football teams ever assembled."

Nebraska has been termed "unemotional and efficient" in its tactical approach, and the two words summarized the Cornhuskers' comebacks, particularly on the last march.

Two Sooner fumbles led to Nebraska scores. But four Cornhusker touchdowns came on respectable marches af 54, 53 and 61 yards in addition to the winning 12-play drive after Harrison's second touchdown reception (17 yards) with 7:05 left had made it, 31-28, Oklahoma.

Twice on important third-down plays, Nebraska managed to avoid technical mistakes and maintain momentum. Kinney, who rushed for 154 yards in the second half, swept 17 yards on third-and-1 at the Cornhusker 35.

The biggest play of the game may have been Jerry Tagge's 11-yard pass to Rodgers on third-and-8 from the O.U. 46. Rodgers caught the ball lying on the ground.

"It's the greatest victory of my career," Coach Bob Devaney said afterward. "When we were down, 31-28, I thought we could score because our offense had been moving the ball in the second half."

In defeat Fairbanks acknowledged that it was a "classic game, the greatest one I've ever been involved in."

The Lost Chance

Oklahoma fans still thought the Sooners had a chance from the 19. But Devaney shifted Joe Blahak, the safety, to cornerback in place of Kosch, who had been victimized by Harrison for four catches and 115 yards.

In fairness to Kosch, it was the first time he had played cornerback in his varsity career. Normally a safety, he was shifted to play Harrison one-on-one in order to put Blahak, a strong tackler, closer to the Sooners' offensive muscle.

Mildren overthrew Harrison deep on first down, kept for 4 yards and was smothered by Larry Jacobson, a 250-pound all-America tackle, for an 8-yard loss before Glover, who was in on 22 tackles, batted the last ball away to send the Cornhuskers to the Orange Bowl with a chance for a second successive national title.

Nebraska	7	7	14	7—35
Oklahoma	3	14	7	7—31

Neb.—Rodgers, 72, punt return (Sanger, kick).
Okla.—FG, Carroll, 30.
Neb.—Kinney, 1, run (Sanger, kick).
Okla.—Mildren, 3, run (Carroll, kick).
Okla.—Harrison, 24, pass from Mildren (Carroll, kick).
Neb.—Kinney, 3, run (Sanger, kick).
Neb.—Kinney, 1, run (Sanger, kick).
Okla.—Mildren, 3, run (Carroll, kick).
Okla.—Harrison, 16, pass from Mildren (Carroll, kick).
Neb.—Kinney, 2, run (Sanger, kick).
Attendance—63,385.

November 26, 1971

STANFORD WINS, 13-12

MICHIGAN IS UPSET

Garcia's 31-Yard Field Goal With :12 to Go Wins Rose Bowl

By BILL BECKER
Special to The New York Times

PASADENA, Calif., Jan. 1—In a Rose Bowl game they'll be talking about for another 70 years, Stanford finally caught up with Michigan today for the 49-0 pasting it took in the 1902 contest, the first of this post-season football series.

The Stanfords used a 31-yard field goal in the final 12 seconds by little Rod Garcia to upset the undefeated Big Ten champions, 13-12, and they accomplished this after virtually handing the game to the Wolverines on a safety a few minutes earlier.

It was the second straight upset victory for the Indians from Palo Alto, Calif., and their coach, John Ralston. Ralston likes to play it cool and loose —but not quite this loose.

103,154 See Game

However, he had Don Bunce, a rifle-armed quarterback, who completed 24 passes for 294 yards to more than match the vaunted Wolverine running attack led by all-America Billy Taylor. Bunce may be a shade behind Jim Plunkett but he did the job almost as well as Plunkett did last New Year's Day against Ohio State.

The loss was the second for Michigan and its coach, Bo Schembechler, in their last two trips. The Wolverines had four consecutive victories here starting with that 1909 inaugural. But they hadn't met Stanford since then.

A crowd of 103,154 was treated to one of the hardest-hitting of the 58 games in the Rose Bowl series. Tough defenses nullified the best thrusts of both teams for three quarters. Dana Coin kicked a 30-yard field goal to give the Wolverines a 3-0 half-time lead before Garcia tied it with a 42-yarder in the third period.

Long Drive at Start

The final period started with Michigan's 71-yard drive producing a 1-yard touchdown plunge by Fritz Seyferth, fullback. Coin's conversion made it 10-3.

But Ralston, a gambler at heart, let his boys run from punt formation on fourth and 10 at their 33-yard line midway in the period. Jackie Brown swept right end for 31 yards and a minute later broke off right tackle for 24 yards and a touchdown. Garcia's conversion tied it, 10-all.

Michigan recovered a Bunce fumble on the Stanford 35 to set up a 46-yard field goal try by Coin, which fell short.

However, Jim Ferguson, a sophomore safety, tried to run the ball back and was knocked back into the end zone by Ed Shuttlesworth's tackle for a safety. Michigan took the lead 12-10, with 3 minutes 18 seconds left.

After one exchange of kicks, the Indians got the ball at their 22 with 1 minute 48 seconds to go. Bunce, the riverboat shifty, passed 13 to Bill Scott, tight end, 16 and 12 to John Winesberry, shifty flanker; 11 to Miles Moore, split end; 14 to Reggie Sanderson, fullback, and there was Stanford on the Michigan 14 with 14 seconds left.

On third down and 7 to go and with Steve Murray holding, Garcia, who led the nation's

United Press International

WINNING POINTS: Stanford's Rod Garcia kicks 31-yard field goal with 12 seconds left against Michigan in Rose Bowl

field goal kickers with 14 in 1971, kicked his biggest. It was a 31-yard bull's-eye requiring only two seconds. A kickoff later, Stanford was returned the 13-12 victor.

Bunce completed 24 of 44, with several near interceptions, but kept the Indians rolling with 22 first downs, compared to 16 for Michigan. Stanford rushed for only four first downs, but the Wolverines got no first downs passing, with Tom Slade, a sophomore, showing more skill as a runner.

Ralston hailed the victory "as just as satisfying" as last year's. This made it three straight for the Pacific 8 over the Big Ten for the first time in this series. Michigan lost, 10-3, to Southern California, in 1970.

Schembechler conceded, "Stanford deserved to win because we didn't get first downs when we needed them."

The Indians made a goal-line stand inside their 5-yard line at the start of the third period, then marched downfield to set up Garcia's first field goal.

They consistently gang-tackled Taylor, the workhorse who carried 32 times for 82 yards, and refused to break under the pounding rush attack of the Wolverines.

The Michigan coach singled out the fake punt as a key play that swung the momentum to Stanford. Ralston said the play was one he had picked up from a fellow coach. The ball was snapped to the fullback, Reg Sanderson, instead of the punter, Murray. Sanderson then

handed it to Brown, who took off.

Ralston also praised Bunce and "all those fine receivers." Especially outstanding was Winesberry, sophomore from Tulsa who caught 8 for 112 yards. Bunce said all the plays on the final drive were audibles. "We were really pulling some plays out of the air," the quarterback told reporters. "I was so excited I didn't even know what I was calling."

Stanford, it should be added, played without Hillary Shockley, fullback hobbled by ankle injury. Sanderson and others took up the slack.

Stanford now has won five games, lost five and tied once in 11 Rose Bowl appearances.

Mich.—FG, Coin, 30.
Stan.—FG, Garcia, 42.
Mich.—Seyferth 1, run (Coin, Rice).
Stan.—Brown, 24, run (kick failed).
Mich.—Safety, Shuttleworth (tackle on Ferguson in end zone).
Stan.—FG, Garcia, 31.
Attendance—103,154.

INDIVIDUAL STATISTICS

RUSHES—Mich.: B. Taylor, 32 carries for 82 yards; Shuttleworth, 13 for 62; Slade, 13 for 41; Doughty, 4 for 56; Seyferth, 3 for 6. Stan.: Brown, 6 for 60; Winesberry, 4 for 15; Bunce, 8 for 2; Sanderson, 5 for 16.
PASSES—Mich.: Slade, 3 completions in 10 attempts for 26 yards. Stan.: Bunce, 24 completions in 44 attempts for 290 yards.
RECEPTIONS—Mich.: Doughty, 2 for 13 yards; Seymour, 1 for 13. Stan.: Winesberry, 8 for 110 yards; Brown, 5 for 30; Scott, 5 for 55; Moore, 3 for 52; and Sanderson, 3 for 45.

STATISTICS OF THE GAME

First downs	22	16
Rushing yardage	23-118	74-290
Passing yardage	290	26
Passes	24-40	3-11
Interdeptions by	1	0
Punts	4-42	7-39
Fumbles lost	4	1
Yards penalized	14	23

Stanford	0 0 3	10—13
Michigan	0 3 0	9—12

January 2, 1972

So. California Rallies to Beat Ohio State, 18-17

Two-Point Play Is Decisive in the Rose Bowl

By WILLIAM N. WALLACE
Special to The New York Times

PASADENA, Calif., Jan. 1 —Pat Haden has thrown hundreds of passes to John McKay, his high school and college classmate, in scores of practices and dozens of games. Their last one, which came today toward the end of the frenetic Rose Bowl game between Southern California and Ohio State, was the best of all.

It was good for a 38-yard touchdown that brought the Trojans up to the edge of a dramatic upset of the Buckeyes, an upset completed on the following successful 2-point conversion pass, from Haden to Shelton Diggs. Those 8 points gave Southern Cal an 18-17 victory before the startled eyes of 106,721 spectators and a national television audience.

Haden, the quarterback who will eschew a pro football—Rhodes scholarship tour in Britain, wound up the No. 1 hero. He was the chief architect of the 8 big points that won the game with such suddenness.

McKay, the slim receiver who is an unlikely candidate for future football, shared with his father, the winning coach, the other parts of the heroics in his final game for U.S.C.

Young McKay caught five big passes from Haden for 104 yards in a contest of rapidly shifting fortunes and eight turnovers. As for the 51-year-old gray-haired coach, he didn't hesitate to try for

the 2-point conversion play following the final touchdown, the difficult play that would bring victory or defeat rather than the easier 1-point kick that, if good, would have brought about a deflating 17-17 tie.

"We always go for the 2 points in a situation like that," said Coach McKay later. "We didn't come to play for a tie. We were a fortuate team to win. They were unfortunate to lose." McKay knew about misfortune. A 2-point conversion play by a Southern California team of his had failed in the 1967 Rose Bowl game won as a consequence by Purdue, 14-13.

Woody Hayes, the Ohio State coach, who in the past has been volatile following defeat, was mild. "We got beaten by a better team," he said. "One point better."

On the Haden-McKay big play, the passer had plenty of time to wait for his buddy, known for his craft rather than his speed, to reach the enemy end zone.

"He knew I'd be there," said young McKay later. "It's our favorite place. He knows I've been there before." The pass was perfect and it was caught in the back of the end zone, with McKay slamming into a wire fence a few steps beyond where fans hugged his maroon helmet.

Did Haden see the catch? "I sure did. I had no doubt he'd get it." The play's designation was 96X Corner and that is where McKay was, in the corner of the end zone.

But Haden had to complete another aerial to win the game. He was less sure that the diving Diggs had held on to the conversion 2-

point pass. "Then I saw the official's arms go up," Haden said of the signal for a score. "I was never so happy in my life."

Ohio State had two minutes left in which to try to score again and the dangerous Cornelius Greene, the Buckeye quarterback, gave it a good try. He got his team up to midfield and on the last play Tom Skladnay's 62-yard field-goal attempt fell short.

It was Greene, more than the acclaimed Archie Griffin, whom the Trojans feared the most because he had been the architect of Ohio State's victory over Southern Cal here a year ago. The fears were justified. Greene ran for 68 yards and one touchdown and he completed 8 of 14 pass attempts, a lot for Ohio State, for 93 yards.

Griffin was less in evidence. The Heisman Trophy winner had gained 100 yards or more in Ohio State's last 22 games. That streak came to an end as Griffin made 76 against a superb Maroon defense. Worse yet he fumbled twice, at the Trojan 5- and 7-yard lines. Ouch!

Anthony Davis, Griffin's counterpart for Southern California, was hurt and left the game in the second period, never to reappear. He had injured ribs but had gained 71 yards in the early going. His replacement, Allen Carter, did very well and led the Trojan ground attack on the victor's two long second-half scoring drives.

Four lost fumbles, one key one by Davis that set up Ohio State's initial touchdown by Champ Henson, contributed to the bizarre game. For example, Coach McKay "returned" 3 points after Chris Limahelu had kicked a 39-yard field goal late in the second quarter.

McKay preferred to accept a 5-yard penalty against Ohio State on the play, which gave U.S.C. a first down and a chance to keep going. Four plays later Limahelu tried a 24-yard field goal, which was no good. That left the Buckeyes with a 7-3 half-time lead and the Trojans in pain.

Haden completed 12 of 22 passes for 181 yards and two touchdowns, the first to the fine tight end, Jim Obradovich. Neal Colzie intercepted two of Haden's passes and he was so elated on the second one that he spiked the ball, meaning he bounced it hard on the turf.

That cost his team a 15-yard unsportsmanlike conduct penalty, from the U.S.C. 9 to its 24 and from there Danny Reece then intercepted a pass by Greene. The Colzie spike was one more way the Buckeyes found to lose the game.

They missed a score on an early 15-yard field-goal attempt. They made nothing out of a blocked Southern Cal punt deep in Trojan territory. And they could not handle Davis's substitute, the unheralded Carter. The victors were hardly guiltless with six errors, two fumbles, two interceptions, the blocked punt and the give-back field goal.

But, as Coach Hayes put it, "Pat Haden made the big play which won the game."

But the elder McKay had the last word. He said, "There were 106,000 people in the stands and no one knew who would win right up until the end. I thought it was a great game between two great teams and in the end we had 18 points and they had 17."

January 2, 1975

Griffin Wins Heisman 2d Time

Ohio State Star Is First to Gain Trophy Twice

By GORDON S. WHITE Jr.

Archie Griffin of Ohio State, one of the smallest athletes to win the annual Heisan Trophy as "the outstanding college football player in the United States," yesterday became the first man to be voted the award twice.

The 5-foot-8½-inch 184-pound tailback was the fifth college junior to win this award when he took it last year and yesterday he succeeded after Doc Blanchard of Army, Doak Walker of Southern Methodist University, Vic Janowicz of Ohio State and Roger Staubach of Navy had failed to repeat as Heisman Trophy winners.

Not the fastest of running backs but certainly one of the best balanced and shiftiest in the college sport, Griffin established a major college varsity career rushing record of 5,176 yards in four seasons with the Buckeyes. This record and his unequaled mark of rushing for 100 yards or more in 31 consecutive regular-season games enabled him to beat out five other running backs by a wide margin in the voting by 888 sports writers and broadcasters throughout the nation.

Earning 454 first-place votes, 167 votes for second and 104 for third, Griffin accumulated 1,800 points to win by a margin of almost 2½ to 1 over Chuck Muncie, the outstanding running back for the University of California.

Muncie, with 145 first-place votes, got 730 points, followed by Ricky Bell of Southern California, 708; Tony Dorsett of Pittsburgh, 616; Joe Washington of Oklahoma, 250, and Jimmy DuBose of the University of Florida, 112.

John Sciarra of the University of California, Los Angeles, was the leading quarterback in the voting that has many times favored athletes at that important position. Sciarra was seventh with 86 points.

Griffin and Sciarra will match talents when the undefeated Ohio State team, ranked No. 1 in the nation, plays U.C.L.A. in the Rose Bowl on Jan. 1.

Members of the Downtown Athletic Club will formally present Griffin with the Heisman Trophy at a dinner in the New York Hilton Hotel on Dec. 11. The Ohio State star flew into New York from Columbus, Ohio, with his coach, Woody Hayes, yesterday morning to be at the D.A.C. when announcement of the first double winner was made at noon.

Griffin, who has won the 40th and 41st Heisman Trophy, is the 38th offensive back to gain the award that was instituted in 1935 when Jay Berwanger of the University of Chicago won it. The two linemen to earn this trophy were both ends—Larry Kelley of Yale in 1936 and Leon Hart of Notre Dame in 1949.

The obviously delighted Ohio State runner said: "There was a lot of pressure this year—more than last year."

Hayes said: "The team stewed and fretted more about Archie winning the Heisman Trophy this year than Archie did."

Janowicz became the third junior to win the Heisman Trophy when Ohio State's single wing tailback took the honor in 1950. However, Hayes succeeded Wes Fesler as the Buckeyes' coach in 1951 and changed the offensive formation from the single wing to the T. Ohio State, which had a 6-3 won-lost record in 1950, dropped to 4-3-2 in Hayes's first season there.

The Buckeyes' coach, who has gone on to much greater success than he had in 1951, said: "It hurt him [Janowicz], I'm sure. If I had to do it over again I'd have kept the single wing for the 1951 season."

The 1951 Heisman Trophy winner was another single-wing tailback, Dick Kazamier of Princeton.

Blanchard became the first junior to capture the Heisman Trophy, in 1945, and did not repeat because his teammate, Glenn Davis, won the award in 1946. As the two running backs went through their varsity careers it became apparent that, barring injury, one would win as a junior and the other as a senior.

Walker won the Heisman Trophy as a junior in 1948 but was plagued with injuries in the 1949 season, the year that Hart became the second lineman to earn the coveted award. Staubach, the only quarterback to win the Heisman Trophy as a junior, did so in 1963. He also was injured much of his senior season and another Notre Dame player, John Huarte, quarterback, took the honor in 1964.

Griffin is the fourth Ohio State player to win the Heisman Trophy, following in the footsteps of Les Horvath, 1944; Janowicz, 1950, and Howard (Hopalong) Cassady, 1955.

Last year Griffin beat out Anthony Davis, the star runner at Southern California, by a slightly larger margin than he won yesterday—1,920 points to 819. Oklahoma's star, Joe Washington, who was fifth yesterday in the voting, was third a year ago when he was a junior.

Michigan's Gordon Bell, a small running back like Griffin, finished eighth in the voting yesterday behind Sciarra with 84 points. Then came Leroy Selman of Oklahoma, the leading lineman in the balloting. He is a middle guard on defense.

In order after Selman were Gene Swick, quarterback at Toledo; Leroy Cook, defensive end at Alabama; Steve Niehaus, defensive tackle at Notre Dame; Jeff Grantz, quarterback at South Carolina, and Nolan Cromwell, running back at Kansas.

December 3, 1975

Who Should Call Signals in College Football?

By GERALD ESKENAZI

Football is said to prepare a college player for the bigger game of life. Football indeed, all sports—are supposed to be as important to a student's development as logic, literature and philosophy.

But the game does not belong to the student any more. In most colleges where football scholarships are given, the coaches run the show.

This question — has the game been taken from the players—is hardly new. But it is especially current, at a time when economics dic-

tate a collegiate policy as surely as the head of the English Department sets a curriculum.

In this college season, which is winding down with the bowl games, visiting teams were limited to dressing only 48 players. This was perhaps the first of only several major rule changes that may wind up once more with one-platoon football. Each change creates different pressures for a head coach, whose motto might have been the well-worn, "The kid's got a four-year scholarship and I've got a one-year contract."

The Background

Football as Americans play it, springs from rugby and soccer and colleges played one-platoon football until 1941. For many, it was an educational experience and the quarterback called the signals.

But in 1941, with the coming of the Armed Forces draft and the resultant shortage of college students, the rules were changed to permit two-platoon football. This allowed teams, short of personnel, to play 11 men on offense and a different 11 to play defense, thus getting

75

Two-time Heisman Trophy winner Archie Griffin picks up yardage against Ohio State's arch rival Michigan in 1974.

more mileage from each player.

Strangely, most coaches didn't utilize the rule they had at their disposal. In 1945, Fritz Crisler at Michigan employed it with a collection of 17-year-olds and had an outstanding season. By 1946, everyone was doing it. And it was then that coaches started to send in plays. Each new player that came in would be permitted to tell the huddle, after one play, what the coach wanted.

In 1953, though, the rule was changed again and reverted to one-platoon football. Sideline coaching was prohibited. The coaches didn't like this. They had become accustomed to running the show. So on some sidelines the coaches looked like baseball's third-base coaches as they gave hand and feet signals.

Others used an assistant coach stationed nearby to do the signaling. Among those who flouted the rules were Forest Evashevski of Iowa and Ara Parseghian of Northwestern.

Finally, two-platoon football returned in 1965, but coaching from the sidelines was prohibited for two more years. In 1973, Bear Bryant of Alabama spurred another rules change. He sent in a player with a field-goal tee, as if to hold for a field-goal attempt against Oregon. The player sneaked out during the huddle, though Oregon played for the field goal, but Alabama threw a pass. En-

ter the rule: A player, on the field must stay in for one play.

The Issues

Should the quarterback, and the defensive captain, call their own game? Is football a "subject" at college, where the answers aren't supposed to be given? Should the coach be permitted to call the shots, either by signals from the sidelines or through a messenger system?

For the Players

A team must have a leader on the field, contends the faction favoring the players. An association and a trust develops with other teammates when the quarterback or the defensive captain is barking orders. Also, some coaches simply believe the player on the field can do a better job. He is more sensitive to the opposition's forces and to his own people's abilities.

Actually, many who favor returning self-reliance to the game would not be satisfied until one-platoon football returns, coupled with the end of coaching from the sidelines. They argue that a boy (or girl) should be responsible for his mistakes. If he fumbles on the 2-yard line, why should he come out and leave the defense with the job of holding the other team? He should stay in and attempt to defend his goal line.

The two-platoon has led to a certain cookie-cutter quality to football players. No one speaks of a "triple-threat" any more. There is a production line element to the game. A player can spend his entire collegiate football career at cornerback or defensive end and know nothing about any other position. And, some say, the coach does not become interested in a player's development. He is interested only in retaining his job.

For the Coaches

A successful leader such as Joe Paterno of Penn State believes he helps the quarterback by relieving him of the responsibility of calling each play. And it is true that quarterbacks are faced with an increasing number of problems in signal-calling. Each club uses at least 12 to 15 basic defensive coverages a game. The player has three or four days to look at films and to prepare for a team. How much, really, can he absorb?

Some quarterbacks have had to be aided by writing on a piece of adhesive tape strapped to their wrist: "third-and-5, slant 34"; "third-and-1, sneak," etc.

But mostly it comes down to the question of a livelihood. A college coach is dismissed for losing just as a pro coach is dismissed for losing. And how many

coaches want to put their careers in the hands of a 17-year-old?

When the pressures to win became greater because winning meant income, it was then the coaches took over the operation completely. With his job on the line, the coach has hired assistants, has more film to look at, spends more time recruiting players. He has years invested in each call.

The Outlook

Money matters, and not philosophical questions of academics and sports, probably will determine which way college football proceeds.

So long as football remains the most important sport for many colleges in helping to pay for its entire athletic program, then the coach will remain supreme at these schools.

But colleges may start to decrease the number of players on the roster, and the number of scholarships a school may give. If this happens, perhaps a modified one-platoon game will evolve. With that more of the players' role will return. It is unlikely, though, that there will be a return to the prohibition in play-calling by the coaches. The players, after all, don't vote on the rule changes.

December 16, 1975

Michigan Beats Ohio State, 14-6, And Gains Berth in Rose Bowl

Record Crowd Sees Buckeyes Stymied by Late Fumble

By GERALD ESKENAZI
Special to The New York Times

ANN ARBOR, Mich., Nov. 19—Amid a constant roar produced by the largest crowd in the history of regular-season college football, Michigan won the Rose Bowl trip today with a 14-6 victory over Ohio State.

The 106,024 fans who filled Michigan Stadium, which has 101,701 seats and is 90 rows high, were part of a spectacle that saw the game end with thousands of Wolverine fanatics dashing onto the field, some climbing the goal posts and tearing them down.

Silently, the 6,000 Ohio State rooters watched from one end of the field, almost all of them wearing red Buckeye jackets.

An Excruciating Fumble

Just a few minutes before, they had had a chance for a tie, which would have sent them to Pasadena, Calif., home of the Rose Bowl. With four minutes remaining Ohio State had moved from its 10-yard line to Michigan's 8, only to lose the ball on a fumble.

Most of the game was also seen by 30 million television viewers, but not the opening seven minutes. Instead, the American Broadcasting Companies showed the historic arrival in Israel of Egypt's President, Anwar el-Sadat. And an ABC official said by telephone from New York, "We received thousands of telephone complaints for missing the kickoff."

What the TV viewers missed was the opening of a Midwestern drama that is played out every year on the last day of the two clubs' season. These teams always meet in their finale, and for eight of the last nine years the trip West for New Year's has been at stake.

This time each wound up with a 7-1 won-lost record in the Big Ten. So the Wolverines go, to meet the champion from the Pacific-8 Conference, on the basis of winning the showdown today. Ohio State accepted a bid tonight from the Sugar Bowl to play Alabama, the Southeastern Conference champion.

The crowd, the players and the bands were at an emotional peak rarely approached in other sports in other places. The TV viewers also failed to see the Michigan players massing in the tunnel on the 50-yard line, leaping faster and faster and higher and higher until they exploded like popcorn from the runway onto the field.

There they jumped under the "Go Blue" banner that, a minute earlier, Coach Woody Hayes and his Ohio State players had sacrilegiously touched.

The unpredictable Hayes, wearing shirtsleeves in the 42-degree chill, had led his players out. Then he suddenly went under the Michigan banner.

Quickly, he and the players were surrounded by fist-waving Michigan students, who shoved some of the players.

Hayes laughed as he took off for the sideline. He wasn't finished, though. He led Ohio State's backers in a pre-game cheer, and then. after his players had left, following the warmups, he gathered his staff of coaches around him for an emotional huddle.

All ths appeared to have worked. For the Buckeyes launched a drive that consumed half the first quarter, and they led, finally, on a 29-yard field goal by Vlade Janakievski, a Macedonian whom Hayes spirited away from Ohio State's soccer team.

The feared option attack was working perfectly, with Rob Gerald, the junior quarterback, befuddling the usually quick Michigan lineman.

Meanwhile, the Wolverines showed no attack in the opening quarter. They ran only five plays from scrimmage in the period, as the Ohio State defense appeared to get to the ball quicker than the Michigan backs did.

Slowly, though, the game turned. The Michigan defense stiffened against the country's leading rushing team, which had entered the game with an average of 332 yards on the ground. Then Roosevelt Smith of the Wolverines, playing for the injured Harlan Huckleby at tailback, scored on a 1-yard burst in the second quarter to cap a 46-yard drive, and Gregg Williner kicked the extra point.

Rick Leach, the Michigan quarterback, was now able to move his backs and hit with his passes.

In the third quarter Ron Springs of State fumbled, giving the ball to Michigan only 20 yards from a score. Leach soon went over, and the extra point extended Michigan's edge to 14-3.

Later in the quarter Janakievski's 44-yard field goal cut the edge to 14-6.

Then came the drama in the last minutes, when a touchdown and a 2-point conversion would have created a tie, left Ohio State unbeaten in conference play and sent the Buckeyes to the Rose Bowl, to be played Jan. 2.

Instead, John Anderson hit Gerald just as he attempted to pitch out to Spring, the ball squirted loose, and it was snared by Derek Howard.

Michigan used up most of the remaining time and then punted, and State could get off only three plays.

"This is by far the best game we ever played and lost," Hays said later, and the statistics tended to support him. The Buckeyes had the edge in first downs (23 to 10), number of plays from scrimmage (74 to 51), rushing yardage (208 to 141) and passing yardage (144 to 55)

Heyes Punches TV Man

That fumble by Gerald sent Hayes into a characteristic tantrum. A TV cameraman put the camera into the coach's face at that critical moment, and Hayes punched him.

"How would you like it if they did this to you all the time?" Hayes said later, putting his fists in a newsman's face.

Haye then signaled that the post-game news conference was over by exiting, not laughing.

He had switched his team to new shoes for Michigan's Tartan surface, which is different from his field's artificial surface. The players had difficulty with the shoes.

"They're not ordinary shoes," said Anderson. "You have to file the edges off them. They were slipping in them."

Bo Schembeckler's Michigan team,

wearing the same old shoes. wound up with a 10-1 record over all, while State was 9-2. But Hayes should not be unduly distressed. Since Schembechler took over here in 1969, Michigan has dropped only two games in its stadium.

The regular-season college record broken by today's crowd was set here two years ago at the Ohio State-Michigan game, attended by 105,543. The overall college football record is 106,-182, set at last season's Rose Bowl, between Michigan and the University of Southern California.

And there is more. Michigan's home average of 104,203 fans a game this season also set a National Collegiate mark. The previous record was 103,159, set here last year. And today's crowd was the 16th straight of more than 100,-000 here.

The intense Schembechler-Hayes rivalry, which began in 1969. is now tied at four games apiece, with one tie.

Michigan was not always this good, and the crowds were not always this large.

"I can remember," said a visitor from Detroit, "when they used to draw only sixty or seventy thousand."

November 20, 1977

College Football Polling Is an Inexact 'Science'

By FRED FERRETTI

A poll is a poll is a poll.

Or is it?

The ways of determining the country's No. 1 college football team are as different as apples are from oranges, often no more scientific than picking fruit off a tree branch.

Some, such as the polls of The Associated Press and United Press International, are attempts to be as dispassionate and universal as possible, although the essential points of view differ—the A.P. polls sportswriters and broadcasters, the U.P.I. asks coaches to pick from among their own.

Others, such as those of the Football Writers Association of America and the National Football Foundation and Hall of Fame, are selections by small committees, and although they award trophies symbolic of a national No. 1 ranking, they are basically public relations gestures.

Importance of Top Rating

Meaningless in themselves, the designations as either the No. 1 team or inclusion in the top 20 teams around the country are important to schools in practical ways. A high ranking makes it easier to recruit players to the school, thus insuring a continuing flow of superior players. A high rank makes it easier to approach alumni for money for athletics-related projects and creates an atmosphere in which the alumni will be more receptive.

Don Coryell, now coach of the professional football St. Louis Cardinals but before that the highly successful coach of San Diego State, says that to be No. 1 "is a tremendous thing."

"It's a great recruiting thing. People say we're in the top 20 and others want to be with a winner," he said yesterday by phone from Mobile, Ala., where he is preparing to coach the Senior Bowl game. "I know kids who'd rather go to U.S.C. or Notre Dame and sit on the bench than play regularly elsewhere. They can say they played for Notre Dame, and that's prestige."

He said "a ranking for the school means it has a good football team, and it will be able to raise money."

Others, such as Wick Temple, sports editor of The Associated Press, say that a ranking has other uses. "They're overrated," he said, "but they can help a coach keep his job."

Dan Devine, coach at Notre Dame, after learning that team was named No. 1 yesterday.

He said that the true way to determine a No. 1 national ranking would be through some kind of championship playoff system, a view shared by Fred McMane, college football editor for U.P.I. "I thank we'd all like to be done with polls and have the championship determined on the field," he said.

The Associated Press poll, the oldest of them all, was begun in 1936. It uses a board of 67 sportswriters and broadcasters, with votes allocated by region and by the number of schools that play what the A.P. considers "representative schedules." The Midwest, the Southeast and the Southwest have the most votes.

Those voting are selected by the chiefs of the various A.P. bureaus, and their votes are collected each Monday and sent by private wire to New York. They are released in midweek.

By Invitation Only

No network broadcasters are included among the voters, the theory being that they move around too much to be effectively critical. A.P. employees are not permitted to vote.

The 67 voters are in the 67 American cities including such diverse places as Los Angeles, San Francisco, Nashville, Baton Rouge, Waco, Detroit, Providence, New Haven, New Brunswick, N.J., New York City, Dallas, St. Louis, Des Moines, Chicago and Corvallis, Ore. Some of those on the panel regard their jobs as so sensitive that they request the A.P. not to release their names.

United Press International's panel is composed of 42 coaches, six each from seven designated regions of the country.

They are invited by U.P.I. to serve as judges and usually remain on the board until they lose or quit their coaching jobs or resign from the board. U.P.I. has had a weekly football ranking since 1950.

The coaches on the board are a cross section of the college coaching stars across the country. They include Woody Hayes of Ohio State, Bear Bryant of Alabama, Dan Devine of Notre Dame, Barry Switzer of Oklahoma and Don James of Washington, all of whom coached in bowl games on Monday. U.P.I. has never disclosed how each member of the board votes each week.

Hayes said he thought Alabama, which beat his team, 35-6, should be No. 1, and Bryant though that was fine. Devine was telling everyone Notre Dame was No. 1 because "I honestly don't feel anyone can beat us, and if they can't beat us, they can't be No. 1." Switzer, whose Oklahoma team lost to Arkansas, suggested, "We might have played the best team." And Don James felt his Washington team, winner in the Rose Bowl, had a claim.

Cooper Rollow of The Chicago Tribune, and president of the Football Writers Association of America, appointed his five-man committee several months ago. Rollow received their votes in Chicago early yesterday and then announced that Notre Dame would receive the Grantland Rice Trophy. Those appointed, according to a past president of the organization, John Mooney, are usually past presidents of the group.

"There is no pressure on us. We think we're pretty fair," he said.

As for the rating, Mooney says, "It doesn't mean a damn except to the guy that gets it. Any of five teams could have claimed it yesterday." The Football Writers' Association has selected a champion since 1954. According to Mooney, one of the reasons it continues to do so is that "the public eats it up."

Rollow agrees.

"The public thinks it's important to have a champion, but you know, college football is the only sport where a championship is not determined on the field of play but by polls. That's a powerful argument for some kind of postseason super tournament."

The National Football Foundation and Hall of Fame also has a panel that votes once a year. Immediately after midnight yesterday it announced for Notre Dame after its 10-man awards committee, a committee that has existed for years with only a few changes, voted.

The committee is a cross section of football all-Americans, coaches, writers and football-related people and has been voting since 1959. Says the group's executive director, Jimmie McDowell, "the idea of No. 1 is so widespread these days, with the fans screaming it, that everybody wants it."

He added, "It's not so hard to pick you know. The teams that go to the bowl games are the same teams, it seems. It's just that each year they go to different bowls."

January 4, 1978

Red Smith

Gaudiest Game In 50 Years

NOTRE Dame and Southern California have met at football 50 times, and now they might as well knock it off. No use trying. If they played another 50 years, they could not match the gaudy theatrics of Saturday's fourth quarter.

What made the implausible downright incredible was the reversal of roles in the second half. For 30 minutes and more, Paul McDonald, Kevin Williams, Frank Jordan, Charles White, Calvin Sweeney and the rest of the U.S.C. Trojans toyed with their visitors. The score was 17-3 at halftime and 24-6 in the third quarter. With the fine running backs, Vagas Ferguson and Jerome Heavens, among the wounded, Notre Dame's attack was null on the ground and the next thing to void in the air. Then without warning, everything turned upside down. Unbelievably, Notre Dame scored three touchdowns and, with 46 seconds on the clock, a game that had been out of reach was won, 25-24. Then with two seconds on the clock, Southern Cal won it back, 27-25. College football's oldest intersectional series produced some rabble-rousers in the past but never one like this.

Bo Schembechler, the Michigan coach, had business in Columbus, Ohio, Saturday and probably couldn't watch U.S.C. on television, but the chances are that films of the game have reached him by now. Maybe between now and Jan. 1, he can discover a route that his pass rushers can follow to reach McDonald, the Southern Cal quarterback, in the Rose Bowl. Secure as a cloistered nun behind the monsters in his offensive line, McDonald took his own sweet time throwing to receivers like Kevin Williams, whom the Notre Dame secondary shunned like a pollution.

And in between passes, McDonald handed off or pitched out to Charles White. A week before the Notre Dame game, with two games to go in the season, White broke the all-time rushing record for the Pacific-Ten, a conference that has rejoiced in running backs like O.J. Simpson, Ricky Bell, Anthony Davis, Mike Garrett and a dozen others. Against Notre Dame, White added 201 yards, and he is only a junior with another full season to build up a conference record worth shooting at. He does it mostly by sheer speed, simply running past tacklers.

White will return to school next fall as the odds-on favorite for the Heisman Trophy, but watching him flash through and around tacklers now, a guy can't help wondering why he isn't a Heisman candidate this year. It is an absurd award, based on the dreamy notion that sportswriters, sportscasters and other "authorities" around the country can compare the talents of players they have not seen and say, "This is the single best college football player in America today."

The election is a triumph of press agentry, and the press agents don't even try to put a candidate forward before his senior year. Watching Charles White, a spectator had to ask himself: "Who could be better than this junior? Billy Sims of Oklahoma? Chuck Fusina of Penn State? That Alexander kid down at Louisiana State? Maybe none of the guys the press agents are pushing."

Then it was the fourth quarter, and the heretical suspicion arose that maybe Joe Montana was better. All of a sudden, Notre Dame's quarterback was a towering figure dominating the field. Time was wasting and the score was still 24-6, but the young man seemed poised and confident as he led his team on what seemed a forlorn march. Six inches short of a touchdown, disaster struck. Montana tried to squeeze into the end zone on a quarterback sneak, and fumbled the ball away.

Not even this discouraged him. Next time Notre Dame had the ball, he fired a bomb to Kris Haines that went 57 yards for a touchdown. (Haines, who looks like a blond choirboy, is Montana's favorite target. In that second half, Montana completed 17 passes for 286 yards, nine of them to Haines for 179 yards.)

Notre Dame had to go 98 yards for a second touchdown, with Montana still at the throttle. He threw long and short, and when he had to run, he showed that White wasn't the only ball carrier who could outdistance tacklers. The clock showed 3:01 when Pete Buchanan went in to make the score 24-19.

U.S.C. plays a possession game, but this time had to yield up the ball with a minute-and-a-half left. There were 48 seconds left when Montana got his troops to the 2-yard line. From there he threw a quickie to Pete Holohan on a slant-in pattern in the end zone.

Southern Cal got the ball on its own 30-yard line with 41 seconds left, and now it was McDonald's turn to show poise. He completed a pass for 10 yards, had an incompletion when several Notre Damers jumped on his wishbone, then pitched to Sweeney, who reached the Notre Dame 25 with 12 seconds to go. McDonald calmly extended six seconds on a run by White to position the ball for Jordan, the kicker. Jordan kicked for 37 yards. It was the whole ball of wax.

November 27, 1978

Coach Hayes Ousted by Ohio State for Punching Player

Gator Bowl Melee Ends His Reign

By PAUL WINFIELD

Woody Hayes was dismissed as Ohio State's football coach the morning after he punched a Clemson player in Friday night's Gator Bowl.

His dismissal was announced by Hugh Hindman, the Ohio State athletic director, in a news conference at 8:30 o'clock yesterday in Jacksonville, Fla., where the game had been played.

"Coach Hayes has been relieved of his duties as head football coach," Hindman said. "This decision has the full support of the president of the university."

Hindman met with the president, Harold Enarson, after the game. "I told him [Hayes] this morning at the hotel about the decision," Hindman said.

The athletic director, when asked if the dismissal had resulted from the Gator Bowl incident, replied, "Yes."

Enarson said last night: "There is not a university or athletic conference in this country that would permit a coach to physically assault a college athlete."

Interception Starts Incident

Hindman said he had asked Hayes if he would resign and Hayes said he would not. But a half-hour after their discussion, at about 8:10 A.M., Hayes telephoned a reporter at The Columbus Dispatch and said he had resigned.

Reports persisted that the school had been looking for a reason to dismiss the 65-year-old Hayes, who has coached at Ohio State for 28 years. He had been on probation in the Big Ten Conference for previous incidents.

After the Florida news conference, the team returned by plane to Columbus, landing at 11:50 A.M. Hayes, who has been unavailable since the incident, left the airport in a police car.

The incident occurred with 1 minute 58 seconds left in the Buckeyes' 17-15 loss to Clemson. Charlie Bauman, Clemson's linebacker, had intercepted an Ohio State pass and was knocked out of bounds on the Ohio State sideline.

Hayes went after Bauman, swinging. An Ohio State player, Ken Fritz, tried to restrain him and was punched in the face by the rampaging coach.

After the game, Bauman first said, "Yeah, he hit me." But when asked about the incident later in the dressing room, he said: "After I was tackled, I just walked away. There was so much excitement, I don't know if he hit me. If it happened, I'm not going to say anything about it."

Leaves With Police Escort

Reached yesterday, Bauman said: "I think he might have hit me. I know he's fired, but I want to see the films before I say anything definite."

One report said Bauman had taunted Hayes by waving the ball in his face.

Hayes stormed off the field with a police escort after the game and asked George Hill, his defensive coordinator, to attend the postgame news conference. Hill said, "I was there, but still couldn't see what happenened at the sideline."

But a national television audience did see, if briefly. ABC, which televised the game, showed only one replay of the melee, and from an angle that obscured Hayes's churning arms. However, replays on television yesterday clearly showed Hayes throwing a punch at Bauman.

Despite the shock of the sudden dismissal, Ohio State was planning for next season, as reports persisted that Lou Holtz of Arkansas would be named the Buckeye coach in a few days.

The reaction to Hayes's ouster ranged from shock to sympathy.

Ron Springs, an Ohio State running

back, and the rest of the team learned of the dismissal on the plane after it had landed in Columbus. "He just got up on the microphone and told us he wasn't going to be head coach anymore," said Springs. "I hope that the next coach is just as good as he is."

Danny Ford, the Clemson coach, said he was sorry about the dismissal.

"He has been a great football coach," said Ford, who replaced Charlie Pell at Clemson after Pell resigned Dec. 10 to become coach at the University of FLorida. "I would have settled for an apology from Coach Hayes, the Ohio State administration and the Big Ten. I didn't expect this big an apology."

In Pasadena, Calif., Wayne Duke, commissioner of the Big Ten, said he had been informed of the decision by Hindman. He expressed regret at "the termination of a great, great career."

In Columbus, callers deluged a radio station with mixed comments. John Bothe, a reporter for WBNS radio, said: "A lot of people said he was completely right in punching out that guy. But most are saying he was a disgrace to the university, that he should have retired a long time ago."

The End of an Era

Chuck Jenkins, a 1965 Ohio State graduate, was among a group who went to the Columbus airport to say hello and goodbye to Hayes. "It's the end of an era," said Jenkins. "We just came out to show the kids that some people really care."

They had a lot of years to care about; Hayes came to Ohio State in 1951. He compiled a glittering 205-61-10 won-lost-tied record, winning national championships in 1954 and 1968. He was named the top college coach in the country in 1957 and again in 1975.

Hayes had only two losing seasons at Ohio State. His overall record in 33 years as a college coach was 238-72-10, including 19-6 at Denison (Ohio) University, his alma mater, over three years, and 14-5 in two years at Miami University of Ohio. Only Paul (Bear) Bryant, among active coaches, has more victories (283).

But controversy won Hayes more headlines than success.

In a 1971 loss to Michigan he broke

United Press International and Associated Press

Woody Hayes, Ohio State coach, throwing a punch at one of his own players, Ken Fritz, as Fritz tried to restrain Hayes during melee that followed incident involving | **Clemson's Charlie Bauman. Hayes pounded on Fritz's face mask, below left, but Fritz persevered and, with the help of others, below right, managed to hold the coach.**

two yard markers across his knee. Two years later he reportedly shoved a camera into the face of a photographer during a practice session for the Rose Bowl.

He was reprimanded by the Big Ten in 1974 for repeated unsportsmanlike conduct in excoriating officials after a 16-13 loss to Michigan State. Hayes was furious at Michigan State and later admitted that he had turned in the school to the National Collegiate Athletic Association for purported recruiting violations. "Did I turn in the team that cheated in the league?" he said at the time. "You're damn right I did. And I'll do it again."

Last season he was reprimanded again and placed on probation after he had hit a television cameraman during a loss to Michigan. That incident occurred after Ohio State had fumbled when in scoring position. The loss cost Hayes and the Buckeyes a trip to the Rose Bowl.

Hayes's regular-season successes were not matched by his teams' recent bowl appearances — four losses in five games.

This season Hayes abandoned his coaching philosophy of staying on the ground and let his freshman quarterback, Art Schlichter, throw passes. The season started with a loss to Penn State

and ended with the frustrating defeat by Clemson and a fourth-place finish in the conference. The Buckeyes had previously won or tied for the conference title six straight times. Twice during the season, Hayes had verbally attacked sports reporters and broadcasters.

To critics who said he was too old and temperamental to continue as a coach, he made it clear after he turned 65 in February that he would not retire until he had reached the university's mandatory retirement age of 70.

December 31, 1978

Alabama Topples Penn State, 14-7, in Sugar Bowl Battle for No. 1

Crimson Tide Stops Lions Twice at 1 in Final Quarter

By GORDON S. WHITE Jr.
Special to The New York Times

NEW ORLEANS, Jan. 1 — The University of Alabama was virtually certain to be named the National Collegiate football champion for 1978 after gaining a thrilling 14-7 victory today over previously undefeated Penn State in the 45th annual Sugar Bowl.

The only obstacle in Alabama's path is the University of Southern California, which beat Michigan in the Rose Bowl and also defeated the Crimson during the regular season. Both contenders finished with 11-1 won-lost records.

Penn State came away from the struggle for the title between the two top-ranked teams certain that it would not get the mythical national championship, which the Nittany Lions have never managed to win in their 92-year history.

The Crimson Tide must await the outcome of the two final wire-service polls tomorrow before being sure of the prize. Alabama, which was ranked No. 2 behind Penn State, left no doubt that it richly deserved the national title for the fifth time in its history — all under its 65-year-old head coach, Paul (Bear) Bryant.

A Game Penn State Wanted

This was only the fifth major bowl matchup in history between the No. 1 and No. 2 ranked teams, and it was the kind of classic confrontation that Joe Paterno had longed for ever since he became Penn State's head coach in 1966.

Paterno and Penn State fans felt slighted when their undefeated teams of 1969 and 1973 were not voted the title. Paterno has long advocated a playoff system for the major-college national title just to avoid such slights. Today's game, played before 76,824 fans in the Superdome and a national television audience, was as close as major colleges can get to a football championship playoff these days.

But when it was over, Penn State's 19-game winning streak through two seasons was ended because Alabama beat the Nittany Lions at their own game — opportunistic defense and the ability to wait for the big breaks. That defense was at its best when Penn State had the ball on the Alabama 1-yard line in the fourth quarter and failed to get the ball over in two plays while trailing by 14-7.

"Alabama has as much a right to the national championship as anyone," Paterno said. "I think they beat an awfully good team today. I'm not disappointed for me. I'm disappointed for

Associated Press

Jeff Rutledge, Alabama quarterback, passing in spite of the effort by Penn State's Chuck Correal in the Sugar Bowl game in New Orleans yesterday.

the players and particularly the seniors."

Linebacker Most Valuable

Barry Krauss, the 6-foot-3-inch senior linebacker for Alabama who was voted the most valuable player of the game, was the hero of the goal-line stand, in which Penn State got the ball within inches of the Crimson end zone on a second-down play. Twice the Nittany Lions went at the middle, and twice the Crimson thwarted the charge by stopping Matt Suhey, the fullback, and then Mike Guman, the tailback. Krauss went underneath to halt Guman on the fourth-down play that left Penn State short of a touchdown and short of the national championship.

The game proved the football maxim that "defense makes champions." Still, the Crimson had to score to win, and Jeff Rutledge directed an 80-yard drive in 71 seconds that gave Alabama the first score in the last minute of the first half. The touchdown came on a 30-yard pass from the senior quarterback to Bruce Bolton, a split end who made a diving catch just over the goal line.

Paterno may have made a serious miscalculation that aided the Alabama drive when he called time twice while

the Crimson had the ball in their territory.

The other Bama score followed a 62-yard punt return by Lou Ikner in the last minute of the third period that set up Alabama at the Penn State 11. The score came when Rutledge, rolling left from the wishbone on the option, pitched back to Major Ogilvie, who scooted 8 yards to break a 7-7 tie.

Interception Leads to Score

Penn State was opportunistic in scoring its only touchdown. Pete Harris, the Lions' safety who led the country in interceptions this season, stole a Rutledge pass at the Alabama 48 midway through the third period. From this beginning, the Nittany Lion quarterback, Chuck Fusina, got Penn State a touchdown by throwing a 17-yard scoring pass to Scott Fitzkee at the back edge of the Alabama end zone.

That score came just 3 minutes 56 seconds before Ogilvie's touchdown run.

During Alabama's 80-yard scoring drive late in the first half, the Crimson Tide swept down field against the nation's No. 1 defense — the Lion defense had given up only 54.5 yards rushing

Associated Press

Joe Paterno, head coach for top-ranked Penn State, after losing to Alabama in the Sugar Bowl.

per game and only 203.9 total yards per game this season.

In six plays, Alabama had its score. The big play prior to Rutledge's scoring pass was a 30-yard run off a sweep right by Tony Nathan. Nathan virtually scorned that No. 1 defense against rushing by picking up 127 yards on 21 carries.

That was more than half of Alabama's impressive 208 yards on the ground. Penn State, which suffered all season from a poor running attack, gained only 19 yards rushing.

In turn, Alabama's defense crippled Penn State's big offensive weapon — the pass. The Crimson intercepted Fusina four times and sacked him five times. That is the same Chuck Fusina who finished second in the Heisman Trophy voting this year to Billy Sims of Oklahoma and the Fusina who Paterno said "is still the best player in the country."

From the opening kickoff — a kickoff that was not witnessed by the television audience because a commercial was still in progress — Alabama kept Penn State bottled up for the next 30 minutes. The Nittany Lions' only move into Alabama territory ended quickly when Murray Legg made the first interception of a Fusina pass.

Penn State got into Crimson land again in the second period when Rich Milot intercepted a Rutledge pass and returned the ball 55 yards to the Alabama 37. But Fusina was sacked for a 15-yard loss into Penn State territory by Byron Braggs on third down.

Braggs, a defensive tackle, was one of the Alabama defenders who consistently forced Fusina out of the pocket. Fusina does not relish scrambling. Nor does he relish interceptions, and the third one hurt a lot. With nine minutes to go in the game, Fusina threw a bomb to Bob Bassett only to have Don McNeal of Alabama come up with the ball for a touchback in the end zone. Bassett and Fusina had little chance on the play as the wide receiver was guarded by two Crimson players.

12-Player Penalty

There was even a touch of irony for the Nittany Lions, who lost their final chance with about six minutes to go. Penn State was apparently about to get the ball at the Alabama 20 after a poor punt, but the Nittany Lions were penalized for having 12 men on the field. That gave the Crimson Tide a first down, and Alabama moved the ball from further danger.

Penn State beat Kansas in the 1969 Orange Bowl, 15-14, to end Paterno's first undefeated season when Kansas had 12 men on the field on a 2-point conversion. Given a second chance, Penn State scored the 2 points to win on the last play of the game.

Today's mixup was almost more em-

barrassing because a 13th player for Penn State barely managed to leave the field before the ball was snapped.

"Our team beat a great football team," Bryant said. "Our entire squad contributed. I have never been associated with a group that did a greater job than our defense did today against Penn State."

This was the 284th victory for Bryant as a head coach since he started his career in 1945 at Maryland. He stands third in college victories behind Amos Alonzo Stagg (314) and Glenn (Pop) Warner (313). This was Bryant's 193d triumph as Alabama's head coach since he began leading the Crimson in 1958 and his second Sugar Bowl victory over Penn State.

Paterno and the Nittany Lions have never won a Sugar Bowl game in three tries, previously losing to Oklahoma and Alabama. Penn State's defeat was its sixth bowl loss and fourth under Paterno, who has gained nine bowl triumphs.

The Penn State coach said last night: "We are a better team than Alabama. I feel we can win."

Yet the No. 1 ranking that Penn State has wanted for so long remained elusive because Alabama had a better defense today

Sugar Bowl Statistics

STATISTICS OF THE GAME

	Penn St.	Alabama
First downs	12	12
Rushing yardage	19	208
Passing yardage	163	91
Passes	15-30	8-15
Interceptions by	2	4
Punts	10-39	10-39
Fumbles lost	0	1
Yards penalized	51	75

INDIVIDUAL LEADERS

RUSHES — Penn.: Suhey, 10 carries for 48 yards, Guman, 9 for 22; Moore, 9 for 6; Fusina, 7 for minus 64. Ala.: Nathan, 21 for 127; Whitman 11 for 51, Ogilvie 14 for 40.

PASSES — Penn.: Fusina, 15 completion of 30 attempts for 163 yards. Ala.: Rutledge 8 of 15 for 91.

RECEPTIONS — Penn.: Guman, 5 for 59 yards, Fitzkee, 3 for 38; Bassett, 2 for 28; Scovill, 2 for 21. Ala.: Bolton 2 for 46, Whitman 2 for 27, Ikner 2 for 5.

January 2, 1979

CHAPTER 2

PRO FOOTBALL

Vince Lombardi, fiery coach of the Green Bay
Packers.

GROWTH OF THE NFL

PRO ELEVENS HURT SPORT, SAYS STAGG

Veteran Coach at Chicago Asks for Preservation of College Football.

STRESSES AMATEUR SPIRIT

CHICAGO, Nov. 1 (Associated Press). —Branding professional football as a "menace," working for the destruction of the college game, Amos Alonzo Stagg, 62-year-old director of athletics at the University of Chicago, tonight addressed a letter "to all friends of college football" urging them to refrain from encouraging the professional sport in any manner.

Stagg, whose reputation for the development of amateur athletics has made him a national figure, declared that to "patronize Sunday professional football is to co-operate with the forces which are destructive of interscholastic and intercollegiate football, and to add to the heavy burden of the schools and colleges in preserving it in its ennobling worth."

Declaring that football when played with the amateur spirit possessed more elements for the development of character and manhood than any other sport, Coach Stagg said: "If you believe in preserving interscholastic and intercollegiate football for the upbuilding of the present and future generations of clean, healthy, right-minded and patriotic citizens, you will not lend your assistance to any of the forces helping to destroy it.

"There is nothing a bunch of gamblers will not do for their purpose, and quite often they carry along with them the support of a group of well-meaning citizens."

Coach Stagg's Statement.

The statement follows:

"It seems like a matter of little consequence for one to attend the Sunday professional football games — nothing more than attending any Sunday event — but it has a deeper meaning than you realize, possibly a vital meaning to college football. Intercollegiate football will live only so long as it contributes to the well being of the students, that is, while the influences of the game are predominantly on the side of amateur principles, right ideals, proper standards and wholesome conditions.

"For years, the colleges have been waging a bitter warfare against the insidious forces of the gambling public and alumni and against overzealous and short-sighted friends, inside and out, and also not infrequently against crooked coaches and managers who have been anxious to win at any cost, and victory has not been completely won. And now along comes another serious menace, possibly greater than all others, viz., Sunday professional football.

"Under the guise of fair play but countenancing rank dishonesty in playing men under assumed names, scores of professional teams have sprung up within the last two or three years, most of them on a salary basis of some kind. These teams are bidding hard for college players in order to capitalize not only on their ability, but also, and mostly, upon the name of the college they come from and in many cases the noised abroad mystery of their presence. The well-known Carlinville and Taylorville incident of 1921 is likely to be repeated in essence on different occasions this Fall. There is nothing that a bunch of gamblers will not do for their purpose and quite often they carry along with them the support of a thoughtless group of business men and well-meaning citizens.

"Cases of the debauching of high school boys not infrequently have come to notice. Also recently one of the well-known Sunday professional teams on which several men are said to be regularly playing under assumed names employed a well-known conference official who officiated under an assumed name.

"The schools and colleges are struggling to combat the various evils connected with football which when played with the amateur spirit possesses more elements for the development of character and manhood than any other sport I know of.

"To co-operate with Sunday professional football games is to co-operate with forces which are destructive of the finest elements of interscholastic and intercollegiate football and to add to the heavy burden of the schools and colleges in preserving it in its ennobling worth.

"To co-operate with Sunday professional football games is to work against the best interests of interscholastic and intercollegiate football and to lend co-operation to forces which are destructive to the finest elements of interscholastic and intercollegiate football.

"If you believe in preserving interscholastic and intercollegiate football for the upbuilding of the present and future generations of clean, healthy, right-minded and patriotic citizens, you will not lend your assistance to any of the forces which are helping to destroy it."

November 2, 1923

'PRO' FOOTBALL IS COMING IN FAVOR

Colleges Cannot Supply the Public Demand, So League of Many Cities Is Formed— Games Average 15,000 Attendance

WHILE professional football seems unlikely ever to overshadow the college game, it has made remarkable strides in the last four or five years and may be regarded as a permanently established Fall sport. The game that was always thought to require a college background has become so firmly entrenched in public esteem that more of a demand for it has arisen than the colleges can supply.

This development has been watched with apprehension. Many college alumni would like to keep the outstanding college sport a sport for amateurs only. Football has been notorious for controversies waged over professionalism when zealous alumni and ambitious institutions are accused of hiring athletes to bolster up their alma mater's eleven. Those that have fought rid the colleges of such "ringers" are alarmed now over the efforts to popularize the game on a commercial basis. They fear that the amateur will vanish.

Brig. Gen. Palmer E. Pierce, in his recent call to the National Collegiate Athletic Association to meet in December, said that efforts to popularize professional football brings the country face to face with even greater difficulties than formerly in keeping up amateur standards. The whole problem of an amateur definition will come before the association and more attention will be devoted to the so-called menace of "pro" football than to any other phase of the subject.

Public Overrules Objections.

Another outspoken opponent of professional football is Major John L. Griffith, Athletic Commissioner of the Big Ten Conference. It was obvious that Red Grange, from the moment that he became a national hero, would be sought as an attraction by one of the numerous "pro" teams. The reports of an offer of $40,000 for three games to the Illinois star brought a prompt protest from Major Griffith.

Even earlier, there were murmurs when some of the stars of other years, such as Walter Koppisch of Columbia and Ducky Pond of Yale, turned professional. These murmurs, however, have not been able to stem the tide of public interest in the game. The colleges cannot supply football enough for all football lovers. Stadiums are limited in size, and students and graduates absorb most of the tickets to the major events, excluding thousands who are keen for the sport.

There are already twenty teams in the Professional Football League, which was formed four years ago, with Joe F. Carr at its head, in Canton, Ohio. In addition there are at least a score of cities that have elevens. The scope of the interest in football is indicated by the cities in which the game is played. New York now has its first team since the ill-fated effort made several years ago by Charles Brickley to launch the game here. There are two teams in Chicago, the Cardinals and Bears, which have worked up a tremendous rivalry that brings out as many as 40,000 spectators.

Kansas City has a league team, as also have Rock Island, Duluth, Milwaukee, Green Bay, Hammond, Ind., Detroit, Cleveland, Canton, Akron, Dayton, Columbus, Buffalo, Rochester, Pottsville, Philadelphia and Providence. Among the teams not in the league around New York are New Britain, Hartford, Newark, Orange and Stapleton.

Post-Graduate Football.

With rare exceptions the players on these teams were once college stars. The Giants, as the New York eleven is known, have a roster that reads like an All-American team. Its squad includes Jappe, Tomlin, Alexander and McBride of Syracuse, Williams and Brennan of Lafayette, Milstead of Yale, Parnell of Colgate, Bomar of Vanderbilt, Hendrian of Pittsburgh, Rooney of Colorado, Benkert of Rutgers, Pottinger of Ursinus, and Hinky Haines of Penn State.

Other famous football names are scattered throughout the league. Buffalo has Koppisch of Columbia and Youngstrom of Dartmouth; the Philadelphia Yellow Jackets have Chamberlain of Nebraska and Beeman of Dickinson; Paddy Driscoll of Notre Dame is with the Chicago Cardinals, as also are John Morhart and Red Dunn; Healey of Dartmouth and Anderson of Notre Dame are on the Chicago Bears;

Akron has Fritz Pollard, the negro star of Brown. The list could be extended indefinitely. It is these great football names that have drawn public attention to "pro" football perhaps more than anything else.

The game is not new. Efforts to establish it have gone on for thirty years. As far as can be learned, it had its beginning in Western Pennsylvania, where the towns of Latrobe and Greenville had powerful teams and big followings at the beginning of the century. Soon after the glory of these teams dimmed, Watertown, N. Y., and Franklin, Penn., developed strong elevens, and they played a so-called championship match in Madison Square Garden, in perhaps the only indoor football game ever played here.

The game gained a foothold in Ohio, where it is strongest now. Massillon, Canton and Akron began keen intercity competition and had the first highly paid teams. The game declined soon after 1905, because gamblers had laid their grip on it.

Great football names of other years appeared on these Ohio teams, such as Bull Smith of Penn, an All-American player; Heston of Michigan, another All-American star; Turner of Dartmouth, Ernst of Lafayette, Stevenson of Penn, Tom Thorpe of Columbia, Andy Farbaugh of Lehigh, Red Salmon of Notre Dame and Charley Moran of Texas A. and M.

But it was not until four years ago that an organized effort was made to put the game on a sound, confidence-inspiring basis. The league was formed on the same principles as the major baseball leagues, with strict rules and regulations. Steps were taken at once to keep the amateur issue clear. Each club posts a forfeit of $1,000 against employing a player before he is through as an amateur. There is also a regulation that each club must have sixteen men under contract and limit its squad to that number. Every precaution is taken to keep the game clear of any influences that would lose the respect of the public.

While the colleges view "pro" football with more or less alarm, The Harvard Crimson recently took a position in its favor. Answering criticisms about the commercialism of college football, The Crimson said that "pro" football should be encouraged, because, if it could be made to attain sufficient prominence, it would soon dwarf the college game and return it again to a strictly sport basis. The editorial cited the case of professional baseball, which has so overshadowed college baseball that no aspersions are ever cast upon the college sport for commercialism or professionalism.

The backers of the professional game also deny that it will adversely affect the college game and, indeed, predict that it will be a benefit instead. Dr. Harry A. March, one of the sponsors of the Giants, himself a college man and a football player, is one of those who believes the amateur sport will be improved instead of harmed.

"In the first place," says Dr. March, "we are very careful not to use any men who have not fully relinquished their amateur status. It isn't as it was in the old days when men played with their college on Saturday and with a 'pro' team on Sunday. Everything, too, is done to keep out the gambling. I believe that with the incentive that they may look forward to a lucrative occupation if they are good enough, the college players will constantly get better. A young man will try his best if, for example, he figures that after college he may make, let us say, the Yellow Jackets or the Giants. Also it will bring the player his due, which he often misses by playing for a small college. Take the case of Parnell, who played one year with Colgate and then three years with Allegheny. He never got his measure of glory, although he is one of the greatest players ever seen.

"Pros" Play Hard.

"The professional game as it is played now is really post-graduate football. It sets a terrific pace, and only one out of three make good in it. The men have had years of football already and know the game in and out. It has been charged that there is not so much zest about the playing as in a college game. As a physician who knows these men and sees them going into action I know that they play as hard as any college team.

"One of the Giants went into a game with a mean boil on his arm and played one quarter. Hinkey Haines's nose was broken in a game. That happened early and we took him out right away. It wasn't any lack of courage; it was just plain sense. A college coach might have felt that such a good man could play a little longer, that he couldn't spare him. Well, it might have disfigured him for life. The injuries that the men have suffered show that they go in there and fight hard. Harry Stuhldreher, a few days ago, suffered a slight brain concussion.

"I became interested in building a New York team last year. I had followed the game for twenty-five years. Our postman was asking me for tickets to the Army-Navy game. He said he would be willing to pay $20, and he brought out that sixty other men in the sub-station where he worked loved football but never got a chance to see it. Not being college men they could not get tickets for any of the big games. Furthermore, they could not get time off on a Saturday, whereas Sundays and holidays were just the times they could go.

"It is this public that we are striving to satisfy. Incidentally, we get a large part of the college public who cannot, for some reason or other, see the college game. Why the colleges should complain I can't see. They do not obect to the baseball player who makes good in the professional game. They are proud of him."

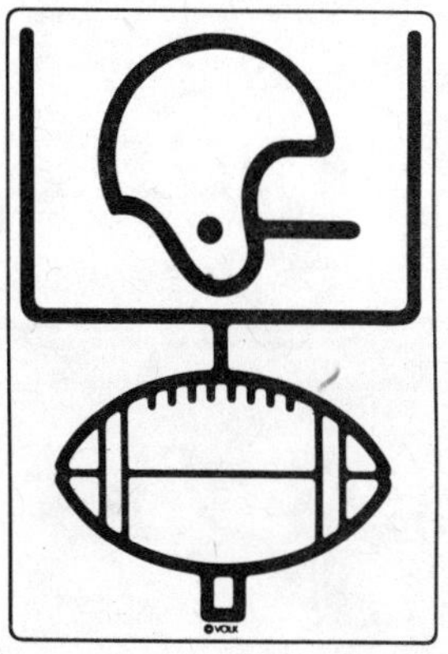

Whether there be a conflict between college and professional football or not, it remains a fact that the "pro" games average an attendance of 15,000. Some cities draw as high as 40,000. The open game has made football more of a spectacle, and the public likes its show

The promoters appear to be doing everything they can to keep the game clean. Their aspirations are to have an Eastern and a Western League, with ultimately a national championship such as there is in baseball.

November 22, 1925

GRANGE WILL PLAY FOR CHICAGO BEARS

Signs Contract and Will Get About $30,500 for First Game on Thanksgiving.

TO APPEAR HERE ON DEC. 6

Plans to Compete in Florida When Northern Season Ends—Pyle Is His Manager.

CHICAGO, Nov. 22 (AP).—Harold (Red) Grange today plunged into the business of capitalizing his gridiron fame by signing to play professional football against the wishes of his father as well as of George Huff, director of athletics of the University of Illinois, Coach Robert Zuppke and others who had hoped he would accept other offers held out to him.

The famous red head contracted with the Chicago Bears to play his first game with them in the Chicago National League Park Thanksgiving Day against the Chicago Cardinals. Grange also signed Charles C. Pyle, a Champaign, Ill., theatrical man, as his manager. Pyle's contract with Grange is for two years. While neither would discuss the terms, it was said that Pyle would receive 25 per cent. of Grange's earnings on the professional gridiron, in motion pictures and other ventures.

Although the terms under which Grange will play professional football were not made public, it was reported that Grange's share of his Thanksgiving Day game alone will amount to about $30,500.

Expect Gate of $80,000.

The contract, it was said, provides that Grange shall receive 10 per cent. of the first $5,000 that comes into the gate, 20 per cent. of the second $5,000 and 40 per cent. of all over this amount. The promoters are figuring on a gate of $80,000. The price of tickets was boosted, and when word spread that Grange would be in the game the scalpers immediately asked from $3 to $5, with indications that the supply would not hold out for forty-eight hours.

Grange will finish the season with the Bears, playing six games, all of them here with the exception of appearances in Philadelphia Dec. 5 and in New York the next day. After these games the Bears, with Grange and additional stars, including Earl Britton, his co-star at Illinois this season, will invade Florida for games during the holidays.

When Grange arrived here today there were so many promoters awaiting him with contracts in their pockets that the crowd looked like a reception committee to the Prince of Wales. There were offers to appear in movies, to write for newspaper syndicates and to do this and that. All were willing to pay Grange whatever he asked.

Grange said that he was leaving the University of Illinois temporarily, but intended to return to finish his course.

"I have received many alluring offers," said Grange, "to enter fields of enterprise in which I have had no training or experience. I believe the public will be better satisfied with my honesty and good motives if I turn my efforts to that field in which I have been most useful in order to reap a reward which will keep the home fires burning.

"I am leaving college temporarily, but will return later. To Messrs. Huff and Zuppke and my teammates, to the student body and alumni, to the public and to the press, I give my thanks out of the depths of a grateful heart for the splendid support and encouragement extended to me throughout my college football career."

Father Gives His Sanction.

Grange's dad, a Deputy Sheriff of Wheaton, Ill., has said from the start he hoped his son would not play professional football, but that he would not interfere with whatever he did.

"I am very sorry that he did not accept the other offers made him," the elder Grange said, "but as long as the boy has decided to play professional football I hope he will be a success and we will make the best of it. Harold is capable of looking out for himself and I have a lot of faith in him. As for selecting Pyle to handle his affairs, if Pyle suits Harold it will be all right with me."

Grange intends to go to Champaign tomorrow night to attend the banquet of the Illinois team, of which he is captain, and at which a captain for 1926 will be elected.

November 23, 1925

70,000 SEE GRANGE IN PRO DEBUT HERE

Famous Red Leads Chicago Bears to Victory Over Giants by 19 to 7.

HIS SHARE ABOUT $30,000

Crowd Is Greatest Ever to Attend Pro Game and All Shout for the Hero.

ADVANCES BALL 128 YARDS

Greatest Single Thrill Comes When "77" Nabs Pass and Runs 35 Yards to Score.

HOW GRANGE EARNED $30,000.

Played all of one quarter and parts of two others.

Gained 53 yards on eleven plays from scrimmage.

Ran back two kicks for total of 13 yards.

Threw three forward passes, two of which were completed for total gain of 32 yards.

Received one forward pass for gain of 23 yards.

Intercepted one forward pass and ran 35 yards for a touchdown.

By RICHARDS VIDMER.

Out of a little Middle Western town came a fiery-haired youth who took the big city by storm. The largest crowd that ever witnessed a professional football game swarmed into the Polo Grounds yesterday to see the far-famed Red Grange in action. It was the first appearance of the Galloping Ghost in this city, and 70,000 made their way to Harlem, streamed into the stadium that lies below Coogan's Bluff, and finally saw the Red Rover lead the Chicago Bears to a 19 to 7 victory over their own New York Giants.

High honors have been heaped on the bright brow of the college football star who turned financier, but none could have attested to his popularity as did the outpouring of New York's citizenry. Seldom, if ever, before has the Polo Grounds, where practically every sport but polo has been staged, accomodated so many persons. There were just so many tickets, and they were all bought. But that didn't stop the overflow that wedged into vacant corners, flooded down the aisles and packed themselves in two and three deep along the rear railings, while hundreds spilled over onto the sidelines.

Had the Chicago Bears played the New York Giants without Red Grange among those on the field it would have been just another professional football game. But with the redhead to be seen in action it was a spectacle that attracted spectators from almost every walk of life.

And the iceman delivered despite the slippery footing of the water-soaked field. He plunged through the line for repeated gains, he hurled passes into waiting arms for further advances, he snatched the ball out of the air while Giants swarmed around him, and finally, to cap the climax, he intercepted a forward pass in the closing period and streaked down the sideline for thirty-five yards and a touchdown.

His Share About $30,000.

There was more than glory and victory in his accomplishments, however, for some $30,000 was added to his rapidly growing bank roll. Altogether Grange advanced the ball, either directly or indirectly, 128 yards. At the rate of reported payment, the turf of the Polo Grounds was worth approximately $230 a yard, which makes it even more valuable than Florida real estate. The New York Exhibition Company probably never realized the value of its holding until Red Grange came to town.

There never was any doubt about what brought forth the great gathering. While Grange was in the game the spectators strained forward eagerly, watching every move he made, waiting for him to break loose from the alert and watchful Giants for one of his famous twisting, squirming runs. They yelled for Gange to get away and they yelled for the Giants to stop him. Every time the ball was snapped into the Chicago back field the throng half arose with the shout of "there he goes!" If a big white "77" showed on the back of the runner they stood up and kept on yelling; if any other number showed they settled back again.

When Grange left the contest in the middle of the second period the thousands watched only with half interest. When he failed to appear at any time in the third quarter an atmosphere of lassitude swept over the stands. And when the final period started with the main attraction still on the sidelines the inevitable chant went up from the bleacherites, gathered force as it was taken up by those in the reserved seats and echoed across the field:

"We want Grange! We want Grange!"

His Return Restores Thrill.

Then Grange came back. Once more excitement and the thrill that the crowd came to get was in the atmosphere and once more the spectators leaned forward in eager anticipation. Their hopes, dreams and desires were fulfilled shortly after the last quarter began.

The Giants, trailing by six points, were struggling desperately, almost frantically, to keep intact their winning streak that had reached seven successive victories. A moment before they had found themselves in the shadow of their own goal posts, forced there by Grange's plunges and passes, and they had managed to shake off those dread symbols of danger that rose white and glaring behind them by a frantic forward pass.

But they passed once too often. The next time they hurled the ball into the air the tall, lean, knock-kneed figure of the Red Rover flashed across the turf, splashed through a puddle and leaped high in the air. His long arms clutched the ball and he was off in the opposite direction, swinging smoothly where the going was rough, breaking into the open and sweeping on thirty-five yards to another touchdown for the Bears.

That one dash over the mud-caked

field was enough to satisfy the throng. That one scamper gave them what they came to see. That one sight of the modern Mercury of the gridiron made old men, young boys and bright-eyed ladies turn to each other and pronounce Grange all that he had been painted. It also cut off the last chance of a New York victory, but nobody seemed to care about that. They all had come to see the phantom in action and they were satisfied.

Grange is not to be blamed for remaining on the sidelines during the third and part of the second periods. He has played six football games in the last fifteen days and he still has contests scheduled for Washington, Boston, Pittsburgh, Detroit and Chicago before next Sunday night. The way to a fortune in football may not be long, but it is extremely exhausting—even for an iceman.

It is estimated that in his five games as a member of the salaried brigade Grange has accumulated something around $82,000. Grange and Charlie Pyle, his manager, both refuse to give out any figures and all that his teammates will say when Grange's share of the gate receipts is discussed is, "He gets plenty." His income tax report will at least prove interesting.

The thousands began assembling in the home of the Giants—baseball and football—the minute that the gates for bleacher tickets were thrown open. The first rush came from a swarm of small boys who had waited long to gain admission and a point of vantage for the game. Red Grange to most of them meant more than President Coolidge. Perhaps Babe Ruth was better known, but even that is questionable.

The bleachers filled in a flash and then the steady stream of reserve-seat ticket holders started pouring in. Gradually the great stands filled. An hour before the game time, long human lines led to every entrance gate and an hour after the game started there still was a steady swarm of spectators finding their way to their seats.

Stands Are Decorated.

The field and stands were decorated for the occasion. Gay bunting floated from the field boxes, gold and blue in honor of the visting Chicago Bears, red and blue in respect for the home town Giants, and green, purple, yellow and scarlet just to add color to the scene. Even the goal posts were decorated with the rival colors and an innovation was introduced when boys changed the pennants on the uprights whenever the teams changed goals.

Overhead it was bright and balmy. No more perfect football day has dawned this season so far as the weather was concerned. Only the rain-soaked, mud-caked field prevented perfection. The storms and rains and drizzles of the past few days left the gridiron wet and slippery and a handicap to Grange, who is at his best on a dry field and in the open. Yesterday, he had to confine most of his activities to line plunging and throwing and receiving passes. Even then he had to travel with extra weight, as his muddy feet looked as if they were wrapped in big, brown bandages after he had been on the field a few minutes.

Only a cheering section was needed to give the spectacle all the trimmings of a big college game. Oh, yes, and they left the goal posts standing at the end of the contest. There was a band! There were the massed thousands and there were the ever-present spectators, demanding two and three times the face value for choice seats. As usual they got their price.

The first appearance of the Bears in golden jerseys caused the first excitement, and every pair of eyes searched the field for the famous "77," which belongs as much to Red Grange as "37" belongs to Mr. Heinz. He was easy to find. All one had to do was follow the course of the photographers. And once the game started the great Grange was never out of sight until he retired from the field of action.

Sternaman Scores First.

The first time the ball came into the possession of the Bears they started a 62-yard march for the first touchdown. Most of these yards were credited to Walquist and Joe Sternaman, who took the ball over the last white line for the score, Grange contributing only nine of them on two plunges.

The redhead played a more prominent part in the second touchdown, however. Starting from his own 40-yard line, he plowed through the Red and Blue line for gains of six, three and two yards; he leaped in the air while three New York players swarmed around him and caught a pass for a gain of 23 yards; he threw a 14-yard pass to Walquist and then led the way for Sternaman to make the score on an end run. It was Sternaman who carried the ball across, but Grange ran the interference and by great body-checking and a last lunge at the last man who barred the way he cleared the path for his teammate.

Before he retired from the game Grange did a few other things worth mentioning. A long pass by the Giants was on its way to a resting place in the arms of a New York player when Grange darted in and knocked it down. He caught a punt and stepped out of a tangled mass to gain nine yards, leaving a heap of disappointed Giants in his wake, and he split the New York line open and swung through for fifteen yards before he was stopped in his longest run from scrimmage during the day.

After that he retired until the fourth quarter; during his absence the Bears could make no progress toward further scoring while the Giants threatened constantly to take the lead with another touchdown, their first having been made in the second period on a sustained advance of sixty-nine yards, most of which was covered by two passes from McBride to Bomar.

But when Grange came back the Bears took up the attack once more and starting from their own 30-yard line they marched down the field to within one yard of the New York goal. There Grange was stopped on a plunge, but he made up for it a moment later when he intercepted a forward pass and wove his way down the sideline while the crowd cheered him to the echo.

The line-up:

CHICAGO (19).		NEW YORK (7).
Hanny (Ind.)	L.E.	Jappe (Syrac.)
Healy (Dartm'th)	L.T.	Milstead (Yale)
And's'n (N. Dame)	L.G.	Carney (Navy)
Trafton (N. Dame)	C.	Alexander (Syrac.)
McMillen (Ill.)	R.G.	Williams (Laf'te)
Murry (Wis.)	R.T.	Parnell (Allegh'y)
Halas (Ill.)	R.E.	Bomar (Vandb't)
J.Sternaman (Ill.)	Q.B.	Palm (Penn State)
Grange (Ill.)	L.H.	Haines (Pa. State)
Walquist (Ill.)	R.H.	Benkert (Rutgers)
E.Sternaman (Ill.)	F.B.	McBride (Syrac.)

SCORE BY PERIODS.

Chicago	12	0	0	7—19
New York	0	7	0	0— 7

Touchdowns—J. Sternaman (2), Grange, White. Points after touchdown—J. Sternaman (drop kick), McBride (place kick).

Substitutions—Chicago: Knop (Illinois) for E. Sternaman, Mohardt (Notre Dame) for Walquist, Smith for Trafton, Trafton for Smith, Scott (Wisconsin) for Healy, E. Sternaman for Knop, Knop for E. Sternaman, Ryan for Grange, Grange for Ryan, Britton (Illinois) for Mohardt. New York: White (Oklahoma) for Benkert, Tomlin (Syracuse) for Williams, Williams for Parnell, Bedner (Lafayette) for Milstead, Reynolds (Georgia) for Jappe, Rooney (Colorado School of Mines) for Haines, Walbridge (Fordham) for Alexander, Nordstrom (Trinity) for Carney.

Referee—Wilmer S. Crowell, Swarthmore. Umpire—Tom Thorpe, Columbia. Field judge—William Hollenback, Pennsylvania. Linesman—Jack Reardon, New Hampshire State. Time of periods—15 minutes.

December 7, 1925

'BIG BILL' EDWARDS PRO FOOTBALL CZAR

Former Revenue Collector and One-Time College Star, Takes $25,000-a-Year Post.

William H. ("Big Bill") Edwards, former Collector of Internal Revenue and Street Cleaning Commissioner of New York, a candidate for Controller on the Hylan ticket in the Fall primary and in his college days a famous Princeton football player, accepted yesterday the Presidency of the American Professional Football League. William Hayward, former United States District Attorney, it was announced at the same time, accepted a place as general counsel of the league, promotion of which was begun several weeks ago by Harold ("Red") Grange and his manager, Charles C. Pyle, and which is expected to include ten large cities.

The announcement of the selection and acceptance of Mr. Edwards and Colonel Hayward for their respective positions was made after a meeting of the league's promoters at the Hotel Commodore. Mr. Edwards, it was announced, was chosen for three years at an annual salary of $25,000, and said he would attempt to have the league provide "football for all" in accordance with the high traditions of the college game. Mr. Edwards, by this appointment, becomes to professional football what Judge Landis is to professional baseball and Will H. Hays is to the moving picture industry.

Mr. Edwards's Statement.

Mr. Edwards's statement regarding his acceptance of the Presidency of the league, in part, follows:

"I have accepted the Presidency because I want to help preserve high-class football as it is played at the colleges. The tradition of our great game is that it is a clean, red-blooded sport—a great character builder—and it must retain these splendid qualities when played professionally.

"The good qualities of the game and the tremendous public interest combine to make it now the property of the public, and it must be played by others than college men and schoolboys.

"There is a great public demand to see the game. Those who are unable, by the constantly increasing limits of football tickets, to see the college game, turn to the professional football team, and the interest has necessarily increased the demand and attendance at professional games.

"The game can best be preserved by proper handling and the greatest and most careful supervision. The future of football rests not only on the shoulders of those who control it, but on the players and the public.

"The league has provided against harm which might come to the high school boy or the undergraduate. No high school or college player is eligible for membership on any team in this league until after his class has been graduated from college. This provision will absolutely prevent the taking away from college of any player before his class graduates. This is an iron-clad prohibition against any college player being eligible, and I shall certainly see the provision enforced."

The league, it was said, has already allocated franchises for New York, where the team will play at the Yankee Stadium under the direction of "Red" Grange; at Newark, Boston and Milwaukee. The New Jersey Athletic Association, of which William Coughlin is President, has the Newark franchise; Robert McKirdy, a sports promoter, the Boston franchise, and Frank Mulhern, also a sports promoter, the Milwaukee franchise.

Applications from nearly a dozen cities, it was stated, have been received for the remaining franchises. One came from Rogers Hornsby, manager of the St. Louis Cardinals and himself a famous baseball player, who has applied for the St. Louis rights in association with Otto Stiefel. Garry Herrmann, owner of the Cincinnati Reds of the National Baseball League, has applied for the Cincinnati permit. Five requests have been received from Chicago and three from Brooklyn, but no decision will be made to whom and to which cities other franchises will be awarded until a general meeting is held later this month.

The league, it was announced, will be patterned after the two major baseball leagues in the contracts made with franchise holders the standards to which they will be held and the discipline exercised over the players. Each franchise applicant must deposit a guarantee of $3,000, which will be held in escrow pending determination of the award in his city and after that retained to cover possible fines and penalties for infraction of the league's rules.

Associated with Mr. Edwards and Colonel Hayward in the direction of the football organization's affairs are, at present, William Coughlin of Newark, who was made Treasurer; Charles C. Pyle, Temporary Vice President, and William Wetzel of Milwaukee, Temporary Secretary. The permanent officials will be chosen at the next league meeting.

Fifteen Games for Teams.

According to Mr. Edwards the league will have a schedule of fifteen games for each team, playing twice a week during a season which will be started immediately after the close of the baseball season and the completion of the world's series. Each of the teams, he said, would have a training season, competent coaching, a training table and absence of "barnstorming" and exhibition games outside its own schedule and would seek in every manner to conduct itself in a manner similar to the teams of the larger colleges, but would not attempt to persuade high school or college men who have won names on the gridiron to leave their studies before graduation as was done by one of the league's founders, "Red" Grange.

Mr. Edwards's Career.

Mr. Edwards's football career began at Lawrenceville, a preparatory school at Lawrenceville, N. J. He made the eleven at Princeton in 1897, and during 1898 and 1899, when he led it as captain, he helped make the years, the team and himself memorable in the college's annals in victory after victory against all rivals, including Yale, bringing the college football championship to Princeton. He coached at Princeton and Annapolis for two years and was an official of many of the greatest games played until 1907.

Then he came to New York to enter business. First he was a Deputy Commissioner of Street Cleaning, next Acting Commissioner of the department. His ability to handle and get results from them after a great snowstorm attracted so much attention that his retiring chief gave him credit for the success of the department and Mayor McClellan appointed him to succeed the Commissioner.

Mr. Edwards' next job was the handling of waste disposal for Newark, but in 1917 he was made Collector of Internal Revenue, a position he held for four years and during which time he collected for the United States Treasury $2,500,000,000. Recently he was made a director of the new police training school, a post which carried no pay and to which he has been giving time from his insurance business.

Colonel Hayward is a native of Nebraska, a lawyer educated at the University of Nebraska and Munich, Germany, a former judge of Otoe County, Neb., and a veteran of the Spanish-American and the World War. He recruited, organized and trained the Fifteenth Infantry, N. G. N. Y., a colored regiment which was later the 369th U. S. Infantry and which was with the first contingent of American forces in France in 1917, earning distinction by being under fire for 191 days, longer than any other American contingent. He has also been prominent in politics in both Nebraska and New York.

In order to stimulate interest among the players and owners, 1 per cent. of the gross receipts of all games will be turned into the league's treasury, half of which will go to the owners of the championship eleven and the other half to the players of the teams finishing among the first four, on the basis of 50 per cent. for the leader, 25 for second, 15 for third, and 10 for fourth place.

March 8, 1926

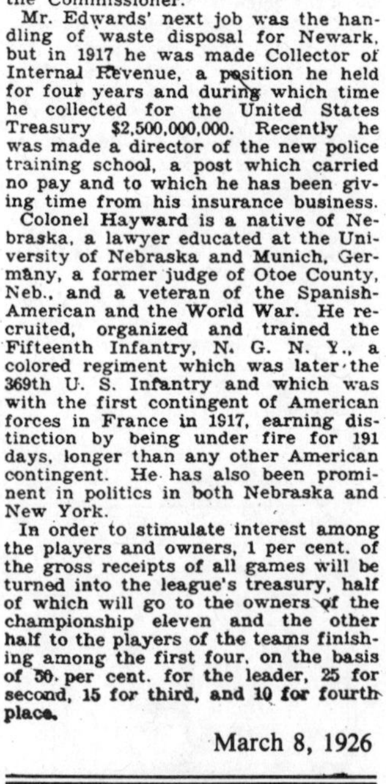

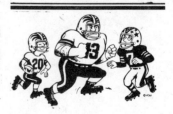

FASTER GAME LOOMS FOR PRO FOOTBALL

Newly Combined National and American Circuits to Have Only 12 Teams.

Professional football in the National League this Fall will be much faster than in previous years, because where there were twenty-nine clubs in the National and American circuits last year, there are now only twelve, the pick of both leagues, according to Dr. Harry A. March, secretary of the New York Giants and representative of the Eastern clubs at the meeting in Chicago, which completed the amalgamation of the rival circuits.

The American League, under William (Big Bill) Edwards, started with eight clubs last season, while the National League opened with twenty-one, scattered through the East and South, with a large number through the Mid-West, where professional football has been popular for a number of years. New York had three clubs, as did Chicago, each having two National and one American eleven.

In the newly combined circuit under the Presidency of Joseph F. Carr of Columbus, Ohio, only the strongest cities have been retained, and with over 300 veteran players and a record number of newcomers who wish to take up professional football, the outlook for a particularly fast game is bright.

Requirements for franchises, guarantees and other financial arrangements in connection with the handling of major league football have been tightened, and with the elimination of the disastrous war between the rival circuits, the owners who dropped thousands of dollars last Fall are hopeful that there is a future of prosperity ahead of them. The abundance of players left as a result of the elimination of seventeen franchises has enabled the owners to cut down on salaries, and increased competition will result in a better brand of football and higher attendance.

The lateral pass and other changes, which will go into effect with the opening of the intercollegiate football season this Fall, also will be adopted in full by the professionals, but with the more experienced set of players the professionals are planning to make use of the innovations which are expected to open up the game, thus presenting a better spectacle for the fans.

August 23, 1927

CHICAGO BEARS WIN PRO FOOTBALL TITLE

Defeat Portsmouth, 9-0, Before 12,000 in Indoor Game at the Chicago Stadium.

Special to THE NEW YORK TIMES.
CHICAGO, Dec. 18.—The Chicago Bears won the National Football League title tonight when they captured the play-off indoors at the Chicago Stadium. The victors rallied in the fourth quarter to defeat the Spartans of Portsmouth, Ohio, 9 to 0, in the only indoor battle of the league season, before a near-capacity crowd of 12,000. Officials announced

that the gross receipts exceeded $15,000.

For three periods the two teams waged a scoreless duel in which the Bears had the better of the ground-gaining. This superiority, however, had availed them nothing. Then in the final session Red Grange grabbed a short forward pass from Bronko Nagurski, to decide the contest.

Grange was standing in the Spartan end zone when he caught the ball, and the touchdown was all the Bears needed to assure them of the professional football championship.

Tiny Engebretsen, who had replaced Bill Buckler at tackle, place-kicked the ball between the wooden uprights and into the mezzanine for the extra point.

Then, just before the end of the battle, Mule Wilson of the Spartans, ready to punt from behind his own goal line, fumbled Clare Randolph's pass from centre, and the ball, rolling out of the end zone, automatically gave the new champions a safety and two more points.

While Grange and Nagurski received the cheers of the crowd for the touchdown, it was Dick Nesbitt who presented the Bears with their scoring opportunity.

Nesbitt raced back from his position at defensive right halfback to leap high into the air and intercept a forward pass by Ace Gutowsky, dashing, with the aid of excellent blocking, to Portsmouth's 7-yard line.

On the next play Nagurski smashed through Portsmouth's left guard for six yards. He came to earth with the goal line within reaching distance. Again Bronko hit the line, but the Spartans, fighting tenaciously, hurled him back with a loss of a yard.

It now was fourth down and the goal to gain. Again Nagurski took the ball, but this time he stepped backward and threw a short pass. Grange caught the ball over the goal line.

The line-up:

Chicago Bears (9).		Portsmouth (0).
Johnsos	L.E.	McKalip
Buckier	L.T.	Davis
Carlson	L.G.	Rodenger
Miller	C.	Randolph
Kopcha	R.G.	Emerson
Burdick	R.T.	Christensen
Hewitt	R.E.	Ebding
Molesworth	Q.B.	Gutowsky
Grange	L.H.	Presnell
Nesbitt	R.H.	Cavosie
Nagurski	F.B.	Lumpkin

December 19, 1932

CHANGE FOOTBALL RULES.

Officials of Pro League Seek to Make Game More Spectacular.

PITTSBURGH, Feb. 26 (AP).— Rule changes designed to pep up the game were made today by the National Professional Football League.

Club owners made the forward pass legal from any point behind the line of scrimmage and moved the goal posts up to the goal line in an effort to increase thrills and reduce the number of tie games.

Joe F. Carr, president of the league, predicted these changes will make the game more spectacular and put the "foot" back in football by encouraging kicking.

The collegiate "5-yard rule," making it permissible to move the ball in 10 yards whenever it is in play within 5 yards from the sidelines, also was approved.

After lengthy discussion, the 25-yard penalty for clipping was retained. The college penalty recently was lowered from 25 to 15 yards.

February 27, 1933

10 CLUBS IN PRO FOOTBALL

CHICAGO, July 8 (AP).—The National Professional Football League today became a ten-club circuit with the admission of Philadelphia, Pittsburgh and Cincinnati, and the

withdrawal of the Staten Island Stapes. The latter organization was permitted to drop out for a year, but must resume in 1934 or lose its franchise.

The Philadelphia team will be coached by Lud Wray, former University of Pennsylvania player and head coach, and will play its games at the Phillies' baseball park.

Jock Dowds, former Washington and Jefferson star, has been named coach of the Pittsburgh club, which will play at Forbes Field. The new Cincinnati entrant will be directed on the field by William Jolley, who played at Marietta College.

Joe E. Carr of Columbus was re-elected president and secretary, and Carl Storck of Detroit again was chosen vice president and treasurer. The executive committee will be composed of Dr. Harry March, New York; Dr. W. W. Kelly, Green Bay, Wis., and George Halas of the Chicago Bears.

July 9, 1933

BEARS BEAT GIANTS FOR TITLE, 23-21

Forward-Lateral, Nagurski to Hewitt to Karr, Brings the Deciding Touchdown.

AIR DUEL THRILLS 30,000

Manders Aids Victors With 3 Field Goals—Newman Completes 12 Passes.

By The Associated Press.
CHICAGO, Dec. 17.—In a sensational forward passing battle the Chicago Bears won the national professional football championship today by beating the New York Giants, 23 to 21. The game was witnessed by 30,000.

The Bears, trailing by 21 to 16, seized victory out of the air in the dramatic closing minutes of the game. Billy Karr, right end, who learned his football at West Virginia, plucked a long lateral pass and, eluding two Giant tacklers who chased him desperately, galloped 25 yards for the deciding score.

The game was a thrilling combat of forward passing skill, desperate line plunging and gridiron strategy that kept the chilled spectators on their feet in constant excitement.

The lead changed hands six times during the furious sixty minutes of play, with first the Bears holding command and then the Giants taking it away from them.

An Offensive Battle.

The struggle was a revelation to college coaches who advocate no changes in the rules. It was strictly an offensive battle and the professional rule of allowing passes to be thrown from any point behind the line of scrimmage was responsible for most of the thrills.

The Bears' attack was led by Bronko Nagurski, former University of Minnesota plunging full-

back, who individually gained 65 yards in fourteen attempts and started the forward-lateral pass that was responsible for the winning touchdown.

A notable performance was turned in also by Jack Manders. The former Gopher kicked three goals from placement, one for 40 yards in four attempts and added a goal after touchdown for a total of ten points.

Newman Passing Star.

Harry Newman, Michigan's all-American quarterback in 1932, was the outstanding star in the Giants' attack. He tossed seventeen passes, completing twelve for a total of 201 yards.

Hailed as the greatest offensive teams in professional football, the rivals did not waste any time in proving it, although the gridiron was slippery, particularly the grassy spots, because of mist and fog that hung over the field as the game started.

Molesworth quick-kicked over Newman's head and gave the Bears their first scoring chance. Strong returned the punt to the Giants' 42-yard line. There Nagurski plucked a pass out of the air and raced to the Giants' 26-yard line. Ronzani slashed right tackle, going to the 15-yard line.

Three plays netted only eight yards, but the ball was placed in a spot for Manders to place kick from the 16-yard line. The ball sailed squarely between the goal posts.

Giants' Defense Tightens.

In the second period, Ronzani tossed a pass to Molesworth, netting the Bears 17 yards and placing the ball on the Giants' 29-yard line. The New York team's defenses tightened, but Manders, called upon for the second time to place kick, booted the oval between the goal posts on a 40-yard effort.

The Giants, stirred to desperation, came back with a touchdown, with Badgro taking Newman's pass and running 29 yards to score. Richards paved the way for the touchdown with a 30-yard drive off left tackle to the Bears' 39-yard line. Strong added the extra tally on a placement kick.

The Bears missed another scoring opportunity just before the half ended, when Grange got away on a 17-yard gallop around left end, going to the Giants' 9-yard line. There Manders attempted another field goal, but this time he failed.

With both teams fighting desperately and using all the strategy at their command, things began to happen in the third period. No sooner did the Bears get the ball than they went right down the field.

Kicks Another Field Goal.

Ronzani gained 15 yards on one play, and a pass, Molesworth to Brumbaugh, brought the ball to Giants' 13-yard line. Once more the Giants' defense stiffened, but Manders again dropped back to the 19-yard line to score with another field goal that gave the Bears a 9-to-7 margin.

The lead did not last long, however, as the Giants, in a sensational display of passing, with Newman heaving the ball to Burnett, Richards and Krause, drove straight down the field for 61 yards and a touchdown, Krause going over. Strong kicked the point.

That score was accomplished in only eight plays. The last pass Newman threw to Krause was caught as the latter was chased out of bounds on the 1-yard line. He went over two plays later.

Then the Bears took a turn at scoring with amazing speed, and in six plays chalked up a touchdown. A pass, Corbett to Brumbaugh,

Bronko Nagurski, powerful fullback of the Chicago Bears in the 1930's, rips through the Philadelphia Eagles' line for a long gain.

that gained 67 yards, provided the spark. It brought the ball to the Giants' 8-yard line, with Nagurski, after two plays, tossing a pass over the goal line to Karr. Manders added the extra point, and the Bears went into the lead again, 16 to 14.

The Giants, however, struck back on the kickoff. They took the ball on the 26-yard line, and with a passing attack carried to the 8-yard line. There Newman wound up the spectacular display by tossing a pass to Strong in the end zone for a touchdown. Again Strong added the extra point, and the Giants led, 21 to 16.

Resume Overhead Attack.

Then came the thrilling climax. The Bears, apparently beaten, took to the air. The first pass, Molesworth to Brumbaugh, brought the ball to the 32-yard line. The next one, hurled from the line of scrimmage, Nagurski to Hewitt, was followed by a long lateral to Karr.

Karr caught it out in the open and started for the Giants' goal. Ken Strong and another Giant tore after him, but Ronzani, formerly of Marquette University, knocked Strong out of the way and Karr raced across the goal with the winning point. The line-up:

CHI. BEARS (23).		N. Y. GIANTS (21).
Hewitt	L.E.	Badgro
Lyman	L.T.	Grant
Carlson	L.G.	Gibson
Miller	C.	Hein
Kopcha	R.G.	Jones
Musso	R.T.	Owen
Karr	R.E.	Flaherty
Brumbaugh	Q.B.	Newman
Molesworth	R.H.	Strong
Ronzani	R.H.	Burnett
Nagurski	F.B.	Molenda

SCORE BY PERIODS.

Chicago Bears	3	3	10	7—23
New York Giants	0	7	7	7—21

Touchdowns — Badgro, Krause, Strong, Karr 2. Field goals—Manders 3 (placements). Points after touchdown—Brumbaugh, Manders, Strong 3 (placements).

Substitutions—New York Giants: backs, Richards, Krause; tackle, Irwin; quarter, Clancy; end, Campbell. Chicago Bears: backs, Manders, Grange, Corbett, Sisk; centre, Pearson; tackle, Richards; guard, Stahlman.

Referee—Tommy Hughitt, Buffalo. Umpire—Bobby Cahn, Chicago. Field judge—Roert Karch, Columbia. Linesman—Dan Tehan, Cincinnati.

December 18, 1933

80,000 SEE BEARS TIE ALL-STARS, 0-0

Collegians Outplay Champions of Pro League, Gaining Six First Downs to Three.

STATISTICS OF THE GAME.
By The Associated Press.

	Bears.	All-Stars.
First downs	3	6
Yards gained rushing	62	136
Forward passed	13	13
Forwards completed	4	3
Yards gained, forwards	62	25
Forwards intercepted by	3	4
Average yards, punts	31.8	34.1
Average yards, run back of	17	9.8
Own fumbles recovered	2	2
Yards lost, penalties	40	35

By The Associated Press.

CHICAGO, Aug. 31.—Eighty-thousand persons saw the Collegian All-Stars of 1933 and the Chicago Bears, champions of professional football, battle to a scoreless tie under the arc lights of Soldier Field tonight.

The result was a moral victory for the All-Stars, who outplayed the National Football League team, outgaining and out-manoeuvring their foes with dazzling speed and coordination. Both teams had chances to score, only to fail because of fumbles and intercepted passes.

The Stars tried to score twice by placement kicks in the third and fourth periods but the attempts failed by wide margins from the 40 and 42 yard lines.

Stage Five Drives.

From the line of scrimmage the All-Stars gained 136 yards to 62 for the Bears, and in first downs, they scored six, two by penalties, to three for the pro champions. The All-Stars made five distinct scoring threats, including their attempts to tally from placements, to two by the Bears in the battle, which was rough and bruising from start to finish.

Five players, three of the All-Stars and two of the Bears, stood out on the floodlighted field. They were Joe Laws of Iowa, Herman Everhardus of Michigan and Mike Mikulak of Oregon, all stars in name and action, and the professional aces, Bill Hewitt and Wayland Becker, who kicked poorly at the start and then saved the day for the Bears with tremendous, well-placed boots.

Laws Starts Advance.

It was a game of costly mistakes. At the outset Laws began what looked like a scoring march when he intercepted Brumbaugh's pass, raced to the Bear's 38-yard line and then to the 21 on sprints around his left wing. Beattie Feathers of Tennessee advanced to the Bears' 14, but on the next play the ex-Tennessee star fumbled and Ookie Miller recovered for the Bears on his 16-yard line.

A passing attack that netted 40 yards on two tosses, from George Corbette to Carl Brumbaugh and Corbett to Gene Ronzani, gave the Bears their first big chance. This time Hewitt fumbled and several Stars recovered on their 18-yard line.

In the second period, with Everhardus doing the passing, the Stars smashed to the Bears' 27, but again a fumble, by Hecker of Purdue, halted the drive.

Stars Gain on Punts.

Getting a big advantage on a punting duel, Laws and Mikulak reached the Bears' 32 and Bill Smith of Washington attempted a placement. The kick was 10 feet wide, but for a time the huge crowd thought it was good.

The Bears had their biggest chance late in the final period when Becker broke through and blocked a punt by Bob Jones, ex-Indiana, and recovered on the All-Star 19½ line. Laws stopped this drive.

Corbett tried a pass but Laws intercepted it on his goal line, ran it back 11 yards and Everhardus got off a beautiful kick of 50 yards to Corbett. That was the Bears' last chance and just before the game ended George Sauer, Nebraska's All-American, intercepted a pass and ran it 20 yards to the Bears' 36. Smith then tried his second placement, missed and it was all over.

World's Fair in Background.

The stadium was a picture of splendor, with 100 powerful lights casting rays upon the lightning-fast greensward, and the World's Fair lights of red, blue and green in the background.

The Bears, heavy favorites, were attired in their regulation uniforms of white jersey and tan silk pants; the All-Stars, selected by a nationwide ballot that attracted 617,000 votes, were dressed in special uniforms of gold jerseys and silvery silk pants.

College playing rules were in effect for the game, except that the goal posts were on the goal line instead of ten yards back. The forward passing rule, forcing passers to throw from at least five yards behind the line of scrimmage, and the college penalty of fifteen yards for clipping, instead of twenty-five, as in the pro code, were enforced.

The All-Stars were introduced to the huge throng in impressive ceremonies. The lights in the big amphitheatre were turned off, and as each player trotted to the field a single beam followed him to the centre of the gridiron as the band played the alma mater song of his college. The line-up:

BEARS (0).		ALL-STARS (0).
Hewitt	L.E.	Manske (N. W.)
Lyman	L.T.	Krause (N. D.)
Carlson	L.G.	Walton (Pitt.)
Miller	C.	Bernard (Mich.)
Kopcha	R.G.	Jones (Ind.)
Musso	R.T.	Schwammel (O. S.)
Johnson	R.E.	Skladany (Pitt.)
Brumbaugh	Q.B.	Griffith (S. Calif.)
Corbett	L.H.	Feathers (Tenn.)
Ronzani	R.H.	Laws (Iowa)
Nagurski	F.B.	Mikulak (Ore.)

Bears' Substitutions—Ends—Karr, Becker. Tackles—Buss. Guards—Zeller, Zizak. Halfbacks—Grange, Westray. Fullback—Manders.

All-star Substitutions: Ends—Gillman (Ohio State), Smith (Washington), Canrinus (St. Mary's). Tackles—Mehringer (Kansas), Gailus (Ohio State), Crawford (Duke). Guards—Hupke (Alabama) Maneikis (Chicago). Krueger (Marquette), Rosequist (Ohio State). Febel (Purdue). Centres—Vuchnich (Ohio State), Gorman (Notre Dame). Quarterbacks—Pardonner (Purdue), Cramer (Ohio State), Montgomery (Columbia), Masterson (Nebraska). Halfbacks—Sebestian (Pittsburgh), Cook (Illinois), Everhardus (Michigan), Lukat. (Notre Dame). Fullbacks — Sauer (Nebraska), Hecker (Purdue).

Referee—James Masker (Northwestern). Umpire—John Schommer (Chicago). Field judge—Wilfrid Smith (Depauw). Linesman—J. J. Lipp (Chicago).

September 1, 1934

37,000 SEE GIANTS ROUT BEARS, 30-13

New Yorkers, Trailing by Ten Points, Drive to 4 Touchdowns in Last Period.

STRONG GOES OVER TWICE

Danowski's Passes Play Big Part in Ending Chicago's Streak in Title Game.

STATISTICS OF THE GAME.

	Giants.	Bears.
First downs	12	10
Yards gained rushing	170	93
Forward passes	13	13
Forwards completed	7	6
Yards gained, forwards	112	76
Forwards intercepted by	3	2
Lateral passes	4	1
Laterals completed	4	1
Yards gained, laterals	54	0
Number of punts	6	9
*Distance of punts, yards	274	366
Run-back of punts, yards	12	46
Fumbles	4	3
Own fumbles recovered	1	2
Penalties	0	4
Yards lost, penalties	0	30

*From point where ball was kicked.

By ROBERT F. KELLEY.

In one of the most wildly exciting periods that any football game has ever seen, the New York Giants scored 27 points in the final session of play at the Polo Grounds yesterday to come from behind and defeat the Chicago Bears, 30 to 13.

Trailing on the short end of a 13-to-3 score when the last quarter opened, the Giants roared through to an amazing victory while 37,000 fans went wild with excitement and for a time threatened to interrupt play as they stormed out on the field.

Four times the Giants crossed the Bears' goal line for touchdowns in that final period as they captured the national professional championship and toppled the Bears from the throne they have occupied since 1932.

Giants' Lead Overcome.

During most of the first half, after the Bears had overcome a first-period lead that Ken Strong gave the Giants with a 38-yard placement goal, the Westerners, undefeated in thirteen National Football League games this year, seemed the certain winners. Then when Jack Manders, the great kicker, shot across a 23-yard field goal late in the third period it was apparently all over but the shouting.

The Bears had come back in the second period with a touchdown when Bronko Nagurski bulled his way across from the one-yard mark. A pass paved the way to this score. Then Manders had made his first field goal, a rifle shot from the 17-yard mark. The third-period goal was apparently the final touch.

But that second score by Manders wasn't the final act in the successful defense of the title by Chicago. Instead it was the final setting of the stage for the frozen drama of the comeback by the Giants.

Little Aids the Winners.

With Lou Little, Columbia's coach, sitting up in the stands and phoning to the bench, Steve Owen directing down there and Strong playing one of the greatest games any back has ever turned in, the Giants came back to win.

The lion's share of the credit goes to Strong, but he had very able assistance. Bill Morgan, at left tackle, played himself out in a superb exhibition of line play; Dale Burnett was, as usual, an amazingly fine back, and Ed Danowski, with some great passing, once more filled to the brim the shoes of the injured Harry Newman.

The Giants returned to the field in the second half with basketball shoes replacing the cleated football shoes. The solidly frozen ground made cleats useless, and the basketball shoes made all the difference in the world.

Starting late in the third period with the kick-off that followed Manders's second field goal, the Giants marched toward the first of the fourth-period scores. Danowski began flipping passes and Ray Flaherty made two good catches that helped tremendously. Then a lateral, Danowski to Strong, gained 15 yards and put the ball on the Bears' 31-yard line as the period closed.

Strong Comes Back.

Strong had been removed from the game in the first half with his left leg twisted. He appeared out of it. But he came back in the second, apparently none the worse for wear.

Starting the fourth period Danowski flipped a long pass to the left and Burnett made a great catch. He was hit hard on the 12-yard line and fumbled, but Strong was there to bat the free ball out of bounds and give the Giants a first down. That New York drive was stopped when Ed Kawal, the Bear centre, jumped up to intercept a short pass from Danowski on the 4-yard line. But Strong promptly brought back Keith Molesworth's punt almost 15 yards to the 30-yard mark and again the Giants were attacking.

Times Wide World Photo.

Nagurski, Bears, being stopped after four-yard gain.

On the first play Danowski sent a long pass down toward the southeast corner of the field. Brumbaugh apparently made the interception over his left shoulder as he raced toward his own goal, but Ike Frankian was there with him and either caught the ball at the same time or wrested it from his hands, for an instant later he was over the goal line with the score.

Strong made the extra point, and it was 13 to 10, the Bears still leading.

The next score came after Molesworth had been hurried on a punt. It was flat and carried only twenty-five yards to the Bears' 48-yard line. Strong jammed through to the 41-yard line. Then, on the next play, he came off his left tackle. Morgan had done a great job there, and Molenda and Danowski blocked well also.

Strong almost hit an official as he came through the line, but dodged and flashed into the open, his sneakered feet flashing under him. Running straight ahead with an amazing burst of speed, he outraced Brumbaugh and Sisk to a touchdown as the crowd poured out on the field in a dance of excitement.

Strong made the extra point with a solid roar going up from the crowd. And so the Giants led at 17 to 13.

But that wasn't the end. The dazed and disappointed Bears were to yield two more touchdowns before the period ended. One followed a brilliant run around right end by Danowski, with Molenda and Strong doing great blocking. It carried twenty yards to a first down on the Bears' 11-yard line.

The touchdown was made by Strong, bringing his total for the day to 17 points. He went off right end and cut in behind fine blocking by Molenda and Tex Irvin to run 11 yards to the score. The try for the extra point failed when Molenda dropped the pass from centre. He attempted a drop-kick, which was blocked.

Lateral Goes to Burnett.

The final touchdown was Danowski's. The stage had been set by Molenda's interception of a Ronzani pass, followed by a lateral to Burnett. The interception came on the Bears' 34-yard line and the play ended on the 22.

Danowski punched out a first down just over the 10. He went off right end on the next play and cut back behind fine blocking to cross the line standing up.

Molenda added the extra point to put the final touch on one of the most amazing comebacks in the history of the game.

The contest was jammed full of excitement from beginning to end, keeping the big, half-frozen crowd in a steady turmoil of excitement. The paid attendance, incidentally, was announced as 35,059.

Strong's placement in the first period came early after a fine Giant march had carried from the New York 36 to the Bears' 9. The Giants clung to that advantage through the period, aided materially by the partial blocking of a Molesworth punt by Irvin and Flaherty.

In the second period, with Nagurski and Molesworth carrying splendidly, the Bears marched from their own 46-yard line to the Giants' 9, and then Manders dropped back to slam across his first field goal.

The Bears definitely had the jump in this quarter. Manders had two more chances, one from the 24-yard line, which went wide when he was rushed, and the other from the 38 at a difficult angle that narrowly missed.

Molesworth Does Well.

Manders's first field goal followed the Bears' touchdown, which was scored early in the period after Molesworth, a great player all during the game, came back almost 20 yards with a punt to the Giants' 37-yard line.

Molesworth and Nagurski jammed through to a first down on the 24-yard line, and then Molesworth threw a long pass which Flaherty almost intercepted, only to bounce it into the hands of Ronzani on the 7-yard line. He was forced out less than a yard from the goal. Nagurski was across at left tackle for the score on the next play and Manders added the point.

The Bears had a great chance a while later when Strong juggled Manders's kick-off and Karr fell on it on the 9-yard line. Nagurski ran off his left end for a touchdown, but the play was called back for off side. Another Bear score later was also nullified by a penalty.

The statistics reveal the superiority of the Giants in this play-off between the winners of the Eastern and Western division league championships. The New Yorkers made twelve first downs to the Bears' ten and gained 170 yards by rushing to their rivals' 93.

Danowski, the ex-Fordham ace, who did all of the Giants' forward passing, completed seven in thirteen attempts for a gain of 112 yards. The Bears also tried thirteen passes and completed six for a gain of 76 yards. The Giants accounted for 54 yards on four laterals, while the one lateral the Chicago eleven attempted resulted in no gain.

The Giants, with their victory, avenged two setbacks at the hands of the Bears during the league season. The scores of those games were 27-7 and 10-9. Eight victories and five defeats constituted the New York record for 1934 league play.

The Bears entered yesterday's game with a brilliant record. They had not been beaten since November of last year, having taken part in thirty-one games, including exhibitions, since then. That last defeat, incidentally, was also handed them by the Giants, 3-0, on a field goal by Strong, N. Y. U.'s gift to professional football.

The line-up:

GIANTS (30).		BEARS (13).
Frankian	L.E.	Hewitt
Morgan	L.T.	Lyman
Gibson	L.G.	Pearson
Hein	C.	Kawa
Jones	R.G.	Carlson
Irvin	R.T.	Musso
Flaherty	R.E.	Karr
Danowski	Q.B.	Brumbaugh
Burnett	L.H.	Ronzani
Strong	R.H.	Molesworth
Molenda	F.B.	Nagurski

SCORE BY PERIODS.

Giants	3	0	0	27—30
Bears	0	10	3	0—13

Touchdowns—Nagurski, Frankian, Strong 2, Danowski. Points after touchdowns—Manders, Strong 2, Molenda (all placements). Field goals Strong, Manders 2 (all placements).

Substitutions—Giants: McBride for Danowski, Richards for Strong, Owen for Irvin, Danowski for McBride, Strong for Richards, Irvin for Owen, Owen for Irvin, Grant for Morgan, Richards for Strong. Bears: Manders for Ronzani, Johnson for Karr, Ronzani for Manders, Karr for Johnson, Buss for Lyman, Manders for Ronzani, Sisk for Manders, Rosequist for Musso, Miller for Carlson, Musso for Rosequist, Ronzani for Sisk, Carlson for Miller, Manders for Nagurski, Masterson for Brumbaugh.

Referee—Bob Cahn, Illinois. Umpire—Bull Lowe, Dartmouth. Linesman—George Vergara, Notre Dame. Field judge—Judge Meyer, Ohio Wesleyan. Time of periods—15 minutes.

December 10, 1934

PLAYER PLAN IS ADOPTED.

Football League Aims to Strengthen Weaker Clubs.

PHILADELPHIA, Feb. 9.—Adoption of a new player plan to strengthen the weaker clubs and a lengthy schedule discussion occupied the delegates at the National Football League meeting which ended tonight.

Club owners received permission to submit the names of eight college stars at the close of the season. The tail-end club will have first call to negotiate with any of the candidates, even those listed by other clubs. The remaining clubs will make selections in the reverse order of the standing at the close of the season.

The league looked with favor upon the franchise application of Los Angeles. A probationary plan was adopted, four or five games to be played on the Coast. Los Angeles was not formally admitted to membership.

February 10, 1936

FRANCHISES ARE AWARDED

Eight Cities to Have Teams In American Football League.

The awarding of franchises to eight cities which will have teams in the American Professional Football League next Fall was announced yesterday by Dr. Harry A. March, president and organizer of the circuit, following a meeting at the Hotel Biltmore.

The cities are Boston, Providence, New York, Jersey City, Syracuse, Cleveland, Pittsburgh and Philadelphia. Dr. March said that the circuit probably would be inaugurated on Sept. 13 or Sept. 20.

A player-limit was set, with twenty-five men allowed each team for the first three contests and twenty-two after that. Night games are planned.

An executive committee and a finance committee were formed, with Judge James E. Dooley of Providence, James Lehrer of New York and Richard Guy of Pittsburgh being appointed to the former group. The finance committee will consist of Harry Newman of New York, John Cutler of New Haven and Boston and Jack McBride of Jersey City.

April 12, 1936

REDSKINS' FRANCHISE GOES TO WASHINGTON
Marshall's Pro Football Team Transferred From Boston to Griffith Stadium.

WASHINGTON, Dec. 16 (AP).—Transfer to Washington of the franchise for the Boston Redskins of the National Football League was announced tonight by George Preston Marshall, majority stockholder.

Marshall said arrangements had been made to lease Griffith Stadium, home of Clark Griffith's American League baseball club, for the 1937 football season.

In transferring the franchise to the capital, the National League Football Club of Boston, Inc., was liquidated to be operated henceforth as Pro Football, Inc., of Washington.

Marshall, holding 51 per cent of the stock, will head the organization, with Edward J. Reeves of New York as vice president.

December 17, 1936

CLEVELAND ELEVEN IS IN PRO LEAGUE

Back in National Football Circuit for First Time Since 1934 Season

By The Associated Press.

CHICAGO, Feb. 12.—The National Football League became a ten-club circuit again today for the first time since 1934 when Cleveland was taken back into the fold.

Club owners, sitting in the first session of their annual two-day meeting, voted Cleveland a franchise after hearing assurances of financial stability from Homer Marshman, president of the Cleveland club, which operated in the American League last year. The admission of Cleveland, which will play in the Western section, will balance the league, with five teams operating in each division.

The magnates also voted to trim the schedule for each team from twelve games to eleven. This was done, President Joe E. Carr said, to close the regular season a week earlier in an effort to assure better weather for the championship play-off battle between the Eastern and Western division leaders.

Competed in 1923

Cleveland is no newcomer to National League warfare. The city was first admitted to the league in 1923, and in 1924 won the championship with a record of seven victories, one defeat and one tie.

Cleveland remained in the league throughout the 1925 campaign, but dropped out the next year. It returned in 1927 for one season, but again faded out of the picture. Another start was made in 1931, but after winning two games and losing eight the franchise again was relinquished.

The expected bid for membership from Los Angeles failed to materialize and petitions from Boston, Minneapolis and Buffalo were tabled.

All officers were re-elected. They are: Carr, president and secretary; Carl Storck, Dayton, vice president and treasurer, and the following, members of the league's finance committee: Carr, chairman; George S. Halas, Chicago; Bert Bell, Philadelphia; L. H. Joannes, Green Bay, Wis., and John V. Mara, New York.

February 13, 1937

BAUGH'S TOSSES WIN FOR REDSKINS, 28-21

Passes Twice to Millner and Once to Justice in Third for Scores to Top Bears

By ARTHUR J. DALEY

Special to THE NEW YORK TIMES.

CHICAGO, Dec. 12.—The passing wizardry of Slingin' Sammy Baugh shot the Washington Redskins into the championship of the National

Football League on the frozen tundra of Wrigley Field today. The Indians, as accustomed as Eskimos to their arctic surroundings, toppled the Chicago Bears, 28 to 21, with a three-touchdown onslaught in the third period.

The gridiron was like a skating rink. The players skidded despite their basketball shoes while some 15,878 citizens who braved frost-bite and chilblains had nothing but the heart-warming exhibition of football skill to ward off the 15 degree cold.

But that hot house flower from Texas, Slingin' Sammy, gave one of the hottest exhibitions of his career. The mighty Cliff Battles was hobbled by the uncertain underfooting. But Baugh pegged passes with either the softness of drifting snow or the fury of a North Pole gale.

Passes Gain 352 Yards

No matter which style, however, he pitched them accurately and well. Half of his passes were completed, 17 of 34, for the prodigious yardage of 352. He twirled one to Wayne Millner for 55 yards and a touchdown, to Millner again for 77 yards and another score and to Justice for 35 and the clincher.

It was amazing, the way Baugh worked. Without him Washington would have been buried deep in the drift of Bear touchdowns. For this was weather and these were conditions that were hand-tailored for Chicago.

The quick-opening Bear plays that had power as their keynote were ideally suited to the situation at hand. It was a day for straight-away running, bullet bursts through the middle of the line, and Jack Manders, Bronko Nagurski and Ray Nolting could gain yard after yard by this method.

These plungers hammered 71 yards for one touchdown in four plays, went 50 more in four plays for the second and 73 in twelve for the third. It was the bludgeon against the rapier, and the more deft weapon of the two triumphed.

Throws While Off Balance

Baugh threw passes that had to be seen to be believed. He pitched them while in full flight and hung them on a nail. He tossed them as tacklers were carrying him to the ground, but so accurate were they that a blind man could have caught them.

The Bears were out to get him. They sent him from the game in the second period, but Slingin' Sam limped back with one sound leg and one injured one in the third quarter and threw the Bears dizzy with his superlative aerials.

And it was Baugh who was the innocent cause of a free-for-all fight in the last quarter, just one more enlivening incident in a spectacular game. Dick Plasman had just caught a pass from Bernie Masterson, and, with a clear field ahead, was dumfounded when the wonder-worker Baugh nailed him from behind and whirled him out of bounds at midfield, plumb in the middle of the Redskin bench.

They spun into a mass of substitutes. Then Plasman injudiciously tossed a gentle punch at Baugh, the idol of the Washington squad. In a flash the Chicago end was pummeled by every one within reach and in a trice Bears and Redskins were pawing away at each other with gay abandon.

A Rough Contest

This was no football game played under the strict code of the football rules committee. It was a bitter knock-'em-down-and-drag-'em-out battle. Slingin' Sammy said after-

ward that it was the roughest game he ever had been in.

But this was Sammy's ball game, the greatest individual triumph any person ever achieved in the history of the National League. At times it almost looked as if he did it with mirrors.

The straw that broke the Bears' back was the touchdown play that brought about the downfall of the Giants the week before. Chicago had been playing for Charlie Malone, the favorite Baugh receiver.

But with the score tied at 21-all in the third period Sammy faded back. Malone cut to the middle, and a cordon of Chicagoans surrounded him. But the smart Mr. Baugh never passed to him. Instead, he whirled a perfect pass to Ed Justice for 35 yards in the right flat, and there it was, the first championship that any Eastern team but the Giants ever gained.

Long Toss From End Zone

The tip-off came on the first play of the game. Baugh, hemmed in by potential tacklers in the end zone, passed 42 yards to Battles. The Bears were routed then and there, even though they did not know it.

This turned the tide, swinging the Washingtonians from a bad spot deep in their own territory right out to midfield. Baugh punted, Nolting punted and the touchdown parade was on. Sammy slung to Riley Smith and to Ernie Pinckert for 32 yards, then to Smith for 6 more, then it was Baugh and Battles along the ground for 21 yards to the end zone, with Battles scoring from the 7 on a sweeping reverse of his left end. Smith converted with the first of four kicks he made.

But the Bears were far from through. They came back from the next kick-off for 71 yards and a touchdown. Manders carried over from the 11 after a plunge through the middle after a Masterson-Manders pass accounted for the major distance of the drive, 51 yards. Manders kicked the extra point and the score was tied.

Then, with the interception of a Baugh-thrown pass, Chicago marched again, this time 50 yards. A Masterson-Manders toss to the right gained 38 yards, and with a placement by Automatic Jack, the Bears were ahead, 14 to 7.

The second quarter saw only two threats, both by the Bears. Manders tried field goals from the 38 and the 40, but was not even close in either instance. Washington never went past midfield in this period because Slingin' Sammy was on the bench.

But Coach Ray Flaherty sent his prize cripple into action in the third quarter, and things began to happen. Within seven minutes three touchdowns were scored. In four plays Washington swept 70 yards.

Redskins-Bears Statistics

	FIRST HALF.		SECOND HALF.		TOTALS.	
	Reds.	Bears.	Reds.	Bears.	Reds.	Bears.
First downs	9	3	6	8	15	11
Yards gained rushing........	19	40	57	100	76	140
Forward passes	23	13	18	12	41	25
Forwards completed	10	4	11	4	21	8
Yards gained, forwards......	133	99	255	109	388	208
Forwards intercepted by......	2	3	1	0	3	3
Number of punts............	4	4	2	2	6	6
*Av. distance of punts, yards.	40	61	40	57	40	58
Run-back of punts, yards.....	0	0	9	0	9	0
Fumbles	1	2	2	1	3	3
Own fumbles recovered.......	0	1	0	1	0	2
Penalties	0	1	1	0	1	1
Yards lost, penalties.........	0	15	5	0	5	15

*From point where ball was kicked.

Chicago Line-Up

REDSKINS (28)		BEARS (21)
Millner	...........L.E....	.......Manske
Edwards	...........L.T....	.......Stydahar
Olsson	...........L.G....	.......Fortmann
Kawal	...........C.....	.......Bausch
Karcher	...........R.G....	.......Musso
Barber	...........R.T....	.......Stjork
Malone	...........R.E....	.......Wilson
R. Smith	...........Q.B....	.......Masterson
Baugh	...........L.H....	.......Nolting
Pinckert	...........R.H....	.......Manders
Battles	...........F.B....	.......Nagurski

SCORE BY PERIODS
Redskins .... 7 0 21 0—28
Bears .... 14 0 7 0—21
Touchdowns—Battles, Manders 2, Millner 2, Manske, Justice. Points after touchdowns—R. Smith 4. Manders 3 (all placements).

SUBSTITUTES
Redskins—Tackles: Bond, Young. Guards: Carroll, Michaels, Kahn. Center: G. Smith. Backs: Justice, Irwin, Krause.
Bears—Ends: Plasman, Karr, McDonald. Tackle: Thompson. Guard: Zeller. Center: Conkright. Backs: Molesworth, Ronzani, Rentner, Buivid, Francis, Feathers.
Referee—W. T. Halloran, Providence. Umpire—E. W. Cochrane, Chicago. Field judge—E. F. Hughitt, Buffalo. Linesman—Bobby Cahn, Chicago. Time of periods—15 minutes.

The last of these shots was a cross-over pass from Baugh to Millner, who outsprinted the secondaries, and finally was thrown by Masterson right across the goal line. Smith obliged, and the score was 14—all.

But these Bears were still hot, even if the day was not. Manders was not to be stopped in shots at the middle of the Redskin line. With Nagurski and Nolting lending able assistance, he slashed and hammered to a first down on the 4.

Play Covers 77 Yards

Two passes were batted down and a Nagurski thrust was stopped at the line of scrimmage by the infuriated Washingtonians. But on the last down Masterson bobbed up with the ball from behind center, jumped and flicked it into the arms of Ed Manske in the end zone. Manders converted, and Chicago was ahead once more, 21 to 14.

The Bears kicked off and Washington returned to the 23. On the first play Baugh passed right down the center alley to Millner, who seized the pigskin at midfield and crossed the goal in the right corner of the gridiron for a 77-yard touchdown advance. With the able assistance of Smith, that made the count 21—21.

It was shortly after this, when Chicago was held at midfield, that the Indians struck the warpath again. Don Irwin drove along the ground and Baugh fired through the air. The turning point was reached on a gamble when Irwin bucked for a yard on the fourth down at the Bear 42 and made it.

No Justice in Sight

Baugh passed to Irwin for 7 yards, then to Justice for 35. And there just wasn't any justice when Chicago tried to halt him. He outraced all Bear defenders to that same right corner and the Redskins were ahead at 28—21.

But this nerve-tingling battle was not quite over. The Redskins went overhead to the 15-yard line after a 61-yard onslaught, only to have Millner lose the ball there on a fumble. Chicago bounced right back to the 24, but Masterson failed on four straight passes.

That still was not all. The Bears advanced 78 yards to the 7 a few moments later, only to have Masterson thrown for a 7-yard loss in attempting one pass and fail entirely on the next. That finished things.

December 13, 1937

GIANTS ANNEX TITLE WITH 23-17 VICTORY

Danowski Fires Two Scoring Passes, Including Winning Toss to Soar in Third

By ARTHUR J. DALEY

The Giants and the Packers delved into the realm of fiction for a storybook football game at the Polo Grounds yesterday. In fact, fiction almost seemed too tame a medium for the thriller that the Eastern and Western champions of the National Football League staged for the world title to the delirious delight of a record play-off crowd of 48,120.

Right to the final seconds of a rousing battle of gridiron titans the tension was such that something seemed bound to snap. But when the final gun cracked the New Yorkers had conquered the ponderous Packers from Green Bay, 23 to 17.

Perhaps there have been better football games since Rutgers and Princeton started the autumnal madness sixty-nine years ago, but no one in that huge crowd would admit it. This was a struggle of such magnificent stature that words seem such feeble tools for describing it.

The Giants, opportunists to the end, blocked two punts for a 9-0 advantage. Back came Green Bay to make the count 9 to 7. The Maramen surged to a 16-7 advantage only to have the Packers reduce that lead to 16 to 14 at the half. Then the mastodons from Wisconsin flashed ahead in the third quarter, 17 to 16, but back came the Giants for 7 more points and the clincher.

Final Period Scoreless

The last quarter was scoreless, but no one dared leave the park. The Packers were hammering along the ground and through the airways, applying terrific pressure to the doughty defense of the pupils of Stout Steve Owen. One long pass could win the game for them, and the Green Bay Monsters were eternally shooting for that tally.

The clock showed a scant five seconds remaining and still the crowd refused to head for the exits. A touchdown was possible, late in the fray as it was. The ball spun through the arc-lighted field in a final desperate attempt for a tally. It missed its target and the Giants were the new champions, the first team in the history of the play-offs to win twice.

At the end the spectators were too emotionally exhausted even to try to rip down the goal posts. These stood untouched, silent sentinels of a magnificent football game.

What a frenzied battle this was! The tackling was fierce and the blocking positively vicious. In the last drive every scrimmage pile-up saw a Packer tackler stretched on the ground. Oddly, however, not one of them really was hurt physically, although the battering their spirits took was tremendous. As for the Giants, they really were hammered to a fare-thee-well.

Johnny Dell Isola was taken to St. Elizabeth's Hospital with a spinal concussion that just missed being a fractured vertebra. Ward Cuff suffered a possible fracture of the sternum.

Mel Hein, kicked in the cheekbone at the end of the second quarter, suffered a concussion of the brain that left him temporarily bereft of his memory. He came to in the final quarter and finished the game. Leland Shaffer sustained a badly sprained ankle.

The play for the full sixty vibrant minutes was absolutely ferocious. No such blocking and tackling by two football teams ever had been seen at the Polo Grounds. Tempers were so frayed and tattered that stray punches were tossed around all afternoon. This was the gridiron sport at its primitive best.

In the first quarter the Giants were as perfect a team as ever had been assembled, a smooth, coordinated machine that made no mistakes. But in the second session the Packers, fired by a 40-yard touchdown pass, caught that same spark and it was hammer and tongs the rest of the way.

The Giants were ready for this game. When the chips were down they had everything. Quickly they fashioned 9 points in the first quarter when Jim Poole and Jim Lee Howell gave one of the finest exhibitions of end play ever seen. They smothered Packer rushes at every turn and then when Clarke Hinkle, an all-league fullback if ever there was one, attempted to punt Howell flashed in, blocked the kick and then caught the ball before it hit the ground.

The Line-Up

NEW YORK (23)		GREEN BAY (17)
Poole	L.E.	Becker
Widseth	L.T.	Seibold
Dell Isola	L.G.	Letlow
Hein	C.	Mulleneaux
Tuttle	R.G.	Goldenberg
Parry	R.T.	Lee
Howell	R.F.	Gantenbein
Danowski	Q.B.	Schneidman
Soar	L.H.	Isbell
Cuff	R.H.	Laws
Shaffer	F.B.	Hinkle

SCORE BY PERIODS

New York ....9 7 7 0—23
Green Bay ....0 14 3 0—17

Touchdowns—Leemans, C. Mulleneaux, Barnard, Hinkle, Soar. Field goals—Cuff, Engebretsen (placements). Points after touchdown—Cuff 2, Engebretsen 2 (placements).

SUBSTITUTES

New York—Ends: Barnard, Gelatka. Tackles: Mellus, Cope. Guards: Lunday, Cole, White. Centers: Johnson, Galazin. Backs: Leemans, Barnum, Karcis, Richards, Gildea, Burnett, Falaschi.

Green Bay—Ends: Hutson, C. Mulleneaux, Scherer. Tackles: Butler, Ray. Guards: Tinsley, Engebretsen. Centers: O. Miller, Svendsen. Backs: P. Miller, Bruder, Jankowski, Uram, Weisgerber, Herber, Monnett.

Referee—Bobby Cahn, Chicago. Umpire—Tom Thorp, Columbia. Linesman—Larry Conover, Penn State. Field judge—J. L. Meyer, Ohio Wesleyan. Time of periods—15 minutes.

Danowski's Pass Short

It was a first down on the Green Bay 7-yard line. The Giants gained a yard in two rushes. Ed Danowski's pass to Cuff was short and the one-time intercollegiate javelin-throwing champion dropped back to the 13 and booted a field goal.

Hardly had the crowd settled back when the harried Packers attempted to kick again. Cecil Isbell was back to punt, but Poole whirled in to block it and Howell made the recovery on the 27. In four plays the Giants were over the goal line. A Danowski-Tuffy Leemans pass picked up 5 yards. Leemans went up to the 6 on an off-tackle dash and then cut back once more off the Packer left tackle for a touchdown with a defender hanging to his jersey. Johnny Gildea missed the extra point.

But the thrills were not ended. In the second quarter Tiny Engebretsen intercepted a Giant pass that he carried to the Green Bay 49. In two rushes Andy Uram went to the New York 40 and then Arnold Herber dropped back and sailed a floater of a pass right down the middle. Carl Mulleneaux plucked the ball out of the air on the 1-yard line right between the goal posts as Gildea missed batting it down. Mulleneaux stumbled across and when Engebretsen booted the extra point the score was 9 to 7.

Not long afterward Hein recovered a fumble at midfield and the Giants were off to town again. The critical play was a pass that Leemans spun to Len Barnum. The Giant freshman caught the ball and fumbled it, but it went out of bounds safely. It was a first down for the Owen men on the 22, although the Packers stormed and raved that Barnum never had gained possession.

Barnum cracked tackle to the 20 and then Danowski, whose passing touched the heights of perfection at the right time, flicked one to Hap Barnard in the end zone for a touchdown. Cuff converted.

Then sensation piled on sensation as Isbell shot a short spot pass to Wayland Becker. He was in the clear when Soar came whirling up to nail him from behind on the 17 after a mad 66-yard gain. Five times in a row Hinkle slammed inside the tackles until he scored from the 2-foot line on a weak-side plunge. When Engebretsen converted again the Packers were back in the ball game.

Tension mounted during the intermission and when play was resumed a 34-yard off tackle romp by Bob Monnett was the backbone of a 63-yard drive that finally was stymied by the Giant defense on the 5. So Engebretsen booted an easy 15-yard field goal to give Green Bay the lead for the first time.

March Covers 62 Yards

Aroused, the Giants stormed back in all their fury, a relentless advance of 62 yards. The clincher was a beautiful pass from Danowski to Soar. The ball was wafted through the air to the 6-yard marker, where Soar, Poole and two Packer defenders leaped for it. But Hank came down with the ball. He had a Packer defender hanging to one leg as he dragged himself across for the last big batch of points. Cuff converted.

Still the dizzy pace of this thriller was not to end. The infuriated Packers struck back, reaching the 32 before Danowski intercepted. In the fourth quarter Green Bay reached the 38 and then the 33. The next play was a Herber-Becker pass that was caught on the 17.

But Cuff flattened the Packer end with such a teeth-rattling tackle that the ball popped out of his hands, Kayo Lunday recovering. The break of the game came soon afterward. A Herber-Gantenbein aerial clicked, but Green Bay was using a spread formation and the flanking back had edged up so much that Gantenbein no longer was eligible.

To the intense dismay and violent chagrin of the Packers a successful play immediately was nullified and it was New York's ball at the point of the foul, the Green Bay 43. So enraged were the ponderous youths from Wisconsin at this ruling that they piled up on the next play to incur a further 15-yard penalty for unnecessary roughness. Cuff finally missed a 36-yard field goal and the Packers had only two chances left.

They fled 38 yards to the Giant 43 before yielding the ball on downs. Then, as the hands of the clock crawled toward the end, the Packers moved 40 yards to the Giant 40 before the gun cracked for the grand finish of a grand game.

Giant heroes were too numerous to mention. There were Poole and Howell at the ends, Widseth, Parry, Cope and Mellus at the tackles, Dell Isola and the hard-working Orville Tuttle at the guards and Hein, magnificent as always, at center. Cuff, Soar, Leemans, Danowski and the rest were great backs.

As for the Packers; they had their stars in Bud Svendsen at center, Buckets Goldenberg, Engebretsen and Will Letlow, guards; Gantenbein and Becker, ends; Hinkle, Herbe Monnett and Joe Laws in the backfield.

December 12, 1938

Giants-Packers Statistics

	FIRST HALF. Giants. Pack.		SECOND HALF. Giants. Pack.		TOTAL. Giants. Pack.	
First downs	5	4	5	10	10	14
Yards gained, rushing	70	24	45	140	115	164
Forward passes	10	5	5	14	15	19
Forwards completed	4	3	4	5	8	8
Yards gained, forwards	53	131	41	83	94	214
Forwards intercepted by	0	1	1	0	1	1
Number of punts	3	6	3	2	6	8
*Av. distance of punts, yards	58	36	46	44	52	38
Run-back of punts, yards	42	3	0	11	42	14
Fumbles	0	1	1	1	1	2
Own fumbles recovered	0	0	0	0	0	0
Penalties	2	1	0	1	2	2
Yards lost, penalties	10	5	0	15	10	20

*From point where ball was kicked.

NOVEL PLAN ADOPTED TO DECIDE PLAY-OFFS
Pro Football Group Title Games on 'Sudden Death' Basis

WASHINGTON, Nov. 18 (UP)—An innovation in football, the "sudden death" system, will be used by the National Football League to decide tie games if play-offs are necessary between teams which may be deadlocked for leadership of each division when the regular 1940 season closes.

This was announced tonight by the league president, Carl Storck, after a special meeting with representatives of teams still in the running for the division titles.

Storck emphasized that the "sudden death" system would be used only in case of a divisional tie and not in the league championship game. In the latter case, league rules already provide that co-champions shall be declared in event the game ends in a tie.

Under the system, borrowed from professional hockey championship play-offs, the team scoring first after the regulation playing time is declared the winner. Storck said that if the teams were tied at the end of the regulation game they would toss a coin, just as at the start of the game.

If neither team has scored in the first "sudden death" period there will be a two-minute intermission and the game will continue until one has scored.

In the Eastern division it is possible for the Dodgers, with six victories and three losses, to finish in a tie for first place with the Redskins, who lead with eight victories and one defeat. Both have two games remaining. In the event of a division tie they will play it off in Washington.

In the Western division, Chicago's Bears have a record of six victories and three losses. Green Bay and Detroit each have five victories and four defeats.

If the Bears and Packers finish in a tie they will play off at Chicago. If the Lions gain a tie, the play-off will be held in Detroit.

The league championship play-off already has been scheduled for the home field of the Eastern winner, either Washington or Brooklyn. If there are no division ties, the championship game will be held Dec. 8; otherwise, Dec. 15.

November 19, 1940

Bears Overwhelm Redskins by Record Score to Capture World Football Title

VERSATILE DISPLAY MARKS 73-0 ROUT

By ARTHUR J. DALEY
Special to The New York Times.

WASHINGTON, Dec. 8 — The weather was perfect. So were the Bears. In the most fearsome display of power ever seen on any gridiron, the Monsters of the Midway won the Ed Thorp Memorial Trophy, which is symbolic of the world football championship, before 36,034 stunned and deriding fans in Griffith Stadium this balmy afternoon.

It being a Sunday, the Washington Humane Society had the day off. So the Bears had nothing to combat in the play-off except the Redskins, who were pretty feeble opposition indeed. Hence it was that the Chicago Bears scalped the Capital Indians, 73 to 0, the highest score in the history of the National Football League.

This was simply dreadful. The only question before the house was whether the Bears could score more points when they were on the offensive or when Washington was on the offensive. It was fairly close competition, Chicago with the ball outscoring the Redskins with the ball, seven touchdowns to four.

Scoring Time Shaved

Before fifty-six seconds had passed the Bears had a tally. Then, when the second half began, they cut that time down, registering another marker in fifty-four seconds. It probably is just as well that the football rules permit only two halves to a game or else George Halas's young men would have been down to fractions of seconds.

There never was anything quite like this. Three weeks ago the Redskins edged out the Bears, 7 to 3. Today it was something else again. Chicago was a perfect football team that played football of such exquisite class that Washington could not have won with a brick wall instead of a line and howitzers instead of backs. The Bears would have battered down everything.

By the time the second half began the Redskins showed a marked improvement. Their defense against points after touchdown had reached such perfection that four out of seven were missed. Washington was the unlucky outfit today. It had the misfortune to have to face a team that could have beaten the other nine elevens in the league just as badly.

Blocking Is Accurate

This was football at its very best. The Bears had the timing for their quick-opening plays down to the hundredth of a second. They riddled the Redskins at will with the overwhelming power of their ground game, rocked them with their infrequent passes and smothered them with their defensive power. The blocking was fiendishly accurate and it almost was a physical impossibility for them to make a mistake.

The Bears registered three touchdowns in the first period, one in the second, four in the third and three in the last. Halas used every eligible man on his squad, thirty-three of them, and fifteen had a share of the scoring. It even reached such a stage that the Bears passed for a point after touchdown by way of variety and by way of adding to Washington's humiliation.

Halas used Sid Luckman, an Old Blue from Columbia, as his first-half quarterback, and no field general ever called plays more artistically or engineered a touchdown parade in more letter-perfect fashion. But the Lion sat out the second half and still the mastodons from the Midwest rolled.

Ray Flaherty's young men were physically in the game, but that was all. After Bill Osmanski had romped 68 yards for the first touchdown, the 'Skins reached the Bear 26, only to have Bob Masterson's 32-yard field-goal effort fail. That was a blow from which George Preston Marshall's lads never recovered. Had they scored, it might have been different.

Go Downhill Speedily

But when they missed they wound up with a minus 10 yards for their first seven passes and went speedily downhill the rest of the way. After a while that descent began to resemble a snowball on the way, picking up power and speed as it heads toward the valley.

The first touchdown was a 75-yard zip to a score. George McAfee picked up 7 yards and then Osmanski, cutting inside Washington's right tackle, went 68 yards more. The tip-off on the Bears came when George Wilson erased two men with the same block to clear the way for the counter.

Then the Bears rolled 80 yards in seventeen plays, the pay-off being Luckman's quarterback sneak from the six-inch line. A moment later Joe Maniaci, the old Fordham Flash, streaked 42 yards for another counter. Jack Manders, Bob Snyder and Phil Martinovich added the extra points and it was 21 to 0.

Redskin fans who had watched their heroes win their first seven games of the league season could not believe their eyes. Yet even they were to become convinced that they were watching one of the greatest football teams of all time in action, a team that had everything.

The Bears reached the 16 in the second quarter and fumbled. Washington made a gesture by going 63 yards to the 18 on ten successive passes, only to lose the ball on downs. The Chicagoans went 56 more to the 24 but Martinovich failed on a field goal try.

Ray Nolting boomed through with one of the eight Bear pass interceptions and the victors were off to the races. Ground plays advanced only 26 yards, so Luckman flipped a 30-yarder to Ken Kavanaugh in the end zone, the freshman from Louisiana State plucking the ball from the grasp of two defenders for another counter. Snyder converted.

The third quarter saw the Redskins give up the ghost. They attempted a pass from the 19, but Hampton Pool, an end, intercepted Sammy Baugh's lateral flick to Jimmy Johnston on the 16 for a marker. Then the Capital crew tried a fourth-down pass from their 33. It was batted down.

So the Bears took over. Nolting gained 10 yards. But he was just warming up. On the next play he burst 23 yards through the middle, feinted Baugh into the middle of the Potomac on the 8 and went across standing up. Dick Plasman missed the conversion, which promptly labeled him an absolute outcast.

Bears-Redskins Game Statistics

	1ST HALF Bears.	1ST HALF Redskins.	2D HALF Bears.	2D HALF Redskins.	TOTAL Bears.	TOTAL Redskins.
First downs	11	9	6	9	17	18
Yards gained rushing	241	31	131	−28	372	3
Forward passes	4	27	4	22	8	49
Forwards completed	3	10	3	11	6	21
Yards gained, forwards	89	162	31	67	120	229
Forwards intercepted by	3	0	5	0	8	0
Number of punts	1	2	1	1	2	3
*Aver. dist. of punts, yards	53	31	51	67	52	49
Runback of punts, yards	18	6	9	0	27	6
Fumbles	4	1	0	4	4	5
Own fumbles recovered	3	1	0	3	3	4
Penalties	0	2	3	5	3	7
Yards lost, penalties	0	10	35	55	35	65

*From point where ball was kicked.

Now Stydahar's Turn

Washington took over again and McAfee intercepted a Roy Zimmerman pass for 35 yards of gorgeous broken-field running for a touchdown. It then was Joe Stydahar's turn and he split the bars with a placement.

The Redskins made an effort to score, reaching the 16 only to lose the ball on downs. When the Bears punted Washington assumed the offensive on its 37. A bad pass from center was recovered on the 21 and Zimmerman's pass was intercepted by Bulldog Turner on the 30. He scored, thanks to a block by Pool. Maniaci's placement was blocked and it was 54 to 0.

The league's champions rumbled 74 yards for their next touchdown in the fourth quarter, Harry Clark going 42 yards on a double reverse for the tally. On this he feinted Frank Filchock into Chesapeake Bay. Gary Famiglietti was elected as the point converter, but failed.

The hapless Redskins later saw Filchock fumble in the shadow of his goal posts. Jack Torrance, the reformed shot-put world record-holder, fell on the ball on the 2. He almost crushed the air out of the ball when his 300 pounds landed on it. So Famiglietti burst across on a quick opener. The crusher was a Saul Sherman-Maniaci pass in the end zone for the extra point.

The last touchdown resulted from a 52-yard drive that was culminated by a 1-yard dance by Clark through the middle. He crossed standing up. A Snyder-Maniaci conversion pass missed. And Maniaci intercepted again just as the Redskins gave promise of threatening.

There was no Redskin hero outside of Flaherty, who had to sit on the bench and absorb it all, too much a beating for so fine a gentleman and coach. The Bears had thirty-three heroes. Luckman, Nolting, McAfee, Osmanski and Maniaci in the backfield were outstanding. So were Lee Artoe, Stydahar, Danny Fortmann, Turner and Plasman in the line.

The day was gorgeous. The crowd was representative, with high government officials scattered throughout the stands. Everything was under the control of the Magnificent Marshall, except the Bears.

At the end the Redskin band played "Should Auld Acquaintance Be Forgot?" If said acquaintance is the Chicago Bears, it should be forgot immediately. At the moment the Bears are the greatest football team of all time.

The line-up:

BEARS (73)		REDSKINS (0)
Nowaskey	...L.E...	Masterson
Stydahar	...L.T...	Wilkin
Fortmann	...L.G...	Farman
Turner	...C...	Titchenal
Musso	...R.G...	Slivinski
Artoe	...R.T...	Barber
Wilson	...R.E...	Malone
Luckman	...Q.B...	Krause
Nolting	...L.H...	Baugh
McAfee	...R.H...	Justice
Osmanski	...F.B...	Johnston

SCORE BY PERIODS

Bears .... 21 7 26 19—73
Redskins .... 0 0   0   0— 0

Touchdowns—Clark 2, Osmanski, Luckman, Maniaci, Kavanaugh, Nolting, Pool, McAfee, Turner, Famiglietti. Points after touchdown—Manders, Snyder 2, Martinovich, Plasman, Stydahar (placements), Maniaci (pass from Sherman).

SUBSTITUTES

Bears—Ends: Siegal, Manske, Plasman, Pool, Kavanaugh. Tackles: Mihal, Kolman, Torrance. Guards: Martinovich, Forte, Baisi. Centers: Bausch, Chesney. Backs: Famiglietti, Clark, Manders, Maniaci, Snyder, Sherman, Masterson, Swisher, McLean.

Redskins — Ends: McChesney, Sanford, Millner. Tackles: Fisher, Russell. Guards: Stralka, Shugart. Centers: Andrako, Parks. Backs: Pinckert, Morgan, Seymour, Zimmerman, Filchock, Moore, Todd, Hare, Hoffman, Farkas, Meade.

Referee—William Friesell, Princeton. Umpire—Harry Robb, Penn State. Linesman—Irving Kupcinet, North Dakota. Field judge—Fred Young, Illinois Wesleyan. Time of periods—15 minutes.

December 9, 1940

EAGLES, STEELERS TRADE FRANCHISES

Bell-Rooney Team to Move to Pittsburgh and Thompson's Eleven to Philadelphia

CHICAGO, April 2 (AP)—Bert Bell announced tonight that he and Art Rooney, co-owners of the Philadelphia Eagles of the National Football League, had traded franchises with Alexis Thompson, owner of the Pittsburgh Steelers.

Bell said no player trades were involved. Thompson will take his Pittsburgh athletes to Philadelphia and the entire Philadelphia squad will move to Pittsburgh.

The league, continuing its efforts to make professional football's rules as equitable as possible, will open its annual meeting tomorrow with its rules committee considering several changes.

While the move had been contemplated for several weeks, observers agreed it was one of the most unusual swaps in sports history. The deal was consummated "by mutual agreement," both parties feeling that they benefited. Thompson, who lives in New York, had long wished to transfer operations closer to his home.

Rooney formerly held the Pittsburgh franchise, but sold out to Thompson last December. Then he purchased an interest in the Philadelphia club.

April 3, 1941

LAYDEN RECEIVES SWEEPING POWERS

Football League Commissioner to Settle Squabbles, Levy and Collect Fines

CHICAGO, April 6 (AP)—The most important meeting in the twenty-one-year history of the National Football League ended today on a harmonious note with the newly inducted commissioner, Elmer Layden, in control of the organization for the next five years.

The powers delegated to the former Notre Dame athletic director and coach are fully as sweeping, if not more so, as the authority held by Kenesaw M. Landis, ruler of baseball.

Layden, who signed the five-year contract last night, presided at today's rules and schedule meeting. The eleven-game schedule for each team was completed except for a few probable changes but will not be released for several weeks.

The new constitution of the league rules that Layden shall have authority on all squabbles between

players and clubs, levy and collect fines, govern conduct of club owners and all their employes in any activity connected with the sport and have complete control of the league finances.

A maximum misconduct fine of $25,000 was set, with Layden having authority to determine the amount. Layden will open league headquarters in Chicago immediately. The New York office will be closed.

April 7, 1941

WASHINGTON TAKES TITLE PLAY-OFF, 14-6

36,006 See 7-1 Underdog Team Dethrone Bears, Winners of 24 Straight Games

STATISTICS OF THE GAME

	Wash.	Bears
First downs	9	10
Yards gained rushing	101	69
Forward passes	13	20
Forwards completed	5	10
Yards gained, forwards	65	130
Forwards intercepted by	3	2
Number of punts	6	6
†Av. dist. of punts, yds.	62.5	52
Run-back of punts, yds.	21	20
Fumbles	1	2
Own fumbles recovered	0	1
Penalties	4	7
Yards lost, penalties	26	47

†From point where ball was kicked.

By ARTHUR DALEY
Special to THE NEW YORK TIMES.

WASHINGTON, Dec. 13—By way of supplying a final madhouse touch to a football season that was noted for its lunacies and upsets, the Redskins soundly trounced the supposedly invincible Bears before an incredulous and deliriously happy gathering of 36,006 spectators in Griffith Stadium today to win the world professional championship.

The Monsters from the Midway, winners of twenty-four straight contests and thirty-nine of their last forty, were beaten in a terrific, teeth-rattling game that never was far from becoming a wild, free-for-all fight.

The capital Braves, giving the Chicagoans a fluke touchdown on a 49-yard run with a fumble recovered by Lee Artoe, 230-pound tackle, came storming back to take a 7-6 lead in the second period and clinched matters with another touchdown in the third for a stunning 14-6 victory.

This was a team that was so much an underdog that the gamblers stopped giving 7-1 odds and handed out as much as 22 points. This also was largely the team that had been beaten, 73—0, in the play-off two years ago. Yet it cracked into the mighty Bears with disregard of the Chicagoans' reputation and handled them as easily as if the Monsters were only P. S. 9.

No Comparison Between Them

The Bears had won two straight championships. They had not been vanquished since the Green Bay Packers edged them out, 16—14, on Nov. 2, 1941. Yet the Redskins were so superior today that there was no comparison.

That tremendous Washington line, which averaged 229 pounds from end to end did a job of pulverizing effectiveness. They held the Bears' vaunted running game to an unheard of 69 yards.

Ray Flaherty's troops were in control of the situation almost all the way. When Artoe missed the extra point after he had scampered to his touchdown, victory slipped from the Bears' clutch. Against the frenzied play of the Redskins, failure to get that one point was a vital mistake.

The 'Skins came back from the impending disaster of that touchdown and whirled 42 yards in three plays. The big one was a pass from Slingin' Sammy Baugh to Wilbur Moore for 38 yards and the tally, and Bob Masterson made the first of his two conversions.

The red-hot Braves went over 43 yards for their second touchdown when Anvil Andy Farkas burst over from the 1-yard line midway in the third quarter.

Luckman Hurled Down

The Redskins were terrific today. The Bears had been handing it out for almost two years but they could not take it when the pressure was on. Sid Luckman, wonder operator of the T-formation, completed five of twelve passes for a total of just 2 yards. He was harried and slammed to earth, treated with such disrespect that one hardly could believe it.

If it had not been for Charlie O'Rourke and the 128 yards gained by the five passes completed of the seven he threw, the Bears would not have had even a presentable statistical average. They had more first downs than Washington and more total yards gained, it is true, but their only score was a fluke.

Never has there been a game of such intensity. Every tackle and block not only could be seen but heard. The officials did a superb job in the face of handicaps.

They had to use a quick whistle to avoid serious trouble. The way these giants slammed into one another was terrifying. Enough punches were thrown to serve for a Madison Square Garden main event as the short-tempered athletes, particularly the Bears, went at it in earnest.

Redskins' Line-Up

WASHINGTON (14)	CHICAGO (6)
Masterson	L.E.	Nowaskey
Wilkin	L.T.	Kolman
Farman	L.G.	Fortmann
Aldrich	C.	Turner
Slivinski	R.G.	Bray
Young	R.T.	Artoe
Cifers	R.E.	Wilson
R. Hare	Q.B.	Luckman
Baugh	L.H.	Nolting
Justice	R.H.	Gallarneau
Farkas	F.B.	Famiglietti

SCORE BY PERIODS

Washington .... 0 7 0—11
Chicago .... 0 6 0 0—6

Touchdowns—Artoe, Moore, Farkas. Points
after touchdown—Masterson 2 (placements).

SUBSTITUTES

Washington — Tackles: Beinor, Davis.
Guards: Shugart, Stralka. Backs: C. Hare,
Moore, Seymour, Todd.
Chicago—Ends: Siegal, Pool. Tackles: Sty-
dahar, Hoptowit. Guards: Drulis, Akin,
Musso. Center: Matuza. Backs: McLean,
Maznicki, Petty, O'Rourke, Osmanski,
Clark.
Referee—Ronald Gibbs. Umpire—Carl Bru-
baker. Linesman—Charlie Bever. Field
judge—Chuck Sweeney. Timer—Harry Robb.

Tackles Stand Out

Redskin stars were many, but it
was the two starting tackles, Wee
Willie Wilkin and Bill Young, along
with Dick Farman and Steve Sli-
vinski, the guards, that did the
damage. Aiding and abetting them
were three sixty-minute players,
Ki Aldrich at center and Masterson and Ed Cifers at the ends. Only
the veteran Joe Stydahar caught
the eye for the Bears.

Mr. Baugh of Washington should
not be overlooked either. He went
the full distance, called all the
plays, punted for an average of
62.5 yards and threw fewer passes
than ever. He completed five of
thirteen for 65 yards. Baugh was
a superlative figure every inch of
the way. That, it might be added,
was more than sufficient.

The Bears had enough chances,
too. They went to the 27-yard line
in the first period, were rocked
back to the 38 and Artoe missed a
46-yard field goal. He was right
on the beam with his kick, but the
ball skidded under the cross-piece.

Then the Bears went to the 28
after an interception, but fumbled.
This was in the first period.

In the last period, with O'Rourke
passing, they traveled 52 yards to
the 12 before the ubiquitous Baugh
intercepted in the end zone. After
that they went 79 yards to the 1,
had a touchdown by Hugh Gallarneau called back because a

back was illegally in motion, and
finally lost the ball on downs.

Todd Fumbles Ball

The Bear touchdown came in
1:29 of the second quarter. Dick
Todd fumbled as George Wilson hit
him. Wilson reached for the ball
but could not hold it. Artoe could,
however, and did. He rumbled 49
yards for a touchdown. The Redskins were offside, but the Bears,
of course, declined the penalty.
Artoe's conversion attempt was
hooked off his foot to the left.

As Chicago drove on again,
Moore intercepted a Luckman pass
to Johnny Siegal and returned it 16
yards to the 42. Cecil Hare gained
4, but a pass from Baugh failed.
Then Sammy faded back and spun
a 50-yarder to Moore.

That worthy made a sensational,
over-the-shoulder catch one step
inside the end zone, with John
Petty on his back, for a dazzling
touchdown. Joe DiMaggio never
made a prettier catch.

Masterson's kick was true and
the Redskins were ahead, George
Preston Marshall, owner of the
club, dropping his cane in the excitement.

The Washingtonians were not
done then, though they lost the
ball on downs after storming up to
the 14, from where two Baugh
passes into the end zone barely
missed connections.

In the third quarter the Braves
clinched matters. Farkas, an in-
different performer earlier, caught
fire. He carried the ball nine of
eleven times in a 43-yard march
overland, going across from the 1.
He fumbled when he hit pay dirt,
but the tally had been called before he dropped the ball. Then he
retired for the afternoon.

O'Rourke was the big gun in two
stabbing Bear aerial assaults in
the final quarter. In one sequence
he pitched for 49 yards of a 52-
yard advance, and then it was for
78 of 79. But after Gallarneau's
touchdown was recalled, the Redskins finally wrested the ball on
downs less than three minutes
from the end of the game.

December 14, 1942

FOOTBALL LEAGUE APPROVES MERGER

Eagles and Steelers Combine —Cards-Bears Union Out —Eight Teams to Play

By The Associated Press.

CHICAGO, June 19—Eight of
last year's ten National Football
League teams elected tonight to
play professional ball in the 1943
season after the club owners had
approved a merger of the Pittsburgh Steelers and Philadelphia
Eagles.

Two other clubs which sought
to merge, the Bears and Cardinals,
both of Chicago, withdrew their
application after the league had
forced through two rules constituting a stiff barrier to such con-

solidation. Then the circuit relaxed
the rules somewhat to allow the
Pennsylvania members to merge.

The team will have no city designation but will play most of its
home games in Philadelphia. The
Eagles will have the one vote in
league business for the combine.

Walter Kiesling of Pittsburgh
and Earle Neale of Philadelphia
will be co-coaches under the new
set-up.

The league will be represented
this fall by these eight clubs:
The Cardinals, Bears, Detroit
Lions and Green Bay Packers in
the West and the New York
Giants, Brooklyn Dodgers, Washington Redskins and the Pitts-
burgh-Philadelphia combine in the
East.

The Cleveland Rams withdrew
from the circuit last April.

Apparently because of the power
that would be concentrated should
the Cardinals and Bears consoli-
date, the league cut off their attempt by passing a rule forbidding
the merging of player talent.
Later, however, this was relaxed,
allowing the Steelers and Eagles

to pool their athletes but at the
same time retain only a single vote
in league affairs. The merger will
be effective only for the 1943 season.

The league's executive committee called in representatives of several groups seeking franchises and
promptly vetoed an application by
Arthur H. Ehlers and Jimmy
Marks of Baltimore. The franchise
was refused because the group had
no coach or players available.

The Eagles and Steelers came to
Chicago seeking a merger, and the
Bears and Cards started a similar
move during the morning session.

Marshall Leads Bloc

A "status quo" group led by
George Marshall, owner of the
Washington Redskins, and believed
to include Earl Lambeau of Green
Bay, Fred Mandel of Detroit, Jack
Mara of the Giants and Pete Caw-
thon, newly employed coach and
"general administrator" of the
Dodgers, immediately forced
through two "conditions of merger" which appeared to be a bar to
such unions.

By a 5-to-2 vote, with Halas
and Bidwell not balloting, the own-

ers decreed that in the event of
two teams merging, the players
could not be a part of the combine; in other words, members of
one team would be thrown on the
league's open market. Also, they
decided the merged clubs would
have a single vote instead of two.

Murray Files Application

Left waiting in the lobby
through all of this were representatives of several groups seeking admittance to the league. In
addition to the five franchise applications received earlier, the
league got a sixth today from
Charley Murray, Buffalo, N. Y.,
promoter who has worked hand
in glove with the league in presenting games in his city for the
last five years.

His franchise bid conflicted with
that of Don Ameche, movie actor,
who also wants to run a team in
Buffalo, while duplicate requests
for the Boston rights were filed
by Ted Collins, manager of Kate
Smith, the singer, and by Frank
Mandel of the Chicago department
store family.

June 20, 1943

Bears Defeat Redskins for Pro Title on Luckman's Five Touchdown Passes

By WILLIAM D. RICHARDSON
Special to THE NEW YORK TIMES.

CHICAGO, Dec. 26—Forced to
stand idly by for four weeks awaiting election returns from the East,
the Chicago Bears vent their pent-
up fury on the Washington Redskins today when they won their
sixth National Football League
championship as easily as
falling off a log.

With Sid Luckman, former Co-

lumbia star, who was singing his
swan song to pro football at least
for the duration, setting a new
play-off-game record by tossing
five touchdown passes, the Bears
smothered the Redskins by the
score of 41 to 21, an achievement
thoroughly enjoyed by the crowd
of 34,320 at Wrigley Field.

The edge was taken off the
Bears' triumph to a large extent
by an injury suffered by Sammy

Baugh in the opening quarter on
the first play he was in.

Sammy did not start the game,
but came in soon after the kick-
off. After punting to Luckman,
the Skins' star passer was knocked
unconscious by a blow from Sid's
knee in making the tackle. Attempts to snap Baugh out of his
fog failed, and he was taken off
the field to the dressing room during the second quarter.

It was not until the third period
that Baugh was able to return to
action. By that time the game was
lost beyond hope, the Bears having
put across three touchdowns during his absence to one for the defending champions.

The crowd, somewhat below expectation, considering that the day
was mild, paid a total of $120,-
500.05, setting a new play-off rec-

Slingin' Sammy Baugh of the Washington Redskins was pro football's first great passer. Here, in a 1938 game with the Giants, he just manages to get one off before being hit.

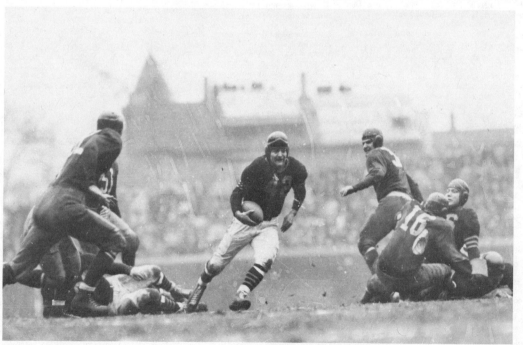

Chicago Bears' quarterback Sid Luckman could pick up yards on the ground as well as in the air. Luckman is shown here gaining 16 yards against the Redskins in the 1943 NFL championship game.

ord. The players' pool amounted to $68,679.58. Of his the Bears received $37,086.98, or $1,135.81 per man, while the Skins' balm was $24,724.65, which meant $754.60 for each man. This, too, set a new mark.

Luckman essayed a new role today, that of running, and gained 64 yards in eight attempts, one of his surprise sprints setting up the second Bear touchdown, but it was his throwing and patrol work that turned the hatchets against wielders, who have been somewhat of a thorn in the Bears' flesh in recent years.

Sid, who goes into the Maritime Service on Jan. 3, terminating an illustrious five-year career in pro football during which he has been such a large factor in the success of the T-formation, completed thirteen out of twenty-four attempts for a total of 276 yards and not one of his tosses was intercepted.

Pilfers Three Tosses

He, on the other hand, pilfered three of Washington's passes, at least two, at critical junctures, which gave him another record to take into the service with him. Up to today the high mark for playoff game interceptions was held by Charley Brock of the Packers with two against the Giants in 1939, a feat duplicated by Joe Maniaci of the Bears against Washington in the 1940 game.

Luckman's feat in completing five touchdown passes cost Baugh a record he had held when he threw three here against the Bears in 1937.

The Bears' quarterback cut in two of his mates on the record-breaking or equaling field day for fleet-footed Harry Clark and the equally fast-stepping Dante Magnani, who scored a brace of touchdowns each during the game after being "hit" by Sid's accurate throws, now are in a tie with Bill Karr and Wayne Millner in that department. Karr scored twice on passes for the Bears against the Giants in 1933 and Millner of the Skins matched the performance against the Bears in 1937.

After a scoreless first quarter, the Bears, with Baugh in the dressing room trying to pull the loose threads in his brain together, scored twice in the second period and then, after Sammy's return to the scene of action, twice in each of the last two periods.

Skins Are Downcast

The Skins, downcast by the calamity that had befallen them, were only able to click for one touchdown per period after they got started in the second stanza.

Coming as early as it did, Baugh's injury cast a pall over the game, robbing it of the thrill that was expected to come when Sammy and Luckman, two of the greatest passers of all time, met in the playoff game. Whether the Skins could have won, even with Baugh in, is a question that never will be answered although it can and probably will be argued for a long time to come.

The Redskins scored first when Andy Farkas went over from only a few inches out in the first play of the second period, but the Bears were quick to retaliate, with Clark taking a screen pass from Luckman and running thirty yards after an unidentified Washington tackler missed him on the line of scrimmage 31 yards from the goal line. Ray Hare, the Skins' quarterback, made a lunge at Clark

Pro Football Champions

1921—Chicago Bears.
1922—Canton Bulldogs.
1923—Canton Bulldogs.
1924—Cleveland.
1925—Chicago Cardinals.
1926—Frankford Yellow Jackets.
1927—New York Giants.
1928—Providence Steam Rollers.
1929—Green Bay Packers.
1930—Green Bay Packers.
1931—Green Bay Packers.
1932—Chicago Bears.
*1933—Chicago Bears.
1934—New York Giants.
1935—Detroit Lions.
1936—Green Bay Packers.
1937—Washington Redskins.
1938—New York Giants.
1939—Green Bay Packers.
1940—Chicago Bears.
1941—Chicago Bears.
1942—Washington Redskins.
1943—Chicago Bears.
*Year play-offs started.

on the goal line but failed to connect.

Subsequently, in the same period, old Bronko Nagurski bashed his way over left guard from the 3 to put the Bears out in front.

Bob Masterson had converted after Farkas' touchdown and Bob Snyder's boots had both been good, so at half-time the score was Bears 14, Washington 7.

It was Luckman who set the stage for Nagurski's touchdown, Sid getting away from Clyde Shugart and racing 24 yards around left end for a first down on the Skins' 21 and then, two plays later, sneaking through the middle for 15 yards and a first down on the 3.

One of Luckman's important interceptions paved the way for the Bears' third touchdown in the third period. Snatching one of George Cafego's tosses, Sid raced 21 yards to the Skins' 42 and then hit Magnani out in the right flat and Dante reversed his field, outfaking Frank Seno and then outrunning Cafego to the corner.

Near the end of the session Sid and Magnani again collaborated on a screen pass play and Dante ran 60 yards all by his lonesome to score. The play itself covered 66 yards. With a minute and a half left in the period, Baugh connected with Farkas in the end zone seventeen yards away.

Luckman, never one to play favorites, in the last quarter gave Jim Benton a chance to score the Bears' fifth touchdown, shooting one that the big ex-Ram end took behind Lee Stasica in the end zone for a 29-yard gain. Later on he got back to Clark again, shooting a 16-yarder to Harry.

Just to show what might have happened had he been able to play throughout the game instead of only in patches of the second half after his early injury, Baugh gave

STATISTICS OF THE GAME

	Bears	R'dskins
First downs	12	11
Yards gained, rushing	168	45
Forward passes	27	22
Forwards completed	13	10
Yards gained, forwards	276	118
Forwards intercepted by	4	0
Number of punts	5	5
†Av. dist. of punts, yds.	42	48.4
Runback of punts, yds.	66	37
Fumbles	0	1
Own fumbles recovered	0	1
Penalties	9	2
Yards lost, penalties	81	20

†From point where ball was kicked.

the Reds their final marker with two consecutive tosses, one to Wilbur Moore, good for 24, and the other to Joe Aguirre from 25 yards out into the Bears' end zone.

It was an interference ruling by Referee Roland Gibbs that was responsible for Washington's opening touchdown. This gave the Redskins a first down on the Chicago 3, from where Farkas went over in two tries.

The line-up:

BEARS (41)		REDSKINS (21)
Benton	L.E.	Masterson
Sigillo	L.T.	Rymkus
Fortmann	L.G.	Shugart
Turner	C.	G. Smith
Musso	R.G.	Slivinski
Hoptowit	R.T.	Pasqua
Wilson	R.E.	Aguirre
Snyder	Q.B.	R. Hare
Clark	L.H.	Cafego
Magnani	R.H.	Seno
Masters	F.B.	Farkas

SCORE BY PERIODS

Bears	0	14	13	14—41
Redskins	0	7	7	7—21

Touchdowns—Magnani 2, Clark 2, Farkas 2, Nagurski, Benton, Aguirre. Points after touchdown—Snyder 5, Masterson 2, Aguirre (placements).

SUBSTITUTES

Bears—Ends: Pool, Berry. Tackles: Steinkemper, Babartsky, Mundee. Guards: Ippolito, Logan. Center: Bray. Backs: McLean, Luckman, Famiglietti, Nagurski, McEnulty, Nolting.

Redskins—Ends: Piasecky, Lapka. Tackles: Wilkin, Zeno. Guards: Fiorentino, Leon. Center: Hayden. Backs: Baugh, Seymour, Moore, Gibson, Akins, Stasica.

Referee—Ronald Gibbs. Umpire—John Kelly. Field Judge—Eddie Tryon. Linesman—Charley Berry. Time of periods—15 minutes.

December 27, 1943

Steelers Merge With Cardinals For 1944 Pro Football Campaign

By The Associated Press.

PHILADELPHIA, April 22—The Pittsburgh Steelers and the Chicago Cardinals agreed late today to merge for the 1944 National Football League season. The league, which had asked the merger as one way to avoid schedule problems attendant upon an eleven-team circuit, immediately gave its blessing to the move.

Pittsburgh-Chicago will play in the Western Division, but the Steelers, who merged last year with the Philadelphia Eagles, made it clear they wished to play as a single team in the Eastern Division after this year.

This development left the league with five teams in each division. Boston, newest member, would have made the eleventh team but for the merger.

"Rover" Plan Not Feasible

George Strickler, league publicity director, announced that the merger was necessary because it was "absolutely impossible" to arrange a schedule for eleven separate teams, even by using the "rover" plan considered last night. This would have exempted one Eastern club from the usual home-and-home arrangements and allowed it to play each other club once. The hitch in this plan was that one club would have had to remain idle each Sunday and satisfactory dates for the "rover" could not be worked out.

The combined team, as yet unnamed, will get the use of any available players from the draft lists of both clubs. The league's waiver rule also was amended so that until the teams have played their first three games, the order of claiming players will be that of the first round of the draft this year. The Boston Yankees thus will get first choice and the Chicago-Pittsburgh team, second, at the beginning of the season. After three games, the clubs will choose according to their positions in current standings.

April 23, 1944

WARD TELLS PLANS FOR FOOTBALL LOOP

New Pro Circuit Will Operate in 1945—Mrs. Lou Gehrig an Owner of New York Team

By The Associated Press.

CHICAGO, Sept. 2—Organization of the All-America Football Conference, a new coast-to-coast professional football league sponsored by "men of millionaire incomes," was announced officially today by Arch Ward, sports editor of The Chicago Tribune and prime organizer of the new loop which will begin operations next year.

Ward said the league will include clubs in eight or possibly ten of the country's key cities, with seven franchises already granted.

Owners of franchises, Ward disclosed, were Chicago, John L. Keeshin, president of a trucking concern; New York, Mrs. Lou Gehrig, widow of the famous Yankee baseball player, and Ray J. Ryan, oil company president; Baltimore, Comdr. Gene Tunney, former heavyweight boxing champion; Buffalo, James Breuil and Will Bennett, oil company executives, and Sam Cordovano, construction company head.

Also Cleveland, Arthur McBride, taxicab magnate; Los Angeles, Don Ameche, actor, and Christy Walsh, former newspaper syndicate director, and San Francisco, Anthony J. Morabito and Allan E. Sorrell, co-owners of a lumber terminal concern, and Ernest J. Turre, construction company manager at Phoenix, Ariz.

In addition, Ward said, prominent business men in Detroit, Philadelphia and Boston are seeking franchises for those cities.

The owners adopted two resolutions which, according to Ward, "are certain to help shape the success of the Conference" and avoid talent raids on the long-established National League. They were:

1. No club will be allowed to employ a coach or player who is under contract to any team in the National Football League.

2. No player will be admitted into the organization who has college football eligibility remaining.

Pointing out that the wealthy owners of the new league "are prepared to engage in a battle of dollars" with the National loop, if necessary, Ward said the restriction on talent raids would avoid such conflicts.

The second resolution, he asserted, was intended to protect college football, since many undergraduate players whose careers were interrupted by war might prefer grabbing "quick money" in football to returning to their studies after the war.

September 3, 1944

LAYDEN QUITS POST; SUCCEEDED BY BELL

Resignation of Commissioner Big Surprise to National Football League Men

NEW CHIEF IN FOR 3 YEARS

Signing $20,000 Contract, He Will Sell Steelers' Stock— Ten-Club Limit Voted

By ROSCOE McGOWEN

Elmer Layden dropped a bombshell into the laps of the National Football League club owners last night by suddenly resigning as commissioner at a special meeting in the Hotel Commodore, where the league's annual session has been under way.

Bert Bell, co-owner with Art Rooney of the Pittsburgh Steelers, was promptly elected to succeed Layden for a three-year term, with a starting salary of $20,000 annually.

At the same time a contract was offered to Layden for an indefinite period, also at $20,000 annually, to serve the league in an advisory capacity. He was "considering this offer."

The retiring commissioner's statement, released by George Strickler, publicity director, follows:

"In view of some plans of my own I today tendered my resignation as commissioner of the National Football League at a special meeting of the club owners. The owners have requested me to ac-

cept a contract to serve in an advisory capacity for an indefinite period. I am considering this offer as mine has been a grand experience with the National League."

Layden made himself "unavailable" some time before the announcement of his resignation. Strickler told newspaper men that Layden had left the hotel and would not return last night.

Report of Ouster Denied

Bell flatly denied a report that Layden had been ousted. "That is not true, not true at all," said the new commissioner. "Elmer resigned."

"I don't think Elmer's personal plans have anything to do with football," said Strickler. Asked whether there had been opposition to renewal of Layden's contract, which would have run until April 1 next, Strickler replied:

"No man could hold a job like that and not find some opposition somewhere." Then he added: "I was the most surprised fellow in the world and I think some of the owners perhaps were more surprised than I."

Strickler said the league offices would be moved from Chicago to New York.

Bell, found at a late dinner in a midtown restaurant, was calm about his elevation to the commissionership.

"I never sought the job," he said, "but I am honored. I will proceed with the job much along the same lines followed by Layden, fairly conservative and not too aggressive. I won't seek any fights, but I won't dodge any that may come my way."

Asked about his half ownership in the Steelers, Bell said "of course" he would dispose of his stock and that Rooney would buy it.

"There'll be nobody else in with him, I think," said Bell. "I'm the only partner he ever had, I believe. Of course, as was announced at the time the Steelers signed Jock Sutherland, he received an option to buy a certain number of shares within a period of five years."

Bell Graduate of Penn

The new commissioner, 52 years old, has been associated with football almost constantly since his youth. Bell attended Penn from 1915 to 1917, then served thirteen months with the United States Army in France. Re-entering Penn he captained the football team in 1919, then after graduation served as backfield coach from 1920 to 1928.

During 1930-31 he was backfield coach for Temple University and in 1933 bought the Philadelphia Eagles, with Lud Wray, former Penn mentor, as his coach. From 1937 through 1940, Bell coached the Eagles himself, then sold the club to Alexis Thompson in 1941. He became co-owner with Rooney of the Steelers in 1941. For the season of 1943 the Steelers were combined with the Eagles and the following season hooked up with the Chicago Cardinals. Last year the team again operated as a separate unit.

Layden, fullback of Notre Dame's "four horsemen," served seven years as head coach of his alma mater, starting in 1933. He resigned on Feb. 3, 1941, to accept the commissionership for a five-year term at $20,000 a year.

During the afternoon, the league voted two drastic changes in its

IN NATIONAL FOOTBALL COMMISSIONER SHIFT

Bert Bell   **Elmer Layden**

constitution. First the owners, meeting as a constitutional committee, voted to limit membership to ten clubs. Second, they ruled that never again would two franchises be allowed to any one city.

As insurance that these two rules would remain, they voted that neither could be abrogated save by unanimous vote. These actions obviously were aimed generally at the new All-America Conference and specifically at the New York Yankees.

"The idea has been advanced," said Strickler, "that one or more of these clubs might seek to affiliate with our league, with the All-America fading out of the football picture. This action slams the door right in their faces."

The move, of course, does not affect the status of the two Chicago clubs, the Bears and Cardinals, since the rule change applies to future action.

January 12, 1946

CLEVELAND RAMS TRANSFER ELEVEN TO LOS ANGELES

CLUB WILL SEEK COLISEUM

By ROSCOE McGOWEN

The National Football League tossed another bomb at the rival All-America Conference yesterday when, in a late afternoon special session of the club owners in the Hotel Commodore, it granted permission to the champion Cleveland Rams to transfer their franchise to Los Angeles.

While no official mention of their infant rival came in this announcement, obviously the NFL boys felt that they had taken another solid belt at the All-America, which already has a club in the Coast metropolis.

The official reason given for the move, as voiced by 33-year-old Daniel F. Reeves, Rams' owner, is that he believes "Los Angeles has the greatest football future of any city in America." The transfer "is effective as of this date," Reeves said.

Reeves said that he is applying for a long-term lease on the giant

Los Angeles Coliseum, which has a seating capacity of 103,000, through his Coast attorney, J. C. Macfarland. The big stadium is controlled by a committee of three representatives, each from city, county and State, and this committee will be met on next Tuesday by the Rams' representatives.

January 13, 1946

Graham Leads Cleveland Eleven to Victory Over Yankees in Title Play-Off

BROWN RALLY TOPS NEW YORKERS, 14-9

Cleveland Touchdown in Last Period Wins All-America Honors Before 40,469

YANKEES FIRST TO TALLY

Johnson Kicks Field Goal in Opening Quarter—Passing of Graham Decisive Factor

STATISTICS OF THE GAME

	Browns	Yanks
First downs	18	10
Yards gained, rushing	102	65
Forward passes	27	20
Forwards completed	16	8
Yards gained, forwards	213	81
Forwards intercepted by	1	1
Number of punts	5	5
†Av. dist. of punts, yds.	47.8	39.2
Run-back of punts, yds.	20	5
Fumbles	3	2
Own fumbles recovered	3	1
Penalties	5	4
Yards lost, penalties	25	20

†From point where ball was kicked.

By WILLIAM D. RICHARDSON
Special to THE NEW YORK TIMES.

CLEVELAND, Dec. 22—It was a case of too much Graham for the Yankees in today's All-America Football Conference play-off in Cleveland's Municipal Stadium as the Browns came from behind in the last quarter to defeat the New Yorkers, 14 to 9, and win the new league's first championship.

Trailing 7 to 9 in the final period before a shivering crowd of 40,469, the Browns made the deciding touchdown with less than five minutes to go.

With the ball on the Yankee 16, Graham, whose throwing had the Yankees baffled most of the day, fired to Dante Lavelli, Cleveland's ace receiver, who had outrun both Jack Russell, end, and Speck Sanders, Yankee fullback. Grabbing the ball only a few steps away from the goal-line, Lavelli sprinted across for winning points.

The touchdown ended a 76-yard drive by the hard-pressed Browns. The local team had a marked advantage over the Yankees in the statistical department up to that point, but was close to being defeated by a courageous rival.

Interception Saves Day

A few minutes later, Graham saved the day for the Browns by intercepting one of Ace Parker's tosses after Sanders had returned Chet Adams' kick-off thirty-five yards. The fast-moving Texan appeared to be on the way to a touchdown when he broke loose and sprinted toward the Browns' goal escorted by a flock of Yan-

kees. He was finally brought down on the Brown forty-six. Eddie Prokop lost twelve on the next play, but Parker got it all back with a pass to Perry Schwartz, who made a great catch. Then Ace tried another. This was the one that Graham intercepted, ending the last chance for the Yankees with time so nearly run out.

The New York eleven was first to score when Harvey Johnson, their ace kicker, booted a field goal from the 21-yard mark with the game only a little more than five minutes old.

The Browns struck back in the next period when Marion Motley, their big Negro fullback, plowed through one and a half yards for a touchdown. Lou (The Toe) Groza, leading point-maker in the league, kicked the point that put the Browns in front, 7 to 3, at the half. This drive covered 74 yards, starting with Graham's 13-yard return of Parker's punt.

The Yankees got the lead back in the third quarter as Sanders crashed 2 yards to wind up an 80-yard drive in which Parker's passes to End Jack Russell gained the most ground.

That looked to be "it" so far as the Yankees were concerned, for they had managed to hold the Browns away from pay dirt. After that first thrust Groza missed three attempted field goal shots and Chet Adams failed in one. They were either too short or wide of the mark.

Groza's first attempt came in the second period when he tried one of 52 yards. It was low and bounced in to the end zone. He had another chance from the 42 in the third period, but it went wide, as did his third attempt early in the fourth period from the 30-yard marker. Adams made his try from the 37.

Jones and Colella Star

The decisive blow by the Browns started with Graham's two-yard run back of Parker's punt to his own 24. The Browns went all the way from there, Graham hitting Edgar (Special Delivery) Jones for a 24-yard gain that gave the Clevelanders a first down on the Yankees' 42. Jones then went to a first down on the 27, after which Tom Colella broke away for 11 and a first down on the 16. The Browns tallied on the next play. Graham pitched the ball to Lavelli, and he just outran the Yankee defenders.

The Browns had a big advantage over the Yankees with 102 yards rushing against 65 and 213 yards passing to only 81.

Graham, who did all the Browns' tossing, completed sixteen out of twenty-seven. This was his best game this year, his first in pro football. In Lavelle and MacSpeedie the Browns had two ends who gave the Yankees trouble all the way. Another thorn in the Yankees' side was John Yonakor, former Notre Dame end, who spent a large part of the time in the Yankee backfield, spoiling several of Parker's passing attempts and making himself otherwise obnoxious.

A third Brown hero was Motley, who, in addition to scoring one of the touchdowns, broke loose for one of the game's longest gains—a 51-yard gallop that put the Browns in position for one of Groza's field-goal shots. Altogether Motley carried the ball thirteen times for a total of 98 yards, making him the day's leading ground gainer with an average of 7.5 yards.

Sanders was the top performer for the losers with 55 yards to his credit in fourteen trips. Parker

completed eight out of eighteen heaves.

All things considered it was a game that measured up to play-off standards. It was played on a field that, although slippery after the tarpaulin covering had been removed, was as good as could be expected.

The crowd, although far below expectations, was an enthusiastic one. Last year when the Rams and the Redskins played here the thermometer was at the zero point, but today it was in the 30's and there was little or no wind to speak of. Except for the playing area, the field was covered with snow, which fell most of yesterday afternoon, scaring off thousands of fans from near-by cities who had planned to attend.

Conference officials had hoped to break the marks set up by the Giants and Bears in the Polo Grounds last week, when 58,346 fans paid $282,955.25.

The line-up:

BROWNS (14)		YANKEES (9)
Speedie	L.E.	Russell
Blandin	L.T.	F. Kinard
Ulinski	L.G.	Baldwin
Scarry	C.	Robertson
Houston	R.G.	Riffle
Rymkus	R.T.	N. Johnson
Lavelli	R.E.	Alford
Graham	Q.B.	Cheatham
Jones	L.H.	Prokop
Greenwood	R.H.	Wagner
Motley	F.B.	Sanders

SCORE BY PERIODS

Browns	0	7	0	7—14
Yankees	3	0	6	0— 9

Touchdowns—Motley, Lavelli, Sanders. Points after touchdowns—Groza 2 (placements). Field goal—H. Johnson (placement).

SUBSTITUTES

Browns—Backs: Schwenk, Saban, Fekete, Smith, Terrell, Colella. Ends: Yonakor, Young, Harrington. Tackles: Adams, Groza. Guard: Willis. Center: Gatski.
Yankees—Backs: Morrow, Kennedy, H. Johnson, Manders, Sweiger, Perina, Parker. Ends: Burrus, Masterson, Schwartz. Tackles: Palmer, Piskor, Bentz. Guards: Karmazin, Yakanich. Centers: Sossamon.
Referee—Thomas Timlin. Umpire—Tommy Hughitt. Field judge—Earl Gross. Linesman—Lou Gordon. Side lines judge—Hal Slutz.

December 23, 1946

Hapes and Filchock Barred Indefinitely by National League

PRO CAREERS END FOR 2 GIANT BACKS

PHILADELPHIA, April 3 (AP)—Merle Hapes and Frank Filchock, New York Giants' backfield stars who became entangled in gamblers' attempts to "fix" the National Football League's championship play-off last Dec. 15, today were suspended indefinitely in the latest chapter of the biggest sports scandal since the 1919 World Series.

Commissioner Bert Bell found the two "guilty of actions detrimental to the welfare of the National League and of professional football." He added: "This suspen-

sion prevents the employment of Hapes or Filchock by any club in the National Football League as player, coach or in any capacity whatsoever."

The commissioner's ruling virtually wrote finis to the playing days of Hapes, who once roamed the backfield at the University of Mississippi, and Filchock, a pro star since leaving the Indiana University campus.

The decision followed by twenty-four hours sentencing of three New York men for attempting to bribe the players to throw the game. David K. Krakauer, Harvey Stemmer and Jerome Zarowitz received prison sentences while a fourth man, Alvin Paris, will be sentenced Monday.

Suspensions Ordered Jan. 8

Testimony at the trial of the four showed that neither Hapes

nor Filchock had accepted the bribes offered. Both were placed on the league's suspended list originally on Jan. 8, the day Paris was convicted in New York on charges of having tried to "fix" the game between the Giants and Chicago Bears.

Hapes was not permitted to play in that game, won by the Bears, 24—14. The former Mississippi star admitted to Mayor William O'Dwyer of New York a few hours before the game that he had received the offer. Filchock, a great passer playing with the Giants for the first season after understudying Sammy Baugh at Washington, denied he had been approached.

During the Paris trial, however, Filchock admitted he had not told the New York Mayor the truth. Paris testified that he had made an offer of $2,500 in cash and a $1,000 bet to Hapes a week before the game and said he had made the same offer to the ex-Indiana player two days later.

Paris also testified that neither player had accepted. During the week before the title game, he said, he had attempted to change their minds but the day before the fray became convinced they would not accept the offers.

Bell, while declining to comment on his ruling, pointed out that he was penalizing the two players the limit—except for a possible fine—under the rules in effect at the time of the bribe attempt. He added, however, that had the code adopted at the league's January meeting been in force, he would have had the power to bar both for life.

"Bit Stiff," Says Hapes

Hapes, who recently accepted a coaching position at the Bryan Consolidated School near Jackson, Miss., felt Commissioner Bell's action "was a little bit stiff."

"It's a bunch of baloney about hurting the league," he added. "All that they got against us is just not reporting the attempt. I don't think we did anything to hurt the league, but I'm through with professional football, anyway."

In Washington, Filchock said:

"I haven't made any future plans simply because I never thought of being out of football. I still want to play football. I guess I always will."

Bell purposely held back his ruling until New York authorities had completed their investigation. He said: "I want publicly to thank them for their cooperation. They did a great job of investigating every angle.

Bell's two-fisted blows at bribery and gambling occurred just short of fourteen months after he had succeeded Elmer Layden as commissioner. At the time the club owners wanted someone "tough" as leader in the fight with the infant All-America Football Conference.

In his first season the league smashed all attendance records, but it was not until the wee, small hours of Dec. 15 that he was called on to make his first important decision—at least so far as the public was concerned.

On hearing of the attempted bribery he ruled that Hapes was ineligible to play but that Filchock could participate in the play-off. At the time Filchock denied he had been approached by gamblers. For a time Bell held back Hapes' share of the players' pool, but later gave it to him when Merle testified he had refused the offered bribe.

The 48-year-old, chunky, black-haired Bell long has been connected with the gridiron sport as player, coach, both college and professional, and owner. He was captain of the 1919 University of Pennsylvania eleven and joined the National League as owner of the Philadelphia Eagles in 1933.

"I never had a tougher decision to make than in this case," he said of the suspensions dealt out to Hapes and Filchock that rate as the most severe punishments ever handed down by a National Football League commissioner. In the past Ken Strong, also of the Giants, and Howie Weiss of the Detroit Lions had been suspended five years each on charges of contract jumping.

The text of Bell's decision:

Professional football cannot continue to exist unless it is based upon absolute honesty. The players must be not only absolutely

honest; they must be above suspicion. In short, the game and its players must be kept free from corruption, from all bribes and offers of bribes, and from any possible "fixing" of games.

I have given Merle Allison Hapes and Frank Filchock a hearing and an opportunity to tell me everything either of them desired to say in connection with the attempts of Alvin Paris to bribe them or either of them. I have carefully considered all of the statements each of these players has made as well as all the testimony in the court case of the people of the State of New York against Alvin Paris and in the court case of the people of the State of New York against David Krakauer, Harvey Stemmer and Jerome Zarowitz.

As commissioner of the National Football League, I find Merle Allison Hapes and Frank Filchock guilty of actions detrimental to the welfare of the National Football League and of professional football and I hereby suspend each of them indefinitely. This suspension prevents the employment of Hapes or Filchok by any club in the National Football League as player, coach or in any capacity whatsoever.

April 4, 1947

ACTS AGAINST GAMBLERS

Bell Orders Advance Notice on Injured Stars' Condition

WASHINGTON, July 15 (U.P.)—Commissioner Bert Bell of the National Football League today directed coaches and publicity directors of all league teams to publish in advance of each game the names of injured players unable to or unlikely to play. He said the new ruling was aimed at protecting the public against professional gamblers.

Bell pointed out that in the past coaches may have withheld injury information for purely strategic reasons. But, he said, such information almost always has been available to professional gamblers through their own agents, with the result they could manipulate betting points and odds to their advantage.

Henceforth coaches and publicity directors must make public before each game the names of injured players who "cannot play" or "may not play." Those withholding such information will be subject to punishment to be prescribed by Bell.

Bell also said he has in his possession the names of all big-time professional gamblers in each National League city.

July 16, 1947

87-Point Total Sets a New Mark As Eagles Top Redskins, 45-42

PHILADELPHIA, Sept. 28 (AP)—The Eagles and Redskins smashed all National Football League scoring records today with the Eagles finishing on the long end of a 45-42 count before a crowd of 35,400 at Municipal Stadium.

In piling up a total of 87 points and topping the previous high of 79 by Green Bay and the Chicago Cardinals in 1942, the Eagles and Redskins each scored six touchdowns, with the Philadelphians winning by the margin of Joe Muha's 40-yard field goal three minutes after the game got under way.

Long Toss by Baugh

The twelve touchdowns also set a National Football League record of most touchdowns scored by two teams. The old mark of eleven touchdowns was first set on Nov. 1, 1942. when the Packers rolled up eight scores and the Cardinals three, and equaled on Oct. 5 by the Packers (eight) and Detroit Lions (three), and again in the 1946 opener here when the Eagles crossed the final marker seven times and the Boston Yanks four times.

The Eagles sprinted away to a 10-0 lead in the first period, held a 24-14 margin at the half and a 38-28 advantage at the end of the third quarter, but they were hard pressed to hold their lead as 33-year-old Sammy Baugh tossed two touchdown passes to Hugh Taylor, rookie end from Oklahoma City University, in the last period.

Taylor also scored the Redkins' second touchdown in the second period, crossing the goal line on the end of a 62-yard pass from Baugh. His touchdowns in the final stanza were on a 36-yard aerial after he had combined with Slingin' Sam to move the ball through the air from the Skins', 29, and an 18-yard pass.

95-Yard Kick-off Return

Baugh completed a total of 21 of 34 passes for 364 yards, to run his total number of completed aerials in eleven years of National Football League play to 1,013.

After Muha had booted his field goal in the first period, the Eagles traveled 62 yards for their opening touchdown with Pete Pihos, first-

year end from Indiana University, catching a 19-yard pass from Tommy Thompson for the score.

The Redskins lost no time taking command in the second period as Baugh passed 25 yards to Bob Nussbaumer for a score and then 62 yards to Taylor for his 1,000th completed aerial.

But Steve Van Buren personally conducted the Eagles back into the lead on a 95-yard kick-off return and before the half ended the Eagles traveled 63 yards for another score. Al Sherman sneaked over from the one-yard line for the marker but the ball was put there on Van Buren's runs and passes from Tommy Thompson to Pihos.

Each team scored twice in the third, the Skins counting on the opening kick-off as Eddie Saenz raced 94 yards with the ball. The Eagles bounded back with Van Buren ending a 70-yard drive in hitting pay dirt from the two-yard stripe and Pihos taking a 21-yard pass from Thompson.

The second Washington touchdown of the period was a 57-yard pass from Baugh to Dick Poillon. Early in the final quarter Neil Armstrong, heralded freshman from Oklahoma A. and M., got into his first program and on the first play took a 29-yard aerial from Thompson to complete the Eagles' scoring.

Poillon and Cliff Patton added all of their extra points from placement. The line-up:

EAGLES (45)		REDSKINS (42)
Ferrante	L.E.	Lockabaugh
Sears	L.T.	Boensch
Patton	L.G.	Peebles
Wojciechowicz	C.	Aldrich
Kilroy	R.G.	Gray
Wistert	R.T.	Adams
Pihos	R.E.	Tereschinski
Kish	Q.B.	Poillon
Van Buren	L.H.	Gaffney
Pritchard	R.H.	Wilde
Muha	F.B.	Jenkins

SCORE BY PERIODS

Eagles	10	14	14	7—45
Redskins	0	14	14	14—42

Touchdowns—Pihos 2, Van Buren 2, Sherman (for Kish), Armstrong (for Green), Nussbaumer (for Wilde), Taylor 3 (for Lockabaugh), Saenz (for Gaffney). Poillon. Points after touchdowns—Patton 6. Poillon 6 (placements). Field goal—Muha (placement).

SUBSTITUTES

Eagles—Ends: Green, Prescott, Armstrong. Tackles: McDowell, Douglas, Campion. Guards: Maronic, Wyhonic, Baisi, Weedon. Center: Williams. Backs: Steele, Steinke, Thompson, Sherman, Hinkle, Doss, McHugh, Mackrides, Macioszcyk.

Redskins—Ends: Taylor, Duckworth, McKee, Turley. Tackles: Avery, Williams, Harris. Guards: Steber, Garzons, Ward. Center: Demao. Backs: Saenz, Baugh, Youel, Nussbaumer, Defruleter, Musiak, Rosato, Ruthstrom, Mont.

September 29, 1947

LUCKMAN, BAUGH SUPREME

Ace Passers Found to Have Set Three Records on Sunday

PHILADELPHIA, Oct. 27 (AP)—Sid Luckman and Sammy Baugh, perhaps the two greatest passers in football history, teamed to establish three new passing marks in Sunday's clash in which the Chicago Bears defeated the Washington Redskins 56—20, league statisticians disclosed today.

Luckman, pitching for the Bears, and Baugh, who teamed with his understudy, Jim Youel, in doing the Skins' chucking, hurled a total

of 84 passes, completed 51 and gained 631 yards. Each figure represents a new total for two teams.

The previous record was established where it was broken, at Washington's Griffith Stadium, and the same Mr. Baugh participated in that hurling marathon on Dec. 1, 1940.

Baugh, however, tossed only seven, completing five, while Davey O'Brien of the Philadelphia Eagles threw 60, completing 33. Thus the pair tossed 67, completed 38 and gained 352 yards.

Incidentally, the Skins won the game 13—6.

October 28, 1947

Major Professional Football Rivals Form 13-Club National-American League

THREE A. A. C. TEAMS ENTER NEW CIRCUIT

49ers, Browns, Colts and All of National League Survive 4-Year Pro Football War

BULLDOGS BUY OUT YANKS

But Giants Will Get 6 Men— Bell Signs for 10 Seasons to Head 2-Division Loop

PHILADELPHIA, Dec. 9 (AP)—Professional football's four-year war was settled across a conference table today. The All-America Conference merged into the National Football League.

Thus ended one of the most costly wars in the history of athletics. Losses to club owners soared upward of $2,000,000 in the protracted battle for players and attendance.

The new league is to be called the National-American Football League—the NAF. It is to be made up of thirteen teams: The complete ten-club National and three from the fledgling conference.

Nobody said so at the hastily summoned press conference at which the report was flashed, but the merger unquestionably was a victory for the older National League, which fought for four years to drive the All-America out of business.

Bert Bell, chubby, affable Philadelphia main liner, remains at the helm of the new league as commissioner. He signed for a new 10-year pact at an undisclosed salary. Bell had been commissioner of the National.

Emil R. Fischer of the Green Bay Packers will become president of the new league's National division. Daniel Sherby of the Cleveland Browns will head the American division.

Commissioner Kessing Out

O. O. Kessing, commissioner of the A.A.C., resigns at the close of the current season. He tendered his resignation some weeks ago.

If there is one man responsible for the merger, it is Horace Stoneham, ruddy-faced owner of the New York Baseball Giants. Stoneham is owner of the Polo Grounds, where two New York National League teams played in 1949 and lost a considerable amount of money.

Bell and J. Arthur Friedlund, representing the conference, revealed Stoneham had started the merger move by summoning Bell and Friedlund to New York last Friday. They talked for a while there and then came to Philadel-

phia two days ago. Round-the-clock conferences ended shortly after noon today when the two men, tired but jubilant, broke the news.

Bell, unshaved but beaming, joined with the dapper Friedlund to announce the new league had been conceived "not only in the interest of the public but also to assure the permanency of professional football."

These are the thirteen teams in the NAF:

From the National: Philadelphia, New York Giants, New York Bulldogs, Washington, Pittsburgh, Chicago Bears, Chicago Cardinals, Detroit, Green Bay and Los Angeles.

From the conference: San Francisco Forty - Niners, Cleveland Browns, Baltimore Colts.

Season to End Dec. 19

The league is to be split into National and American divisions, with the winners meeting in a world football championship. Makeup of the divisions has not yet been determined. The new league will become official on Dec. 19, the day after the N.F.L. championship game.

The complication in the merger is what will happen to the players on the three conference teams liquidated in the move and to the college players already drafted by clubs in the two circuits for the 1950 season.

The A. A. C. and N. F. L. draft meetings were canceled. All of these players will be tossed into a giant pool when the N. A. F. gets together at its first meeting, tentatively arranged for January. It will take approval of 11 of the 13 teams for any player to be assigned to a new club.

Bell said that the only players not affected by the formation of the new league are the 32 players on each of the rosters of the 13 teams in the new league.

The two New York teams are special cases, however. Dan Topping's New York Yankees of the A. A. C. were purchased outright by Ted Collins, owner of the New York Bulldogs. Collins acquired the right to deal with all except six of the players on the Yankees.

Those six will go to the New York Giants. Names of the six players were not disclosed.

Hornets Broken Up

In addition to the Yankees, the Buffalo Bills, Los Angeles Dons and Chicago Hornets of the A. A. C. are going out of business. The Hornets are to be broken up completely, while the Dons merge with the Los Angeles Rams and the Bills with the Cleveland Browns.

James Breuil, owner of the Buffalo club of the A. A. C., acquired what Bell and Friedlund said was "a substantial interest" in the Browns and exclusive rights of that club to present exhibition games at Buffalo.

Professional football was born in 1895 in a game at Latrobe, Pa. Connie Mack, owner-manager of the Athletics, organized a team in 1902.

The National Football League was organized in 1921, although it wasn't known by that name until a year later. Its first name was

the American Professional Football Association. The league was reorganized in 1927 and six years later was split into eastern and western divisions with the winners playing for the world championship.

In 1946, however, eight teams got together and organized themselves as the All-America Conference. It was at that point that the war started.

Salaries of players soared into astronomical figures as teams from the two leagues fought a battle of dollars for their services. Competition between the leagues and owners' costs rose sharply, but there was no comparable rise in receipts.

Some club owners, notably Alexis Thompson of the Philadelphia Eagles in the N. F. L., quit the fight, saying it was costing too much. Others grumbled.

Last winter it appeared as if the two leagues would get together. Representatives met for three days at Philadelphia, but they couldn't

agree on a merger plan.

Hints of peace were dropped sporadically ever since then, but it wasn't until Stoneham got Bell and Friedlund together that something concrete was done.

Friedlund is general counsel and secretary of the baseball New York Yankees and the football Yankees. He and Bell and George Weiss, vice president and general manager of the baseball Yankees, conferred briefly in New York at Stoneham's invitation before the confab moved here and Weiss dropped out.

The merger plan had been a closely guarded secret. It was announced with unexpected suddenness.

"We do things in a hurry when we do them," Bell remarked.

"Especially when there's a lot of money involved," someone suggested.

Chortled Bell: "You're right."

December 10, 1949

Bears Down Cardinals, 52 to 21, As Lujack Passes for Six Scores

Quarterback Connects on 24 of 40 Aerials for 468-Yard Gain, New League Record —Kavanaugh, Hoffman Tally Twice

CHICAGO, Dec. 11 (AP)—Playing his finest game in two years as a Chicago Bear quarterback, Johnny Lujack flipped six touchdown passes and set a National Football League record with an aerial gain of 468 yards as his team routed the Chicago Cardinals, 52—21.

A Wrigley Field throng of 50,101 sat through a drizzle to watch the crosstown rivals battle in their fifty-seventh meeting on a slippery, muddy gridiron. It was the Bears' thirty-eighth victory in pro football's oldest rivalry and their ninth in twelve league starts this season.

Today's score also was the most decisive since the Northsiders hoisted a 53-7 verdict over the Cards in 1941.

Baugh's Record Smashed

Lujack's fancy aerial work bested by 22 yards the record gain of 446 registered by Washington's Sammy Baugh against Boston on Oct. 31, 1948. Lujack completed twenty-four out of forty tosses and connected for four touchdowns in the first half to give the Bears an overwhelming 31-7 edge.

The former Notre Dame star, who is on the Bear payroll for about $20,000 per season, missed by only one touchdown pitch of matching the league mark set by the Bears' Sid Luckman against the New York Giants in 1943.

As it was, Johnny nearly had three more pay-off pitches to his credit. In the first quarter, he hit

Statistics of the Game

	Bears.	Cards.
First downs	24	17
Yards gained, rushing	128	48
Forward passes	42	31
Forwards completed	24	19
Yards gained, forwards	468	280
Forwards intercepted by	2	3
*Av. dist. of punts, yds.	43.6	44.7
‡Runback of kicks, yds.	161	131
Rival fumbles recovered	2	1
Yards lost, penalties	102	50

*From line of scrimmage
‡Includes punts and kick-offs

Julie Rykovich for 12 yards only to have the receiver fumble on the 1-yard line. Ken Kavanaugh was brought down from behind on the Cardinal 2 after taking a 10-yard pass in the third. And in the fourth, Kavanaugh also was caught on the Card 12 after a 58-yard toss from Lujack.

Blanda Kicks Field Goal

The Bears clinched the game with two touchdowns in the first five minutes on Lujack's 52-yard toss to George McAfee and one for 17 yards to Kavanaugh.

In the second, Lujack connected with Kavanaugh for 37 and a third counter then hit Jackrabbit Boone for 18 and a fourth. George Blanda added a 25-yard field goal in the final minute of the second period.

The Bears struck again on the ground for an 80-yard touchdown parade at the outset of the third. George Gulyanics went over from the 2.

In the finale, Lujack's aerials paid off for 6 yards to John Hoffman and 65 to Hoffman. Lujack converted after each score.

The Cardinals, gaining 280 yards by passing, counted on Paul Christman's 3-yard flip to Charlie Trippi in the first, his 49-yard connection with Mal Kutner in the third, and his 19-yard completion to Trippi in the fourth.

Pat Harder converted, raising his scoring tally to 102 points for the season.

The line-up:

CHICAGO BEARS (52)
Left Ends—Kavanaugh, Milner, Dugger.
Left Tackles—Connor, Davis, Bauman.
Left Guards—Drulis, Preston, Flanagan.
Centers—Turner, Clarkson, Szymanski.
Right Guards—Bray, Serini.
Right Tackles—Stenn, Stickel.
Right Ends—Keane, Sprinkle.
Quarterbacks—Lujack, Blanda.
Left Halfbacks—Gulyanics, Boone, Dreyer, Magnani.
Right Halfbacks—Rykovich, McAfee, Perina, Deonrevont.
Fullbacks—Hoffman, Kindt, Cody.

CHICAGO CARDINALS (21)
Left Ends—Ravensberg, Dewell, Wham, Dove.
Left Tackles—Fischer, Goldsberry.
Left Guards—Petrovich, Coomer.
Centers—Blackburn, Banonis, Campbell.
Right Guards—Ramsey, Angiskis, Nichols.
Right Tackles—Andros, Zimny.
Right Ends—Kutner, Cain.
Quarterbacks—Christman, Hardy, Nussbaumer.
Left Halfbacks—Trippi, Davis, Cochran.
Right Halfbacks—Angsman, Self, Schwall.
Fullbacks—Harder, Clatt, Dimancheff, Yablonski.

SCORE BY PERIODS
Chicago Bears .... 14 17 7 14—52
Chicago Cardinals .... 7 0 7 7—21
Touchdowns—McAfee, Trippi 2 Kutner, Kavanaugh 2, Boone, Gulyanics, Hoffman 2. Field goal—Blanda. Points after touchdown—Lujack 4. Harder 3.

December 12, 1949

Sports of the Times
By ARTHUR DALEY
End of an Era?

THE loyalties of football coaches usually are neither as deep as the ocean nor as high as the sky. They flit hither and yon in ardent pursuit of the almighty dollar. Hence it comes as a distinct shock to discover that Curly Lambeau has brought to an abrupt termination his connection with the Green Bay Packers. After thirty-one years as the chief mahout of the Ponderous Pachyderms, the Bellicose Belgian has transferred his allegiances, his energies and his skills to the Chicago Cardinals.

The length of his tenure with the Packers would be sufficient of itself to make his switch a monumental one. But this was no ordinary relationship. The Green Bay team was Curly's baby. He founded it. He was present at its birth. It could also be that he left it on its deathbed. Lambeau and the Packers were virtually synonymous. Now Curly is gone and Green Bay may find the pro football pace so swift that the parade has passed it by.

The Packers were an anomaly, anyway. The Wisconsin city entered pro ball even before the National Football League was organized and it became a charter member when the league was still a whistle-stop circuit. The other small towns fell by the wayside until only Green Bay was left, a stark testimonial to the driving force and talents of just one man, Lambeau. He not only kept them on a par with bigger rivals but actually made them one of the game's standout attractions. For the past couple of years they've slipped greivously, and they may very well continue their precipitous descent until they drop out of the bottom of the league.

Romantic Story

The love affair between Curly and the Packers is a rather romantic story. He was born in Green Bay and matriculated at Notre Dame in 1918, serving as the fullback of Knute Rockne's first team and as a team-mate of the immortal George Gipp. But balky tonsils felled him when he returned home for the Christmas holidays and the ensuing tonsillectomy left him so overcut in his classes that he never did go back to South Bend. He went to work for the Indian Packing Company, his football dreams at an end. Or were they?

But Curly was as restless and as furiously infatuated with football then as he is today. He suggested to his bosses that they sponsor a team. The cost would be only $500; he could buy the Canton franchise for $50 and he would even condescend to have the word "packers" emblazoned on the shirt-fronts. Lambeau was just 20 years old when his contagious enthusiasm met favorable response. He thus became the coach, captain and star. So successful a venture was it that each player received as his share of the profits that the season's end the munificent sum of $16.75.

Unique Set-Up

A year later the city of Green Bay took over

the sponsorship of the Packers and they were to become the most glamorous advertising medium that any town ever had, their fame spreading from coast to coast. The Packers became a quite unique organization, a community undertaking which certainly must have ranked near the top of sportsdom's Seven Wonders.

It's quite possible that Curly was even ahead of his time. He was exploiting the forward pass long before anyone else. His original passer was Curly Lambeau. Then came Red Dunn, and the Packers began to roll in high when they got Arnie Herber to throw and the extraordinary Johnny Blood to receive. But just as the phenomenal Blood began to slow down a bit along came Don Hutson. The Herber-Hutson combination was without equal until Cecil Isbell replaced long-throwing Arnie at the pitching end. The Isbell-Hutson pair set records by the bushel basket.

Try as he would, however, Lambeau never did bob up with an Isbell replacement, a deficiency which might not have been so costly if it hadn't been for the fact that the incomparable Hutson began to wear out at the same approximate time. Packer fortunes simultaneously began to sag, and the behind-the-scenes bickering, which the hard-crusted Lambeau blithely ignored while he was winning, gained vocal power. He quit as coach last September, but won the post-season internal battle for control. Not until then did he quit of his own volition in order to bring peace back into the family.

Opening the Gates

One of the secrets of Lambeau's success was that he never was satisfied. Even perfection left him unmoved, and his nagging search for that perfection was occasionally irritating to his hired

hands. One day in 1928 he blistered his athletes between halves of a Packer-Cardinal game for the shoddiness of their passing attack. Since no improvement was immediately forthcoming, Curly substituted himself in the backfield.

"I'll show you guys how to pass," he raged and walked angrily away from the huddle.

Cal Hubbard, the umpire who then was football's mightiest tackle, spoke up.

"Let's open the gates on him," he drawled mischievously.

Lambeau dropped back to pass. The ten other Packer players stepped aside and let eleven Cardinal players hit Curly at once. Reproachfully he glanced at them as he staggered to his feet. He then limped to the sidelines, never to play again.

Yet that didn't rank as his most startling misadventure. This one came in a fray with the Giants at the Polo Grounds. Lambeau decided to do his coaching from the press-box eyrie. He even timed himself beforehand, clocking his journey from press coop to dressing room for his half-time instructions. It took four minutes.

Lost, Strayed or Stolen

But Curly had forgotten that a crowd of 50,000 will mill about during intermission. He had to fight his way frantically through the multitude as minutes ticked away. In desperation he sought a shortcut by ducking outside the park to the dressing room. The outer door was locked. He pounded, screamed and shouted. No one heard him. Finally two friendly policemen boosted him up to a window. "Good luck, fellers," he gasped in the shortest between-halves speech of his career.

Once more he is on the outside, looking in. But this has had a degree of permanence to it that the other lacked. Curly will miss the Packers, of course. He could not be human without so doing. However, the Packers are going to miss him a great deal more. So peculiar was their relationship that he leaves a gap impossible to fill.

February 12, 1950

National Football League Keeps Name, Designates 2 'Conferences'

Combination Title Assumed After 'Merger' With All-America Is Dropped—Group Winners to Meet for Championship

PHILADELPHIA, March 3 (AP)
In a roundabout way, the National Football League admitted today that it didn't merge with the All-America Conference. Instead, it merely gobbled up the A. A. C.

Commissioner Bert Bell didn't put it that way in announcing that professional football would operate next season as the National Football League and not the National-

American Football League.

But the implication was clear. He said 1950 marks the thirty-first continuous year of the N. F. L.

Last December, Bell, in announcing the "merger," described the National-American as a "new league." It expired today without one football game having been played.

Bell said the decision to stick

by the old name was made upon advice of counsel and unanimous consent of the thirteen club owners.

In 1950 the league will have thirteen instead of ten teams and a new designation for its two branches.

Ten Teams Last Year

Last year there were five teams each in the league's divisions, labeled "Eastern" and "Western."

In 1950 the divisions become "conferences," to be known as the National and American.

This step obviously is aimed at putting pro football on the same basis as major league baseball with two leagues and a world series of football.

The conferences are made up this way:

American — Chicago Cardinals, Cleveland Browns, New York Giants, Philadelphia Eagles, Pittsburgh Steelers and Washington Redskins.

National—Baltimore Colts, Chicago Bears, Detroit Lions, Green Bay Packers, Los Angeles Rams, New York Bulldogs and San Francisco 49ers.

The three teams which played last year in the All-America Conference are Cleveland, Baltimore and San Francisco.

Schedule Is Explained

The schedule will be played in this manner:

The six teams in the American Conference and six of those in the National—Baltimore is the exception—will play twelve games. Each team will play home-and-home games with the other five clubs in its conference, one with a "traditional rival" and one against Baltimore.

The Colts are the league's "swing" team, playing each of the other twelve clubs once during the season.

The winners in the two conferences will meet in a championship game at the end of the regular season.

Each conference will have its own president, with Dan Sherby of Cleveland head of the American Conference and Emil R. Fisher of Green Bay president of the National.

March 4, 1950

BAN ON FILCHOCK REMOVED BY BELL

Giants' Star Suspended in '47 Is Eligible to Play Again— Hapes Asks to Return

PHILADELPHIA, July 13 (AP)— Bert Bell, National Football League commissioner, today ended the indefinite suspension of Frank Filchock, New York Giants' star, barred from the league three years ago after he was offered a bribe.

Filchock and a team-mate, Merle Hapes, were suspended after a hearing before Bell in 1947. They admitted that they received and rejected a bribe offer and did not report it to their club or the league.

Three men were convicted and sentenced to jail for offering money to Filchock and Hapes to "fix" the N. F. L. championship game between the Giants and the Chicago Bears.

Neither Filchock nor Hapes was accused of accepting any money.

Bell said he lifted the suspension on Filchock after a thorough investigation showed the 33-year-old backfield star "has at all times conducted himself in a manner reflecting the highest standards of sportsmanship."

On Montreal Eleven

Filchock has been playing with the Montreal professional football club in Canada. Bell said Filchock "has made a real contribution to the promotion and development of clean sports in Canada."

No action was taken today on Hapes. Bell said he had just received an application from Hapes seeking lifting of the suspension and had not had time to study it.

While Filchock now is eligible to return to the N. F. L., Coach Lew Hayman of the Montreal Alouettes said Frank would return next fall to the Canadian Big Four League.

Jack Mara, owner of the Giants, who no longer have rights to Filchock's services, said he was "glad to hear that Frank has been reinstated, that his name has been cleared."

"We do not plan to make him an offer because we are stressing youth," Mara said. "But he certainly would be a handy man for some club."

Filchock's Conduct Lauded

Lifting of the suspension followed a hearing during which Filchock and Leo Dandurand, president of the Montreal club, presented testimonials from clergymen, businessmen and sportsmen lauding Filchock's conduct.

New York's Mayor William O'Dwyer and Assistant District Attorney George Monaghan also urged lifting of the suspension.

The bribe offer was made shortly before the 1946 championship game. Hapes was barred from the game but Filchock played and the Bears won, 24 to 14.

July 14, 1950

Browns Win Pro Football Title on Groza's Field Goal in Final 20 Seconds

CLEVELAND DOWNS LOS ANGELES, 30-28

STATISTICS OF THE GAME

	Browns	Rams
First downs	22	22
Yards gained, rushing	73	95
Forward passes	33	32
Forwards completed	22	18
Yards gained, forward	298	312
Forwards intercepted by	5	1
Number of punts	5	4
*Av. dist. of punts, yds.	38.2	50%
Run-back of punts, yds.	22	14
Fumbles	3	0
Own fumbles recovered	0	0
Penalties	3	4
Yards lost, penalties	25	48

*From line of scrimmage.

By LOUIS EFFRAT

Special to The New York Times.

CLEVELAND, Dec. 24—It was the day before Christmas and all through the house 29,751 rabid rooters hoping for a miracle, while gazing gloomily at the clock, all but gave up on the 'Cleveland Browns in their National Football League championship play-off against the Los Angeles Rams today.

But the Browns, who never have lost a play-off, did not give up on themselves and with a successful last-gasp effort became monarchs of all they survey in the gridiron world.

The seemingly impossible—impossible because of the time element—came to pass when, with only twenty seconds remaining in a spectacularly fought contest over Municipal Stadium's frozen turf, Lou Groza booted a perfect 16-yard field goal. Groza's specialty—he did it twice against the Giants last week—turned an almost certain 28—27 setback into a glorious 30—28 victory for the Browns.

All of a sudden it was a "joyeux noel" for Paul Brown's charges, who despite the herculean efforts of Otto Graham, spent most of the cold afternoon trailing Joe Stydahar's Pacific Coast representatives. In the end, it was somewhat ironic that so flashy an aerial duel between Graham and Bob Waterfield should be decided by a placement kick from the very same distance at which Waterfield had barely missed a 3-pointer in the second period.

Passes Gain 298 Yards

Between intermittent snow flurries, a 28-mile-an-hour wind that blew in from Lake Erie and the 29-degree temperature, Graham completed 22 of 32 passes, four for touchdowns and an over-all 298 yards. Waterfield fired only one 6-pointer, but his 18 completions in 31 attempts gained 312 yards.

Four of Waterfield's thrusts were intercepted by the victors.

It will be recalled that before peace came to professional football, the Browns, under the guidance of their canny coach, annexed every All-American Conference crown.

There were some who attempted to discredit Brown's accomplishments on the basis of a weak league. "Just wait until he gets into the National League," they said.

After four years of monotonous winning in the A. A. C., Brown and his Browns joined the National. This, the first season, was a rough one, but aside from two defeats by Steve Owen's Giants, whom they conquered, 8—3, in the American Conference play-off a week ago, it was not rough enough to make a difference. Nor was it tough enough to stymie them today.

That the Rams, with Waterfield a threat every inch of the way, almost turned the trick, was a credit to themselves and their coach. Disdaining rubber sneakers—only four Rams wore them, while every Brownie was so equipped for better footing—the Californians scored on their very first offensive maneuver. This was an electrifying 82-yard-pass play from Waterfield to Glenn Davis. Waterfield's toss went 30 yards and Davis galloped 52 for the score. The contest was only 27 seconds old when Waterfield kicked the extra point and Los Angeles had a 7-0 lead.

Rugged and Well-Played

Between this and Groza's field-goal at 14:40 in the fourth quarter, it was, in spite of discouraging weather conditions, one of the best-played and most rugged clashes of the campaign, as six play-off records were surpassed and three tied.

As the minutes passed, every indication was that the Rams, who, as the Cleveland Rams in 1945 took the championship in the play-off that year, would be crowned in Bert Bell's circuit. Trailing, 28—20, the Browns appeared to be out of the running when the final period started. There was a slight chance when Graham's running and passing brought the home club to the Los Angeles 14-yard line.

Then Graham flipped a 14-yard aerial to Rex Bumgardner in the end zone and Groza converted. Now only one point separated the teams, and time was running out.

Twice they exchanged punts and when with five minutes to go, Tom Thompson intercepted a Waterfield pass at midfield and Graham hit Dub Jones with a 22-yard toss, the Cleveland fans went wild. Then Graham bootlegged to the 21, but he fumbled and Milan Lazetich made a timely recovery for the Rams.

It looked bad for Cleveland, even if the visitors were held to a minor gain and Waterfield was forced to punt. Bob got off a long one which Cliff Lewis caught on his own 14 and returned to the 32. This meant the Browns, in possession 68 yards away from the goal-line, had exactly 1 minute 48 seconds in which to produce a tally.

Plays Against the Clock

Graham, trying to spot a receiver, found none and ran for 14, stepping out of bounds to stop the clock. On the next play Otto clicked with a 15-yarder to Bumgardner in the left flat, the latter running outside and again stopping the clock. The tension mounted when Graham found Jones in the right flat and the Browns had a first down on the 22. Again Graham reversed the pattern, passing to the left flat, where Bumgardner made the catch on the 11 and stepped out. Everything that was being done by the Browns was being dictated by time.

Thus, when Graham looked up and saw 40 seconds remaining, he tried a quarterback sneak. Unmindful of gaining, Otto's plan was to run diagonally in order to put the ball nearer to the center. He gained only a yard, but his principal purpose had been served.

It was only second down, but Graham refused to gamble on another pass. He was confident that Groza's talented toe, which had kicked fifteen field goals this year, would do it again. A hush fell over the stadium as the teams lined up for the most important play of the game. Earlier, Tom James, the holder for Groza's placements, had been unable to handle a low pass from center following the second Cleveland touchdown. A similar occurrence would be ruinous.

This time, however, everything went smoothly. James took the perfect pass from center, spotted it perfectly on the 16 and Groza booted it perfectly between the uprights. There was little that the Rams could do in the twenty seconds that remained and their dying gesture, a 55-yard pass by Norm Van Brocklin, was intercepted by Warren Lahr as the game and season ended.

Score Is Quickly Tied

The story-book finish dwarfed all that had happened earlier. Off winging on Waterfield's record-breaking pass, the Rams were tied at 3:10 in the first when Graham fired 31 yards to Jones for a touchdown and Groza converted. At 7:05, the Rams, after an 80-yard advance on eight plays, scored again as Dick Hoerner plunged over from the 3 and Waterfield kicked the point.

A 35-yard aerial from Graham to Dante Lavelli produced the next Cleveland touchdown at 2:20 in the second. Then it was that James was unable to put down the ball for the attempted placement by Groza. James recovered and tried to pass to Tony Adamle in the end zone, but the latter dropped the ball and Los Angeles was ahead 14—13.

It became Cleveland's turn to lead at 4:00 in the third when Lavelli snared his second touchdown pass, a 39-yarder from Graham, and Groza made it 20—14, but the Rams rebounded quickly and scored twice within twenty-one seconds. They drove 71 yards in eleven plays, Hoerner going over for his second tally from the 1 and Waterfield converting. Then a fumble by Marion Motley was recovered by Larry Brink of the Rams and he ran seven yards into end zone. Again Waterfield made the point and the picture was black, despite the white background, for the Browns.

Then it was that the Browns, overcoming every obstacle, including the clock, marched to victory.

The line-up:

CLEVELAND BROWNS (30)
Left Ends—Young, Speedie, Gillom.
Left Tackles—Palmer, Groza, Kissell.
Left Guards—Agase, Humble, Gibron.
Centers—Herring, Gatski, T. Thompson.
Right Guards—Willis, Houston.
Right Tackles—Grigg, Rymkus, Sandusky.
Right Ends—Martin, Lavelli, Ford.
Quarterbacks—Gorgal, Graham, C. Lewis.
Left Halfbacks—Lahr, Baumgardner, Carpenter, Moselle.
Right Halfbacks—James, Jones, Phelps.
Fullbacks—Adamle, Motley, Cole.

LOS ANGELES RAMS (28)
Left Ends—Fears, Brink, Keane.
Left Tackles—Huffman, Champagne.
Left Guards—Finlay, Vasicek.
Centers—Statuto, Naumetz, Paul.
Right Guards—West, H. Thompson, Stephenson, Lazetich.
Right Tackles—Reinhard, Bouley.
Right Ends—Hirsch, Zilly, Boyd, Smyth.
Quarterbacks—Waterfield, Van Brocklin.
Left Halfbacks—Davis, Williams.
Right Halfbacks—Smith, Kalmanir, Barry, W. Lewis.
Fullbacks—Hoerner, Towler, Younger, Pasquariello.

SCORE BY PERIODS
Cleveland Browns .... 7 6 7 10—30
Los Angeles Rams .... 14 0 14 0—28
Touchdowns—Davis, Jones, Hoerner 2, Lavelli 2, Brink, Baumgardner. Points after touchdown—Waterfield 4, Groza 3 (placements). Field goal—Groza (placement).
Referee—Ronnie Gibbs. Umpire—Sam Wilson. Linesman—Charlie Berry. Back Judge—Norman Duncan. Field judge—Lloyd Brazill.

December 25, 1950

Rams Defeat Browns for Pro Football Title Before Record 59,475 on Coast

LOS ANGELES WINS ON LATE PASS, 24-17

STATISTICS OF THE GAME

	L. A.	Cleve.
First downs	20	22
Rushing yardage	81	92
Passing yardage	253	280
Passes attempted	30	41
Passes completed	13	19
Passes intercepted by	2	3
Number of punts	5	4
Punting average, yds.	43.4	37
Fumbles lost	1	1
Yards penalized	25	41

LOS ANGELES, Dec. 23 (AP)—Los Angeles' spectacular Rams, with a tie-breaking 73-yard pass play in the final quarter, captured the National League championship today from the Cleveland Browns in a battle that ended the visitors' five-year rule in professional football. The score was 24—17.

Left End Tommy Fears of the Rams, racing down the field, gathered in a tremendous pass thrown by Norman Van Brocklin, the Rams' alternate quarterback, and tore on to complete the day's longest play that sent the Rams off the field with their first championship since the club moved here from Cleveland in 1946.

That throw ended the Browns' domination of the old National League and marked their first defeat in a title game in a string stretching back to 1946, when they became the rulers of the now-defunct All-America Conference.

It culminated a series of breaks, thrills and spills which left the record-breaking crowd of 59,475 limp with excitement and must have provided an equal thrill to the millions of television followers across the nation.

First Victory in 4 Tries

It also marked the first victory in four tries for Los Angeles over the precision-built machine from Cleveland, and the first time the Ram coach, Joe Stydahar, outfoxed Paul Brown, the talented young master from Massillon, Ohio, in five coaching duels, including last year's pro bowl.

Once again the Rams were not without a nod from Lady Luck. A fumble by Cleveland's quarterback wizard, Otto Graham, when 240-pound defensive end Larry Brink hit him on a pass attempt was picked up by End Andy Robustelli in the third quarter and turned into a touchdown that put the Rams ahead, 14—10.

That break and the Van Brocklin-Fears touchdown pass play erased a brilliant performance by Graham and a 52-yard field goal by Lou (The Toe) Groza that set a new record for the play-off.

The pay-off was a personal triumph for the Rams' No. 1 quarterback and captain, Bob Waterfield, who had led the club to its only other N. F. L. title in 1945.

The Rams scored first on a 55-yard drive in the second period that ended with Fullback Dick Hoerner crashing over from the 1-yard mark.

Groza's marvelous place-kick put the Browns on the scoreboard and then Cleveland struck quickly for a touchdown to take a 10-7 lead at half-time. The combination of Brink and Robustelli took advantage of the Graham fumble to put the Rams in front, 14—10, in the third quarter. Early in the fourth Waterfield's 17-yard field goal made it 17—10.

Graham Sparks Drive

Graham gathered his forces together for an explosive punch that netted 70 yards in ten plays, Automatic Otto contributing a 34-yard run down the sideline. Ken Carpenter went over right tackle for a yard, and when Groza added the point, the game was tied at 17—17 and the fray headed into its final eight minutes.

The Browns never stopped threatening, and it appeared they might duplicate their victory in the final twenty-eight seconds of the championship game with the Rams in Cleveland last December — a 30-28 decision, accomplished on a Groza field goal.

The Rams were not to be denied this time before the largest crowd ever to see an N. F. L. title contest. The old record was 58,346 in the Polo Grounds between the New York Giants and the Chicago Bears in 1946.

Twice the Rams missed, or the Browns stopped, scoring chances. Fears caught an arching pass and fought his way to a 48-yard gain to the Brown 1. Soon afterward Marvin Johnson intercepted a Graham pass and ran it back 35 to the Brown 1.

Altogether, the Rams had seven cracks at the Cleveland line, failed to cross the goal and on the second try had to settle for Waterfield's field goal.

Cleveland had its heartbreaks, too. The Browns took the opening kick-off and marched from their 23 to the Rams' 16. The drive stalled and Groza stepped back for a field goal from the 23. There was a groan from the outnumbered Brown supporters when it sailed to the left for a miss.

In the third period, with the Rams leading, 14—10, Graham fired a strike to Mac Speedie, who was in the clear and ran to a touchdown, but the play was called back because a Browns' lineman was detected holding.

Cleveland's first score was a study in Graham perfection. He hit Speedie for 14, Marion Motley for 23, and Dub Jones for the final 17 of a swift 54-yard scoring sequence.

Waterfield guided the Rams on their first scoring series, passing for 18, to Vitamin T. Smith, for 15 to Hoerner and barging deep into the Browns' territory. Pass interference was called on Cleveland's Tommy Thompson on the 12 and the Rams hammered across, with Dan Towler making a big 6 to reach the 1. Hoerner went over from there.

Fears last year's all-pro end who was on the injured list much of the season, climbed back to renown with his performance. Tommy earned 146 yards in four catches, including the winning touchdown. He overshadowed Elroy Hirsch, this year's league leader who had 56 yards in four receptions.

The Groza field goal eclipsed the old title-game distance of 42 yards, held jointly by Ward Cuff of the Giants and Ernie Smith of Green Bay. Cuff set his against Green Bay in 1938 and Smith tied it against the Giants the next year.

Local fans, who had seen the Rams win eight games and lose

Otto Graham, great quarterback of the Cleveland Browns, is about to have a violent encounter with a member of the Los Angeles Rams in the 1950 NFL title game. Note the extra bit of mayhem going on at the upper right.

Lou "The Toe" Groza was the man who made the field goal an integral part of the pro game. In this shot the Cleveland Browns' booter scores against the Baltimore Colts.

four in the regular season and were well aware that Cleveland had lost just one game and had won eleven straight going into the match, mobbed the Rams as the gun sounded.

Even Stydahar—275 pounds or more—was lifted bodily and carried off the field in triumph.

The Rams collected $2,108.44 apiece and each Cleveland player got $1,483.12 as the players' pool totaled $156,551.42 from a paid attendance of 57,540. It is based on 70 per cent of the net receipts. Gross receipts, including $75,000 for television and radio rights, were $325,970.

The gross and the players' share topped the previous high for the title game, set in 1946 between the Bears and Giants at the Polo Grounds. Gross receipts in that contest, for which no video or radio rights were sold, were $282,955.25. The winning Bears got $1,975,82 and the Giants $1,295,57.

The line-up:

LOS ANGELES RAMS (24)
Left Ends—Fears, Brink, Hecker, Keane.
Left Tackles—Simenson, Winkler.
Left Guards—Daugherty, West, Finlay.
Centers—McLaughlin, Paul, Reid.
Right Guards—Lange, Thompson, Collier.
Right Tackles—Dahms, Toogood, Hallichy.
Right Ends—Hirsch, Robustelli, Boyd.
Quarterbacks—Waterfield, Van Brocklin.
Left Halfbacks — Towler, Davis, Williams, Johnson.

Right Halfbacks—Younger, Smith, Kalmanir, Lewis, Rich.
Fullback—Hoerner.

CLEVELAND BROWNS (17)
Left Ends—Speedie, Young, Gillom.
Left Tackles—Groza, Kissell, Palmer.
Left Guards—Gibron, Thompson, Agase.
Centers—Gatski, Herring.
Right Guards—Gaudio, Willis, Houston.
Right Tackles—Rymkus, Sandusky, Grigg.
Right Ends—Lavelli, Ford, Oristaglio.
Quarterbacks—Graham, Lewis, Shula.
Left Halfbacks—Carpenter, Lahr, Baumgardner.
Right Halfbacks—Jones, James Taseff.
Fullbacks—Motley, Adamle, Cole, Jagade.

SCORE BY PERIODS
Los Angeles Rams............0 7 7 10—24
Cleveland Browns...........0 10 0 7—17

Touchdowns—Hoerner, Towler, Fears, Jones, Carpenter. Points after touchdowns—Waterfield 3, Groza 2. Field goals—Waterfield, Groza.

December 24, 1951

BALTIMORE MEETS GOAL SET BY N. F. L.

15,000 Season Tickets Sold by City, So Bell Indicates It Will Get Franchise

PHILADELPHIA, Jan. 6 (AP)—Commissioner Bert Bell of the National Football League said tonight that Baltimore fans had "lived up to their end of the bargain" by buying 15,000 season tickets for 1953 and "I'm ready to live up to mine" by approving a franchise for the Maryland city.

Bell promised Baltimoreans on Dec. 3 they could have the franchise if they bought $250,000 worth of tickets by Jan. 22. That figured out

to be 15,000 season tickets for six home games.

Individual Baltimoreans had bought more than 13,000 up to today. Tonight, an oil company announced it would buy any of the 15,000 not sold by the deadline.

Baltimore is to get the Dallas Texas squad whose backers quit in midseason. The team, which formerly was the New York Yankees, finished the season under league administration with only one victory.

The commissioner expects to announce within the next few days the name of the new Baltimore franchise owner. He has every hope, that man will be Carroll Rosenbloom, a 45-year-old clothing manufacturer who played football at the University of Pennsylvania while Bell was coaching there.

Whoever does get the franchise at Baltimore will have to pay $200,000 for it. The new owner will acquire, along with the franchise, the players

from the defunct Texas team.

It will be the second professional football franchise for Baltimore. It had one for three years in the All-American Conference and for one year, 1950, when that loop merged with the National Football League.

In case Rosenbloom doesn't want the franchise, Bruce Livie of Baltimore is felt ready to ask for it. Livi, owner of a thoroughbred racing stable, was chairman of the season ticket selling campaign. He said he had been approached by several business men who wanted him to head a syndicate of buyers.

"All of them are well-to-do and are more interested in keeping a team here than merely making money out of the venture," Livie said. He told the interested financiers he was "in no position to discuss anything" until Bell made a move.

Bell also said earlier that he was backing Keith Molesworth for the Baltimore coaching job. Molesworth

was backfield coach of the Pittsburgh Steelers last season and formerly coached at Navy. He once played quarterback for the Chicago Bears.

Bell said that if an owner was not decided upon by next Monday he would proceed to name a two-man coaching staff. He said that would be necessary so somebody could start planning for Baltimore's draft choices at the league meeting Jan. 23.

Livie said that the oil company probably would not have to buy a single ticket, but that its action in underwriting the remainder permitted Baltimore to inform Bell it had completed its part of the deal.

Livie said, "I'm hoping we can walk into the league meeting Jan. 23 and tell them we sold 20,000 tickets."

Asked what would happen if Bell failed to come up with an owner, Livi replied: "there will be a team."

January 7, 1953

Court Limits Pro Football's Control of Television to the Area of Home Games

LEAGUE FORBIDDEN TO RESTRICT RADIO

N.F.L. Can Bar TV of Its Other Contests Only in Area Where a Game Is Being Played

PHILADELPHIA, Nov. 12 (UP) —A Federal judge ruled today that the National Football League could continue to restrict television broadcasts of games only in its teams' home areas but could not interfere with any other telecasts or any radio broadcasts of its games.

The decision was made by United States District Judge Allan K. Grim in a twenty-one-page opinion in the Government's anti-trust suit against the league and its member clubs.

The decision boiled down to a ruling that the league could restrict telecasts that would inter-

fere with gate receipts of a specific game but that it could not interfere with telecasts on radio broadcasts that would not affect attendance.

In effect, the jurist ruled that the league could forbid any telecast of its games within seventy-five miles of a game in progress, but it must not interfere with telecasts outside the seventy-five-mile limit.

Gate Receipts Factor

Under the decision, if the New York Giants are playing the Chicago Bears at New York, the league can black out the New York area to all telecasts of any of its games while the game is in progress. It could not forbid the telecast of that game or any other area of the nation because gate receipts of the New York game would not be affected.

The decision also took away the powers of Bert Bell, the league commissioner, to approve or disapprove all contracts made by the league teams for the telecasts or broadcasts of their games.

Judge Grim rejected the contention of the league that it was not subject to the anti-trust laws because it was not a business engaged in interstate commerce. The

United States Supreme Court ruled last Monday that big league baseball could continue to enforce its reserve clause in players' contracts because it was not an interstate business.

TV Interstate Industry

However, Judge Grim pointed out that whatever the status of the league, radio and television is an interstate industry and the league's policies interfered with the conduct of its business.

The jurist said his decision then was whether or not the restraint of trade was reasonable, because only unreasonable restraints are barred by the Sherman Anti-Trust Law.

Judge Grim held that the restriction of television broadcasts in the territory of a game was necessary for the league's existence and therefore was not an unreasonable restraint. He said a drop in gate receipts could mean financial disaster for clubs and possibly failure of the league because a circuit cannot exist without member teams.

Both sides claimed victory. The Government attorneys said the decision prevented the N. F. L. from unlimited restrictions of telecasts of its games. Bell said professional football "won the most im-

portant part of its case because the league's most vital need is the protection of our home gate if we are to continue our existence."

In banning radio restrictions, Judge Grim pointed out they obviously did not interfere with gate receipts because most of the leagues permitted broadcasts of their games even in their home areas.

The ruling did not include any specific injunction. Government and N. F. L. attorneys have been directed to submit briefs in the next thirty days. The briefs will be used in formulating a formal decree of Judge Grimm's findings.

November 13, 1953

Lions Defeat Browns Again for Second Straight Pro Football Championship

BOOT BY WALKER DECIDES, 17 TO 16

Detroit Back Converts After Doran Ties Score on Layne Pass Before 54,577

STATISTICS OF THE GAME

	Lions	Browns
First downs	18	11
Rushing yardage	129	182
Passing yardage	179	9
Passes attempted	25	16
Passes completed	12	3
Passes intercepted by	2	2
Number of punts	4	5
Punting average, yds	49	42
Fumbles lost	2	2
Yards penalized	50	30

By LOUIS EFFRAT
Special to THE NEW YORK TIMES.

DETROIT, Dec. 27—They didn't have a place-kicker like Lou Groza. Nor did they have a runner like Chick Jagade. But the Detroit Lions did have the spirit, the determination and the weapons to come from behind in the closing minutes and upset the Cleveland Browns, 17—16, for the professional football championship at Briggs Stadium today.

They also had Bobby Layne, who clearly outshone renowned Otto Graham, the peerless passer of the National Football League. Then, there was little-known Jim Doran, a gentleman farmer from Boone, Iowa, who captured the aerial that set the stage for the tie-breaking, title-winning extra point. And, when they needed him most, the Lions had Doak Walker to boot the placement that brought the crown to the Motor City for the second straight year and for the third time since 1935.

Two minutes and 8 seconds remained in the contest, which, for one half, had been a drab, sloppily played, boring game to most of the 54,577 fans, when Doran fashioned the tying touchdown on a 33-yard toss from Layne.

This put it squarely up to Walker. The former Southern Methodist ace, until Doran's tally, had scored all the Detroit points, via a first-period touchdown and conversion and a 22-yard field goal in the second quarter. Along the way, Walker had failed to click with field-goal attempts from the 45 and the 33.

Kick Prevents Overtime

In pro football, it is almost a sin for anyone to miss a try for the extra point. However rare such a failure may be, though, the tension was obvious when the rivals lined up. If Walker, with Layne holding the ball, missed, the game probably would have ended in a 16-16 deadlock and, in accordance with Commissioner Bert Bell's ruling for title games, the first "sudden death" overtime in league history would have been invoked.

But Walker did not miss. His placement kick was firm, high and, most important, accurate. The ball sailed true between the uprights. Some two minutes later, the Browns, for the third straight year, had bowed in the championship play-off.

Paul Brown's lads were downed, 24—17, by the Los Angeles Rams in 1951 and by the Lions, 17—7, last season.

Played in 31-degree temperature but on a gridiron that was soft enough to cause numerous slips and lots of slides, the game, for thirty minutes, left much to be desired. Fumbles, traffic jams and collisions between teammates made it difficult to believe that these were the best football players in the land.

Graham, who led the loop in passing with a 64.77 percentage of completions, ran into trouble the first time he tried to pass. The Browns, having received the kick-off, were in possession on their 24, where it was second down. Graham attempted to pass, but before he was able to raise his right arm in dashed Detroit's Joe Schmidt to hit Otto's hand, causing a fumble. Les Bingaman pounced on the loose ball for the Lions, who started to attack 13 yards away from the goal.

Score on Six Plays

Six plays were all the Lions required to effect the game's first score. After Gene Gedman, Hunchy Hoernschemeyer and Layne had taken turns running, Walker took the ball over his left tackle from the 1. Walker also converted and at 4:05 in the opening period, Buddy Parker's athletes enjoyed a 7-0 spread.

It is doubtful whether Brown's squad, once the scourge of the All-America Conference, a title finalist in two leagues for eight consecutive years and a 3½-point favorite to win this afternoon, ever had performed so ineffectually as in this quarter. By the same token, it is doubtful whether Graham, the former Northwestern All-America player ever had suffered through so trying a contest.

Until a Hoernschemeyer fumble, recovered by Len Ford on the Detroit 6, gave them the ball, the Browns had not passed midfield in this quarter. But the Ohioans, unable to move, had to be content with 3 points, via a 14-yard field goal by Groza. Later he was to attempt three more, succeeding with two.

Following Groza's scoring boot, the Lions lost the services of Notre Dame's Leon Hart, the big right end. A knee injury after the kick-off put Hart out of action and, though there was no way of knowing it at the moment, it was this accident that made Doran available. For Doran, primarily a defensive end, had to be used on offense because of Hart's injury.

Aside from a 73-yard punt by Detroit's Yale Lary and a missed 45-yard field-goal try by Walker, there was little to rouse the spectators until late in the second period. Then Jim David intercepted a Graham aerial and returned 35 yards to the Cleveland 20. On the next play, Layne pitched out to Walker, who then flipped a short pass to Layne. The latter, making the catch on the scrimmage line, ran to the 15, feinted Tom James out of position and went over for what appeared to be a touchdown.

The ball had been placed on the 2 and the Lions were ready to try for the point when Warren Lahr and Ken Gorgal called to the officials' attention the fact that Layne, on that maneuver, had been an ineligible receiver. Into a long huddle went the five arbiters and finally the touchdown was disallowed. The Lions are a T-team and Rule 7, Section 5, Article 2, Item 1, Notice D, clearly states that "an ineligible receiver is one who, while behind center receives a hand to hand pass from him." The play had started with Layne directly behind the center.

Victors Lead at Half, 10—3

However, it was not a complete loss. A couple of plays later Walker place-kicked a 3-pointer from the 22 and half-time found the defending champions, albeit underdogs, enjoying a 10-3 bulge, after Groza had missed with a 51-yard field-goal attempt.

Precisely what Coach Brown, who now has won a game from Coach Parker, told his charges during the intermission, is not known. However, the change in the Browns was noticeable shortly after action was resumed. Gorgal intercepted a Layne pass and the visitors followed with their first sustained advance. It was a good ground offensive that covered 51 yards in eight plays and brought a touchdown.

The scoring maneuver was a 9-yard plunge by Jagade. Graham, after faking a pitchout to Billy Reynolds, handed-off to Jagade, who bulled his way inside his right guard and tallied standing up. At 6:57, Groza kicked the tying point.

The Lions then appeared to threaten until Don Colo, the game's outstanding defensive lineman, helped Cleveland by recovering a Layne fumble.

The Browns, with Jagade ripping off yardage on traps, seemed on their way to another touchdown in the same quarter, which ended with the visitors on the 7. There was no further advance as the fourth got under way and Groza kicked a 15-yard field goal for a 13-10 lead.

Into the air went the Lions and Layne completed two passes for sizable yardage. Hoernschemeyer, Gedman and Layne contributed some good running and the home side reached the 26. Stymied there, Detroit tried for 3 points on a 33-yard place-kick by Walker. He was wide.

Groza Kicks 43-Yarder

Then the Browns attacked. A 30-yard plunge by Jagade brought a first down on the opposite 39. Again Jagade carried, good for 8 yards. But the Lions tightened and Cleveland had to try for another field goal. This one, by Groza for 43 yards, gave the Cleveland eleven a 16-10 advantage.

Now only 4 minutes and 10 seconds were left to play. Even while some of the fans were heading toward the exits, Layne was starting an aerial bombardment from the 20. Three completions, two to Doran and one to Cloyce Box, carried the Lions beyond midfield. Two plunges, by Hoernschemeyer and Layne, brought a first down on the Cleveland 33.

And then it happened. Doran, who had not scored a point all season, his second campaign with the Lions, darted toward the end zone. It seemed as if Lahr, the defender, had the intended receiver well covered. Somehow, though, Doran got ahead of Lahr and took Layne's 33-yard toss, going away, in the end zone. Walker's placement followed.

The gross receipts, including $101,000 for television and radio, totaled $358,693, a record. A $2,424.10 pay-off for each winning share also resulted. Each losing share was worth $1,654.26.

The big surprise of the day was the ineffective passing of Graham, who completed 2 of 15 aerials. As a result, the Browns concluded with only 9 yards gained in the air. Layne, on the other hand, succeeded with 12 of 25 for 179 yards. In the running department, Jagade's 102 yards were tops, with Hoernschemeyer's 51 high for Detroit. Doran received four passes for 95 yards, including the big touchdown.

The line-up:

DETROIT LIONS (17)
Left Ends—Dibble, Box, Gandee.
Left Tackles—Creekmur, McGraw.
Left Guards—Sewell, Martin, Bingaman.
Centers—Ane, Banonis, Torgeson.
Right Guards—Stanfel, Schmidt.
Right Tackles—Spencer, Miller, Prchlik.
Right Ends—Hart, Doran, Cain.
Quarterbacks—Layne, Lary.
Left Halfbacks—Walker, Girard, David, Christiansen.
Right Halfbacks—Gedman, R. J. Smith, Karilivacz.
Fullbacks—Hoernschemeyer, Cline, L. Carpenter.

CLEVELAND BROWNS (16)
Left Ends—Brewster, Young, Atkins.
Left Tackles—Groza, Colo.
Left Guards—Gibron, Donaldson, Steinbrunner
Centers—Gatski, Catlin.
Right Guards—Noll, Houston, Willis.
Right Tackles—Sandusky, Palmer, Helluin.
Right Ends—Lavelli, Gillom, Ford.
Quarterbacks—Graham, Ratterman, Gorgal.
Left Halfbacks—Renfro, K. Carpenter, Lahr.
Right Halfbacks—Jones, Reynolds, Konz, James.
Fullbacks—Jagade, Motley, Michaels, Howard.

SCORE BY PERIODS

Detroit Lions	7	3	0	7	—17
Cleveland Browns	0	3	7	6	—16

Detroit scoring—Touchdowns: Walker, Doran. Conversions: Walker 2 (placements). Field goal: Walker (placement). Cleveland scoring—Touchdown: Jagade. Conversion: Groza (placement). Field goals—Groza 3 (placements).

Referee—Ronald Gibbs, St. Thomas. Umpire—Samuel Wilson, Lehigh. Back Judge—James Hamer, California State Teachers. Linesman—Dan Tehan, Xavier. Field Judge—Carl Rebele, Penn State.

December 28, 1953

Pro Football League Outlaws Electronics as Medium for Coaches' Messages

REACTION OF FANS CITED AS REASON

Their Objection to Electronic Devices Used by Coaches Brings Season's Ban

PHILADELPHIA, Oct. 18 (AP) —The National Football League is going back to the old-fashioned style of having quarterbacks either think for themselves or receive instructions by messengers on foot.

Commissioner Bert Bell said today that electronic devices used by some of the league teams for communication between the coaches on the sidelines and the quarterback had been outlawed for the balance of the season.

The action was taken in a telephone poll of N. F. L. teams and Bell said there was not one dissenting voice. Even Paul Brown, coach of the Cleveland Browns, who first supplied receiving sets to his quarterbacks, was happy to go along with the ban.

Permanent Action Expected

The commissioner said: "By unanimous consent of the twelve member clubs * * * all electronic devices, including walkie talkies * * * must be eliminated for the remainder of the season."

Bell thinks the action will become a permanent one. "All the clubs were cooperative and it is my opinion that at the next annual meeting something will be put in the league book to outlaw the things permanently," he said.

Bell said flatly that the action was initiated because reaction to the use of these coach-to-quarterback radios or transistors was bad. He said the fans, through the mail, and press, radio and television reporters had expressed disapproval. "I did not read or hear any favorable comments on it," Bell said.

Giants Snare Signals

The operation became almost a joke last Sunday when the New York Giants said they intercepted Brown's orders to his quarterbacks in the Browns-Giants game. According to the Giants, they had a coach stationed on the sidelines with an interceptor set and relayed the Cleveland plays to their defense.

Brown used the electronic system only for a few plays, as the roar of the crowd drowned out his voice in the quarterback's helmet receiving set.

The directive does not exclude a telephone line to the bench from the press box or scouting positions, or a telephone line with extra footage used by a coach on the sidelines.

October 19, 1956

'Pro Football Is Better to Watch'

By JOHNNY LUJACK

STOPGAP—New York Giant blockers (left and right) show how pros open a hole for a ball carrier. Mel Triplett (33), plowing through, finally is downed by a rival line backer.

THE college football season is all but ended and the professional season is approaching its "world series"—the playoff for the championship between the Eastern and Western Divisions of the National League. This, then, is a good time to consider the question: which is better to watch, pro football or collegiate?

The tremendous growth in popularity of the pros is evidenced in the latest figures from the office of Bert Bell, high commissioner of professional football. In 1955 the pros drew a total attendance of 2,521,836, compared to 2,190,571 the year before. The current rate of attendance indicates another record season, with the crowd figure going over 2,750,000.

Of course, these figures fall far short of the total collegiate attendance, since there are so many more college teams and leagues than there are pros. But it also should be borne in mind that the collegians have an advantage at the gate because they play on Saturdays, whereas the pros operate on Sundays. It is my opinion that if, say, in cities like New York, Chicago, Philadelphia, Washington, Los Angeles and Detroit, the pros were Saturday instead of Sunday players, they would outdraw competing collegiate games.

Another advantage the collegians have is what in the broadcasting industry is called a "captive audience." The old school tie, and nothing else, dragoons a large portion of the crowd to many a collegiate game.

I do not intend to find fault with the collegiate game, for I enjoyed my three years of football at Notre Dame. But having also played four years with the Chicago Bears, I think I'm in some position to judge the merits of pro versus college football. And, again, I want to emphasize that I'm speaking from the viewpoint of the spectator, which is strictly what I am now.

So, with the possible exception of watching my alma mater—and this, I might add, has been something of a trial this season—I would rather see one pro football game than six played by top-ranking collegiate teams. First, let us take a look at the typical collegiate game.

THERE is the kickoff and the game is on. The receiving team returns the ball to about the 25 or 30-yard line, where there is a big pileup when the carrier is downed. After this is untangled there is the first play, known as the bread-and-butter play, that feels out the opposition. Second down, now, and six yards to go. Another play for about three yards. Then the quarterback sneak on the third down leaves about a yard to go for a first down. This means a punt. The other team, putting the ball into play for the first time, goes through about the same sequence of plays and there is another punt.

A seesaw like this goes on until, suddenly, you look at the clock and there are three minutes left to play in the first quarter. In perhaps fifteen or eighteen plays the ball may have been thrown twice because one quarterback or the other is the "daring" type who likes to keep the defense guessing.

The next collegiate game you see try a little test. Watch that third down play for short yardage and see how much time is lost untangling the pileup. Of course, the referee thinks he can get to the bottom so soon that he doesn't need to call time out — which he could do. The result is that precious seconds that might produce an additional play are lost. Such a loss subtracts substantially from the number of plays over the course of a game and so robs it of much of the action the fans come to see.

BY contrast, see how many more plays the pros cram into their sixty minutes. On the average, they run twenty to twenty - five more per game than the collegians do. What is more, the pros offer far more variety. No time is wasted on feeler plays. Besides spectacular dashes and long and beautiful passes, you may be treated to a field goal or so—all in the first quarter. No wonder a fan leaves the park saying to his buddy, "Brother, that's real football!"

Well, you are going to say now, why shouldn't it be? Don't the pros get the cream of the college teams each year, guys who have played four years of high school ball and three years of varsity ball? That is true; 98 per cent of the pros come from college teams. Moreover, those collegians are just blossoming into manhood and, athletically, their prime.

Consider my Notre Dame class. Out of twenty-two first-string men on the champion teams of 1946 and 1947, twenty went into pro football. George Connor and I joined the Bears. I found, and I'm sure that George found, that we had a lot to learn. And some things to unlearn, too.

LET me show you. When I was at Notre Dame, I was a two-platoon man; that is, I was used both on the offense and defense. (The colleges, you may recall, were platooning

then, but later abolished that system.) When I joined the Bears, the first thing their coach, George Halas, did was to give me defensive duty. After all, I was rated as high on defense as on offense back in college. But I soon learned what a bewildering number of decoys, all as fast as the potential receiver, the pros could send downfield to lead a defending back astray on a pass. I also learned how much deeper into the secondary defense solid blocking went in the pro game. It was rough.

George and I also had to relearn tackling techniques. In college football, the ball was down, or dead, the moment one knee of the carrier touched the ground. Not so in pro football, at the time we joined the Bears; a man momentarily tumbled or stopped could get up again and run. We soon found out that tackling which had stopped collegians, merely interrupted pro carriers. We had to retrain ourselves to hit with finality on the first tackle; there were no second chances. Now, though the pro rule on when a ball carrier is down conforms to the collegiate one in the interest of reducing injuries, no half-baked tackling is tolerated.

Furthermore, the necktie tackle, so frowned upon even though legal in collegiate football, has been made both spectacular and respectable in pro football. And George, an All-American at Notre Dame, learned that a pro lineman who, like a collegian, smashed in as hard as he could all the way, was dumped fast by the vicious side block known as the trap play. So, the hard way, George learned to charge a few yards, pause until he was sure where the play was going, then go after the ball carrier.

MOST colleges, these days, have about eight basic plays with variations that make the attack add up to eighteen or twenty plays. That's the way it was when I was quarterback at Notre Dame. When I got into the Bears' offensive backfield I found out that we had to learn seventy-five to 100 *basic* plays. From these there were variations to fit different defenses that made the number of plays add up to 400. Not only that, but I had to learn the each and every assignment of the linemen and other backs on every play.

For example, the signal for a typical play was 29—0—Round George—3—6. Translated, here's what the signal meant. Number 2 back (left halfback) would carry the ball to the Number 9 hole (around right end). The 0 told the left guard to pull out of the line and lead the play; round meant the right halfback was to block the opposing left end;

George meant the right guard also was to pull out and block the opposing line backer; 3 meant the fullback would go into motion and 6 that the ball would be snapped on the count of six,

SUCH plays put a responsibility on the pro quarterback unlike anything that he has to shoulder in college. For he not only must choose the correct one, but must make sure he calls the best blocking into action. Blocking assignments, incidentally, change with each defensive line-up. It's no wonder to me that Paul Brown and other pro coaches felt they had to wire their quarterbacks for sound.

Another thing I had to unlearn in the pro ranks was when to pass. At Notre Dame, after the ball was snapped from center, you had three seconds to fade back, spot the receiver, then let fly with the ball. After you had done that as often as I had at college it became almost reflex action. When I started throwing for the Bears I found that they figured five seconds for the play to unfold. It took me a full week of hard practice, to get out of the three-second habit—or so I thought.

But in a pre-season exhibition game I was getting rushed hard on every pass and, in order to avoid being thrown for a loss, I was anticipating the receiver's break and throwing. The result was a string of incomplete passes, and Halas called me out of the game. "You're throwing too soon again," he growled. "You know by now that you have five full seconds to throw." "Yes," I said, to the annoyance of the boss, "but you better tell those guys rushing me, because they don't seem to know anything about your rule."

It has been accurately said that the pros put the foot back in football. A punt in pro football is a thing of soaring beauty; it's rare that one is rushed, flubbed or blocked. Then there is the field goal. You usually can count on the fingers of one hand the number of collegiate games won in a season with a field goal. But scarcely a Sunday goes by that not one, but several field goals win or are a vital part of pro victories.

Now in fairness to the collegians, it must be said that their rule putting the goal posts ten yards back of the goal-line works against the try for the field goal by placement or drop-kick. It makes it, in nine out of ten games, a desperate gamble.

But even before their goal posts were moved back, the collegians treated the field goal attempt as at best a marginal weapon. Not so the pros. To them, it is as much an offensive weapon as the pass or the run, and it probably would be so even if pro goal posts were not on the goal-line—where goal posts belong.

ONE of the first things I noticed when I joined the Bears was the great superiority of line play over that of collegiate football. Seldom do you see even the best pro line open up a big gap in the center of the opposing line. This is because a pro lineman is hard to feint out of position, hard to trap with a side block. He never commits himself until he knows where the ball is going, then he hits like a ton of bricks.

Conversely, on the offense, pro blocking has that essence of the perfect football play timing. The hole opened up may not be as wide as it was in college, but it will be there for the split second the ball carrier needs to

111

sprint or squirm past a tackler's outstretched hands.

One of the main reasons for the better line play in the pros is the absence of what I call refereeitis. All too often, on the first play or so, college players will sense that they've got an overzealous referee who is going to blow the whistle on the slightest bit of overaggressiveness. The result is that the collegians, not wanting that 15-yard penalty, begin to pull their punches, figuratively speaking. The game not only slows down, as a result, but becomes more dangerous to the player. For if there is one thing you learn early in football it is the truth of this axiom: the fellow who hits is the one who doesn't get hurt.

The pros suffer from no such referee domination. I can remember one game when, in a pile-up, an enemy lineman swung an elbow at one of my team-mates, but didn't connect. I called the incident to the referee's attention, thinking that, as would have happened in college, we'd get a penalty out of it. All the referee said was: "He missed, didn't he? Now get back and play ball."

WHEN I was at Notre

Dame I thought the time spent in practice and "skull" sessions was rugged enough. And, of course, I had to keep up with my studies. In the pro game, though, you have much more time for practice—and you get it. A typical week for a pro team goes like this: Three-hour practice sessions Tuesdays through Fridays and a short session on Saturday. Before each practice there are forty - five - minute blackboard meetings and, in addition, two-and-a-half-hour skull sessions three nights a week. For the quarterback there is one additional meeting at night.

One night, when the offensive coach had finished and it was getting late, Hunk Anderson, the defensive coach, took over. About that time big Alf Baumann, an All-American from Northwestern, dozed off. Connor, sitting next to his slumbering teammate, elbowed him in the ribs and whispered: "Block the tackle, block the tackle." Baumann came to with a shout: "I block the tackle, coach!"—obviously unaware that the offensive session had ended.

Everyone got a laugh out of poor Baumann's embarrassment except Halas and the victim. Halas fined him $25 for snoozing on the job and Baumann paid it. Moreover, he didn't doze the rest of the

year, on or off the field.

I COULD give many other situations pointing up the difference between pro and college football. I think, though, that one final note will do.

Last New Year's Day, the bowl game that seemed the best to watch was the Maryland-Oklahoma contest at Miami, which Oklahoma won 20 to 6. The game was far more interesting than the score suggests. Why? Because Oklahoma, as the sports writers put it, was a "team in a hurry." The Sooners came out of their huddles fast and kept the game moving, always moving. No time lost between plays. The Sooners had borrowed a lesson from the pro game, as they are doing again this season. When more colleges do likewise, college football may get back on a par with the pro game in spectator appeal.

December 2, 1956

Bell, National League Commissioner, Hits Court Ruling as Discriminatory

'Pro' Football Placed Under Antitrust Law

By LUTHER A. HUSTON
Special to The New York Times.

WASHINGTON, Feb. 25— The Supreme Court today, in a 6-to-3 ruling, placed professional football under the antitrust laws.

The crux of the high court's decision was that the volume of interstate business involved in organized football brought it within the purview of the Sherman Act, the basic antitrust statute.

Professional baseball was thus left in lonely grandeur as the only professional sport specifically held by the court to be outside the antitrust laws. In 1922, the high tribunal, in the case known as Federal Baseball, held that the diamond game was a sport, not a business, and therefore immune from prosecution under the anti-monopoly statues. The court reaffirmed that decision in 1953 in the case known as Toolson against the New York Yankees.

In 1955 the court ruled that professional boxing was within the scope of the Sherman Act. Today's decision adhered more closely to the boxing ruling than

to the historic baseball opinion.

Justice Tom C. Clark delivered the opinion of the court. He was joined by Chief Justice Earl Warren and Justices Hugo L. Black, Stanley F. Reed, William O. Douglas and Harold H. Burton.

Justice Brennan Dissents

Justices Felix Frankfurter, John M. Harlan and William J. Brennan Jr., the newest member of the court, dissented.

The decision was in the case of William Radovich, formerly a guard on the Detroit Lions. He sued the National Football League, Bert Bell, the commissioner of the league; J. Rufus Klawans, the commissioner of the Pacific Coast League, and the clubs that made up the National League.

These were, at the time the suit was filed, the New York Giants, Boston Yanks, Philadelphia Eagles, Los Angeles Rams, Pittsburgh Steelers, Washington Redskins, Chicago Bears, Chicago Cardinals, Detroit Lions and Green Bay Packers.

Radovich contended that the defendants entered into a conspiracy to monopolize and control organized professional football in the United States in violation of the Sherman Act. He claimed also that he had been blacklisted and prevented from earning a living in his profession.

Radovich asked $35,000 damages. The law provides that any person injured in his business or property by reason of anything forbidden in the statute may recover "threefold the damages by him sustained." This would mean that Radovich could receive an award of $105,000, plus costs and attorney's fees.

Team Sports Treated Alike

The high court did not award damages, however. It sent the case back to the Federal Court of Appeals for the Ninth Circuit, in San Francisco, to determine whether the defendants actually had violated the antitrust laws. A decision as to that could be months or years away.

The lower Federal court had dismissed Radovich's complaint on the basis of the ruling in the Toolson case, reaffirming the immunity of baseball from the antitrust laws. The court below applied the doctrine that football was a team sport, the same as baseball.

Justice Clark said that in the Toolson case, involving a player who was under contract to the Yankees and was placed on the ineligible list when he refused to report to a club to which his contract was assigned, the high court had "continued to hold the umbrella over baseball that was placed there some thirty-one years earlier by Federal Baseball."

That was the case in which the Federal League, which flourished for a brief period, sued the National and American Leagues as an illegal monopoly. The "umbrella" referred to by

Justice Clark was the court's ruling that the interstate phase of organized baseball was so minor that the sport could not be considered in interstate commerce and thus subject to Federal regulation under the antitrust laws.

Justice Clark's opinion was, however, a tacit invitation to Congress to revise the laws so as to include baseball. He noted that the court had "intended to isolate" the baseball cases by "limiting them to baseball" but said that the doctrine laid down in those cases continued only at the sufferance of Congress.

The court had not extended the doctrine to football or boxing, he said, because the volume of interstate business involved in each "was such that both activities were within the act."

This ruling might be "unrealistic, inconsistent or illogical," Justice Clark acknowledged, but the answer was that "were we considering the question of baseball for the first time upon a clean slate, we would have no doubts."

No Other Business Exempt

Baseball had been ruled outside the scope of antitrust, Justice Clark noted, but "no other business claiming the coverage of those cases has had such an adjudication."

The orderly way to eliminate "error or discrimination," he asserted, was by "legislation and not by court decision."

Justice Frankfurter asserted that he had heard no arguments to lead him to think that the baseball rulings were not

"equally applicable to football:"
Justice Harlan, joined by Justice Brennan, also said he was unable to distinguish football from baseball and could "find no basis for attributing to Congress a purpose to put baseball in a class by itself."

The Radovich case was argued on Jan. 16. Maxwell Keith of San Francisco spoke for Rado-vich. Philip Elman of the Department of Justice, argued for the United States as a "friend of the court". Bernard I. Nordlinger, of Washington and Marshall E. Leahy of San Francisco represented the National Football League and other defendants.

February 26, 1957

Jim Brown Sets Rushing Mark For Cleveland in 20-10 Game

Browns' Player Sprints 152 Yards at Washington for 1,163 in Eight Tests

By GORDON S. WHITE Jr.

Special to The New York Times.

WASHINGTON, Nov. 16 — Jim Brown, fullback; Paul Brown, coach, and all the other Browns—Cleveland variety—are again sitting by themselves on top of the Eastern Division of the National Football League.

Jim Brown, though, may be somewhat further up in the clouds, possibly on top of the world. For the sophomore professional set a league rushing record for a season as he paced the Browns to a 20-10 victory over the Washington Redskins today. The victory, achieved before a sellout crowd of 32,372 at Griffith Stadium, put the Browns a game ahead of the New York Giants.

Charging on defense and trying hard to outguess Cleveland's moves, the Redskins managed to hold Brown to 60 yards gained in the first half. But the former Syracuse University star wore down his tacklers and picked up enough yardage in the second half to total 152 yards for the day and 1,163 for the season. He scored both Cleveland touchdowns against the Redskins.

Brown's ground gaining for eight games this year broke the former mark of 1,146 for a twelve-game season set by Steve Van Buren of the Philadelphia Eagles in 1949. At his current pace of 144.2 yards a game, Brown, with four games remaining, should read a season high of about 1,750 yards.

Though Brown worked hard, along with Lew Carpenter, who also ran well, and Milt Plum, the quarterback, who passed well, the Browns let many chances escape them. They lost ground on some plays, had passes intercepted at key spots, fumbled and were penalized 60 yards. As a result, the victory didn't come easily and it wasn't until Lou Groza kicked his second field goal of the game late in the fourth period that the Browns appeared assured of the decision.

Eddie LeBaron, Washington's No. 1 quarterback, didn't play until the second half. During the first two periods, Ralph Guglielmi quarterbacked the Skins to a 10-10 tie. LeBaron

Statistics of the Game

	Browns	Redsk.
First downs	20	11
Rushing yardage	237	75
Passing yardage	186	150
Passes attempted	27	21
Passes completed	12	9
Passes intercepted by	2	3
Punts	2	3
Av. dist. of punts, yds.	35	48
Fumbles lost	1	3
Yards penalized	60	11

suffered a high fever and cold during the past week and wasn't up to par when he did see action in the third and fourth periods.

Cleveland appeared to be en route to a walk-away at the start. Plum hit Preston Carpenter with a pass good for 74 yards on the second play of the game. This put the ball on Washington's 6.

Lew Carpenter failed to get the ball over in three straight line bucks, so Plum called on Brown for the first time in the afternoon. Brown went over from the 1 on the fourth down before two minutes had gone by.

In the middle of the fourth period, Brown, going through the middle, running the ends and generally wearing down the hitherto tough Washington defense, led a long march by Cleveland to a point where Groza kicked his winning points. Carrying the ball nine times on the charge, Brown picked up from 5 to 10 yards each time, moving the ball to Washington's 19.

Groza kicked from the 25 and Cleveland went ahead, 13—10. Cleveland's Don Paul intercepted a Redskin pass seconds later and brought the ball back to the Washington 11. In two running plays, Brown went over for the final touchdown at 13:58 of the fourth period.

Cleveland Browns	7	3	0	10—20
Washington Redskins	7	3	0	0—10

Cleveland scoring—Touchdowns: Brown 2 (1, plunge; 5 run) Field goals: Groza 2 (10, 25). Conversions: Groza 2.
Washington scoring—Touchdown: Podoley (84, pass from Guglielmi). Field goal: Baker (35). Conversion: Baker.

November 17, 1958

Colts Beat Giants, Win in Overtime

23-17 Game Tied With 7 Seconds Left in Regulation Time

By LOUIS EFFRAT

Time and fortune finally ran out on professional football's Cinderella team, the New York Giants, yesterday at the Yankee Stadium. And so it was that the Baltimore Colts, with a 23-17 victory, won the championship of the National Football League.

With a couple of minutes to go in the fourth period, the Giants seemed to have the triumph in their grasp. But with seven seconds to go, Baltimore tied the score at 17—17 on a field goal.

Then, in a sudden-death overtime period, the Baltimore team coached by Weeb Ewbank fashioned the winning touchdown after 8 minutes 15 seconds.

The excitement generated by football's longest game left most of the 64,185 spectators limp. Aside from an experimental exhibition contest, it was the first sudden-death game (with victory going instantly to the first team to score) in the league.

Alan (The Horse) Ameche, who had plunged for a 2-yard touchdown in the second quarter, drove over from the 1 for the tally that crushed the New Yorkers.

Ameche was a hero, but he was not THE hero. The 15,000 fans who had made the trip from Baltimore could have pointed to any one of a number of outstanding Colts.

Johnny Unitas was the man who engineered the dynamic offensive that moved the visitors from the shadow of defeat to the glory of their ultimate success. Then there was Steve Myrha, who kicked a 20-yard field goal at 14:53 in the fourth quarter.

Not to be ignored was the spectacular pass-catching of Ray Berry, the end, who captured twelve of Unitas' aerials for a gain of 178 yards. The receptions and yardage were championship play-off records. And votes would not be difficult to get for Lenny Moore, L. G. Dupre, Jim Mutscheller and members of Baltimore's defensive unit.

The Giants, too, had their share of standouts in what was easily the most dramatic, most exciting encounter witnessed on the pro circuit in many a season.

Some voiced the opinion that it was the "greatest game I've even seen." Among those who expressed that sentiment was Bert Bell, the commissioner of the N.F.L.

Each side had its ups and downs. The Giants, after it appeared that they had fumbled away their chance for the championship, stormed back from a 14-3 deficit at the half. With the 37-year-old Charley Conerly turning in a magnificent job of passing and quarterbacking the New Yorkers made an almost incredible comeback.

Triplett Goes Over.

Mel Triplett scored on a dive play from the 1 for the Giants' third-period touchdown. A 15-yard aerial from Conerly to Frank Gifford accounted for the touchdown that moved the Giants ahead early in the fourth quarter.

It was fitting that Gifford recorded the 6-pointer. Two fumbles by Gifford were recovered by the Colts and led to two Baltimore touchdowns earlier in the game.

To report that the Giants were unimpressive while the favored Colts were taking charge during the first half would be an understatement.

The outlook did not become brighter immediately after the intermission, either. The Colts, with Unitas hitting receivers with amazing regularity, moved to the 1-yard line and it seemed that Cinderella was about to be chased out of the park.

Something had to happen—fast. It did. The New Yorkers won nearly everyone's admiration with a wonderful goal-line stand. Cliff Livingston, on fourth down, dropped Ameche on the 5 and the fine effort of the defense seemed to ignite a fire under the local offensive unit.

Gifford plunged for 5 and Alex Webster for 3. Then occurred a big play. Conerly clicked with a long pass to Kyle Rote, who gained 62 yards before he fumbled on the 25. There Webster scooped up the ball and raced to the 1, where Carl Taseff forced him out of bounds. It was then that Triplett scored. Pat Summerall, who had booted a 36-yard field goal in the opening quarter, converted for the first of his two extra points.

Conerly's Passes Click.

Early in the fourth period, pass from Conerly to Bob Schnelker was good for 46 yards. Then Conerly fired to Gifford, who carried Baltimore's Milt Davis over on his back. Summerall added the point and the Giants were on top, 17—14.

Along about this time the Colts might have been regretting their decision to pass up a virtually certain field goal, before the Giants had made their inspired goal-line stand. But there was a job to be done

113

The Giants' Frank Gifford was a runner and pass catcher of great skill. His passing on the option play made him a triple threat. The Philadelphia Eagles' Tom Brookshier watches as this pass, a bit too long, rolls off Gifford's finger tips.

and Unitas went about his chores calmly and effectively. His passes carried the Colts to the 38, where Bert Rechichar's attempt for a field goal was short.

Later a fumble by Phil King allowed the Colts another opening and they advanced to the 27. There, however, Andy Robustelli and Jim Katcavage did yeoman work in throwing Unitas for successive big losses and it appeared that the Giants were home free.

But the Colt defense stopped the Giants. On third down, Gifford's run was a foot short of a first down. Don Chandler had to punt and the Colts took over on their 14-yard line.

STATISTICS OF THE GAME

	Colts	Giants
First downs	27	10
Rushing yardage	138	88
Passing yardage	322	178
Passes attempted	40	18
Passes completed	26	12
Passes intercepted by	0	1
Punts	4	6
Av. dist. of punts, yds.	51	48
Fumbles lost	2	4
Yards penalized	62	52

When the visitors put the ball in play they were 86 yards from the goal. They had 1 minute 56 seconds to go the distance. Unitas missed with a toss to Dupre, losing four seconds. Then he hit Moore with an 11-yarder at the cost of twenty-two seconds.

Another aerial failed, but the next, to Berry, was good for 25 yards. Then, twice in succession, it was Unitas to Berry for 16 and 21 yards. Suddenly the Colts were on the 13-yard line.

The seconds continued to tick away. When Myhra put his toe to the ball on the 20 and sent the ball between the uprights, only seven seconds remained.

Chandler Punts to Colts

That, of course, made it 17—17 and necessitated the sudden-death finish. The Giants won the toss and elected to receive. Again the Giants were held by the defense. On third down, Conerly's option run was inches short of a first down and Chandler punted to the Colts. That was the last time the Giants handled the ball.

Starting on the 20, the Colts drove 80 yards in thirteen plays. Unitas, the quarterback no one seemed to want several years ago, hit with four of five passes. At the 1, Unitas handed off to Ameche and The Horse rammed over the right side to the championship. There was no try for the extra point.

At one stage during the campaign the Giants trailed the Cleveland Browns by two games. Coach Jim Lee Howell's squad upset the Colts and the Browns in succession and wound up tied with the Browns for the Eastern Conference crown. They beat the Browns in a play-off and took their ninth division championship a month after the Colts had wrapped up their first Western Conference title. Baltimore is "west" because of the crazy-quilt geographic set-up in the N. F. L.

Each Colt earned a record $4,718.77 share yesterday. Each Giant share was worth $3,111.33, also a record.

December 29, 1958

A Persevering Passer

Johnny Unitas

The New York Times

Three years ago he couldn't get a job in pro football
(Unitas talking with newsmen in dressing room after game)

DURING the extra period at Yankee Stadium yesterday, it was risky to pass, but Johnny Unitas passed. This was to be expected from the Baltimore Colts' quarterback, who couldn't get a job in pro football three years ago. Unitas, whose name is prounced "You-night-us," is as cocky on the field as he is off.

Man in the News

In the dressing room he said, "Why shouldn't I have passed then? After all, you don't have to risk anything when you know where you're passing."

Five passes by Unitas, including four completions, helped move the Colts the distance required to gain the winning touchdown.

Unitas, a 25-year-old 6-foot 1-inch blond of Lithuanian ancestry, has known where he's been headed for a long time. Disappointments haven't stopped him nor setbacks discouraged him.

Johnny gained most of his determination from his family, particularly his widowed mother. She raised a family of four children in Pittsburgh after her first husband, Leonard Sr., died in 1938. Unitas' mother, now 55, remarried four years ago.

That was long after Mrs. Helen Unitas had kept Leonard Unitas' coal delivery business going in the late Thirties. When spring and summer came and the demand for coal dropped off, she got a job cleaning offices in downtown Pittsburgh at night.

Her children seldom wanted and she taught them that desire, courage and spirit were the principal factors in making progress against adversity.

James Carey, Unitas' coach at St. Justin's High in Pittsburgh, saw the potential in Unitas some years ago. However, letter-writing and in-person demonstrations by Unitas couldn't prove to college coaches that Johnny was valuable football material.

Through a Notre Dame alumnus, Carey saw to it that Unitas got a chance to show his wares at Notre Dame. Bernie Crimmins, then an assistant to the Irish head coach, Frank Leahy, saw the 145-pound high school boy enough to decide that Unitas was too small and not good enough for Notre Dame.

The University of Indiana gave Unitas the same treatment and the player, anxious to get to college for football, was aware of his first phase of not being wanted. The University of Louisville gave a scholarship to Unitas and Johnny enrolled there in 1951. He was graduated in 1955 and again was not wanted for football in the fall of 1955.

The Pittsburgh Steelers drafted Unitas, but didn't keep him. "We don't have any use for four quarterbacks," they said. Unitas was the fourth man and the forsaken one.

Married then and with his second of three children on the way, Johnny went to work with a pile-driving gang in what he describes as a "temporary job." It was temporary because he was determined to make a professional football team. He started by asking at the top.

He wrote to Paul Brown,

the coach of the Cleveland Browns. Brown answered that he didn't need Unitas in 1955, but told Johnny to try again in the training season of 1956. Brown never got the chance to see Unitas in a Browns' uniform.

Don Kellett, the general manager of the Colts, signed Unitas in February of 1956 after hearing reports of the fine quarterback playing for a sandlot team in Pittsburgh called the Bloomfield Rams. Johnny was getting $6 a game for playing with the Rams.

Asked yesterday why he signed Unitas, Kellett said, "When you get a quarterback for nothing, sign him." Unitas was a free agent after his release by the Steelers. The value of the Colts' investment was shown last season when Johnny was voted the most valuable player in the league.

Unitas carries his calm approach onto the field, where he can snap a quick pass a split second after getting the ball or saunter about in the backfield taking his time looking for receivers while dodging 250-pound linemen. He has the assurance of that rarity in pro football—a player with all his teeth. He calls 70 per cent of the Colts' plays and has a cool daring that has paid off handsomely.

During the Colts' last march of the season, yesterday's final drive for a touchdown, Unitas saw a receiver on his left who was clear. The Colts needed 8 yards for a first down and Ray Berry, the potential receiver, was only about 5 yards beyond the line of scrimmage.

Unitas could have flipped the Ball to Berry who was all alone and hoped that the end would carry another 3 for the first down. Instead, the quarterback rolled slowly to his left, motioned Berry to move farther downfield and then, when the end was in first-down territory, Unitas tossed a strike.

The cocky touch adds to the luster of a star who can virtually call plays while they're in progress. He does this by verbal signals after approaching the line and noting the offensive alignment.

Unitas didn't get much of a chance with the Colts until the fourth game of the 1956 season. Baltimore's regular quarterback, George Shaw, was carried out in the second period of a game against the Chicago Bears. Unitas replaced Shaw and he's been the No. 1 man since.

Quiet and retiring Unitas turned down $750 in fees for TV appearances scheduled for last night and this morning. Johnny said, "I want to be with the team on the big night and I want to get home."

Home is a modern split-level house in Towson, Md., where he lives with his wife, Dorothy Jane, and Janice Ann, 3; John Jr., 2, and Bobby, 7 months.

During the off-season he's a salesman for a container company and also does promotion work for a sporting goods corporation.

He's $4,718.77 richer for his efforts of yesterday. That's a trifle better than his pay with the Bloomfield Rams.

December 29, 1958

Lombardi of Giants to Coach Packer Eleven

General Manager's Post Also Included in Five-Year Pact

By GORDON S. WHITE Jr.

Vince Lombardi, the offensive coach of the New York Football Giants since 1954, was named yesterday as the head coach and general manager of the Green Bay Packers.

Lombardi will sign a five-year contract at a meeting with the Green Bay directors in the Wisconsin city Monday. He said at the Manhattan Hotel:

"I'm both happy and sad. Happy about getting the new job and sad because I'm leaving the Giants and a fine group in the Mara family, which owns the Giants."

However, it was hard to see sadness showing through his big grin as he talked of his plans.

Of Fordham Fame

The 5-foot 11-inch Lombardi, who in the Thirties was a member of the famed Fordham line known as the Seven Blocks of Granite, will succeed Ray (Scooter) McLean as the head coach at Green Bay and Verne Lewellen as the general manager.

McLean resigned last month after only one season with the Packers, during which the club won one game, lost ten and tied one. Lewellen was dropped as general manager simultaneously with Lombardi's appointment.

"I was first approached (by the Packers) at the National Football League draft meetings in Philadelphia recently," Lombardi said. "I made final arrangements with the club last Monday in Green Bay and I was notified today that the directors had voted for me."

Dominic Olejniczak, the Packer president, did the contact work with Lombardi.

Lombardi, who hasn't been a head coach since his term at St. Cecilia's High School in Englewood, N. J., thirteen years ago, joins Paul Brown of the Cleveland Browns as the only coach and general manager in the league. George Halas, the coach, owner and president of the Chicago Bears, is the only other coach in the league who holds another position as well.

A complete change for Lombardi and his family and a complete change for the Packers are in the offing, according to the husky, Brooklyn-born coach. Raised in the metropolitan area and now living with his wife and two children in Fair Haven, N. J., Lombardi said, "We'll move lock, stock and barrel soon."

Referring to what's about to happen to the Packers, he said, "I'll take the Giant offense with me and use it with the Packers as personnel permits."

Lombardi became the Giants' offensive coach in 1954, after Jim Lee Howell had succeeded Steve Owen as head coach. Lombardi's plan of attack was based on a power offense, using what he called "the close-end attack" instead of the league's more popular slot-T formation. The Giants' attack had the ends closer, with a wide flanker, instead of placing a halfback between tackle and a wide end.

Lombardi said, "My attack is harder to defend against and I'm going to stick with what has been successful for the Giants." Under Howell and Lombardi the Giants won the 1956 league title and last season won the Eastern Conference championship, only to lose to the Baltimore Colts in the league championship game.

Lombardi admitted he wasn't

too familiar with the Packer players. "Since they're in the Western Conference I haven't had much chance to see them while I've been with the Giants," he said. "But in a month or so, after seeing all the movies of their games last year, I'll be able to form plans on who will have what jobs in the team I plan to field."

Staff to Be Picked

All of McLean's assistants have been released by the Packers and the 45-year-old Lombardi will pick his own staff. He didn't mention names, but said he would choose from among nine or ten possibilities.

Though his work for years has been with the offense, Lombardi said, "I'll put the Packers' best players on defense. It's best for a team and good for its morale." Defense always has been a Giant strong point.

The new coach hopes he'll not have to use two quarterbacks constantly, as he did with the Giants. "That was a thing peculiar to the Giants," Lombardi said. "I'd like to have just one man there."

The Packers, as bottom team in the league, had first draft choice this year and picked Randy Duncan of Iowa, one of the nation's best college quarterbacks last season. It will be Lombardi's job as general manager to sign Duncan and then his job as coach to see if Duncan is the one quarterback he wants.

Vito Parilli and Bart Starr were the Green Bay quarterbacks last season.

Man He Leaves Behind

Lombardi spoke wistfully about leaving behind Frank Gifford, the Giant halfback, who was a key man in many of the coach's plays. In particular, Lombardi wanted "a guy like Gifford for that option pass play he did so well."

As a player at St. Francis Prep in Brooklyn, Lombardi was a fullback. At Fordham he was a guard on the most feared line in college football from 1934 through 1936.

He went to law school at Fordham and then took the coaching job at St. Cecilia's in 1939, where he stayed until 1946. At the Englewood school, Lombardi's teams won six New Jersey State championships and in one stretch won thirty-six games in a row.

From that job, Lombardi went to the freshman coaching post at Fordham in 1947, where he installed the T formation for the freshmen. In 1948 he assisted the varsity coach, Ed Danowski. From 1949 until he got this sassurance from Lombardi assisted Earl (Red) Blaik at Army.

The Packer fans, always among the most enthusiastic, got this assurance from Lombardi: "I've never been with a losing team in my life and I don't think I'll start now."

Lombardi will resign a job he holds with the Federation Bank and Trust Company in New York.

The New York Times

Vince Lombardi, new head coach and general manager of the Green Bay Packers, in his room at Manhattan Hotel.

January 29, 1959

New Pro Football League Formed

FRANCHISES GIVEN TO 2 TEXAS CITIES

Dallas, Houston and Denver in New American League —Expansion Possible

CHICAGO, Aug. 14 (UPI)—A second professional football league, to be called the American Football League, was formed tonight and franchises were announced for six cities.

Lamar Hunt of Dallas said teams would be formed in Dallas, Houston, Minneapolis-St. Paul, Denver, New York and Los Angeles.

Hunt said Barron Hilton, a son of the hotel owner, Conrad N. Hilton, would head the Los Angeles franchise.

Hunt, the founder of the league, said it planned to begin play in 1960.

Hunt said the league might expand to eight teams, with the other two coming from Seattle, Buffalo, San Francisco, Miami or Kansas City. It was also reported that New Orleans was a possibility.

12 Teams in N. F. L.

The National Football League is the only major circuit now in operation. It has twelve teams —two in Chicago and one each in New York, Baltimore, Washington, Philadelphia, Pittsburgh, Cleveland, Detroit, Los Angeles, San Francisco and Green Bay, Wis.

Draft plans will be drawn for this fall and committees are at work on the constitution, by-laws and working agreements, Hunt said.

K. S. (Bud) Adams, a Houston oilman and owner of the Houston franchise of the new league, joined with Hunt in conducting the organizational meeting.

The Denver franchise was represented by Robert Howsam of Rocky Mountain Empire Sports, Inc. Max Winter and Bill Boyer were the representatives from Minneapolis-St. Paul.

Harry Wismer, the radio and television sports broadcaster, represented the New York franchise.

No Headquarters Yet

Hunt said, "We'll try to beat the National Football League on their draft" in the race to secure top college players for the new league.

"No headquarters have been set up yet," Hunt said.

Hunt said the league would hold another meeting within two weeks, probably in Dallas, where a constitution would be drawn up.

"We have definite commitments," he said. "A kitty is being set up to assure the financial success of the league."

August 15, 1959

Football Giants Steal a Half-Step

New Man-in-Motion Series Is Designed to Slow Pursuit

By ROBERT L. TEAGUE

Followers of the New York Football Giants will see something new this fall: A man-in-motion series. Its purpose is to slow defensive pursuit.

Repeated matinee and evening showings of game movies shot in 1958 convinced the coaches that something had to be done to discourage pursuers. For even a jet-propelled, deceptive-gaited halfback cannot break away if the cutback area is overpopulated. Pursuit being what it is in the pro league, he might as well be a lead-footed oaf.

A backwash of tacklers from the side of the field farthest from the hole of impact will engulf him almost immediately, holding a potential romp to a picayune gain.

There is nothing in the Giants' regular patterns to prevent defenders on the far side from clogging the secondary. The blockers on that side check the men nearest them only momentarily before sprinting to keep appointments downfield.

Al Sherman, the assistant coach in charge of the Giants' offense, thinks the man in motion will turn the incurable suspicion that is common to defenders into an advantage for his team.

"Primarily, he puts mental pressure on the defense," Sherman said. "They can't afford to ignore him, because his position determines our strong side, and that's the side we can hit them hardest."

So the defenders begin leaning in the moving back's direction before the ball is snapped; and, once the play gets under way, they begin "flowing" with him.

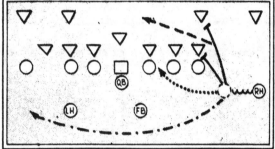

The New York Times   Sept. 9, 1959

Diagram shows maneuvers of the back in motion (RH) in new series to be used by the 1959 Giants. He is alternately a blocker (solid lines), a pass receiver (dashes), runner (dots) and key man in reverse (dot-dashes).

"If we run another back to the opposite side," Sherman said, "they're too far off balance to be as quick to pursue as they normally are."

The ball carrier thus may gain a half-step advantage, enough to make his cutback and scram.

The man in motion also keeps the defense from digging in. His movement draws them out of their foxholes. They thus are less difficult for other blockers to budge.

The accompanying diagram, made from a drawing by Sherman, shows the various maneuvers of the nomadic halfback in this series as a runner, blocker, pass receiver and flim-flammer. The drawing shows the right half set on the right flank, but the series works as well with the left half set wide on the left.

When the Giants break from the huddle, the designated back goes 8 to 9 yards wide of his end and about a yard behind the line. As the quarterback starts his long count, the flanker starts jogging (wavy line) toward the other backs.

The broken circle represents his position at the time of the snap from center. There, he is, in effect, an eighth lineman at a spot that has three men opposing two.

On running plays, he has good blocking angles on the corner defender and the nearest safety man (solid lines).

On the pass play (dashes), he fakes a block on the near safety and cuts over the middle to take a pitch. This is an area that the Giants' receivers rarely were able to infiltrate on their regular patterns last year, Sherman said.

The moving back can be a decoy or a ball carrier in a sequence that sends him between guard and tackle (dotted line). With the defense flowing toward that hole, another back, going around end or through the line, has a chance to get the jump on his pursuers.

Another sequence sending the man in motion behind his backfield mates (dots and dashes) also starts the defense flowing. He can be a decoy on runs hitting the weak side, a pass receiver in the flat, a ball carrier or the key man in a double reverse.

He also has a pass route straight down the field, breaking from a stationary start on a quick count.

September 9, 1959

Ram Official Heads Pro Football League

By LOUIS EFFRAT
Special to The New York Times.

MIAMI BEACH, Jan. 26—In a sudden switch that brought to an end seven days of bitter wrangling among the twelve club-owners, a new commissioner of the National Football League was elected tonight.

He is Alvin Ray (Pete) Rozelle, the 33-year-old general manager of the Los Angeles Rams.

Elected on the twenty-third round of balloting, Rozelle was named to a three-year term at an annual salary of $50,000 by the professional circuit.

The new commissioner said he planned to operate for the present from the suburban Philadelphia office that Bert Bell used until his sudden death last Oct. 11. Rozelle said he would eventually move his headquarters to New York.

Until the sudden and dramatic announcement of Rozelle's victory, his name had not been mentioned among the dozen or so proposed for the big job. Through most of the voting the leaders had been Marshall G. Leahy, a San Francisco lawyer, and Austin H. Gunsel, the former F. B. I. man who had been acting commissioner.

That the pros and cons had been hot and heavy right to the

end was evidenced by the actual tally of the final ballot.

Eight clubs voted for Rozelle. The San Francisco 49ers, for whom Leahy had served as counsel, remained committed to him. The Detroit Lions, Chicago Bears and Los Angeles Rams abstained. A three-quarter majority of those voting was needed to elect.

Rozelle said he hoped to keep the N. F. L. office staff. A few minutes later it was announced that the 50-year-old Gunsel had been re-elected treasurer of the league, one of the several posts he held.

Gunsel's salary was increased from $10,000 to $15,000 a year and he was voted a $10,000 bonus for his services as acting commissioner.

When it became obvious that the bloc favoring Leahy, nick-named the "solid seven," and the "fearless four" who supported Gunsel would not budge, a compromise was reached. It was Carroll Rosenbloom, the owner of the champion Baltimore Colts and a Gunsel supporter who proposed Rozelle.

Rozelle said, "I would be silly to consider myself anything but a compromise commissioner. I only hope that I will be able to live up to the confidence that

has been shown in me."

Expansion Is Favored

Rozelle said he favored expansion of the league. He also said that, the newly organized American Football League and the N. F. L. "will get along if there is a mutual respect of contracts."

Rozelle will be in the chair at 9:30 tomorrow morning when the league resumes the forty-first annual meeting. Now that the question of the commissioner has been resolved, expansion and other matters will be dealt with. Commitments for franchises have been made to Dallas and Minneapolis-St. Paul. How and when these will be granted are matters for conjecture.

Rozelle, a soft-spoken, 6-foot 1½-inch 180-pounder, is married and the father of a 16-month-old daughter, Ann Marie. He played high school basketball and dabbled a bit in tennis, but most of his extra-curricular career at Compton Junior College and the University of San Francisco was devoted to sports publicity. He served for a while as assistant director of athletics at the university under Joe Kuharich.

He insists his chief claim to fame is that he "played basketball with Duke Snider at Compton High School."

From 1952 through 1954 he

Associated Press
ELECTED: Pete Rozelle, general manager of the Los Angeles Rams, who was chosen as Commissioner of National Football League.

was the public relations man for the Rams, a job he quit to join an advertising agency. In the spring of 1957 he returned to the Rams as general manager.

An odd twist is that it was Bell who used his influence to place Rozelle in the big job with the Rams. Five squabbling partners needed someone to keep peace and Bell felt Rozelle was the man to do it.

Sixth Head of League

Rozelle is the sixth head of the league. Dating back to 1920, the others were Jim Thorpe, Joe F. Carr, Carl Storck, Elmer Layden and Bell, who died of a heart attack at 65 while watching the Pittsburgh Steelers play the Eagles at Philadelphia's Franklin Field.

Rozelle was present at a meeting this afternoon, but only as a member of the Rams' brass, when Bill MacPhail, sports director of the Columbia Broadcasting System, gave an informal report on a proposed package television deal.

MacPhail's network would pay the league approximately $3,000,000, to be divided as the league sees fit, for exclusive rights to televise all games except the championship play-off.

January 27, 1960

National Football League Admits Dallas for '60 and Twin Cities for '61

RANGERS WILL GET HELP FROM RIVALS

By LOUIS EFFRAT
Special to The New York Times.

MIAMI BEACH, Jan. 28—Immediate expansion, regarded as hopeless ten days ago by some National Football League owners, became a reality tonight. By a vote of 11-0, with the Chicago Cardinals abstaining, the league admitted the Dallas Rangers.

The thirteenth club in the forty-year-old league is owned by Clint Murchison Jr. and Beford Wynne and coached by Tom Landry, formerly of the New York Giants. Dallas will be a "swing team." It will be assigned to the Western Conference for 1960 and meet every club in the Eastern and Western divisions once. The Rangers will play their home games in the Cotton Bowl.

Alvin Ray (Pete) Rozelle, the new Commissioner of the N. F. L. also announced shortly after 6 P. M. that a franchise to become operative in 1961 had been granted to Minneapolis-St. Paul.

"Furthermore," the 33-year old Commissioner added, "if conditions are practical, two more teams will be added within the next three years. We feel that two eight-team divisions would be ideal."

Murchison and Wynne, each 36 years old and each a multimillionaire, had been waiting for more than a week. "This was well worth waiting for," Wynne said. "We're ready to go."

The cost of the franchise was $50,000, which goes into the league treasury. There is, however, a catch.

Because the Rangers are to be permitted to "buy" player-contracts, three from each established N. F. L. team, the new owners will be obliged to pay an additional $550,000. This sum is to be handed over to the Commissioner, as trustee for the member clubs. He will divide it among the twelve other outfits.

While details are yet to be arranged, it is expected that the twelve other clubs will provide some talent for the new member. After protecting their "untouchables," each club will present a list of ten players who were active at the end of last season. From each list, Landry will be permitted to take three players.

Among the conditions imposed on new franchises is one that requires the Texans to pay $200,000 of the $600,000 to

the league upon being admitted to membership. The remainder is to be paid in installments. Since Murchison and Wynne already had $25,000 in "earnest money" on deposit, they will have to turn over a check for $175,000. "We'll do that tomorrow," Murchison said.

Another condition makes it imperative that in the event the new owners desire to sell their franchise within the next three years, it must be offered to the league at the price it cost—$600,000. Also, the commissioner and the other owners retain the right to approve management contracts.

Murchison and Wynne were so happy to enter the fold that they readily agreed to the provision that "new franchises will have no voting rights until the annual meeting following their admission."

Also, they agreed that the Eastern Conference of the league would have the right, after the 1960 season, to choose which of the new clubs—Dallas or Minneapolis-St. Paul—would join it.

The Minneapolis-St. Paul eleven will play its home games at Metropolitan Stadium, between the Twin Cities. The arena can accommodate about 26,000 fans now, but the stands will be enlarged to handle 40,000.

Halas Offers Motion

The motion that paved the way for immediate expansion

was made by George Halas of the Chicago Bears and seconded by Joseph A. Donoghue of the Philadelphia Eagles.

Dallas, despite the uncertainty surrounding a franchise for 1960, has been "working" steadily. Landry, the defensive genius, and Tex Schramm, the general manager of the Rangers, have lined up about thirty college players. Among the best are Don Meredith, a Southern Methodist quarterback; Don Perkins, a New Mexico halfback, and Jim Mooty, an Arkansas halfback.

That Dallas apparently is to house two professional football teams does not frighten Murchison and Wynne. Another group, this one headed by Lamar Hunt and called the Dallas Texans, is in the rival American Football League and also will play its home games in the Cotton Bowl.

"Dallas," Murchison said, "is a big-league city that will back big-league pro football. We will have the big-league team, because we will be playing the established big-league teams, backed with established big-league players. The other team will have to start as a minor-league outfit. Perhaps it will be supported, but we, the Rangers, will prosper."

The population of Dallas is 750,000. Within a fifty-mile area, however, the Rangers hope to draw from another 250,000.

January 29, 1960

CARDINALS' ELEVEN TO SHIFT THIS YEAR

CHICAGO, March 29 (UPI) —The Chicago Cardinals today informed the National Football League that their franchise would be moved to St. Louis for the 1960 season.

Managing Director Walter Wolfner confirmed the shift to the meeting of league club owners after they had officially approved the language of a resolution in which the league will pay the club $500,000 for moving.

The move originally was announced at the league's recent meeting in Los Angeles, but Wolfner had until April 2 to make a final decision. Commissioner Pete Rozelle said the delay was granted to permit him to arrange a lease for Busch Stadium and arrange other details.

Wolfner said:

"We have a favorable lease now and when this move is permanent."

Rozelle refused to make public how and when the $500,000 would be paid to the Cardinals, but said the Chicago Bears, who will receive the right to televise road games into Chicago with the Cardinals gone, will play the largest portion.

March 30, 1960

EAGLES WIN, 17-13, TO TAKE PRO TITLE

58-Yard Return of Kick-Off Helps Defeat Packers

By JOSEPH M. SHEEHAN
Special to The New York Times.

PHILADELPHIA, Dec. 26 — The National Football League championship, as well as baseball's supreme crown, now reposes in the Commonwealth of Pennsylvania.

With a comeback worthy of the Pittsburgh Pirates, the Philadelphia Eagles defeated the Green Bay Packers, 17—13, in the title play-off today. A sellout crowd of 67,325 saw the game at Franklin Field.

Coach Buck Shaw's Eastern Conference champions beat the favored Packers at the Packers' game—running. The normally pass-minded Eagles went overhead only once in driving 32 yards in seven plays to score the winning touchdown at 5:21 of the final period.

Ted Dean, a fleet, powerful rookie halfback from near-by Radnor, Pa., slammed across for the deciding points from 5 yards out on a sweep around Green Bay's right end behind a crushing block by Gerry Huth.

Dean had set the winning drive in motion by sprinting 58 yards to Green Bay's 39-yard line with a kick-off. That followed the touchdown that put the Packers in the lead for the second time.

Dominant in the early going, Green Bay scored on field goals of 20 and 23 yards by Paul Horning in the first two periods.

On the pinpoint passing of their great Norm Van Brocklin, the Eagles struck back late in the second quarter. A 35-yard pass from Van Brocklin to Tommy McDonald moved Philadelphia ahead, 7—6, at 8:08 of the second period.

Before the half ended, Van Brocklin also had passed his team into position for a 15-yard field goal by Bobby Walston.

The Eagles' embattled defense, which checked the Packers in scoring territory five times, held firm through the third period. Then it yielded at 1:53 of the last quarter to a 7-yard touchdown pass from Bart Starr to Max McGee.

Time Runs Out on Packers

Philadelphia's offensive unit quickly recouped on Dean's touchdown. The Eagle defenders hung grimly on the rest of the way, with the clock as an ally. They stopped a last-ditch Packer drive on the Eagle 10-yard line as time ran out.

The result sent the partisan onlookers into a state of delirium. The enthused Eagle adherents leveled the goal posts in a jiffy as soon as the police had lifted their guard and still were whooping it up in the near-by streets two hours later.

The game started at noon, earlier than usual for a professional contest. This was done to allow for a sudden-death overtime, which was planned had regulation time ended with the score tied. Franklin Field has no lights.

It was Philadelphia's first National League championship since Greasy Neale's Eagles of 1949 defeated the Los Angeles Rams, 14—0, in the second of two consecutive victories.

Coach Vince Lombardi's Packers, whose Western Conference victory was as great a surprise as that of the Eagles in the East, had all the best of the statistics. Green Bay outgained Philadelphia from scrimmage, 401 yards to 296, and piled up twenty-two first downs against thirteen.

Packers Lack Decisiveness

With their powerful running game, which accounted for 223 yards, the Packers controlled the ball for long intervals. But they lacked decisiveness when opportunity beckoned. The Eagles, who ran only forty-eight scrimmage plays to the Packers' seventy-seven, did the better job of the cashing in on their chances.

Having Van Brocklin on its side helped Philadelphia immeasurably. The 34-year-old quarterback, who confirmed his decision to retire, has had better days passing, but he called a magnificent game.

Sharing honors with Van Brocklin, Dean, McDonald and Walston, who also place-kicked 2 extra points, was Chuck Bednarik, the 35-year-old Eagle center. Doubling on offense and defense, he was on the field every scrimmage play.

Among other things, Bednarik knocked Paul Hornung, Green Bay's league scoring leader, out of action with a rib-rattling tackle early in the third period; recovered a fumble that stopped a promising Packer march in the fourth period and made the game-ending tackle that assured victory for the Eagles.

Muddy Spots on Field

The weather was fine—sparkling clear and surprisingly warm, with the temperature ranging up to 48 degrees. The field was a bit treacherous, though, frozen hard underneath and soft on top, with muddy spots where icy patches had melted.

The Eagles won the toss, elected to receive and promptly put themselves in a deep hole. On their first scrimmage play, Van Brocklin flipped a lateral to Bill Barnes, who had flared to the left. The ball bounced off Barnes' reaching hands into those of Bill Quinlan, Green Bay's defensive right end.

This break set up the Packers on Philadelphia's 14. Jim Taylor, Green Bay's admirable fullback, whose line-cracking activities netted 105 yards, smashed to the 9 on the first play. But the Eagles dug in, held three more rushes to 3 yards and took the ball on downs on their 6.

Almost immediately, the Eagles gave away the ball again. On the third play, Barnes, after breaking loose for what would have been a first down, fumbled when tackled. Bill Forester recovered for Green Bay on the Philadelphia 22.

Two power thrusts by Hornung and Taylor produced a Packer first down on the 12. Then Hornung ripped through to the 8. But Green Bay went offside on its next rush, and two passes by Starr missed connections. So the Packers settled for a field goal by Hornung from the 20.

Late in the first period, Green Bay got rolling from its 37 on a march that carried to Philadelphia's 17 at the start of the second quarter. But after Taylor had reached the 12, the Packers again were guilty of an offside. Again two passes failed, and again Hornung kicked a field goal, from the 23.

On this movement, the Packers missed a glowing chance to score a touchdown on the first play of the second quarter. Hornung, on a halfback option pass, failed to get the ball to Boyd Dowler, in the clear behind the last Packer defender. The underthrown pass was knocked down.

A few minutes later, Van Brocklin had the same chance and didn't fail. The elusive McDonald broke loose from his right flanker post, and Van pitched a strike to him for a 22-yard gain. On the next play, the same combination clicked again for a 35-yard touchdown.

The next time the Eagles had the ball, Van Brocklin hung a 41-yard pass on a handle for Pete Retzlaff. This put Philadelphia on Green Bay's 33. Dean picked up 3 yards, Van Brocklin missed once, then hit Dean for a 22-yard gain to the Packer 8.

Green Bay balked Van Brocklin's next three passes, but the Eagles were in position to take a 15-yard field goal by Walston that stretched their lead to 10—6.

From the kick-off that followed, the Packers roared 72 yards to a first down on Philadelphia's 7. But time was running out in the half. After Starr had failed to gain when trapped behind his line on an attempted pass, the Packers tried a field goal. Hornung's boot from the 12 was wide to the left.

Early in the third period, the Packers, on 15-yard runs by Horning and Taylor, reached Philadelphia's 34. But, after yielding 5 yards to Hornung's next thrust, the Eagles clamped down and took the ball on downs just inside their 25. On this sequence Hornung's shoulder was reinjured. Except to kick the point after Green Bay's touchdown, he played no more.

Symank Intercepts Pass

From this point, the Eagles swiftly moved to Green Bay's 5, with passes by Van Brocklin to McDonald and Walston accounting for most of the yardage. But on second down, John Symank ended the threat by intercepting a pass by Van Brocklin in the end zone.

An enterprising play by McGee got Green Bay started on the touchdown drive that followed. After the interception, the Packers were stalled on their 20.

Back to punt on fourth down with 10 yards to go, McGee spotted the Eagle defense dropping back and ran instead. He raced 35 yards to Philadelphia's 45 before being hauled down.

A pass by Starr to Gary Knafelc moved the ball to the Eagle 34 as the third period ended. From there, Tom Moore, standing in for Hornung, and Taylor advanced to the 7. Then Starr switched to the air and hit McGee, who cut in sharply from the left flank, with a perfect pass on the goal line.

Philadelphia retaliated explosively. Taking the kick-off on his 3, Dean raced back to Green Bay's 39, where Willie Wood fought through two blockers to knock him out of bounds.

Runs Replace Passes

Green Bay was penalized 7 yards for defensive holding on Philadelphia's first play, a pass by Van Brocklin that never got airbound. From the 32, Van Brocklin crossed the Packer defense by calling running plays.

Hitting hard on off-tackle plays, Dean and Barnes punched out a first down on the 20. The Packer line then spilled Van Brocklin for a 7-yard loss. He recouped it with a couple of yards to spare on a screen pass to Barnes.

Then the cagy Philadelphia signal-caller caught the Packers off guard again. On third down with 8 to go, they were looking for a pass. He sent Barnes off tackle and the stumpy halfback slashed and squirmed to a first down on the 10.

From there, Dean hit off tackle to the 5 and then circled end for the score. Huth's crushing block got him around the corner but he still had to drive through a couple of tacklers on his own.

Green Bay moved past midfield from the following kickoff, but on-the-spot Bednarik was there to grab the ball when McGee fumbled a pass from Starr on Philadelphia's 48.

Packers Make Final Bid
Nothing was accomplished by

either side in the next couple of exchanges. Then, with 1 minute 15 seconds to go, the Packers aroused themselves. From their 35, they stormed to Philadelphia's 22 on Starr's passing to various receivers.

But they couldn't break anyone completely loose and there was time for just one more play. Again Starr had no free deep receiver. So he threw short—just over the line to Taylor.

Bednarik quickly clamped the Green Bay fullback in a bear hug and, with the assistance of another tackler, wrestled him to the ground on the 10. That was the ball game.

PHILADELPHIA EAGLES (17)
Left Ends—Retzlaff, Robb.

Left Tackles—McCusker, Keys, Gossage.
Left Guards—Huth, Wittenborn, Richardson, Gunnels.
Centers—Bednarik, Lapham, Weber.
Right Guards—S. Campbell, Khayat.
Right Tackles—Smith, Wilcox, M. Campbell.
Right Ends—Walston, Reichow, Lucas, Baughan, Nocera.
Quarterbacks—Van Brocklin, Jurgensen, Freeman.
Left Halfbacks—Barnes, Brown, Carr, Jackson.
Right Halfbacks—McDonald, Brookshier.
Fullbacks—Dean, Burroughs, Sapp.
GREEN BAY PACKERS (13)
Left Ends—McGee, Currie, R. Kramer.
Left Tackles—Skoronski, Masters, Davis, Beck, Miller.
Left Guards—Thurston, Cvercko, Hanner.
Centers—Ringo, Iman, Nitschke, Bettis.
Right Guards—J. Kramer, Jordan.
Right Ends—Knafelc, Meilinger, Forester.
Quarterbacks—Starr, McHan, Symank, Wood, Pesonen.
Left Halfbacks—Hornung, Moore, Winslow, Gremminger, Hackbart.
Right Halfbacks—Dowler, Carpenter, Whittenton.
Fullbacks—Taylor, Hickman, Tunnell.
Philadelphia Eagles......0   10   0   7—17
Green Bay Packers.......3   3   7   0—13
G.B.-FG, Hornung, 20.

G.B.-FG, Hornung, 23.
Phil.—McDonald, 35, pass from Van Brocklin (Walston, kick).
Phil.—FG, Walston, 15.
G.B.-McGee, 7, pass from Starr (Hornung, kick).
Phil.—Dean, 5, run (Walston, kick).
G.B.-McGee, 7, pass from Starr (Hornung, kick).
Referee—Ron Gibbs. Umpire—Joe Connell. Linesman—John Highberger. Back judge—Sam Giangreco. Field judge—Herman Rohrig.
Attendance—67,325.

STATISTICS OF THE GAME

	Eagles	Pack.
First downs	13	22
Rushing yardage	99	223
Passing yardage	197	178
Passes	9-20	21-35
Interceptions by	0	1
Punts	6-40	5-45
Fumbles lost	2	1
Yards penalized	0	27

December 27, 1960

Giants Beat Redskins, 49-34, as Tittle Hurls 7 Touchdown Passes Here

NEW YORK GAINS 505 YARDS IN AIR

Tittle Hits on 12 Passes in Row and 27 of 39—Snead Hurls 4 Scoring Tosses

STATISTICS OF THE GAME

	Giants	'Skins
First downs	25	19
Rushing yardage	97	58
Passing yardage	505	316
Passes	27-39	17-40
Interceptions by	3	0
Punts	4-47	6-31
Fumbles lost	0	1
Yards penalized	127	35

By ROBERT L. TEAGUE

As if the league-leading Washington Redskins weren't even there, Y. A. Tittle of the New York Giants played catch with fleet-footed friends yesterday afternoon at Yankee Stadium. The results were a record-equaling seven touchdown passes for Tittle and a 49-34 triumph for New York.

Only twice before had any National Football League quarterback wreaked so much havoc with his throwing arm in a single joust. Eons ago, Sid Luckman of the Bears established a league high of seven scoring passes in one game. Later that was matched by Adrian Burk of the Eagles.

Yesterday, a vociferous throng of 62,844 saw the Giants abruptly halt Washington's unbeaten streak at six, and re-establish New York's ranking as the club most likely to succeed in the Eastern Conference.

Joe Walton crossed the goal line three times with Tittle's passes. Joe Morrison scored with two and Frank Gifford and Del Shofner sprinted into the end

zone with one apiece for the 1961 conference champions.

All told, the 35-year-old Tittle made connections on 27 of 39 passes—and 12 of the completions came in succession. He thus accounted for 505 yards, more than any of his predecessors on the Giants ever had.

A Necessary Achievement

As the final score suggests, Tittle was virtually compelled to reach the apogee of his 15-year career as a pro. Norm Snead turned in his greatest performance to date as Washington's second-year quarterback. He made four touchdown throws. Two of these went to Bobby Mitchell on plays covering 80 and 44 yards.

Shofner was Tittle's primary target although it was Gifford who was in on the longest Giant pass of the day—63 yards. The lanky Shofner gained 269 yards on 11 catches which equaled Gifford's club record for receptions in one game. Shofner also eclipsed the Giants one-day mark of 212 yards gained by a pass catcher set by Gene Roberts in 1949.

At times, Tittle and Shofner seemed oblivious of the Redskins, as if warming up for a big game at some later date. Again and again, Del embarrassed Claude Crabb, Washington's rookie defensive back, in the secondary.

What made the Tittle-Shofner combination so effective, of course, was the stubbornness of New York's forward blockers—Ray Wietecha, Darrell Dess, Roosevelt Brown, Jack Stroud and Reed Bohovich. They gave Tittle plenty of time and room to study the field, and gave the receivers time to bamboozle or outrun their shadowers.

Redskin Attack Halted

On the other hand, Snead was hard pressed more often than not, and frequently was flattened by the Giants before he could get a pass off. The tacklers in most of these instances

were Jim Katcavage, Rosey Grier, Andy Robustelli and Dick Modzelewski.

The same quartet also stood out in thwarting Washington's rushing game, holding the Skins to 58 yards.

Erich Barnes of the Giants did a notable job of guarding the elusive Mitchell, although he twice was charged with pass interference. Only one of those penalties helped the Redskins score. The important thing was that Barnes allowed Mitchell to catch only five pitches and batted down that many himself.

In addition, the Giants' corner back intercepted one of Snead's passes to set up New York's second touchdown. A teammate, Jim Patton, twice halted Redskin threats in the second half by picking off passes near the New York goal line.

Coach Allie Sherman's Giants had stumbled into a 7-0 hole late in the first quarter when Johnny Counts of New York fumbled a fair catch on his 40. Vince Promuto recovered for the Redskins on the 44. Snead immediately collaborated with Mitchell on a touchdown pass.

The Giants struck back at once with an 81-yard scoring drive. They flew most of the way on Tittle's passes to Gifford, Shofner and Walton. A 22-yard pitch to Morrison wound it up, and Don Chandler kicked the first of seven extra points.

New York went ahead to stay early in the second period after Barnes had stolen the ball at the Giant 44. Tittle and Shofner teamed on passes of 34 and 11 yards to advance to the 9. Shortly thereafter, Tittle hit Walton in the end zone from the 4.

Following the next kickoff, Snead guided the Redskins 80 yards to a touchdown. He completed first-down passes to Don Bosseler, Bill Anderson and Fred Dugan along the way. From the Giant 24, Snead threw to Dugan again for the score.

Bob Khayat might have booted the tying point, but Sam Huff charged in from his line-

backing position and blocked the kick. That left the Giants in front, 14-13.

With time running out in the first half, Tittle and Shofner combined on a 53-yard pass play that set up another Giant score. This time, Tittle capped the march with a deceptive rollout pass to Morrison from the 2. That made the count 21-13 at the intermission.

Washington again came within a point of squaring the match on the first play from scrimmage in the third quarter. Here, the Redskins came up with perhaps the most beautifully executed play of the day.

It started like an end sweep at their 20, with Snead faking a handoff. Then he passed to Mitchell, who was a step behind Barnes on the New York 45. The fleet flanker back went the rest of the way. Khayat's kick made it 21-20.

By the time the third period ended, however, there was no doubt about the outcome. The Giants widened the gap to 42-20 as Tittle completed touchdown tosses to Shofner (32 yards), Walton (26 yards) and Gifford (63 yards).

The final Giant score, in the fourth period, was just so much frosting on the cake. It came on a 6-yard pass from Tittle to Walton.

In the final period, Dick James of Washington returned a kickoff from his 7 to the Giant 28. Snead capped this advance with a 1-yard plunge for the touchdown. Later, Snead ended an 86-yard drive with a scoring pass to Steve Junker from the Giant 35.

October 29, 1962

Pass Masters of Football

The pros have pulled off some record-breaking tosses this season as the game shifts steadily from a ground operation to aerial maneuvers.

By ARTHUR DALEY

WHEN Johnny Unitas and Raymond Berry were the dominant forward-passing combination in professional football a few seasons ago, their artistry with this most spectacular weapon in the gridiron arsenal propelled the Baltimore Colts into two successive world championships. No one has better described the peculiar affinity between passer and receiver than Berry, the target for the Unitas sharpshooting.

"It's almost like a marriage," he said. "You have to make allowances and understand each other. You get to know each other so well that you know instinctively what to expect in any situation."

The football marriage brokers have been busy since then with other glittering pairings. Among them have been Y. A. Tittle and Del Shofner of the New York Giants; Norm Snead and Bobby Mitchell of the Washington Redskins; Sonny Jurgensen and Tommy McDonald of the Philadelphia Eagles, and a host of others.

They are all masters at their trade, so proficient that on occasion they crash the record book. The Tittle-Shofner combination had such an explosive afternoon against the Washington Redskins earlier this season. Tittle—he prefers to be called Y. A. or Yat rather than by his given name of Yelberton Abraham—threw seven touchdown passes to equal a league record. He completed 27 of 39 tosses, an efficiency ratio that has never been matched, and his passes gained 505 yards, second best in pro annals. Shofner equalled a Giant mark with 11 catches and set a new club standard for yardage gained at 269.

IN spite of the public awareness nowadays of the value to a football team of perfectly mated passing combinations, it should be pointed out that such pairings are not exactly new. A quarter of a century ago, the Green Bay Packers had Cecil Isbell and Don Hutson, the latter the greatest pass catcher who ever lived. Things are different now from what they were when Hutson caught more passes for more touchdowns and more yards gained than any player in football history. Refinements in techniques have lifted the aerial plays to plateaus considered unattainable in the old days. Yet one principle remains unchanged. "For every pass I caught in a game," Hutson once said, "I caught a thousand passes in practice."

Practice still makes perfect, even though Hutson was a generation ahead of his time. He performed before the

ARTHUR DALEY writes a daily column for this newspaper called "Sports of The Times."

two-platoon system, one for offense and one for defense, was introduced. Two of every three plays in Hutson's day were running plays and the technique of the forward pass was so sketchily outlined that it often showed evidence of the impromptu.

Today more than half the plays are passes. Rarely does the impromptu work any more. Pass patterns—the routes a receiver follows—are as carefully plotted as the approach lanes to an airport. Deviation can cause a crack-up.

"A RECEIVER must follow his pass patterns precisely," says today's strategist. "He takes so many steps one way and changes his direction at the exact point he's supposed to. If he breaks a yard too soon or a yard too late, it can make a tremendous difference when the ball is thrown to where he should have been—but isn't."

As a group, the receivers and passers of today are infinitely superior craftsmen to the operatives of a generation ago—except for two notable exceptions: Hutson, as a receiver, and Slingin' Sammy Baugh of the Washington Redskins, as a passer. Each was the absolute best and no one since has offered serious challenge to either.

Before letting them fade back into the past, two illustrative stories will be offered, one probably apochryphal and the other real.

When Slingin' Sam first joined the Redskins, a pass play was outlined on the blackboard for him by Ray Flaherty, the coach. "When the receiver gets here," explained Flaherty, marking the spot in chalk with an X, "then you throw. And I want you to hit him in the eye with the ball."

"Which eye?" drawled Sammy, a stickler for accuracy.

The other tale is guaranteed to be true—although it smacks of fiction. Just before a game between the Packers and the Rams, the swiftest Ram runner, Dante Magnani, was assigned the task of covering Hutson by coach Dutch Clark.

"Dante," said Dutch, "you're the only man in the league who is fast enough to stay with Hutson. Just make sure you never let him get between you and the goal line."

Magnani covered the Alabama Antelope like an adhesive plaster. Suddenly it happened. Hutson broke away from his left-end position with a lazy, deceptive lope, heading in a diagonal course for the right upright of the goal posts. Magnani stayed with him.

HUTSON quickened his pace. Magnani stayed with him. Hutson shifted into high gear and Magnani still stayed with him. Then Hutson gave it the jet propulsion. Magnani matched him

stride for stride as they tore at unbelievable speed toward the goal posts, hewing to the same diagonal course.

Hutson headed for the outside of the post, hooked it with his left arm as he shot past and let his momentum swing him around just as Isbell floated a pass to him. Hanging onto the post with his left hand, the Packer phenomenon made a one-handed catch with his right for a touchdown.

Baugh and Hutson were individualists. But the passing combinations of today need that "marriage" that Berry mentioned. This is an age of specialists in a sport that has become complex. Today's players devote two and three times as many hours to their preparations as did the one-platoon 60-minute players of a generation ago, when life—and plays—were simpler. It takes specialists to beat specialists.

THE motion picture camera has reduced the human element and narrowed the margin for error. The players study films for hours. It has reached such a point of ridiculous efficiency that the kick-off platoon of the Giants, also known as the Suicide Squad, will study a spliced film that shows nothing but kick-offs. The offensive platoon scans enemy defenses and the defensive platoon watches enemy offenses.

A Del Shofner, or any great pass catcher, will pay exclusive attention to the mannerisms, quirks and reactions of the man who will guard him. He might think in this fashion: "He gives you room on the short ones but not on the long ones. He can be suckered by a head fake. He comes in fast on the buttonhook, but can be beat on the stop-and-go." *Et sic ad infinitum.*

Meanwhile, each crack defender will be making observations on the man he will guard. He might think: "He goes better to his right than to his left. He usually feints left and goes right. He's fast and murder on the long ones. Hit him hard on the short passes and he starts looking for you instead of the ball. Watch out for the criss-cross he pulls with the split end." And so it goes.

Game movies have helped

PROFITABLE PARTNERSHIP—Del Shofner of the New York Giants (left) grabs a pass thrown by teammate Yat Tittle (right).

In a recent game Tittle threw seven touchdown passes (equaling a league record) and completed 27 of 39 throws (setting a new mark).

remove the human element, but they have not eradicated it. And the sport has become so scientific, with its delicate system of checks and balances, that what works one week won't necessarily work the next. Nor are football players automatons. They have good days and bad days. It is consistency, in the long pull, that distinguishes the champion.

Before Tittle joined the Giants a year ago and formed his happy "marriage" with Shofner, the Bald Eagle had pitched plenty of passes for the San Francisco 49ers. Who had been his pet target there?

"Billy Wilson," said Yat.

Was there any particular reason?

"Certainly," said Yat. "Billy was the best receiver we had. There is nothing mysterious about this business. It follows all the rules of logic. A passer prefers throwing to his best

receiver rather than to someone who isn't as clever. When the defense clamps down on him, I switch to someone else. The trick is in finding and playing the hot hand. The defense will always control the availability of your receivers."

IT is clear from that exposition that Tittle — the kidding of his teammates notwithstanding — doesn't throw to Shofner because Del is his roommate, but because Del is his best receiver.

When Frank Gifford, the glamour boy of the Giants, retired at the end of the 1960 season—he has since unretired himself after a year's sabbatical—it meant that Charlie Conerly, then the New York passer, lost not only a favorite receiver but his roommate as well. The whimsical Kyle Rote moved in.

"I like to catch passes," was Rote's tongue-in-cheek expla-

nation, "and I thought it would help to room with Conerly. But then we got Tittle in a trade and he likes to throw to Shofner. That's when I discovered I was rooming with the wrong quarterback."

Rote was being funny. No conscious effort is made by the football clubs to make a star passer and a star receiver room together. When a conscious effort is made to pair players off, the more normal practice is to bring together two of a kind—two quarterbacks, maybe, or two receivers or two defenders.

Norm Van Brocklin of the Philadelphia Eagles at one time roomed with Sonny Jurgensen, his quarterbacking understudy. Then, when the Dutchman departed to become coach of the Minnesota Vikings, Jurgensen moved in with his closest friend, Tommy McDonald—who also happens to be his favorite receiver. This

pair and Tittle and Shofner are the only passing combinations known to room together.

THE dedicated Raymond Berry of Baltimore has polished up his catching techniques in the off-season by making unique use of his permanent roommate, his wife Sally. He has taught her how to throw a football. She can't match Johnny Unitas in accuracy or distance, but she doesn't do badly.

"Throw one over my head, honey," Raymond will say. "Now one at my feet, dear." He doesn't speak that tenderly to Unitas.

But Unitas and Berry are simpático. When the Colts beat the Giants in sudden-death overtime for the 1958 world championship in "The Greatest Game Ever Played," Baltimore had to travel 66 yards in less than two minutes just to get the tie that led to an extra period. Of the 66 yards traversed, 62 were gained on passes from Unitas to Berry.

The howling mob of 64,185 people in the Yankee Stadium saw only the end result. The fans saw nothing of the countless hours of practice which had made it all possible.

The passer must learn to disregard his receiver's fakes and feints, designed to delude the defenders. He must have an absolute knowledge of the pass pattern. He must have peripheral vision — Otto Graham of the Cleveland Browns almost seemed to have eyes in the back of his head.

EACH pass play calls for a specific receiver, a primary target. Meanwhile, other receivers flood downfield on carefully plotted courses that are designed to confuse and disrupt the defense. Essentially these men are decoys. Whenever the primary target is too well covered, however, the passer searches quickly for the man who serves as his secondary target. If he, too, is covered, then the passer flips a short one to his "out" man —**sometimes a blocker, sometimes a flanker.**

**Graham gained miles of ground over the years with little quickies to the huge Marion Motley, his chief blocker. This would happen when his pet receivers, Mac Speedie and Dante Lavelli, were covered. The Cleveland quarterback used to whipsaw the defenses with passes to

Passing, Fancy

No forward-pass play has spanned the full length of the gridiron in more than four decades of National Football League history. But there have been plays measured from the line of scrimmage that have come awfully close to the final chalk marks—at both ends of the field.

The longest was a 99-yard swoop that was engineered by Frank Filchock, the passer, and Andy Farkas, the receiver, for the Washington Redskins against the Pittsburgh Steelers in 1939. The shortest was a toss from

Speedie at one sideline or to Lavelli at the opposite sideline.

"Speedie has practically everything Don Hutson had," said coach Paul Brown in a rare moment of enthusiasm. "And he has other assets besides—including Lavelli."

When the aerial circus of the Los Angeles Rams ruled supreme a decade ago, the Rams were overloaded with talent. As passers they had Van Brocklin and Bob Waterfield, and they also had Tom Fears and Elroy (Crazylegs) Hirsch as receivers.

"None of us roomed together," said Hirsch not long ago, "and we weren't especially close, even though we were good friends. But we worked endless extra hours after prac-

Eddie LeBaron to Dick Bielski of the Dallas Cowboys against the Redskins in 1960. The distance was carefully measured: it was two inches.

The oddest pass plays of all, however, involved three of the top aerial artists—Johnny Unitas of the Baltimore Colts, Y. A. Tittle, then with the San Francisco Forty-Niners, and Milt Plum of the Cleveland Browns. Charging linemen deflected passes as they threw. So each quarterback caught his own pass and ran with it. Unitas gained one yard, Tittle four and Plum a fancier 20.—A. D.

tice was over, polishing our techniques. We ran until we didn't have the strength to run any more. Lawdy, how we worked!

THE strangest part of it all, perhaps, was that we were interchangeable. We seemed to click, regardless of who was involved. Both Fears and I caught passes from both Waterfield and Van Brocklin. No one had a favorite. The season I equaled Don Hutson's record of 17 touchdown passes. I caught nine from one of them and eight from the other. Right now I don't even remember which was which."

The experts are agreed on one thing, though. As far as the relationship between passer and receiver is concerned, familiarity breeds effi-

ciency. The longer a gifted pair work together, the better they get.

When Van Brocklin was traded from Los Angeles to Philadelphia, he instantly began to have trouble with the best Eagle receiver, the ebullient Tommy McDonald. That carefree character gave way to impulse far too often and failed to stay in the pass patterns.

"McDonald makes me throw interceptions," said the hot-tempered Dutchman angrily. But he learned to go with Tommy's unpredictability and even was able to turn weakness into strength.

The Eagles were in a jam one day, backed against the goal line. In the huddle, Van Brocklin pointed to the mercury-footed McDonald.

"Sprint downfield as fast as you can, Tommy," he ordered. "I'll find you."

McDonald sprinted downfield. Van Brocklin found him. The pass was perfect. The reception was perfect. The touchdown play spanned 90 yards.

The best forward-passing combinations represent a wedding of skills. As is the case in real matrimony, the two parties involved must work at it in order to make it click. They learn to adjust, compensate and make allowances until reactions to situations become almost instinctive. The rewards in each field of endeavor are most satisfying.

December 2, 1962

Dallas Beats Houston, 20-17, for Title

BOOT BY BROOKER BREAKS 17-17 TIE

24-Yard Field Goal Decides the Game for Dallas After 17:54 of Overtime Play

HOUSTON, Dec. 23 (AP)—Tom Brooker's 24-yard field goal in the second overtime period brought Dallas a 20-17 victory over Houston in the American Football League championship game today.

Houston, league champions for the first two years of A.F.L. history, came from behind a 17-0 halftime deficit to tie the game and send it into sudden death overtime.

The first 15 minute overtime period was scoreless. Brooker's winning field goal came 2 min-

utes, 54 seconds deep into the second overtime.

The only other overtime game in professional history involved the Baltimore Colts and New York Giants in the National Football League championship game in 1958, the Colts winning, 23-17.

Brooker Kicks Field Goal

Sparked by Len Dawson's passes 9 and 14 yards to Abner Haynes and Jack Spikes, Dallas moved 44 yards to the Houston 8 from where Tommy Brooker gave the Texans a 3-0 lead with 16 yard field goal in the first period.

The drive began after E. J. Holub ended a 52-yard Houston threat to the Texan 5 by intercepting a George Blanda pass and returning—43 yards. Houston later advanced from its 28 to the Dallas 40, from where a fourth down field goal attempt by Blanda was wide.

Dallas struck 80 yards for one touchdown in the second period and cashed in on a pass interception for another to take a 17-0 halftime lead.

Spikes started the long drive

with a 33-yard run, and Dawson ended it by passing 28 yard to Haynes for the score. Late in the period, Dave Grayson intercepted a Blanda pass and returned 20 yards to the Houston 29.

Seven plays later, Haynes carried over from the 2. Brooker kicked both extra points.

A 49-yard kick off return by Bobby Jancik permitted Houston to threaten at the Dallas 25 but the Texans held and took over by slapping down two Blanda passes.

Houston took the second half kickoff and moved 67 yards on Blanda's passes and the running of Charlie Tolar for a touchdown, Blanda passing the final 15 yards to Willard Dewveall.

Blanda, who completed three or four passes for 51 yards in the drive, also converted.

Houston, meanwhile, prevented Dallas from crossing its 41 yard line and the Oilers got another chance when they recovered Hayne's fumble at the Texas 20. On the next play, however, Johnny Robinson intercepted a Blanda pass and

returned 37 yards.

In the fourth period Blanda's passes led Houston on drives of 41 and 49 yards. Blanda kicking a 31-yard field goal after the first drive and Tolar scoring from a yard out on the second to gain a 17-17 tie and force a sudden death playoff.

In the first overtime period Dallsas used pass interceptions by Robinson and Bill Hull to stop Houston drives. Dallas moved to the Houston 38 after Robinson's interception but the Houston defense swarmed Dawson and forced the Texans to kick from their 49. The second Houston drive moved 53 yards to the Texans' 35 before Hull intercepted.

Dallas	3	14	0	0	0	3—20
Houston	0	0	7	10	0	0—17

Dallas—FG, Brooker, 16.
Dallas—Haynes, 28, pass from Dawson (Brooker kick).
Dallas—Haynes, 2, run (Brooker kick).
Houston—Dewveall, 15, pass from Blanda (Blanda kick).
Houston—FG, Blanda, 31.
Houston—Tolar, 1, run (Blanda kick).
Dallas—FG, Brooker, 25.
Attendance 37,981.

December 24, 1962

Football Stars Banned for Bets

Hornung and Karras Are Suspended by National League

By GORDON S. WHITE Jr.

Two outstanding professional football players—Paul Hornung of the Green Bay Packers and Alex Karras of the Detroit Lions—were suspended indefinitely by the National Football League yesterday for betting on league games and associating with gamblers or "known hoodiums."

Five other players were fined for betting on the 1962 league championship game and the Detroit club was fined for failing to heed reports of its players' gambling activities.

Pete Rozelle, the league commissioner, said Hornung, a star halfback, was penalized for "his pattern of betting and transmission of specific information concerning N.F.L. games for betting purposes." Karras, an all-league defense tackle, made at least six significant bets on league games since 1958, the commissioner said in a report.

The commissioner said he had notified all the clubs and players involved, just before he announced the penalties. He reported Karras expressed anger at the suspension. Hornung was reported to have said he now realized he had made a mistake and that he was sorry.

Mr. Rozelle said that the league was continuing an investigation into reports that Carroll Rosenbloom, the president of the Baltimore club, had bet on league games. The commissioner said "completion of this investigation can be expected in the near future."

The five players, who were fined $2,000 each, are with the Detroit Lions. They are John Gordy, a tackle; Gary Lowe, a defensive halfback; Joe Schmidt, a linebacker; Wayne Walker, a linebacker and place-kicker, and Sam Williams, a defensive end. All seven players penalized have been in the league at least four years.

Mr. Rozelle's report said the five fined players were punished because they had bet $50 each on the outcome of the championship game between the Packers and the New York Giants last Dec. 30 at Yankee Stadium.

The report stated that Karras had bet $100 on the Packers in that game and that his five teammates had placed their bets through a friend of Karras. The Packers, favored by 6 points, won 16-7.

Paul Hornung at interview yesterday in Louisville.

Associated Press Wirephotos

Alex Karras as he discussed the suspension in Detroit.

In football wagering, a bettor is allowed a certain number of points if he is backing the underdog. If he is betting on the favorite, he gives that many points. The point spread is determined by the nations leading odds-makers.

With a 6-point spread, the final betting score on the championship game was 16—13, so that those who had bet on the Packers won their wagers.

Mr. Rozelle emphasized that there was no evidence that the players ever had bet against their own teams, sold information to gamblers, or had given less than their best efforts in a game. But the report stated that the players did carry on undesirable associations which led to their betting on their teams to win and that they also had bet on other league games.

Club Fined on 2 Counts

Mr. Rozelle explained that the indefinite suspension to Hornung and Karras meant: "There will be no possible reconsideration for lifting the suspension until after the 1963 season." A league season ends when the championship game is played, on the Sunday between Christmas and New Year's Day.

The commissioner said the fines to the other players would be taken from their pay during the 1963 season. The Detroit Club said it would abide by the rulings. Presumably, the club will pay its $4,000 fine in the near future.

The Detroit club was fined $2,000 on each of two counts of violating league rules. Mr. Rozelle's announcement stated that the Lions' head coach, George Wilson, minimized information he had received concerning undesirable associations of some of his players.

Also, the club was punished for permitting unauthorized persons to sit on the Detroit bench during games.

In releasing his report at

league headquarters here. Mr. Rozelle said that Hornung and Karras had admitted to him that they had placed bets on league games.

In reference to Hornung, Mr. Rozelle said: "What he said was this [betting] started in 1959 and it was a weekly pattern. There was no evidence he bet against the Packers."

The investigation of players' gambling was conducted by Austin Gunsel, the league treasurer. It traced Hornung's and Karras's associations with gamblers and "hoodlums", in the case of the Green Bay star, to 1956, and in the case of Karras, to 1958.

The commissioner said that reports of Hornung's gambling activities had reached the league office as early as the spring of 1962. A broad investigation of rumors about gambling by other league players began after the 1962 championship game.

Hornung, known as the golden boy from Notre Dame, was the league's most valuable player in 1961, when the Packers won the crown for the first time in 17 years. Last season he was on the sidelines much of the season because of a leg injury.

Hornung's Kick Decides

One of the games Karras reportedly bet on was the contest between Detroit and Green Bay last Oct. 7. The Packers won the game, 9-7, though Karras won his bet because he got more than 2 points in betting on the Lions. Oddly, Hornung won the game by kicking a field goal with 33 seconds remaining.

Hornung also bet on college games, the report said, through the person with whom he is said to have placed bets on league games.

Mr. Rozelle said that Hornung and Karras were "legally free to play in any other professional league." The suspended players, as far as the league

is concerned, would still belong to their original teams.

Milt Woodard, the assistant commissioner of the American Football League, said his league would "cooperate" with the National League. Presumably, American League teams will not try to sign Hornung or Karras to contracts.

Mr. Rozelle's report specifically cleared Bob St. Clair of the San Francisco 49ers and Rick Casares of the Chicago Bears of any wrongdoing. These players had been reported to have associated with undesirable persons.

Karras admitted last January that he had bet on Detroit games. However, in a television interview, he said the bets were only for cigarettes. Mr. Rozelle's report specifically named $50 and $100 as amounts Karras had bet on N. F. L. games.

Hornung bet as much as $500 a game, the report said.

Mr. Rozelle, who succeeded the late Bert Bell as commissioner in 1960, said: "I reached the decisions on the suspensions and fines myself. The club owners were advised in summary form within the last hour."

Bell, who did much to develop the league rules against gambling, suspended two players in 1946 after reports of an attempt to fix the outcome of the championship game between the New York Giants and the Chicago Bears. The suspended players were Merle Hapes and Frank Filchock, both of the Giants.

Hapes' suspension was not lifted till 1954; Filchock's ended in 1950.

Mr. Rozelle said that in pursuing his current investigation he had received cooperation from the Senate permanent subcommittee on investigations. This subcommittee, headed by Senator John L. McClellan, a Democrat from Arkansas, is scheduled to hold hearings on football and other professional sports.

April 18, 1963

The Great TV Bonanza

Pro Football Sitting Pretty as Networks Pay More Than $64 Million for Games

By WILLIAM N. WALLACE

Jimmy Brown can run the wrong way. Y. A. Tittle can wear a hair piece if he wants. They can have a seven-way tie for first place and six sudden-death periods in a championship game. No matter what happens in professional football next season, the year will be commemorated by the great television 10-strike that made January a joy.

Television has committed $64,100,000 for the rights to transmit future pro football games and to sell advertising on the programs. On Jan. 24, the Columbia Broadcasting System won the rights to the 98 regular-season games of the National Football League, paying $28.2 million in open competitive bidding for a two-year contract. Last Wednesday, the National Broadcasting Company successfully bid $36 million for the American League schedule of 56 games over a five-year period beginning in 1965.

The first contract will mean an annual income from television of $1 million to each of the 14 N.F.L. teams, a jump from $325,000 in 1962 and 1963, and a jump from nothing in the years before television's arrival in 1946.

The American League, aged 4 to the National League's 44, will have the TV income of its eight teams rise from an estimated $261,000 this year to $900,000 in 1965. The A.F.L.'s five-year contract with the American Broadcasting Company runs out next season.

The broadcast bonanza, which made pro football the television industry's favorite sport, may bring about the following changes in the social-economic life of America:

Football players will be the financial elite in professional sports, their salaries and bonuses rising in a ratio similar to the added television revenue. That means an A.F.L. guard drawing $8,000 in 1964 will ask for $27,000 in 1965. Who's to say he won't get it?

Overhead Up to $1 Million

Franchise owners will scream louder than ever about surging expenses and the high cost of talent. At present the annual overhead of a pro team is between $800,000 and $1 million, most of it in salaries. This means the new television contracts can pay the overhead, leaving stadium gate receipts for net profit. It will not be that way for long with the players demanding their share of the cornucopia.

The war between the rival leagues could end rather quickly. The N.F.L. has bitterly opposed the A.F.L., but the owners of the clubs in the older league must now realize that the young organization is here to stay. The N.B.C. contract, a non-cancellable one, assures that.

The way for franchise owners to keep their new profits would be to halt the interleague war for promising college players who in turn will be asking for higher and higher bonuses. A common draft of the leagues would save hundreds of thousands of dollars.

Once economics dictate a common draft, interleague exhibition games will come and eventually a "world series" game or games between the league champions. N.B.C., by dragging the A.F.L. up to financial parity with the N.F.L., will be the responsible party for these developments.

Advertisers will have to pay considerably more for the privilege of hawking their products in between the exploits of a Clemon Daniels or a Cookie Gilchrist.

The going rate for a commercial minute on a C.B.S.-N.F.L. telecast will go from $45,000 to $70,000, according to some estimates.

Some 15 million persons watch Sunday N.F.L. telecasts (6.2 million see A.F.L. games, according to ratings), and the cost-per-thousand ratio is not relatively attractive. But pro football is considered to be a prestige buy on Madison Avenue.

Ratings Gain in Importance

The philosophy of ratings, which so infests the entertainment side of television, may come to bear upon pro football. Certainly the A.F.L. will outdo itself to compare favorably with the N.F.L. in the Nielsen ratings. Rather than throw more passes, the trend will likely be to intimacy, such as wiring quarterbacks for sound and televising half-time strategy meetings.

Some old pros will be on guard against such revelations. When it was suggested recently to Wellington Mara, vice president of the New York Giants, that some day soon he could expect to find a TV camera scanning the team locker room, he said, "Over my dead body!"

Sunday the day of rest, will undergo a transformation in the American home. C.B.S., with a lot of football to sell, proposes to telecast double-headers, meaning an East Coast game followed by a West Coast one, for instance. This can mean five hours of televiewing for the pro football buff on 14 Sunday afternoons of the year. Mrs. Buff and all the little Buffs had best learn up on blitzes, drops, influences, down-and-outs and keys. The blend of the game and television has become too potent to oppose. Pull up a chair.

February 2, 1964

Pro Football Ban on Hornung and Karras Lifted After 11 Months

BOTH MAKE PLANS TO REJOIN TEAMS

Hornung to Go to Green Bay for Workouts—Karras to Train With Lion Rookies

By WILLIAM N. WALLACE

Paul Hornung of the Green Bay Packers and Alex Karras of the Detroit Lions were reinstated yesterday by Commissioner Pete Rozelle of the National Football League following 11-month suspensions for betting on games. Their coaches, Vince Lombardi of the Packers and George Wilson of the Lions, warmly welcomed the players back to the active rosters and put to rest rumors they would discard them.

"Hornung will not be traded," said Lombardi in Green Bay, without being asked, and Wilson said there was no thought of trading Karras.

"He's the best defensive tackle in the league," said Wilson, "the best pass rusher in a long time."

The athletes violated their player contracts by betting. Hornung wagered sums of $100 to $500 on dozens of contests between 1956 and 1961 (most often backing the Packers), and Karras $50 to $100 at least six times between 1958 and 1962. Although football ranks behind only horse racing and basketball as a medium of betting, N.F.L. players are forbidden to wager on it.

As he had when the suspensions were first made, Rozelle emphasized yesterday that there was no evidence that either Hornung or Karras "ever bet against his own team or performed less than his best in any football game."

In reviewing the case, the commissioner attempted to fit the penalty to the offense and decided that an 11-month suspension, which included one season of play, was good enough. When the suspensions were announced last April 17, they were called "indefinite." Rozelle ended the sentences after interviewing Hornung March 7 and Karras last Saturday in his office here "to explore their attitude and thinking."

Hornung had been repentant all along.

"I did wrong," he had said many times. "I should be penalized."

Karras, however, was at first indignant, asserting he had done nothing wrong, and it took him some months to change. Last December he announced the impending sale of his interest in the Lindell A.C., a bar frequented by "known hoodlums," according to Detroit police.

Karras was contrite yesterday. Interviewed in Detroit, he said the suspension "may have been the best thing that ever happened to me. Pro athletes get lulled into thinking their sports careers will last the rest of their lives. You don't know how much you miss something until you have it taken away."

A league statement yesterday said, "Personal discussions with Hornung and Karras have established to the satisfaction of the Commissioner that each now has a clear understanding of the seriousness of the offenses and of the circumstances that brought them about."

Rozelle said that he believed both players understood "the double standard that applies to people who are in the public eye. They must be above reproach."

Rozelle was unable to reach the players by telephone yesterday morning to tell them the news and both were informed by reporters. Hornung, a bachelor, was awakened in a Miami Beach hotel. He said he was "very, very happy," and wanted to thank the commissioner "for all the kindness he has shown me in this."

Lombardi, in Green Bay, passed a hint to his star halfback. The coach said, "We're happy to have him back, but I don't know what kind of shape he's in."

Hornung seemed to get the message. He said he would go to Green Bay immediately to start workouts under Lombardi's direction.

"I'll have to get my legs back in shape," said Hornung.

7th Season for Hornung

The former Notre Dame all-

America is 28 years old. Next season will be his seventh in pro football.

The Green Bay halfback was the league's leading scorer for three years and set a season record with 176 points in 1960. In 1961 he was voted the league's most valuable player. The Packers won three championships with him—in 1960, '61 and '62 — and lost the title without him in 1963.

Karras, the son of a Gary, Ind., physician, went to the University of Iowa. His older brother, Lou, played for the Washington Redskins and a younger brother, Ted, is a guard

with the Chicago Bears. In recent months, Alex has been living with his wife's family in Clinton, Iowa, and teaching his 4-year-old son how to swim at the Y.M.C.A.

He said yesterday he weighed 250 pounds, five below his playing weight and would report to training camp with the rookies.

"That's what I am now," he said. "I only wish I were that young."

Karras, 29, is heading into his sixth pro campaign.

March 17, 1964

bonus money, and the Internal Revenue Service. The circle goes around this way.

The best teams attract the largest television ratings and justify the spiraling TV income. The best players, who all come from the colleges, go to make up the best teams. It is incumbent upon a team to sign its choices if it is to stay competitive and someday win a title.

The champion Browns, for example, have such stars as Jim Brown, Paul Warfield and Ryan, who sell tickets and turn on TV sets. But the A.F.L.'s Denver Broncos, whose players are unknown to the majority of football fans, do not rank as an attraction comparable to the Cleveland team, at the box office or on TV.

JIM BROWN SETS RUSHING RECORD

Fullback Gains 149 Yards to Become First N.F.L. Star to Break 10,000 Barrier

STATISTICS OF THE GAME

	Browns	Stlrs.
First downs	24	16
Rushing yardage	250	165
Passing yardage	162	86
Passes	15-28	8-23
Interceptions by	2	0
Punts	2-45	4-46
Fumbles lost	1	0
Yards penalized	70	30

PITTSBURGH, Nov. 1 (UPI) — Jimmy Brown became the

first National Football League player to break the 10,000-yard rushing barrier today in pacing the Cleveland Browns to a 30-17 victory over the Pittsburgh Steelers.

The all-pro fullback gained 149 yards in 23 carries to lift his career total to 10,135. It was the 47th time Brown rolled up more than 100 yards a game.

A crowd of 49,568—the second largest in Steeler home-game history—saw the game under ideal weather conditions at Pitt Stadium. The temperature was in the high 60's.

Their sixth victory enabled the Browns to solidify their lead in the Eastern Conference. Pittsburgh handed Cleveland its only defeat last month and the St. Louis Cardinals fought the Browns to a 33-33 tie.

Lou Groza kicked field goals of 36, 22 and 16 yards and kicked three conversions. Frank

Ryan hurled a 25-yard touchdown pass to Clifton McNeil and Ernie Green scored two touchdowns. That accounted for all the Browns' scoring.

The teams were tied 10—10 at half-time. Cleveland went ahead, 10—0, but the Steelers drew even in the closing seconds of the second period. Bob Harrison, a linebacker, recovered Ryan's fumble with 38 seconds remaining and Mike Clark kicked a 26-yard field goal. Clarence Peaks ran 5 yards to cap a 79-yard drive for the Steelers' first score.

Cleveland Browns ....0 10 10 10—30
Pittsburgh Steelers ...0 10 0   7—17
Clev.—FG, Groza, 36.
Clev.—McNeil, 25, pas from Ryan (Groza, kick).
Pitt.—Peaks, 5, run (Clark, kick).
Pitt.—FG, Clark, 26.
Clev.—Green, 7, run (Groza, kick).
Clev.—FG, Groza, 22.
Clev.—FG, Groza, 16.
Pitt.—Johnson, 1, run (Clark, kick).
Clev.—Green, 13, run (Groza, kick).
Attendance—49,568.

November 2, 1964

Both Claim Victory

In the current race to sign a bumper crop of potential stars from the college ranks, both leagues claim victory. The eight-team A.F.L. says it needs to sign only 37 per cent of its top draft choices to maintain parity with the 14-team N.F.L. This time it has signed 56 per cent. The N.F.L. points to its record of signing 11 of its 14 choices in the first draft round, where the stars lie, plus many other "name" players

Namath's $405,000 contract for a five-year period made the quarterback from Beaver Falls, Pa., the money champion by far. John Huarte's estimated $200,000 pact, also with the Jets, placed him in an apparent tie for second with Craig Morton, the California quarterback signed by the Dallas Cowboys, and Dick Butkus, the Illinois linebacker now the property of the Chicago Bears.

Fred Biletnikoff, the split end for Florida State, will cost the Oakland Raiders about $150,000 over two to three years. The

Cost of Players Held Peril to Football

By WILLIAM N. WALLACE

When Frank Ryan, the Cleveland Browns' quarterback with the sense of humor of a pixie, suggested that he was worth a million dollars now that Joe Namath, the rookie quarterback from Alabama, had signed with the Jets for $400,000, not everyone in pro football laughed

The cost of signing new players from the college ranks in recent weeks had been deplored in many front offices, but no one is able to present a solution to a dilemma that threatens the solvency of a thriving professional sport.

The 22 teams of the National and American leagues have committed themselves to more than $4 million in contracts for next year's rookies, over half of whom will not be good enough to make their new varsities. The average payroll of a pro team next season will exceed $1 million for the first time.

"It's become ridiculous," said Arthur Modell, president of the National League's new champions, the Cleveland Browns. "Contracts, like the one Namath got, can be the ruination of the game."

"If the bonuses keep going up," said Wellington Mara, vice

president of the New York Giants, "some of the teams are going to find themselves priced right out of the market."

Free Farm System

Pro football, unlike baseball, has a balance of team strengths built into its operations through the annual draft of college players with the weakest teams entitled to choose first from the talent pool. The hundreds of college squads serve as a free farm system for the pros.

Mara's point is that the delicate balance can be upset if some teams do not have the big money required to sign stars like Namath.

The two pro leagues, American and National, are engaged in a war without profit. The competition for players is driving the prices up and so is the increasing television revenue.

"We seem merely to be passing along to the college boys a big slice of our TV money," said one executive.

The 14 N.F.L. teams each received $1,000,000 from the Columbia Broadcasting System this year for television rights, up from $325,000 in 1962 and 1963. The National Broadcasting Company made available to the eight A.F.L. teams $250,-

000 each for signing players and five accepted the advance. (The New York Jets, who averaged 42,710 fans for their seven games in Shea Stadium last fall, did not.)

The solution would be for the two leagues to hold a common draft of the college athletes. But such is the animosity between the circuits that this obvious compromise seems far off, especially for Pete Rozelle, the N.F.L. commissioner and adamant enemy of the A.F.L. However, as Mara admitted, simple economics may drive the rivals into concert with regard to signing new talent.

"Prestige is no longer at stake," said Don Klosterman, the talent man for the Kansas City Chiefs. "A common draft has to come quickly. The N.F.L. people know this as well as we do. This year's prices have proved it."

"I don't know what's going to happen," said Modell. "But I do know that it's economic suicide for us to continue at this rate. That television money isn't guaranteed for life, you know."

The two leagues are caught in a vicious circle that benefits the college boys they sign; the automobile dealers from whom the youngsters buy cars with their

Records of Signings On Pro Football Clubs

The following chart shows each professional team's record to date in signing its top 10 draft choices.

NATIONAL FOOTBALL LEAGUE

	Signed	Lost to A.F.L.	Unsigned
Baltimore	4	2	3*
Chicago	4	2	4
Cleveland	5	3	1**
Dallas	8	1	1
Detroit	4	1	5
Green Bay	4	2	4***
Los Angeles	4	1	4
Minnesota	8	1	1
New York	7	0	3
Philadelphia	1	4	5
Pittsburgh	5	0	5
St. Louis	3	1	6
San Francisco	6	2	2
Washington	4	1	5
Totals	67	20	51

Futures (players drafted in 1963 for 1965 season): 76 selected, 30 signed, 7 lost to A. F. L.

AMERICAN FOOTBALL LEAGUE

	Signed	Lost to N.F.L.	Unsigned
Boston	2	1	7
Buffalo	4	3	3
Denver	5	3	2
Houston	3	5	2**
Kansas City	4	2	4
New York	5	1	4
Oakland	6	2	2
San Diego	4	4	2
Totals	33	23	23

Futures: 76 selected, 9 signed, 33 lost to N.F.L.

*Baltimore lost player to Canadian Football League.
**Neeley, Oklahoma, signed with both Dallas and Houston.
***Los Angeles had only nine players eligible to be signed.

New York Giants are believed to have assured Tucker Frederickson, the Auburn fullback, of $100,000 in a three-year pact.

Although teams do not announce their terms, beneficiaries in the $50,000 and over bracket are believed to be Larry Elkins, Baylor end with Houston; Malcolm Walker, Rice linebacker; Jerry Rhome, Tulsa quarterback, and Bob Hayes, Florida A. & M. halfback, all signed by Dallas; Jack Snow, Notre Dame split end who now belongs to Los Angeles; and Gale Sayers, Kansas halfback who went with the Bears.

Not everyone spent a lot of money. The Browns will have a conservative outlay for new players, perhaps no more than $100,000. "We drafted to fill needs," explained Modell, "not to acquire stars. We have the stars We avoided drafting some players because we suspected we might end up in a bidding war for their services."

Modell abhors big contracts that upset the older players on more modest pay scales. The players themselves do not seem to mind the large bonuses going to the 1964 collegians. But they do mind the concomitant no-cut contracts. Klosterman, however, feels that most of the seasoned personnel will demand big raises and with justice as they equate their proven value to that of untried rookies.

The Boston Patriots of the A.F.L. have hardly spent anything at all, with only one player of their first 10 draft choices signed so far.

The Giants have been the most successful of any team, having signed 12 men with only one loss to the A.F.L. The commitment to the franchise is about $400,000, which means the Giants acquired a dozen players for the price of one Namath.

Modell, in disagreement with the philosophy of the star system followed by Sonny Werblin, Jet president, asserts that at least 21 other good players besides the quarterback are necessary on a successful pro team.

The quarterback syndrome flourishes in pro football. Many teams sign quarterback after quarterback, as the Jets have done, and the reserves languish on the bench for years, on full salary.

Some contend that it is better to stay with one quarterback and develop him rather than sign new ones season after season. They cite Rudy Bukich, who became a regular with the Bears this season at the age of 32 in his 10th pro season, and Cleveland's Ryan, a star in his seventh pro year after previous failures.

The Dallas Cowboys rival the Jets for surplus quarterbacks. They will have $275,000 invested in Rhome and Morton for next year and they recently got rid of Sonny Gibbs, a 1963 rookie who signed a three-year pact at $20,000 a season. Morton and Rhome will compete with the incumbent, Don Meredith; a 1964 rookie, Jake Jacobs, who was farmed to the minor United League; and perhaps Ernie Kellerman of Miami of Ohio and Brig Owens of Cincinnati, two more quarterbacks on the draft list but as yet unsigned.

The American League, 5 years old last season, proved how hard it is to find young quarterbacks.

A.F.L. teams last fall used such seasoned performers as George Blanda of Houston and Tobin Rote of San Diego, both 36; Babe Parilli of Boston, 34; Cotton Davidson of Oakland, 30; Jack Kemp of Buffalo, Dick Wood of New York and Len Dawson, of Kansas City, each 28. All at one time played in the N.F.L., and only Rote in the status of a regular.

And everyone of them wishes he was younger, to qualify for the big money now coming to their young successors from the colleges.

January 10, 1965

Atlanta Club Named Falcons

ATLANTA, Aug. 28 (UPI)—The new Atlanta entry in the National Football League adopted tonight the Atlanta Falcons as its official nickname. The Falcons' owner, Rankin H. Smith, in a prerecorded announcement, disclosed the name of the team during pregame ceremonies at the Baltimore Colts-Pittsburgh Steelers exhibition game in the new 57,000-seat Atlanta stadium when they begin league play in 1966.

August 29, 1965

Packers Beat Colts on Hornung's 5 Touchdowns

GREEN BAY GAINS 42-TO-27 VICTORY

STATISTICS OF THE GAME

	Packers	Colts
First downs	18	21
Rushing yardage	144	74
Passing yardage	222	190
Passes	10-17	20-41
Interceptions by	3	1
Punts	3-44	4-33
Fumbles lost	2	0
Yards penalized	68	37

By WILLIAM N. WALLACE
Special to The New York Times

BALTIMORE, Dec. 12—Gary Cuozzo, young and impetuous, tried to fool the Green Bay defense, mature and disciplined, but failed today when Dave Robinson intercepted the Baltimore quarterback's little flip pass and ran 88 yards.

This big play late in the second period turned the game around and the Packers went on to defeat the Colts, 42-27. Paul Hornung, the Golden Boy who had been returned to the starting lineup for this big game, scored five touchdowns.

The victory jumped the Packers over the Colts into first place—by half a game—in the Western Conference of the National Football league.

The turning point came today in the fog of Baltimore Stadium when the 23-year-old Cuozzo, playing the biggest game of his life as a stand-in for the injured Johnny Unitas, went up to the line of scrimmage with his offensive unit. The Colts were 1 point behind, 14-13, and had a second down on the Green Bay 2-yard line, thanks to a recovered fumble.

Moore Fakes to Inside

It was an enviable situation. Cuozzo faked Lenny Moore, his halfback, to the inside. Jerry Hill, the fullback, tried to sneak outside to his right and Cuozzo lofted the football toward Hill.

But Willie Davis, the Packer right end, knew a pass was coming because the tackle opposite him, George Preas, had tipped it off. Robinson, the big linebacker playing just outside Davis, also had diagnosed the daring play.

Davis almost intercepted the pass, which went by his fingertips, and Robinson did, the ball hitting him chest high. Said a dejected Cuozzo later, "Robinson dropped off. I should have thrown the ball higher."

The Green Bay linebacker then raced 88 yards to the Colt 10-yard line. On the first play from there, with 19 seconds to go before half-time, Bart Starr passed deep to Boyd Dowler, his flanker, in the back of the end zone—and the Packers went to their locker room with an 8-point lead.

Less than a minute before they had been about to fall 6 points behind. So it goes in pro football.

In the third quarter, Green Bay opened up a 35-14 lead and the 60,238 Baltimore adherents in the stands were quiet as mice.

Returns After Injury

Cuozzo was hurt for one series and a halfback named Tom Matte had to play quarterback. Cuozzo's left shoulder was taped and he went into the locker room to be given a painkilling shot.

Then he came back and attacked the Packers with a series of good passes. The youth with an injured shoulder completed 13 of 22 passes and took his team in for two touchdowns that closed the gap to 8 points with six minutes left to play.

It was a thrilling rally that had the fog-blanketed stadium in an uproar. But it all came to naught when Starr, the sound Green Bay quarterback, ended the nonsense by throwing a 65-yard touchdown pass to Hornung at 10:30 of the fourth period. That closed the scoring at 42-27.

On a third-and-9 situation, Hornung went up the middle against a blitzing Colt defense while Jimmy Taylor, the fullback, stayed back to block for Starr. Bart hit Hornung 15 yards downfield and he went all the way. Hornung was wide open because the blitzing middle linebacker, Dennis Gaubatz, had vacated the area.

In the first period, a similar play of 50 yards — Starr to Hornung — had given Green Bay a 14-3 lead. The Packers trailed only after a 14-yard field goal by Lou Michaels of the Colts had opened the scoring at 4:29 of the first quarter.

Hornung also scored on runs of 2, 9 and 3 yards, all off-tackle cutbacks in the typical Green Bay power style.

This was an old-fashioned Green Bay game — Hornung running outside and Taylor inside, with Starr throwing occasionally. It was elemental, fundamental football designed to destroy the other team's defense, which it did. On defense, Green Bay was sound and conservative, not even blitzing.

This was the best offensive game of the year for Green Bay, which has had a lot of trouble moving. Hornung, who was not a starter the last two games, had scored only three times and gained merely 231 yards. He got 61 yards running and 115 catching passes today.

The Colts? They show a tie and two losses for their last three games after winning eight in a row, and the bottom appears to have dropped out of their team.

Baltimore's best player today was Raymond Berry, the incomparable split end who caught 10 of Cuozzo's passes against the tight coverage of Doug Hart, but Berry could not do it alone against the mighty Packer defense that has carried Green Bay such a long way this season.

Green Bay Packers	14	7	14	7—42
Baltimore Colts	3	10	0	14—27

Balt.—FG. Michaels, 14.
G. B.—Hornung, 2, run (Chandler, kick).
G. B.—Hornung, 50, pass from Starr (Chandler, kick).
Balt.—FG. Michaels, 45.
Balt.—Moore, 3, run (Michaels, kick).
G. B.—Dowler, 10, pass from Starr (Chandler, kick).
G. B.—Hornung, 9, run (Chandler, kick).
G. B.—Hornung, 3, run (Chandler, kick).
Balt.—Hill, 1, run (Michaels, kick).
Balt.—Berry, 5, pass from Cuozzo (Michaels, kick).
G. B.—Hornung, 65, pass from Starr (Chandler, kick).

INDIVIDUAL STATISTICS

RUSHES—G. B.: Taylor, 17 for 66 yards; Hornung 15 for 61. Balt.: Moore, 15 for 42; Hill, 9 for 24.
PASSES—G.B.: Starr, 10 of 17 for 222 yards; Balt.: Cuozzo, 20 of 38 for 212; Matte, 0 of 3.
RECEPTIONS—G.B.: Dowler, 4 for 40 yards; Hornung, 2 for 115; Taylor, 2 for 39; McGee, 1 for 14; Fleming, 1 for 14. Balt.: Berry, 10 for 125; Orr, 3 for 22; Moore, 2 for 14; Matte, 2 for 23.
Attendance—60,238.

December 13, 1965

Sayers Gets 6 as Bears Win

49ERS Vanquished In Chicago, 61-20

CHICAGO, Dec. 12 (AP)—Gale Sayers scored six touchdowns today, raising his season total to 21—a National Football League record—as the Chicago Bears routed the San Francisco 49ers, 61-20.

Sayers established a Bear scoring record for one game and also matched the single game N.F.L. mark for touchdowns set by Ernie Nevers in 1929 and matched by Dub Jones in 1951.

Sayers's season total bettered the league record of 20 by Lenny More of the Baltimore Colts and matched this year by Jimmy Brown of the Cleveland Browns.

The triumph, avenging an opening-game 52-24 defeat at San Francisco, kept alive the Bears' chances of sharing the Western Conference title. They now have a 9-4 won-lost mark.

STATISTICS OF THE GAME

	Bears	49ers
First downs	21	19
Rushing yardage	183	58
Passing yardage	401	272
Passes	17-33	23-44
Interceptions by	2	0
Punts	3-33	6-49
Fumbles lost	0	0
Yards Penalized	30	14

The remarkable rookie from Kansas scored in the first quarter, taking a screen pass from Rudy Bukich and running 80 yards.

In the second period, Sayers scored on runs of 21 and 7 yards.

Sayers cut through tackle and raced 50 yards in the third period. Later in this quarter, he dived over from the 1. His final touchdown, in the fourth quarter, came on a punt return of 85 yards.

Chicago Bears	13 14 13 21—61
San Francisco 49ers	0 13 0 7—20

Chi—Sayers, 80, pass from Bukich (pass failed).
Chi.—Ditka, 29, pass from Bukich (Leclerc, kick).
S.F.—Parks, 9, pass from Brodie (Davis, kick).
Chi.—Sayers, 21, (Leclerc, kick).
S.F.—Crow, 15, pass from Brodie (kick failed).
Chi—Sayers, 7, run (Leclerc, kick).
Chi.—Sayers, 50, run (Leclerc, kick).
Chi.—Sayers, 1, run (run failed).
S.F.—Kopay, 2, run (Davis, kick).
Chi.—Jones, 8, pass from Bukich (Leclerc, kick).
Chi.—Sayers, 85, punt return (Leclerc, kick).
Chi.—Arnett, 2, run (Leclerc, kick).
Attendance—46,278.

December 13, 1965

Dawson Leads Chiefs to 25-20 Triumph Over Oilers

KANSAS CITY STAR SETS PASS RECORD

HOUSTON, Sept. 9 (AP)—Len Dawson set a pro football record with 15 consecutive pass completions tonight while leading the Kansas City Chiefs to a 25-20 American Football League victory over the Houston Oilers. It was the season opener for both teams.

Dawson's incomplete sideline pass in the fourth quarter broke the string.

Tied once but never behind, the Chiefs moved after a scoreless first quarter to control a Houston team that came up with a surprising ground game in their 13th straight loss.

Mike Garrett opend scoring with a 2-yard run to end a Chiefs' drive covering 85 yards in seven plays. The longest gains were Dawson's passes of 10 and 8 yards to Chris Burford and Garrett.

With Jacky Lee at the helm, Houston responded with a drive starting with an 18-yard run by Hoyle Granger. Sid Blanks gained 35 yards of the 80-yard march, with Granger scoring from the 4.

The Chiefs' tallied next on Jan Stenerud's 54-yard field goal, one yard shy of the A.F.L. record held by Oakland's George Blanda.

A 39-yard pass interference call against Kansas City helped Houston to its next touchdown, made on a 7-yard run by Blanks. Granger and Blanks

STATISTICS OF THE GAME

	Chiefs	Oilers
First downs	20	17
Rushing yardage	141	178
Passing yardage	167	158
Return yardage	90	148
Passes	19-17	25-16
Interceptions by	1	1
Punts	4-38	2-40
Fumbles lost	1	0
Yards penalized	117	128

gained the other 41 yards of that drive. After John Wittenborne's second point-after kick, the 28,203 fans gave the Oilers a standing ovation.

Dawson retaliated with six passes in a row, including tosses of 12 and 19 yards to Garrett and a 16-yard touchdown throw to Fred Arbanas.

Two interceptions were the second-half highlights. Bobby Bell went 32 yards with one of Jacky Lee's passes for a Chiefs' touchdown and Dawson's pass

to Reg Carolan supplied the 2 points after.

In the fourth quarter, a Houston rookie, Ken Houston, picked off Dawson's pass in the end zone, and returned it 77 yards with the help of key blocks by George Webster and Miller Farr. On the next play, Granger took Lee's short pass 27 yards for a touchdown.

For the game Dawson completed 17 of 19 passes for 189 yards.

Kansas City Chiefs	0 17 8 0—25
Houston Oilers	0 14 0 6—20

K.C.—Garrett, 2, run (Stenerud, kick).
Hou.—Granger, 4, run (Wittenborn, kick).
K.C.—FG, Stenerud, 54.
Hou.—Blanks, 7, run (Wittenborn, kick).
K.C.—Arbanas, 16, pass from Dawson (Stenerud, kick).
K.C.—Bell, 32, interception (Carolan, pass from Dawson).
Hou.—Granger, 28, pass from Lee (pass failed).
Attendance—28,003.

September 10, 1967

THE SUPER LEAGUE

National and American Football Leagues Will Merge Into 26-Team Circuit

UNIFICATION SET FOR 1970 SEASON

By JOSEPH M. SHEEHAN

Professional football's heated money war has ended. The 47-year-old National Football League and seven-year-old American Football League announced yesterday plans to merge into a single league of at least 26 teams in 25 cities.

It will take until 1970, after their present, separate multi-million dollar television contracts expire, for the leagues fully to implement the merger by playing a unified schedule. Meanwhile, the leagues will retain their present identities.

But the merger agreement will have many immediate benefits to the clubs of both present leagues and professional football's legion of followers— if not to the players.

Under the pact, there will be a world championship game next January between the 1966 champions of each league. This will provide the first interleague confrontation on the playing field. There also will be interleague preseason play starting in 1967.

The leagues also have agreed

to conduct a common draft of graduating players next January. This means that one team in either league would get exclusive negotiation rights with the players it selected in the college draft.

Up to now, the leagues have conducted separate drafts, allowing players to negotiate with one team in each league — and to play them off against each other.

This gave rise to a costly

EXPLAINING THE MERGER: At news conference here are, from left, Tex Schramm, president of Dallas Cowboys of N.F.L.; Pete Rozelle, the N.F.L. commissioner, who will head unified league when merger is fully effective, and Lamar Hunter, founder of A.F.L.

The New York Times (by Carl T. Gossett Jr.)

bidding war between the leagues for prime prospects and was a major factor in the move for peace. Interleague competition for top college stars resulted in bonus package-deals ranging up to the $600,000 reported to have been paid last winter to Tommy Nobis, a University of Texas linebacker, for signing with the new Atlanta Falcons of the National League.

The common draft will drastically cut bonus payments and should appease the colleges, which have rallied against the in-season solicitation and premature signings of college players attributable to the scramble for talent.

It also raised a possible restraint-of-trade issue under the antitrust laws. In Washington, the Justice Department said it would "take a close look" at the merger plan to see if it violates antitrust laws. A department spokesman said the agency "had been given some advance notice" of the merger.

$18-Million Involved

The agreement requires the nine present American League clubs to pay the 15 present National League clubs a total of $18-million in principal and interest over a 20-year period.

The National League clubs also will receive the franchise fees to be paid by two new clubs—one in each present league—to be added by 1968. On the basis of going franchise rates, this could add $15-million to $18-million to the National League coffers.

In addition, the American

League will supply the players to stock the new club that will play within the American League through 1969.

Following are other major provisions of the merger:

¶Pete Rozelle of the National League will be the commissioner of the unified league when the merger becomes fully effective. Meanwhile, Rozelle will administer all interleague affairs. Al Davis, the newly appointed American League commissioner, is free to continue in his present post "if he so desires."

[Davis, who is understood to have been opposed to the cessation of hostilities, declined immediate comment on the merger or his immediate plans.]

¶All existing franchises in both leagues will be retained and none will be transferred from its present location.

¶Two additional franchises will be granted as soon after 1968 as practicable, with the ultimate aim of bringing the unified league to 28 teams. This number is needed to achieve a balanced schedule, with all teams playing each week over a 14-week period.

¶Two-network television will continue.

Two Hurdles Cleared

¶Interleague player trades will be barred until after final unification because of contractual and pension considerations.

The $2-million-per-club American League payment to the National League and the American League's waiver of

a share in the franchise fees paid by the next two expansion clubs were the chief stumbling blocks in the merger negotiations.

Apparently, the American League owners accepted the terms as a reasonable franchise fee for the security of guaranteed inclusion in an expanded, unified league.

The National League made concessions, too. It was the more solidly established and financially secure circuit and, in the merger, its strength aids the junior league, whose long-term prospects still were cloudy.

The National League also yielded on its one-team-to-a-city stand, in permitting the American League Jets to remain in New York in addition to the National League Giants and in allowing the American League Raiders to stay in Oakland, in the same metropolitan area as the National League Forty-Niners of San Francisco.

Two Clubs Compensated

At a news conference at the Hotel Warwick here last night, Rozelle said that the Giants and the Forty-Niners would get a large pro-rated share of the American League payments to compensate them for the loss of exclusive territorial rights in the unified league.

Present also at the conference were Lamar Hunt of the Kansas City Chiefs, who founded the American League, and Tex Schramm, the president of the National League Dallas Cowboys. These men had head-

ed the negotiating teams of their respective leagues, which have been working on the merger conditions since early April.

Rozelle said the N.F.L. owners were unanimous when the final vote was taken on whether or not to merge.

Hunt said A.F.L. owners were not unanimous and it was learned that the vote was 7-2 in favor of the merger. The Jets voted against the merger.

The rapidly escalating television fees received by both leagues helped fan the player-recruiting war that brought this newest merger.

In the last few years, both leagues have been guilty of player-recruiting activities that have enraged the colleges. The National League organized a vast "baby-sitting" operation, in which field representatives in central locations held college stars incommunicado during the draft until they could be persuaded to commit themselves to the National League.

In at least two years, the American League admittedly held advance secret drafts in which the owners staked out negotiating priorities.

Both leagues have been guilty of in-season approaches to college players, in defiance of their own league rules, and of signing players before their college seasons had ended.

Rising attendance also helped swell the rival leagues' war chests. The National League drew a record total of 4,634,021 paid admissions to its 98 regular-season games in 1965, up 70,972 from 1964, averaging 47,286 per game (which was 83 per cent of available park capacity).

The American League also reached a new peak last year, drawing 1,773,784 to 56 regular-season games, up 325,909 from 1964, averaging 31,675.

Season ticket demand has reached a stage in the National League where at least half the member teams already are assured of capacity crowds for all their home games this year.

Some American League teams, most notably the Jets here and the Bills in Buffalo, also are approaching the point of guaranteed home sellouts.

June 9, 1966

UNITAS SETS MARK AS COLTS WIN, 17-3

LOS ANGELES, Oct. 30 (UPI) —Johnny Unitas became the National Football League's leading passer today and celebrated by connecting on an 89-yard touchdown play to John Mackey while leading the Baltimore Colts to a 17-3 victory over the Los Angeles Rams.

The Baltimore quarterback bettered Y. A. Tittle's career mark of 28,339 yards on the final play of the third period. He hit Ray Berry with a 31-yard pass to give him 231 yards to that point.

In addition to his 89-yard pass to Mackey, Unitas hit the

same receiver for a 17-yard scoring pass in the second period. Lou Michaels kicked a 31-yard field goal for the other Colts' points.

Bruce Gossett kicked a 12-yard field goal for the Rams in the second period.

Unitas completed 13 of 22 passes for 252 yards and has a total of 28,375 yards. Gabriel hit on 11 of 22 for 153 yards. His replacement, Bill Munsen, clicked on 12 of 17 for 118 yards. The Rams gained 386 yards to 344 for Baltimore.

Baltimore Colts 10   7   0   0—17
Los Angeles Rams 0   3   0   0— 3
  Balt.—Mackey, 89, pass from Unitas (Michaels, kick).
  Balt.—FG, Michaels, 31.
  L.A.—FG, Gossett, 12.
  Balt.—Mackey, 17, pass from Unitas (Michaels, kick).
  Attendance—57,898.

October 31, 1966

New Orleans Eleven To 'March In' as Saints

NEW ORLEANS, Jan. 9 (UPI)—The new National Football League team, in New Orleans, will be named the Saints. Al Hirt, the famed trumpeter who is part owner of the new club, made the announcement today.

Hirt, who is also entertainment chairman of the Saints, will be on hand to pipe the team onto the field for its first game with his rendition of "When the Saints Go Marching In."

There is some opposition to the name from people who feel that using the name for an athletic team is somewhat irreverent, but by and large Saints is a popular choice.

January 10, 1967

GREEN BAY WINS FOOTBALL TITLE

By WILLIAM N. WALLACE
Special to The New York Times

LOS ANGELES, Jan. 15 — Bryan Bartlett (Bart) Starr, the quarterback for the Green Bay Packers, led his team to a 35-10 victory over the Kansas City Chiefs today in the first professional football game between the champions of the National and American Leagues.

Doubt about the outcome disappeared in the third quarter when Starr's pretty passes made mere Indians out of the American League Chiefs and Green Bay scored twice.

Those 14 points stretched Green Bay's lead to 28-10 and, during the final quarter many of the spectators in the crowd of 63,036 left Memorial Coliseum, which had been only two-thirds filled.

The outcome served to settle the curiosity of the customers,

who paid from $6 to $12 for tickets, and a television audience estimated at 60 million, regarding the worth of the Chiefs.

The final score was an honest one, meaning it correctly reflected what went on during the game. The great interest had led to naming the event the Super Bowl, but the contest was more ordinary than super.

McGee Catches 7 Passes

Starr, methodical and unruffled as ever, completed 16 of 23 passes, six producing first downs on key third-down plays. Seven completions went to Max McGee, a 34-year-old substitute end who was in action only because Boyd Dowler, the regular, was hurt on the game's sixth play.

McGee scored two of Green Bay's five touchdowns, the first one after an outstanding one-handed, hip-high catch of a pass thrown slightly behind him.

The Packers, who had been favored by two touchdowns, knew they were in a challenging game for at least half of the 2½-hour contest.

Kansas City played very well in the first two quarters and the half-time score, 14-10, made the teams just about even. Green Bay's offense was sluggish. Kansas City had stopped the Packer rushing game and Starr had not exploited the Chiefs' defensive men — Fred

Williamson and Willie Mitchell —who looked vulnerable. Bart was to take care of that matter in the second half.

The Chiefs, with Lenny Dawson running the offense at quarterback, had found they could pass on Green Bay, so three times the team was in scoring range. Out of that came one touchdown, scored by the fullback, Curtis McClinton, on a 7-yard pass from Dawson, and a 31-yard field goal by Mike Mercer.

But that was all for Kansas City. In the second half the mighty Packer defense shut out the Chiefs, who were in the Green Bay half of the field only once—for one play. And they were only four yards into Packer territory.

The Packers changed their defensive tactics for the second half. They had not blitzed their linebackers during the first two periods and the four rushing linemen were unable to get at Dawson.

But the blitz came in the third period and Dawson found himself harassed.

Three times he was dropped for losses and once, under blitzing pressure, he threw a weak pass that Willie Wood intercepted for Green Bay and ran back 50 yards to the Kansas City 5-yard line.

Elijah Pitts, the halfback, scored on first down from the 5, running off left tackle behind

a power block from Bob Skoronski, a tackle. That gave the Packers a 21-10 lead and they were in command for good.

The pass rush that led to Wood's interception was the key play. The Chiefs and Dawson never recovered. The Kansas City quarterback later left the field and Pete Beathard took his place in the fourth quarter.

Richest Sports Event

For their efforts the 40 Packer players won $15,000 each, with $7,500 going to each Chief. Gate receipts were estimated at $750,000 and the two television networks — the Columbia Broadcasting System and the National Broadcasting Company — paid $1-million apiece for the TV rights. So this was a $2,750,000 event, the richest for any American team sports event.

Starr was worth every cent of his $15,000. In the first period he took his team 80 yards in six quick plays for the opening score. The sixth play, on third down, was the 37-yard pass to McGee on which Max made his great catch.

Kansas City tied the score at 7-7 in the second quarter with a six-play, 66-yard drive featuring three passes by Dawson to Mike Garrett, Otis Taylor and McClinton, the one to McClinton for a touchdown.

Starr connected on a 64-yard touchdown pass play to Carroll

Associated Press Wirephoto

PULLING IT IN: Max McGee of Packers snares first-quarter pass from Bart Starr as Willie Mitchell (22) and Fred Williamson try to stop him on the Chiefs' 20-yard line.

Offensive linemen are often unsung heroes. Jerry Kramer (number 64) of the Green Bay Packers is about to provide Jim Taylor with some running room.

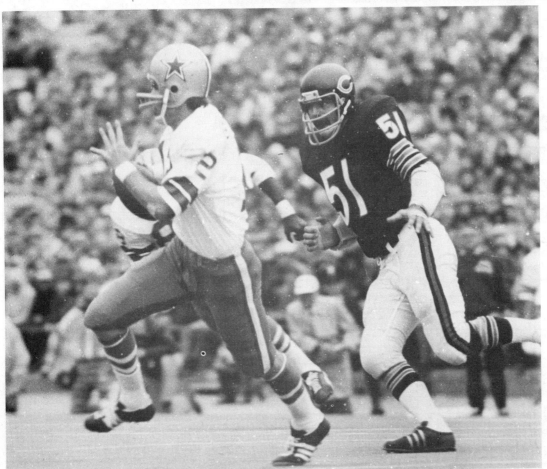

Roger Staubach, Dallas quarterback, may have heard Chicago Bear linebacker Dick Butkus closing in on him. If so, it would have given him good incentive to run a little faster.

Dale (on third down), but a Packer lineman was illegally in motion and the play was called back. That failed to bother Starr, who after 11 subsequent plays had the Packers over the Kansas City goal line.

It was a beautiful series of plays. On four third-down situations, Starr passed successfully for the first down. The score was made from 14 yards out by hard-running Jim Taylor on a sweep behind blocking by the guards, Fred Thurston and Jerry Kramer.

Just before the half, Kansas City drove to the Green Bay 31, but a pass to Garrett failed to pick up a first down and Mercer kicked a field goal that cut the N.F.L. team's lead to 14-10.

In the second half Starr concentrated on Mitchell, the cornerback who had had so much trouble covering McGee and Dale. Bart had great protection and on two touchdown drives that featured the pass, he probed at Mitchell's position successfully five times.

On these drives, one of 56 yards in the third quarter and one of 80 yards in the fourth, Starr completed seven of eight passes with cool precision. The Chiefs were helpless to stop him.

The first score was made by McGee from 13 yards out. He casually bobbled the ball, then caught it for six points, performing as if he were back in Green Bay during a routine practice on a Wednesday afternoon. McGee had caught only four passes during Green Bay's regular 14-game season.

The second touchdown went to Pitts, who slid off left tackle from a yard out as the Packer line closed down to the inside.

The Green Bay execution was as impeccable as ever. The only mistake was a harmless interception by Mitchell of a pass by Starr. It was the first interception against Starr since last Oct. 16. He had thrown 173 passes without an interception.

The Packer defense held the elusive Garrett to only 17 yards and Kansas City's offense had a net gain of only 239 yards. At the end the Packers were playing substitutes, but Paul Hornung never got in the game.

The Super Bowl games will now go on year after year, but it may be some time before an American League team will be good enough to win one, especially if the National League champion comes from Green Bay.

GREEN BAY (35)

Ends—Dale, Fleming, Davis, Aldridge, Long, Anderson, B. Brown.
Tackles—Skoronski, Gregg, Kostelnik, Jordan, Wright, Weatherwax.
Guards—Thurston, Kramer, Gillingham.
Centers—Curry, Bowman.
Linebackers—D. Robinson, Nitschke, Caffey, Crutcher.
Quarterbacks—Starr, Bratkowski.
Offensive Backs—E. Pitts, J. Taylor, Dowler, McGee, Anderson, Mack, Vandersea, Grabowski.
Defensive Backs—Jeter, Adderly, T. Brown, Wood, Hart, Hathcock.
Kicker—Chandler.

KANSAS CITY (10)

Ends—Burford, Arbanas, Mays, Hurston, F. Pitts, Carolan, A. Brown.
Tackles—Tyrer, Hill, Rice, Buchanan, DiMidio.
Guards—Budde, Merz, Reynolds, Biodrowski.
Centers—Frazier, Gilliam.
Linebackers—Bell, Headrick, Holub, Corey, Abell, Stover.
Quarterbacks—Dawson, Beathard.
Offensive Backs—Garrett, McClinton, O. Taylor, Coan, Thomas.
Defensive Backs—Williamson, Mitchell, Hunt, J. Robinson, F. Smith, Ply.
Kickers—Mercer, Wilson.

Green Bay Packers	7	7	14	7—35
Kansas City Chiefs	10	0	0	0—10

G.B.—McGee, 37, pass from Starr (Chandler, kick).
K.C.—McClinton, 7, pass from Dawson (Mercer, kick).
G.B.—Taylor, 14, run (Chandler, kick).
K.C.—FG, Mercer, 31.
G.B.—Pitts, 5, run (Chandler, kick).
G.B.—McGee, 13, pass from Starr (Chandler, kick).
G.B.—Pitts, 1, run (Chandler, kick).
Attendance—63,036.

INDIVIDUAL STATISTICS

Rushing—G. B.: Taylor, 16 attempts for 53 yards; Pitts, 11 for 45; Anderson, 4 for 30; Grabowski, 2 for 2. K. C.: Dawson 3 for 24; Garrett 6 for 17; McClinton 6 for 16; Coan 3 for 1.
Passing—G. B.: Starr, 16 completions in 23 attempts for 250 yards; Bratkowski, 0 in 1. K. C.: Dawson 16 in 27 for 211; Beathard 1 in 5 for 17.
Receiving—G. B.: McGee, 7 receptions for 138 yards; Dale, 4 for 59; Fleming, 2 for 22; Pitts, 2 for 32. K. C.: Burford, 4 for 67; Taylor, 4 for 57; Garrett, 3 for 28; McClinton, 2 for 34; Arbanas, 2 for 30; Carolan, 1 for 7; Coan, 1 for 5.

STATISTICS OF THE GAME

	Packers	Chiefs
First downs	21	17
Rushing yardage	130	72
Passing yardage	228	167
Passes	16-24	17-32
Interceptions by	1	1
Punts	4-43	7-45
Fumbles lost	1	1
Yards penalized	40	26

January 16, 1967

Pro Football Going Electronic

By WILLIAM N. WALLACE

The television analysts make football sound so complicated. Vince Lombardi, one of the sport's demi-gods, maintains it is a simple game won by those who block and tackle best. Ara Parseghian says it is a game of emotion.

Simple or complex, sterile or emotional, football is a subject for the computer like so many aspects of American life.

Pro football, which can afford the bill, is taking a long look at computer applications and 14 of the teams, all except one in the National Football League, stand to benefit this season.

There are two distinct applications. One concerns a system to speed up the breakdown of scouting films of the upcoming opponent. The other assimilates the mass of information on 1,500 college players scouted by the pros each year.

Old Hat for Tigers

The use of the computer in football is, not new. When Charlie Caldwell was the coach, Princeton began using punch-card data processing in the late nineteen-forties. The effectiveness of the Tigers' complex single-wing offense was recorded play-by-play, game-by-game so that Caldwell knew what plays worked against whom.

As in the case of so many elements of football, the pros took the computer idea from the colleges. One system now in vogue had its origin three years ago at the University of Maryland when Tom Nugent was the coach there.

Nugent, an imaginative football man, asked an outfit called Computer Applications Inc., of Silver Spring, Md., to look into the tedious process of breaking down opponent game films. Howard I. Morrison, a vice president and a football buff, took up the challenge and worked out a program without charging a fee.

In preparing to play their next foe, all serious football teams at the college and professional level attempt to take from films the probabilities—called frequencies—of the opponent's offense and defense. Football teams are creatures of habit and they like to do what they know they can do best.

Siwash U. has a great passer, Boley Smith. On third down and long yardage situations, Boley is going to throw nine times out of 10, and six times out of those nine he will throw to Joe Goodhands, his split end, on a down-and-out pattern.

Such information is invaluable and it comes from painstaking repetitive study of Siwash game films by blinking assistant coaches in dark rooms.

Pain Is Alleviated

The computer has taken much pain out of the extraction of frequencies. A film need only be run through once with the proper information extracted and programmed. Into a computer it goes and four hours later a book dissecting a team's offense—and defense if requested—is available with the frequencies coded on wide sheets.

Two years ago Bill McPeak, then coach of the Redskins, learned what Nugent was doing at Maryland. The Redskins bought a system and Ed Hughes, a defensive assistant, became its biggest booster.

This season six N.F.L. teams, Washington, Dallas, Los Angeles, Minnesota, Chicago and Detroit, plus Miami of the American League, are using computer systems for offense

							PASS RECE_		
PLAY NO.	DOWN AND DISTANCE	TERR. AND YARD LINE	OFFENSIVE FORMATION	RUNNING B H PLAY	PASS PLAYS	PRIM. R PAT.	2ND R PAT.	3RD R PAT.	
27	1ST AND 10	-22	BR L Y	2 0 FULLTON					
31	1ST AND 10	-24	FL R L	3 9 NRAD					
32	2ND AND 10	-24	SP L		GR	X STOP	8 CURL	9 GO	
33	3RD AND 10	-24	SP L Y	4 1 CO	GR	9 CB	X CRX2	8 SQIN	
34	4TH AND 10	-24	PUN T Y						
35	1ST AND 10	-15	SP L Y		GR	8 SQIN	X CRX1	9 CRX1	
38	3RD AND 16	-20	SP R Y	2 0 CO	GR	9 CURL	X CRX2	8 CB	
40	2ND AND 05	-25	BR L Y	2 5 FLATE	GR	3 FAST	9 GO	X CRX7	
41	3RD AND 15	-15	SP L Y	4 9 18	GR	8 CB	X CRN	9 SQIN	
46	3RD AND 03	-13	SG R Y		BL	8 HITCH	X SHALW	2 FLAN	
57	1ST AND 10	-21	BR R Y	3 5 HALFA					
58	2ND AND 08	-23	BR R Y	4 1 FULLTON					
59	3RD AND 10	-21	SP R Y		GR	8 CB	9 SQIN	X SLOW	
60	4TH AND 10	-21	PUN T Y						
61	1ST AND 10	-16	I H	3 8 FAN					
62	2ND AND 08	-18	BR L Y	2 0 FULLTON					
63	3RD AND 04	-22	STG L Y		GR	R X DRAG	8 GO	2 FLC?	
69	1ST AND 10	-20	STG L Y	2 4 COA					
70	2ND AND 09	-21	STG L Y	4 5 HALFMO					
71	3RD AND 10	-20	SP L Y	0 2 MOTIONLT	GR	R 8 SQIN	2 TRAIL	4 CK+?	
72	4TH AND 17	-13	PUN T Y						
73	1ST AND 10	-14	STG R Y	2 4 HALFMO					

PLAYS EXECUTED BETWEEN THE -11 AND -25 YARD LINES

This is how computer outlines game analysis. Terms, format change according to teams.

or defense. Computer Applications does not have all the business — competitors appeared— but it remains foremost in the field.

Art Rooney Jr. of the Pittsburgh Steelers asked if the computer could be put to use in college playing scouting. It could. Computer Applications worked out a compact system to replace the bulky black notebooks of handwritten scouting reports.

There are three scouting combines in the N.F.L. called Blesto V, Troika and Cepo. Blesto V, which has five clubs in its membership, and Cepo, with seven, computerized their information. There is a sheet

of ability grades supplied by scouts for each pro prospect, like Boley Smith and Joe Goodhands of Siwash.

The computer reports give each player a ranking in relation to all the other prospects playing that position. Joe Goodhands, for example, might be rated the seventh best split end in the nation.

After the first two rounds of the draft have gone by, the pro teams have only 15 minutes each to decide upon their next selection. The computer rating information is then invaluable.

A pro team using offense and defense systems will spend up to $7,000 a season while a scouting system can run up to $20,000, depending upon the volume of information required.

But the human element remains, and the computer is merely an auxiliary tool. Scouting reports are only as good as the scouts.

An example came up this year, when the college guard rated fourth best in the nation by the computer ranking was not drafted. Two scouts reported he was too small to be considered. He was signed as a free agent, made the varsity of one of the N.F.L. teams and is now considered to be an outstanding prospect.

Who was he? Sorry, that information is classified. The pro teams make secrets out of much of their computer information.

October 22, 1967

trius Synodinus, raised in Steubenville, Ohio.

When his mother died, his father took him to Greece. There he attended American University at Athens for two years. His best subjects, he says with a smile, were mathematics and history. Returning to Ohio, he was an executive in a coal-stripping firm.

"Later on, I drilled for oil near Denver," he said, "but after 22 consecutive dry wells, I came to Vegas in 1956."

He's an Author, Too

In quoting odds for a living, he operated in the Santa Anita Turf and Sport Club here before free-lancing. In addition to his column in the Las Vegas Sun, he supplies a few West Coast newspapers with his pro football point spreads. He also writes magazine articles and is working on a book.

"The news media trusts me," he said. "The guy making a bet in a bar deserves to know the proper point spread, because these guys make 99 per cent of the bets on pro football."

His annual income, he said, fluctuates "between $17,000 and $25,000," a substantial sum for the support of his wife and five children. But it is a one-car family, a '65 blue Oldsmobile. Despite his reputation, he realizes that he is only as good as his most recent selection.

"I'm giving everybody the Bears this week," he said, propping the collar of his shirt, "but suppose they lose?

"The people all say then that The Greek gave them a loser. If the Bears win the bet, they figure that they liked the Bears anyway, they would have bet them anyway, but if they lose, I got to take the rap.

"Wherever I go, though," he said, "everybody wants to know how The Greek has it figured."

November 19, 1967

Vegas Analyst Dopes Out the Line

Jimmy (The Greek) Snyder Sets Point Spread on Games

By DAVE ANDERSON
Special to The New York Times

LAS VEGAS, Nev., Nov. 18 —Not far away, in the gaudy gloom of the casino, the green felt dice tables and the tinkle of coins spewing out of slot machines accented the atmosphere as Jimmy (The Greek) Snyder, self-titled "sports analyst," strolled through the lobby of Caesars Palace.

Every few steps, he was stopped. It might be by a bellhop, an executive, a cocktail waitress.

"Hey, Jimmy," each of them invariably said, "give me a team for Sunday, give me a winner."

And late last night, as Jimmy The Greek, in his soft blue shirt with the rolled show-biz collar and expensive dark blue sports jacket, answered them, his reply was always the same.

"The Bears," he said in his gravel voice. "Take the Bears."

He Makes 'The Line'

According to Jimmy The Greek's figures, the Chicago Bears were a one-point underdog to the St. Louis Cardinals for tomorrow's game in Chicago. But the Bears were his best bet. And when Jimmy The Greek advises, "Take the Bears," people listen.

Throughout most of the nation, the "line" that lists the point spread in each week's pro football games is established by Jimmy The Greek.

"I make it up every Sunday night in my home," he was saying now over a cup of coffee. "I have my own rating system of each team. Quite often the point spread

is dictated simply by the difference in points in the rating system. Right now the Colts are my top team in the National Football League, with a 93 rating. The Packers are 91. In the other league, Oakland is 91, the Jets and Chiefs 89."

But in forming a pointspread, he also takes into consideration several factors.

Two Five-Point Men

"Over-all team speed is the first factor with me," he explained. "Then comes the front defense, the front four. Next, the back defense, especially the cornerbacks. Then the quarterback, the passing offense, I give X amount of points to a better quarterback and then I have to consider the intangibles."

The mental attitude of a team is an important intangible but, he acknowledges, "you have to try to guess it."

Another intangible is the coach. He respects Vince Lombardi of the Packers the most, but the second coach he mentioned was Blanton Collier of the Cleveland Browns.

Regarding quarterbacks, he puts Joe Namath of the Jets in a class with Johnny Unitas of the Colts in importance.

"Namath and Unitas are both worth five points if they're out," he said, "but that's a relative thing. It depends on the No. 2 quarterback. As good as Bart Starr is, if he's hurt, the Packers aren't wrecked because Zeke Bratkowski has won for them. He's not as good as Starr, but he's a good No. 2 quarterback."

In other years, the point spread on the Packers often depended on the availability of Paul Hornung and Jim Taylor.

"Not last year," he said, "Hornung didn't mean anything last year, but a few

years ago, Hornung and Taylor combined were worth four or five points in a game."

Jim Brown, however, never was as important to Jimmy the Greek as he was to the Cleveland Browns as their fullback.

"Brown was great against the Redskins or the Eagles," he said, "but in a real big game he wasn't the exceptional back. He used to be corralled pretty good by [Sam] Huff when the Giants were real good several years ago."

Another intangible to Jimmy the Greek is the home team. Although the Bears rate high at Wrigley Field, the Denver Broncos impress him as the strongest home team in either league.

"Notice what happens in the final quarter of their home games," he said. "Every time they seem to do well in the final quarter. As far as I'm concerned, it's a matter of their players being more used to the elevation there. The visiting teams poop out."

Although his specialty is pro football, "because it has so much exposure you can really stay up on it," he also quotes the odds on the baseball pennant races, the World Series, and the major golf tournaments.

"But the Red Sox won't be favored next season, the Orioles will," he said. "They finished strong and they got their pitching straightened out. In the other league, the Cardinals will be favored unless the Pirates make some phenomenal trades for two pitchers and a bull pen."

At the recent Sahara golf tournament here, Arnold Palmer shot a 76 in the opening round.

"After that 76," he recalled, "I made Palmer 300 to 1 to win the tournament. And I had to prove my opinion by laying $1 to $300 to about four guys."

Palmer didn't win, a professional triumph for Deme-

The Man to Watch Is ...The Middle Linebacker

By J. KIRK SALE

THE DEFENSE'S MAN-WHO-DOES-EVERYTHING

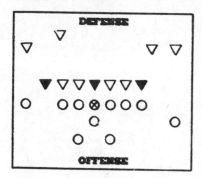
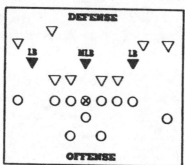

The linebacker positions (right) evolved out of the old seven-man line (left) with three men dropping back to give better protection against passes.

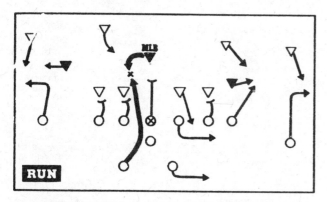

The middle linebacker must be big enough to stop runners...

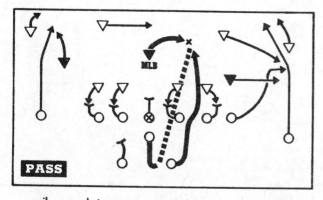

...agile enough to cover pass receivers over the middle...

"This great game of ours has gone so far and fast those pinkos can't touch it."

—RIP MILLER, Assistant Athletic Director, U.S. Naval Academy.

YOU remember the great names of professional football. Johnny Blood. Ken Strong. Cliff Battles. Ward Cuff. Names you could savor. Greasy Neal. Howard Buck. Bulldog Turner. Chug Justice. Ernie Steele. And today, today who are the heroes that dreams are made of? Milton Plum. Bob Lilly. Francis Tarkenton. Merlin Olsen. No savor, not even an aftertaste. Lester Shy. Billy Glass. Brian Piccolo. Theron Sapp.

Theron Sapp?

Those old, honest names of football greatness—are they all gone now, gone with the flying wedge and cardboard shoulderpads? Well, not entirely. But today it seems that most of them are borne by men playing one position only: linebacker. Men like Dick Butkus, Tommy Nobis, Ray Nitschke—together they sound like a head-on train crash; Bob Tubbs, Andy Bowling, Sam Huff, Bill Jobko—names that have the very ring of bellicosity; and Steve Stonebreaker—even if he weren't 6 foot 3, 230 pounds and mean besides, he'd give ulcers to the calmest quarterback.

It is no doubt only a happy accident that linebackers are the inheritors of the violent names of pro football. But it is a fact that the single most rugged position in all of that rugged game, the most specialized and brutal job in that sport of specialized brutality, is the linebacker's. And it's not enough that he has to *be* tough, plowing into a ton of flesh every single Sunday afternoon for an entire fall—even more important, he has to *feel* tough, with a bottom-of-the-barrel bitterness that no one on the other side can miss. A name helps.

"Being in politics is like being a football coach. You have to be smart enough to understand the game ... and dumb enough to think it's important."

—EUGENE MCCARTHY, United States Senator.

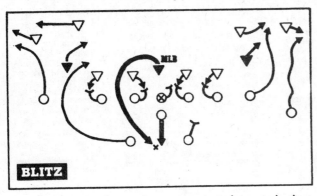

BLITZ

...and fast enough to charge unprotected quarterbacks.

LINEBACKERS? Linebackers. Back in the days of Johnny Blood, of course, they didn't have any, for those were the unsubtle sock-'em days of football's adolescence. But as the sport matured and offenses blossomed with mortar-armed quarterbacks, Olympic-fast flankers and untippable running backs, defenses had to grow to meet them. And so were born the linebackers—men who were expected to stop them all.

It was the New York Giants' Steve Owen in the early fifties who first saw the real potential of the defensive part of football and invented the linebacker to build it around. To counter the increasing use of the pass, but still retain some check on the run, Owen decided to drop three men back from the usual seven-man line to get them closer to the passing zones (see diagrams, top left).

Owen required only one thing of these three men: everything. They had to be big enough to move forward and stop the charging fullbacks, yet fast enough to keep up with the speedy ends and flankers on the pass plays; they had to be bright enough to figure out which way the play was going—and quick enough to get to it. With that single change, Owen turned the game into something of an art.

He was so successful with the art that a few years later Tom Landry, then Giant defensive coach and now head coach of the Dallas Cowboys, came along and turned it into a science. He gave specific assignments to the linebackers—"keys" they're called in the trade—telling them how they're expected to react in any given situation. He plotted out extensive and complicated defensive plays for the entire squad, almost the first time a coach had spent as much care on the stoppers-of-points as he had on the getters. And then he put the responsibility for carrying it all out on the man in the eye of the vortex: the middle linebacker.

December 10, 1967

Packers Beat Cowboys, 21-17, for N.F.L. Title on Score in Last 13 Seconds

STARR'S PLUNGE ON 3D DOWN WINS

Quarterback Also Passes for 2 Scores as Packers Gain Record 3d Title in Row

STATISTICS OF THE GAME

	Cowb.	Packers
First downs	11	18
Rushing yardage	92	80
Passing yardage	100	115
Return yardage	43	44
Passes	11-26	14-24
Interceptions by	0	1
Punts	8-39	8-29
Fumbles lost	1	2
Yards penalized	58	10

By WILLIAM N. WALLACE

Special to The New York Times

GREEN BAY, Wis., Dec. 31—There had never been a football game like this one. Everyone agreed—Vince Lombardi, the winning coach; Tom Landry, the losing coach; Chuck Howley, the Dallas linebacker who symbolized the losers; Bart Starr, the quarterback who scored the winning touchdown with 13 seconds left to play.

The Green Bay Packers, frustrated and punished for 40 of the 60 minutes it takes to play these games, won their third straight championship of the National Football League by defeating the Dallas Cowboys, 21-17, before a capacity crowd of 50,861 at Lambeau Field.

The temperature was 14 degrees below zero at the start of the game and 12 degrees below at the end. And on top of that there was a 14-knot northwest breeze blowing down from the Yukon.

"It was terrible out there," said Landry, "terrible for both sides. That in itself made this game distinctive from any other."

A Game of Distinction

The fact that the teams, champions of the Western and Eastern conferences of the N. F. L., were able to play such capable football was remarkable. It was remarkable too that the stadium was filled and nobody went home before the outcome was decided. The customers, who paid as much as $12 for their tickets, received full worth.

No team in the 47-year history of the N.F.L. has ever before won three straight championships. But the Packers came within 13 seconds of missing this achievement. On third down from the 1-yard line Starr drove over right guard behind Jerry Kramer's block to score the winning touchdown.

This touchdown came at the end of an exciting 68-yard drive against the gallant Cowboys and the clock. Football players are mortal like the rest of us and they have fear. "I was scared we had thrown it all away," said Henry Jordan, the Packers' defensive tackle who played a magnificent game.

The Packers won $8,000 apiece today and now they move on to the Super Bowl at Miami on Jan. 14 to play the American League champion.

Jordan Paces Defense

Jordan and his mates on the defensive unit kept the Packers in the game by holding the rampant Cowboys numerous times in the second half. They made victory possible. The Green Bay offense was in trouble most of the time and had ground to a halt after opening a 14-0 lead in the first 12 minutes.

Starr, pressured relentlessly by the Cowboy front four, was thrown eight times, while attempting to pass, for losses totaling 76 yards.

But Bart and all the Packers have come back so many times from the depths of adversity. They did so again by mustering that last scoring drive.

The temperature was too cold for the "electric blanket" —the heating system under the

Green Bay Scoring

Dallas Cowboys	0	10	0	7—17
Green Bay Packers	7	7	0	7—21

G.B.—Dowler, 8, pass from Starr (Chandler, kick).
G.B.—Dowler, 46, pass from Starr (Chandler, kick).
Dal.—Andrie, 7, return of fumble recovery (Villanueva, kick).
Dal.—FG, Villanueva, 21.
Dal.—Rentzel, 50, pass from Reeves (Villanueva, kick).
G.B.—Starr, 1, run (Chandler, kick).
Attendance—50,861.

INDIVIDUAL STATISTICS

RUSHES—G.B.: Anderson, 18 for 35 yards; Mercein, 6 for 20; Williams, 4 for 13; Wilson, 3 for 11; Starr, 1 for 1. Dal.: Perkins, 17 for 51; Reeves, 13 for 42; Baynham, 1 for minus 1; Meredith, 1 for 9.
PASSES—G.B.: Starr, 14 of 24 for 191 yards. Dal.: Meredith, 10 of 25 for 59; Reeves, 1 of 1 for 50.
RECEPTIONS—G.B.: Dowler, 4 for 77 yards; Anderson, 4 for 44; Dale, 3 for 44; Mercein, 2 for 22; Williams, 1 for 4. Dal.: Hayes, 3 for 16; Reeves, 3 for 11; Clarke, 2 for 24; Rentzel, 2 for 61; Baynham, 1 for 3.

turf—to work and the field became progressively harder and harder. This was to the Packers' advantage.

Starr began to throw short wide passes to his backs, Donnie Anderson and Chuck Mercein. The linebackers covering them, Dave Edward and Howley, who is an All-Pro performer, could not react swiftly enough to tackle the attackers in the open field. "There was no traction," said Howley. "The advantage had gone to the offense."

Starr passed to Anderson for 6 yards, to Anderson again for 12 to the Dallas 39 and then

at the beginning of the game and seemed to worry less about the cold. Boyd Dowler scored on two touchdown passes from Starr, the first worked against Mike Johnson, the Dallas cornerback who is half a foot shorter than Dowler and proved a big one to Mercein for 19 to the Cowboy 11. Mercein, a fullback, who was a New York Giants' reject, stormed to the 3. Anderson was stopped twice and then Starr tried the quarterback sneak to score.

If he had failed would the Packers have had time to kick a field goal on fourth down to tie the score and send the game into a sudden-death overtime? Their time-outs were used up.

"It would have been close," said Lombardi. "We didn't want a tie. We had compassion for those spectators. We wanted to send them home right then."

The Packers seemed to have a much more positive attitude to be a weak link in the early going. The first scoring pass was short, 8 yards, the second long, 46 yards.

Dallas scored to trail, 14-7, when Willie Townes dropped Starr for a 19-yard loss and Bart fumbled the football. George Andrie, the defensive end, picked it up and ran with it for a score from the 7. But Dallas in the first half gained only 42 yards and Don Meredith completed only four of 13 pass attempts. Meredith's passes for the most part were dreadful.

Halfback Throws a 'Bomb'

But Dallas made 3 points just before the half on a 21-yard field goal by Dan Villanueva after Willie Wood of Green Bay had fumbled away a punt.

Meredith and his offense finally began to show something in the third period. A big play at the top of the fourth quarter suddenly put the Cowboys ahead, 17-14. It was the halfback pass, Dan Reeves to Lance Rentzel for 50 yards. Rentzel, the flankerback was wide open, and the Packers—rarely tricked—had been fooled completely.

By then it looked as if Dallas could win because Townes, Andrie, Jethroe Pugh and Bob Lilly were dropping Starr as often as he tried to pass.

With five minutes left in the game, the Green Bay offense, so sorely tried all season and weakened by injuries, began the winning drive. It was to be a fatal one to the Cowboys and one that would enable the Packers to remain as champions once more.

"Those last five minutes are what the Packers are all about," said Lombardi. "They do it because they respect each other. They are selfless."

January 1, 1968

Brightest One of All

Bryan Bartlett Starr

IF the cumulative effect of being violently tossed to the frozen ground eight times by gigantic enemy linemen bothered Bryan Bartlett Starr yesterday, he would have been the last man to let on.

For as Bart Starr, the Green Bay Packers' quarterback, he has learned to not only live with pain and self-effacement, but also to show the opposition — and the public — that he couldn't care less. When he charged over from the 1-yard line, squirming underneath two Dallas Cowboys, he brought, with 13 seconds left to play, the Packers their third consecutive National Football League title.

Man in the News

This was the season that Starr once and for all shook off the sobriquet, said with a sneer, of "automaton." His Packer team was not the best he has played with, and often he became a "scrambler," a quarterback who leaves the protective pocket formed by his linemen when a play has broken down.

Yesterday's victory was a case in point. Starr was tackled eight times for losses by the Cowboys, threw two touchdown passes. And when the championship was at stake, he took the ball over.

Injury Proves Handicap

In the huddle before the winning play, Starr took extra time explaining what he wanted. He said he wanted the same blocking as always except that he wouldn't hand off to either the halfback or the fullback. And he said, "We darn well better make it."

Darn is Bart's strongest expletive. A friend has described him as "one of the nicest people I've ever known —but far from the most exciting."

Over the years his public posture changed little. A non-smoking, nondrinking man who answers "yes, sir," he took his role good-naturedly, subordinating his own thoughts of how to play the game for the grind-it-out Green Bay style hammered home by coach Vince Lombardi.

And early this season, when his passes had been intercepted nine times in the first two games, both Lombardi and Starr discounted reports that anything was wrong with Starr. Last season, his passes were intercepted only three times in 14 games.

But Lombardi suddenly disclosed (on his own TV show) that Starr was indeed injured, (bruised ribs, suffered in a preseason game), and a shoulder injury suffered against Atlanta further added to the Packers' troubles. Starr never said a word. The injuries healed (or at least the pain was overcome) and Starr went on to complete a season in which 55 per cent of his passes found their mark.

Starr is in his 12th season, but he was the lowest quarterback in Green Bay's estimation until Lombardi took over the team in 1959—Starr had been the fourth-string passer.

Pressure has always been Starr's strong suit. As a freshman quarterback he helped engineer his college team, the University of Alabama, to a 61-6 victory over Syracuse in the 1953 Orange Bowl.

Crimson Tide Marks Set

He was born in Montgomery, Ala., on Jan. 9, 1934, went to high school there and was to set records at the university that would be broken later by a player named Joe Namath.

At Green Bay, when Lom-

bardi's reign began, Starr was considered the best of a mediocre lot. But he has been the quarterback as the Packers have won six conference titles and he has led the league's passers three times.

Starr reached his peak last January, when Green Bay won the first Super Bowl game. He was named the outstanding player.

A coach of a rival club said of him, "He is probably the best quarterback in football and before he gets

through—which I hope is soon—he may be recognized as the best of them all."

Typically, the 6-foot, 1-inch 195-pound Starr praised his teammates and scolded himself after yesterday's victory, which again put the Packers in the Super Bowl.

"A few times I should have thrown the ball away," he said, referring to the times he was tackled for a loss. "But," he said, "I just had to eat the ball."

January 1, 1968

N.F.L. Players Group Votes To Register as Labor Union

HOLLYWOOD BEACH, Fla., Jan. 7 (UPI)—The National Football League Players Association will take formal action this week to register as a labor union with the United States Department of Labor, Mike Pyle of the Chicago Bears announced today.

Pyle, the president of the association, also announced that Daniel S. Shulman, a Chicago labor lawyer, had been retained as chief negotiator and labor relations counsel.

Shulman will handle all labor negotiations and is formulating proposals for presentation to the club owners.

"Major pledges of support have been received from all teams in the National Football League," Pyle said.

The association is now meeting at the Hollywood Beach Hotel with all N.F.L. teams. All players in the league will be notified officially of the association's action.

Pyle said the 16 player representatives had voted unanimously to reject efforts by the Teamsters Union to organize the players.

"The association will take a militant attitude to protect its members and to undertake all appropriate action to see that the players' demands are met," Pyle said.

Creighton Miller, who for 11 seasons has been legal counsel to the players, has resigned to take a new post as representative of the nation's top college players. He will be associated with James Morse of Muskegon, Mich., also a lawyer, in the new venture.

Miller also will represent professional players who are playing out their options in negotiations with N.F.L. and American Football League clubs next season.

January 8, 1968

GREEN BAY BEATS OAKLAND, 33 TO 14, IN THE SUPER BOWL

Chandler of Packers Kicks 4 Field Goals—Adderley Tallies on Interception

---

75,546 AT GAME IN MIAMI

Starr Throws for 62-Yard Score—Lamonica Passes for 2 Raider Touchdowns

By WILLIAM N. WALLACE
Special to The New York Times

MIAMI, Jan. 14—The Green Bay Packers, a splendid collection of football players who have made a habit of winning the big games, won another one today and enriched themselves by $15,000 each.

The Packers, champions of the National Football League, trounced the Oakland Raiders of the American league, 33-14, before a crowd of 75,546 in the Orange Bowl and thus exceeded expectations. They had been favored by 14 points.

This was the Super Bowl game, watched by a television audience estimated at 50 million, but only in the first half did it approach being a super game. The Packers led a half-time, 16-7, and the Raiders had made the mid-afternoon interesting by challenging Green Bay in both offense and defense.

Game Slips Away

But the game slipped away from the American League team in the second half much as it did for Kansas City in the first Super Bowl contest a year ago in Los Angeles when Green Bay routed the Chiefs in the last two periods and went on to win, 35-10.

Although he kicked four field goals, Don Chandler of the Packers was put into position to swing his right leg for $15,-000 through the more important contributions of several of his teammates. These were Bart Starr, the impeccable quarterback; Gale Gillingham, the guard who neutralized Tom Keating, the outstanding Oakland tackle; plus Herb Adderley, Ron Kostelnik and Ray Nitschke of the magnificent defensive

unit. Chandler's field goals, which ranged in length from 20 to 43 yards, came at the end of Green Bay drives in the first, second and third periods. These 3-point kicks gave the Packers leads of 3-0, 6-0, 16-7 just before half-time, and 26-7.

Adderley, the cornerback, stepped into a weak pass thrown by Daryle Lamonica toward Fred Biletnikoff, intercepted and streaked 60 yards for a touchdown. That was the final Packer score and along the way Adderley was aided by two tremendous blocks by Henry Jordan and Kostelnik.

Lamonica was a producer for Oakland, which had a limited offense, on two touchdown passes. He passed twice for 23 yards to Bill Miller, a slot back lined up on the strong side inside of Biletnikoff. This somewhat unorthodox offensive formation was the only Oakland weapon that bothered the Packers.

The Super Bowl prize money was set at $15,000 for each of the winners and $7,500 for each of the losers. Keating, one of the losers, certainly warranted every dollar. Playing with a sprained ankle, this small-sized (247 pounds) defensive tackle from Michigan was the only Raider to put pressure on Starr, who was Mr. Cool as usual.

Starr Sprains Thumb

Starr completed 13 of 24 passes for 202 yards and one touchdown (62 yards to Boyd Dowler in the second period) before leaving the game in the last quarter because of a sprained thumb. Starr also made good on six of 11 third-down plays while Lamonica gained the first down only four times on nine third-down situations.

Lamonica found his receivers covered most of the time and completed 15 of 34 attempts. He did enjoy good pass protection until late in the game, when Kostelnik and Willie Davis of Green Bay began to bore into him through tiring linemen.

The Oakland defense, as with Green Bay the strongest half of the team, put up a stout fight. But the Packers nibbled away at this defense, as is their custom, and put the points on the scoreboard in every quarter. The Packers' only big offensive play was the strike by Starr to Dowler that made the score 13-0 in the second period. Dowler, who is 6 feet 5 inches tall, ran to the inside and past Kent McCloughan, the covering cornerback. Dowler was beyond the last man when he caught the ball.

Outcome Sealed Early

Oakland then courageously mounted a quick two-minute touchdown drive of 78 yards in nine plays. Four plays were completed passes, two to Miller.

The Raiders did not score again until almost six minutes

had passed in the fourth quarter and Green Bay was ahead, 33-7. The outcome had by then been sealed by the wealthy minions of Coach Vincent Lombardi.

One of the troubles of Lamonica and his coach, John Rauch, was their insistence in trying to run around Green Bay flanks. No teams do this successfully and Nitschke, the ferocious middle linebacker, wound up tackling Hewritt Dixon, the Raider fullback, for no gain.

Starr moved his plays around the Oakland defense and found no glaring weakness, but he did find several little inadequacies. It was a typical, thorough Packer job and if this was Lombardi's last game as a coach, he went out with a good one to remember.

GREEN BAY PACKERS (33)
Ends—Dowler, Dale, Fleming, Davis, Aldridge, Long, McGee, Capp, B. Brown.
Tackles—Skoronski, Gregg, Kostelnik, Jordan, Weatherwax.
Guards—Gillingham, Kramer, Thurston.
Centers—Hyland, Bowman.
Linebackers—Robinson, Nitschke, Caffey, Crutcher, Flanigan.
Quarterbacks—Starr, Bratkowski.
Offensive Backs—Anderson, Wilson, Williams, Mercein.
Defensive Backs—Adderley, Jeter, T. Brown, Wood, Rowser, Hart.
Kicker—Chandler.

OAKLAND RAIDERS (14)
Ends—Miller, Biletnikoff, Cannon, Lassiter, Davidson, Wells, Kocourek, Herock, Oats.
Tackles—Svihus, Schuh, Birdwell, Keating, Kruse, Archer, Sligh.
Guards—Upshaw, Hawkins, Harvey.
Center—J. Otto.
Linebackers—Laskey, Conners, G. Otto, Williamson, Budness, Benson.
Quarterback—Lamonica.
Offensive Backs—Banaszak, Dixon, Todd, Hagberg.
Defensive Backs—McCloughan, W. Brown, Grayson, Powers, Williams, Bird.
Kickers—Blanda, Eischeid.

Green Bay Packers	3	13 10	7—33
Oakland Raiders	0	7 0	7—14

G.B.—FG, Chandler, 39.
G.B.—FG, Chandler, 20.
G.B.—Dowler, 62, pass from Starr (Chandler, kick).
Oak.—Miller, 23, pass from Lamonica (Blanda, kick).
G.B.—FG, Chandler, 43.
G.B.—Anderson, 2, run (Chandler, kick).
G.B.—FG, Chandler, 31.
G.B.—Adderley, 60, return of interception (Chandler, kick).
Oak.—Miller, 23, pass from Lamonica (Blanda, kick).

INDIVIDUAL STATISTICS
RUSHES—G.B.: Wilson, 17 for 65 yards; Anderson, 14 for 48; Williams, 8 for 36; Starr, 1 for 14; Mercein, 1 for 0. Oak.: Dixon, 12 for 52; Todd, 2 for 37; Banaszak, 6 for 16.
PASSES—G.B.: Starr, 13 of 24 for 202 yards. Oak.: Lamonica, 15 of 34 for 208.
RECEPTIONS—G.B.: Dale, 4 for 43 yards; Fleming, 4 for 35; Anderson, 2 for 18; Dowler, 2 for 71; McGee, 1 for 35. Oak.: Miller, 5 for 84; Biletnikoff, 2 for 10; Banaszak, 4 for 69; Cannon, 2 for 25; Dixon, 1 for 3; Wells, 1 for 17.

STATISTICS OF THE GAME

	Packers	Raiders
First downs	19	16
Rushing yardage	163	105
Passing yardage	162	186
Return yardage	144	139
Passes	13-24	15-34
Interceptions by	1	0
Punts	6-39	6-44
Fumbles lost	0	2
Yards penalized	12	31

January 15, 1968

Papa of the Bears
George Stanley Halas

I^N the fall of 1919, a young engineering graduate from the University of Illinois founded a professional football team in Decatur, Ill.

One year later, the team—the Decatur Staleys — moved north and became the Chicago Bears of the newly formed National Football League. The graduate student, George Stanley Halas, played end, coached, handled administrative details, collected tickets, wrote publicity releases and nurtured through its early years a team that became one of the most successful and legendary institutions in modern sports history.

Yesterday, when George Halas announced his retirement as head coach, the news was carried in streamer headlines across page one of the Chicago afternoon papers.

So thoroughly had the 73-year-old perfectionist taskmaster impressed his image on the team over a 49-year span, that the Bears have become known as "Halas U."

Reunions Held Each Year

Every season, after the final home game, Halas throws a reunion party for Bear "alumni." As many as 600 people who have been

Associated Press

Coached some of the best
(Halas watching his 1963 championship team)

associated with the team dine, dance and recall the many moments of glory that they shared with Halas.

His record as a coach is the greatest in N. F. L. history. His 321 victories are 91

Man in the News

more than those of the late Curly Lambeau of the Green Bay Packers, whose record is second on the list of winning coaches.

The reason Halas gave yesterday for retiring—an arthritic hip—dates back to an injury he suffered in his brief baseball career with the New York Yankees in 1919. He hurt the hip sliding into third base in an exhibition game and never completely recovered.

Although his baseball career was undistinguished, he has noted that in 1920 the Yankees found an excellent replacement for him in right field—Babe Ruth.

The hip injury did not keep him from playing a hard and speedy game as an end for the Bears until 1929, when he retired as a player. He still holds the N.F.L. record for the longest run with a recovered fumble—98 yards.

Jim Thorpe, who had fumbled the ball, caught up with Halas near the goal line and smashed him into the end zone with a vicious tackle, but Halas held on to the ball.

Notable Backs on Squads

As a coach, Halas attracted some of the greatest. He brought Red Grange to the professional game in the nineteen-twenties and afterward coached such notable backs as Bronko Nagurski, Sid Luckman, Johnny Lujack and Gale Sayers.

The team he assembled in 1940, when the "Monsters of the Midway" demolished the Washington Redskins, 73-0, in the N.F.L. championship game, was perhaps Halas's strongest squad.

Halas has retired three times before, causing some critics to call him the Sarah Bernhardt of football. In 1929, 1942 (to enter the Navy) and in 1955, he put down the coaching reins, but he could not find happiness away from the bench and returned.

The sight of Halas marching up and down the sidelines, baiting the officials and shouting to his players, became a sentimental delight to fans at Wrigley Field. He wore a business suit and a battered hat that he often threw to the ground and kicked indignantly when fortune was running against the Bears.

Supporting "Papa Bear," as he is known, in his crusades against N.F.L. opponents were his late wife, Min, and his two children, George Jr., and Virginia, who often imitated his antics in the stands.

George Jr. is now the president and general manager of the Bears and Virginia's husband, Ed McCaskey, has become a vice president and the treasurer of the club.

Born in Chicago on Feb. 2, 1895, Halas, the son of a Czechoslovak tailor, was a 6-foot 170-pound star in baseball and football at Illinois before serving in the Navy during World War I. After the war, he worked briefly as a railroad engineer before his unsuccessful try at professional baseball.

His next project was professional football and since then, George Halas and the N.F.L. have grown rich and powerful.

The last of his six championship teams was the one in 1963. He gained much publicity (mostly bad) after the 1965 season, however, when he took George Allen, an assistant coach, to court rather than let him move to the head coaching job with the Los Angeles Rams.

Allen Finally Released

After establishing early in the proceedings that Allen and he had a firm contract that was binding on Allen, Halas suddenly released Allen from his obligations.

The episode was characteristic of Halas's tenacity and the devotion to duty that he demanded of the Bears.

After the trial, in a terse conversation with Allen, Halas instructed his former assistant:

"Bring back those books."

He was referring to the Bears' playbooks—books containing all of the Chicago offensive and defensive alignments, the books that Halas will now pass on to his successor. Papa Bear has become a spectator.

May 28, 1968

Sports of The Times
By ARTHUR DALEY

The Lombardi Mystique

MARIE LOMBARDI groped for the proper words to describe her husband, Vince, and it immediately became evident that the many-faceted qualities of the genius of Green Bay do not lend themselves to a vest pocket summation.

"He's kind of a mystery," she said hesitantly. "He eludes you. But to me he's the most wonderful man in the world."

If Vince, the devoted family man, can seem mysterious and elusive to Marie after 27 years of happy matrimony, it must be evident that he is much more of an enigma to everyone else. Not all the veils surrounding this complex man are torn aside by the Columbia Broadcasting System in its dramatic study of the retired Packer coach, which will be a television special tonight, pre-empting the Ed Sullivan Hour.

But it provides a deeper understanding of Lombardi and the dynasty he created at Green Bay. The two are so intertwined that they are inseparable. In 1959 he arrived to take over a moribund franchise that had "no direction, no future, no morale." And he supplied the driving force to transform the Packers into the mightiest football power on earth with six division championships, five league titles and two Super Bowl victories.

No Substitute

Illuminating glimpses of the man are to be found in the comments of various people, including Marie, his wife; Paul Hornung, the playboy; Bart Starr, the straight arrow; Jerry Kramer, the amazingly articulate blocking demon; Ray Nitschke, the hard-boiled linebacker; Willie Davis, the whimsical defensive captain, and Red Blaik, Lombardi's coaching preceptor at West Point. It was at the Point that Vince learned from Blaik, who had learned it from his idol,

The New York Times
Vince Lombardi
Founder of the Green Bay dynasty

General Douglas MacArthur, "There is no substitute for victory."

Insatiable has been Lombardi's quest for victory. Deeply religious in his personal life, Vince brought that same religious fervor to football. He found willing converts at Green Bay, imparting to the Packers his own football fanaticism, even if he had to whip some of the more reluctant into becoming true believers. He showed the way to salvation in his first game as coach when the Packers upset the mighty Chicago Bears.

"We were so elated," commented Starr, "so excited at having won this game for our new coach that we just swept him up

on our shoulders."

Blaik described his prize pupil thusly:

"He is volatile, enthusiastic and given to degrees of emotion not likely to be found in coaches."

A sideline camera constantly gives the viewers a clear idea of Lombardi's emotional involvement during various segments of spectacularly shot football footage. Shown are his cowering rages.

"What the hell kind of football are we playing out there?" he screams during some bad moments of one game. "We're grabbing, not tackling." Shown also his his blissful reaction to a sensational long-distance run by Travis Williams.

"What a man!" he exclaims, fetching Travis a whack on the rump. Shown also is his very human remark to an official just before one game.

"After all these years, Mike, you'd think I'd be nice and relaxed. I'm a nervous wreck."

That is one thing that the TV special achieves. It humanizes Lombardi and gives fans sharper appreciation of what makes him tick.

Down the Alley

In one segment he outlines a play on the blackboard and draws a heavy vertical line through the right tackle position. Another line is drawn farther to the outside to form an alley.

"We seal it off to the inside here," he indicates. "And we seal off the outside here." Then he revealed one secret of his success as a coach.

"Not only must I show them how," he said. "I must also show them why. Once they understand a play they can do it."

The Lombardi mystique even has his tough, battle-hardened players thinking like the impressionable youngsters of an earlier generation and not like the cynics of today.

"You grow in stature under Vince," says Starr.

"He has taught us the values of life," says Davis.

Maybe it sounds corny, but their sincerity absolves them of that. If the TV people had thought of it, they might have asked Jerry Kramer to quote a line from his marvelous new book, "Instant Replay"—more on the book another day—because no one described the man more accurately. Wrote Kramer:

"Vincent Thomas Lombardi, a cruel, kind, tough, gentle, miserable, wonderful man whom I often hate and often love and always respect."

September 15, 1968

Jets Cut for 'Heidi'; TV Fans Complain

By THOMAS ROGERS

Fans of Heidi, the diminutive Swiss orphan girl in the story by Johama Spyri, were happy, but professional football followers were irate last night when the National Broadcasting Company terminated its telecast of the New York Jets-Oakland Raiders game with one minute left to play and the outcome still to be decided.

At 7 P.M., New York time, N.B.C. abandoned its coverage here of the American Football League game in Oakland to begin a two-hour movie, "Heidi." Viewers on the West Coast, however, saw the final minute of action, in which the Raiders rallied for two touchdowns to win, 43-32. A spokesman for N.B.C. in New York said that when an attempt was made to return to the game, it was over.

Thousands of angry fans flooded the N.B.C. switchboard with calls complaining of the decision to cut off the game. The load of calls, according to an N.B.C. operator, caused the switchboard to break down.

Many callers, unable to reach N.B.C., called the Police Department and tied up the emergency police number for several hours. Operators at The New York Telephone Company and The New York Times were also deluged with calls.

At approximately 8:20 P.M., WNBC-TV in New York ran a streamer under the movie's pastoral, Alpine setting that gave the final score, explained that the Raiders had made two touchdowns to win and advised viewers, "Details on the 11th Hour News."

At 8:30 P.M., Julian Goodman the president of N.B.C., issued a statement that said:

"It was a forgivable error committed by humans who were concerned about the children who were expecting to see 'Heidi' at 7 P.M. I missed the end of the game as much as anyone else."

Another spokesman for the network added, "N.B.C. made a mistake. It regrets it deeply."

He also said that the policy of N.B.C. is generally to show athletic events "to their conclusion."

It was the second time during the day that N.B.C. abandoned its television coverage of a game before it was completed. Earlier, the network had left the San Diego-Buffalo game in the final minutes to show the beginning of the Jet-Raider game at 4 P.M.

The game at Oakland started at 4:03 and ended at about 7:10. It was slowed by 19 time-consuming penalties and by numerous time-outs called by both teams.

The average professional football game lasts about 2½ hours.

November 18, 1968

JETS UPSET COLTS BY 16-7 FOR TITLE IN THE SUPER BOWL

A.F.L. Club Wins for First Time as Namath Pierces Baltimore Defense

By DAVE ANDERSON
Special to The New York Times

MIAMI, Jan. 12—In a memorable upset that astonished virtually everyone in the football realm, the New York Jets of the American League conquered the Baltimore Colts, the supposedly impregnable National League champions, 16-7, today for the Super Bowl prestige and paycheck.

Joe Namath, the quarterback whose optimism proved to be contagious to his teammates, directed the Jets to a 4-yard touchdown run by Matt Snell, the workhorse fullback, and field goals by Jim Turner from 32, 30 and 9 yards.

Equally important, the Jet defensive unit dominated the Colt offense. Led by Gerry Philbin, the Jet pass-rushers hurried Earl Morrall, selected as the N.F.L.'s most valuable player, into throwing three interceptions in the first half.

Midway in the third quarter, Morrall was benched and Johnny Unitas, the sore-armed master, took over at quarterback. With about 3½ minutes remaining in the game, the Colts scored on a 1-yard run by Jerry Hill, but by that time the Jets were in command.

In the A.F.L.'s ninth season, the Jets convinced 75,377 stunned spectators in the Orange Bowl and a television audience of perhaps 60 million that they deserved parity with the best teams in the N.F.L. and that Namath had developed into pro football's best quarterback.

In the two previous Super Bowl games, the Green Bay Packers had maintained the N.F.L. aura of invincibility by decisively defeating their A.F.L. opponents — 35-10 over the Kansas City Chiefs two years ago, 33-14 over the Oakland Raiders a year ago. And the

The New York Times (by Meyer Liebowitz)

HANDOFF: Joe Namath, giving the ball to Matt Snell, left foreground, his fullback, for a short gain on a first-half play. Snell also scored the Jets' only touchdown of the game.

Colts had been expected to continue that supremacy.

In the point-spread type of betting, the Colts were favored by 18 to 20 points. Without a point spread, the Colts were a 7-to-1 choice.

The outcome put the Jets on a plateau with such other famous upsetmakers in sports as Cassius Clay, knocking out Sonny Liston for the world heavyweight title as an 8-1 underdog in 1964, and the racehorse, Upset, defeating Man o' War in 1919 for that thoroughbred's only loss.

But the upset did not surprise Namath, the Jets' positive thinker. Despite his reputation as a playboy, he also is a serious student of football. As he observed the Colts in game films during the week, he noticed weaknesses in their vaunted zone pass-defense that he hoped to exploit. It is one thing to see the weaknesses as the film is flashed on a hotel-room wall, it is quite another to penetrate that defense on the field.

Namath accomplished it with his lariat arm, a scientific split end named George Sauer Jr. and a fullback, Snell, whose power running established the ground game that enabled the celebrated $400,000 quarterback to keep the Colts uncertain as to what play he would call next.

Namath, Sauer and Snell accumulated impressive statistics, but the members of the Jets'

offensive line—Winston Hill, Bob Talamini, John Schmitt, Randy Rasmussen and Dave Herman—provided the blocking that produced those statistics.

Protected from the vaunted Colt pass-rush as if he were a rare jewel, Namath completed 17 of 28 passes for 206 yards. Sauer caught eight for 133 yards, a significant statistic because the Jets' other wide receiver, Don Maynard, was shut out. Snell rushed for 121 yards and caught four passes for 40 more.

In earning $15,000 apiece, double the reward for each Colt, the Jets kept their poise in moments of crisis as demanded by their coach, Weeb Ewbank, once dismissed by Baltimore.

Late in the scoreless first quarter, Sauer fumbled a sideline pass when tackled by Lenny Lyles, and the loose ball was pounced on by Ron Porter, a Colt linebacker, at the Jets' 12-yard line. On third down at the 6, Morrall's pass bounced high into the air off his intended receiver, Tom Mitchell. Randy Beverly, the Jets' cornerback who had been outmaneuvered by Mitchell, intercepted. Touchback. Jet ball.

Starting at the Jets' 20, Namath used Snell on four consecutive running plays aimed at the Colts' right side. Ordell Braase, the end, and Don Shinnick, the linebacker, were victimized for a total of 26 yards, providing Namath with a first down at the Jets' 46, good field position.

After an incompletion and a short pass to Bill Mathis, a third-and-4 situation confronted Namath, but he drilled a 14-yard pass to Sauer, who had fooled Lyles, for the first down.

Another pass to Sauer moved the Jets to the Colts' 23. Then

a 2-yard gain by Emerson Boozer, a 12-yard pass to Snell, a 5-yard gain by Snell and Snell's sweep produced a touchdown.

Sample Makes Interception

Not long after that, Tom Matte, who ran for a total of 116 yards, put the Colts at the Jets' 16 with a 58-yard dash down the right sideline.

On first down, Morrall threw toward Willie Richardson, his flanker, but Johnny Sample, once a Colt, zipped across to intercept the pass at the 2.

In the final minute of the first half, Morrall committed his worst mistake. At the Jets' 45, he handed off to Matte, who turned and tossed a backward pass to Morrall as the split end, Jimmy Orr, drifted beyond Beverly toward the end zone.

Orr was alone near the goal-line, with no Jet within 20 yards, but Morrall apparently never saw him. He threw toward Jerry Hill, his fullback, who was in front of the goal posts, but Jim Hudson, the Jets' strongside safetyman, intercepted at the 12, assuring a 7-0 half-time lead.

Another mistake, a fumble by Matte on the first play from scrimmage of the second half, turned the ball over to the Jets at the Colts' 33, in position for Turner's first field goal.

After three unsuccessful passes by Morrall on the next Colt series, Namath hit Sauer for two 14-yard gains to set up

Super Bowl Scoring

NEW YORK JETS (16)

Ends—Sauer, Maynard, Lammons, B. Turner, Rademacher, Philbin, Biggs.
Tackles—Hill, Herman, Richardson, Walton, Rochester, Elliott, McAdams.
Guards—Talamini, Rasmussen.
Centers—Schmitt, Crane.
Linebackers — Baker, Atkinson, Grantham, Neidert.
Quarterbacks—Namath, Parilli.
Offensive Backs—Boozer, Snell, Mathis, Smolinski.
Defensive Backs—Sample, Beverly, Hudson, Baird, Christy, D'Amato, Richard, Dockery.
Kickers—J. Turner, Curley Johnson.

BALTIMORE COLTS (7)

Ends—Orr, Richardson, Mackey, Perkins, Hawkins, Mitchell, Bubba Smith, Braase, Michaels.
Tackles—Vogel, Ball, J. Williams, Billy Ray Smith, Miller, Hilton.
Guards—Ressler, Sullivan, Cornelius Johnson.
Centers—Curry, Szymanski.
Linebackers—Curtis, Gaubatz, Shinnick, S. Williams, Porter.
Quarterbacks—Morrall, Unitas.
Offensive Backs—Matte, Hill, Brown, Pearson, Cole.
Defensive Backs—Boyd, Lyles, Logan, Volk, Stukes, Austin.
Kicker—Lee.

New York Jets .... 0 7 6 3—16
Baltimore Colts .... 0 0 0 7— 7

N. Y.—Snell, 4, run (Turner, kick).
N. Y.—FG, Turner, 32.
N. Y.—FG, Turner, 30.
N. Y.—FG, Turner, 9.
Balt—Hill, 1, run (Michaels, kick).
Attendance—75,377.

STATISTICS OF THE GAME

	Jets	Colts
First downs	21	18
Rushing yardage	142	143
Passing yardage	206	181
Return yardage	34	139
Passes	17-29	17-41
Interceptions by	4	0
Punts	4-39	3-44
Fumbles lost	1	1
Yards penalized	28	23

GETTING IT OFF: Joe Namath (12) of the Jets throwing a pass over the heads of Baltimore defenders. Rushing for the Colts are Ron Porter (55), Lou Michaels (79) and Lenny Lyles (43), Bill Mathis (31) blocks for his quarterback.

Super Bowl Comparison

INDIVIDUAL PASSING

	Att.	Comp.	Yds.	Td.	Int.
Namath, N. Y.	28	17	206	0	0
Parilli, N. Y.	1	0	0	0	0
Morrall, Balt.	17	6	71	0	3
Unitas, Balt.	24	11	110	0	1

RECEIVING

	Caught	Yds.
Snell, N. Y.	4	40
Lammons, N. Y.	2	13
Mathis, N. Y.	3	20
Sauer, N. Y.	8	133
Mackey, Balt.	3	35
Mitchell, Balt.	1	15
Richardson, Balt.	6	58
Matte, Balt.	2	30
Hill, Balt.	2	1
Orr, Balt.	3	42

INDIVIDUAL RUSHING

	Att.	Yds.	Avg.	Td
Boozer, N. Y.	10	19	1.9	0
Snell, N. Y.	30	121	4.1	1
Mathis, N. Y.	3	2	0.7	0
Morrall, Balt.	2	−2	−1.0	0
Matte, Balt.	11	116	10.5	0
Hill, Balt.	9	29	3.2	1
Unitas, Balt.	1	0	0.0	0

Interceptions—Beverly, N.Y., 2; Sample, N.Y., 1; Hudson, N.Y., 1.

Turner's second field goal for a 13-0 lead with about 4 minutes remaining in the third quarter.

When the Colt offensive took the field, Unitas had replaced Morrall. Unable to throw long because of his tender right elbow, Unitas misfired twice on short passes to Matte and Orr.

When the third quarter ended, Namath was guiding the team to Turner's final field goal and the Colts had been limited to only eight plays, including two punts, in that period.

But early in the final quarter, Matte and Hill moved the Colts to the Jets' 25, but Unitas was unable to deliver. After overthrowing Richardson, the 35-year-old quarterback found Orr in the end zone, but the pass was intercepted by Beverly.

In his next opportunity, Unitas generated an 80-yard drive, sparked by a fourth-down pass to Orr from his own 20.

After the Colts avoided a shutout on Hill's touchdown, they recovered an onside kick-off at the Jets' 44. When Unitas hit Orr and Richardson to move the ball to the 24, the Jets began to wonder if Unitas would work the magic he had performed for so many years when his right arm was healthy.

But again, the Jet pass-defenders, not the Colt pass-receivers, made the big play. Sample tipped away a pass intended for Richardson. After the Jet rush harassed Unitas into throwing short to Orr and then too longs a fourth-down pass intended for Orr was batted beyond his reach by Larry Grantham, the linebacker.

After that, Snell carried on six consecutive plays, providing a needed first down that enabled the Jets to exhaust the final 2 minutes 21 seconds and frustrate the Colts.

Namath was awarded a Dodge Charger by Sport magazine as the game's most valuable player, but Snell appeared to be equally deserving. So did all the offensive linemen. In the most significant victory in A.F.L. history, the battle had been won where it usually is in football—in the trenches.

January 13, 1969

United Press International

SUPER PASS NEEDED: With Bubba Smith of the Colts about to smother him, Joe Namath of the Jets looks for a receiver before passing in the second quarter of the Super Bowl.

Football's Super Star

Joseph William Namath

PEOPLE talk about Joe Namath. He excites comment. Today he is provoking more than ever, because, after an all-America career at the University of Alabama and four years as the quarterback of the New York Jets, he sits supreme at the top of the hard-nosed world of professional football. Namath, the ultra - publicized individualstic quarterback from Beaver Falls, Pa., yesterday led the New York Jets to an astounding 16-7 victory over the Baltimore Colts in the Super Bowl game at Miami. He intended to do it and, last week, in preparation for the game, said he would do it. Few believed him.

Man in the News

The victory, which elevated the American League to an equal level with the older National League, marks the high point of Namath's success-studded career.

"What we like about him is that he is a winner, he doesn't know about losing," commented Webb Ewbank, the coach of the Jets, a few seasons ago.

Sonny Werblin, the former owner of the Jets, who signed Namath for a bonus of $387,-000 and a Lincoln convertible, found another quality in Namath that he thought valuable. He said, on signing the sleepily handsome 6-foot-2-inch black-haired star:

"Namath has the presence of a star. You know how a real star lights up a room when he comes in. Joe has that quality."

Namath, who sparkled on the football field for Beaver Falls High School and at Alabama has become a legendary figure since moving to New York in 1965.

His penthouse apartment at 76th and First Avenue with its famous white llama rug is often the scene of get-togethers and parties. ("A get-together is when the guys come over to eat steaks and play cards; a party is when there are girls," he has said.)

Namath has pursued pleasure in the saloons and discotheques of the East Side, often in the company of beautiful young women. During one early-morning jaunt, he allegedly had a dispute with a sports writer that is still awaiting legal adjudication.

Joseph William Namath, the fifth child of a Hungarian steelworker, was born in Beaver Falls on May 31, 1943, and started playing football with his three older brothers when he was hardly able to hold the football.

The Golden Arm

After a splendid career in high school, he was offered scholarships by 52 colleges and universities. He also was offered $50,000 to play baseball with the Chicago Cubs.

Under Coach Paul (Bear) Bryant, Namath developed into one of the most sought-after passers in college football. Bryant called him, "the greatest athlete I ever coached."

His signing by Werblin and the Jets represented a great triumph for the A. F. L. and many observers contend led the way for the merger of the A. F. L. and N. F. L.

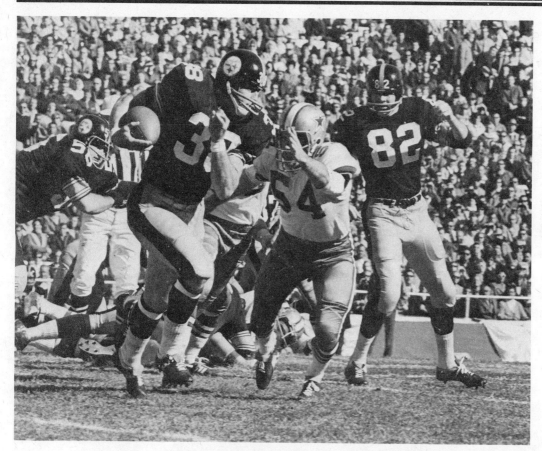

The Dallas Cowboys' superb linebacker, Chuck Howley (54), is about to bring down Pittsburgh's Earl Gros.

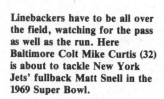

Linebackers have to be all over the field, watching for the pass as well as the run. Here Baltimore Colt Mike Curtis (32) is about to tackle New York Jets' fullback Matt Snell in the 1969 Super Bowl.

Although many people scoffed at the huge investment in the weak-kneed Namath and predicted he might never be able to complete one season because of his delicate underpinnings, he quickly established himself as one of the greatest passing quarterbacks.

Although the Jets were not able to win a league championship with Namath until this season, he set a pro record for the most yardage in a single campaign in 1967 by passing for 4,007 yards.

This year, although he threw significantly fewer passes for fewer touchdowns, he was voted the most valuable player in the A.F.L.

At Miami, while training for the Super Bowl, he was bedeviled by sports writers, who eagerly quoted him saying that the Jets would win the game, that the A.F.L. was equal to the N.F.L., that Earl Morrall of the Colts was not as good a passer as several in Namath's league. Most writers expected Na-

math to eat his words yesterday.

Instead, Namath said of the writers in a post-game interview: "I hope they all eat their pencils and pads. We won!"

January 13, 1969

Pro Football's Broken Men

By BILL SURFACE

JOHNNY UNITAS, the Baltimore Colts' venerable quarterback, has just called the Colts' Yellow-66 play and cocked his right arm while waiting for a flanker to sprint six more yards, then fake and spin left. Before the flanker reaches the place where he should pivot and take the pass, however, Unitas is clearly in trouble. Deacon Jones, the Los Angeles Rams' 260-pound, all-pro defensive end has knocked aside one of Baltimore's blockers and is charging menacingly toward Unitas's blind side. An intense man with an affinity for "racking up guys and sending them home early," Jones is now in the position of sending Unitas prematurely to the dressing room. Drawing back his fists, which are taped and soaked as tight as plaster casts, Jones lunges toward Unitas.

Instead of landing on Unitas, however, he collides with Bill Curry, the Colts' 230-pound center, who has slipped quickly in front of his path. Swinging furiously to get around him, Jones throws his weight into Curry's chest, then pounds his right fist on the sensitive earhole of Curry's helmet. Stepping laterally, Curry resembles a dazed boxer unable to strike back as he meekly slaps at Jones's hands. His ears buzzing, his head suddenly aching, he is so infuriated that he would like to kick his opponent. But, as Jones lowers his head and pushes even harder, Curry remains passively in his path for another 2.5 seconds before telling himself that he is unable to resist any longer. Fortunately, as he feels Jones slide past him, Curry realizes that Unitas has thrown the ball.

It was an excellent job. The more punishment that Curry is able to absorb without being knocked aside by defensemen, the higher he is graded by coaches. While he sees only larger, abusive defensemen during a game (and never sees the ball

BILL SURFACE, a frequent contributor, is the author of a book about Appalachia, to be published next year.

once it is snapped), Curry is fulfilling what just may be pro football's most demanding specialist role. He is, like the center and four offensive guards and tackles on each team, a body guard whose sole purpose on passing plays is to sacrifice himself so that defensemen cannot maul the quarterback. The job carries no illusions of heroism. "They call me a tackle, but I'm here to ride shotgun for the most valuable player in the game," volunteered Winston Hill, a New York Jets body guard, as he motioned toward quarterback Joe Namath's locker. "He's my only security. 'Cause if he goes, I'll have to go."

A lot of body guards do go. Relying upon exceptional agility, temperament and heavily muscled legs, shoulders and backs, they must be able to keep themselves diagonally between defensemen and their backpedaling quarterback for four to six seconds, thereby forming what is known as a 5-by-8-yard "pocket" around him. There is less margin for failure than in any other assignment. A flanker can catch seven of ten perfectly aimed passes and be considered sensational. A body guard on a winning team can fail on just two of thirty-five assignments and be blamed for losing a game or the team's quarterback for an entire season. "That pocket's got to be sealed up like a balloon," said John Sandusky, the 250-pound coach of Baltimore's body guards. "Just one hole in it and the whole thing blows up."

A BODY GUARD'S responsibility has been further compounded by the unprecedented emphasis on well-paid defensemen crashing into quarterbacks so forcibly that they either throw erratically, lose yardage, fumble or are physically unable to continue playing. The trend is so disquieting that, already this season, quarterbacks Len Dawson and Jackie Lee of Kansas City, Greg Cook of Cincinnati, Craig Morton of Dallas, Bob Berry of Atlanta, Bart Starr of Green Bay, John Hadl of San Diego, Gary Cuozzo of Minnesota, Steve Tensi of Denver, Dick Shiner of Pittsburgh and Jim Harris of Buffalo have left the field with disabling injuries. If the pattern continues, more quarterbacks will be hurt this fall than in 1968, when 21 of 26 men who began the season as starting quarter-

backs in the American and National Football Leagues were incapacitated with concussions, broken arms, legs and collarbones, and torn ligaments or cartilages.

Being able to protect quarterbacks from such brutality has made dependable body guards as valuable as most players who pass, catch or carry the ball. Plainly, teams with first-rate quarterbacks and second-rate body guards seldom win consistently, while teams with adequate quarterbacks and first-rate body guards are consistently in championship games. The Colts dramatized that fact last season when, through a trade, they acquired Earl Morrall, one of the New York Giants' expendable quarterbacks, after Unitas was unable to play because of a sore elbow. Although Morrall had been a substitute with five different teams in all but two of his twelve years in professional football, he was protected so well by Baltimore's body guards that he led the N.F.L. in passing with 2,909 yards and 26 touchdowns, was voted its player of the year, and passed the Colts to a league championship.

"Those guys in front of me give me the confidence that I could set up and throw without getting belted," Morrall recalled the other day. "Nobody passes as well if you're hurrying to throw before losing the ball, getting knocked dizzy or stepped on."

Not even great quarterbacks can compensate for the disadvantage of playing behind weak body guards. Poorly guarded Sonny Jurgensen, for example, not superbly guarded Joe Namath, has long been considered by many coaches as pro football's shrewdest, most accurate passer. Yet, while Jurgensen has played for losing teams in Philadelphia and Washington, Namath was able to pass the Jets to the 1968 pro football championship largely because his body guards kept opposing defensemen away on all but 15 plays during the entire season. By contrast, the Atlanta Falcons, winners of only two games last season, saw their quarterbacks thrown for losses 70 times —and forced to rush many more passes that were subsequently intercepted — in order to escape hard-charging defensemen. In one game alone this season, Bob Berry, the Falcons' quarterback, was tackled 10 times. If Namath played behind the same body guards, some coaches contend, he probably would have been injured or, at best, be just another quarterback.

Even Namath is quick to recognize his body guards' value. After the Jets-Giants exhibition game, he shook his head in astonishment as he recalled how Fran Tarkenton, the Giants' quarterback, ran across the field eluding defensemen who had overpowered his body guards. While Tarkenton is conspicuously faster than the stiff-legged, heavily taped Namath, he was scrambling more out of necessity than avocation. "If I had a line like that in front of me, I'd be scrambling, too," Namath said, "or else get killed. If Tarkenton had a line like mine, he wouldn't have to scramble."

It isn't easy to develop offensive lines like the one guarding Namath or any other successful quarterback. Unlike defensemen, body guards must theoretically block opposing players on passing plays by keeping both fists near their chests, and not even appearing to hold, hook or strike them (but they can slap away punches). Merely dropping one arm around a defenseman can bring a 15-yard penalty for "holding."

Moreover, if a body guard throws himself against a defenseman away from the line of scrimmage while the defenseman's back is turned, the offensive team is similarly penalized. On the other hand, if a defenseman hits a ball-carrier from behind so forcibly that the player breaks an arm, that is considered hard-nosed football. And since defensive linemen can charge, push, strike, pull or grab

There's a reason some players are called "body guards"—they are essential to the survival of the quarterback. Mashed and battered, they don't often volunteer for their job, which requires them to stem a murderous tide to let the quarterback do his thing. But, as one practitioner of the art said, "When you pop your man right, you get a helluva warm feeling."

offensive linemen, body guards must discipline themselves not to retaliate against defensemen who hit them so violently that, at times, they break their face mask, nose or teeth. In trying to become body guards, countless players have been unable to accept a defenseman's abuse without fighting, grabbing or angrily attempting to push him back, only to be slung aside and, in turn, see the defenseman sprint toward the quarterback.

"You can start out with a busload of defensemen who can dish out the tough stuff and go after people," says Sandusky. "But you'll only need a cab to haul back the guys who can sit back on an offensive line and take it without teeing off."

Even many first-rate body guards who have repeatedly proven they can take it must continue to practice controlling their temper as carefully as a quarterback practices throwing the ball. Winston Hill, the Jets' 285-pound offensive tackle, neglected to prepare himself mentally for an abusive opponent just once in the last five years, and ended up being ejected from the game for fighting.

"You start out knowing that they all—even the faking and finesse guys—will hit you in the face," Hill says. "But then you also play against what we'll just call 'overly aggressive types' who crank up on passing plays and let you have it a lot harder from your head to your toes—then taunt you to death while you're hurting. They want you to hit 'em or push 'em back and you're fighting yourself not to. When I know my next game is against an overly aggressive type, I psyche myself up all week that I'm gonna be punished, kicked and cussed, but I don't care. I let people hit me in practice. No matter how hectic things get at home or any-

where, nothing makes me mad. I don't even pay any attention to things that ordinarily cause me to blow my stack. So when this overly aggressive type guy gives me everything he can think of, man I'm passive."

At the same time, body guards must be generally smarter than their opponents. While hulking defensemen need only to react by pursuing the player with the ball, body guards must know their teams' 100 or more plays and be considerably more agile and coordinated than other players. "Pass blocking is no place for the big fat guy who just dares people to run over him," emphasizes Weeb Ewbank, who developed solid pockets for quarterbacks as coach of the Colts and Jets. "You need fast, smart, coordinated men who can react as a unit and each switch to a different man if, say, the defense stunts" by having each man charge a different body guard than the one they're facing and try to get two offensive linemen blocking one defense man and the other tackling the quarterback.

That coordination was apparent when Johnny Unitas recently walked up behind Curry, his center, and stared at the Rams' defensemen who tackle opposing quarterbacks an average of 13.9 per cent of the times they attempt to pass. When Unitas barked "Set!" the Colts' body guards set one hand on the ground and adjusted their feet so that their weight was evenly distributed and their stance the same one they would use if they had to open a space between a guard and tackle for the fullback to run, pull back to run interference for a halfback, or raise up and form a pocket around Unitas.

Since the Rams were playing what is called a four-three defense, the four men in the front row knelt opposite Bob Vogel, Glenn Ressler, Dan Sullivan and Sam Ball, the Colts' body guards. Sometimes the Rams place a fifth lineman directly in front of Curry, but on this play only the linebacker was in front of him. As Unitas counted in cadence, the motionless body guards guessed that the Rams were unlikely to use the same technique as in the previous play. Deacon Jones, who had just rammed into Ball's chest, might fake left, pound his hammerlike fists into Ball's helmet, then sidestep him. Diron Talbert, another defensive end, could spring forward, then swerve around the body guard.

Regardless of how the Rams moved, the body guards were prepared. As Unitas suddenly straightened up and backpedaled with the ball, the two lines collided so hard that they caused a thumping sound like a speeding automobile striking a cow. The body guards held their feet so firmly that three Rams bounced nearly a foot, then recoiled. As the Rams hit again, the body guards moved in a boxerlike shuffle as they yielded only inches of ground. A defenseman who hit Vogel seemed momentarily stunned (but Vogel also injured his ankle). Simultaneously, Curry, as he later recalled, saw a linebacker "going hell bent for election" toward Unitas. Backtracking, Curry seemingly lunged toward the linebacker's shoulders but surprised him by landing just above the knees, spilling him awkwardly on the ground. Only 3.8 seconds had elapsed, but, by the time the first Ram was past a bodyguard, Unitas had thrown a short pass.

Apart from their ability to work together, body guards must also be so individually motivated that they work hour after hour each week to be sure that the man opposing them the following Sunday will not, at any price, "beat them." One technique that keeps outstanding body guards from getting beaten is the ability to surprise defensemen with different types of blocks. If a body guard opposes a particularly elusive guard, he may just shuffle to remain in front of him for one play, then bump him under the chin on the next. If a body guard is blocking a slower or stronger 285-pound tackle, he may attempt only to slap his hands on second down but fall against his ankles on third down, and

knock him to the ground. As a result, well-known defensemen seldom get past healthy, all-league offensive linemen such as Vogel, Ralph Neely of Dallas, Bob Brown of Los Angeles, Gene Hickerson of Cleveland, Mick Tingelhoff of Minnesota, Ron Mix and Walt Sweeney of San Diego, Jim Tryer of Kansas City, Gene Upshaw and Jim Otto of Oakland and Dave Herman and Winston Hill of the Jets.

CONSIDER, for example, Herman. A high-strung, 255-pound guard, he received an exceptionally high grade of 94 per cent on his blocking assignments from Jet coaches last season, even though he was moved to an unfamiliar tackle position both in the A.F.L. championship and Super Bowl games in order to block two tough defensemen whom other players couldn't stop. Yet, he is neither fast nor athletically inclined. While many of the Jets are outstanding basketball or softball players, Herman knows that he is too awkward to compete against them. "I can't even shoot pool," he maintains.

An asset that Herman does possess, however, is a determination that he isn't going to oppose a defenseman unless he knows more about his playing habits than his own. He starts each Tuesday by studying the Jets scouting report, which is compiled by watching players and questioning their former teammates or coaches. The report catalogues his opponent's known weaknesses and strengths, his favorite method of hitting blockers and any probable injuries or sore places that might be considered "key points" for him to block. Then, hour after hour, Herman watches movies of his opponent's two most recent games and compares his play with the last time he opposed him. Even after the game starts, Herman subtly studies the position of his opponent's chin, fingers, palms, shoulder and feet as he adjusts his stance.

"I can tell exactly what at least three men plan to do by the way they get down in their stance," Herman says confidently. "These are just tiny things, but they tell me if my man plans to bull right over me, fake and loop around me, or go inside. Even their own coaches haven't noticed these habits or, of course, they'd correct them."

When Herman cannot anticipate what the defensive guard he opposes will do, he seems almost infuriated as he mentally says, "You ———, there are only three ways for you to get through me—on the inside, outside or over the top of me—and you're not going any way." Once the defenseman charges, Herman has several techniques, but he prefers to ram his helmet into the guard's stomach, reasoning that he is getting his "hardest shot" in the center of his body. It has turned out to be sound reasoning. Herman has repeatedly been able to block his man for four or more seconds, and, as coaches say, also "get a piece of somebody else blitzing through the line."

FEW plays have been more important to the Jets than the time they faced a third down, with 18 yards to go for a first down. Sensing a pass, the defensive team used a "safety blitz," in which a shallow safetyman charged through a gap in the line instead of remaining in his normal position to stop a runner or short pass. Although the defense risked having a fullback run through the middle of the line, it guessed correctly. The Jets were passing, all five body guards were blocking linemen, and the safetyman was sprinting toward Namath as he watched for a receiver to get into the open. The safetyman, however, was too close to Herman. Though still butting a guard with his helmet, Herman shifted so adeptly that he also hooked the safetyman's throat before the umpire could see him.

"I clotheslined* the blitzer right in the throat," Herman said quietly. "If I'd been caught and the team penalized 15 yards, it would have been a bad play on my part. But since I didn't get caught, it has to be a successful play. Instead of being clobbered, Namath was able to throw for a touchdown. There was a lot of cussing, but this is the name of the game."

Herman, though, goes beyond cursing to maintain his reputation as a body guard who scrupulously avenges any

---

*Clotheslined is the players' term for ramming a fist or elbow into someone's nose, mouth or throat and attaining approximately the same results as if a player's throat struck a taut clothesline while running at full speed.

play that he considers unethical. Calling himself an "ornery type," he frequently draws back his fists when he feels that he has been unnecessarily roughed up, only to see John Schmitt, the Jets' calm center, tell the officials and players that he's "just a little sore and doesn't mean anything by all this." Though Herman has ostensibly regained his composure, he is merely awaiting an opportunity for revenge.

In a game against the Kansas City Chiefs he once drove his elbow so quickly into a defensive man (whom he knew from playing on the same college team) that the defenseman swung back at him, but was ejected from the game because an official thought he had started the fight. "You have to let people know that if they rough you up too much they're going to get it twice as bad," Herman says. "You got to go ahead and play a good game. But sooner or later our line has to open a hole for our backs to carry the ball and, when we do, the guy who got me is in that pile and out of sight. I got two fists and two feet. I get my licks in."

The surreptitious use of hands isn't limited to the times that linemen are piled up after a play. Several body guards are also skilled at holding defensemen they block without being caught. The risk of penalties at crucial times generally makes such practices so unsound that coaches tend to tolerate "holders" only until they find adequate replacements. Coaches have a higher tolerance of holders, though, if they conceal their hands from the umpires.

Such body guards have found that holding is their biggest asset. For example, charging into Jim Otto, the Raiders' 255-pound All-A.F.L. center, is like hitting a telephone pole and then being entangled once you are able to start slipping past it. According to several defensemen, Otto holds their pads, jersey, belt, neck or skin without being penalized more than a few times each year. "He not only is just about the worst holder I've ever seen," maintains one Jet, "but he has you wondering if he isn't kin to all the officials, even though you know better." Like any such body guard, Otto seems indignant when asked about holding in order to avoid drawing closer attention from the umpire. "Holding!" he fumes. "The only person I hold is my wife."

THERE is no argument about the price that Otto, as well as many body guards, have to pay. To start with Otto looks like somebody who was in the front seat of a bad automobile wreck and was then treated by an old country doctor. His lips have been cut so frequently that he has a crooked smile, and his nose broken so often ("nine or ten times") that the bridge appears to be mashed. When his fingers have been dislocated during a game they haven't been manipulated back into place until his offensive team has left the field. And broken bones in his fingers haven't usually been set in plaster casts until after the game, leaving him with fingers that protrude in grotesque positions.

Otto's invisible scars may be more dangerous. He must wear (1) a rubber cushion around his neck to minimize having nerves pinched again, and (2) a specially lined helmet to reduce his chances of further concussions that have left him looking so stunned that some frightened rookies were cautioned not to look at him.

The variety of injuries isn't uncommon for a body guard who has played pro football as long as Otto. While offensive linemen suffer fewer broken ankles or torn ligaments than running backs, they probably lead all positions in the number of broken fingers, noses and teeth, cuts, sprains, or severe bruises. Yet most body guards seldom feel good after a game if they escape injuries. Ron Mix, San Diego's offensive tackle, has said that his head doesn't stop aching until four days after playing a particularly hard-hitting team. Bill Curry's condition is more noticeable. "You get so you don't like to look at yourself after some games," he said. "Your body's full of cleat marks."

ALL of the bodyguards' injuries are negligible in comparison with what it costs a team if defensemen cannot be blocked until a quarterback has thrown and regained his balance sufficiently to dodge would-be tacklers. Many defensemen have perfected the art of hitting a quarterback precisely after he passes or, if he has clearly thrown the ball, running past him ostensibly to avoid colliding with him. In the process, defensemen hook the quarterback's passing arm or inflict some other form of torture. "If some defensemen aren't kept out for that extra split second," quarterback Earl Morrall said while feigning a punch to the neck, "then they'll give your arm a good hook or clothesline you and leave you spitting blood."

Still, it is even more costly if defensemen overpower body guards so methodically that the guards can, as many do, only shout; "Look out!" Apart from causing quarterbacks to lose yardage or throw wildly, many emotional defensemen tackle them while a teammate tackles the ball and, if necessary, resorts to pinching, gouging, mashing, biting, kneeing in the groin or back, or bending an arm, leg or finger in order to accomplish what is called "forcing a fumble." Even if defensemen can't get the ball, they are expected to wear down the quarterback either by wallowing on him or by putting all of their weight on a sensitive part of his body as they raise themselves up after a tackle.

As sadistic as it may seem, many defensemen feel that they can expect an increase in salary if they charge so brutally into a quarterback that he is knocked unconscious or incoherent, or, as they say, "hears footsteps the next time he passes." There are some defensemen players say, who actually want to break a quarterback's arm, collarbone, leg or fingers and, particularly, to damage Joe Namath's scarred knees.

"Rack him up! There are characters in his game who want to build a reputation of knocking out Joe for good." says Dave Herman, shaking his head for emphasis. "Some decent guys get past a lineman and just throw their chest against quarterbacks and maybe knock the wind out of 'em or bruise 'em a little. But these characters I'm talking about are in the second and third year in the league—and some a little older—who want to tear up his legs—twist the legs that have been operated on.

"I know exactly who these guys are. In fact, there's practically one whole team that'll tear him up. So if these guys ever get past me and zero in on Joe I may look like a rookie by getting our team penalized 15 yards down by the goal line. But I'm going to get them one way or another before they get to him—legal or illegal. Even if you cost the team a 15-yard penalty it's worth it to keep your quarterback from going off on a stretcher. It's worth 1,000 yards."

NONE of the players in question have harmed Namath so far this season. But any doubts that such brutality isn't intentional or highly motivated have been dispelled almost every time he is knocked down.

In the Jets' opening game, Bob Tatarek, a tackle for Buffalo, caused Winston Hill to stumble into Namath, in turn causing the quarterback to bend his right heel against his back. As Namath jerked off his helmet and grimaced, Tatarek applauded himself. In the second game against Denver, end Dave Costa rammed his head under Namath's ribs, then tapped his own chest while Namath seemed to be unconscious.

Yet for sheer brazenness, nothing surpasses what occured last December when rumors circulated that the Oakland Raiders would "get" Namath in the A.F.L. championship game. Among the first things that some Raiders did was to mash Namath's left hand and dislocate a finger. Then, as he winced in pain, Namath recalled, Ike Lassiter, a 270-pound defensive end, laughed, "Hey, look at that finger, wouldya?"

Several Raiders were even more jubilant in the second quarter when Lassiter and 280-pound Ben Davidson, the other defensive end, charged into Namath. He couldn't expect anything less than what the Raiders call their "best shot." A year earlier Davidson had charged so strongly into Namath's head that he knocked off his helmet, fractured his cheekbone and caused the referee to penalize the Raiders 15 yards for unnecessary roughness. This time, as Davidson and Lassiter slowly raised themselves up, Namath was obviously stunned and unable to stand, where upon Lassiter, pointing to Namath and looking at his bench, was overheard to exclaim in tones usually reserved for winning a championship, "We got 'im! We got 'im'! He's hurt!"

Even though Namath was tackled four times in the first two games, the Jet's blocking does not appear weaker this season. One member of the team, when asked about the incidents, countered that there is "such a thing as a quarterback drifting too much" and thereby leaving his pocket. Coach Weeb Ewbank was more specific. "Why were they getting to Joe in the first two games?" he mused. "Well, one guy [tackle Sam Walton] was hurt and the back-up man [Dave Foley] at that position tore up his knee, and we had to go with the hurt man. But he's OK. and our blocking is straightened out. This same fellow that let 'em through in the first two games had a great adjustment in the third. We called an all-out pass against San Diego. It was pass or nothing else, and they sent a blitzer after Joe. But Sam bumped his man, then bounced over and bumped the guy blitzing just enough to enable Joe to throw. That's blocking."

Few of the men blocking for the Jets or any other team envisioned that they would become body guards although, as standouts, they take fierce pride in their work. Dave Herman wanted to tackle quarterbacks instead of protecting them. But, as about the 300th player chosen in the college draft, he was told that the Jets' only "open slot" was in the offensive line.

Winston Hill thought he had the height and hands to be a tight end until Alexander Durley, his coach at Texas Southern University, told him, "Even if you catch the ball, we'd have to call time out for you to cross that goal line." Played as both an offensive and defensive tackle at Texas Southern, Hill found the experience useful in seeking a job in pro football for which there are not many volunteers.

A body guard's salary is lower than that paid an outstanding quarterback, running back or pass receiver who helps a team sell season tickets. But there are other compensations. "It's never fun," says Bob Vogel of the Colts, "but when you get your man right, you get a helluva warm feeling." ■

October 26, 1969

Oakland Raider defensive end Ben Davidson had a reputation for being very tough on the opposition. Joe Namath found this out when a bone-crunching Davidson tackle put him out of action. Shown here (at left) is Buffalo quarterback James Harris running for his life as the 6'7'', 265-pound Davidson (number 83) is about to make contact.

Detroit Lion quarterback Greg Landry would like to throw a pass. Alan Page (88), Minnesota Vikings tackle, has other ideas.

Pass-Catching Record Set By Alworth; Chargers Win

SAN DIEGO, Dec. 14 (AP)—Lance Alworth set a pass-catching record today as the San Diego Chargers rolled to a 45-6 victory over the Buffalo Bills in the American Football League.

Alworth caught a 9-yard pass from John Hadl in San Diego's second offensive series to break Don Hutson's record of receptions in 96 consecutive games. Hutson, of Green Bay, set the mark 27 years ago.

Alworth finished with seven catches for 122 yards, gaining more than 1,000 for the seventh straight season. A 27-yarder in the second quarter was his 453d, moving him into ninth place in the all-time reception list.

The Chargers poured it on with Dick Post, the league's rushing leader, scoring on runs of 34 and 3 yards. He gained 106 yards in 19 carries.

It was the fifth game in which the 5-foot-9-inch, 190-pounder had rushed for more than 100 yards.

The rookie quarterback, Marty Domres of Columbia, replaced Hadl and scored the

STATISTICS OF THE GAME		
	Charg.	Bills
First downs	30	15
Rushing yardage	242	58
Passing yardage	305	180
Return yardage	74	46
Passes	19-32	18-35
Interceptions by	2	0
Punts	2-54	8-45
Fumbles lost	1	0
Yards penalized	21	55

Chargers' sixth touchdown on a 9-yard run before Buffalo got on the scoreboard in the waning moments.

The Chargers ended the season with eight victories and six defeats. The Bills were 4-10.

O. J. Simpson, Buffalo's rookie back, managed only 27 yards in seven carries. He lost 8 yards on three pass receptions.

San Diego Chargers ..10 14 7 14—45
Buffalo Bills ....0 0 0 6—6
S.D.—Garrison, 41, pass from Hadl (Partee, kick).
S.D.—FG, Partee, 33.
S.D.—Ever, 30, pass from Hadl (Partee, kick).
S.D.—Alworth, 1, pass from Hadl (Partee, kick).
S.D.—Post, 34, run (Partee, kick).
S.D.—Post, 3, run (Partee, kick).
S.D.—Domres, run (Partee, kick).
Buf.—Grate, 19, pass from Sherman (kick failed).
Attendance—47,582.

December 15, 1969

KANSAS CITY BEATS MINNESOTA BY 23-7 IN THE SUPER BOWL

Dawson of Chiefs Shatters Vikings' Defense, Passes for 46-Yard Touchdown

By WILLIAM N. WALLACE
Special to The New York Times

NEW ORLEANS, Jan. 11—Kansas City was all Chiefs and no Indians on the field today as the American League champions upset the Minnesota Vikings, 23-7, in the Super Bowl game before 80,998 fans at Tulane Stadium.

The mightiest Chief of all was Len Dawson, the quarterback who attacked and cracked the Vikings' defense that had yielded only 10 points a game in winning the National Football League title.

Dawson, 34 years old and a failure with two NFL teams early in his career, triumphantly ended a season in which he had missed six games because of a knee injury and had been tenuously linked five days ago with a gambling investigation in Detroit. Completing 12 of 17 pass attempts, Dawson exploited the perimeters of the Minnesota zone defense and pitched one 46-yard touchdown pass to Otis Taylor.

That was the big play of a game that was never close but full of expectation that the Vikings might finally bestir themselves. They did, just once.

Vikings Sport Brief

Behind, 16-0, and thoroughly outplayed in the first half, the Vikings drove 69 yards for a touchdown, scored by Dave Osborn early in the second half, showing their offensive talents for the first time. But hope was short-lived.

With a first down on the Minnesota 46 in the following series, Dawson started his play on a short count without the usual shift out of the I formation. He quickly threw a pass to Otis Taylor, who was covered alone at the sideline by Earsell Mackbee, the Viking cornerback.

Playing Taylor closely and without help from the inside, Macbee attempted a tackle as the receiver caught the ball. It was not good enough. Taylor broke free and ran 40 yards for a score.

Mackbee said, with reference to Taylor's pass pattern: "He had used a hitch [a pause] and go earlier. This was just a hitch. I had gone up tight on him a lot. Earlier I had a pinched nerve in my shoulder and as I hit him my shoulder went numb and I lost him."

The play had come with 82 seconds remaining in the third quarter and it was apparent that the Vikings, down by 16 points, would not have time to catch up against a defense as strong as the Chiefs, even if everything went right.

Nothing went right in the final quarter for the Vikings. Joe Kapp, the heralded Minnesota quarterback, threw two poor passes that were intercepted and his successor, Gary Cuozzo, threw one.

Kapp, an admitted tough guy believed to be indestructible, was knocked out of the game when tackled hard by Aaron Brown, the Kansas City defensive end. The Chiefs liked that added touch.

"We socked it to them," said Mike Garrett, the little Kansas City halfback. "We felt if we could outhit them we could beat them," added Jerry Mays, the giant defensive end.

In the first half the Chiefs came close enough to the Minnesota goal so that Jan Stenerud, their Norwegian-born soccer-style kicker, could kick field goals of 48, 32 and 25 yards.

After the third field goal, Charlie West of the Vikings fumbled the kickoff and Kansas City recovered at the Minnesota 19-yard line.

Grant Praises Chiefs

Dawson ran Wendell Hayes on a draw play past the over-eager Alan Page, the charging Minnesota tackle, and then threw a pass to Taylor, who beat Mackbee at the 5. On third down Garrett scored behind a block by Mo Moorman that split Page and Paul Dickson at the goal-line defense. It was only the fifth touchdown the Minnesota defense had given up on the ground in 17 games.

The touchdown was doubly significant because the Vikings were not moving the ball. They had crossed midfield only twice and never past the Kansas City 38. About that fumble, Coach Bud Grant of the Vikings later said: "They got a break and scored. We played a great team and they beat us. Why? They made the big plays and didn't make any errors."

The victory for the Chiefs proved that there is some value in being second in pro football as in automobile rentals. Kansas City, which had an 11-3 regular-season won-lost record compared with Minnesota's 12-2, finished 1½ games behind the Oakland Raiders in the Western Division of the A.F.L.

(Oakland fans paraded here near the end of a game with a banner reading, "Raiders Still No. 1).

	Chiefs	Vikings
First downs	18	13
Rushing yardage	151	67
Passing yardage	122	172
Return yardage	79	97
Passes	12-17	17-28
Interceptions by	3	1
Punts	4-49	3-37
Fumbles lost	0	2
Yards penalized	47	67

Then the Chiefs began the uphill climb defeating the Jets, the Eastern winners, in New York and the Raiders in Oakland for the league title. For the first and last time, the second-place team in each division qualified for the A.F.L. playoffs. Kansas City thus won three pressure games in a row and no wonder Hank Stram, the coach said, "I'm really proud of our team."

The Chiefs were well rewarded. Each will receive $15,000 for today's victory to go with the $7,000 apiece they gained in the A.F.L. championship. The Vikings settle for $14,800, $7,500 from today's contest and about $7,300 for the N.F.L. title game.

It would be hard to single out individual Chiefs, but Dave Hill, an offensive tackle, plus the two cornerbacks, Emmitt Thomas and Jim Marsalis, deserve citations. Hill played Carl Eller, the feared defensive end, to a standstill, which means a victory for the offense. "He's good but not that good," said Hill.

Hill, Moorman and the others on the offensive line—Ed Budde, E. J. Holub and Jim Tyrer—were stubborn in protecting Dawson. Eller and the other Viking end, Jim Marshall, were often double-teamed. The Viking pass defenders had always been suspect but N.F.L. quarterbacks had a hard time working against Mackbee and Sharockman because they were always so harassed by the Minnesota pass rush that could not reach Dawson today.

Marsalis and Thomas covered the Viking wide receivers all the way and held Gene Washington, the best one, to one catch. Thomas, Johnny Robinson, who played despite sore ribs, and Willie Lanier, the middle linebacker, made the interceptions.

The game brought to an end the rivalry between the National and American Leagues because next season all 26 pro teams will be under one umbrella, the newly constituted N.F.L.

The Super Bowl score ended at two victories for each league but the A.F.L. won the last two in a row. Not only did the American Leaguers end up even with the National, they got in the last punch.

Kansas City Chiefs 3 13 7 0—23
Minnesota Vikings 0 0 0 7— 7
K.C.—FG, Stenerud, 48.
K.C.—FG, Stenerud, 32.
K.C.—FG, Stenerud, 25.
K.C.—Garrett, 5, run (Stenerud, kick).
Minn.—Osborn, 4, run (Cox, kick).
K.C.—Taylor, 46, pass from Dawson. Stenerud, run, kick).
Attendance—80,998.

January 12, 1970

Unitas Voted Top Star Of 60's in Pro Football

Johnny Unitas of the Baltimore Colts was named pro football athlete of the decade yesterday in a special poll taken by The Associated Press.

The Colts' quarterback, the leading passer in pro football history, easily outpolled three other stars of the nineteen-sixties — Bart Starr, Jimmy Brown, and Joe Namath.

Unitas received 223 votes from the sports writers and broadcasters participating in the poll. Starr, Green Bay quarterback, was second with 124½. Brown, who played for Cleveland and is retired, received 105 votes and Namath, of the New York Jets, 71.

Unitas, whose career spans 14 years, was picked off the sandlots by Baltimore after the club received a fan letter heralding his ability.

February 4, 1970

Pro Football Club Owners and Players Agree to 4-Year Pact, Ending Strike

ROZELLE ASSUMES ROLE OF MEDIATOR

$19.1-Million Is Allotted for Pensions, Other Benefits After 22 Hours of Talks

By DAVE ANDERSON

After 22 consecutive hours of negotiations mediated by Commissioner Pete Rozelle, the National Football League Club owners and players settled their labor dispute yesterday in an unhappy but relieved atmosphere.

Throughout the nation, nearly 1,300 experienced players, who had been on strike as members of the Players Association began reporting to the 26 training camps. Ten exhibition games scheduled for this weekend will be played.

Under the four-year contract, which assures labor peace in pro football until 1974, the owners and players agreed to a $19.1-million package, an $11-million increase based on 1969 levels. But neither side was completely satisfied.

"There wasn't any winner," said John Mackey, the Baltimore Colts' tight end who is president of the players' group. "We have an agreement, that's the important thing."

Only 21 Players Reported

Mackey, who had emerged as one of the nation's most famous labor leaders in recent weeks, praised the Players Association members for their support in the impasse. Only 21 players (only three of stature) crossed the invisible picket lines at the training camps.

The players' firmness created the showdown with the owners because of the imminence of the exhibition games.

When the settlement was attained, the owners quickly dispersed. One of them, requesting anonymity, said:

"I'm not happy with the settlement, but it's done and I didn't think it was possible. I'm just exhausted."

The owners had convened at about 12:30 P.M. on Sunday at N.F.L. headquarters at 410 Park Avenue and except for a dinner break by some, they remained there until 10:30 A.M. yesterday when the truce was announced. Mackey and his associates had arrived at about 1:30 and remained until the settlement.

Rozelle's role as mediator was particularly significant since the players, in their initial demands, had attempted to restrict the commissioner's authority. But, except for the inclusion of an arbiter in injury-grievance cases, the commissioner's power was unaffected by the settlement.

The players withdrew their demand that Rozelle be labeled a "joint employer" with the owners, and that an umpire be required in non-injury-grievance cases, such as last year's controversy involving Joe Namath, the New York Jets' quarterback, and alleged "undesirable" customers in his East Side bistro.

"The power of the commissioner is undiminished," commented George Halas Sr., owner of the Chicago Bears and the president of the National Conference. "The fight for principle was upheld."

The players' group also credited J. Curtis Counts, director of the Federal Mediation and Conciliation Service, for helping to guide the settlement that resulted in the owners providing an annual contribution of $4,535,000 to the pension plan, plus another $250,000 annually for other benefits.

For the first time, the players obtained disability payments, widow's benefits, maternity and dental benefits.

The pension-benefits sum increased from $2.8-million this year, but, in providing one source of the money, the players agreed to joint licensing with the owners in regard to trading-card and picture-premium rights.

The players obtained guaranteed sums for competitors in the conference championship games — $8,000 for the winners, $6,000 for losers—as compared with a share of the gate that depended on the stadium's size, as in the past.

The shares for the members of the conference all-star teams in the postseason Pro Bowl game were increased by $500-$2,000 to winners, $1,500 to losers. In addition, a 40-man roster will be named, with six coaches.

Per-diem meal allowance on road trips was increased to $16 from $12 in the N.F.L. and $11 in the American Football League.

Agreement had been established previously on preseason game pay and training camp per diem. The game payment for a five-year player is now $280, with the per-diem payment at $12.

Despite the apparently lucrative settlement for the players, their demands will increase in 1974, judging by the reaction of Ken Bowman, one of the association's vice presidents.

"I still don't think either side is happy," said Bowman, the center for the Green Bay Packers. "I'd estimate that we came down about 60 per cent from our original requests and they were up about 40 per cent. We got the best contract we could, but it's still not representative of what it should be."

August 4, 1970

Pro Football: 63-Yard Field Goal

By MURRAY CHASS

Although Tom Dempsey was born with half a right foot and a stub for a right hand, he doesn't consider himself handicapped. "I've always been able to do anything anybody else did," he says.

In New Orleans' game against the Detroit Lions yesterday, Dempsey did something better than anyone in pro football ever had done.

Using that half foot, he kicked a 63-yard field goal, which is 7 yards farther than the previous longest field goal in pro history, Bert Rechichar's 56-yarder for Baltimore in 1953.

And since it would have been a shame to waste such a prodigious feat on just any old 3 points, the 6-foot-1-inch, 264-pound Dempsey kicked it on the last play of the game and gave the Saints a 19-17 upset victory.

Special Shoe Helps

"I knew I could kick the ball that far, but whether or not I could kick it straight that far kept running through my mind," said Dempsey, who wears a special kicking shoe approved by the league.

The 23-year-old Saint, who booted the ball from the New Orleans 37-yard line—that's 3 yards farther back from the kickoff spot—said he couldn't see the ball clear the crossbar, which it did by inches.

"I saw the referee's hands go up and heard everybody start yelling and I knew it was good," he said. "It's quite a thrill. I'm still shook up."

Just 11 seconds before Dempsey's fourth field goal of the game, Errol Mann kicked an 18-yarder that gave the Lions a 17-16 lead. After the ensuing kickoff, Bill Kilmer completed a pass to Al Dodd, who went out of bounds at the Saints' 45 with two seconds left.

Dempsey, who succeeded on four of five field goal attempts yesterday, was five for 15 going into the game.

AT NEW ORLEANS

Detroit Lions .... 0 7 7 3—17
New Orleans Saints .3 3 3 10—19
N.O.—FG, Dempsey, 29.
Det.—Farr, 10, run (Mann, kick).
N.O.—FG, Dempsey, 27.
Det.—Sanders, 2, pass from Munson (Mann, kick).
N.O.—FG, Dempsey, 8.
N.O.—Barrington, 3, run (Dempsey, kick).
Det.—FG, Mann, 18.
N.O.—FG, Dempsey, 63.
Attendance—66,910.

	Saints	Lions
First downs	15	18
Rushing yardage	131	135
Passing yardage	141	143
Return yardage	42	51
Passes	15-28	13-25
Interceptions by	2	0
Punts	6-44	3-31
Fumbles lost	0	3
Yards penalized	124	31

November 9, 1970

Baltimore Field Goal in Last 5 Seconds Defeats Dallas in Super Bowl, 16 to 13

By WILLIAM N. WALLACE
Special to The New York Times

MIAMI, Jan. 17—The Baltimore Colts beat the Dallas Cowboys, 16-13, and won the Super Bowl game today. The National Football League headquarters will soon be sending the winners their $15,000 checks. But it will be difficult to convince the Cowboys and many of the viewers that anybody won this game, the climactic contest of the pro football season.

The contest was full of errors made by both offensive teams and one Baltimore touchdown play, a 75-yard pass-run, John Unitas to John Mackey, was controversial if not illegal.

The winning points were scored with only five seconds to play when Jim O'Brien, a Baltimore rookie, kicked a 32-yard field goal, breaking a 13-13 tie and eliminating the possibility of a sudden-death overtime period.

It might have been a good idea to start all over again with everyone even.

The Cowboys led, 13-6, at half-time, but the Colts scored a touchdown and a field goal in the fourth quarter. Interceptions set up both scoring opportunities. Those were two of the 11 turnovers, resulting from an intercepted pass or a lost fumble, in the game, seen by 80,055 in the Orange Bowl and an estimated 64 million on television.

The Colts lost four fumbles to the Cowboys and had three passes intercepted. Two of these were thrown by Unitas and one by Earl Morrall. Unitas was hurt (bruised ribs) in the second period and Morrall took over.

There is an adage that a team cannot win when it turns the ball over to its opponent half a dozen times or more. But this game defied a lot of adages. Three Cowboy passes,

Jim O'Brien kicking the 32-yard field goal that won the Super Bowl for Baltimore Colts. Earl Morrall holds ball.

United Press International

all by Craig Morton, were also intercepted, and Dallas lost a fumble on the Baltimore 1-yard line. The ball was knocked loose from Duane Thomas's grip in a pile-up.

"We beat ourselves," said Tom Landry, the Dallas coach.

all by Craig Morton, were also intercepted, and Dallas lost a fumble on the Baltimore 1-yard line. The ball was knocked loose from Duane Thomas's grip in a pile-up.

The fumble and two interceptions, killed us."

Did Cowboys Touch Pass?

So did some kind of fate. The Dallas defense was outstanding, and the Colts, with Unitas, made no early progress. Then Unitas threw a pass 20 yards deep and high to Eddie Hinton, who got his finger tips on the ball but could not hold it or stop it. The ball passed over or through a Dallas player's finger tips and into the hands of Mackey, who ran 45 yards for a score that tied the game at 6-6 in the second quarter.

A pass is incomplete if two offensive players touch the ball successively without a defensive player intervening. The ruling on this play was that a Dallas defender had touched the football. Which defender?

"Not me," said Charlie Waters, the safetyman. "I was 10 yards away," said Cornell Green, the other safety. "I don't know," said Mel Renfro, the cornerback. "I didn't think I did," he added, and then to another questioner, he said, "maybe my finger nail."

The replay shown on television was inconclusive because of a poor camera angle. The official's instant decision was that the ball had been touched by a Cowboy and the call will stand.

Another pass grazed the finger tips of Walt Garrison, the Cowboy fullback, when Dallas was ahead, 13-6, in the fourth quarter and comfortably in control.

Rick Volk, the Colt's safety, made the interception on the Dallas 33 and ran to the 3. Tom Nowatzke scored on second down and the game was tied, 13-13, with half the period still to play.

With a minute left more fingers came into play. Morton's pass to Dan Reeves, the halfback, bounced off his hands when he was hit by Jerry Logan. The football careened into the hands of Mike Curtis, the Baltimore linebacker, and he returned this interception 13 yards to the Dallas 28.

The Colts ran two plays and then O'Brien, a nervous 23-year-old, came in and kicked his field goal. It represented the $7,500 difference between a winning and losing share for himself and his 39 teammates.

Interception by Howley

The Colts failed on three prior scoring chances. Hinton fumbled after catching a pass from Sam Havrilak, a halfback, in the final period. The ball rolled from the Dallas 5 through the end zone and out of bounds. Because the Colts were the last team to have possession, the play resulted in a touchback and Dallas took over at its 20.

Chuck Howley intercepted a pass by Morrall in the Cowboy end zone at the start of the fourth quarter and the Colts failed to score in four downs at the Dallas 2 just before the half-time intermission.

Dallas missed its touchdown chances early in the game. Recovery of a Baltimore fumble—Ron Gardin dropped a punt—put the Cowboys on the Colt 9, but Morton overthrew Reggie Rucker in the end zone. Dallas settled for a field goal by Mike Clark.

Morton missed on two more passes a little later from the

STATISTICS OF THE GAME

	Colts	Cowboys
First downs	14	9
Rushing yardage	69	104
Passing yardage	260	113
Return yardage	159	65
Passes	11-25	12-26
Interceptions by	3	3
Punts	4-42	9-39
Fumbles lost	4	1
Yards penalized	44	120

Baltimore 7 and, following a penalty, Clark kicked a 30-yard field goal for a 6-0 lead.

The Colts tied the game when Mackey scored on the controversial play and O'Brien's attempted conversion kick was blocked by Mark Washington.

A fumble by Unitas at his 28 set up the Cowboy touchdown, scored on a 7-yard pass by Morton to Thomas in the second period.

The Colt defense tightened in the second half and the Cowboys' big runner, Thomas, gained only 37 yards in all.

Curtis was the outstanding defender.

Morton again left much to be desired as a passer. So did Unitas, who completed only three of nine passes and made only two first downs. Morrall was the best quarterback, although he had little to do

INDIVIDUAL STATISTICS

RUSHES—Balt.: Nowatzke, 10 for 33 yards; Bulaich, 18 for 28; Unitas, 1 for 4; Havrilak, 1 for 3; Morrall, 1 for 1. Dal.: Garrison, 12 for 65; Thomas, 18 for 37; Morton, 1 for 2.

PASSES — Balt.: Morrall, 7 of 15 for 147 yards; Unitas, 3 of 9 for 88; Havrilak, 1 of 1 for 25. Dal.: Morton, 12 of 26 for 127.

RECEPTIONS — Balt.: Jefferson, 3 for 52 yards; Mackey, 2 for 80; Hinton, 2 for 51; Havrilak, 2 for 27; Bulaich, 1 for 5; Nowatzke, 1 for 45. Dal.: Reeves, 5 for 46; Thomas, 4 for 21; Garrison, 2 for 19; Hayes, 1 for 41.

with winning the game apart from holding the ball for O'Brien's field goal.

Somebody upstairs seemed to take care of the winning and losing. "You can say that again," said Renfro.

Baltimore Colts. 0 6 0 10—16
Dallas Cowboys 3 10 0 0—13
Dallas—FG, Clark, 14.
Dallas—FG, Clark, 30.
Baltimore—Mackey, 75, pass from Unitas (kick blocked).
Dallas—Thomas, 7, pass from Morton (Clark, kick).
Baltimore — Nowatzke, 2, run (O'Brien, kick).
Baltimore—FG, O'Brien, 32.
Attendance—80,055.

January 18, 1971

Gallup Poll on Spectator Sports

Here are the results of the Gallup Poll announced yesterday and a comparison with previous polls.

Question: What is your favorite sport to watch?

	1972	1961	1948
Football	36%	21%	17%
Baseball	21%	34%	39%
Basketball	8%	9%	10%
Bowling	4%	5%	1%
Wrestling	3%	5%	1%
Hockey	3%	3%	2%
Skiing and skating	2%	1%	Under 1%
Boxing	1%	3%	3%
Golf	1%	3%	3%
Swimming	Under 1%	1%	2%
Horse racing	1%	Under 1%	4%
Others	10%	18%	12%

Results from yesterday's survey broken down by men and women:

Football	Men 44%	Women 18%
Baseball	Men 24%	Women 17%
Basketball	Men 6%	Women 10%
Bowling	Men 2%	Women 6%

The No. 1 Sport? It's Now Football

At a time when television experts are predicting that some 65 million United States viewers will watch today's Super Bowl game, the latest Gallup Poll revealed yesterday that football had now become America's No. 1 spectator sport.

Baseball, long considered the major spectator sport, has fallen behind football as the game Americans are most likely to mention when asked which sport they watch.

The results of the poll show 36 per cent of American adults naming football as their favorite sport to watch and 21 per cent naming baseball. In a Gallup Poll sports survey reported in January, 1961, the figures were 34 per cent for baseball and 21 percent for football.

Basketball remains the third most popular sport, but it ranks considerably behind football and baseball.

Yesterday's results reveal that football has made its greatest gains in popularity with American men. Basketball and bowling, however, remains more likely to be named as the favorite spectator sport of women.

Interest in football has no

doubt been affected by the steadily increasing coverage the sport has received from the major television networks. The Super Bowl, for example, will be viewed not only by almost one of every three Americans, but it will also be relayed live to Canada, Mexico and Puerto Rico and by delayed satellite transmission to most of Europe.

The Gallup Poll results were obtained at a time in the year similar to other Gallup sports surveys, thus assuring that no sport would benefit from seasonal bias. The findings were based on personal interviews with over 1,000 adults, 18 and older,

January 16, 1972

Dallas Routs Miami in Super Bowl, 24-3

By WILLIAM N. WALLACE
Special to The New York Times

NEW ORLEANS, Jan. 16—The Dallas Cowboys completed the trip to a Super Bowl championship today, a voyage they had begun but never finished five straight times before. The Cowboys were methodical and merciless as they turned back the Miami Dolphins, 24-3, in what amounted to a rout.

The margin of victory, 21 points, was 4 points fewer than in Green Bay's 35-10 triumph over the Kansas City Chiefs in the first Super Bowl game five years ago. But the manner in which the result was achieved today proved more decisive than any of the previous Super Bowl contests, the National Football League's championship event.

Dallas missed a fourth touchdown by a yard with two minutes to play when Calvin Hill fumbled on the Miami 1-yard line. It was the only mistake of the game for the winners.

The Dolphins, meanwhile, were guilty of two fumbles and one interception, which helped the Cowboys to score 10 points.

Dallas had qualified for the N.F.L. playoffs every year since 1966 but never before had won a championship, coming close a year ago when the Cowboys lost the Super Bowl in Miami to the Baltimore Colts in the last five seconds, 16-13.

They looked like winners all the way on this cold afternoon (39 degrees) in Tulane Stadium before a crowd of 81,023. The Cowboys established and maintained a crushing ground-gaining game, which the coaches, Tom Landry of Dallas and Don Shula of Miami, had said

would be the key to the contest. Both were right.

But the Cowboys had the running game and the Dolphins did not. Duane Thomas gained 95 yards, with one touchdown, and Walt Garrison 74 as Dallas ran for 252 yards, a Super Bowl record. Miami managed only 80 yards, 40 each for Jim Kiick and Larry Csonka.

Said Landry afterward: "I can't describe how we feel. We fought so hard, came so close so many times. It's great for players like Bob Lilly and Chuck Howley who have been with the team for so long."

Lilly and Howley were stalwarts on defense, Howley intercepting Bob Griese's pass in the fourth quarter. The 35-year-old linebacker, who joined the Cowboys with Lilly in 1961, ran the ball back 40 years to the Miami 10 and three plays later Mike Ditka scored from the 7 on a pass from Roger Staubach. That was the final score of the game.

Staubach, who became a regular only last October, was singled out by Sport magazine as the outstanding player and he will receive a new automobile as a prize. It was a reasonable choice but Sport might easily have given away 40 cars to all 40 Cowboys.

Staubach, the 29-year-old one-time Naval Academy hero and Navy lieutenant, was confused in the early going. But he settled down and threw two touchdown passes that were impeccable.

The first came 75 seconds before the half-time intermission with the ball on the Miami 7, first down. Lance Alworth, the wide receiver, went down into the corner where there was almost no room. He was also guarded by Curtis Johnson, the Dolphin cornerback.

Staubach drilled his pass to Alworth, who made a quick grab at chest-level and

THE FIRST 3 POINTS OF SUPER BOWL: Mike Clark of Dallas kicking a 9-yard field goal over the outstretched hands of Bob Heinz (72) of Miami in the first quarter at New Orleans, yesterday. Dan Reeves (30) was the holder.

Chuck Howley, Dallas linebacker, intercepting a pass in right flat at midfield intended for Jim Kiick of Miami in the fourth quarter. He ran ball back to Dolphins' 10-yard line.

stepped into the end zone for a touchdown. Johnson had no chance to bat the ball away. That touchdown gave Dallas a 10-0 lead because Mike Clark had kicked a 9-yard field goal in the first quarter.

Miami came back and Garo Yepremian, the little Cypriot soccer-style kicker, booted a 31-yard field goal 4 seconds before the half ended for the Dolphins' only points.

As the second half began with Miami behind by a touchdown, there was still a chance for an exciting game worth the huge Super Bowl promotion. The Cowboys were not interested in excitement.

They received the kickoff and smashed 71 yards in eight plays for a decisive touchdown. Hill, in relief of Thomas, caught a swing pass for 12 yards but all the other plays were blasting runs: Thomas for 7, Thomas for 23, Bob Hayes for 15 on an end-round play and finally Thomas for 3 and into the end zone. The lead became 17-3.

The Cowboy offensive line, led by John Niland and Blaine Nye, the guards, blocked decisively. Seldom seen was Nick Buoniconti, the Dolphin middle linebacker, the key man of their defense and a particular Cowboy target.

"The drive that started the second half killed us," said Bill Stanfill, the Miami defensive end.

Also in trouble was Griese, the Dolphin quarterback who won so many honors this season. Griese could never get anything going and wound up with 12 pass completions in 23 attempts for only a net of 104 yards. He tried to scramble once in the first quarter and went back and back, finally tackled by Lilly and Larry Cole for a 29-yard loss at his 11.

Staubach, by contrast, completed 12 of 19 passes for 119 yards but said: "When the Cowboys run, everything else opens up. I guess I gave Coach Landry a few gray hairs at the beginning when I didn't see open receivers."

Shula may have had the last word. He said: "We played poorly. Dallas played a near-perfect game."

Super Bowl Scoring

Dallas Cowboys .... 3 7 7 7—24
Miami Dolphins .... 0 3 0 0— 3

Dal—F.G., Clark, 9
Dal—Alworth, 7, pass from Staubach (Clark, kick).
Mia—F.G. Yepremian, 31.
Dal. Thomas, 3, run (Clark, kick)
Dal: Dika, 7;, pass from Staubach (Clark, kick).

INDIVIDUAL STATISTICS

RUSHES—DAL.: D. Thomas, 19 for 95 yards: Garrison, 14 for 74; Hill, 7 for 25; Staubach, 5 for 18; Hayes, 1 for 16; Reeves, 1 for 7; Ditka, 1 for 17; Mia.; Csonka, 9 for 40; Kick, 7 for 40; Griese, 1 for 0.

PASSES—Dal.: Staubach, 12 of 19 for 119 yards. Mia.: Griese, 12 of 23 for 134.

RECEPTIONS—Dal.: D. Thomas, 3 for 17; Alworth;, 2 for 28; Ditka, 2 for 11; Hill 1 for 12, Mia.: Warfield, 4 for 39; Kicks, 3 for 21; Csonka, 2 for 18; Fleming, 1 for 27; Twilley, 1 for 20; Mandich, 1 for 9.

Attendance—81,023.

STATISTICS OF THE GAME

	Cowboys	Dolph.
First downs	23	10
Rushing yardage	48-252	20-80
Passing yardage	119	134
Passes	12-19	12-23
Interceptions by	1	0
Punts	5-37	5-40
Fumbles lost	1	2
Yards penalized	15	0

January 17, 1972

Miami Wins in Bowl for Perfect Season

United Press International

Referee signaling touchdown, scored by Howard Twilley of the Dolphins on a pass play, in the first quarter of the Super Bowl. Pat Fischer of Redskins is at right.

By WILLIAM N. WALLACE

Special to The New York Times

LOS ANGELES, Jan. 14—The big scoreboard in the Coliseum flashed the message over and over, "The Dolphins Are Super," at the end of the Super Bowl contest today, and indeed the Miami team had played an almost perfect game in defeating the Washington Redskins, 14-7, for a perfect season and the championship.

The game was watched by millions on national television.

[Many television sets in the metropolitan New York area were affected by atmospheric disturbances that interrupted the program.]

The score of the undefeated Dolphins' 17th victory could easily have been a more decisive 21-0 or 17-0 except for a single botched Miami play near the end of the game. That play featured little Garo Yepremian, the soccer-kicking specialist from Cyprus, attempting the skills of the big fellows, passing and tackling. Yepremian tried futilely to throw a pass after his 42-yard field-goal attempt had been blocked.

This pass was intercepted by Mike Bass, the cornerback, who ran 49 yards for the Redskins' only touchdown with 2 minutes 7 seconds left to play. The 155-pound Yepremian missed the tackle. This score put some suspense into a game that otherwise had generated little excitement because Miami was the dominant team from the start.

The Redskins had the ball one more time with 74 seconds remaining, but the Dolphin defense harassed Bill Kilmer, the Washington quarterback, and the final play was symbolic. Kilmer was dropped by Bill Stanfill and Vern Den Herder for a 9-yard loss on his 17-yard line.

Larry Csonka ran for 112 yards for Miami, 9 short of the Super Bowl record set by Matt Snell of the New York Jets in 1969, while Larry Brown, the Redskins' No. 1 carrier, scratched out 72 in 22 carries. His average was 3.3 yards, a yard below his standard during the regular season. Brown's longest run was for 11 yards while Csonka had one of 49 yards, the most yards the Redskins' defense had given up on a single ground play all season.

Csonka's running mate, Jim Kiick, scored the second Miami touchdown on a 1-yard run in the second period and Howard Twilley, the wide receiver, made the first on a dazzling play in the opening quarter. Twilley, cutting inside and then outside, caught a pass from Bob Griese on the 5 and scored to complete a 28-yard play. Twilley turned the defending back, Pat Fischer, all the way around on his fake.

Jake Scott, the Miami free safety, won the automobile when he was voted the game's outstanding player by a panel on the basis of his two interceptions. The choice of Scott was hardly a clear-cut one because all 11 players on the Dolphin defense were outstanding.

George Allen, the Redskin coach, had anticipated his defense giving Miami 14 or even 17 points, but his hope for victory expired because his offense was shut out rather than scoring the expected 21 or 24 points.

Allen said: "We felt we had to get on the board early against them because when they get ahead they have the talent to hold the ball and ground it out." That is what happened before the crowd of 81,706.

Allen added: "There was great pressure on Kilmer because we were unable to run as we would have liked to. It was a difficult day for him. But he brought us where we are today. They stopped our running better than I thought they would."

This attack, with Brown held in check, never moved into Miami territory until the third quarter began. That drive failed when Curt Knight's 33-yard field-goal try went wide.

The Redskins' only other drive, in the final period, ended when Kilmer's pass on third down to Charlie Taylor was

Associated Press

An attempted field goal by Garo Yepremian is bounced back to him, above. He then tried to pass the ball, right. Ball was deflected to Mike Bass (41), below, who then ran for Redskins' only touchdown.

intercepted by Scott in his end zone.

Kilmer had little luck when attempting to pass into the middle of the Miami zone defense. His first effort in the second quarter was intercepted by Scott and his second, in the same period, was picked off by Nick Buoniconti.

Washington had four turnover errors, the three interceptions and a lost fumble, to just one, an interception, for Miami. This interception, of a Griese pass by Brig Owens in his own end zone, prevented a Miami touchdown late in the third quarter that would have put the game out of Washington's sights with a 21-0 lead.

The early Miami touchdowns came after a six-play, 63-yard drive, which ended with the Twilley score, and a 27-yard drive following Buoniconti's interception and 32-yard return. Kiick slammed over the goal from the 1 behind a block by Csonka to make it 14-0 at half-time.

So Miami became the first team in the 53-year history of the National Football League to go through a season undefeated and untied. For the coach, Don Shula, a Super Bowl victory had been some time in coming. His two earlier qualifiers, the 1969 Baltimore Colts and last year's Dolphins, had lost, to the Jets and to the Dallas Cowboys.

I'm 0-2," said Shula last week, "and on Sunday night I intend to be 1-2." He made it.

For Allen and the Redskins, there was disappointment at the end of a glorious season that had carried the coach and the Washington entry to the Super Bowl for the first time.

Form held up. The Dolphins were the fourth team to win the Super Bowl on the second try after losing on the first. The

others were Kansas City in 1970, Baltimore in 1971 and Dallas last year.

In the locker room, Shula said: "There is no empty feeling this year. This is the ultimate."

Griese added: "I'm really happy for Don Shula. This year we won it for him."

Each of the 40 Dolphins also won for themselves $15,000, the Super Bowl prize money. The Redskins will receive half as much.

A downcast Allen commented: "It doesn't do any good to play in the Super Bowl if you don't win. We just lost to a team that played a better game."

Allen said the Redskin kicking game "was not up to par," a reference to Mike Bragg's weak 31-yard punting average and Knight's missed field-goal attempt.

Then Allen said: "I can't get out of here [Los Angeles] fast enough. There will be a lot of hours of agony tonight." George will start working on next season tomorrow.

Shula will linger to savor the victory. "This team," he said of the Dolphins, "is the greatest I have been associated with. It went undefeated and won at the end and they have to be given credit for their achievement."

Miami Dolphins . . . . 7 7 0 0—14
Washington Redskins . . . 0 0 0 7— 7
  Mia.—Twilley, 28, pass from Griese (Yepremian, kick).
  Mia.—Kick, 1, run (Yepremian, kick).
  Wash.—Bass, 49, fumble recovery return (Knight, kick).
  Attendance—81,706.

INDIVIDUAL STATISTICS
RUSHES Mia.: Csonka, 15 for 112 yards; Kiick, 12 for 38; Morris, 10 for 37; Kilmer, 2 for 18.
PASSES—Mia.: Griese, 8 of 11 for 88 yards. Wash.: Kilmer, 14 of 28 for 104.
RECEPTIONS—Mia.: Warfield, 3 for 36 yards; Kiick, 2 for 6; Twilley, 1 for 28; Mandich, 1 for 19; Csonka, 1 for minus 1. Wash.: Jefferson, 5 for 50; Brown, 5 for 26; C. Taylor, 2 for 20; J. Smith, 2 for 11; Harraway, 1 for 3.

January 15, 1973

Senate Votes, 76-6, to Restrict TV Blackouts of Sports Events

By JOSEPH DURSO
Special to The New York Times

WASHINGTON, Sept. 6—The Senate voted today to forbid television blackouts of professional sports events that are sold out 72 hours in advance.

The bill was passed, 76 to 6, only 11 days before the opening of the regular professional football season and was sent to the House of Representatives, where a similar measure was being hurried toward a floor vote. President Nixon, who has called for an end to television blackouts of home games in the past, was expected to sign the bill should it clear Congress.

The Senate acted while members of a House subcommittee were hearing a dissent by Pete Rozelle, the commissioner of the National Football League, which for years has refused to televise games within 75 miles of the home site.

Mr. Rozelle was flanked by the owners of two teams — Edward Bennett Williams of the Washington Redskins and Art Modell of the Cleveland Browns —as he warned that an end to the blackout would hurt the clubs financially. But he conceded that Congressional action was imminent, saying:

"We weren't exactly even money going in, we are realistic enough to think that some action will be taken by Congress. But it is beyond question that the bills being considered will be damaging to professional football, and we hope that in a year's time the full impact will become known. Jimmy the Greek didn't have to take this one off the board for us to realize it was a sure thing."

Representative Torbert H. MacDonald, Democrat of Massachusetts, an old Harvard halfback and chairman of the House subcommittee, agreed only that final action indeed seemed a "sure thing." He indicated that the Senate and House versions could be reconciled in time for the kickoff of the N.F.L. season on Sunday, Sept. 16. But he disagreed on Rozelle's dire prediction.

"You're a monopoly," he told the commissioner of the 26 professional teams. "You are the only game in town. I never said this wouldn't hurt you financially. It will. But I believe you have enough fat so that some could be cut off and you'd still have the pot of gold."

The word "monopoly," in

fact, has been underlying recent Federal inquiries into professional football, baseball, basketball and hockey. They were granted immunity from the antitrust laws 12 years ago when Congress permitted them to negotiate collectively — as leagues — for television coverage.

They also were allowed to prohibit the televising of games within the local territory of a team when it was playing at home, even if the stadium was sold out. The immunity was given when football was considered in a shaky financial position and when baseball was being protected as "the national pastime." But since then, football has become 90 per cent sold out, and the home-town fans have protested that they often could neither buy tickets nor watch the team on television.

Even the Super Bowl game was blacked out in Los Angeles last January, though 90,182 tickets were sold far in advance. Under public pressure, the blackout was lifted there 10 days before the game. And, the N.F.L. has been quick to point out 8,478 persons then skipped the game even though they had bought tickets.

While Rozelle was repeating this "lesson" in the Rayburn House Building, however, the Senate was overwhelmingly striking its blow for open TV.

The bill, sponsored by Senator John O. Pastore, Democrat of Rhode Island, would apply to any professional sports event, though football clearly was the prime target. It was rated the "toughest" of three bills being drafted in both chambers, but it was modified by a voice vote on the floor. It originally required that blackouts be lifted if all seats were sold 48 hours in advance, but the "deadline" was lengthened to 72 hours to give the teams more time.

Rozelle apparently won one other point: The law would last one year, then would be evaluated to see if the teams had lost customers at the gate while gaining an audience on television.

"The concessionaires tell us that they average $1.50 to $2 for each ticket sold, and that could be lost," Rozelle argued before the House subcommittee on communications and power. "The business of professional football is in fact very small business indeed. The entire football industry in an economic sense, ranks with the American rope-and-twine manufacturing industry."

When he added that the home team also would lose the emotional advantage of a full house, MacDonald replied: "I know it's an emotional game, but there's more emotion at a high school Thanksgiving Day game than at the Super Bowl."

"I would like you to be my guest on the sidelines of the next Super Bowl game," Rozelle commented.

"That's the best offer I've had," the chairman said.

"It's a crowd-psychology thing," Rozelle persisted. "You will someday see empty stands."

One of the committee members, Representative Lionel Van Deerlin, Democrat of California, said at another point: "I think you hit bottom in presenting all this evidence when you included a letter from the head of the Pinkerton guards in Baltimore saying they'd hire fewer men."

Rozelle laughed and quipped: "We were hoping there'd be a Congressman from Baltimore on the committee."

"It would be disastrous to us," Modell testified later. "We have 55,000 tickets sold for the Browns' game against Baltimore next Sunday, but we would find it logistically impossible to sell 30,000 tickets over the counter in two days. We accept the fact that some law will emerge, but we urge you to give us the earliest possible point of determining a sellout.

"I feel like a fourth-string quarterback coming into the game with the score 35-0 against us," said Williams, the prominent lawyer who has headed the Redskins for eight years. "We got Washington the best team in the world at a cost of many millions of dollars. But now we're tapped out of revenue."

"We understand your problems to a point," the chairman replied. "But we'd like everybody to see your team, and where in the world are kids in the inner city going to raise the $8 for a ticket?"

September 7, 1973

Simpson's 250 Yards Set N.F.L. Rush Mark

By THOMAS ROGERS

O. J. Simpson, a Heisman Trophy winner as a running back at Southern California, started his fifth season in the National Football League with explosive power yesterday, gaining 250 yards as the Buffalo Bills whipped the New England Patriots, 31-13, at Foxboro, Mass.

The total broke the league record of 247 set in 1971 by Willie Ellison, then of the Los Angeles Rams. Simpson also pushed his total career yardage to 3,428 yards to break the Buffalo club record of 3,268 set by Wray Carlton.

Simpson, who led the N.F.L.

in rushing with 1,251 yards last season, carried the ball 29 times. He broke loose for touchdown runs of 80 and 22 yards. He set the record on a 7-yard advance with 70 seconds remaining in the game.

"It looked like Grant going through Richmond." said Chuck Fairbanks, the New England coach, who lost in his debut. "We were helpless and couldn't slow him down. We'd have a hole blocked up, but O. J.'s natural ability got him away from the hole."

"He had more yardage than Secretariat," said Edgar

Chandler, the Patriot's linebacker, who played four seasons with Simpson at Buffalo. "He has that deceptive speed. You think you have the angle on him, then he's gone. It was embarrassing."

"I was tired when they said 15 more yards, I went back in and they kept calling my number," said Simpson. "I don't think anybody will ever criticize our line again. They were just blowing them out of there. The guys have been telling me they are going to get me 1,700 yards this season. They certainly went out and played like they meant it."

"I'm glad he got the record," said Lou Saban, the Buffalo coach. "You don't find many like him. He's a man, a great team man."

September 17, 1973

New Pro Football League Plans to Start in 1974 With 12 Teams

By WILLIAM N. WALLACE

Plans were announced yesterday for a new 12-team professional football league that would attempt to play at a major league level beginning next year. Its name would be the World Football League and eventually it would have teams abroad. It would have a team in New York to succeed the Giants at Yankee Stadium.

The league is the concept of Gary L. Davidson, who has experience in this line of work. Davidson, a 38-year-old California attorney, was a founder of the American Basketball Association and the World Hockey Association, both of which have survived against established competitors like the National Basketball Association and the National Hockey League.

Davidson is also an organizer of World Team Tennis, a 16-unit league beginning its first season next May, although so far it has signed only a few stars, including Mrs. Billie Jean King.

Speaking from Newport Beach, Calif., where he directs the W.H.A. as its president, Davidson said six football franchises were definite and he named owners. These would be in New York, Boston, Anaheim, Calif.; Vancouver, British Columbia; Toronto and another site to be determined.

He also spoke of teams in Mexico City, London, Rome, Dusseldorf, Germany; Tokyo and Osaka, Japan, but those would be in the future.

More likely sites at the start would be Chicago, Seattle, Tampa-St. Petersburg,

Fla.; Memphis, Birmingham, Ala., and Honolulu, according to Davidson.

"We're going to try to loosen everybody up a little with a bright new look to the sport," he said. Possible rule differences from the N.F.L. would be the 2-point conversion option, kickoffs from the 35-yard line and mandatory punt returns rather than fair catches.

Where would the players come from?

"There's no shortage," said Davidson. "There are 7,000 in colleges. We would also take some from the semipros, some from the Canadian League, some who had been cut and some who played out their options in the N.F.L."

The last reference indicated that the new league, as did the A.B.A. and W.H.A., would be ready to raid the old league.

N.F.L. players would welcome a competing league, hoping salaries would rise. Players feel their salaries compare unfavorably with basketball and hockey athletes.

"We want to go from the outhouse to the penthouse," said one Giant player at practice yesterday. Another said he was ready to form a syndicate and bid for a W.F.L. franchise.

The initial price for a franchise was said to be $250,000, which would be about $18-million less than the fee the N.F.L. will set for its two or four expansion franchises next year.

Davidson named these principals: Robert Schmertz, New York; Nick Mileti,

Cleveland; John Bassett Jr., Toronto; Howard L. Baldwin, Boston, and Steve Arnold, New York. Schmertz is chief executive of the Boston Celtics of the N.B.A. and the New England Whalers of the W.H.A.

He has planned before to put a football team in Yankee Stadium, but does not know where the games would be played while the stadium is rebuilt.

Mileti is head of the Cleveland Indians baseball team, the Cleveland Cavaliers of the N.B.A., a team with over $1-million in debts, and the Cleveland Crusaders of the W.H.A. His football club would play in a city other than Cleveland.

Baldwin is part-owner of the Whalers. Bassett heads the Toronto Argonauts of the Canadian League, which would be threatened. Arnold is a player agent and personnel director of the W.H.L. Davidson, too, would take a franchise at the start, as he did in the basketball and hockey leagues, and sell it later.

High start-up costs and obtaining television exposure are the foremost of many obstacles facing such an enterprise, Davidson acknowledged.

October 4, 1973

Simpson Breaks Mark as Bills Rout Jets, 34 to 14

O.J. Gains 200 Yards for Total 2,003–Ewbank Says Good-by

By MURRAY CHASS

On a day that combined the happiest moments of O. J. Simpson's career and the most emotional of Weeb Ewbank's, the Buffalo Bills defeated the Jets yesterday, 34-14, at Shea Stadium.

Simpson was happy because he had shattered Jim Brown's rushing record and become the first runner in the National Football League to gain over 2,000 yards in a season. Ewbank was emotional because he retired after 20 years of coaching pro football.

As the outcome indicated, the emotion stirred by Ewbank's retirement was no match for the offense ignited by Simpson's magnificent running.

In gaining 200 yards on a snow-covered field and leading the Bills to their ninth victory against five defeats (the Jets finished with a 4-10 record) Simpson reached that lofty yardage level for a record third time this season (Brown did it twice in 1963).

With the rest of the Buffalo offensive unit geared to make sure O. J. got the record—he needed 61 yards—Simpson ran for 200 on 34 carries. He wound up the season with 2,003, well ahead of the 1,863 Brown amassed in 1963.

In addition, the indomitable Simpson surpassed Brown's record for the number of carries in a season—332 to 305. He also helped the Bills set a league record for total yards rushing by a team, 3,088 to 2,950 the Miami Dolphins gained last season.

As for the significance of Simpson's yardage in the game itself, he ran for 57 of the team's 71 on the first touchdown drive and scored the second touchdown on a nifty 13-yard burst through the left side of the line.

"We tried to mix our defenses like always, but we weren't successful," Charlie Winner, Ewbank's designated successor, said. "We were embarrassed that he got so much yardage against us. We gun." The Jets had such little success stopping Simpson that he gained the record on the first play after Bills got the ball for the second time.

With Joe DeLamielleure, the rookie right guard, knocking Mark Lomas, the right end, out of the way, Simpson broke through the left side and gained 6 yards before John Little tackled him from behind with 10:34 gone in the first quarter.

The game was stopped, the other offensive players pounded Simpson on the back and hugged him. An official handed the ball to Simpson, who took it to the Bills' bench, where he was mobbed.

"We thought they'd give the ball to the fullback more, figuring we would key on O.J.," explained Ralph Baker the linebacker who calls defensive signals. "But they didn't. They came right out to get the record."

"We were saying let's get it in the first quarter," said Simpson, who also experienced his record, 11th 100-yard game of the season and surpassed the 5,000-yard mark for his five-year career. "But after we got it, we relaxed and I fumbled."

The fumble came on the play immediately after the one on which he broke the record. Two plays after that, Joe Namath—who may have been playing his last game — connected with Jerome Barkum for the tying touchdown on a 48-yard pass play.

But Simpson's 13-yard scoring burst with 1:12 left in the first half snapped the tie, and 48 seconds later Bill Cahill took Julian Fagan's 26-yard punt and scooted 51 yards for another Buffalo touchdown.

The Bills then spent the second half focusing on the attempt to raise O. J. to the unheard-of plateau of 2,000 yards. At one point early in the fourth quarter, Simpson related, "Joe Ferguson [the rookie quarterback] came in and said I needed 50 yards for 2,000. We broke 20 off right away and we were going after it then."

With 6:28 left in the game, Simpson reached the mark on a 7-yard smash through left guard to the Jet 13. This time he went to the sideline and was lifted to the shoulders of his excited teammates. He did not return to the game.

The clock, meanwhile, ticked off the final minutes of Ewbank's noted career. When it was over and the Jets were in the seclusion of their locker room, away from the onslaughts of Simpson, they held a ceremony of their own.

First, Winston Hill led the team in the traditional post game prayer. Kneeling and with his hefty arm around the roly-poly coach, the tackle said: "Thanks, Lord, for our rich relationship with Weeb. We want to thank you for Weeb."

Then, another long-time Jet, Dave Herman, gave Ewbank a gold watch.

"When you look at this watch, just think of what you have meant to us," Herman said in his brief presentation. As he finished, the players crowded together in a semi-circle, applauded heartily and Ewbank began crying profusely. The players cried, too.

"It's a great game, it's a great life," the 66-year-old coach responded in a broken voice. "I let you down. It's been good to me. Don't let things like this get you down. We've had good days here and we've had bad days. You're still great. Come back

Photographs for The New York Times by BARTON SILVERMAN
Simpson hitting a hole in the first quarter against the Jets to break Jim Brown's record of 1,863 yards. Simpson carried the ball 34 times for 200 yards.

next year and win 'em all."

Then Ewbank, tears still rolling down his chunky face, walked around the room, stopping at each locker to hug and shake hands with each player.

"I don't like to cry," Namath said later. "But I coulda cried. I had to fight back the tears."

"I'm really disappointed,"

Ewbank said of the game, his eyes red and moist "I'm sorry we didn't do better. But the kids tried. I wouldn't fault anybody. We just have to take our hats off to a great halfback. That guy is fabulous."

Buffalo Bills .... 7 14 7 6—34
New York Jets .... 7 0 0 7—14
Buff.—Braxton 1, run (Leypoldt, kick).
N.Y.—Barkum, 48, pass from Namath (Howfield, kick).
Buff.—Simpson, 13, run (Leypoldt, kick).

Buff.—Cahill, 51, punt return (Leypoldt, kick).
Buff.—Braxton, 1, run (Leypoldt, kick).
Buff.—FG, Leypoldt, 12.
Buff.—FG, Leypoldt, 11.
N.Y.—Caster, 16, pass from Namath (Howfield, kick).
Attendance—47,740.

INDIVIDUAL STATISTICS
Rushes—Buff.: Simpson, 34 carries for 200 yards; Braxton, 24 for 98; Watkins, 2 for 6; Ferguson, 2 for 0. N.Y.: Boozer, 7 for 32; Adamle, 3 for 6; Bjorklund, 1 for 1.
Passes—Buff.: Ferguson, 3 completions of 5 attempts for 70 yards. N.Y.: Namath, 13 of 30 for 206.
Receptions—Buff.: Chandler, 2 catches for 55 yards; Braxton, 1 for 15. N.Y.:

Barkum, 4 for 102; Caster, 3 for 58, Knight, 2 for 23; Boozer, 2 for 12; Bell, 1 for 11; Adamle, 1 for 0.

	Bills	Jets
First downs	21	12
Rushing yardage	304	39
Passing yardage	70	184
Passes	3-5	13-30
Interceptions by	0	0
Punts	2-35	7-33
Fumbles	1	0
Yards penalized	10	0

December 17, 1973

Dolphins Rout Vikings, 24-7, to Win 2d Super Bowl in Row

M.V.P. Car Given to Csonka

By WILLIAM N. WALLACE
Special to The New York Times

HOUSTON, Jan. 13 — On the scoreboard it was not the most one-sided Super Bowl victory of all, the Green Bay Packers retaining that distinction for their 25-point triumph over the Kansas City Chiefs in the first of pro football's extravaganzas seven years ago. But the flow of the play on the artificial turf of Rice Stadium today was the most decisive in Super Bowl annals as the Miami Dolphins annihilated the Minnesota Vikings, 24-7, to win the championship of the National Football League for the second year in a row.

The Dolphins followed exactly the formula for success devised by their coach, Don Shula, who has walked off the field a winner 32 times in the last 34 games, including successive Super Bowls.

The Miami offense ground out the yards, led by that astounding 238-pound former farmboy, Larry Csonka, who set a Super Bowl record by rushing for 145 yards. Bob Griese, the quarterback, threw only seven no-risk passes, completing six, and the Minnesota attackers were left standing on the sideline waiting for a chance to try their stuff.

By the time Francis Tarkenton, the Minnesota magician, had some room in which to maneuver, the Dolphins were ahead, 17-0, and smug. That was midway through the second quarter.

Csonka won a car, a football and universal plaudits. The car was for being the most valuable performer of the 75 players in action, and

he received one of two game balls, the symbols of victory, given out by the Dolphins. The other went to Bill Arnsparger, the defensive coach, as a farewell gesture. Shula said, "The Giants are getting a great coach," confirming the hiring of Arnsparger, whose appointment will be announced officially in New York on Wednesday.

Following the Shula formula further, the Dolphins made no mistakes—no lost

fumbles, no intercepted passes and only one penalty for a loss of 4 unimportant yards. They tackled in teams of twos and threes. They covered receivers in group fashion and left Tarkenton with only one type of play that worked at all. That was the pass to the tight end, of which there were four completions.

Stu Voigt caught three of them for 46 yards and he was the leading gainer for

Associated Press
Larry Csonka of the Dolphins scoring in the third quarter after plowing through three Viking defenders.

the Vikings, which said a lot.

Following the opening kickoff, the grinding process began. Mercury Morris gained 4 yards on the first play, Csonka 2 on the second and Griese hit Jim Mandich for 13 on the third. That achieved the first of Miami's 21 first downs and the drive went on for five more minutes.

Csonka carried on five of the 10 plays for 36 of the 62 yards. He scored the touchdown from the 5 with a full bore blast up the middle, Paul Krause and Jeff Siemon of the Vikings bouncing off him like handballs off the wall.

The second drive, starting the next time Miami got the ball, came out of the same cutter—56 yards, 10 plays, 5:46 of playing time, Csonka carrying three times for 28 yards. His buddy, Jim Kiick, scored from the 1 on an inside blast, the first touchdown of the season for him in the final game.

So Miami was ahead, 14-0, with the first period not yet completed. Another drive of 44 yards set up a 28-yard field goal by Garo Yepremian for a 17-0 lead and the Vikings, the National Conference Champions who had won 12 of 14 regular-season games as the Dolphins of the American Conference had, were comatose.

Tarkenton kicked some life into them but the first of a series of small disasters befell Minnesota. The Vikings drove 74 yards to the Miami 6. On fourth down Coach Bud Grant waived a field-goal attempt and Oscar Reed was sent into the line in search of a yard and a first down. He never got it.

Nick Buoniconti hit Reed so hard he fumbled a yard short and Jake Scott recovered for Miami. That would have been a good place for the Vikings to score and keep the television audience of 60 million interested for the second half.

The last 30 minutes began inauspiciously for the Vikes. John Gilliam returned the kickoff 65 yards to the Miami 34 but Voigt was penalized for clipping and Minnesota was on its 10 rather than in Miami's backyard.

Miami took over next at its 43 and there was more of the same, an eight-play touchdown drive with Griese passing 27 yards to Paul Warfield for the big play. Csonka made the victors' last touchdown drive from the 2.

The Vikings, behind, 24-0, then scored early in the final period as Tarkenton ran round right end from the 4, culminating a 57-yard drive. Tarkenton completed five of seven pass attempts in the 10 plays. The pass was all he had left. For the game he tried 28 and completed 18, the latter figure setting a Super Bowl record.

Said Grant: "Tarkenton faced many difficult situations and under the circumstances did well. When you fall 14 points behind it's pretty hard to overcome that against a good team."

The Vikings' last shot was also wiped out by a penalty. Fred Cox artfully achieved a short kickoff covered by Terry Brown, his teammate, on Miami's 48, which would have kept the ball in Minnesota's hands and out of Csonka's. But Ron Porter was offside and Cox had to kick over, this time deep.

The game concluded on a dull note. Tarkenton's last pass was intercepted under the Miami goal post by Curtis Johnson when Jim Lash, the receiver, slowed up on the pattern. Then the Dolphins, again in their fashion, took over and killed the last 6 minutes 24 seconds of playing time. It was dull but decisive football.

Are the Dolphins the best team of all time? Shula said, "It's not my job to say, although I feel that way."

Super Bowl at a Glance

Mia.	Minn.	
7	0	**FIRST QUARTER** Csonka 5-yard run at 5:27. 62-yard drive in 10 plays. Key gains: Mandich 13-yard pass from Griese; Csonka 16 and 8 yard runs. Yepremian kick.
14	0	Kiick 1-yard run at 13:38. 56-yard drive in 10 plays. Key gains: Csonka 12 and 8 yard runs. Yepremian kick.
17	0	**SECOND QUARTER** Yepremian 28-yard field goal at 8:58. 44-yard drive in 7 plays. Key gains: Morris 10-yard run, Csonka 9-yard run. Key play: 15-yard penalty against Minnesota's Hilgenberg, unsportsmanlike conduct.
24	0	**THIRD QUARTER** Csonka 2-yard run at 6:16. 43-yard drive in 8 plays. Key gain: Warfield 27-yard pass from Griese. Yepremian kick.
24	7	**FOURTH QUARTER** Tarkenton 4-yard run at 3:09. 57-yard drive in 10 plays. Key gains: Voigt 15 and Lash 9 yard passes from Tarkenton. Cox kick.

INDIVIDUAL STATISTICS

RUSHES—Mia.: Csonka, 33 for 145 yards; Morris, 11 for 34; Kiick, 7 for 10; Griese, 2 for 7. Minn.: Reed, 11 for 32; Foreman, 7 for 18; Tarkenton, 4 for 17; Marinaro, 1 for 3; Brown, 1 for 2.

PASSES—Mia.: Griese, 6 completions of 7 attempts for 73 yards. Minn.: Tarkenton, 18 of 28 for 182.

RECEPTIONS—Mia.: Warfield, 2 for 33 yards; Mandich, 2 for 21; Briscoe, 2 for 19. Minn.: Foreman, 5 for 27; Gilliam, 4 for 44; Voigt, 3 for 46; Marinaro, 2 for 39; Kingsriter, 1 for 9; Lash, 1 for 9; B. Brown, 1 for 9; Reed, 1 for minus 1.

STATISTICS OF THE GAME

	Dolphins	Vikings
First downs	26	14
Rushing yardage	196	72
Passing yardage	63	166
Passes	6-7	18-28
Interceptions by	1	0
Punts	3-40	5-42
Fumbles lost	0	1
Yards penalized	4	65

Miami Dolphins ......14 3 7 0—24
Minnesota Vikings .....0 0 0 7— 7

Mia.—Csonka, 5, run (Yepremian, kick).
Mia.—Kiick, 1, run (Yepremian, kick).
Mia.—FG, Yepremian, 28.
Mia.—Csonka, 2, run (Yepremian, kick).
Minn.—Tarkenton, 4, run (Cox, kick).
Attendance—68,142.

January 14, 1974

negotiations and we assumed the Dolphin management would sit down and try to get them settled. Even when the Toronto team drafted us, nothing happened. I don't think they took the new league seriously."

"We felt we had to take this offer rather than wait for Robbie's offer," Kiick said. "We didn't know if this offer would be the same if we didn't take it now. And we couldn't imagine the Dolphins coming up with money anywhere near this. We're guaranteed this money. If we get hurt, if we die, if the W.F.L. doesn't get off the ground, we still get it."

Asked if they were concerned about reprisals from Shula during the coming season, Csonka said:

"No, because he takes one season at a time. He wants to win the Super Bowl again, and we do, too. I like Shula. I like playing for him. I like playing for the Miami Dolphins. But you don't always do what you want to do. I felt I had to make this move. So did Paul and Jim."

Asked if they felt the Dolphins fans would resent their decision to desert them, Warfield commented:

"I don't think so. After the Toronto team drafted us, many Dolphin fans in Miami told me that they realized that it was in my best interest to explore the situation. We plan to give the Miami fans 100 per cent effort this season, so I assume they'll hold no grudges against us."

Keating negotiated the deal as a package, but Kiick disclosed that the three contracts were not identical. The 27-year-old Csonka, a 240-pound running back who gained a record 145 yards when the Dolphins won the Super Bowl for the second consecutive year, presumably has the most lucrative contract of the three. Warfield is a 31-year-old sleek wide receiver. Kiick is a 27-year-old running back. Each earned about $60,000 annually under their Dolphin contracts.

"It gives us a great deal of satisfaction," Kiick said, "to know that we're pioneers in a way, that with us joining the new league, it might open the way for other ballplayers to join in, too. Some people didn't believe that this new league existed but now I think most people will begin to take it a lot more seriously."

Csonka predicted that the two leagues would "level off in three or four years" if an influx of N.F.L. players occurred.

"We got a lot of fringe benefits in our contract," Kiick said. "Homes, cars, things like that. But there's no way I would have agreed to play in Toronto if my fam-

Csonka, Warfield and Kiick to Go to W.F.L.

3-Year Pacts for $3-Million Total Signed

By DAVE ANDERSON

For a total of approximately $3-million, three stars of the Super Bowl champion Miami Dolphins—Larry Csonka, Paul Warfield and Jim Kiick—provided the new World Football League with instant credibility yesterday by signing three-year contracts with the Toronto Northmen, beginning in 1975.

The trio will compete for the Dolphins this year under the option clause of their National Football League contracts.

Csonka, Warfield and Kiick were chosen by the Toronto team two weeks ago in the W.F.L.'s draft of current pro players. They arrived in Toronto over the weekend with their business representative, Ed Keating, of International Management, Inc., a Cleveland-based firm, and discussed a reported $3-million offer from John Bassett Jr., owner of the Northmen franchise.

"The $3-million figure is pretty accurate," Kiick said during a telephone interview with the three players from Toronto after the announcement there. "If anything, it's a little low."

According to Kiick, the other 11 franchises in the W.F.L., which is to begin its first season in July, contributed $1-million to the highest-priced player contracts in pro football history. Joe Namath, the New York Jets' quarterback, is the highest salaried N.F.L. player at $250,000 a season. Only his option year remains.

"We notified the Dolphins what was going on about 18 hours before the contract was finalized," Csonka said. "But the Dolphins didn't make any specific counter offer. Joe Robbie finally told Ed Keating that he needed two days. Keating told them he had two hours but Robbie told him he didn't want to negotiate over the telephone."

Csonka had phoned Don Shula on Saturday and the Dolphin coach informed Robbie, the club's principal owner, of the situation.

"But we hadn't heard from the Dolphin management since the Super Bowl game," Warfield said. "All three of our contracts were up for

ily wasn't happy. My wife, Alice, is with me and we've been treated great up here."

Csonka's wife also was in Toronto for the negotiations. Warfield has been there on several other occasions.

"I want to get into TV and radio broadcasting when I'm through playing football." Warfield said. "I'll have that opportunity now. Mr. Bassett owns one of Toronto's biggest TV stations."

Kiick, depressed because Eugene (Mercury) Morris had supplanted him in the Dolphin backfield, had planned to exercise the option clause in his Dolphin contract before the Toronto offer materialized.

Csonka, Warfield and Kiick are the most notable players signed by the W. F. L. even though a one-year embargo exists on their availability.

Of the other W. F. L. teams, the New York Stars, who hold, the negotiation rights in their league to Namath, have signed John Elliott, once an all-pro defensive tackle with the Jets, and the Chicago Fire has signed Virgil Carter, a quarterback with the Cincinnati Bengals last season.

In addition to their Toronto news conference, Csonka, Warfield and Kiick appeared on network TV shows of the American Broadcasting Company and the Columbia Broadcasting System yesterday. On the A.B.C. show, Csonka indicated that another Dolphin star, Manny Fernandez, a defensive tackle, was exploring a W.F.L. offer from the Portland, Ore., franchise.

In six seasons, Csonka has run for 5,151 yards and scored 32 touchdowns for the Dolphins while Kiick has run for 3,370 yards, accumulated 2,055 yards with 203 pass receptions and scored 29 touchdowns. Warfield, with the Cleveland Browns for six seasons before joining the Dolphins in 1970, has career totals of 344 receptions for 7,165 yards and 75 touchdowns.

April 1, 1974

Nine Football Rules Amended by Pros To Enliven Games

By WILLIAM N. WALLACE

Sweeping rules changes were made yesterday in an effort to enliven the National Football League games. Not since 1933 has the sport been so drastically altered.

The new rules discourage field goals by returning the goal posts to the end line of the end zone, as in college football, and having missed field goals returned to the line of scrimmage if it is beyond the 20-yard line.

Forward passing will be encouraged by restricting the defensive tactics. Sudden-death overtime periods will be played in an effort to reduce the number of ties in regular season games as well as playoffs.

The goal posts were moved in 1933 from the end line of the end zone to the goal line to encourage field-goal kicking. That same year, the league permitted passes to be thrown anywhere behind the line of scrimmage to spur the aerial game.

Commissioner Pete Rozelle denied that the changes were being made because of the incursions threatened by the new World Football League but said the new league might have hastened them.

Speaking of the committee of owners that voted the changes, Rozelle, said, "I think they were reacting to the Super Bowls," alluding to the rather dull character of most of the N.F.L. championship games played before huge television audiences

Rozelle thought significant alterations had been ordered before the World Football League was founded. The W.F.L.'s rules incorporate the 35-yard line kickoff, which the N.F.L. will do, and sudden death to eliminate tie scores.

The initial consensus was that the changes would require more intelligent thinking by coaches, more risk taking on third and fourth downs, which most coaches dislike, and new versatility to the kicking game. The punter, for example, will become more important, the field-goal kicker less.

The package of nine revisions generally, is as follows:

1. One sudden death period of 15 minutes duration will be played at the end of any tie game in the regulation 60 minutes to help break ties. The first team to score in the extra period wins. If there is no score, the tie stands. In 182 regular season games over the past five years, the number of ties have averaged six per year.

2. Kickoffs are now to take place from the kicking team's 35-yard line rather than the 40, which puts an added burden on the kicker trying to reach or go beyond the opponent's end zone. The purpose is to bring out more running returns of kickoffs rather than the no return and the static touchback that puts the ball on the receiving team's 20-yard line.

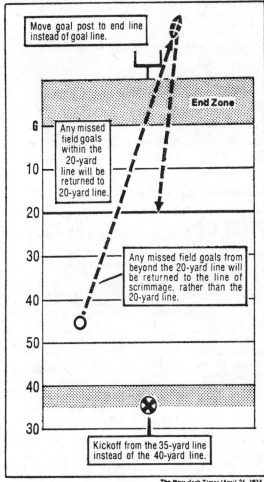

Move goal post to end line instead of goal line.

End Zone

Any missed field goals within the 20-yard line will be returned to 20-yard line.

Any missed field goals from beyond the 20-yard line will be returned to the line of scrimmage, rather than the 20-yard line.

Kickoff from the 35-yard line instead of the 40-yard line.

The New York Times/April 26, 1974

3. Goal posts move to the back of the end zone adding 10 yards to both field-goal attempts and the point-after-touchdown kick. The latter becomes a 19-yard field-goal attempt rather than one from only 9 yards out.

4. If a field goal attempt is no good, the ball goes back to the line of scrimmage or the 20-yard line, whichever is farther from the goal line. Heretofore the ball returned to the 20 after all failures. Random field-goal attempts from 40 yards out and beyond fourth down will be far less while the out-of-bounds punt inside the opponent's 10-yard line (the coffin corner kick) will increase.

5. Members of the kicking team cannot run downfield until the ball is kicked. This holding action at the line of scrimmage will make kick returns more popular and the no-return fair catch less so.

6. To enhance a wide receiver's ability to get free to catch a pass, he cannot be cut down by a block below the knees—the so-called roll block or cut.

7. Once the receiver is downfield by more than three yards from the line of scrimmage, he can be hit only once by any defending player. This change, in effect, rules out the bump and run technique whereby the defending back continually hit into the receiver, ran with him and then hit him again to knock him out of the pass pattern.

8. The wide receiver, however, can no longer return to the line of scrimmage and block a defender below the waist. This eliminates the crackback block on the linebacker. The most famous case of this tactic in recent seasons was delivered in 1972 by Charlie Taylor of the Redskins on Chuck Howley of the Dallas Cowboys, injuring Howley so that his season was finished.

9. The penalty for holding by an offensive blocker was reduced from 15 yards to 10. The purpose here is to give the offensive team a little better chance to move the ball after the penalty has been assessed.

The rules changes were presented to the owners of the 26 teams by the league's competition committee in a bloc to be approved or refused. The competition committee is made up of Tex Schramm of Dallas, Paul Brown of Cincinnati, Al Davis of Oakland and Jim Finks of Minnesota.

This committee was given a mandate a year ago by the owners to come up with significant rules changes that would retain in general the balance between offense and defense, which is the heart of football. They are at the same time intended to add zest to the game, meaning more offense.

April 26, 1974

Players Halt Strike

WASHINGTON, Aug. 11 (AP) — National Football League regulars decided today to suspend their strike for 14 days, effective Wednesday, in an effort to resolve their labor dispute with the 26 club owners.

The N.F.L. Players' Association, which has been on strike since July 1, said it would ask its members to report to training camps Wednesday so that, as union officials put it, "a cooling-ff period could take place."

In New York, it was reported that most of the Jets' regulars would report tomorrow to the team's training camp at Hofstra University in Hempstead, L. I.

Ed Garvey, executive director of the association, said W. J. Usery Jr., the Federal mediator working on the dispute, recommended that the strike be suspended for two weeks in an effort to resume productive talks. Negotia-

tions were recessed last night without agreement.

The decision to report to camp "was a tough one," according to Garvey, and apparently was not unanimous among the union's executive committee and the 26 team representatives.

One player, as he left the news conference where the announcement was made, made an obscene gesture and said, "and if we don't get this one, the Federal Government is to blame."

Usery has been involved in the negotiations for the past two weeks, meeting with both the N.F.L. Management Council and the players' association in extended negotiations at the Labor Department. He has met with the two sides jointly and separately in an effort to resolve the dispute which began March 16 when the players presented their demands.

August 12, 1974

Pro Football Reserve Rule
Held Illegal by U.S. Judge

By HENRY WEINSTEIN
Special to The New York Times

SAN FRANCISCO, Dec. 20—In a sweeping decision that almost certainly will be appealed, Federal District Judge William T. Sweigert ruled today that the National Football League's contract and player-reserve system was illegal.

In an antitrust suit brought by a former Minnesota Vikings quarterback, Joe Kapp, Judge Sweigert held that the league's so-called Rozelle rule is "patently unreasonable and illegal." Under the rule, the league can perpetually restrain a player's employment choice

(even after he has otherwise become a free agent by fulfilling his contract with a league team).

Judge Sweigert also held that the N.F.L.'s "draft" rule is "patently unreasonable and illegal" insofar as it enables the league to exert control over a player's employment even though the drafting club fails to sign him.

The decision means that unless the N.F.L. can get an immediate stay of the option, players such as Joe Namath, the New York Jets quarter-

back, who played out their options are now free agents who can negotiate with any other team in the league.

College Stars Affected

Additionally, the decision means that college stars, such as Anthony Davis of the University of Southern California, are free to sign with any N.F.L. team unless the league modifies its draft rule before the Jan. 28 draft. Presumably, this could be done along the lines of major league baseball, which has a six-month limitation on a team having sole rights to a player after a draft, or in some other fashion, so long as the player is not indefinitely restrained from signing with another team.

Baseball is the only major sport exempt from the antitrust laws. It would take an Act of Congress to change that status.

In Washington, the decision was hailed "as the most exciting development in the history of professional sports" by the head of the N.F.L. Players Association, Ed Garvey.

Mr. Garvey added that the ruling would not necessarily mean the better players would go to a few, wealthy teams.

The termination of the Rozelle rule, named for N.F.L. Commissioner Pete Rozelle, was one of the key issues in the players' bitter strike during last summer's training season.

Would this now mean a lessening of loyalty of players, who know they can get up and go whenever their contracts expire?

"We discussed this possibility with the players," said Mr. Garvey. "And the feeling is that not that many would change teams. They've moved to a city, bought a home there, found a job. You don't always go looking for new jobs if you're happy. If not, you'll move. I think in the first two years there'll be a lot of movement, then it will taper off."

Rozelle, reached in San Francisco after his arrival to attend tomorrow's playoff game between Oakland and Miami, would not comment on the decision.

"Naturally, we've had no chance to go over it," he explained. "I'll go over it with our lawyers this weekend."

At a news conference held in the office of one of his attorneys, Moses Lasky, after the decision was announced Kapp said, "I'm extremely pleased. It's been a long battle." Asked if it had been worth the wait, Kapp said, "I don't know if it ever could be worth the time I lost in the prime of my career, but I felt it was important to do this. I reported

Associated Press
Judge William T. Sweigert, who ruled against N.F.L.

to Boston. They threw me out of camp. I was forced to go to legal proceedings."

As for plans to play again, Kapp, who is now 36 years old, said, "I had hoped all along I could play, but it's been four years and after a while I could take a hint." Then Kapp was asked if he still thought it possible that he could play. Lasky interrupted before Kapp could answer, saying it was an issue that would be relevant to the amount of damages that could be awarded in an impending trial. Lasky would not give a definite figure, but said that based on a treble damages formula the minimum would be $2-million and the maximum might run to "eight figures," meaning as much as $10-million. Lasky said that unless Judge Sweigert's decision was overturned the structure of pro football was "going to have to change pretty radically."

Judge Sweigert also knocked out three other rules insofar as they were used to interpret league regulations "restricting free employment choice." These are: the league's "one-man rule" policy under which Commissioner Pete Rozelle is given final say over disputes and grievances; the "tampering" rule under which fines and other penalties are imposed on rules violators, and the Standard Player Contract rule that requires all league players to sign a certain type contract as a condition of eligibility to perform.

Judge Sweigert ruled, however, that the league's rule which provides that a team has an option for a players' services for an additional one-year period at 90 per cent of the prior year's salary is not unreasonable on its face and that its reasonableness must be determined by a full trial, rather than by summary judgment as was the case with the rest of the issues.

The league's principal defense to the suit—that all its rules had been accepted by players such as Kapp under a collective bargaining contract—was rejected by Judge Sweigert.

Kapp, who also played for the Boston Patriots and sued that team for breach of contract, will have to have a separate trial on that issue and the amount of damages he may have been caused as a result of any breach or "tortious inducement" of any breach by the league.

Judge Sweigert stated in the opinion that he felt that sports leagues, such as the N.F.L., cannot simply be treated like any other business in regard to Kapp's antitrust contentions. He said sports league activities have a "unique nature" and that "there must be some degree and kind of restriction on the right of clubs to hire and sign players as they please."

The opinion does not take issue with the league's contention that some restrictions are necessary "because the very purpose of a professional sports league is to provide reasonably matched teams for field competition to attract and sustain the interest and patronage of fans," and that if there were "free-for-all competition for the best or better players, then the most strongly financed or otherwise better advantaged club would be able to sign up and monopolize the best or better players."

However, the judge said that the Rozelle rule went too far. The Rozelle rule applies when a player "plays out" his option and joins another team. His new team must pay compensation to the team he left.

The essence of the rule is that the league members have the power to make any player stay on the team for which he is currently playing.

If the two teams cannot agree on a settlement price, the commissioner steps in and imposes a settlement. Since the commissioner can set an arbitrarily high price, this possibility effectively scares off potential negotiators for the services of a man who has played out his option.

Judge Sweigert concluded that such a rule "imposing restraint virtually unlimited in time and extent goes far beyond any possible need for fair protection of the interest of the club-employers or the purposes of the N.F.L. and that it imposes upon the player-employes such undue hardships as to be an unreasonable restraint." He added that such a rule "is not susceptible of different inferences concerning its reasonableness; it is unreasonable under any legal test and there is no genuine issue about it to require or justify a trial," and therefore the judge ruled against the league by summary judgment.

The suit originated in a dispute among Kapp, Rozelle, and the Boston Patriots more than four years ago. After a successful college career in which he led the University of California Bears into the Rose Bowl, Kapp played eight years in the Canadian Football League. He had been drafted by the Washington Redskins on the third round of the N.F.L. draft in 1959, but they never made him a satisfactory offer. Kapp then signed in 1966 with Houston of the American Football League, which was just merging with the National League. His Canadian contract had an option year for 1967, and his agreement with Houston included the possibility that he might not be able to report until 1968.

However, when Kapp obtained a release from his Canadian team, Rozelle ruled that his Houston contract was invalid because it had been negotiated before his Canadian contract expired. (This point has since been resolved in favor of the players by various court decisions.) Kapp was allowed to sign with Minnesota in the N.F.L. and in 1969 led them into the Super Bowl.

After playing out his Minnesota option in the 1969 season, he was theoretically a free agent and signed with Boston. Minnesota received a player and a No. 1 draft choice as compensation. But Kapp refused to sign a standard player contract because it said the player agrees to the special powers granted to the commissioner and Kapp did not believe the commissioner should have so much power, particularly after the Houston contract conflict.

Kapp's personally negotiated regular business contract with Boston covered 1970, 1971 and 1972, and was for $600,000. He played under it for 11 of the 14 games in 1970 and received $154,000 of the contracted amount.

Then Rozelle ruled that Kapp could no longer play unless he signed a standard contract. Kapp refused, and the antitrust suit began—in essence for having been blacklisted by the league (no other team would negotiate with him) when he would not abide by the commissioner's ruling concerning his contract, and for damages because he was not allowed to fulfill the contract he had signed.

The league contended that Kapp, through the N.F.L. Players Association, had accepted the standard player contract because it was part of a collective bargaining agreement signed by the league and the association on June 17, 1971, and by its terms made retroactive to Feb. 1, 1970.

However, Judge Sweigert rejected this argument. He said that the league and the

Patriots "brought their pressure to bear" on Kapp to sign the standard player contract between January and May 28, 1971, when Rozelle sent a letter to the Patriots "to the effect that no player could play in a game or even practice with a member club unless an executed standard contract was on file with the commissioner."

Today's decision also noted that "according to the record" of the case Kapp was never told that the collective bargaining agreement required him to sign the standard player contract, "only that" this was "required by the N.F.L. constitution and bylaws."

The judge added that, "even if the N.F.L. standard player contract had been accepted through collective bargaining" this did not resolve the thorny legal question of "what are the limits to the antitrust violations to which labor and management can agree," an issue raised by Justice Thurgood Marshall of the United States Supreme Court in his dissent in Curt Flood's antitrust suit against major league baseball, which challenged the reserve clause binding a player to one club.

The decision did not hold that the draft was illegal as a means of selecting players. It held that the draft was illegal only "insofar as it permits virtually perpetual boycott of a draft prospect even when the drafting club refuses or fails within a reasonable time to reach a contract with the player." The opinion did not spell out what would be a reasonable time.

Kapp has not played football since 1971. Since then, he has made an income from business interests in Canada, a few roles in motion two years has been a radio broadcaster for University of California football games.

December 21, 1974

Steelers Beat Vikings, 16-6, in Super Bowl

By WILLIAM N. WALLACE
Special to The New York Times

NEW ORLEANS, Jan. 12—The ninth Super Bowl game today had a lot of firsts as the Pittsburgh Steelers won, 16-6, to become the champions of the National Football League for the first time.

The Minnesota Vikings became the first team to lose in the Super Bowl for the third time. Franco Harris of the Steelers became the first back to gain over 150 yards rushing in a Super Bowl contest and the first to carry the ball as many as 34 times.

The first safety in a Super Bowl game was scored by Pittsburgh after Fran Tarkenton, the Vikings' quarterback, wound up recovering a fumble in his own end zone. And Bobby Walden, the Steeler punter, had his first kick of the season blocked and the result was the Minnesota touchdown, scored by Terry Brown, who recovered the loose ball in the Pittsburgh end zone.

Apart from these firsts, the Steelers became the third team to win a Super Bowl game on the first try. The others were the Green Bay Packers, who won the first one in 1967, and the New York Jets, who won the third in 1969.

Bud Grant, the disappointed Minnesota coach whose teams lost in the Super Bowl in 1970 to Kansas City and a year ago to Miami, said of today's contest, "It wasn't a very good game."

Grant managed a sly dig at the officials, for which he will probably be fined by Commissioner Pete Rozelle, when he described the game as "a succession of errors by all three teams." The third team had to be the officials'

team headed by Bernie Ulman, the referee.

Grant was alluding to some judgment calls that went against the Vikings and possibly could have affected the outcome. But Tarkenton had the more accurate perspective when he conceded, "The better team won."

Except for the zaniness of the turnovers, eight in all, with five in Pittsburgh's **favor, the flow of the game was predictable. The Steelers did establish a running game and Minnesota could not. So the Vikings had to pass and the risk of eventual intercep-**

Franco Harris of the Steelers scoring in the opening moments of the third period after Vikings fumbled kickoff

Associated Press

tions was realized when the Steelers picked off three of Tarkenton's aerials in key situations.

So one of football's oldest and most fundamental axioms was realized. The team that can control the ball with a strong running game usually walks off with the victory.

Harris was sensationally strong. The big 230-pound fullback churned his way through the purple-shirted Vikings much like Larry Csonka of the Miami Dolphins against the same team a year ago. He carried the ball one more time than Csonka and gained 158 yards, or 13 more than Csonka last year. Franco had a lot of help from people like Gerry Mullins, the pulling right guard who blocks linebackers so well on the sweeps.

The figures told the story. The Steelers gained 333 yards in all, 249 on the ground, to 119 for the Vikings and only 17 by rushing.

Dave Osborn carried eight times for a total gain of minus 1 yard and Chuck Foreman had 12 carries for just 18. They could make no headway against the Steeler defense, led by Joe Greene and L. C. Greenwood on the front line. The Minnesota offensive line could create no running room.

Another telling figure was

the total number of offensive plays, 73 for Pittsburgh and almost half as many, 47, for Minnesota. The Vikings had their opportunities. "But we couldn't cash 'em in," Tarkenton said. The Steelers missed some, too, and were repeatedly penalized, for a total of 107 yards to 18 for Minnesota.

Because of the effectiveness of Harris, Terry Bradshaw, the Steeler quarterback, did not have to do much or take risks. He tried 14 passes and completed 9 for 96 yards and one touchdown, the latter on a 4-yard pass to Larry Brown, the tight end, in the last quarter to seal the decision. Those figures of Bradshaw were circumspect enough, similar to those of Bob Griese of Miami against Minnesota last year when he completed six of only seven pass attempts.

Tarkenton, therefore, had "to peek and peck" at the Steeler defense as he had predicted. He completed 11 of 27 pass attempts and he threw many of them on a rollout run to the right or left to escape the pressure of the Pittsburgh pass rush. Greene, Greenwood and the others never did sack him, although they deflected four of his passes, three by Greenwood and the other by Dwight White. One of Greenwood's

deflections resulted in an interception by Greene.

Another resulted in a hilarious play that was scored as a completed pass, Tarkenton to Tarkenton. Greenwood tipped this one and the ball bounced back into Tarkenton's hands. So Francis tried again and flung a long pass down field to John Gilliam for a 40-yard gain. But it was called back and ruled a penalty play because a team cannot throw two forward passes on the same play.

That's how hard it was for the Vikings to do something right on this cold, blustery day. It was their kind of weather, meaning cold with a chill factor of 22 degrees. The stadium was not full. The attendance in Tulane Stadium was announced as 79,997, about 1,000 less than capacity. All the $20 tickets were sold so there were 1,000 no-shows who elected to stay away and watch on local television.

They saw a first half in which only 2 points were scored. The safety resulted when Tarkenton tried to pitch the ball out to Dave Osborn, the halfback, on his 6-yard line. The ball slipped out of his hands and rolled backwards. Tarkenton recovered the fumble in the end zone but he had left his feet and was downed there.

That gave the Steelers 2 points.

The Vikings had poor field position throughout the first half, the offense putting the ball in play on its 33, the 14, the 21, the 23, the 6 and the 20.

Minnesota did, however, have two scoring opportunities in the first two quarters. The first came when Rocky Bleier fumbled and Randy Polti recovered for Minnesota at the Steeler 24. Four plays later Fred Cox tried a 39-yard field goal but the kick was wide to the right.

The Vikings, just before half-time, mounted a drive that ended when Gilliam failed to hold onto a Tarkenton pass on the Pittsburgh 5 after being hit hard by Glen Edwards. The ball came out of his hands and went up in the air. Mel Blount grabbed it for an interception.

In that first half the Vikings gained only 76 yards and merely 11 by rushing.

Matters did not improve much for the National Conference champions in the second half as the Steelers kept the Vikings pinned in the Minnesota half of the field most of the time. The Vikings could not even score when a pass intereference penalty against Mike Wagner for fouling Gilliam put them on the Steeler 5. On the first

Joe Greene chasing Fran Tarkenton in the backfield

Vikings' John Gilliam after pass for him was intercepted

play Foreman fumbled when he carried into the line and Greene recovered for the Steelers.

Four plays after that Walden went back to punt for the Steelers. The kick was blocked at the 5 by Matt Blair and the ball bounded backward into the Steeler end zone. Terry Brown, a reserve defensive back, recovered it there for a Viking touchdown. But the conversion kick by Cox failed when the ball hit the left upright of the goal post.

This was not the best kind of season for the veteran Minnesota kicker. On eight other occasions he failed to make the conversion kick. So Minnesota's only points today were scored by a special teams unit and the Steel-

ers' defense had in effect accomplished a shutout.

The Steelers played most of the second half with two new linebackers, Ed Bradley and Loren Toews, who replaced two injured regulars, Andy Russell and Jack Lambert.

That Minnesota touchdown left the Vikings trailing by just 3 points with half of the final quarter remaining.

The Steelers then locked up the game by driving down the field, 66 yards in 11 plays, with Harris running on six of them. On the last play Bradshaw rolled out to

his right and threw a hard pass to Larry Brown, the tight end, who was in the end zone. That amounted to the clinching score. The Vikings had only three more offensive

plays after that.

A pass by Tarkenton for Gilliam going deep was intercepted by Wagner and the Steelers kept the ball until only 41 seconds were left. Tarkenton threw two more short passes from his 23 and the contest was over.

The Steelers went ahead in the early part of the third quarter when Minnesota made a costly mistake. Bill Brown, the seasoned fullback, fumbled the kickoff. He could not pick up the rolling, bouncing football and

Marv Kellum recovered it for Pittsburgh at the Minnesota 30.

The Steelers moved right in for the kill. Harris ripped to the 6 for a 24-yard gain. After a loss of 3 yards, big Franco went round left end for the touchdown, with Mullins throwing the key block on Wally Hilgenberg.

That put the Steelers ahead, 9-0 and they were on their way to the first N.F.L. championship it had ever won in 42 years of trying.

January 13, 1975

FOOTBALL TEAMS END THEIR STRIKE

By WILLIAM N. WALLACE

The strike in the National Football League ended yesterday and the season will open on schedule this Sunday. A temporary agreement was reached between the N.F.L. Players Association and management early yesterday and the five striking teams agreed

to go back to work, which meant practicing for Sunday's games.

But the New England Patriots, who started the strike by refusing to play in a preseason game last Sunday, were stubborn. It took William J. Usery, the Federal mediator, five hours yesterday afternoon at Foxboro, Mass., to persuade the Patriot players to accept the truce proposal.

Contract Offer Pledged

The key to the truce was a promise by the N.F.L. Manage-

ment Council, representing the 26 owners, to make a substantial contract offer by Monday. The last contract expired Jan. 31, 1974, and the last offer by the council was rejected by the players three weeks ago by a vote of 906 to 11.

"We are now willing to go back to play this weekend," said Randy Vataha, the player representative of the Patriots. "However, we are still completely committed to the principles that we started with.

"Mr. Usery has stuck his feelings out for us. He feels that

after discussions with the management council in New York something meaningful will come on Monday. Heaven forbid if it's not meaningful.

Ed Garvey, the executive director of the players association, had signed a no-strike pledge good for two weeks on behalf of four of the striking teams. The Patriots were not included. But Tom Neville, one of the team's tackles, said that if there was a good proposal on Monday "we will enter into a no-strike agreement until Oct. 1."

Apart from the Patriots, the

other striking teams were the Giants and Jets, the Washington Redskins and the Detroit Lions, although the Lions say all they did was boycott for a day.

Eleven teams had voted not to strike while the other 10 had made no commitment.

One of the terms of the agreement was a promise by management that there would be no reprisals taken against the Patriots. They now have two days rather than the usual five to prepare to play the Houston Oilers in Foxboro on Sunday. The Oilers had voted, 43 to 0, not to strike and have practiced all week.

The settlement process became intensive at midnight in the management council's offices at 580 Madison Avenue. Usery, Garvey and Sargent Karch, executive director of the council, were the key people. There were also five players present—Doug Van Horn and Dick Enderle of the Giants; Richard Neal and Dick Anderson of the Miami Dolphins.

That meeting broke up at 9 A.M. upon the agreement to halt the strike and to play

the games pending management's new offer on Monday. Then Usery, Garvey, Karch and Neal took a plane to Boston to present the proposal to the Patriots, the most militant of the 1,118 players in the N.F.L. Van Horn, the Giants' player representative, missed the plane.

Van Horn, after the 13-hour marathon meeting, said the players had been won over by Usery's assurances that management would move off its intractable position, which had so upset the players. With a third party such as Usery the head of the Federal Mediation and Conciliation Service, offering support, the athletes were ready to halt the walkout.

Usery, a former welder from Georgia who likes to watch pro football games on television and admits to making a bet occasionally, was praised by Terry Bledsoe, the assistant executive director of the management council. "He held on at several points even though it looked like we were at an impasse," said Bledsoe.

The players on Monday

will send their representatives here to consider management's proposal. Of particular interest will be the way the management council treats the "Rozelle rule," which has been a stumbling block in the negotiations that began 16 months ago.

The owners want to bargain over the rule, which determines a system of compensation when a player leaves one team and switches to another by his own volition. The players association says that the rule is illegal and that its future should be determined in the courts rather than in collective bargaining.

The other elements of the contract concerned payments by the owners into the player pension fund; medical payment, insurance and preseason pay. These economic factors were of more importance to many of the players than the Rozelle rule. But debate over the latter had stalled all the bargaining.

The strike left some teams, which had largely ignored it, in a position to play at their

maximum potential on Sunday.

But others had been split by close voting on the issue to strike in support of the Patriots. The Vikings vote was 21 to 19 not to strike, a vote that so angered three key defensive players that they walked out of practice. They were Alan Page, Jim Marshall and Bobby Bryant. The Cleveland Browns' vote was also close, 23 to 19.

Participation by the players in the long night meeting here was voluntary. Van Horn and his teammate, Dick Enderle, had led a delegation of Giants down from their training site at Pleasantville, N.Y., last evening to the management council's offices.

Neal, the player representative who said he had lost "three days sleep and eight pounds," and Winston Hill came in from the Jets' site at Hempstead, L.I.

Anderson, coming from an antistrike team, the Miami Dolphins, was on crutches, out for the season following knee surgery.

September 19, 1975

The New York Times/Barton Silverman

In Hempstead, L.I., it was business as usual, with the Jets working out after ending their two-day-old strike

Money Ills Force W.F.L. to Disband

By STEVE CADY

Unable to sustain itself without television or season-ticket support, the World Football League went out of business yesterday.

"Our product was exciting but fragile," said Chris Hemmeter, the Hawaiian businessman who reorganized the financially troubled league this year after a disastrous opening season. "We couldn't withstand bad weather or the National Football League or media skepticism."

Hemmeter, speaking at a

hastily called news conference here, said termination of operations would take effect immediately. The 10-team league was to have played the 12th round of games in its 20-week schedule this weekend.

"There were no problems that 20,000 people in every stadium wouldn't have solved," said Hemmeter, "but we found it's harder to renovate an old house than to build a new one."

The vote to disband reportedly was 6-4, leaving 380 players without jobs.

In the wake of the announcement, there was confusion over the status of a number of top players lured from the N.F.L. by big-money deals with the new league. The stranded group includes Larry Csonka, Paul Warfield and Jim Kiick, former Miami Dolphin stars.

Ed Keating, business agent for the three former Dolphins, said they had received $1.6-million so far from the Memphis Grizzlies. He estimated the whole package, including extras, at $3.6-million, and he said over the phone from Cleveland that the three players were now "free agents."

However, other sources indicated Csonka, Warfield and Kick had signed "personal services" contracts with John Bassett of the Memphis franchise, and were still under obligation to him. Memphis and the Birmingham franchise, known as the Vulcans, plan to apply for admission to the N.F.L.

Pete Rozelle, commissioner of the N.F.L., issued a statement saying that teams in his league would be permitted to sign players from the defunct league if the players were free from all contractual obligations. Such signings, he ruled, must be completed before the trading deadline of 4 P.M. next Tuesday.

The New York Jets hold the N.F.L. rights to Anthony Davis, the former University of Southern California all-American who has been the W.F.L.'s leading ground-gainer.

In Cleveland, the owner of the Browns, Arthur B. Modell, said he was interested in picking up "any quality players" to beef up a team with a 0-5 won-lost record.

"I would be insane to say I wasn't interested in Csonka and Warfield," Modell said.

Don Shula, coach of the Dolphins, refused to say whether he would actively seek the return of his three former stars.

Since its inception last year, the W.F.L. has teetered on a fiscal tightrope. It reportedly lost $20-million its first season as a number of franchises failed to meet payrolls, shifted to other cities or went bankrupt. The deficit this year was said to have reached $10-million.

Average attendance through last week's games had declined to 13,371 for the season, a slump of 28 per cent over the last five weeks. Apparently, yesterday's decision was a case of the board of directors deciding not to throw good money after bad.

"They say pro sports can take a grown man and make a child out of him in a matter of minutes," Hemmeter said. "But prudence prevailed in our decision. Seven of our board members are directors of banks."

According to the league president, it would have taken a two-year expenditure of $25-million to $40-million

to make the W.F.L. a success.

"In light of an unstable economy, continuing inflation, no assurance of national television rights and a softening market for new sports leagues," Hemmeter said, "we considered this enormous expenditure an unwise investment."

Hemmeter broke the news of his league's demise at a conference in a small office on the 39th floor of the Time-Life Building. Stapled to the wall behind him, like bright-colored college banners, were the pennants of the W.F.L. teams: Grizzlies, Vulcans, Philadelphia Bell, Portland Thunder, San Antonio Wings, Charlotte Hornets, Shreveport Steamer, Jacksonville Express, Southern California Sun and The Hawaiians.

The use of singular nicknames such as "Bell" and "Sun" was popular from the start of the W.F.L. But the frequent changing of names reflected the league's instability and its lack of fan-appeal tradition.

For example, the Charlotte Hornets were the Charlotte Stars last year after the New York Stars shifted their franchise in midseason to Charlotte. In Charlotte last night, the club's president,

Upton Bell, said the league "would have prospered" if it had made it through the 1975 season.

"We just ran out of time," Bell said. "We never were able to overcome the problems we had the first season."

Hemmeter promised that the league would pay all its outstanding debts, but that individual team debts would be a matter for the various franchises to settle. He defended the "Hemmeter Plan" —the incentive program he developed in which players shared in the gate receipts.

"The plan worked beautifully," he said. "But it was never intended to develop a market. What we needed was a strong marketing plan. You can have an exciting product, but if doesn't have customer appeal on the shelf, it's worthless."

Calling his league's failure "a serious comment" on the world of professional sports, Hemmeter suggested the default would have "a dramatic effect on the acquisition of new franchises."

October 23, 1975

N.F.L. Stocking Plan Set

By WILLIAM N. WALLACE

In determining how the Seattle Seahawks and the Tampa Bay Buccaneers will acquire their players next winter, the owners of the 26 existing National Football League teams yesterday were generous in comparison to the plans adopted for the three most recent expansion clubs—Atlanta, 1966; New Orleans, 1967, and Cincinnati, 1968.

"We have created the largest pool of quality players ever available in football expansion," said Pete Rozelle, the N.F.L. commissioner. The alleged acts of generosity are based on the premises that from quantity will come quality and that the newcomers should be helped for the good of the competitive balance of the league.

The pool of established N.F.L. players, from which Seattle and Tampa Bay are to select 39 athletes each on Jan. 23 and 24, will have in it more than 500 names. The existing teams will be allowed to freeze their best 30 players from current rosters of 43 plus two more

from their injured reserve lists. Those lists now have 139 names and by season's end the total should be close to 200.

For each player selected from that pool, an established team can freeze one more.

As for the draft of college talent on Feb. 4, Seattle and Tampa Bay will alternate first and second choices in each of the 17 rounds. In addition, each will have two extra selections at the end of the second, third, fourth and fifth rounds for a total of 25.

So the heart of the new squads will be 39 seasoned N.F.L. players plus 25 drafted rookies. Beyond those 64, free agents and nondrafted rookies will be available.

The tricky part concerns the present teams' two lists of reserved players, those injured and out for the season and those not under contract, meaning they signed in the Canadian or World Football Leagues or retired.

Take Miami. The Dolphins at last count had six players on injured reserve and three are important—Dick Anderson, the safety; Nick Buoniconti, the linebacker, and Bob Heinz, the defensive tackle. On their other reserve list there is Larry Csonka, Jim Kiick and Paul Warfield, supposedly under contract to the Memphis Southmen of the late W.F.L., an outfit seeking admission to the N.F.L., which is an unlikely development.

The Dolphins can freeze only two of these six, probably Anderson and Csonka, and thus expose the others to selection by the two expansion teams.

Then there is Anthony Davis, signed to play in Canada. Will the Jets freeze him? Mike Reid, the Bengals' fine defensive tackle, retired this year at age 28. He may wish to play again. Does Cincinnati let him go into the pool or find a place for him on the precious protected list of 30?

John Jennings, one of the Tampa Bay owners, said he was pleased with the plan and so did John Thompson, the Seattle general manager.

November 20, 1975

Pittsburgh Defeats Dallas by 21 to 17 In the Super Bowl

By WILLIAM N. WALLACE
Special to The New York Times

MIAMI, Jan. 18—The Super Bowl justified its existence today. The most heavily promoted and lavishly staged sports extravaganza of all presented to the 80,187 fans in the Orange Bowl and the vast television audience a well-played and exciting football game that was unresolved until the last play. The Pitts-

burgh Steelers won, 21-17.

The Dallas Cowboys were ahead by 10-7 early in the final quarter. Then Pittsburgh rallied. But the Cowboys were only 38 yards from the potential winning touchdown when the last play began.

That final play wound up with Glen Edwards, the Steelers' safetyman, intercepting a pass by Roger Staubach, the Cowboy quarterback, in the Pittsburgh end zone, and it was typical of what had gone on in the 60 minutes of action. Super Bowl games have been characterized in the past by sluggishness and ennui, but not this one.

The interception was the third of Staubach's passes. He had no choice but to risk these passes in the second half because the Steeler defense had proved impenetrable to any other means of attack. That defensive unit has been the heart of the Pittsburgh team and it was tested to the utmost by Staubach and his clever companions right to the end.

The Steelers thus won the Super Bowl, the championship game of the National Football League, for the second season in a row. This was the 10th Super Bowl game, which matches the champions of the American and National Conferences. Two other teams had won consecutive Super Bowl contests, the Green Bay Packers, 1967 and 1968, and the

Miami Dolphins, 1973 and 1974.

Blocked Kick Key Play

A lot of action, strategy and heroism was packed into the final quarter, which had a variety of elements seldom produced in 15 minutes of a football game. The Steelers, trailing 10-7, scored 14 points in that period on a safety, two field goals and a touchdown. And the Cowboys got 7 back two minutes before the end.

The key play was a blocked kick. Reggie Harrison, a Steeler reserve running back who plays on the special teams, blocked a punt by Mitch Hoopes at the Dallas 9. The ball hit Harrison in the face and bounced backward so hard it went all the way out of the Dallas end zone.

The ruling in such cases is a safety, giving the attacking team 2 points. That made the score 10-9, Dallas still ahead. The Cowboys then had to execute a free kick from their 20-yard line and Hoopes punted 50 yards. But a good return is easy on free kicks and Mike Collier of the Steelers raced back to the Cowboy 45.

Seven plays later the Steelers were on the Dallas 20 and Roy Gerela kicked a 36-yard field goal to put Pittsburgh ahead for the first time, 12-10, with 8 minutes 41 seconds to play. Gerela earlier had missed field-goal attempts of 36 and 33 yards.

Tom Landry, the Dallas coach, said: "The blocked punt changed the momentum.

It cost us 5 points and that was the difference."

Landry also said: "That Lynn Swann was really something. He made two big catches when he was covered."

The coach thus cited the Pittsburgh wide receiver, who caught four passes for 161 yards, scored one touchdown, was given the game ball, the traditional symbol of victory, and also was voted the game's outstanding player.

The last-named honor wins for him a new automobile in addition to $15,000 as a member of the winning squad. (Each Cowboy will receive $7,500.)

The first of Swann's two big catches came in the opening period on a pass from Terry Bradshaw, the play covering 32 yards and moving Pittsburgh to the Dallas 16.

Three plays later Bradshaw passed 7 yards to Randy Grossman, the tight end, for a touchdown that tied the score, 7-7.

Swann's second catch was the game's gem. It was a 64-yard touchdown play, Bradshaw's pass covering 59 yards in the air. That was the Steelers' final score, giving them a 21-10 lead.

Swann certainly was cov-

Associated Press

Teammates and trainers helping Terry Bradshaw off the field after he was injured in the fourth quarter.

ered well on both plays. Mark Washington, the cornerback, was right with Swann, but the second-year receiver from Southern California, who is now an all-pro performer, made remarkable, leaping catches of perfectly thrown passes.

Bradshaw was knocked silly on the 64-yard touchdown pass play by a safety blitz and did not play again. Terry Hanratty was the quarterback for the team's last offensive series, one in which the Steelers took a risk and got away with it.

They had fourth down and 9 to go at the Dallas 41 with 88 seconds left. They chose not to punt and made 2 yards, turning the ball over to the Cowboys, who had just scored to trail by 21-17.

But Dallas had no more time-outs to stop the clock and the time did run out after five plays.

Chuck Noll, the Pittsburgh coach, explained that he elected not to punt because he feared the chance of a disastrous blocked kick, the Cowboy rush having come close all afternoon. Also, he didn't think there would be time enough for Dallas to go 61 yards to score a touchdown. "If all they needed was a field goal to tie or win, we'd have punted," said Noll.

He also knew the Cowboys had not been going anywhere against his defense. They had never been in Pittsburgh territory until they had fallen behind by 11 points.

Staubach did manage an 80-yard drive previously, but it was too little, too late. Preston Pearson said, "They shut everything down on us in the second half and got away from us."

The Cowboys indeed tried hard. They had dazzling sets of formations and plays, including the shotgun formation for Staubach in every long-

yardage passing situation. Mike Wagner, the Steeler safety, was certainly fascinated. He said: "Their game is so interesting, so calculated. They gave us a good run for our money today."

"Pittsburgh is the best," said Staubach. The Steelers dropped him seven times while he was trying to pass (a Super Bowl record) for losses totaling 42 yards and intercepted three of his passes. The Cowboys' net yardage passing was 162 on 15 completions of 24 attempts for an average per pass play of only 5.4. The Pittsburgh figure was 9.0, mostly attributable to Swann, as Bradshaw completed 9 of 19 attempts for a modest 209 total.

The Steelers fired their cannon, Franco Harris, at the Cowboys 27 times. Dallas did not reel. The 230-pound fullback gained only 82 yards or just 3.0 a carry. The Cowboys kept him out of the end zone and stopped him numerous times on third down.

The defensive players on both sides were outstanding. The hardest hitters were Jack Lambert, the Steeler middle linebacker, and Cliff Harris, the pugnacious Cowboy safety.

Harris and D.D. Lewis, the linebacker, knocked Bradshaw out on the blitz and if they had reached him a split second sooner he never would have got the touchdown pass off to Swann.

As it was, Bradshaw didn't see the catch. He later acknowledged that he was in such a daze that he didn't know it was a touchdown until he came to in the locker room.

Steelers Alert to Play

Another play that said it all was an intercepted pass by Wagner in the final quarter, which led to Gerela's second field goal and a 15-10 Pittsburgh lead.

Drew Pearson, the wide re-

Associated Press

Drew Pearson scores for Dallas in the first quarter.

ceiver, was the intended receiver. He started the play as a man-in-motion, running from the outside along the scrimmage line and then cutting sharply across the middle of the Pittsburgh secondary once Staubach had the ball. That was the play on which the Cowboys had first scored with Pearson wide open on a beautiful 29-yard touchdown pass production.

This time the Steeler secondary closed like a claw. Three defenders were around Pearson and Wagner stole the ball.

"That's been our bread-and-butter play all year," said Pearson. "This was the first time it didn't work.'"

That was a suitable epitaph for a fine football game.

January 19, 1976

Raiders Rout Vikings, 32-14, in Record Super Bowl Performance

Oakland Runs to Left Side; Gains Total of 429 Yards

By WILLIAM N. WALLACE
Special to The New York Times

Associated Press

Dave Casper of the Raiders catching pass for first touchdown yesterday.

PASADENA, Calif., Jan. 9—The shows at the Super Bowl today were better than the game. With shows? Pregame, halftime and postgame. These shows were unpredictable, spontaneous and efficient with the audience of 100,421, plus a resonant band from the Los Angeles United School District, serving as the actors in the Rose Bowl.

As to the other actors, the football players, the Oakland Raiders were predictable, planned and efficient. But it takes two to make a contest. The Minnesota Vikings were inefficient, inept and, at the end, inexcusable. The Raiders won, 32-14.

Only one other Super Bowl game, of 11, was comparable as to decisive sting. That was the first one a decade ago when the Green Bay Packers destroyed the Kansas City Chiefs, 35-10.

First Viking Disaster

The hope for a contest, the hope of the one-tenth of a million watchers within the stadium and an estimated 75 million before television sets, disappeared in the sixth minute of the game. Fred McNeill had blocked a punt by Ray Guy and McNeill then recovered the rolling football on the Raider 3-yard line.

The Vikings were jubilant. However, on their second attempt to get into the Raider end zone, the first of a series of disasters for the people wearing purple took place. Brent McClanahan, the Viking fullback, fumbled and Willie Hall recovered for Oakland. McClanahan had help in the act of fumbling, which was to cost himself and his 42 teammates the difference between a $15,000 Super Bowl reward and a $7,500 consolation prize, because Phil Villapiano stripped the football out of his hands.

Then the Raiders rolled. They went 90 yards to set up a field goal by Errol Mann to score the first 3 points of 16 in the first half and of 16 more in the second.

Yardage Records Set

The Raiders rolled and rolled as if they were going down the San Diego Freeway to Tijuana with no traffic. They gained the most yards, 429, and the most by rushing, 266, that any team had ever achieved in pro football's ultimate contest. And they almost always went to the left.

Francis Tarkenton, half-naked, told the nation's television audience the truth after the game when he said: "They totally dominated us. We have no excuses."

The geniuses had figured out before the kickoff that Oakland would run to the left behind the blocking of Art Shell and Gene Upshaw, tackle and guard, respectively, who weigh a collective 550 quick-moving pounds. The Raiders did not disappoint those experts.

They went to their left against Jim Marshall, Alan Page, Wally Hilgenberg and Bobby Bryant, defenders of the Minnesota right perimeter, on 15 key plays in the first half beginning with the first one. That one gained only 1 yard.

There was more to come, 6.0 yards gained on an average of the 73 plays when all was done. Minnesota ran 71 plays. Their average gain 2.7.

All the Vikings knew this would happen. The vulnerable left-right matchup had to be proved and it was. Those victimized Vikings played to the best of their ability but it was not good enough.

Bud Grant, the Minnesota coach, tried new people at those positions: McNeill for Hilgenberg after Wally was caught a step behind Clarence Davis, the Oakland halfback, on a pass reception from Stabler; Nate Allen for Bryant, and Mark Mullaney for Marshall. That made no difference.

Clarence Davis, the Oakland runner, gained 137 yards in 16 carries, almost a third of the Raiders' 52 rushing plays.

Fred Biletnikoff, one of four Raiders who remain from this team's only other Super Bowl appearance back in 1968, caught four passes for 79 yards but

Super Bowl XI Scoring

Oak.	Minn.	
		SECOND QUARTER
3	0	Mann, 24-yard field goal at 0:48. 90 yards in 12 plays after Hall recovered McClanahan's fumble at Raider 3. Key plays: Davis, run, 35; Stabler, pass to Garrett, 11, and pass to Casper, 25.
10	0	Casper, 1-yard pass from Stabler at 7:50. Mann, kick. 64-yard drive in 10 plays. Key plays: Stabler, pass to Casper, 19, on third down; Garrett, run, 13.
16	0	Banaszak, 1-yard run at 11:27. Mann's kick wide. 35-yard drive in 5 plays after Colzie's 38-yard punt return. Key plays: Stabler's pass to Biletnikoff, 17, to 1.
		THIRD QUARTER
19	0	Mann, 40-yard field goal at 9:44. 54-yard drive in 5 plays after Colzie's 12-yard punt return. Key plays: Davis, run, 18; Stabler, pass to Branch, 10.
19	7	White, 8-yard pass from Tarkenton at 14:13. Cox, kick. 58-yard drive in 18 plays. Key plays: roughing-kicker penalty against Oakland; 4 Tarkenton passes to Voigt, Rashad and Foreman twice.
		FOURTH QUARTER
26	7	Banaszak, 2-yard run at 7:21. Mann, kick. 54-yard drive in 4 plays after Hall intercepted Tarkenton pass and returned 16 to Minnesota 32. Key play: Stabler, 48-yard pass to Biletnikoff to 2.
32	7	W. Brown, 75-yard return after intercepting Tarkenton pass at 9:17. Mann's kick wide.
32	14	Voigt, 13-yard pass from Lee at 14:35. Cox, kick. 86-yard drive in 9 plays. Key plays: 4 Lee passes, 2 to White for 37, 2 to S. Johnson for 9.

no touchdown. The catches were key ones and they attracted the ballots of the press box incumbents who voted him the game's most valuable performer.

However, Dave Casper also caught four, for 70 yards and one touchdown.

Stabler threw all of those passes. He completed 12 of 19 attempts for 180 yards and one touchdown, that one to Casper, which made the score 10-0 in the second quarter.

When Stabler came back to the bench he said to Coach John Madden: "Don't worry. There is more where that came from."

He was correct. When the Raiders moved next, 35 yards in five plays within the same quarter, there was a key pass, Stabler to Biletnikoff for 17 yards to the Minnesota 1, Pete Banaszak, another of the four Raiders who played in Super Bowl II nine years ago scored the first of his two touchdowns from there.

Before the pass to Biletnikoff, there was an offensive Oakland huddle in which the following conversation took place.

Stabler said to Biletnikoff, who has a history of speechlessness at these moments, "Do you want anything?"

Biletnikoff said one word: "Post."

Post means a pass thrown to a receiver

cutting toward the goal posts.

The play evolved. Biletnikoff caught the football around his ankles at the Minnesota half-yard line with a Viking on top of him, Nate Wright.

In describing it later, Stabler said: "He [Biletnikoff] never likes to say anything. I have to beat it out of him.

Also later, Biletnikoff made an acknowledgement. "It's the first time all year I said anything."

He paused. Then he said, "Kenny throws the ball where I can catch it—and away from people."

January 10, 1977

Cowboys Triumph in Error Filled Super Bowl, 27-10

By WILLIAM N. WALLACE

Special to The New York Times

NEW ORLEANS, Jan. 15—Hand it to the Denver Broncos. They made Tom Landry, the Dallas coach, use every conceivable weapon in the Cowboy arsenal to secure the Super Bowl XII victory here tonight.

Intercepting passes, grabbing fumbles and seizing advantages wherever they found them, the favored Cowboys defeated the Broncos, 27-10, to capture the championship of the National Football League.

It was professional football's most analyzed, advertised and aggrandized event, but much of it turned out to be a decidedly unspectacular spectacle. Both teams fumbled repeatedly and were set back by numerous penalties; Craig Morton, the Denver quarterback, was sacked again and again and intercepted four times in the first half, which ended with a 13-0 Dallas lead.

But two big plays in the second half broke the back of the Denver defense. Both were passes for touchdowns, one in the third quarter and one in the fourth.

Staubach-to-Johnson

On the first big play, Roger Staubach hit Butch Johnson for 45 yards. It took an exceptional end-zone catch by Johnson, an alternating wide receiver, and it put Dallas ahead, 20-3. With Denver wallowing in blunders, lost fumbles and intercepted passes, it appeared the victory was sealed for Dallas.

But the Broncos stormed back to score a touchdown and close the deficit to 20-10. Then, another lost Denver fumble set up the second back-breaker for Dallas, a play from the Landry arsenal no one had seen before. Robert Newhouse, a running back, threw it and Golden Richards, the other alternate wide receiver, caught it to put the count beyond Denver's reach at 27-10.

The game—a national prime-time phenomenon seen by 85 million Americans on television and 76,400 persons in the Superdome in New Orleans—capped weeks of promotional hoopla

that left sports fans awash in statistics and steeped in such strategic esoterica as the texture of the turf and the religious inclinations of the quarterbacks.

Jitters in First Quarter

The Cowboys had been 5½-point favorites, a spread indicating that the oddsmakers, at least, had expected a close contest. But after some first-quarter jitters by both teams, the outcome was rarely in doubt, though sloppy play and turnovers continued through much of the game.

Many of the turnovers were forced by tough, alert defensive play by both sides—Dallas's "Doomsday Defense," top rated in the National Football Conference, and Denver's "Orange Crush," rated third in the American Football Conference.

In addition to the two second-half touchdown passes, Dallas scored a touchdown in the first quarter on a short plunge by Tony Dorsett. Efren Herrera added two field goals and three conversions.

Denver scored on a field goal by Jim Turner and on an off-tackle plunge by Rob Lytle, all in the third quarter.

It was the Cowboys' second Super Bowl victory—the other was a 24-3 victory over Miami in 1972 in four trips to the championship game. It was Denver's first Super Bowl appearance.

By any standard, inept play notwithstanding, it was a big money contest: CBS paid $4.5 million to televise it; a panoply of corporations paid up to $325,000 for a minute of air time to sponsor it; fans at $30 a ticket paid $2.3 million at the Superdome gate; the N.F.L. paid $18,000 to each of the winning players and $9,000 to each of the losers, and bettors put up untold millions to play the odds.

Avalanches of statistics and background had inundated armchair quarterbacks in the past week's promotional binge, but it all added up to a single final score tonight in the $160-million Superdome.

For the final score of the game, Dallas's coach dipped into the Landry bag of tricks for the play requiring Newhouse, the stumpy fullback, to run a left-end sweep, stop and throw a pass

downfield. The pass by a running back is one of football's most vexing plays for defensive backs. Do they come up to stop the run? Or do they stay back to defend against the wide receiver, who is heading into their territory?

Bill Thompson and Bernard Jackson stayed back. Newhouse's pass wobbled but came down in Richards's hands in the Denver end zone.

So Richards and Johnson, sharing the same position, had made excellent catches that almost alone won Super Bowl XII for the Cowboys. That is what they were trained to do, paid to do and almost but not quite expected to do.

If the Broncos had not lost the ball so many times on turnovers, seven times in the first half and once in the second, the outcome might have been different and certainly the style in which the game was played—sloppy—would have been different.

Morton? The Cowboy scouting report had stated succinctly that he "rattled easily." He rattled enough, what with four of his passes being intercepted, that his coach, Red Miller, benched him and turned to Norris Weese, a much more mobile quarterback, late in the third quarter as the Broncos reached for a rally when behind, 20-10.

Weese did his best, but he fumbled once when hit by Harvey Martin, who had previously been zeroing in on Morton. This fourth lost Bronco fumble was recovered by Aaron Kyle of the Cowboys on the Bronco 29 and served as the prelude to the Newhouse-to-Richards pass.

Weese drove Denver down the field near the end of the game, but a fourth-down play failed and Dallas took over on its 25-yard line with 3 minutes 14 seconds to play. The Bronco offensive players never got their hands on the ball again.

Broncos Made It Game

The best team had won. But the second-best team made it a game all the way, a good game that cannot be included in the long list of previous Super Bowl contests labeled as dull or conclusive far too early for spectators.

Super Bowl Statistics

	Cowboys	Broncos
First downs	17	11
Rushing yardage	143	121
Passing yardage	182	35
Passes	19-28	8-25
Interceptions by	4	0
Punts	5-42	4-38
Fumbles lost	2	4
Yards penalized	94	60

INDIVIDUAL STATISTICS

RUSHES—Dal.: Dorsett, 15 rushes for 66 yards; Newhouse 14 for 55; White, 1 for 13. Den.: Lytle, 10 for 35, Armstrong, 7 for 27; Weese, 3 for 26.

PASSES—Dal.: Staubach, 17 completions of 25 attempts for 183 yards; White 1 of 5; Newhouse 1 of 1 for 29. Den.: Morton 4 of 15 for 39; Weese 4 of 10 for 22.

RECEPTIONS—Dal.: P. Pearson 5 for 37 yard; DuPree 4 for 66, Johnson 2 for 53, Richards 2 for 38, Dorsett 2 for 11. Den.: Dolbin 2 for 24, Odoms 2 for 9, Moses 1 for 21.

Attendance—76,400.

The most important statistic about the Broncos was negative, eight turnovers from four lost fumbles and four intercepted passes—seven of the turnovers coming in the first half. A team seldom wins any kind of game, let alone a championship one, after committing eight turnovers.

The Broncos were fortunate to go to their locker room at halftime behind by a score of merely 13-0. But the Cowboys had squandered their scoring chances in the second period.

In the Broncos' halftime locker room, Coach Miller put a message up on the blackboard that said: 'Setle down. Break the ice," meaning the score.

They did.

The first Denver points came in the third quarter on a 47-yard field goal by Turner, a field goal a yard short of a Super Bowl record. The second score, a touchdown run from a yard out by Lytle, came after Rick Upchurch had returned a Dallas kickoff 67 yards, an outright Super Bowl record for distance and for excitement.

Turner said, "Good kickers come only once in a while." This was in the losing locker room afterward. Turner, 36 years old and a hero of the New York Jets' Super Bowl victory nine years ago, put his head down, then looked up and said, "I'm a good kicker." Unfortunately, Turner never had further chances to prove that.

There were no more Denver points after the Lytle touchdown, and Turner's routine conversion kick that made the score 20-10. The Cowboys took firm command, although they felt some pain doing so. Staubach suffered a fractured right index finger and was replaced at one point by Danny White. And Johnson suffered a broken right

United Press International

thumb, although it did not stop him from making his big, fingertip catch of Staubach's pass.

As for Morton, he had an unfortunate day. It was typified in the first quarter when he let go a pass he should never have thrown because there was a posse of Cowboys surrounding him. The Cowboys had him but Morton let go with a short push of the arm anyway. The pass carried only a few feet, into the

lap of Randy Hughes of the Cowboys, who was on his knees.

After that first interception, the Cowboys moved to their first touchdown, and shortly thereafter they had their second interception of a Morton pass, this one by Kyle. It led to an Herrera field goal and a 10-0 lead, a disadvantage the Broncos never were able to overcome.

Dorsett's touchdown was the first score of the game and came on a three-yard run five plays after the interception. Dallas kicked two field goals and led at the half, 13-0. In the second half, Dallas scored twice on passes and won, 27-10.

January 16, 1978

Steelers Conquer Cowboys, 35-31, in Super Bowl

By WILLIAM N. WALLACE

Special to The New York Times

MIAMI, Jan. 21 — Finally, a Super Bowl.

The 13th such professional football championship produced a game worthy of superlatives. The Pittsburgh Steel-

ers defeated the Dallas Cowboys, 35-31, today to become the first team to win three Super Bowls — IX, X and XIII — in the highest scoring, most exciting game of the series.

It was a game with everything a football fan could want. It had the excellent passing of Terry Bradshaw, the Pitts-

burgh quarterback who set Super Bowl records for most passing yardage, 318, and most touchdowns thrown, four. It had the utter frustration of Jackie Smith, the Dallas reserve tight end — a veteran of 16 professional seasons — who dropped a certain touchdown pass in the end zone that would have given

Steelers' Terry Bradshaw, top, left, picked the Dallas secondary apart with four touchdown passes, including 28-yarder to John Stallworth, right, in first quarter, and 7-yarder to Rocky Bleier shortly before first half ended

his team a 21-21 tie in the third period. It had the acrobatic catches of Lynn Swann and John Stallworth. It had the running of the cagey Tony Dorsett and stubborn Franco Harris. It had a lost fumble by the Cowboys on a kickoff. It had a penalty call — Benny Barnes interfering with Swann — that will be debated endlessly.

It was a game for all seasons.

Air Attack Benefits Steelers

The 66 points scored at the Orange Bowl were exactly double the average number of points scored in the previous 12 Super Bowl games. Neither team

could establish a dominating running offense, so they both resorted to passing, an attack that went a lot of places, good places for Pittsburgh.

Rocky Bleier, the Steeler running back who caught Bradshaw's third touchdown pass on the next-to-last play of the first half, summed up the game witnessed by 78,856 fans in the stadium and by uncounted millions who watched on television.

He said: "The Steelers and the Cowboys have played the two most exciting games ever in the Super Bowl. I give credit to Dallas because they didn't quit. They kept our defense out there in

the fourth quarter. They really gave us a scare."

Steelers Score Twice in 19 Seconds

Bleier was referring to the Pittsburgh victory over Dallas here three years ago, also by 4 points, 21-17, and to the Cowboys' late comeback today from an 18-point deficit that the Steelers had accumulated suddenly in the middle of the last period.

After the National Football League's two best teams had battled for three periods they were only 4 points apart, Pittsburgh ahead, 21-17. The Steelers led, 21-14, at the end of the first half in which Bradshaw completed 11 of 18 passes for 253 yards and three touchdowns, two to John Stallworth, the wide-ranging wide receiver.

Stallworth developed a leg cramp and saw almost no action in the second half. He had, however, already done his damage and Bradshaw had already broken Bart Starr's 12-year-old record for most yards passing (250) in a Super Bowl game.

The Cowboys lost the game within 19 seconds midway through that final period as Pittsburgh scored 14 points. Bradshaw, under a big rush by the Dallas defenders, who sacked him four times during the game, threw a soft pass high in the air toward Swann. The Steeler receiver and his defender, Barnes, were far down the field and they became entangled.

Judge Rules for Pittsburgh

"He tripped me," said Swann.

"He pushed me," said Barnes.

Fred Swearingen, the field judge, ruled that Barnes was guilty of pass interference, and the Steelers had a 33-yard penalty gain on the incomplete pass.

"It was a judgment call on a pass play," Swearingen said candidly.

The penalty put the Steelers on the Dallas 23-yard line and from the 22 Harris, otherwise contained throughout the game, blasted to the end zone on a typical Pittsburgh inside trap-block play. That touchdown put the Steelers ahead by 11 points, 28-17.

The following kickoff by Roy Gerela was so short that it went to Randy White, a defensive tackle who plays with his fingers wrapped in tape. White could not scoop up the ball and a wild rush for the fumble resulted. Dennis Winston of the Steelers recovered on the Cowboy 18 and then Bradshaw's passing skill made 6 points more.

On the first down, Bradshaw rifled a pass toward the back of the end zone that seemed too high to be caught. But the graceful Swann jumped, reached, and grabbed the ball for the touchdown, the picture play of the game that was filled with big plays.

The Cowboys, now trailing by 35-17,

Game Statistics

	Cowboys	Steelers
First downs	20	19
Rushing yardage	141	66
Passing yardage	228	318
Passes	17-30	17-30
Interceptions by	1	1
Punts	3-43	5-40
Fumbles lost	2	2
Yards penalized	89	35

INDIVIDUAL LEADERS

RUSHES — Pitt.: Harris, 20 carries for 68 yards; Bleier, 2 for 3; Bradshaw, 2 for minus 5. Dall.: Dorsett, 15 for 96; Newhouse, 8 for 3; D. Pearson, 1 for minus 13; Staubach, 4 for 37; P. Pearson, 1 for 6; Laidlaw, 3 for 12.

PASSES — Pitt.: Bradshaw, 17 completions of 30 attempts for 318 yards. Dall.: Staubach, 17 of 30 for 228.

RECEPTIONS — Pitt.: Stallworth, 3 for 115 yards; Grossman, 3 for 29; Harris, 1 for 22; Swann, 7 for 124; Bleier, 1 for 7. Bell, 2 for 21. Dall.: B. Johnson, 2 for 30; Hill, 2 for 49; P. Pearson, 2 for 15; Dorsett, 5 for 44; DuPree, 2 for 17; D. Pearson, 4 for 73.

Attendance: 78,656.

then mounted two scoring drives of 89 and 52 yards in the last seven minutes, their final touchdown coming with only 22 seconds left to play. From their standpoint they did not lose the game. They ran out of time.

"They played their hearts out," said Tom Landry, the Dallas coach.

But they wound up 4 points short.

Those 4 points were lost when Smith, the 38-year-old second-string tight end, failed to catch a pass from Roger Staubach in the Pittsburgh end zone in the third period. Smith slipped on the damp, yellow-painted grass and the pass, low and wobbly, hit him in the shoulder pads and fell to the turf. Dallas had to settle for a field goal.

Staubach Good, Bradshaw Better

"I was wide open and I missed it," said Smith. That play cost the 45 Cowboy players $405,000 because each of the 45 Steelers received $18,000 for winning the game and each of the Cowboys $9,000.

Staubach said later, "I could have thrown Jackie a lot better pass." The Dallas quarterback, playing in his fifth Super Bowl game, was good. Bradshaw

was better. Staubach completed 17 of 30 pass attempts for 228 yards and three touchdowns, one to Billy Joe DuPree late in the game, and had one intercepted pass as did Bradshaw Staubach was dropped five times by the Steelers and fumbled once. Bradshaw fumbled twice, one bobble resulting in a Dallas touchdown.

That happened in the second period when Mike Hegman, the Cowboy linebacker, stripped the ball from Bradshaw ball and kept going for 37 yards and 6 points.

Bradshaw seemed unphased by his record performance. When told of his record day he said, "Did I do all that?"

Cliff Harris, the Cowboy safetyman who knew full well that the defenders had to hold Bradshaw down, expressed admiration. "We didn't stop him the way we had to," Harris said. "I told Bradshaw he had a hell of a game. He did a great job and deserved the most valuable player award. It's really where he puts the ball for them [Stallworth and Swann]. He throws it so they can catch it."

Most Yards, Most Records

Of the 674 yards gained in the most productive Super Bowl game in the series, 467 were net passing yards (546 yards minus the number of yards lost in quarterback sacks). Harris garnered only 68 rushing yards on 20 attempts and Dorsett ran for 96 on 15 tries.

Bradshaw, who called all the Steeler plays, went to his strength, passes to Stallworth and Swann, for 239 yards and three touchdowns.

The Cowboys, who were forewarned, failed to stop the trio, in a Super Bowl filled with records on offense.

Records broken included most points scored, 66; most touchdowns, 9; most touchdown passes, 7; most yards gained by passing in one game, 467; most yards by passing, Bradshaw, 318; most touchdown passes thrown, Bradshaw, 4.

The next Super Bowl game will be played in 364 days in Pasadena, Calif.

January 22, 1979

CHAPTER 3

FOOTBALL AND SOCIETY

Woody Hayes leads the Ohio State cheering
section at the 1974 Rose Bowl. He was dismissed
five years later when he punched a rival player in
the waning minutes of a game where the
Buckeyes were headed for a loss.

FOOTBALL UNFIT FOR COLLEGE USE

President Eliot Talks of Athletics in His Report on Harvard for Last Year.

In his report upon Harvard University for the academic year 1893-4 President Eliot says that the year has wrought only one favorable change in the conduct of athletic sports. The men who took part in the highly-competitive sports were not this year brought to the principal events in the state bordering on exhaustion in which they were brought to them in former years. He says:

"The evils of the intercollegiate sports as described in the President's report of last year continue without real redress or diminution. In particular, the game of football grows worse and worse as regards foul and violent play and the number and gravity of the injuries which the players suffer. It has become perfectly clear that the game as now played is unfit for college use. The rules of the game are at present such as to cause inevitably a large number of broken bones, sprains, and wrenches, even during trial or practice games played legitimately; and they also permit those who play with reckless violence or with shrewd violations of the rules to gain thereby great advantages.

"What is called the development of the game has steadily increased its risks, until they have become unjustifiable. Naturally the public is losing faith in the sincerity of the professed desire of coaches, Captains, and promoters to reform it.

"It should be distinctly understood, however, that the players themselves have little real responsibility for the evils of the game. They are swayed by a tyrannical public opinion—partly ignorant and partly barbarous—to the formation of which graduates and undergraduates, fathers, mothers, and sisters, leaders of society, and the veriest gamblers and rowdies all contribute.

"The state of mind of the spectators at a hard-fought football match at Springfield, New-York, or Philadelphia cannot but suggest the query how far these assemblages differ at heart from the throngs which enjoy the prize fight, cock fight, or bull fight, or which, in other centuries, delighted in the sports of the Roman arena. Several fatal accidents have happened this year to schoolboys and college students on the football field; and in every strenuous game now played, whether for practice or in an intercollegiate or other competition, there is the ever-present liability of death on the field.

"It is often said that by employing more men to watch the players, with authority to punish instantly infractions of the rules, foul and vicious playing could be stopped. The sufficient answer to this suggestion is that a game which needs to be so watched is not fit for genuine sportsmen. Moreover, experience indicates that it would be hard to find trustworthy watchers.

"Extravagant expenditure for the teams throughout the season and by the spectators at the principal games continues to disgust the advocates of simple and rational manly sports."

Prof. Eliot, however, draws attention to the fact that much wholesome physical exercise is taken and much genuine athletic sport enjoyed in the university. "The athletic sports and exercises which commend themselves to sensible teachers and parents," he says, "are those which can be used moderately and steadily, and which remain available in some measure in mature life."

January 31, 1895

LIKENS FOOTBALL TO WAR.

Walter Camp Compares the Gridiron to Battlefield.

"Football is, in a sense, something like the game of war," says Walter Camp, the Yale gridiron mentor, in a discussion of the pigskin game in The American Boy. "Football is a game in which the opportunity for real genius is almost unlimited.

"The gridiron is the battlefield. The two teams are the opposing armies. The Captain and the coaches and the players are the brains that plan the attack and prepare the defense. Moreover, there is a rapidity approaching similarity between the theory of modern war and the theory of football. In old time war, the privates and humbler officers were there only to obey. In modern warfare, individual initiative is becoming more important—yet obedience and united action are imperative.

"So in football, the humblest player may plan a play that may rout his team's dearest enemy—yet instant obedience and discipline must govern the team's movements. The devising of plays and the perfecting of defenses for other plays—these are the two points that have meant phenomenal success for some coaches and dismal failure for others.

"It must not be thought," continues Mr. Camp, "that the strategy of football is only for the experts. Any boy who starts to study football early enough ought to develop a thoroughly sound judgment of the game. Then, if he has sufficient imagination, he may build up plays, plays of such real character that they leave their mark on football. The field of planning and devising is still practically unlimited."

November 4, 1917

College Sports Tainted by Bounties, Carnegie Fund Finds in Wide Study

Survey of 130 Schools Shows One in Seven Athletes Subsidized— N. Y. U., Fordham, Columbia, Harvard and Princeton Are Accused—'Slush Funds' and 'Recruiting' Indicted.

One athlete out of every seven engaged in intercollegiate competition is "subsidized" to a point bordering upon professionalism, says a report on "American College Athletics," made public yesterday by the Carnegie Foundation for the Advancement of Teaching after a survey which has consumed more than three and a half years and entailed visits to 130 colleges and secondary schools. The granting of bounties to athletes for no other consideration than athletic ability whether it be in the form of "athletic scholarships," "slush funds," supplied by loyal alumni and local tradesmen, or in the shape of sinecure campus jobs, constitutes "the darkest blot upon American college sport," the report asserts. Those engaged in "the nation-wide commerce," of recruiting and subsidizing—alumni, athletic directors and in some cases college administrative officers — are "the Fagins of American sport and higher education," according to the report.

At the very root of the manifold defects of American college athletics, in the view of the authors of the report, are "two fundamental causes": the commercialization of intercollegiate competition on the athletic field and "a negligent attitude toward the educational opportunity for which the American college exists." The responsibility for these conditions and the means of correcting them rest with the trustees and presidents of colleges and universities where abuses exist, the report contends.

"Bulletin 23," as the report is called, represents the first comprehensive study of American college athletic practices and their effect upon the minds, morals and physical well-being of undergraduates. Making its appearance in the midst of the football season, it is certain to become a centre of a controversial storm for, while it purposely disclaims any attempt to rate institutions according to prevalance or absence of abuses, the names of colleges, universities and preparatory schools are used freely as examples of specific practices.

For instance, at New York University, it is said, coaches award most of the limited number of scholarships to athletes with the administrative officers of the university acting as "recording agents." This institution, too, the report asserts, has maintained promising athletes in preparatory schools until they were ready to enter the university and compete on its teams.

At Fordham University, the report asserts, forty scholarships are provided from athletic funds to provide the cost of tuition, board and room for needy athletes who sometimes receive additional assistance from individual alumni. Well organized systems of recruiting were noted at Columbia University, but there, it is pointed out, both athletes and non-athletes were included among the beneficiaries of loans and scholarships on "equal terms."

Only 28 Institutions Cleared.

Out of 112 educational institutions visited and studied specifically for traces of professionalism, only twenty-eight were listed as entirely free of subsidized athletes. Of the so-called "Big Three" of the Eastern universities — Yale, Harvard and Princeton—only Yale was acquitted. Cornell, Chicago, Illinois, Wesleyan, Williams and the United States Military Academy, however, were found free of professionalism, and it is explained that only minor taints, which are being eliminated, kept Harvard and Princeton outside the fold.

Various forms of subsidy exist in the Catholic colleges and universities, the report says, and are "at least as objectionable" as elsewhere. Notre Dame, it is said, does little more than provide jobs to pay for tuition, board and room in return "for very nominal services." In some cases, it is said, "an outright allocation of funds without return except in athletic participation" may be made, as at Georgetown. Athletes in need of assistance at Boston College sometimes are maintained through "arrangements" effected by priests "among their own parishioners, members of the faculty or friends of their college." At Holy Cross, an effort is made to balance awards among athletes and non-athletes, so that no student will "feel that his muscles alone are sufficient to get him through," and at Marquette, no more assistance is rendered to job-hunting athletes than to other students.

In the matter of athletic scholarships, awarded wholly or in part on a basis of an applicant's value to an institution's team, the foundation's report provides much interesting data. It disclosed that seventy-five such scholarships are available at Pennsylvania State College and New York University, while Colgate has twenty-five. Syracuse values its total of such scholarships at $14,000, while Southern California valued its at $40,000.

The presiding officers of Catholic institutions, it is said, are "not so closely in touch" with campus affairs as the heads of other institutions, but recently there has been a change of attitude on their part, until now they are less willing to follow the advice of alumni and athletic directors without examining the facts themselves.

The fact that even twenty-eight institutions were free of paid athletes, the report declared, disproves "the notion that intercollegiate competition is impossible or at least impracticable without subsidies."

In making public the report estimating the number of subsidized college athletes at one out of seven, Dr. Savage explained that this was "a modest, conservative figure." The number of subsidized players on first class varsity football teams throughout the country, probably would run as high as fifty per cent, he said.

Survey Authorized in 1926.

The survey was authorized by the foundation on Jan. 8, 1926, after it had been requested by such bodies as the Association of American Colleges, the Association of Colleges and Secondary Schools of the Southern States, the National Collegiate Athletic Association and many individuals interested in educational problems. Bulletin 23 was compiled by Dr. Howard J. Savage, staff member of the foundation, and Harold W. Bentley, John T. McGovern and Dr. Dean F. Smiley, secretary of the American Student Health Association. A preface to the report was written by Henry S. Pritchett, president of the foundation, who offers a drastic remedy for the conditions disclosed.

Answering the question, "What ought to be done?" the foundation's president says:

"The paid coach, the gate receipts, the special training tables, the costly sweaters and extensive journeys in special Pullman cars, the recruiting from the high school, the demoralizing publicity showered on the players, the devotion of an undue proportion of time to training, the devices for putting a desirable athlete, but a weak scholar, across the hurdles of the examinations—these ought to stop and the intercollege and intramural sports be brought back to a stage in which they can be enjoyed by large numbers of students and where they do not involve an expenditure of time and money wholly at variance with any ideal of honest study.

"The compromises that have to be made to keep such students in the college and to pass them through to a degree give an air of insincerity to the whole university-college régime. We cannot serve every cause—scholarship, science, business, salesmanship, organized athletics—through the university. The need today is to re-examine our educational régime with the determination to attain in greater measure the simplicity, sincerity and thoroughness that is the life blood of a true university in any country at any age."

Report Deplores Trend.

The report itself does not go so far as to advocate the abolition of paid coaches and gate receipts, although it does deplore the trend toward coach-controlled athletics, mammoth stadia and games played in cities far from the college campus for the sake of bigger profits. The report points out that "ringers" and "tramp athletes" virtually have disappeared from intercollegiate sports and points to the growing tendency of undergraduates to regard sports as not the only important phase of college life as an indication of "a general reappreciation of its place in undergraduate affairs."

In conclusion the report sets forth "two prime needs of our college athletics—one particular and one general":

"The first is a change of values in a field that is sodden with the commercial and the material and the vested interests that these forces have created. Commercialism in college athletics must be diminished and college sport must rise to a point where it is esteemed primarily and . . . v for the opportunities it affords to mature youth under responsibility to exercise at once the body and the mind and to foster habits both of bodily health and of those high qualities of character which, until they are revealed in action, we accept on faith.

"The second need is more fundamental. The American college must renew within itself the force that will challenge the best intellectual capabilities of the undergraduate. Happily, this task is now engaging the attention of numerous college officers and teachers. Better still, the fact is becoming recognized that the granting of opportunity for the fulfillment of intellectual promise need not impair the socializing qualities of college sport. It is not necessary to 'include athletics in the curriculum' of the undergraduate or to legislate out of them their life and spirit in order to extract what educational values they promise in terms of courage, independent thinking, cooperation, initiative, habits of bodily activity and, above all, honesty in dealings between man and man. Whichever conception of the function of the American college, intellectual or socializing agency, be adopted, let only the chosen ideal be followed with sincerity and clear vision, and in the course of years our college sport will largely take care of itself."

In only two instances did the foundation's investigators encounter anything but "full cooperation." At Oglethorpe University permission was refused field representatives to examine books and records or interview members of the faculty or student body. At the University of Georgia "promises of one officer to send complete data and materials as requested" were not fulfilled. Elsewhere, the foundation's investigators reported every assistance was afforded, even to opening the files of correspondence with schoolboys seeking subsidies. Many of these letters, with the names of individuals and institutions disguised, are printed in an appendix to the 311-page report, which deals with every phase of the problem from the competition among rival institutions for matriculates to the influence of publicity and the daily press upon college sports.

Conclusions Reached in Study.

Chief among the conclusions reached as a result of the survey are the following:

That what is needed to correct the defects is not "more law but a more genuine regard for existing law," for no matter how lofty the ideals of eligibility, amateur standing and standards of scholarship set forth in conference and association agreements the tendency in most cases is to observe the letter, but not the spirit of the rules.

That in Canada, the English influence of the sportsman's code of "playing the game" has worked against the encroachments of professionalism through evasions of conference rules, while "in the United States all too few influences have hitherto been strongly exerted."

That with the spread of commercialism in intercollegiate sports, the needs of the many for athletic training have been sacrificed for the exaltation of a few members of a team, many of whom are subsidized.

That methods of training often are unscientific and equipment unhygenic to the point where actual harm results to participants in college and school athletics.

Schoolboys "Shop Around."

That the practice of recruiting has induced schoolboys to "shop around," offering their services on the football field, baseball diamond, basketball court and track to "the highest bidder."

That gross revenues from gate receipts totaling $1,119,000, such as were reported at Yale University, result in extravagances in the purchase of equipment and the hiring of paid personnel which are harmful to students and college sports as well.

That of the thousands of instances of recruiting and subsidizing reported, alumni were responsible for 30 per cent, college administrators for 8 per cent and athletic officers in 50 per cent, and that "correspondence" leads all other methods of establishing contacts with promising athletes.

That only from 18 to 25 per cent of the students in the institutions considered in the survey engage in intercollegiate athletics, although the number participating in intramural athletics runs between 50 and 63 per cent.

Lowering of Standards.

That the making of special concessions to athletes almost always is followed by a lowering of academic standards so that members of teams can keep up in their marks and remain eligible to play despite the hours they are required to spend under the tutelage of coaches.

That coaches, who sometimes receive larger salaries than deans, seldom are "consistently, actively and practically concerned with the sportsmanship of their athletes" and often are active in recruiting promising material for future teams.

That the coach has come to play so large and important a part in directing the moves of his charges in competition that the player has "opportunity to exhibit little more initiative than a chessman."

That newspapers should have "an enlightened" sports news policy by drawing a sharp distinction between amateur and professional sport and in leading public opinion "to esteem the true value of the amateur status," and ceasing to view "with a kind of cynical admiration evasion or open defiance of the amateur convention."

Recruiting Is Defined.

The chapter dealing with "The Recruiting and Subsidizing of Athletes" probably will provoke the bulk of comment. Recruiting is defined as "the solicitation of school athletes with a view to inducing them to attend a college or university." In its manifestations it may range "from rare an daccasional contacts" made or directed by an individual in the athletic association, as at Chicago University, University of Colorado, Cornell and Washington State College, to "an intensively organized, sometimes subtle system that may utilize or coordinate numbers of agents on or off the campus." This latter system, "which gives to recruiting its most insidious form," is typical of the methods in use at Michigan, Northwestern, Oglethorpe, Southern California and Wisconsin, says the report.

Soliciting and bidding for athletes is "especially keen," the report asserts, "in the Midwest and South and on the Pacific Coast," while in the Rocky Mountain Conference "the practice, although not general, is spreading." It is "less strenuous in the Southwest, and with one or two exceptions in New England," than it is in the other Eastern and Middle Atlantic States.

Several institutions, the report says, have not yielded to the temptation to obtain a winning team by recruiting methods. These institutions include Bowdoin, Lehigh, Massachusetts Agricultural, Middlebury, Trinity, Tufts, Tulane, College of Wooster, Emory, Reed and Massachusetts Institute of Technology. Occasional instances of acts of individuals officially connected with Amherst, Chicago, University of Colorado, Cornell, Oberlin and Vanderbilt were not considered sufficient to place those institutions in the category of colleges where recruiting is an established practice.

According to the report, recruiting activities are chiefly under the direction of the departments of athletics at Alabama, California, Columbia, Denver, Drake, Michigan, Montana State College, New York University, Ohio Wesleyan, Oregon Agricultural, Pennsylvania, Rutgers, Southern California, Vermont, Washington, Washington and Jefferson, Washington State College and Wisconsin. The correspondence to or about promising schoolboy athletes vary "from the most innocuous and casual to the most purposive and systematized," the report says.

At most small colleges and at California, New York University and the University of Pennsylvania the head football coach acts as director of athletics and can "set the policy respecting the treatment of correspondence."

How Rules Are Evaded.

In view of the universal expressions of disapproval by both athletic and academic officers concerning the commercializing attitude of the "shopping athlete," says the report, "it is astonishing not to find in replies to inquiries a similarly universal effort to correct this attitude." Instead, the answers sometimes are "so laudatory or solicitous" that the schoolboy who values the answer "in dollars and cents" swells with self-importance and "thinks not at all of his offense against amateurism in offering his athletic skill at a price." An example of how conference rules against recruiting are skirted is provided in the report by a sample letter from an athletic director to a promising schoolboy athlete, pointing out that rules forbid the director's making overtures, but adding "the lid is off if any one makes inquiry."

But athletic directors, coaches and graduate managers are not the only recruiting agents. Alumni secretaries at Drake, Georgia School of Technology, Michigan, Northwestern, Oregon Agricultural, Southern California, Vermont and Washington and Jefferson have become involved in recruiting, says the report. Alumni dinners "in honor of victorious teams," to which preparatory school seniors are invited, have been found valuable aids to recruiting at Brown, Dartmouth and Rutgers, the report asserts. Fraternity entertainments for prospects and secondary school athletic contests in college stadia often provide the means for establishing contact between likely looking candidates for varsity teams and athletic officers of the higher institutions.

Definition of Subsidy.

The report defines a subsidy as "any assistance, favor, gift, award, scholarship or concession, direct or indirect, which advantages an athlete because of his athletic ability or reputation and which sets him apart from his fellows in the undergraduate body." Prevalent as they are, these subsidies can be controlled by the university authorities unless the solicitation, the procuring of funds and the actual award are entirely under the supervision of agencies outside the jurisdiction of the college authorities—a condition which exists where tradesmen more interested in booming their town and boosting their own sales volume than in academic standards take a hand in the granting of bounties. Rare as such cases are, they have been reported at Arizona, University of Colorado, Ohio State and Wyoming, and in one instance grew "out of impatience on the part of business men with the meager encouragement given to athletes at the local institution."

Subsidizing was found to exist at 81 of 112 colleges and universities subjected to scrutiny. At only twenty of these institutions was a single agency responsible for the practice. The institution was the sole dispenser of subsidies in one instance, the alumni alone in one and the athletic association alone in one. At fifty institutions, or 62 per cent of the whole number, the athletic department or some member of the staff was a party to the arrangement.

Following is a list of the only institutions studied where no evidence of subsidizing was found:

Blates	Reed
Bowdoin	Rochester
Carleton	University of
Chicago	Saskatchewan
Cornell University	Toronto
Dalhousie	Trinity
Emory	Tufts
Illinois	Tulane
Laval	United States Military
Marquette	Academy
Massachusetts	University of Virginia
Agricultural College	Wesleyan
Massachusetts Institute of Technology	Williams
	College of Wooster
Ottawa	Yale
Queen's	

"In this list," the report declares, "stand colleges and universities of all sizes, sections of the continent, conferences and unions. At some the temptations to subsidize are less strong than at others. At some there has been subsidizing in the past. Of any one it is impossible to say that there will be no subsidizing in the future. Possibly also at the time of the field visit subsidizing existed without being discovered, but in our inquiry an apparent absence of subsidizing inevitably occasioned the closest scrutiny. Whatever may be the rights and wrongs of athletic subsidies, the conditions encountered at this group of institutions, especially at those enjoying keen intercollegiate competition, should encourage those who feel that subsidies ought to be eliminated from American college athletics."

Four Ways of Financing.

College athletes are subsidized through four main instrumentalities, jobs and work of various kinds, loans, scholarships and miscellaneous assistance, the report explains.

In the matter of jobs, the report goes on, there is a vast difference between honest work for which fair wages are received and the "sinecures" often reserved for athletes and paid out of all proportion to the value of services rendered as a means of dodging conference rules, which proscribe "financial assistance."

That such special privilege is entirely unnecessary, the report asserts, is demonstrated at colleges where applicants for jobs are referred to the university employment office and do not obtain employment through special arrangements with the athletic department. Among the institutions named as exemplifying this are Beloit, Stanford, Bowdoin, Cornell, Tulane, Brigham Young, Columbia and Yale.

At a large number of institutions the responsibility for finding jobs devolves upon the person or agency which induced the work-seeking athlete to matriculate. In this category are Brown, Alabama, Amherst, Chicago, Arizona, Colgate, Columbia, Dartmouth, Denver, Drake, Georgia School of Technology, Idaho, Michigan, Missouri in part; Montana State College, Northwestern, in part; Oglethorpe, Oklahoma, Oregon Agricultural, Purdue, Rutgers, Queens, South Dakota, Southern Methodist, Tennessee, Utah, Vermont, Washington State College, University of Washington and Wisconsin.

Coach Gives Out Jobs.

Sometimes, as at Arizona, Chicago, Missouri and Utah, the coach apportions the paid tasks of caring for athletic equipment among the more promising members of his squad. Sometimes, as at Idaho, Oklahoma, Oregon Agricultural and South Dakota, athletes have almost "a complete monopoly" of the more lucrative campus jobs. The system that left Harvard out of the list of subsidy-free institutions is the practice of allotting concessions at athletic contests exclusively to athletes, a practice which the foundation has been assured will be corrected when conditions permit.

At Brown, Denver, Northwestern, Purdue and Wisconsin, says the report, "a more specialized development" is found. There a member of the athletic staff or some other individual has had little to do but recruit and subsidize athletes. Freshman coaches are employed similarly in off seasons at Alabama, Colgate, Dartmouth and to some extent at Columbia.

Remuneration is based sometimes as much upon athletes' needs as upon the value of their services and it is not uncommon for them to shirk their tasks, or to leave them for substitutes to fill, when the jobholder is responsible to the athletic department, although under other conditions his work may be satisfactory.

Jobs off the campus, where the athlete is compelled to "give services commensurate with his wages," the report says, may not be considered as subsidies except when such employment is obtained through "an organized attempt, directed, perhaps, by a paid official, to provide and assign" such work.

Loans to Athletes.

Pointing out that "little good flows from accustoming any young man to slack at his work," and declaring that the "self-respecting American undergraduate does not solicit charity," the report takes up the subject of "loans," which reflect "a conscientious attempt to compromise between athletic scholarships or cash payments, on the one hand, and the withholding of all financial assistance to athletes on the other."

Individuals, alumni and business men friendly to the institution, luncheon clubs and other organizations, have been willing to advance funds to needy athletes. Students at Southern Methodist, Texas, Drake, Georgia School of Technology, Ohio Wesleyan, Vermont and Baylor have found it convenient to avail themselves of this form of subsidy, although the practice is dropping off, according to the report, which adds:

"Unfortunately, it appears that the notes of athletes are collectible in comparatively few instances, even when the fund is administered through a local bank in order to create a sense of responsibility on the part of athlete borrowers. The fact is that loans from funds provided by groups of persons and controlled or administered by athletic organizations or departments are practically the equivalent of gifts, and borrowers tend to regard them as subsidies, feel little responsibility for repayment and appear not to fear prosecution for default."

Requirements on Scholarships.

In connection with the large numbers of "athletic scholarships" at many institutions, the report makes this interesting observation:

"No single factor has contributed more directly to the use of athletic scholarships in American colleges than the second qualification set by the will of Cecil Rhodes for recipients of the Oxford scholarships that bear his name. Certain American institutions—Dartmouth, Rutgers and Swarthmore, for examples—award scholarships upon what is termed an all-around basis, including, besides scholastic excellence, qualities of 'leadership,' interest in undergraduate activities, usually physical vigor, and, perhaps, value to the student body. Obviously all of these qualifications except the first point in the direction of athletic ability. When, in awards, intellectual achievement is underrated, and qualities of character and 'leadership,' thereby are given undue emphasis, an 'all-around scholarship' is in reality granted on the basis of athletic skill and attainment. Examination of academic records of such scholarship holders usually bears out this view."

In addition to regular athletic scholarships, the report explains, Columbia, Hobart, the undergraduate division of the New York University School of Commerce, Southern California, Southern Methodist, Stanford and Ursinus have at their disposal certain special funds which are awarded as scholarships, usually to athletes.

In this connection the report says:

"Most of the personal recommendations appear to come from the alumni, coaches and recruiting agents who are interested in the athletic success of the institution. Indeed, for the actual appointments, or the nominations that are their practical equivalents, made by alumni or coaches, the officers of a university may merely act as recording agents (New York University, Southern California, Stanford, Catholic institutions). Even when the actual appointments are made by the duly constituted scholarship agencies, the recommendations of recruiters may be influential (Columbia)."

Other Methods of Awards.

The report continues:

"Only one step removed from this practice is the procedure by which a regular committee on scholarships appoints incumbents after the receipt of recommendations from persons intimately acquainted with candidates (Southern Methodist; proposed method at Stanford; Ursinus). A dean may permit a coach to dispose of a number of scholarships upon official approval of the dean (New York University), or the alumni who provide the necessary funds may merely inform university officers that certain candidates are to receive credit for specified sums of money (Stanford). Even though appointments be nominally annual, is is usually understood that, once made, they will continue while the holder remains in residence.

"The sources and value and the numbers of such special scholarships vary greatly among the institutions that make use of them. The principal sources are two: university funds allocated by presidents or trustees to provide a certain number of scholarships or amount of assistance (Drake, neither specified—converted into loans; New York University, seventy-five scholarships; Southern Methodist, twenty scholarships; Southern California, $40,000; Ursinus, twenty scholarships; certain Catholic institutions); or alumni contributions (Stanford, approximately fifty scholarships). If funds or numbers of scholarships available are limited, most of the awards usually go to football players (New York University, Southern Methodist, Ursinus) but keenness of interest in other sports may bring a wider distribution (Columbia, Stanford). In no instance are awards of special scholarships confined exclusively to athletes. The popularity of this method of assistance probably flows from the convictions, first, that it is fairer than other methods to both athletes and non-athletes; second, that under it the athletic situation is more nearly controlled and the interests involved are better subserved, possibly on a basis of compromise; and, third, that, if athletics are to be subsidized at all, the institution itself should dispense the subsidies.

Funds of Another Type.

"Another type of scholarships is hardly distinguishable from that just described. It includes those honor awards which, named from the donor, source, or purpose of the fund that provides them, almost invariably are bestowed upon athletes and are currently regarded by many as athletic scholarships (Brown, one scholarship; Des Moines, fifteen scholarships; University of Georgia, forty scholarships; Lehigh, one scholarship; Montana, five scholarships; Princeton, eight scholarships; Southern California, two scholarships). If a traditional practice of awarding such scholarships to athletes exists, it may be in part due to the influence of alumni in urging the appointment of athletes whom they have encouraged to attend the university (Princeton). Again, the scholarship funds may have been specially earmarked by their donors for athletes (Brown, Lehigh, Montana, Southern California); or a university may remit all or part of the tuition for an unspecified number of athletes as a tapering-off of a more extensive system (Des Moines); or a special fund may have been created by alumni (Georgia School of Technology, University of Georgia) in the hope of ultimately eliminating subsidies (Universty of Georgia). Although such controlled and duly recorded awards may represent a step in advance of extensive and indiscriminate subsidizing by outside agencies, the policy is not to be compared for firmness and courage with the action of the University of California in advocating a conference rule to deprive itself of a gift that would have established what would have proved to be an athletic scholarship.

"We turn now to those forms of aid which are frankly and unequivocally termed athletic scholarships. The amounts or numbers of such awards available and the bases of award at the time of each field visit varied considerably (Blue Ridge, twelve; Colgate, twenty-five; Geneva, thirty-five; Georgetown, unspecified; Gettysburg, thirty; Fordham, forty; Lebanon Valley, sixteen; Muhlenberg, unspecified; Pennsylvania State College, seventy-five; Syracuse, $14,000; West Virginia Wesleyan, twenty; Ursinus, sixteen).

"The benefit is rarely paid in cash. The partial or complete remission of tuition through athletic scholarships generally involves and often takes place in the offices of the institution, which devise methods of award to suit local conditions and the needs of athletes. Values of athletic scholarships range from part or full tuition at the lower end of the scale (Colgate), to allotments graduated in amount according to the number of teams for which the recipient is selected (Blue Ridge). In the first instance, athletic scholarships represent a step away from even graver forms of subsidizing; in the second, a step toward them."

Miscellaneous Methods.

Discussing forms of subsidy other than those provided by scholarships, the report continues:

"The practice of 'caring for' a more or less definite number of athletes, ranging from twenty-five to fifty (Bucknell, Gettysburg, Muhlenberg, Oglethorpe, Pennsylvania State, Pittsburgh, West Virginia Wesleyan), is a somewhat less formal matter than the award of athletic scholarships. Its excuse is the competitive bids of rivals, and its limit is usually 'all college expenses.' Sometimes (Boston College, Holy Cross, Notre Dame) no definite promises are made; the athlete is merely assured that he will be 'cared for.' Neither procedure necessarily entails cash payments, although these may be present. The sources of the necessary funds or credits may include, singly or in combination, subscriptions from alumni as individuals or as groups and from local merchants, appropriations from the athletic treasury and the remitting of tuition by the institution. Although the probable success of a candidate at athletics is usually a prerequisite to such arrangements, a further obligation of some sort is occasionally imposed: the performing of odd tasks about the campus, or recruiting—indeed, an athlete successful at recruiting may even be valued at his full college expenses without any other requirement than attendance at the university (Oglethorpe). As is to be expected under a system that links the institution, through the bestowal of athletic scholarships, with other agencies and sources of provision, recommendations and appointments to subsidies are made by persons intimately acquainted with the institution's athletic affairs: coaches, graduate managers, athletic directors, the president's assistant (Gettysburg), or the president himself (Oglethorpe)."

The report asserted the "element of barter entered more frequently into the recruiting and maintenance of athletes" than in the awarding of scholarships. In such cases alumni subsidies are dispensed from "a slush fund" or "black box fund," and thus, says the report, a close supervision may be maintained.

Amounts of Funds Vary.

Continuing, the report declares: "The amounts available in slush funds vary (Carnegie Institute of Technology, $13,000; Centre, $600; Grove City, $8,000; Lafayette, $3,000) with the interest of contributors; but the number of beneficiaries varies less with the size of each fund than with the cost of living at the institutions (Carnegie Institute of Technology, thirty-two; Centre, eleven; Dickinson, twelve; Grove City, thirty-five; Lafayette, twelve; Lebanon Valley, sixteen; Northwestern, sixteen; Western Maryland, six).

"The intensity of the practice depends upon conditions in the section or Conference in which the college is situated and which may license, retard or even stop the practice. Ordinarily, an interview between the recruiter—be he coach or agent—and the prospect settles the prospect's approximate need, which in at least one instance was supplemented on instructions from the recruiter's 'superiors' to 'match anything up to tuition, board and room.' The bargaining that results sometimes taxes the wits of both parties; one subsidizer personally and closely examined every candidate for assistance to ascertain his precise needs. Cooperation from fraternities in providing food and lodging and from the athletic organization in supplying jobs, is, of course, very helpful. At no institution are all of the athletes thus subsidized, and at none also is it customary to grant subsidies in excess of the cost of tuition, food, lodging, books, supplies and incidental fees.

"In an extreme case of subsidizing alumni and business men made contributions ranging from $10 to nearly $1,000 annually to a fund aggregating from $25,000 to $50,000 a year. From this the college expenses of all football players were paid and additional sums, termed 'pay checks,' were disbursed to leading performers (Washington and Jefferson). Later the practice was modified to provide only tuitions, board, room and fees, without cash payments. The essentials of the practice may be the same, even though the fund be small (Franklin and Marshall).

"In at least three instances the practices at the time of the field visits were explained as a tapering-off of more extensive operations (Centre, Lafayette, Northwestern)."

When food is provided without charge at the training table to athletes, the training table itself becomes a subsidy, the report asserts, pointing to Colgate, Columbia and Pennsylvania as colleges where the practice is countenanced. Fraternities sometimes lend a hand in providing free board and lodging to athletes at Franklin and Marshall, New York University, Penn State and Ohio Wesleyan. The value of complimentary tickets to football games is exemplified, the report points out, by one varsity man on the Pacific Coast who sold his allotment at a profit of about $100 each for various major games of the season.

Games of bodily contact such as football, basketball, hockey and lacrosse, in which the greatest numbers of fractures and sprains are suffered, are worthless to college men after graduation, according to the report, and yet since they are the chief box-office attractions they receive more emphasis than sports which would provide amusement through life.

College athletics should develop inherent traits of courage, perseverance, honesty and a sense of fair play, but instead, as intercollegiate sports are conducted today, they fail in that function because of the deceit and chicanery that surrounds them, the report asserts.

From the standpoint of the physical well-being of participants, the observations of the foundation's investigators are interesting. The result of a survey of 43,923 participants in intercollegiate and intramural athletic contests is given in the following table:

Type of Injury or Accident.	Total	Intercollegiate Athletics.	Intramural Athletics.
Chronic sprains disabling for more than three weeks	523	405	118
Dislocations	318	237	81
Concussions	240	205	35
Fractures	188	153	35
Collapse	30	24	6
Internal injuries	21	21	0
	1,320	1,045	275

Another table showed that football maintained its reputation as the "most hazardous of college games," with boxing, lacrosse and soccer following in order. Out of 5,400 students engaged in football games it was found that 649 sustained "serious injuries" in a year and of this number 525 were hurt in intercollegiate competition.

Following are the colleges and secondary schools visited by field agents of the foundation:

New England States.

Amherst College
Bates College
Boston College
Bowdoin College
Brown University
Dartmouth College
Deerfield Academy
Harvard University
Holy Cross College
Groton School
Mass. Agricultural
M. I. T.
Saint Mark's School
Middlebury College
Middlesex School
Phillips Academy
Trinity College
Tufts College
Vermont
Wesleyan University
Williams College
Yale University
Y. M. C. A. College

Mid-Atlantic States.

Allegheny College
Bellefonte Academy
Bucknell University
Carnegie Institute
Colgate University
Columbia Universtiy
Cornell University
De Witt Clinton H. S.
Dickinson College
Erasmus Hall H. S.
Fordham Universtiy
Franklin and Marshall
Geneva College
Gettysburg College
Groton Public H. S.
Grove City College
Hamilton College
Hobart College
Ithaca Public H. S.
Kiskiminetas Springs School
Lafayette College
Lawrenceville School
Lebanon Valley Col
Lehigh University
Manual Training H.
Morris High School
Muhlenberg College
New Utrecht H. S.
New York Universi
Pennsylvania
Pennsylvania State
Univ. of Pittsburgh
Princeton University
Univ. of Rochester
Rutgers University
Susquehanna University
Syracuse University
U. S. Military Acad
Ursinus College
Washington and Jefferson

South Atlantic States.

Blue Ridge College
Emory University
University of Georgia
Georgia Technology
Georgetown Univ.
North Carolina
Oglethorpe Univ.
Univ. of Virginia
West Virginia Univ
W. Va. Wesleyan
Western Maryland

East North Central States.

Ann Arbor Public H. S.
Beloit College
Univ. of Chicago
Univ. of Illinois
Marquette University
Univ. of Michigan
Northwestern Univ.
Notre Dame
Oberlin College
Ohio State Univ.
Ohio Wesleyan
Purdue University
Wisconsin
College of Wooster

West North Central States.

Carleton College
Coe College
Des Moines University
Drake University
Haskell University
University of Iowa
Minnesota
Missouri
South Dakota

East South Central States.

University of Alabama
Centre College
University of Tennessee
Vanderbilt University

West South Central States.

Baylor University
University of Oklahoma
Southern Methodist
University of Texas
Tulane University

Rocky Mountain States.

University of Arizona
Brigham Young University
University of Colorado
University of Denver
University of Idaho
Montana State College
University of Utah
University of Wyoming

Pacific States

University of California
Oregon State Agricultural
Reed College
Southern California
Stanford
University of Washington
Washington State College
Los Angeles H. S.
San Bernardino H. S.

Dominion of Canada.

Dalhousie University
Laval University
McGill University
University of Ottawa
Queen's University
Saskatchewan
University of Toronto

Field visits usually occupied three or four days, the report explained, adding that these were supplemented by correspondence. Copies of the report may be had without charge by writing to the foundation at 522 Fifth Avenue.

HAWKES'S VIEW OF REPORT.

No Discrimination for Athletes, Columbia Dean Asserts.

Dean Herbert E. Hawkes of Columbia, chairman of the scholarship committee, commenting yesterday on the report of the Carnegie Foundation for the Advancement of Teaching, said:

"Charges that Columbia College scholarships are awarded primarily for proficiency in football are absurd. As chairman of the scholarship committee every scholarship passes over my desk, and I know that there is no discrimination in favor of athletes. The trouble with such charges of general corruption is that the men who make them usually lean to the other extreme and really discriminate against athletes. And that we will never do. It is possible to stand so straight as to lean over backwards and bump your head.

"The Columbia Club scholarships are awarded on the recommendation of a committee which has no connection with the alumni or the athletic office. A professional athlete would never pass this board. Of the twelve freshmen now holding club scholarships, only three, as far as I know, are playing football. Only four first-stringers on the varsity football team are holding scholarships—Scott, Tys, Campbell and Bleeker.

"The records and documents here are open for any properly authorized person to examine. I welcome such an examination."

N.Y.U. OFFICIALS SILENT

Decline to Comment Until They Have Studied Carnegie Report

No official comment on the report of the Carnegie Foundation for the Advancement of Teaching was made yesterday at New York University, and officials of the university refused to make any individual statements until they had an opportunity to study the report.

John F. (Chick) Meehan, head football coach; Albert B. Nixon, graduate manager, and Giles L. Courtney, chairman of the Board of Athletic Control, had not seen the report late last night, but said that a meeting was to be held today and that the report n o doubt would be discussed.

Harold O. Voorhis, secretary of the univrsity, said that a special committee of three, headed by Dean John B. Munn, was named some time ago to handle the report when it became public and their statement would reflect the university's attitude.

HARVARD ACTED ON ABUSE

Field Concessions Now Under Employment Office, says Bingham

Special to The New York Times

CAMBRIDGE, Mass. Oct. 23—Asked to comment on the report of the Carnegie Foundation. William J. Bingham, director of athletics at Harvard, made the following statement today:

"When I became director of athletics the concessions at Soldiers' Field were run by one undergraduate. To be certain that abuses would not arise the concessions were placed under the supervision of the assistant director of athletics, and in 1928 102 students received remuneration, about half of who were non-athletes. The amounts of money which each received were small. When it was pointed out to us that this system was open to possible abuse we turned over all the concessions at Soldiers' Field to the university employment office.

YOST DENIES CHARGES

University of Michigan Coach Says "Recruiting" Accusation Is False.

Special to The New York Times

ANN ARBOR, Mich., Oct. 23—An assertion in the Carnegie Foundation's report that the University of Michigan uses an "intensely organized, sometimes subtle, system" in recruiting athletes was vigorously denied tonight by Fielding H. Yost, athletic director, and by others familiar with alumni activities.

"I know of no such intensely organized system of agents, operating on or off the campus, to recruit athletes for the University of Michigan," said Mr. Yost. "If it does exist, I would like information regarding it."

Wilfred B. Shaw, director of alumni relations, said, that "certainly the fact that a boy has athletic ability should not prevent his forming legitimate contacts with representatives of the university."

SILENCE AT PENNSYLVANIA

Officials Appear Shocked at Parts of Carnegie Report

Special to The New York Times.

PHILADELPHIA, Oct. 23.—No statements were forthcoming from officials of the University of Pennsylvania tonight on the report of the Carnegie Foundation for the Advancement of Teaching. Officials of the university appeared shocked when they read portions of the report aimed at their institution.

On behalf of Provost Josiah H. Penniman, it was said he would not make any comment until he had time to make an adequate study of the report if then.

Lou Young, head coach of the varsity football team, merely smiled as sections of the report were shown to him. He nodded his head as he thumbed over the pages of the report and said. "That's the extent of my talking."

The attitude of Pennsylvania may be defined with the return of Sidney Emlen Hutchinson, chairman of the council on athletics. Mr. Hutchinson, also chairman of the football committee has been abroad since late in August, but is expected to sail for home in a few days.

H. Jamison Swartz, acting graduate manager, and James Gorman, treasurer of the council on athletics, had nothing to say about the Carnegie report.

STANFORD MEN SILENT

Athletic Officials Not Ready to Discuss Carnegie Report.

Special to The New York Times.

SAN FRANCISCO, Oct. 23—Both Bob Masters graduate manager, and Dr. Thomas Story, head of the department of physical education at Stanford University declined to-night to comment on the report.

"Until such time as I have had opportunity to digest the report of the Carnegie Foundation," said Dr. Story. "I do not believe it would be wise for me to enter into this discussion. I am sure the report will offer much interesting reading, and doubtless, when the opportunity is ripe, there will be an official statement from the Stanford officials."

COLLEGE ADMITS CHARGE

Lebanon Valley President Says It is Forced to Give Scholarships.

ANNVILLE, Pa., Oct. 23. (AP).—Dr. G.D. Gossard, president of Lebanon Valley College, said tonight that "athletic scholarships" are given at that institution, as alleged in the Carnegie Foundation report.

"What is said is true," Dr. Gossard asserted. "Practically all colleges do it. We are compelled to. Here we give a certain number of scholarships, fifteen in all, to athletes, in addition to the other college scholarships. They are given to men who are good athletes as well as good students. These scholarships are valued at $200 a year and they are continued if the recipient proves worthy in athletics and scholarship."

CHARGES BREAKING OF FAITH.

Bucknell Official Says He Was Told Names Would Not Be Revealed

LEWISBURG, Pa., Oct. 23 (AP) Professor B.W. Griffith, graduate manager of athletics at Bucknell University, declared tonight that the Carnegie Foundation had "broken faith" with American colleges and universities in mentioning "specific names" in its report on the subsidizing of athletes.

Professor Griffith made it clear that his statement was personal and should not be construed as an official view of the college.

"The Carnegie people assured us," he said, "that specific names would not be mentioned. We gave them our help on that basis. They said they wanted the data for a general study. Now they have broken faith.

"So far as I know, we are doing about the same thing as other colleges and universities. Our means, perhaps, would indicate that we do less."

Professor Griffith explained that athletes were helped at Bucknell as their needs require, sometimes by the payment of tuition, sometimes by the payment of board and room. Such men are not taken, however, solely for their athletic ability, he asserted. They must enter the institution without scholastic conditions.

"We have to do this," he added, "to meet competition. We consider that we restrain this practice sufficiently to make this aid a legitimate performance."

BELIEVES LEHIGH IS "CLEAN."

Dean McConn Says, However, Alumni May Subsidize Athletes.

BETHLEHEM, Pa., Oct. 23 (P).—Athletic scholarships were abolished at Lehigh University three years ago, Dr. C. M. McConn, dean of the university, declared tonight in commenting on the Carnegie Foundation report.

"So far as I know," Dr. McConn said, "there is nothing of that sort here. I will say, however, that what a man of my position doesn't know about such things may be everything.

"But three years ago we abolished all athletic scholarships. No athletic prowess is taken into consideration when scholarships are awarded. I know this because these matters are handled by a faculty committee of which I am a member.

"What some alumnus or group of alumni may offer some student to attend Lehigh is beyond our knowledge. We have no way of knowing these things and probably we could not stop it if we did know of it.

"Aside from the possibility of that sort of thing, I believe Lehigh is clean."

NO COMMENT AT DARTMOUTH.

Significance of Survey Doubted—Hopkins Cites Boston Speech in 1926

Special to The New York Times.

HANOVER, N. H., Oct. 23.—Harry R. Heneage, supervisor of Dartmouth athletics, had no comment to make on the classification of Dartmouth among other colleges said to subsidize preparatory schools for future football stars. Mr. Heneage was re-

luctant to attach significance to the survey.

When questioned, President Hopkins of Dartmouth referred to his views as given in his speech before the Boston Alumni Association on Jan. 30, 1926. In that speech he said:

"I pass over as inconsequential at this time the fact that on the basis of statistics carefully compiled it would appear that Dartmouth attracts men of athletic ability in rather less degree from the great schools than do several others of the Eastern colleges. I proceed at once to the assertion that, as a result of the selective process, it might easily be true that we should have an increased number of men of athletic ability. I confess to a hope that this may come to be so."

On the selective process at Dartmouth President Hopkins said, in the same speech: "There is nothing obscure or hidden in regard to its principles. It is not a smoke-screen behind which anything is being done or attempted beyond what we would gladly publish in detail. Given a group of men of scholastic qualifications sufficiently above the average, as evidenced in scholastic work, we prefer the man who has demonstrated in addition to his interest in curriculum, that he has other interests, whether these be in art, in music, in literature, or the participation in school athletics."

DEFENDS BIG TEN POLICIES.

F. L. Griffith Says Carnegie Report Gives an Unfair Picture.

Special to The New York Times.

CHICAGO, Oct. 23—Major John L. Griffith, commissioner of athletics in the Big Ten (actually the big nine since the technical eviction of Iowa) issued tonight an informal statement, without trace of an apologetic note.

"I have not had an opportunity to read the report," he said, "but judging from the excerpts I don't believe the Carnegie investigators have given a fair picture of Big Ten conditions.

"We have nothing to be ashamed of. I think that I am better informed of Big Ten athletic conditions than any investigator for the Carnegie Foundation. And I honestly believe that the Western Intercollegiate Conference universities are cleaner in regard to proselyting and subsidizing athletes than are any

other ten universities any one may name.

"When the Carnegie report relies upon the facts uncovered by an agent in a twenty-four hour visit to a university, it seems to me that it is evident that the report cannot be always fair to the institution."

DR. WARD DENIES CHARGE.

Western Maryland Head Says There Is "No Taint of Professionalism."

WESTMINSTER, Md., Oct. 23 (P).—"There is not a taint of professionalism in any of our sports," Dr. Norman A. Ward, president of Western Maryland College, one of the colleges mentioned as subsidizing athletes in the report of the Carnegie Foundation.

"It would be impossible for the institution to support athletes, simply because it does not have enough money," Dr. Ward declared. "Of course, it could be possible that they received aid from outside sources, but such a condition has never been brought to my attention. I would not stand for anything of the sort."

Western Maryland has one of the few undefeated and untied football teams in the country this season.

REPORT ATTACKED AT BROWN.

Chairman of Athletic Board Calls It Misleading and "Partly False."

Special to The New York Times.

PROVIDENCE, R. I., Oct. 23.—On behalf of Brown University, Norman S. Taber, chairman of the Athletic Council of that institution, attacked tonight the report of the Carnegie Foundation in its references to sports at Brown.

"In part false and in toto so misleading as to make it difficult to believe that the authors could present it as the result of a bona fide survey or that the Carnegie Foundation could allow its name to be attached to it," was Mr. Taber's condemnation of the foundation's indictment of Brown.

To the assertion that Brown had appointed "alumni advisory committees to various branches of athletics," Mr. Taber replied: "That statement is simply and utterly false. Brown has no alumni advisory committee to any branch of athletics."

He charged that Harold W. Bent-

ley, representative of the foundation, had been fully informed of the true conditions when he visited Providence.

"I cannot understand such bungling of a report," Mr. Taber exclaimed.

BLUE RIDGE ENDED FOOTBALL.

College Forced Out of Field by Competition, Says Dr. Bixler.

NEW WINDSOR, Md., Oct. 23 (P).—Dr. E. G. Bixler, president of Blue Ridge College, said tonight the institution had had to cut out football when the competition of other schools made it prohibitive to give away scholarships, as had been the practice. He was replying to the charges of the Carnegie Foundation that athletes were subsidized.

"We have since dropped football, cut out all forms of athletic scholarships," Dr. Bixler said. "Formerly when we heard of a good athlete we tried to get him. We offered only tuition and board and never paid any salaries. We had to cut out football because we had to get in too many extra players for the size of the school."

Denies Athletes Are Subsidized.

LANCASTER, Pa., Oct. 23 (P).—Subsidization of college athletes has been eliminated at Franklin and Marshall College, if such a practice ever existed, Dean Howard R. Omwake declared tonight. "This is our fourth year in the Eastern Collegiate Athletic conference, of which we were a charter member," Dean Omwake said, "and we know of no instances in which the practices outlined in the Carnegie Foundation report are carried on at Franklin and Marshall. Neither is there any private subsidization to my knowledge."

Says Albright Gives Scholarships.

READING, Pa., Oct. 23 (P).—While Albright College was not mentioned in the Carnegie Foundation report as one of the colleges which subsidizes its athletes, Dr. Warren F. Teel tonight said scholarships were awarded to athletes. Dr. Teel said no other help was given to athletes, asserting there was no indication of professionalism in Albright athletics.

October 24, 1929

Army-Notre Dame Football Game of 1947 Will Be Last for Indefinite Period

BREAK IS DECREED IN CLASSIC RIVALRY

Army-Notre Dame Battles on Gridiron to Suspend in '47 After South Bend Game

DE-EMPHASIS IS PURPOSE

By JOHN RENDEL

The Army-Notre Dame football game will not be held after 1947 for an indefinite period and next fall's contest will not be at its traditional location, the Yankee Sta-

dium here, but in South Bend, Ind.

Announcement of the break in a rivalry that has come to transcend almost everything else in the game was made simultaneously yesterday at West Point by Maj. Gen. Maxwell D. Taylor, superintendent of the United States Military Academy, and at South Bend by the Rev. John J. Cavanaugh, C. S. C., president of the university.

The joint statement said:

"Two reasons led to the decision. The first was the conviction of the authorities of both schools that the Army-Notre Dame game had grown to such proportions that it had come to be played under conditions escaping the control of the two colleges, some of which were not conducive to wholesome intercollegiate sport.

"The second reason was the desire of West Point as a national institution to greater flexibility in the scheduling of intersectional op-

ponents throughout the country.

Rivalry Will Continue

"In coming to the decision to interrupt the series, both Army and Notre Dame avow the intention of renewing the traditional rivalry from time to time when resumption will serve the interests of both institutions and of intercollegiate athletics. Out of consideration for the cordial relationships which have always existed between West Point and Notre Dame, the Army team will travel to South Bend in 1947 for the game on Nov. 8."

Although there was no elaboration of this formal statement, it was believed that a factor in this rift in a series that goes back to 1913 was that authorities at both schools were dissatisfied because highly prized tickets got into the hands of speculators. There was concern, also, over the ever-increasing gambling on football games.

From South Bend came a report that the gridiron giants might meet again soon after 1950, ostensibly when the ticket-buying public cooled off a bit and the betting fraternity was not so free with a dollar.

Football schedules for both schools have been completed through 1950, so there can be no resumption of the rivalry until 1951. A South Bend spokesman said that the interruption would have no bearing on the Navy-Notre Dame relationship. He pointed out that Navy and the Irish have contracted to play through 1949 and that a "gentleman's agreement" exists to continue the series after that date. The Navy-Notre Dame contests never have attracted the nationwide attention or hysteria attaching to those in which the Army was involved.

While the statement did not say so, it was accepted in sports circles

END FOOTBALL TIES

Maj. Gen. Maxwell D. Taylor
Associated Press

The Rev. John J. Cavanaugh
The New York Times

that moving the 1947 game to a college campus, was a step in the process of de-emphasizing sports in general and football in particular in the Midwest. The game has been played in the Yankee Stadium for the last fifteen years, always before capacity crowds and always surrounded by considerable hubbub from the "subway alumni" of both institutions.

Letters of Criticism

The zealots who attached themselves to the game had become a source of embarrassment, West Point receiving letters of horrid criticisms for the bad beatings administered to Notre Dame in 1944 and 1945. This was seen as one of the reasons behind the statement that the game had got out of control.

As for tickets, there had been reports for months that officials of both schools were somewhat mys-

tified and considerably upset over the fact that speculators had got hold of tickets in large numbers. This came to a head this season when both teams came up to their game unbeaten and the clash resolved itself into a national championship one. Thousands poured into New York from all parts of the country to see this big game.

The speculators got the tickets despite every precaution to distribute them only to students, school officials, alumni and, as in the case of South Bend residents, friends of the colleges. Speculators advertised openly that they had tickets and a few days before the game were getting as much as $200 for a single one.

While there never has been a hint of gambling scandal attached to the Army-Notre Dame game, it had become the medium for a tremendous amount of betting and here, again, was a sore point with the officials. Bookmakers estimated that last fall's scoreless tie involved the betting of $5,000,000 or more throughout the country.

Favored by Half Point

Under the point system of setting odds, the Irish were installed as half-point favorites for the game. This changed to even-up a few days before the game, probably because of a sprained ankle suffered by Notre Dame's ace quarterback, Johnny Lujack, bringing about a fresh onset of Army money.

It was noted that both General Taylor and Father Cavanaugh were undoubtedly thinking of gambling when they said conditions surrounding the Army-Notre Dame game were not conducive to wholesome intercollegiate sport.

This reading of the evils of gambling and ticket speculation into the statement was general among sports followers last night and a poll of sports writers taken by the Associated Press agreed almost unanimously that the temporary demise of the series was a good thing.

Besides the evils that had grown up around the game, some observers believed that a factor behind the break was that Notre Dame would be "loaded" with football talent for the next several seasons, while the cadets, losing Doc Blanchard and Glenn Davis, might slip considerably.

De-emphasis on Football

Others saw in the decision an aftermath of the Big Nine-Pacific Coast Conference Rose Bowl agreement. The new set-up to be inaugurated with tomorrow's game, was aimed partly to de-emphasize the commercial aspects of big-time football. At the same time, it was seen as a drawing back of Army into the "Ivy League."

Army was regarded as a member of this unofficial conference before the war, but the war-time powerhouses developed at West Point rolled over the rest of the "Ivy" schools and there was none to match them.

Announcement of the interruption had an immediate reaction, indicating that far from losing interest in the game, next season's would be fully as eagerly sought after by fans. Within a few minutes of the statement, the Notre Dame ticket office was deluged with telephone calls for tickets. Robert Cahill, Notre Dame ticket manager, immediately said that tickets for Army's first appearance

at the 56,000-seat Notre Dame Stadium would not go on sale until next summer.

None of the athletic officials at either institution was available for immediate comment. Colonel L. M. (Biff) Jones, graduate manager of athletics at West Point, was "out and not expected back until tomorrow." Father Cavanaugh was expected to make official comment today, while Coach Frank Leahy was in New Orleans for the Sugar Bowl game.

December 31, 1946

Georgia Tech to Play In Sugar Bowl Game

ATLANTA, Dec. 5—The Board of Regents of Georgia's university system turned down today Gov. Marvin Griffin's move to take Georgia Tech out of the Jan. 2 Sugar Bowl game against the University of Pittsburgh.

It banned Georgia teams, however, from participating in any future bowl contest in the South that do not follow the segregation laws and customs of the host state.

The Governor had asked the board to bar Georgia teams from games that involve mixing of the races. Pittsburgh has a Negro on its squad, Bobby Grier, a reserve fullback. Sugar Bowl officials also have permitted the university to sell its tickets on a nonsegregated basis.

The Board of Regents in its decision cleared the way for state-supported Georgia teams to play in games outside the South where segregation is not practiced. The board's "declaration of policy" resolution was approved by a 14-to-1 vote. The University of Georgia, a second major football power in the state, also would be restricted.

In a prepared statement, Governor Griffin said the Regents had decided to permit Tech to play in the Sugar Bowl "due to a prior contract." He complimented the Regents for having "adopted a strong resolution of policy" governing future athletic events.

Griffin Backs Down

At a news conference shortly before the Regents met in special session, Governor Griffin backed down somewhat on his demand of last Friday. At that time he asked for a racial segregation policy that not only would have barred Tech from the Sugar Bowl but also would have prohibited any Georgia state college or university team from playing against Negroes or before unsegregated spectators in any state.

The board announced its action after a session of two and a half hours. When the compromise was reached, newsmen were called in and the resolution was read to them by Regent Charles Bloch of Macon, chairman of the board's education committee.

The Regents' resolution, which

was adopted "after prayerful consideration, thoughtful deliberation and careful study," stated:

"1. This policy is adopted in the sure knowledge it represents the wishes and sentiment of the masses of the people of Georgia, and, in so doing, we commend Gov. Marvin Griffin for his courageous stand in upholding his oath as Governor and for his inspiring leadership in protecting inviolate the sacred institutions of our people. He has kept the faith by placing conscience and principle above all other considerations. We pledge him full support and continuing esteem.

"2. This directive of policy shall apply to all athletic teams of, or affiliated with, units of the university system of Georgia and shall be applicable to all future agreements or contracts for athletic contests of such teams.

"All contests held within the State of Georgia shall be held in conformity with the Constitution, laws, customs, and traditions of the state. No athletic team of, or affiliated with, units of the university system shall be permitted to engage in contest in the State of Georgia with other teams where the races are mixed on such teams or where segregation is not required among spectators at such events nor shall any facility of the university system of Georgia be used where the foregoing provisions are not observed.

"Athletic teams of, or affiliated with, units of the university system of Georgia, in all contests entered into in the future in which they participate outside the state shall respect the laws, customs and traditions of the host state. No contract or agreement shall be entered into for an athletic contest in any state where the circumstances under which it is to be fulfilled are repugnant to the laws, customs and traditions of the host state."

Regent Bloch told newsmen that the last section applied specifically to the Sugar Bowl in New Orleans. No team of the university system, he said, could take part in a nonsegregated game there after Jan. 2, because Louisiana laws and customs call for segregation.

The only opposition to the resolution came from Regent David Rice of Atlanta. Earlier he had called the Governor's request "asinine and ridiculous."

The Regents, in another resolution, also directed Dr. Blake R. Van Leer, president of Georgia Tech, to attempt to fix responsibility for the demonstrations early Saturday of Tech students, in denunciation of Governor Griffin's position. Two thousand persons, mostly students, burned several effigies of the Governor and demonstrated in front of his mansion and smashed into the State Capitol. State patrolmen were summoned to stop the crowd.

The Georgia Tech president was directed to prescribe "proper disciplinary action" if responsible students were found and to report back to the Regents Dec. 14.

Robert O. Arnold, Regents chairman, opened the meeting with prayer. He said that the Governor had brought no pressure on him or on any of the other Regents on the issue.

At Emory University, a private school here, about twenty-five unidentified persons tonight burned an image of the Governor and posted a sign reading "To hell with Griffin" on the steps of the university library.

In his plea to the Regents last Friday, Governor Griffin said "it is my request that athletic teams of units of the university system of Georgia not be permitted to engage in contests with other teams where the races are mixed on such teams or where segregation is not required among spectators at such events."

The Governor's action raised a storm of protest. Thousands of letters and telegrams swamped the offices of the Governor, Board of Regents and Georgia Tech officials over the week-end, the majority of them strongly assailing Mr. Griffin's stand and urging the Regents to override him.

December 6, 1955

Syracuse Athletics Charged With 'Chronic Racism'

By NEIL AMDUR

The suspension of eight black athletes who boycotted football practice at Syracuse University last spring was "an act of institutional racism unworthy of a great university," a special investigative committee at Syracuse has concluded.

In a 38-page report prepared after 10 weeks of testimony and published yesterday in a student-owned newspaper, the 12-member committee declared that "racism in the Syracuse University Athletic Department is real, chronic, largely unintentional, and sustained and complicated unwittingly by many modes of behavior common in American athletics and long-standing at Syracuse University."

The committee noted that "the personnel of the athletic department showed unwarranted insensitivity to attempts by black players to question such [discriminatory] treatment."

The committee's report was presented yesterday to Dr. John E. Corbally, the Syracuse chancellor. It is expected to be released officially by the chancellor's office this afternoon, and a news conference has been called for tomorrow afternoon by Dr. Corbally, presumably to comment on its contents.

Committee Edited Text

The report was published in Dialog by Alan Stamm, the editor and publisher, and one of the members of the committee. Stamm, 21 years old and a senior journalism major from New York City, said the text published in Dialog was reviewed and edited by the committee last week.

The committee made nine recommendations, of which the following three are the most significant:

¶Suspended black players should not be punished for focusing attention on the need for a racially diversified coaching staff, and requests should be made to allow the athletes an additional year of eligibility.

¶The present administrative board on athletics should be dissolved as soon as possible and replaced by an Athletic Policy Board. This new board of faculty members, students, alumni and administrators should have the responsibility for overall policy and direction, control and supervision of intercollegiate and intramural athletics at Syracuse.

¶A new code for Syracuse athletes should emphasize that athletes enjoy the same basic personal rights as all other students at Syracuse, and thus such things as personal appearance, social activities and political expression are matters of individual choice insofar as they do not interfere with the rights of others.

The committee of three trustees, five professors, three students and one administrator was formed on Sept. 24 by Dr. Corbally to study the events that prompted the boycott of spring practice by the eight blacks and led to their suspension from the team by Ben Schwartzwalder, the head coach.

"The definition of the spring boycott merely as an issue of violating coaching authority, and the penalizing of black athletes without taking into consideration the broader context of their protest was an act of institutional racism unworthy of a great university," the report stated.

No Blacks Return to Team

The blacks were officially reinstated after Dr. Corbally's intervention, but none actually joined the team and several were academically ineligible to compete. Among those eligible to return were Al Newton, a fullback, and Greg Allen, a halfback, who were the team's two leading ground-gainers during the 1969 season. Syracuse lost its first three games this year and finished with a 6-4 won-lost record.

The 61-year-old Schwartzwalder, pictured as "insensitive to changing student concerns" by the committee, has declined comment. But one member of the athletic department, who asked for anonymity pending an official release of the report, said the material published in the student paper failed to define the problems.

"Maybe something's the matter with my thinking," the source said. "But I don't see how one side can be exonerated completely and the other side condemned so completely."

Problems in the athletic department, the committee concluded, are hampered by ineffective communications between players and coaches and between coaches and administrators. The report also said that coaches on Schwartzwalder's staff had a "negligible awareness" of players' interest in decisions governing their lives, education and careers.

The committee studied various allegations made by the black athletes. These areas included name-calling, poor medical treatment, uneven academic advisement and assistance between blacks and whites, recruiting, coaching harassment and the failure of the athletic department to hire black assistant coaches.

A black coach, Carlmon Jones, was hired at Syracuse last August, but the report said that the "legitimate request; made as early as the spring of 1969, that a black assistant football coach should be hired, was ignored; that the athletic department was grossly insensitive to the legitimacy and meaning of this request; that signs of increasing estrangement between the black football players and the white coaching staff were ignored; and that an effective corrective measure—the hiring of a black assistant—was not taken until after the black athletes boycotted spring practice.'

"It is the opinion of the committee that the disappointment and frustration over the black coach issue were the primary substantive causes of the boycott of spring practice," the report said.

The report also said that "the lines of authority within the athletic department were poorly structured."

"Further," the report continues, "it [the committee] finds a totaly unsatisfactory response on the part of the athletic director [James Decker] to the year-long crisis."

The committee recommended that Chancellor Corbally review the functions of the athletic director with the purpose of strengthening the authority of the office.

The committee conducted 28 hearings and questioned more than 40 witnesses, including current and former players, all football coaches, the athletic director, administrators and Dr. Corbally. Stamm said the complete testimony totaled 604 pages.

December 9, 1970

Sports of The Times

Out of Their League—I

By ROBERT LIPSYTE

Seven years ago, a St. Louis Cardinal reserve linebacker earned $35 a night at Rotary meetings and high schools sports banquets where he showed a highlight film with beer commercials and explained to his admirers: "Football is just like life. Those of you who work the hardest and are the most dedicated will be the most successful. The competitiveness of football is excellent preparation for the competition of life." He would end his speech by emphasizing that playing football developed the right values and attitudes.

By 1969, Dave Meggysey was no longer in demand on the straight circuit, although he was getting more playing time. He reports: "I found that being in condition was really great for smoking dope—with my lungs in shape, I could really inhale a tremendous volume of smoke. I also found I could go out the next day and run without experiencing any bad after effects. I had smoked cigarettes on and off throughout

Dave Meggyesy of the St. Louis Cardinals tackles Pittsburgh's Dick Hoak after a pass reception. Meggyesy made even more news off the field with his criticism of the way that football is played.

college and in the pros and found they really cut down my wind, but smoking marijuana or hashish didn't affect me at all."

Superpsych

It will be argued in the months to come that Meggysey's 1969 advocacy of dope was as hypocritical and self-serving as his 1963 propagandizing for football. This argument may be true. But there's no question in the radicalization of Meggysey and the distance he has traveled from crew-cut "coaches' dream" to a bearded activist for social change who returned to his alma mater, Syracuse, two weeks ago and told nearly 1,000 students that "symbolically and metaphysically, big-time football represents our violent culture and the mode of authoritarianism. It has as its keynote competition and militaristic, organized violence."

Meggysey was born 29 years ago in Cleveland and grew up humiliatingly poor on an Ohio farm. In high school football he found approval and recognition as a brutal, fanatical player. On scholarship at Syracuse, his teammates ridiculed his aggressive hustle and called him "Superpsych." In his book, "Out of Their League" (Ramparts Press, $6.95), he emerges as an outsider, first through his poverty, later through his inability to completely accept the values of his football life. At Syracuse, he says, players were treated as a "commodity" and discarded after use: Of the 26 freshmen who arrived with football scholarships in 1958, Meggysey was one of only three who was graduated in 1963.

At Syracuse, he says, Coach Ben Schwartzwalder warned him against "hanging out with those beatniks," friends he had made among liberal arts and graduate students who laughed at football and called the short, war-hero coach the "pigmy paratrooper." Other players questioned the morality of Meggysey's living with the girl he later married, a "sinful" relationship and abnormal compared to the more "healty and manly" practice of getting drunk and roughing a pickup.

The Clinic

He had some trouble, he says, getting used to taking money from alumni or coaches after a good game, but eventually accepted $30 a week in an envelope. He feels he was one of many whose body was abused by medical practices that were sometimes faulty and always directed toward getting him back into the game. When his team finally revolted, it was perfectly in keeping with the system: The players threatened to boycott the Liberty Bowl, from which the school would get television money, unless they got wrist watches.

Meggysey's devotion to the game kept him in the pros through a rookie season in which he was an expendable on the "bomb squads," the kick-off and punt-return teams. He had planned at that time to enroll in medical school after a few years in the league, and he took an offseason job as a medical research assistant in a St. Louis hospital. It was here, Meggysey once said in an interview, that he began "to get his head together."

He met medical researchers who had given up the opportunity to earn much more money in private practice, and he writes that he saw "the poor women who would come into the free clinic and wait, many times four to six hours, to get medical treatment for their sick children. I couldn't help but realize the perversity of spending thousands of dollars on a football player with a sprained ankle while many poor kids were not getting adequate medical care."

December 21, 1970

Sports of The Times

By ROBERT LIPSYTE

Out of Their League—II

Wally Lemm, coach of the Houston Oilers, was asked recently about a linebacker named Dave Meggysey he coached several years ago at St. Louis. Lemm said: "He was strictly a borderline football player. Nobody would pay any attention to him if he had not been a football player, and yet he is ripping the game now. He is down on the capitalistic society, but you can bet he'll get paid for this story. Meggysey is just a hippie and St. Louis is better off without him. In looking back, I can see he was an agitator all the time he was there and I was coach.

I don't see how a guy who admits to dropping acid and the other things he does in the story can have any pride in himself, and if he doesn't have any pride in himself, he won't have any pride in football or anything else."

After seven years with the Cardinals, Meggysey quit the game to write "Out of Their League" (Ramparts Press, $6.95), the first important, serious, radical insider's attack on the morality of football.

A Football Freak

Meggysey writes, " . . . . it would be impossible for me not to see football as both a reflection and reinforcement of the worst things in American culture. There was the incredible racism which I was to see close up in the Cardinals' organization and throughout the league. There was also the violence and sadism, not so much on the part of the players or in the game itself, but very much in the minds of the beholders—the millions of Americans who watch football every weekend in something approaching a sexual frenzy.

"And then there was the whole militaristic aura surrounding pro football, not only in obvious things like football stars visiting troops in Vietnam, but in the language of the game—'throwing the bomb,' being a 'field general' etc., and in the unthinking obligation to 'duty' required of the players. In short, the game has been wrapped in red, white and blue. It is no accident that some of the most maudlin and dangerous pregame 'patriotism' we see in this country appears in football stadiums. Nor is it an accident that the most repressive political regime in the history of this country is ruled by a football-freak, Richard M. Nixon."

Meggysey wrote this book with help from Jack Scott, director of the Institute for the Study of Sport in Society in Oakland, Calif. Scott is a former athlete and college instructor who is less radical and more reform minded than Meggysey. During a recent visit to New York, Scott expressed this basic thesis: The athletic department, usually unable to justify its existence educationally or economically, has promoted itself as a moral guardian. In exchange for money and a free hand, the coach will impose discipline on the most physical students, and set a norm of conduct for all. The pros support this system because it supplies them with players, and the political administration helps glorify it.

Two Scandals

Meggysey's life is a thread through Scott's fabric. His brutal, fanatical play in high school won him recognition and a college scholarship. Ashamed of his poverty, unrecognized at home, Meggysey became one of "the good people" at high school, who submitted to the system, avoided "certain girls" and wore prescribed clothing. Although he began to doubt the system's values at Syracuse, he was good enough on field to reap its benefits: Cash gifts for good games, exam answers, a reprimand instead of a jail sentence for 55 unpaid parking tickets.

Meggysey was more vocally doubting as a pro, where he was nowhere near being the star he had been in high school and college. He feels he was able to get away with his peace activities only because the Cardinal ownership, rocked by racial dissention, didn't want two scandals in one season. When he quit after the 1969 season, he became deeply involved in the drug culture and in movements for social change.

The book is not subtle or witty or particularly entertaining; there are very few of the gossipy details that tickle fans, and even fewer descriptions of game action. Meggysey's style is polemical, and he offers no specific answers. But the questions he raises are rooted in basic American issues. For example, he suggests that the players should have struck against "dehumanizing conditions" rather than for more money last season; had the Players' Association negotiated their own television contract, rented stadiums and played games, he writes, it could have cut out the owners' "tremendous profits" and made possible a "drastic reduction in the price the fans must pay for tickets."

December 24, 1970

Athletes Separate, but Unequal

DALLAS, Aug. 31 (UPI)—Southern Methodist University moved 36 students out of one of its best dormitories on the campus today so football players can use the dormitory exclusively. The dispossessed students were not happy about it. "We feel like we really got shafted," Cy Rosenblatt and Bruce Boguez, two of the students, said.

The athletes also have been assigned a separate cafeteria line. Six hundred students use one line while 125 athletes use another. The football coach, Dave Smith, said separate dormitory and eating facilities are necessary for "control, morale and a prideful atmosphere."

September 1, 1973

N.F.L. to Check Redskins on Drug Report

By NEIL AMDUR

The National Football League said yesterday it would investigate a report that one-third of the Washington Redskins players use amphetamines to help charge themselves up before games.

Commenting on the estimate by George Burman, a 30-year-old reserve center for the Redskins, Pete Rozelle, the N.F.L. commissioner, said, "We plan to discuss the matter with him in keeping with our policies as outlined to Congressman [Harley] Staggers's committee early last summer."

"If the N.F.L. calls me, I'll be glad to cooperate," Burman said by telephone last night after returning from a Washington workout in which he addressed the squad at a team meeting. "But I'm not going to call them up."

Rozelle's statement came after Burman, who is in his eighth season in the N.F.L., had said the figure for the number of Redskin players who used amphetamines was about the same as it was throughout the league.

Other sources close to the Redskins, however, believe that between 50 and 60 per cent of the team were amphetamine users last season. when Washington reached the Super Bowl before bowing to Miami, 14-7.

When questioned about the extent of drugs being taken by Washington players this year, one starter on the Redskin defense said recently, "Nothing has changed. Everybody is just as dapped as before."

"Dapped" is a shortened form of Daprisal, one of the two amphetamines believed to have been used by Redskin players last year. The other drug was Dexedrine. Amphetamines are used as stimulants for the central nervous system.

The use of drugs to aid performance or ease pain is not new to pro football. Various types of stimulants and pep pills were dispensed reg-

NOTICE

It is League policy that the use by NFL players of any drugs which have not been specifically prescribed, recommended, or approved by your team doctor or personal physician is not in your interest, the interest of your team, or the interest of the National Football League.

The use or distribution of "pep pills" or "diet pills" by members of this team is not condoned by the League or by the management of this Club. The taking of these drugs, regardless of amount, has never been shown to improve performance on the athletic field. Furthermore their use should not be viewed as a matter without medical consequence. To the contrary, significant side effects can occur on the heart, pulse, and blood pressure, as well as in connection with withdrawal or "coming down" from the drug, especially with repeated or prolonged usage. Added medical risks can be encountered if one is injured and requires anaesthesia for surgery.

Should there be any questions about this policy, or about the use of drugs of any character either on or off the playing field, the team doctor will be happy to discuss them in private with individual players.

A warning posted in all locker rooms of N.F.L. teams

ularly in training rooms and by team physicians for many years, until league officials began a crackdown.

The N.F.L. now has a special medical consultant, Dr. Walter Riker of the Cornell University Medical College, who evaluates bills of drug purchases submitted by various clubs. Spot checks for drug abuses are also made by security personnel attached to the league.

In discussing the availability of drugs, the 6-foot-3-inch, 250-pound Burman, who has a Ph.D. in economics from the University of Chicago, said the Redskins had complied with rules for dispensing amphetamines but that players still managed to obtain them on their own.

"George Burman's comments confirm what our investigation has indicated, namely that amphetamines are not being dispensed, either directly or indirectly, by club management," Rozelle said.

"It is obvious now, however, if his statements regarding players are true, that we are going to have to have the active cooperation of the players themselves in elimi-

nating outside sources. It is unfortunate that George has seen fit to label his teammates anonymously."

Washington currently is tied with Dallas for first place in the Eastern Division of the National Football Conference. The Redskins are home against Baltimore Sunday.

Burman said he had discussed the matter with George Allen, the Redskin coach, on Tuesday. "He didn't make any specific comments one way or another," Burman said of Allen's reaction.

"Burman got up and talked to the team before practice today," one Redskin player said. "He said he felt like he did the right thing in talking about it, and if anybody had any problem over it he should come talk to him and don't go talking behind his back."

Mrs. Marianne Burman said her husband's comments came up at a luncheon of wives of the Redskins' players yesterday in Washington.

"I was anticipating a barrage of either negative or positive comments," Mrs. Burman said. "But people I

talked with said their husband's were very positive about the article [which appeared in The Washington Post] for being honest."

Reaction among Redskin coaches and players to Burman's comments appeared to be divided.

"I'm positive there's no drug problem," Allen said. "I know we don't have a drug problem. I'm not worried about it. My only concern is the Baltimore Colts."

"It's bad timing, that's all I can say," one member of the Redskin defense said, reached at home after practice.

Reports about drug use among the Redskins was not limited to players, according to some sources. A wife of one of the players reportedly used a supply of amphetamines, obtained from her husband, to keep her awake while driving from Washington to Los Angeles for the Super Bowl game.

One player said the reluctance of Dr. P. M. Palumbo, the team physician, to dispense drugs had "dried up" easy access, but other sources were available to players who wanted them.

The player said that one member of the offense "arranged everything for everybody" with medical contacts away from the club because another player, on the defense, had said that when the supply had shut down in other cities for players, "they got it off the street."

"Everything's legitimate, there's nothing crooked about it or illegal about it at all," said the player, an admitted user.

Asked about the adverse reaction to taking drugs, the player said, "the worst reaction is being so tired you can't perform and getting put on waivers."

Could you do without them? the player was asked.

"I don't want to find out," he replied.

November 15, 1973

The Football Phenomenon And Its Place on Campus

By IVER PETERSON

Millions of armchair quarterbacks saw some good college football during the annual New Years' Day bowl-game binge, but they probably did not see the best. After all, the University of Oklahoma's Sooners trounced both Cotton Bowl teams — Nebraska and Texas—during the regular season, and tied Southern California, which lost to Ohio State in the Rose Bowl.

The reason for their absence, as college sports fans know, is that the Big Red team from Norman, Okla., is under a two-year ban from playing televised bowl games. The ban was imposed by the National Collegiate Athletic Association and Oklahoma's Big Eight Conference after the Sooners fielded two players with doctored high school transcripts.

The illegally altered class standings, which made the two players appear eligible for the football scholarships that the University of Oklahoma had pressed upon them, pointed up an important element in the controversy over big time college sports. The intense demand for blue-chip athletes and a winning team has apparently presented too much of a temptation to coaches and players to go beyond the strictly limited inducements for prospective players permitted by the N.C.A.A.—free tuition, room and board, some laundry and book money, and some transportation expenses.

Other Offers Reported

And the college sports scene is rife with reports that many other inducements, including money, cars, clothes and a job, are offered under the table.

"I used to think everything I heard was exaggerated," Darrell Royal, coach of the Texas Longhorns and athletic director of the University of Texas, told the Chronicle of Higher Education, "but we've had too many people come here that told us what people have offered them. You're out there trying to sell yourself and your school, and the guy ain't hearing a word you're saying. All he's wondering about is when you're going to start talking money."

To its credit, the University of Oklahoma, like other important sports colleges, acted quickly if not entirely openly to correct these abuses when they were discovered, and the attitude among officials there seems to be that the growing venality of college sports can be contained by good faith and constant vigilance.

But the question that skeptics have long been asking is not just how major colleges should contain the greed and excesses of college sports, but what business does an institution of higher learning have in producing and promoting multimillion-dollar public spectacles in the first place.

A stranger at the University of Oklahoma who poses that question comes away with the realization that probably came to the men who run the country's public colleges and universities a long time ago. It is that, in more ways than just sports, there is a vast gap between the ideals of higher education and the realities of life at a large, state-supported public university.

The notion that sports should be a pleasant interlude from their studies for energetic young gentlemen has no more to do with these realities in today's America than the Heidelberg and Oxford traditions of turning out refined young men to move smoothly into positions of power have to do with the true goals of American public institutions.

"We are not the linear descendants of Oxford and Heidelberg," said Paul Sharp, president of the University of Oklahoma, in the tone of a man who is tired of explaining the difference. "It is in the context of the realities of American life that we measure the reality on the academic level."

Dr. Sharp and others in his position know that these realities are that American public education has drawn its support from the public by providing what the public needs and wants. Land grant colleges were founded to produce agriculturalists and technicians when intensive farming began after the Civil War; after 1957, campuses produced scientists in response to Sputnik, and today the emphasis is on cheap, informal and easily accessible two-year community colleges. And on sports.

Last season, for example, more than 400 million fans watched nearly 3,000 college football games. About 30 million of the fans paid an estimated $150-million—not including bowl games—to attend in person. The television networks spent another $13.5-million for broadcast rights, and will pay more next season.

And as Wade Walker, the University of Oklahoma's athletic director, points out, sports—and especially football—is a lot more than a game. Being a real fan almost means believing in a particular way of life.

"Athletics is still one of the true free enterprise areas of the American democracy," Mr. Walker said in his friendly Western drawl. "It doesn't make any difference what color your skin is, or what your social status is, because you just got 11 youngsters out there, nose to nose and toes to toes, and the guy who really wants to qualify can make it. That's the way this country began, and this is still one place where a guy can be rewarded by what he does. And it's not like that in any other area anymore."

Anyone who has ever watched the Rose Bowl parade or gone through the annual Oklahoma and University of Texas pre-game drinking and partying brawl (278 arrested in 1972) knows that sports is not just a game, that it involves more than a contest between two teams. At the University of Oklahoma, students and faculty members on both sides of the controversy agree that sports—especially football—goes much deeper.

"Football is everything; it's just the life here," said Stephanie Miller, a graduate student in journalism at the University of Oklahoma.

William Maehl, professor of history at the university and president of the Faculty Senate, described the importance of football to Oklahoma in a way that might be applied to many other states, or indeed, to much of the country.

"This is a young state," he said. "It has no real traditions, and football provides a kind of focus of values that is much more important to people here than it would be, perhaps, to people in an Eastern state."

Mr. Walker, the Oklahoma athletic director, sees it clearly:

"If you only had one toy when you were a youngster, but it was a good toy, you could still go out in the neighborhood and stick your chest out and say, 'that's mine!'

"Well, this is a rural state, and our football gives John Doe Q. Public, wherever he lives, something to identify with—it gives him something to stick out his chest about, and say, 'Boy, I'm a Sooner! I'm part of the Big Red!' It gives him something wholesome."

There is nothing abstract in Mr. Walker's view of the connection between sports and American ideals. "We're teachers," he said of himself and his coaching staff. "We teach a philosophy, we teach a skill, and we danged sure also teach a little bit of religion. And we teach discipline—this is one of the last areas where true discipline is taught, where love for the American flag and respect for the American President is taught, through discipline."

Mr. Walker spends most of his time, he said, promoting support for the Sooners by making this kind of appeal and urging fans to "get a piece of the action, be a part of the Big Red." And they respond.

'We Teach Discipline'

Those who can afford the $1,000 annual dues may join the Winning Edge, the university's élite booster club, which raises money for athletic scholarships. By contributing a carcass of beef for the training tables, one can join the Sooner Beef Club. And there are the Sooner Club and the Touchdown Club, established like the others to raise money for the nearly $3-million self-supporting annual athletic budget at the University of Oklahoma.

Last year, these supporters contributed $220,000 toward operating expenses, not including capital gifts, which is a fairly modest sum compared with the more than $800,000 similarly raised last year for the University of North Carolina teams, or the $700,000 contributed to the University of South Carolina athletic program.

Not everyone, of course, shares Wade Walker's view of the wholesomeness of this kind of fan loyalty. Michael Vitt, a senior who is editor of the student-run Oklahoma Daily, gave what might be described as the underside of Mr. Wade's explanation for football's popularity at the university.

"If it wasn't for O. U. football," he said, "there wouldn't be anything else that O. U. students could identify with, because in everything else, O. U. is a loser."

What about the nonstudent fans— the alumni and nonalumni boosters who make up most of the team's support?

"When you think about what the history of this state is," Mr. Vitt, a native Oklahoman, said, "you realize it's Indian murders and claim-jumping and people who were so down and out somewhere else that they came here. So if you have a football team that's a winner, well, everybody can identify with a winner. They don't have a damn thing to do with that team going out and winning, but it's something they can be proud of."

Fan loyalty has its pitfalls, however, and officials at big time sports schools have learned that they have to tread gingerly between promoting the enthusiasm of loyal supporters and resisting the demands that seem to accompany the support.

When Chuck Fairbanks ended the 1966-'67 season at Oklahoma with a 6-3-1 record—a disaster for a team that is used to being top or near the top in the country—"Chuck Chuck" stickers appeared on the bumpers of Oklahoma cars, and the coach did leave, to take over the New England Patriots in the National Football League.

Then, when the Big Eight and N.C.A.A. probation was announced, along with a prohibition against the

Sooners appearing on television for two seasons, Gov. David Hall of Oklahoma won political points by appealing for a lifting of the TV ban and by threatening to go to court when the appeal failed. The episode made some friends for Governor Hall, but it angered and embarrassed members of the university.

Dr. Sharp, the university's president, said his administration had to resist "constant external pressures to use [football] for political or commercial purposes." He added, "We resist these pressures because we feel that they are an intrusion into the academic purpose of the university."

When he made this comment in an interview just before Christmas, Dr. Sharp was in the midst of a battle with the Oklahoma Legislature and the State Board of Regents for additional funds to cover the university's rising costs. In Oklahoma, student radicalism and the growing popularity of two-year community colleges continue to tempt legislators and regents to give a larger share of public funds for education to community colleges and the more

placid Oklahoma State University, formerly called Oklahoma A. & M.

Relations with the Legislature "understandably are eased" when the Sooners have a good season, Dr. Sharp said, but he insisted that success on the gridiron was not all that important in terms of money.

"Relations with the Legislature are always friendlier when we are able to be successful in bringing the state this kind of credit," Dr. Sharp said. "They don't icepick us to death on all the little issues or questions that a legislature could raise if they wanted to." He also said that he would be "more afraid of nit-picking questions of accountability and the management of public funds," rather than questions of funding, if the Sooners started losing.

"But remember, I haven't been through a losing season," he added, "and I would have to go through a losing season before I could make a final judgment on that."

He made it sound like something he would just as soon avoid having to do.

January 16, 1974

An Anthropologist Looks at the Rituals of Football

By WILLIAM ARENS

The attitude toward the football player has obviously changed since Shakespeare's time. Today the once "base football player," as Shakespeare described him in "King Lear," occupies the hearts, minds and television screens of millions. He is emulated and sought after, and the stratagems he uses in the game are often followed at the highest levels of government and business.

As an anthropologist I would contend that football, although only a game, tells us much about who and what we Americans are as a people.

If an anthropologist from another planet visited here, he would be struck by the American fixation on this game and would report on it with the glee and romantic intoxication anthropologists normally reserve for the exotic rituals of a newly discovered tribe. This assertion is based on the theory that certain significant symbols are the key to understanding a culture; football is such a symbol.

America Brand Unexportable

Football has emerged as an item of our cultural inventory that we share with no other country except Canada, where it is of minor interest. We share our language, kinship system, religions, political and economic institutions and a variety of other traits with many nations, but our premier spectator sport remains ours alone. This is important when we consider that other societies have taken up baseball, which is derived from cricket, and basketball, a domestic product. Like English beer, the American brand of football is unexportable, even to the colonies.

Football, in contrast to our language and many of our values, was not forced upon us. We chose to accept it. Our

society, like any other complex one, is divided by race, ethnicity, income, political affiliation and regionalism. Yet 79 percent of all the households in the country tuned in the first Super Bowl on television, implying that the event cut through many of these divisive factors.

The game does not represent Middle America, as is so often claimed, but rather the whole of America. A love of football is one of the few interests we share with few outside our borders, but with almost everyone within them.

The salient features of the game reflect some striking similarities to the society that created and nourished it. More than any other sport, football combines the qualities of group coordina-

tion through a complex division of labor with highly developed specialization.

Violence is one of our society's most obvious traits, and its expression in football, where bodily contact and territorial incursion are essential, clearly accounts for part of the game's appeal.

To single out violence as the sole or even primary reason for the game's popularity is a tempting oversimplification. Boxing, for example, allows for an even greater display of legitimate blood spilling. Yet boxing's popularity has waned over the last few decades, an indication, perhaps, that reliance on naked individual force has less appeal for us than aggression acted out in a more tactical and sophisticated context. Football's violence is expressed within the framework of teamwork, specialization, mechanization and variation, and this combination accounts for its appeal. But we cannot explain football's popularity on the basis of violence alone because we are not unique in this respect. There have been many other violent nations, but they did not enshrine football as a national symbol.

Although baseball—the national pastime—has not suffered the same fate as boxing, interest in this game has also ebbed. Like boxing, baseball is not in step with the times. Its action does not entail the degree of complexity, coordination and specialization that now captures our fancy. The recent introduction of players who only bat or run bases, and who never field, are moves to inject specialization and heighten the game's appeal to modern America. Baseball, however, belongs to a past era when life was a bit less complicated.

Game a Male Preserve

While football, representing the typical American outlook, overshadows class, race and economic differences in our society, it emphasizes the division between the sexes. The game is a male preserve that manifests and symbolizes both the physical and cultural values of masculinity. Entrance into the arena of football competition depends upon muscle power and speed, which only a very few males and probably no females possess. Women can and do excel in a variety of other sports, but football to-

185

tally excludes them from participation.

In an informal game between females in a Long Island community, the husbands responded by appearing on the sidelines in women's clothes and wigs. The message was clear. If the women were going to act like men, then the men were going to transform themselves into women. These "rituals of rebellion" involving an inversion of sex roles have often been recorded by anthropologists. It is not surprising that this symbolic rebellion in our culture involved a bastion of male supremacy.

If this argument seems farfetched, consider the extent to which football gear accents the male physique. The donning of the required items results in an enlarged head and shoulders and a narrowed waist, with the lower torso poured into skintight pants accented only by a metal codpiece. The result is not an expression but an exaggeration of maleness. Dressed in this manner, players can engage in hand holding, hugging and bottom patting that would be disapproved of in any other context, but which is accepted on the gridiron

without a second thought.

Admittedly , there are good reasons for wearing the gear, but that does not mean that we should dismiss the symbolic significance of the visual impression. The game could just as easily be played without the major items such as the helmet, shoulder pads and cleats. They are as much offensive as defensive in function. Indeed, in comparison, Rugby players seem to manage quite well in the flimsiest of uniforms.

November 16, 1975

FOOTBALL is a field game between two teams, played with an inflated oval-shaped ball that is advanced to a goal by running, passing, or kicking. Among the most ancient of ball games and known by a variety of names, modern football divided into two forms in the mid-19th century. One version of the game ruled that the ball could be advanced only by kicking and that all players except the goaltender were prohibited from handling the ball. This version was formalized by the London Football Association, founded in 1863 in England, and was known as association football, or soccer. This is the form most extensively played throughout the world. In most countries "football" denotes the game of soccer.

The other version, called rugby, formalized by the Rugby Football Union in London in 1871, permitted touching the ball with the hands—carrying it as well as kicking it. It stemmed from a game played at Rugby School in England, when, in 1823, a player illegally picked up a ball and ran with it.

From soccer and, more directly, from rugby evolved the games played today under the names of American, Canadian, and Australian football. These games, which in one degree or another permit running with and throwing as well as kicking a ball, also include blocking, which permits a ballcarrier's teammates to make contact with, knock down, or ward off opposing players seeking to tackle the player running with the ball.

The most distinctive aspect of the American and Canadian games is the principle of possession. Through a series of plays, or downs, the team possessing the ball can sustain an attack, mixing its plays on the ground and in the air until it either scores or is forced to relinquish possession to the opposing team. In the Australian game, play is continuous; the ball goes back and forth between the teams until a goal is scored, a foul is committed, or the ball goes out of bounds. Another marked difference among the games is substitutions—unlimited in the American and Canadian games; disallowed in Australian play.

The games are played on fields of varying sizes and under complex rules that define what a player may or may not do, with penalties imposed for infractions detected by officials who supervise the play. The common objective of all football games is to advance a ball over the opposing team's goal line or to kick it between the goalposts, the winner being the team that scores the greater number of points under a system assigning values to each scoring procedure.

The rules and eligibility of players are administered by national organizations. In the United States, control of amateurs and professionals is separate. Only on military service teams may amateurs and professionals play together. Amateur control is divided among the National Collegiate Athletic Association (NCAA), which numbers among its members all the large universities; the National Association of Intercollegiate Athletics (NAIA), to which many smaller col-

leges belong; the National Junior College Athletic Association; and the National Federation of State High School Athletic Associations. For rules making, the last three are combined as the National Alliance Football Committee. Control of professional football is vested in the National Football League (NFL), which merged in 1970 with the rival American Football League (AFL).

In other countries the national organization makes the rules for all participants and sponsors development at all playing levels. Their games have some similarities and marked differences that will be discussed in detail, along with the offshoots of American football called six-man football and touch football.

American Football

American football is a rough, even violent, body contact sport. More than most games, it has been subjected to rules revisions as new techniques and tactics are devised to give the offense or the defense the upper hand. The rules makers strive for balance, though obviously the offense has a built-in advantage in knowing what play it will use and its direction. Football is often compared to mimic warfare in its strategy and tactics, its disciplines and rigors.

Football is generally an outdoor sport, though the advent of domed stadiums may encourage more indoor football in communities prosperous enough to afford such arenas. It is played on a grassed surface or on composition grasslike material.

RULES AND GAME PROGRESS

The objective of the game is to score more points than the opponent within the allotted time. The clock-running time is 60 minutes in professional and college football and 48 minutes in high school contests. There are two halves, with a 15-minute intermission after the first half for rest and a discussion of second-half strategy. The halves are divided into quarters. At the end of each quarter the teams change goals. NFL rules provide for a sudden-death overtime period when games end in a tie.

Field and Goal. The playing area is 120 yards long from end line to end line and 53⅓ yards (160 feet) wide. Within this area is the field of play, 100 yards long. Ten yards from each end line and parallel to it is the goal line. The 10-yard-deep space between the goal line and the end line is the end zone. It is in this area that a player must carry or catch the football to make a touchdown, the basic score of the game. White stripes run across the field from sideline to sideline at 5-yard intervals.

The midfield stripe is the 50-yard line. From that point, going in both directions, the lines are designated as the 45-yard line, 40-yard line, and so on to the goal line. The two lines on the field parallel to the sidelines (53 feet 4 inches inside in the college game, 70 feet 9 inches in the professional game) are the inbounds markers, or hash marks. Whether the ball is carried out of bounds (over the sideline) or is downed outside the inbounds boundary, the ball is always put in play on this line.

An H-shaped goalpost stands at each end of the field. The posts are centered on the end lines. A crossbar joins the posts 10 feet above the ground. The posts are 20 feet high, but for scoring purposes the goal area is the vertical plane of the posts extended indefinitely above the crossbar. The posts are set 18 feet 6 inches apart in professional games and 23 feet 4 inches apart in college and high school games.

Positions of Players. A team comprises 11 players. Their positions traditionally have been called left end, left tackle, left guard, center, right guard, right tackle, and right end (the linemen or forwards); and quarterback, left halfback, right halfback, and fullback (the backfield players or backs). With the modern use of separate teams for offense and defense (the two-platoon system), the positions of the players on offense generally retain these designations. Members of the defensive team are called guards, tackles, and ends, if they play on the scrimmage line; linebackers, if they play immediately behind the line; halfbacks, or cornerbacks, if they deploy wider and slightly deeper than the linebackers; and safeties, if they are the deepest defensive players.

Conduct of the Game. Before a game begins, the captains of the two teams meet with the referee for a toss of a coin. The winner of the toss chooses either to kick off or receive the kickoff, or to pick the goal his team will defend. The loser has the remaining option and first choice of the options for the second half.

A kickoff puts the ball into play at the start of each half. This takes place from the kicking team's 40-yard line in college games and 35-yard line in professional contests. The receiving team spreads out on its side of the 50-yard line. Once the kicker sends the ball in the direction of the receiving team (usually trying to kick it as deep into the opponent's territory as possible), the kicking team races downfield in an attempt to tackle (bring down) the receiver of the ball or force him out of bounds. The receiver, meanwhile, tries to run back, or return, the ball as deep into the opponent's territory as he can. If he can "take it all the way"—that is, carry the ball over the opponent's goal line—he scores a touchdown. At the point the kick receiver (ballcarrier) is stopped, his team prepares for offensive play. (If the ball goes out of bounds on the kickoff, it must be kicked again, but from a point 5 yards farther back, unless the receiving team declines the penalty.)

The offense is permitted a series of four plays called downs, in which to advance the ball at least 10 yards or else relinquish possession to the defense. Anytime the ball is advanced 10 or more yards during the course of the series, and after the ballcarrier or pass catcher is halted, the team is credited with a first down. This entitles the team to a new series of four more plays to make another 10 yards. If the first play in the series fails to result in a 10-yard gain, the next play becomes second down, with the remaining yardage of the 10 to be gained.

The ball changes hands immediately, however, if a defensive player recovers a dropped (fumbled) ball, "steals" the ball from the ballcarrier, or intercepts the ball in flight. Otherwise, the offensive team retains possession until it scores or elects to give the ball up (usually on the fourth play of the series, with a yard or more needed to earn a first down) by kicking, or punting. (The punt is the offensive team's way of exchanging distance for loss of possession.) Once the offense loses possession, the defensive team takes the offensive and tries to advance the ball and score.

On every down at least seven offensive players (linemen) must be on the scrimmage line—that is, on an imaginary line parallel to the goal line and passing through the forward point of the ball. (A player is considered on the line if he faces the opponent's goal line, with his shoulders parallel to the line and his head within one foot of it.) Although the defense is not restricted in its alignment, it does have a scrimmage line—the nearer point of the ball. The area between the two imaginary lines thus established (the length of the ball) is the neutral zone into which neither side may encroach until the ball is in play.

The offensive center starts the action of each play by a snap—that is, by passing or handing the ball between his legs to a teammate in the backfield. (In the standard offense alignment, or formation, a quarterback stands directly behind the center to receive a hand-to-hand snap. This is the basic T formation, so called because the position of the quarterback and his three backfield teammates form a T.) After the snap, the quarterback, or any back who receives the snap, may hand the ball to another back or any lineman who has (by turning 180 degrees) assumed a backfield position one yard behind the line. Or he may run with it, or pass it in various ways to make forward progress. The defensive players deploy (spread out) for prearranged assignments and try to halt the ballcarrier. Once a defender stops a ballcarrier, or if a forward pass fails—that is, if the ball is grounded—the ball becomes dead (out of play), and a similar procedure starts again.

Under professional rules, a defender may run with a recovered fumble. Under college and high school rules he may not (unless he catches the ball in midair), but his team restarts play at the spot of recovery. Under all rules an offensive player may run with a recovered fumble.

Scoring. The prime unit of scoring is the touchdown, which is worth 6 points in school, college, and professional games. A touchdown occurs whenever either team takes the ball over the opponent's goal line or when the defense recovers the ball in the opponent's end zone. The offense can score a touchdown by running the ball over the goal line, by passing it to an eligible receiver (an end or backfield player) in the end zone, or by passing it to a player who then carries it over the goal line. A pass receiver, however, must catch the ball while it is in the air; if it touches the ground before it is caught the pass is incomplete and the down is lost. A player who receives a kickoff on the field of play or in the end zone, or who catches any other kick on the field of play, can score a touchdown if he carries the ball across the opponent's goal line.

Once a touchdown is made, the scoring team may try for a conversion—that is, for 1 or 2 additional points. To try for this score the team lines up parallel to and three yards from the goal line and may kick (not punt), pass, or run for the score. A kick over the crossbar and between the posts scores 1 point. Rules for the scoring of a pass or a run vary. The NFL and schools score a successful pass or run as 1 point, the same as for a kick, which is the standard conversion try. College rules provide for the option—2 points for a successful run or pass and 1 point for a kick.

Any time a team has the ball (except on the kickoff) it may try to score a goal by kicking the ball from the field of play over the crossbar of the opponent's goal, either by a placekick or a dropkick. A goal from the field, or field goal, scores 3 points.

Another method of scoring is the safety, which is worth 2 points to the team forcing the safety. A touchback often looks like a safety but has no scoring value. It is a safety when the ball becomes dead (downed or out of bounds) behind a team's own goal line, provided the impetus came from a player of that team. It is a touchback in a like situation when the impetus came from the opposing team. After a safety, the team scored upon is awarded a free kick from its 20-yard line (the restraining lines being 10 yards apart as on a kickoff). After a touchback, the defending team puts the ball in play on its 20-yard line.

A punt that crosses the goal line is a touchback. After a missed field goal in which scrimmage was beyond the 20-yard line, the defensive team takes possession at the scrimmage line. If the attempt was from within the 20-yard line, the ball is put in play on that line. After an incomplete forward pass on fourth down from inside the 20-yard line, the ball is returned to play at the line of scrimmage.

Officials and Infractions—*Officials.* In a National Football League game, seven officials supervise play: referee, umpire, head linesman, line judge, back judge, side judge, and field judge. In college games four to six are used.

The *referee* is the overall supervisor. He keeps score and is the final authority on the rules. He decides whether the ball is in play or dead and puts it into play for the next down. For plays from scrimmage, he stands behind the offensive team. Other officials report infractions to him, which are indicated by the dropping of a weighted handkerchief (flag) to the ground. The referee then identifies the offending team or player (by number) and the kind of foul, and explains the options (accepting or declining the penalty) to the offended team's captain. To convey the information, the referee uses a uniform code of signals involving hand, arm, and leg movements.

The *umpire*, stationed behind the defensive line, checks on the players' equipment and oversees their conduct and actions on the line of scrimmage. The *head linesman*, in position at one end of the scrimmage line, rules on blocks and sideline action, assists the referee in keeping track of downs, and supervises the 10-yard chain in determining first downs. The *line judge*, on the opposite end of the line, rules on the legality of the passer's position relative to the scrimmage line and on the actions of blockers and defenders in his area. The *back judge*, stationed downfield, rules on pass receptions, defensive infractions, and sideline action of pass receivers or ball carriers in his area. The *side judge* has similar functions but keys on the wide receiver. The *field judge*, taking the deepest position and keying on the tight end, rules on various actions on that side. He also times intervals between plays on the 30-second clock and intermission between periods.

Infractions. Infractions bring about loss of yardage, loss of down, award of automatic first down, or eviction of players. If a team is penalized on the same play in which it scores, the score is nullified. The penalties almost always call for loss of down or loss of yardage.

Yardage penalties are set at 5, 10, or 15 yards, depending on the seriousness of the infraction. The 5-yard penalties include offside; illegal formation, shift, or motion; delay of game; excessive time-outs; running into the kicker; defensive holding or illegal use of hands; out-of-bounds kickoff; and more than 11 players on the field. The 10-yard penalties are assessed for offensive pass interference, offensive holding or illegal use of hands, ineligible receiver downfield, and tripping by either team. Among the 15-yard penalties are clipping, unnecessary roughness, roughing the kicker or passer, grabbing an opponent's face mask, piling on, illegal blocking below the waist, and unsportsmanlike conduct. Certain infractions, such as defensive holding or illegal use of hands, roughing or running into the kicker, roughing the passer, and piling on, result in an automatic first down for the offensive team.

If a team scores while a penalty is called on the opponent, or if it gains more yardage than the penalty awards for the infraction, the team may refuse to accept the penalty and let the play stand. If the penalty is such that the yardage awarded puts the ball into the end zone, the officials mark off a distance halfway between where the infraction occurred and the goal line. If a potential pass receiver is fouled as he tries to catch the ball in the end zone, the ball is placed on the one-yard line. When both teams are in violation on the same play, the penalties and the play are nullified. If a team fouls twice on one play, the offended team may choose the penalty that would be more advantageous.

SKILLS AND FUNDAMENTALS

Although size, power, and speed are attributes that coaches look for in football players, the game's fundamental skills can be learned and perfected only through practice. Many a slower or smaller player becomes outstanding because he has mastered blocking, tackling, kicking, running, passing, and receiving.

Blocking. Blocking is the way an offensive player makes contact with, wards off, or knocks down a defensive player who is trying to get to the ballcarrier. Whether a player is running with the ball or throwing a forward pass, blockers are essential to protect him or clear a path for him to follow. In blocking, a player may use any part of his body except the hands and feet. A blocker need not knock down an opponent to prevent him from reaching the ballcarrier. Often simple contact (brush block) or interposition of his body (screen block) is sufficient. More often than not, however, a well-executed shoulder block or body block is required.

The shoulder block is most often used on plays from scrimmage, and thus linemen do most of the blocking. The player assumes a three-point stance—that is, he crouches with feet spread apart, one foot slightly to the rear of the other, and with one hand on the ground, knuckles down. The free arm rests across the bent knee. The blocker is thus ready to spring forward and jam a shoulder into the player on the other side of the scrimmage line as his center snaps the ball. The blocker attacks low, taking short, driving steps, and aims at the opponent's midriff. Then he continues his charge. If he pulls in his hands toward his chest he widens his shoulder area, and thus the contact with the opponent is easier to maintain. The shoulder block is useful in the open field, also, once the play is under way.

To execute a body block, the blocker must twist sideways just before he hits the opponent. He drops to the ground upon making contact and, if he slams into the opponent's thighs, he can send the defender tumbling to the ground. In any event, he can keep him away from the ballcarrier. The blocker must not hit an opponent (other than the ballcarrier) from behind or he will be penalized for clipping.

Blocking is not solely an individual effort. It requires cohesive effort, for just one breakdown in the line may cause a loss of yardage. Often two players are needed to obstruct an opponent. Sometimes a blocker "pulls" from the middle of the line—that is, turns and goes into his own backfield—to lead a ballcarrier around the end or through the line.

Tackling. In tackling, a defensive player uses his body and arms to bring a ballcarrier to the ground or stop his forward progress. In a tackle from the front, the tackler hits the opponent with his shoulder a few inches above the knees, at the same time wrapping both arms around him, lifting him, and then driving him to the ground. Many time the tackle is made from the side or by grabbing a ballcarrier by the arm or the leg as he races by. Sometimes it takes more than one tackler to stop a strong and powerful ballcarrier. When such is the case, the effective way to bring him down or stop his forward progress is for one tackler to hit him high and the other, low.

Kicking. Kicking—a punt, a place-kick, or a dropkick—is a skill that only a few members on each team need master. The punt is generally used when a team, unable to make a first down in three plays, chooses to kick the ball out of its own territory on the fourth down. The punter sends the ball as far and as high as possible into his opponent's territory, or out of bounds when the distance to the goal is short of the punter's range. Speed and accuracy in punting are essential. The punter, awaiting the ball about 15 yards behind the scrimmage line, catches a direct pass from the center, positions the ball in his hands, lets it drop, and kicks it with a quick leg-snap. To position the ball properly, a right-footed punter places his left hand on the front of the ball on its left side and his right hand to the rear of the ball on its right side. As the punter prepares to drop the ball he takes the first of several steps forward to gain momentum. When he drops it, the instep of his right foot should meet the ball just to the left of center before it touches the ground and send it in a spiral flight about 35 to 40 yards or more from the scrimmage line. (A left-footed kicker reverses this procedure.)

The place-kick is used on the kickoff, on a free kick after a safety, or from scrimmage. It can also be used on a try for a field goal. For a place-kick the ball must be set nearly upright on the field or on a tee of prescribed height (2 inches in the college game, 3 inches in the professional). For field goal tries, a teammate kneeling by the spot where the ball is to be set receives the snap from the center and positions the ball for the kick. To kick the ball, the kicker takes one forward step and, with a fast leg-snap, meets the ball between its middle and bottom, lifting it high over the charging defensive players. In place-kicking, the ball is hit with the toes, not the instep.

The dropkick, archaic though still legal, is executed by letting the ball fall to the ground point foremost and kicking it quickly as it rises. The toe meets the ball slightly below the middle, resulting in an end-over-end flight.

Running with the Ball. In running with the ball, the prime consideration is to gain yardage and to avoid fumbling or having the ball stolen. The ballcarrier protects the ball by placing the palm of his hand around the front part of the ball and tucking it against his side, his elbow firmly placed against it. The ball should be carried in the arm away from a potential tackler whenever possible, freeing the other arm for warding off (straight-arming) tacklers. Runners follow the paths opened up by their blockers, shifting directions quickly, changing pace, and forcing their way past opponents to gain yardage.

Passing. Passing, or throwing, the ball is one of football's more difficult skills. The quarterback throws nearly all of the passes in standard offensive systems. Occasionally a halfback or fullback throws a pass, after first feinting a running play; he generally has to throw on the run. In rare instances an end, dropping into the backfield, will throw.

To be legal, a pass must be thrown from behind the line of scrimmage. The passer grips the ball with four fingers across the laces; his thumb is spread. With the elbow out in front and the ball held behind the ear, the passer releases the ball with a quick snap of the wrist. The ball must spiral, rather than proceed end over end, in order to move swiftly through the air and be easy to catch. For short passes, both feet should be firmly planted. For a long pass the player must rear back somewhat and bring one foot forward, making certain that the body follows through after he releases the ball.

Pass Receiving. A pass receiver must have speed to get down the field and be shifty to escape opponents. A good sense of timing—knowing when the quarterback will release the ball—is essential. A pass receiver must catch the ball on the fly in midair for a legal catch. He literally "looks the ball into his hands"—that is, he keeps his eyes on the ball until it is firmly in his grasp. To make the actual catch, the receiver forms a pocket with his hands, palms out. Sometimes he may have to catch the ball on his chest or over his shoulder, while running at full speed. Only after considerable practice between the passer and his receivers can a successful passing attack be developed.

FORMATIONS AND STRATEGY

Modern football is a highly technical game. For reports about opposing teams, coaches use scouts for a personal evaluation, films of games played for a check on tactics and skills, and even computers for help in determining player talent. Hundreds of offensive plays are available, and complicated defense systems to halt the opposing attack are designed.

To decide which play the offense or defense will use, the eleven players form a huddle (group together) a few yards behind the line of scrimmage. On offense, the quarterback selects the play. On defense, a linebacker usually calls the formation.

Offensive Formations. The intricate plays used on offense today evolved from simple mass formations, such as the V and the flying wedge. In the early days, though opponents had to be 10 yards removed from a kickoff, the rules did not require that the ball be kicked—the kicker could merely touch foot to ball and then pass it to a teammate. In a game with Pennsylvania in 1884, the Princeton quarterback arranged his seven-man line like a V, and the player who received the pass on the kickoff placed himself inside the V. Though the play was successful in that game, the "V-trick" did not become the standard means of putting the ball in play until 1888. Called the wedge, the formation massed interlocked players who pulled or pushed the runner in the mass attack launching each half. In 1892,

Harvard added momentum to the wedge in the game against Yale. With the kicker poised at midfield, the remaining 10 players deployed in two groups in diagonal files up the field. At the signal the files converged on the run toward the kicker. As they reached him, he "footed" the ball, then passed it to the runner who stepped inside the wedge. Called the flying wedge, this violent method of providing interference for the ballcarrier led to many injuries. All wedge plays were outlawed between 1894 and 1896. Other formations which pulled tackles, guards, or ends back and sent them into motion before the snap to generate mass momentum assaults at defensive positions, wreaked havoc with the players. For example, 18 deaths and 159 serious injuries were cited in 1905. In 1906 the Football Rules Committee legalized the forward pass and prohibited the more dangerous mass plays. The forward pass opened up the game and ended the era when brawn was the determining factor in football competition. Early pass plays, however, amounted to little more than delegating an end to race downfield to receive the pass.

About 1910 the single wingback formation, which emphasized power and speed, was developed by Glenn S. (Pop) Warner, then coach at Carlisle Indian School. He stationed a backfield player (wingback) behind and outside an end, using either a balanced or unbalanced line. (A balanced line has three linemen on either side of the center; an unbalanced line has four or more linemen on one side of the center. The latter side is called the strong side, and most plays are run toward this side.) With the single-wing method most of the passing and running is done by the halfback, called the tailback, and fullback, called the plunging back. The quarterback serves as a blocker. The wingback may be a blocker, runner, passer, or pass receiver, or merely a decoy to lead the defense astray.

Sometimes the ends play far out to the side. With this variation of the single wing, called the split-end formation, either end is in a position to break down the field to receive a pass. This formation forces the defense to watch both ends as well as the wingback and the ballcarrier.

In the double wingback formation, also originated by Warner, each of the halfbacks, or wingbacks, stands behind and outside an end. The quarterback plays behind the strong-side tackle (or guard) and the fullback, behind the center. The fullback handles the ball first on most of the plays.

Knute Rockne, famed coach of Notre Dame and one of football's earliest pass receivers, introduced a unique arrangement that also stressed precision and speed rather than brute force. The players lined up first in a T (a balanced line, with the left halfback, fullback, and right halfback about 4 to 5 yards behind the center and the quarterback directly behind the center) and then shifted to a box formation—the backs deployed to either the left or right side of the center, two about a yard behind the line and two rear backs between 4 and 5 yards behind the line. Called the Notre Dame box, this formation was widely used during the 1920's and 1930's.

The short punt formation, popularized in the 1920's at the University of Michigan, enabled the team to play a passing game because the punter was also in position to pass or run. A halfback stood about 5 to 7 yards behind the center, which was normally the position assumed by a punter. The passing plays were simple, with the ends going out toward the sidelines or criss-crossing.

As knowledge about the game accumulated, the single-wing offense was exploited to include reverses (a player coming from one side of the backfield, taking the ball, and running around the opposite side, while his teammates deceive the defense on the direction of the play), and "buck" laterals (a fullback handing the ball to the quarterback who in turn sends a lateral pass—to the side or backward—to a halfback). Some teams developed plays in which four or five men handled the ball on a single play. Each offensive system had its vogue in various guises.

The T formation, however, has been in the game almost from its beginnings. But not until 1940 did a modernized version capture the imagination of coaches. The success of the T is based on quick-striking halfbacks plunging through quickly opened holes in the defensive line and a quarterback who keeps the ball hidden until he runs with it, hands it off, or passes it. The T sometimes features a man in motion—that is, one offensive back (usually a halfback) who can take a lateral pass from the quarterback and dash around the end or cut around the end and race downfield to receive a forward pass. In the modern T the quarterback always takes the ball from the center on a direct handoff (a hand-to-hand snap).

Variations of the T include the split-T and the wing-T. In the split-T, devised by Don Faurot of the University of Missouri, the linemen and backs are stationed (split) farther apart at the start of the play than they are in the regular T lineup. This split enables the quarterback to take the ball around end or through tackle, or send a lateral pass to a trailing halfback, depending on the movement of the defensive lineman, who is the main target of the attack. The wing-T stresses elements of single-wing blocking by employing a halfback on the flank, who can assist his end in blocking a defensive tackle, or run reverses, or catch a pass.

In professional and some college football, player positions have distinct designations in the standard T. One end, separated from the rest of the line is called the split end; the other, the tight end. One halfback, stationed out to the side, is the flankerback; he is vital to the modern passing game. Two backs (halfback and fullback), called running backs, are entrusted with running the ball, blocking for the quarterback and each other, or taking short passes from the quarterback when his primary receivers are closely covered.

Defensive Formations. Defensive formations vary with the coaching systems and with the position of the ball on the field. Some of the most common defenses include the 6-2-2-1, the 7-diamond, and the professional 4-3-2-2. The 6-2-2-1, an all-purpose formation, has six players (guards, tackles, and ends) on the line of scrimmage; these players shift to meet the offensive shifts. Two linebackers protect the zone immediately back of their linemen; these players usually stand behind the defensive tackles. The halfbacks, or cornerbacks, are 4 to 10 yards behind the linebackers and about one yard outside their own ends. Behind these secondary defensemen stands the deepest player, the safety man. He may be about 20 yards back of the scrimmage line unless the attacking team is likely to kick. Then he stands 30 to 40 yards back.

The 7-diamond defense calls for seven men on the scrimmage line, one linebacker, one halfback on each side behind his own end, and a safety. This alignment was used primarily against expected running plays and fell into disfavor as the passing game expanded.

Professional teams often use a 4-man line and a 3-2-2-secondary (three linebackers, two halfbacks, or cornerbacks, and two safeties, one of whom roams at will). Experimentation proved that this alignment serves the defense best. Similarly, many college coaches prefer a 5-3-2-1, depending on their personnel. Static defenses are avoided.

College and high school teams tend to use more players on the line because there is less skillful passing. But most teams cannot afford to keep six or seven men on the scrimmage line if the opponent has a good passer. Because defensive units are not so restricted by rules as the offense, there is more latitude in arrangements and shifting just before the ball is snapped.

EQUIPMENT

As the rules of play, football equipment has undergone many changes through the years. Most of these changes are the result of improved materials and the needs of the players.

Ball. The ball is in the shape of an elongated sphere tapered at both ends, with a four-panel, pebble-grained natural tan leather cover enclosing a rubber bladder. (At night, a white or striped ball is used.) It must be 11 to 11½ inches in length (long axis). The circumference around the short axis is 21¼ to 21½ inches and 28 to 28½ inches around the long axis. The ball is inflated to a pressure of 12½ to 13½ pounds of air.

Player Equipment. Each player wears a helmet, usually of unbreakable plastic, fitted with a face mask or bar and webbing on the inside to lessen shock. He usually wears pads that protect the shoulders, thighs, hips, knees, and ribs. Some of the pads are sewn into the football pants. The shoe has cleats attached to the sole for improved traction. On frozen fields, players may wear shoes without cleats to aid in traction. Some players have a specially designed mouth guard to protect against injuries to the lips and teeth. All player equipment is designed for the safety of the opponent as well as of the wearer. Each player's jersey shows his number on both the front and back. (For the television audience, this number may also appear on the helmet and shoulders.)

To facilitate identification by officials and spectators, numbers assigned players are systematized as follows: 10-49 for backfield men; 50-59, centers; 60-69, guards; 70-79, tackles; and 80-89, ends. Because of changing defensive alignments, however, the numbering system is difficult to maintain.

Officials' Equipment. Officials wear striped shirts and billed caps. All carry a red handkerchief used to call rules violations; the referee must have a whistle, while the other officials carry horns or whistles. The linesman's device for measuring the yardage gained on downs consists of two poles separated by 10 yards of sturdy small-mesh chain.

GLOSSARY OF FOOTBALL TERMS

Automatic. A play called by a quarterback at the line of scrimmage that is different from the play originally designated in the huddle.

Behind. In Australian football, a post on the goal line. Also, a point awarded the attackers if the ball goes over the line between the goalpost and behind post.

Blitz. A defensive charge by one or more secondary backfield players, usually linebackers, in an effort to tackle the quarterback before he can launch his play. See also *Red-dog.*

Bomb. A long forward pass designed for a quick touchdown.

Bootleg. A deception play executed by the quarterback, who hides the ball on his hip after faking a hand-off and then runs around end with no primary blocking.

Buttonhook. A pass pattern (maneuver) by a receiver who runs downfield and pivots quickly, facing the passer.

Clipping. Blocking from behind an opponent who does not have the ball; illegal beyond the line of scrimmage and subject to a penalty.

Conversion. One or more points scored after a touchdown; also called extra point(s).

Counter. A deceptive running play in which a ballcarrier runs opposite to the direction of most of his blockers.

Dead Ball. A ball not in play.

Dead Line. In Canadian football, the line parallel to and 25 yards behind each goal line.

Down. A unit of play. It starts with a snap and ends when the ball is declared dead. In U.S. play, a team is permitted four downs to advance the ball 10 yards; in Canadian play a team is permitted three.

Draw. A fake pass that entices defensive linemen into the offensive backfield, after which the quarterback hands off to a fellow back for a run through the vacated area. See also *Mousetrap.*

Fair Catch. A catch of a kicked ball that is beyond the neutral zone, after the receiver signals such intent by raising one arm overhead. The receiver forfeits the right to advance the ball, and the kicking team forfeits the right to tackle or block him. However, the ball is free if fumbled.

Flanker. A halfback who sets wide on offense, deploying as a prime passing target.

Flat. The area, right and left, of the scrimmage zone.

Free or Loose Ball. A live ball, other than a forward pass, that is not in the possession of a player.

Free Kick. A kick taken under conditions that prohibit either team from advancing beyond established restraining lines until the ball is kicked. A kickoff and the kick after a safety are free kicks.

Fumble. The dropping or mishandling of the ball by the player in possession.

Gridiron. The playing field, so called because of its 5-yard line markings parallel to the goal line.

Hand-off. A hand-to-hand exchange of the ball between teammates after the snap from center.

Holding. Illegally grasping of any opponent not carrying the ball.

Interception. A defensive player's catch of an opponent's pass, forward or lateral.

Kickoff. A free kick that puts the ball in play at the start of each half of the game or after a touchdown and conversion attempt or after a field goal.

Lateral. A ball (pass) thrown parallel to the scrimmage line or toward the offense's own goal line. Unlike a forward pass, it can be thrown anywhere on the field and is a free ball if it touches the ground.

Live Ball. A ball in play. A passed, kicked, or fumbled ball is live until it touches the ground or goes out of bounds.

Man in Motion. An offensive back who legally moves parallel to, or away from, the line of scrimmage before the snap. No one else on the offense, after assuming a set position, may move before the snap.

Marking. In Australian football, catching a kicked ball in midair. Players leap 4 or 5 feet in the air to hold spectacular marks. A player who marks the ball has the privilege of a free kick without opposition.

Mousetrap. A play that entices a defensive lineman into the offensive backfield to make him vulnerable to a block from the side. See also *Draw*.

Naked Reverse. A counter play by a ballcarrier without benefit of blockers ahead of him.

Offside. The status of a player on the line of scrimmage who, when play begins, is farther advanced toward his opponent's goal than the rules permit. A player is offside if he is in the neutral zone or makes contact with an opponent before the snap. In Canadian football, an offensive player ahead of a fumbled ball or completed pass is also offside.

Platoon. A specialized unit of a team employed only for offense or defense.

Punt. A method of kicking the ball by dropping and striking it before it touches the ground. The punt is the offensive team's way of exchanging distance for loss of possession.

Quick Kick. A punt (on 1st, 2d, or 3d down) not in regular punt formation, designed to gain more distance by surprising the defense.

Red-dog. To rush the passer. See also *Blitz*.

Reverse. A counter play that reverses the original direction of an attack.

Rollout. A quarterback pattern of running the ball toward the sideline for an optional pass, run, or hand-off.

Rouge. In Canadian football, a kick over the opponent's deadline or goal-area sideline. A rouge scores 1 point.

Ruck. In Australian football, three players who are permitted to roam anywhere on the field of play during the game.

Safety. A scoring play (2 points for the opposition) that occurs when a team is downed in its own end zone, or when a punt from the end zone goes out of bounds in that team's end zone.

Screen Pass. A pass into the flat to a receiver with several blockers lined up ahead of him.

Scrimmage. The action that ensues between the teams during a down, which begins with a snap of the ball and continues until the ball is dead.

Shepherding. In Australian football, obstructing or blocking, permitted only within 5 yards of the ball.

Slant. A diagonal run directed at the tackle positions.

Slot. The opened space between a tackle and an end, or an end and a flanker, in which another back is lined up. A slot formation uses such an alignment.

Snap. The pass sent by the center between his legs to a back, starting all scrimmage plays.

Spoiling. In Australian football, preventing a player from marking, usually by punching the ball.

Sudden Death. An overtime period assigned in professional championship games to break a tie score. The game ends when a score is made.

Tailback. The deep back in single-wing formation. Not a term used in T formation.

Touchback. A nonscoring play that occurs when the ball is downed in the end zone by the defense, provided it was not responsible for putting the ball there.

Bibliography

American Football League, *Official Guide* (St. Louis, current ed.).

Andrew, Bruce, *Australian Football Handbook* (Adelaide, current ed.).

Canadian Football League, *Official Record* (Toronto, current ed.).

Daley, Arthur, *Pro Football's Hall of Fame* (New York 1968).

Higdon, Hal, *Pro Football USA* (New York 1968).

Kramer, Jerry, *Instant Replay* (New York 1968).

Maule, Tex, *The Game,* rev. ed. (New York 1967).

Maule, Tex, *The Players: The Great Pros and How They Play* (New York 1967).

National Collegiate Athletic Association, *Official Football Guide* (Phoenix, current ed.).

National Federation of State High School Athletic Associations, *Football Handbook, Six Man Football,* and *Touch Football* (Chicago, current eds.).

Sporting News, *Football Register* (St. Louis, current ed.).

Treat, Roger, *The Official Encyclopedia of Football,* 6th rev. ed. (New York 1968).

College Football

1902 Michigan 49, Stanford 0	1936 Stanford 7, So. Methodist 0	1955 Ohio State 20, So. California 7
1916 Wash. State 14, Brown 0	1937 Pittsburgh 21, Washington 0	1956 Mich. State 17, UCLA 14
1917 Oregon 14, Pennsylvania 0	1938 California 13, Alabama 0	1957 Iowa 35, Oregon St. 19
1918–19 Service teams	1939 So. California 7, Duke 3	1958 Ohio State 10, Oregon 7
1920 Harvard 7, Oregon 6	1940 So. California 14, Tennessee 0	1959 Iowa 38, California 12
1921 California 28, Ohio State 0	1941 Stanford 21, Nebraska 13	1960 Washington 44, Wisconsin 8
1922 Wash. & Jeff. 0, California 0	1942 Oregon St. 20, Duke 16	1961 Washington 17, Minnesota 7
1923 So. California 14, Penn State 3	(at Durham)	1962 Minnesota 21, UCLA 3
1924 Navy 14, Washington 14	1943 Georgia 9, UCLA 0	1963 So. California 42, Wisconsin 37
1925 Notre Dame 27, Stanford 10	1944 So. California 29, Washington 0	1964 Illinois 17, Washington 7
1926 Alabama 20, Washington 19	1945 So. California 25, Tennessee 0	1965 Michigan 34, Oregon St. 7
1927 Alabama 7, Stanford 7	1946 Alabama 34, So. California 14	1966 UCLA 14, Mich. State 12
1928 Stanford 7, Pittsburgh 6	1947 Illinois 45, UCLA 14	1967 Purdue 14, So. California 13
1929 Georgia Tech 8, California 7	1948 Michigan 49, So. California 0	1968 Southern Cal. 14, Indiana 3
1930 So. California 47, Pittsburgh 14	1949 Northwestern 20, California 14	1969 Ohio State 27, Southern Cal. 16
1931 Alabama 24, Wash. State 0	1950 Ohio State 17, California 14	1970 Southern Cal. 10, Michigan 3
1932 So. California 21, Tulane 12	1951 Michigan 14, California 6	1971 Stanford 27, Ohio State 17
1933 So. California 35, Pittsburgh 0	1952 Illinois 40, Stanford 7	1972 Stanford 13, Michigan 12
1934 Columbia 7, Stanford 0	1953 So. California 7, Wisconsin 0	1973 So. California 42, Ohio State 17
1935 Alabama 29, Stanford 13	1954 Mich. State 28, UCLA 20	1974 Ohio State 42, So. California 21

1975 So. California 18, Ohio State 17
1976 UCLA 23, Ohio State 10
1977 So. California 14, Michigan 6
1978 Washington 27, Michigan 20
1979 So. California 17, Michigan 10

Orange Bowl, Miami

1933 Miami (Fla.) 7, Manhattan 0
1934 Duquesne 33, Miami (Fla.) 7
1935 Bucknell 26, Miami (Fla.) 0
1936 Catholic U. 20, Mississippi 19
1937 Duquesne 13, Miss. State 12
1938 Auburn 6, Mich. State 0
1939 Tennessee 17, Oklahoma 0
1940 Georgia Tech 21, Missouri 7
1941 Miss. State 14, Georgetown 7
1942 Georgia 40, TCU 26
1943 Alabama 37, Boston Col. 21
1944 LSU 19, Texas A&M 14
1945 Tulsa 26, Georgia Tech 12
1946 Miami (Fla.) 13, Holy Cross 6
1947 Rice 8, Tennessee 0
1948 Georgia Tech 20, Kansas 14
1949 Texas 41, Georgia 28
1950 Santa Clara 21, Kentucky 13
1951 Clemson 15, Miami (Fla.) 14
1952 Georgia Tech 17, Baylor 14
1953 Alabama 61, Syracuse 6
1954 Oklahoma 7, Maryland 0
1955 Duke 34, Nebraska 7
1956 Oklahoma 20, Maryland 6
1957 Colorado 27, Clemson 21
1958 Oklahoma 48, Duke 21
1959 Oklahoma 21, Syracuse 6
1960 Georgia 14, Missouri 0
1961 Missouri 21, Navy 14
1962 LSU 25, Colorado 7
1963 Alabama 17, Oklahoma 0
1964 Nebraska 13, Auburn 7
1965 Texas 21, Alabama 17
1966 Alabama 39, Nebraska 28
1967 Florida 27, Georgia Tech 12
1968 Oklahoma 26, Tennessee 24
1969 Penn State 15, Kansas 14
1970 Penn State 10, Missouri 3
1971 Nebraska 17, Louisiana St. 12
1972 Nebraska 38, Alabama 6
1973 Nebraska 40, Notre Dame 6
1974 Penn State 16, Louisiana St. 9

1975 Notre Dame 13, Alabama 11
1976 Oklahoma 14, Michigan 6
1977 Ohio State 27, Colorado 10
1978 Arkansas 31, Oklahoma 6
1979 Oklahoma 31, Nebraska 24

Sugar Bowl, New Orleans

1935 Tulane 20, Temple 14
1936 TCU 3, LSU 2
1937 Santa Clara 21, LSU 14
1938 Santa Clara 6, LSU 0
1939 TCU 15, Carnegie Tech 7
1940 Texas A&M 14, Tulane 13
1941 Boston Col. 19, Tennessee 13
1942 Fordham 2, Missouri 0
1943 Tennessee 14, Tulsa 7
1944 Georgia Tech 20, Tulsa 18
1945 Duke 29, Alabama 26
1946 Oklahoma A&M 33, St. Mary's 13
1947 Georgia 20, No. Carolina 10
1948 Texas 27, Alabama 7
1949 Oklahoma 14, No. Carolina 6
1950 Oklahoma 35, LSU 0
1951 Kentucky 13, Oklahoma 7
1952 Maryland 28, Tennessee 13
1953 Georgia Tech 24, Mississippi 7
1954 Georgia Tech 42, West Virginia 19
1955 Navy 21, Mississippi 0
1956 Georgia Tech 7, Pittsburgh 0
1957 Baylor 13, Tennessee 7
1958 Mississippi 39, Texas 7
1959 LSU 7, Clemson 0
1960 Mississippi 21, LSU 0
1961 Mississippi 14, Rice 6
1962 Alabama 10, Arkansas 3
1963 Mississippi 17, Arkansas 13
1964 Alabama 12, Mississippi 7
1965 LSU 13, Syracuse 10
1966 Missouri 20, Florida 18
1967 Alabama 34, Nebraska 7
1968 LSU 20, Wyoming 13
1969 Arkansas 16, Georgia 2
1970 Mississippi 27, Arkansas 22
1971 Tennessee 34, Air Force 13
1972 Oklahoma 40, Auburn 22
*1972 (Dec.) Oklahoma 14, Penn State 0
1973 Notre Dame 24, Alabama 23
1974 Nebraska 13, Florida 10
1975 Alabama 13, Penn State 6

1977 (Jan.) Pittsburgh 27, Georgia 3
1978 Alabama 35, Ohio State 6
1979 Alabama 14, Penn State 7
* Penn St. awarded game by forfeit

Cotton Bowl, Dallas

1937 TCU 16, Marquette 6
1938 Rice 28, Colorado 14
1939 St. Mary's 20, Texas Tech 13
1940 Clemson 6, Boston Col. 3
1941 Texas A&M, 13 Fordham 12
1942 Alabama 29, Texas A&M 21
1943 Texas 14, Georgia Tech 7
1944 Randolph Field 7, Texas 7
1945 Oklahoma A&M 34, TCU 0
1946 Texas 40, Missouri 27
1947 Arkansas 0, LSU 0
1948 So. Methodist 13, Penn State 13
1949 So. Methodist 21, Oregon 13
1950 Rice 27, No. Carolina 13
1951 Tennessee 20, Texas 14
1952 Kentucky 20, TCU 7
1953 Texas 16, Tennessee 0
1954 Rice 28, Alabama 6
1955 Georgia Tech 14, Arkansas 6
1956 Mississippi 14, TCU 13
1957 TCU 28, Syracuse 27
1958 Navy 20, Rice 7
1959 TCU 0, Air Force 0
1960 Syracuse 23, Texas 14
1961 Duke 7, Arkansas 6
1962 Texas 12, Mississippi 7
1963 LSU 13, Texas 0
1964 Texas 28, Navy 6
1965 Arkansas 10, Nebraska 7
1966 LSU 14, Arkansas 7
1967 Georgia 24, So. Methodist 9
1968 Texas A&M 20, Alabama 16
1969 Texas 36, Tennessee 13
1970 Texas 21, Notre Dame 17
1971 Notre Dame 24, Texas 11
1972 Penn State 30, Texas 6
1973 Texas 17, Alabama 13
1974 Nebraska 19, Texas 3
1975 Penn State 41, Baylor 20
1976 Arkansas 31, Georgia 10
1977 Houston 30, Maryland 21
1978 Notre Dame 38, Texas 10
1979 Notre Dame 35, Houston 34

Professional Football

National Football League Champions

Year	East Winner (W.L.T.)	West Winner (W.L.T.)	Playoff
1933	New York Giants (1-3-0)	Chicago Bears (10-2-1)	Chicago Bears 23, New York 21
1934	New York Giants (8-5-0)	Chicago Bears (13-0-0)	New York 30, Chicago Bears 13
1935	New York Giants (9-3-0)	Detroit Lions (7-3-2)	Detroit 25, New York 7
1936	Boston Redskins (7-5-0)	Green Bay Packers (10-1-1)	Green Bay 21, Boston 6
1937	Washington Redskins (8-3-0)	Chicago Bears (9-1-1)	Washington 28, Chicago Bears 21
1938	New York Giants (8-2-1)	Green Bay Packers (8-3-0)	New York 23, Green Bay 17
1939	New York Giants (9-1-1)	Green Bay Packers (9-2-0)	Green Bay 27, New York 0
1940	Washington Redskins (9-2-0)	Chicago Bears (8-3-0)	Chicago Bears 73, Washington 0
1941	New York Giants (8-3-0)	Chicago Bears (10-1-1)	Chicago Bears 37, New York 9
1942	Wash. Redskins (10-1-1)	Chicago Bears (11-0-0)	Washington 1, Chicago Bears 6
1942	Wash. Redskins (6-3-1)	Chicago Bears (8-1-1)	Chicago Bears, 41, Washington 21
1944	New York Giants (8-1-1)	Green Bay Packers (8-2-0)	Green Bay 14, New York 7
1945	Wash. Redskins (8-2-0)	Cleveland Rams (9-1-0)	Cleveland 15, Washington 14
1946	New York Giants (7-3-1)	Chicago Bears (8-2-1)	Chicago Bears 24, New York 14
1947	Philadelphia Eagles (8-4-0)	Chicago Cardinals (9-3-0)	Chicago Cardinals 28, Philadelphia 21
1948	Philadelphia Eagles (9-2-1)	Chicago Cardinals (11-1-0)	Philadelphia 7, Chicago Cardinals 0
1949	Philadelphai Eagles (11-1-0)	Los Angeles Rams (8-2-2)	Philadelphia 14, Los Angeles 0
1950	Cleveland Browns (10-2-0)	Los Angeles Rams (9-3-0)	Cleveland 30, Los Angeles 28
1951	Cleveland Browns (11-1-0)	Los Angeles Rams (8-4-0)	Los Angeles 24, Cleveland 17
1952	Cleveland Browns (8-4-0)	Detroit Lions (9-3-0)	Detroit 17, Cleveland 7
1953	Cleveland Browns (11-1-0)	Detroit Lions (10-2-0)	Detroit 17, Cleveland 16
1954	Cleveland Browns (9-3—0)	Detroit Lions (9-2-1)	Cleveland 56, Detroit 10
1955	Cleveland Browns (9-2-1(	Los Angeles Rams (8-3-1(	Cleveland 38, Los Angeles 14
1956	New York Giants (8-3-1(	Chicago Bears (9-2-1)	New York 47, Chicago Bears 7
1957	Cleveland Browns (9-2)	Detroit Lions (8-4-0)	Detroit 59, Cleveland 14
1958	New York Giants (9-3-0)	Baltimore Colts (9-3-0)	Baltimore 23, New York 17(b)
1959	New York Giants (10-2-0)	Baltimore Colts (9-3-0)	Baltimore 31, New York 16
1960	Philadelphia Eagles (10-2-0)	Green Bay Packers (8-4-0)	Philadelphia 17, Green Bay 13
1961	New York Giants (10-3-1)	Green Bay Packers (11-3-0)	Green Bay 37, New York 0
1962	New York Giants (12-2-0)	Green Bay Packers (13-1-0)	Green Bay 16, New York 7
1963	New York Giants (11-3-0)	Chicago Bears (11-1-21)	Chicago 114, New York 10
1964	Cleveland Browns (10-3-1)	Baltimore Colts (12-2-0)	Cleveland 27, Baltimore 0
1965	Cleveland Browns (11-3-0)	Green Bay Packers (10-3-1)	Green Bay 23, Cleveland 12
1966	Dallas Cowboys (10-3-1)	Green Bay Packers (12-2-0)	Green Bay 34, Dallas 27

Super Bowl

Year	Winner	Loser
1967	Green Bay Packers, 35	Kansas City chiefs, 10
1968	Green Bay Packers, 33	Oakland Raiders, 14
1969	New York Jets, 16	Baltimore Colts, 7
1970	Kansas City Chiefs, 23	Minnesota Vikings, 7
1971	Baltimore Colts, 16	Dallas Cowboys, 13
1972	Dallas Cowboys, 24	Miami Dolphins, 3
1973	Miami Dolphins, 14	Washington Redskins, 7
1974	Miami Dolphins, 24	Minnesota Vikings, 7
1975	Pittsburgh Steelers, 16	Minnesota Vikings, 6
1976	Pittsburgh Steelers, 21	Dallas Cowboys, 17
1977	Oakland Raiders, 32	Minnesota Vikings, 14
1978	Dallas Cowboys, 27	Denver Broncos, 10
1979	Pittsburgh Steelers, 35	Dallas Cowboys, 31

INDEX

Adams, Arthur, 47
Adderley, Herb, 137
Alabama, University of, 26–27, 50–51, 82–83
Albright College, 178
All-American Football Conference, 99–100, 103
Allen, George, 153–54, 183
Allen, Greg, 180
All Stars football, 91
Alworth, Lance, 148, 151
Ameche, Alan, 49, 113–15
Ameche, Don, 97
American Football League, 88, 92, 117, 128–29
amphetamines, use in football, 183
Anderson, Bob, 52–53, 60–62
Anderson, Dick, 164
Anderson, Donnie, 135–36
Anderson, Heartley, 23–24
anthropology and football, 185–86
anti-trust laws and football, 112–13
Arkansas, University of, 68
Army: vs Columbia University 1947, 39–41; lonesome end play, 58–59; losses to Notre Dame, 15; vs Michigan 1949, 41–42; vs Navy 1946, 36–39; 1950, 44–45; 1959, 60–62; vs Notre Dame games disbanded, 178–79; vs Notre Dame 1913, 7–8; 1929, 20–22; 1946, 35–36; 1957, 52–53; record 1944–1947, 40; vs Yale 1929, 18–20
Arnold, Claude, 43
Arnold, Steve, 155
Artoe, Lee, 96
Associated Press football poll, 78–79
athletes, college subsidies for, 177–78
Azzaro, Joe, 65–66

Baker, David, 58
Baker Field, 12
Baldwin, Howard, 155
Baltimore Colts, 113–15, 127, 139–41, 150–51
Baltimore, Maryland, 108
Barabas, Al, 25–26
Barnes, Erich, 120
Barnum, Len, 94
Barrett, Bill, 44
Baugh, Sammy, 29–30, 93, 95–99, 102, 121–23
Bass, Mike, 153
Bassett, John, 155, 158
Bauman, Charlie, 80–81
Baysinger, Reaves, 38–39
Beathard, Pete, 62
Beban, Gary, 63–64
Becker, Wayland, 91
Beirne, Jim, 66
Bell, Bert, 16, 96, 100–105, 108, 112–13
Bellino, Joe, 60–62
Berry, Raymond, 113–15, 121–23, 127
Bertelsen, Jim, 68–71, 72
Berwanger, Jay, 28, 75
Biletnikoff, Fred, 167–68
Bingham, William, 177
Bixler, E. G., 178
blacks in football, 179–80, 182
Blaik, Earl, 35–36, 53, 138
Blanchard, Felix (Doc), 35–36, 38–39, 40, 75, 179
Blanda, George, 103–4, 123
Bleier, Rocky, 170
Blue Ridge College, 178
body guards, football, 143–46
Booth, A., 18–20

Boston Redskins, 92
Bourland, Dave, 52–53
bowls, football, 12–13, 68–70; see also specific Bowls
Bradshaw, Terry, 162, 166, 169–71
Bramlett, Leon, 38–39
Brennan, Terry, 35–36
Brickley, Charles, 86
broadcasts, football, 18, 31–32
Brooker, Tom, 123
Brown, Jim, 57, 113, 126
Brown University, 8–9, 178
Brumbaugh, Carl, 89–92
Bruno, Al, 46
Bryan, Bucky, 27–28
Bryant, Paul, 27, 82–83
Bucknell University, 177
Buffalo Bills, 156–57
Buivid, Ray, 30
Bukich, Rudy, 49
Bulger, Jim, 71–72
Bunce, Don, 73–74
Burman, George, 183
Bushnell, Asa, 48

Cagle, Chris (Red), 20–21
Cain, Jim, 41–42, 45
Caldwell, Joe, 60–62
California, University of. See UCLA
California, University of Southern. See USC
Cameron, Bob, 45
Camp, Walter, 5, 10–12, 174
Carlisle Indian football team, 7
Carnegie Fund Study of football, 174–78
Carpenter, Bill, 60–62
Carpenter, Lew, 113
Carr, Joe F., 86, 89
Cavanaugh, John, 178–79
Cavender, Regis, 64–66
Champi, Frank, 67
Chandler, Don, 115, 137
Chewning, Lynn, 38–39
Chicago Bears: vs All Stars 1934, 91; Grange on, 87–88; Halas as coach, 137–38; vs New York Giants 1925, 87–88; 1933, 89–91; 1934, 91–92; vs Portsmouth Spartans 1932, 89; vs St. Louis Cardinals 1949, 103–4; vs San Francisco 49ers 1965, 128; vs Washington Redskins 1937, 93–94; 1940, 95–96; 1943, 97–99
Chicago Cardinals, 119
Chicago Hornets, 103
Chicago, University of, 11, 32
cleats, rubber, 17
Cleveland Browns, 93, 101, 105–9, 113
Cleveland Rams, 100
coaching, college football, 8–10, 75–77
coaching, pro football, 110
Colella, Tom, 101
Colgate University, 57
colleges, 12, 13, 32, 34, 174–78; see also football, college; specific colleges and universities
Collins, Ted, 97, 103
Columbia University, 12, 25–26, 39–41, 177
computers in football, 132–33
Conerly, Charley, 113–15, 122–23
conversion, 2-point, football, 58
Cotton Bowl 1937, 29–30; 1954, 50–51; 1970, 70–71; 1971, 71–72
Corbally, John, 180
Corbett, George, 91

Cornell University, 7
Cowhig, Gerry, 35–36
Crisler, H.O., 49–51, 77
Cross, George, 48
Csonka, Larry, 151–54, 157–59, 162, 164–65
Cuff, Ward, 94
Cuozzo, Gary, 127
Curry, Bill, 143–46
Curtice, Jack, 63

Dallas Cowboys: *vs* Baltimore Colts *1971*, 150–51; *vs* Denver Broncos *1978*, 168–69; *vs* Green Bay Packers *1968*, 135–36; *vs* Houston Oilers *1962*, 123; *vs* Miami Dolphins *1972*, 151–53; *vs* Pittsburgh Steelers *1976*, 165–66; *1979*, 169–71
Dallas Rangers, 118
Danowski, Ed, 91–92, 94
Dartmouth College, 178
Daugherty, Duffy, 63–64
Davidson, Gary, 155
Davis, Anthony, 74–75
Davis, Glenn, 35–36, 38–39, 40, 75, 105–6, 179
Davis, Willie, 138
Dawson, Len, 128, 130, 148
dead ball, football, 25
Dean, Ted, 119–20
deaths, football, 5
defense, college football, 2–3, 23–25, 53–54
defense, pro football, 134–35
Dicus, Chuck, 68
Dempsey, Tom, 149–50
Denver Broncos, 168–69
Detroit Lions, 109
Dodds, Harold, 47
Dorais, Charley, 7–8
Doran, Jim, 109
Dowling, Brian, 67
drugs and football, 180–83
Dudley Stadium, 12
Dufek, Don, 41–42
Duke University, 30–31

Earl, Bill, 38–39
Edwards, Glen, 165
Edwards, William H., 88, 89
elbow pads, football, 16
Elder, Jack, 20–21
electronics, use in football, 110, 132–33
Eliot, Charles W., 174
Ellis, Clarence, 70–72
Enderle, Dick, 164
equipment, football, 17, 25
Erdelatz, Eddie, 62
Everhardus, Herman, 91
Ewbank, Weeb, 113–15, 146, 156–57

fans, football, 28
Farkas, Andy, 99
Faurot, Don, 51
Fears, Tommy, 106–8, 123
Fenstemaker, Leroy, 51
field goal, football, 149–50, 159
Filchock, Frank, 101–2, 105, 123
films, football, 10–11
Fischl, Frank, 41–42, 45
Flaherty, Ray, 95–96, 121
Foldberg, Dan, 42, 45
Ford; Danny, 80–81
formations, football, 51; I formation, 59; T formation, 34, 51, 53
Fordham University, 31–32
Four Horsemen, 15–16
franchise, AFL, 92
Franklin and Marshall College, 178
free agents, football, 160–61

Friedlund, J. Arthur, 103
Fritz, Ken, 80–81
Fusina, Chuck, 82–83

Galiffa, Arnold, 40–42
gambling, football, 101–2, 124–26, 133, 179
Garcia, Rod, 73–74
Garrett, Mike, 148
Garvey, Ed, 160, 163–64
Gaspar, Phil, 30–31
Gater Bowl, 80–81
Gatewood, Tom, 71–72
Gehrig, Mrs. Lou, 99
Georgia Tech, 18, 54–55, 179–80
Gerald, Rob, 78
Gifford, Frank, 113–15
Gill, Barney, 58
Gillian, John, 162–63
Gladieux, Bob, 65–66
goal posts, college football, 16–17, 60
goal posts, pro football, 159
Gossard, G.D., 177
Graham, Otto, 101, 105–9
Grange, Harold (Red), 13, 87–89
Grant, Bud, 161
Grayson, Bobby, 25–27
Green Bay Packers: *vs* Baltimore Colts *1965*, 127; *vs* Dallas Cowboys *1968*, 135–36; *vs* Kansas City Chiefs *1967*, 130–32; Lambeau on, 104; Lombardi as coach, 116, 138–39; *vs* New York Giants *1938*, 94; *vs* Oakland Raiders *1968*, 137; *vs* Philadelphia Eagles *1960*, 119–20
Greene, Cornelius, 74
Grider, Dallas, 63–64
Grier, Bobby, 54–55, 179
Griese, Bob, 66, 151–54, 156–57
Griffin, Archie, 74–75
Griffin, Marvin, 179–80
Griffith, John, 86, 178
Griffith, R.W., 177–78
Groza, Lou, 101, 105–9, 113
Gustafson, Bill, 40–41

Haden, Pat, 74
Halas, George, 51, 137–38
Haluska, Jim, 49
Hamilton, Tom, 25–26, 38–39, 47
Hanratty, Terry, 65–66
Hapes, Merle, 101–2, 105
Harris, Franco, 161–63, 170–71
Harrison, Reggie, 166
Harvard Stadium, 13
Harvard University, 67, 174, 177
Hawkes, Herbert, 177
Hawkins, Bill, 38–39
Hayes, Wayne (Woody): and Griffin, 75; as Ohio State coach, 47; ousted from football, 80–81; at Rose Bowl *1975*, 74; *1977*, 77–78
Hayward, William, 88
Hein, Mel, 94
Heisman Award, 75
Heisman, John W., 11
Hemmeter, Chris, 164–65
Hempel, Scott, 70–72
Heneage, Harry R., 178
Herman, Dave, 145–46, 156
Hewitt, Bill, 91
Hill, Harry, 45
Hill, Jerry, 139–40
Hill, Winston, 156
Hirsch, Elroy, 123
Hoffman, John, 104
Hoover, Herbert, 25
Hornung, Paul, 119–20, 124–27, 138
Houston Oilers, 128

Howell, Jim Lee, 94
Howell, Millard, 26–27
Howley, Chuch, 151–52
huddle, football, 161
Hunt, Lamar, 129
Hutson, Don, 27, 43, 121–23

Illinois, University of, 13
injuries, football, 25, 143–46
Intercollegiate Football Rules Committee, 5, 7; see also rules, college football
Iowa, University of, 12, 13
Ivy League and football, 47–48

Jamerson, Wilbur, 46
Jamison, Al, 57
Janowicz, Vic, 75
Jefferson, Bernie, 29
Johnson, Butch, 168
Johnson, Harvey, 101
Johnson, L.B., 70
Joint Rules Committee, football, 8; see also rules, college football
Jones, Carlmon, 180
Jones, Deacon, 143, 145
Jones, Edgar, 101
Jones, Howard, 18, 24–25
Jones, L.M. (Biff), 179
Juday, Steve, 63–64
Jurgensen, Sonny, 121–22

Kaiser, Dave, 55
Kansas City Chiefs, 128, 130–32, 148
Kapp, Joe, 160–61
Karch, Sargent, 164
Karras, Alex, 124–26
Karr, Billy, 89–91
Kavanaugh, Ken, 103–4
Keating, Ed, 158, 164–65
Kellum, Bill, 41–42
Kentucky, University of, 46
Kessing, O.O., 103
kick, college football, 5, 7, 17, 25
kickoffs, football, 159
Kiesling, Walter, 97
Kiick, Jim, 158–59, 164–65
Kinney, Jeff, 72
Kirk, Grayson, 47
Knox, Ronnie, 55
Koceski, Leo, 42
Koppisch, Walter, 86
Kovatch, John, 29
Kowalcyk, Walt, 55
Koy, Ted, 70
Kramer, Jerry, 138–39
Krause, Barry, 82–83
Krueger, Al, 30–31
Kuckhahn, Karl, 41–42
Kusserow, Lou, 40–41

labor union, football players as, 136
Lambeau, Curly, 104
Lamonica, Daryle, 137
Landry, Tom, 135, 151–53, 166, 168
Lansdell, Grenville, 30–31
Lassiter, Ike, 146
Lavelli, Dante, 101, 106, 123
Laws, Joe, 91
Layden, Elmer, 13, 15–16, 96, 100
Layne, Bobby, 109
Leahy, Frank, 34, 43–44
Lebanon Valley College, 177
Lehigh University, 178
Leland Stanford Jr. University, 13; see also Stanford University

Lemm, Wally, 182
Lewisohn Stadium, 12
Lewis, Tommy, 50–51
Lilly, Bob, 151–52
Little, Lou, 25–26, 49–51, 91
Livie, Bruce, 108
Lombardi, Vince, 116, 138–39
Lom, Benny, 18
Los Angeles Coliseum, 12
Los Angeles Rams, 105–8, 144–45
Luckman, Sid, 95–99, 102
Lujack, Johnny, 35–36, 103–4, 179
Lytle, Rob, 168–69

McAfee, George, 30–31
McCall, Scott, 29–30
Maccioli, Mike, 43–44
McConn, C.M., 178
McCully, Al, 38–39
McDonald, Paul, 79–80
McDonald, Tommy, 119–23
MacDonald, Torbert, 154–55
McGee, Max, 130
McKay, John, 74
Mackbee, Earsell, 148
Mackey, John, 149
Mackmull, Jack, 40–42
McNeill, Fred, 167
Magnani, Dante, 99, 121–23
Malott, Deane, 47
Mandel, Frank, 197
Manders, Jack, 89, 91–93, 95–96
Maniaci, Joe, 95–96
March, Harry, 86, 89, 92
Marine Corps, 13
Marquette University, 29–30
Masterson, Bernie, 93
Masterson, Bob, 99
Matal, Red, 25
Meggysey, Dave, 180–83
mergers in football, 97, 99, 103, 128–29
Meyer, L.D. (Monk), 28–30
Miami Dolphins, 151–54, 157–59
Michigan, University of: vs Army 1949, 41–42; Big 10 rating 1926, 16; football revenue of, 9; vs Illinois 1924, 13; vs Notre Dame 1966, 64–66; vs Ohio State 1921, 10; 1977, 77–78; 1978, 80–81; slush funds for athletes, 177; vs Stanford 1972, 73–74; vs UCLA 1956, 55; 1966, 63–64
Mikulak, Mike, 91
Mildren, Jack, 72
Mileti, Nick, 155
Miller, Creighton, 136
Miller, Red, 168–69
Minneapolis-St. Paul club, 118
Minnesota, University of, 28–29
Minnesota Vikings, 148, 157–58, 161–63
Mintz, Barney, 27–28
Modell, Arthur B., 165
Moegle, Dicky, 50–51
Molesworth, Keith, 89–92
Momsen, Tony, 42
Montana, Joe, 79–80
Montgomery, Bill, 25–26, 29–30, 68
Moore, Bernie, 48
Morrall, Earl, 139–40, 143, 150
Morton, Craig, 150–51
Moscrip, Monk, 27
Motley, Marion, 106–8, 123
Murchison, Clint, Jr., 118
Murray, Carley, 97
Myrha, Steve, 113–15

Nagurski, Bronco, 89–93, 99
Namath, Joe, 126, 139–46, 156–57
National-American Football League, 103

National Collegiate Athletic Association, and football, 15, 47, 68–70, 184–85; *see also* rules, college football

National Football League (NFL): admission of new teams, 118; and Baltimore club, 108; championship *1943*, 97–99; *1950*, 105–6; *1951*, 106–8; *1953*, 109; and Cleveland club, 93; and drugs in football, 183; Eastern-Western divisions of, 104–5; and Hapes-Filchock scandal, 101–2; and Layden, 96, 100; merger with AFL, 128–29; merger with All-American Conference, 103; player plan, 92; player-reserve system, 160–61; players as labor union, 136; players' strike, 160, 163–64; Rozelle as commissioner, 117–18; stocking plan, 165; suspension of players, 124–26; and WFL, 164–65

Nave, Doyle, 30–31

Navy football team, 36–39, 44–45, 60–62

Neale, Earle, 97

Neal, Richard, 164

Nebraska, University of, 13, 33, 72

Newman, Harry, 89–91

New Orleans Saints, 130

Newton, Al, 180

New York Giants, 87–92, 94, 113–15, 120

New York Jets, 139–43, 156–57

New York University, 177

New York Yankees, 101

night game, football, 17

Nitschke, Ray, 138

Nixon, Richard, 68, 154, 182

Noll, Chuck, 166

Nolting, Ray, 95–96

Northwestern University, 28–29

Notre Dame: *vs* Army games disbanded, 178–79; *vs* Army *1913*, 7–8; *1929*, 20–22; *1946*, 35–36; *1957*; 52–53; *vs* Michigan *1966*, 64–66; *vs* Nebraska *1924*, 13; *vs* Oklahoma *1957*, 57–58; *vs* Purdue *1950*, 43–44; records, 15, 23–24, 44; *vs* Stanford *1925*, 15–16; *vs* Texas *1970*, 70–71; *1971*, 71–72; T formation, 34; travels of football team, 8; *vs* USC *1931*, 23–24; *1978*, 79–80

numbers, football, 7

Oakland Raiders, 137, 139, 146, 167–68

O'Brien, Jim, 150–51

offense, college football, 5, 16–17, 23, 33–34, 53–54

Ohio State: Hayes as coach, 47; *vs* Michigan *1921*, 10; *1977*, 77–78; *1978*, 80–81; *vs* USC *1975*, 74

Okeson, Walter, 33–34

Oklahoma, University of, 57–58, 72, 184–85

Olympic Games, 12

Omwake, Howard, 178

O'Rourke, Charlie, 96–97

Ortmann, Charley, 41–42

Otto, Jim, 145–46

Out of Their League (Meggysey and Scott), 182–83

Owen State, 135

Parseghian, Ara, 70–72

pass, college football, 5, 7, 16

pass, pro football, 89, 121–23, 148

Pastore, John, 154

Paterno, Joe, 82–83

Pearson, Drew, 166

penalties, football, 16, 159

Pennsylvania, University of, 12, 16, 82–83, 177

periods, football, 7

Peschel, Randy, 68

Peters, Reeves, 48

Philadelphia Eagles, 96, 97, 102, 119–20

Philbin, Gerry, 139

Phillips, Eddie, 71–72

Pierce, Palmer, 86

Pietrosante, Nick, 52–53, 58

Pittsburgh Steelers: *vs* Dallas Cowboys, *1976*, 165–66; *1979*, 169–71; franchise trade, 96; merger with Cardinals, 99; merger with Eagles, 97; *vs* Minnesota Vikings *1975*, 161–63

Pittsburgh, University of, 17–18, 54–55

Planutis, Gerry, 55

plays, football: lonesome end, 58–59; ride series, 53; short side option, 60

poll, public opinion, 78–79, 151

Pond, Ducky, 86

professional football, 84–171

Princeton University, 9, 11

Prothro, Tommy, 63–64

Purdue University, 43–44, 66

Pyle, Charles C., 88

Pyle, Mike, 136

racism and football, 179–80, 182

radio broadcast, football, 18, 108

Ralston, John, 73–74

ratings, football *1926*, 16

Raye, Jimmy, 65–66

Reagan, Frank, 59

records, college football, 57, 62, 63

records, pro football: Bradshaw, 171; Brown, 126, 128; field goal, 149–50; pass-catching, 148; rushing, 126, 128, 155; Simpson, 156–57; Super Bowl *1977*, 167–68

recruiting, pro football, 174–78

Reeves, Daniel, 100

reform of football, 2

revenue, football, 10

Reynolds, Frank, 52–53, 58

Rhome, Jerry, 63

Rice Memorial Stadium, 12

Rice University, 50–51

Richards, Golden, 168

Ridlon, Jim, 57

Riegels, Roy, 18

riots, football, 28

ritual of football, 185–86

Robbie, Joe, 158–59

Rockne, Knut, 24: Army game *1913*, 7–8; portrait of, 22; record wins *1924*, 15; Stanford game *1925*, 15–16

Rollow, Cooper, 79

Ronzoni, Gene, 89–92

Roosevelt, Theodore, 2

Rose Bowl *1928*, 18; *1933*, 25–26; *1934*, 26–27; *1939*, 30–31; *1940*, 33; *1953*, 49; *1956*, 55; *1963*, 62; *1966*, 63–64; *1967*, 66; *1972*, 73–74; *1975*, 74; *1977*, 77–78

Rowan, Rip, 36, 39, 40–41

Royal, Darrell, 68, 70–72

Rozelle, Alvin (Pete): football strike, 149; merger with AFL, 129; NFL head, 117–18; player-reserve system, 160–61; and rules change, 159–60; and Super Bowl *1975*, 161; and suspension of players, 124; and TV blackouts, 154–55; and WFL, 165

Ruffa, Tony, 30–31

rules, college football: change in, 2–9, 16–17, 25; goal posts widened, 60; side line coaching, 9–10; speedier offense, 33–34; two-platoon system, 49–50, 63; 2-point conversion, 58

rules, pro football, 89, 159–60

Rutgers, University, 9, 60

Ruttledge, Jeff, 82–83

Sadat, Anwar el-, 77

St. Louis Cardinals, 99, 103–4, 119, 182

salaries, football, 115, 126–27

Samuels, Dale, 43–44

San Francisco '49ers, 128

Sauer, George, Jr. 140

Sayers, Gale, 128

Schlembeckler, Bo, 78

Schmertz, Robert, 155

Schramm, Tex, 129

Schwartzwalder, Ben, 180

Sciarra, John, 75

scoreboard, football, 16

Scott, Jack, 182

Senate, U.S., 154–55
Shakespeare, Bill, 28
Sharp, Paul, 184–85
Shaughnessy, Clark, 32–34, 51
Shaver, Gaius, 23–24
Shofner, Del, 120–23
Shula, Don, 151–54, 157, 165
signal-calling, football, 75–77
Simons, Monk, 27–28
Simpson, O.J., 71, 155–57
Skoglund, Bob, 35–36
slush funds, college athletic, 174–78
Snead, Norm, 120–23
Snell, Matt, 139–41
Snyder, Jimmy (The Greek), 133
Southeastern Conference, 70
Southern Methodist University, 183
Speedie, Mac, 123
Speyrer, Charles, 70–71
Stabler, Ken, 168
stadiums. *See* bowls, football
Stagg, Amos Alonzo (Lonnie), 8, 48, 86
Stallworth, John, 170–71
Stanford University: *vs* Alabama *1934*, 26–27; *vs* Columbia
    1933, 25–26; *vs* Michigan 1972, 74–75; *vs* Nebraska *1940*,
    33; *vs* Notre Dame, *1925*, 15–16; *vs* Pittsburgh *1927*, 17;
    1928, 18; slush funds, 177; T formation, 34; *vs* UCLA
    1924, 15
Starr, Bart, 51, 130–32, 135–38
Stassen, Harold, 48
Staubach, Roger, 75, 151–53, 165, 168, 171
Sternaman, Joe, 88
Stevens, Mal, 20
Stickles, Monty, 52–53, 58
Stiegman, John, 60
Stiles, Bob, 63–64
Stout, Elmer, 42, 45
Street, James, 68–70
Strickler, George, 99, 100
strike, football, 149, 160, 163–64
Strong, Ken, 91–92
Stydahar, Joe, 105–6, 108
subsidies, college athletic, 177–78
substitution, college football, 25, 33–34, 49–50, 63
sudden death, football, 95, 159
Sugar Bowl *1935*, 27–28; *1951*, 46; *1956*, 54–55, 179–80; *1979*,
    82–83;
Super Bowl *1968*, 137; *1969*, 139–41; *1971*, 150–51; *1972*,
    151–53; *1973*, 153–54; *1974*, 157–58; *1975*, 161–63; *1976*,
    165–66; *1977*, 167–68; *1978*, 168–69; *1979*, 169–71
Supreme Court on football, 112–13
Swann, Lynn, 166, 170–71
Swearingen, Fred, 171
Sweigert, William, 160–61
Swiacki, Bill, 40–41
Symank, John, 119–20
Syracuse University, 57, 180

Taber, Norman, 178
tackle, football, 7
Tarkenton, Fran, 144, 157–58, 161–63, 167–68
Taylor, Maxwell, 35, 38, 178–79
Taylor, Otis, 148
television college football games on, 31–32, 47, 70, 77–78; pro
    football games on, 108, 125, 139, 154–55
Temple University, 27–28
Texas Christian University, 29–30
Texas, University of, 68, 70–72
Tharp, Corky, 51
Theismann, Joe, 70–72
Thomas, Clendon, 58
Thompson, Tommy, 102
Thorpe, Jim, 7, 43
Tibbott, Dave, 9

Tipton, Eric, 30–31
Tittle, Y.A., 120–23
Todd, Dick, 97
Toronto Northmen, 158–59
Toth, Steve, 28–29
Triplett, Mel, 113–15
Truman, Bess, 38
Truman, Harry, 36, 38, 44–45
Tucker, Arnold, 35–36, 38–39, 40
Tulane University, 27–28
Tulsa, University of, 63

UCLA, 12–13, 15, 55, 63–64
union, labor, football, 136
Unitas, Johnny, 113–16, 121–23, 129–30, 139–41, 143–45, 149
United Press International poll, 78–79
universities and football, 2, 12–13; *see also* colleges; football,
    college
USC: *vs* Duke *1939*, 30–31; *vs* Georgia Tech *1928*, 18; Jones as
    coach, 24–25; *vs* Notre Dame *1931*, 23–24; *1978*, 79–80; *vs*
    Ohio *1975*, 74; *vs* Purdue, *1967*, 66; *vs* Washington and
    Jefferson *1922*, 10; *vs* Wisconsin *1953*, 49; *1963*, 62
Usery, W.J., Jr., 160, 163–64

Van Brocklin, Norm, 119–20, 122–23
Van Dellen, Buck, 25–27
Van Horn, Doug, 164
Vanderbilt University, 12
Villanova, 59
Vogel, Bob, 145, 146
Voight, Stu, 157–58

Wagner, Mike, 166
Walden, Bobby, 161–63
Walker, Doak, 75, 109
Walker, Jimmy, 23
Walker, Wade, 184–85
Walton, Joe, 120
Ward, Arch, 99–100
Ward, Norman, 178
Warfield, Paul, 158–59, 164–65
Warner, Glenn, 24, 43
Washington and Jefferson University, 10
Washington Redskins: *vs* Chicago Bears *1937*, 93–94; *1940*,
    95–96; *1942*, 96–97; *1943*, 97–99; *vs* Cleveland Browns
    1958, 113; and drugs, 183; *vs* Miami Dolphins *1973*,
    153–54; *vs* New York Giants *1962*, 120; *vs* Philadelphia
    Eagles, *1947*, 102; transfer from Boston, 92
Washington State, 8–9
Waterfield, Bob, 105–6, 123
Waynesburg, University of, 31–32
Weese, Norris, 168
Western Maryland College, 178
White, Charles, 79–80
Widseth, Ed, 28–29
Williams, Bob, 58
Williams, Kevin, 79–80
Williams, Pete, 38–39
Wisconsin, University of, 12, 13, 49, 62
World Football Championship, 95–96, 96–97
World Football League, 155, 158–60, 164–65
Worster, Steve, 70–72

Yablonski, Ventan, 40–41
Yale University, 18–20, 67
Yankee Stadium, 12–13
Yepremian, Garo, 152, 153, 157–58
Yoder, Jim, 70–72
Young, Len, 177
Yost, Fielding, 177
Yowarsky, Walt, 46

Zaranka, Ben, 46
Zastrow, Bob, 45
Zuppke, Bob, 16, 22, 87